The Bhagavad Gita
A Text and Commentary for Students

The Sussex Library of Religious Beliefs and Practices

This series is intended for students of religion, social sciences and history, and for the interested layperson. It is concerned with the beliefs and practices of religions in their social, cultural and historical setting. These books will be of particular interest to Religious Studies teachers and students at universities, colleges, and high schools. Inspection copies available on request.

Published

The Ancient Egyptians   Rosalie David
The Bhagavad Gita: A text and commentary for students   Jeaneane Fowler
Buddhism   Merv Fowler
Chinese Religions   Jeaneane Fowler and Merv Fowler
Christian Theology: The Spiritual Tradition   John Glyndwr Harris
Gnosticism   John Glyndwr Harris
Hinduism   Jeaneane Fowler
Hindu Goddesses   Lynn Foulston
Humanism   Jeaneane Fowler
Islam   David Norcliffe
The Jews   Alan Unterman
The Protestant Reformation: Tradition and Practice   Madeleine Gray
Sikhism   W. Owen Cole and Piara Singh Sambhi
T'ai Chi Ch'üan   Jeaneane Fowler and Shifu Keith Ewers
Zen Buddhism   Merv Fowler
Zoroastrianism   Peter Clark

Forthcoming

You Reap What You Sow: Causality in the Religions of the World
Jeaneane Fowler

Published and of related interest

Chanting in the Hillsides: Nichiren Daishonin Buddhism in Wales and the Borders
   Jeaneane Fowler and Merv Fowler
An Introduction to the Philosophy and Religion of Taoism: Pathways to Immortality
   Jeaneane Fowler
Perspectives of Reality: An Introduction to the Philosophy of Hinduism
   Jeaneane Fowler
World Religions: An Introduction for Students   Jeaneane Fowler, Merv Fowler,
David Norcliffe, Nora Hill and Diane Watkins

The Bhagavad Gita
A Text and Commentary for Students

Jeaneane Fowler

sussex
ACADEMIC
PRESS
Brighton • Chicago • Toronto

2 4 6 8 10 9 7 5 3 1

First published in 2012 by
SUSSEX ACADEMIC PRESS
PO Box 139
Eastbourne BN24 9BP

Distributed in North America by
SUSSEX ACADEMIC PRESS
Independent Publishers Group
814 N Franklin St, Chicago, IL 60610, USA

British Library Cataloguing in Publication Data
A CIP catalogue record for this book is available from the British Library.

Library of Congress Cataloging-in-Publication Data

Fowler, Jeaneane D.
The Bhagavad Gita : a text and commentary for students / Jeaneane Fowler.
p. cm.
Includes bibliographical references and index.
ISBN 978-1-84519-520-5 (h/b : alk. paper) —
ISBN 978-1-84519-346-1 (p/b : alk. paper)
    1. Bhagavadgita—Commentaries. 2. Hinduism. I. Title.
BL1138.66.F69 2012
294.5′924047—dc23
                                                                    2011033897

Typeset and designed by Sussex Academic Press, Brighton & Eastbourne.
Printed and bound by CPI Group (UK) Ltd, Croydon, CR0 4YY
This book is printed on acid-free paper.

Contents

Preface and Acknowledgements

The *Bhagavad Gita* is a multi-layered text with many avenues of exploration for the post-modern individual who is caught up in the fast pace of present living. Its *sitz im leben* is something of a time capsule on a battlefield where armies are drawn up ready to fight, conch shells have sounded to herald the commencement of war, and the psychological tension of conflict fills the air. And then there is a very, very long pause in which Krishna the God takes time to teach Arjuna the man the answers to fundamental questions about life – What is the nature of the self? What is the nature of God? What is the relationship between the self and God? From where did the world come? And what is the relationship between God and the world? What should the proximate goals of life be for a living being? What is the ultimate aim of life and what are the means for achieving such an aim? It is this long pause that is the context of the *Gita*. While primitive ideas are to be found in its pages, the gently-paced *Gita* has much that provides perspectives on some of the philosophical questions that are just as applicable in today's world, providing we, too, pause to peruse its contents.

I began the first layer of this text many years ago when my students needed a commentary on the *Gita* that was not studded with Sanskrit grammar on the one hand and overtly esoteric on the other. Subsequent publishing commitments meant a long pause before the second layer was attempted a few years ago, and the layers have been deepened since then resulting in the present work, which has been a joy to do. While the text of the *Bhagavad Gita* is explained by way of a detailed commentary, there are generic aspects of early Hinduism that underpin the content, in particular the *Vedic* and *Vedantic* traditions that have informed the practices, philosophy and metaphysics of the *Gita*. Rather than infuse such material into the commentary, I have supplied a lengthy *Introduction* that sets the historical and religious background to the text and the reader is advised to peruse this since, once done, no further preliminary knowledge will be necessary before embarking on the chapters of the *Gita*.

The cover of the book has been designed by two excellent artists, Masae Takeuchi and Mark Medcalf. Their work is always innovative and inspiring and covers a broad spectrum of artistic media with a particular interest in Eastern cultures. Mark and Masae also provided the logo that appears before the colophons at the close of each of the chapters. The cover of the book is replete with symbolism. Krishna is always represented as blue in colour, hence the colour of the hands in the cover design. The chariot of Krishna and Arjuna is to be seen in the motif at the base, while the triple motif symbolizes the triple paths of the *Gita* – action without desire for results, knowledge and devotion. There are also three strands that make up all phenomena – light and radiance, energy, and inertia, as well as three aspects of the divine in the *Gita* – the totally transcendent Absolute, the manifest deity that is also the essence of all things, and the personal God to whom devotion can be given. The main image of Krishna is superimposed on the roots of the *ashvattha* tree that features in chapter 15: its branches reach down into the earth and its roots ascend upwards and it represents phenomenal existence. All these aspects Mark and Masae have captured admirably in their design, for which I am extremely grateful.

It is with particular pleasure that I am able to thank Anuradha Roma Choudhury for her assistance with some of the romanization of Sanskrit terms. Anuradha is one of those rare individuals who radiates a quiet charisma and who one is privileged to call a friend. She is greatly accomplished. A graduate in Indian music, Anuradha specialises in *Rabindra Sangeet*, the singing of the poems of Rabindranath Tagore. She has written a book in Bengali about his songs and their particular notation, which has become standard for those studying the songs. She has also contributed to books on Hinduism in the English language. Her workshops on *alpana*, Indian floor paintings constructed in rice powder, are well known, and her life is sufficiently remarkable for her to have been featured in a television production – *A Day in the Life of Roma Choudhuri*. I have known her for many years and she has delighted my students with her excellent talks on Hinduism and with demonstrations of art. To me, and I am sure to many others, she is a *devi*. I also wish to thank Professor Pratap Bandyopadhyay for his assistance in the romanization of Sanskrit *anusvara*. Now retired, Professor Bandyopadhyay was Professor of Sanskrit at the University of Burdwan in West Bengal, India. Following his retirement, he has taken on the huge task of editing the *Vishnu Dharmottara Purana* as General Editor for the VDUP Project with the Asiatic Society in Calcutta. I should also like to thank the team at Sussex Academic Press. The Press has continued to be supportive to what I write and I am especially grateful to Anthony Grahame for his friendly dialogue and expertise. Sarah Norman at the Institute of Oriental Philosophy European Centre at Taplow Court, near Maidenhead, Berkshire, has been of invaluable support. Sarah has provided rare sources quickly with her usual efficiency and friendly assistance. Readers are advised to explore the exceptional library at Taplow Court, which is situated in an oasis of calm in exquisite surroundings.

Finally, mentioning family always seems somewhat unacademic. However, on this occasion I owe an enormous debt to my husband Merv for his support with this book. I occasionally lost track in between the layers and had to regain mastery a number of times. For the final layer, he gave me unfettered time by undertaking all the mundane chores in the home and garden and by cultivating culinary skills to greater heights. Having six or seven hours a day to devote to the text was a writer's dream and it is thanks to him that the text was completed. Thus, it is to Merv that this book is so deservedly dedicated with immense love.

Jeaneane Fowler
AUTUMN 2011

From the unreal lead me to the real,
from darkness lead me to light,
from death lead me to immortality.

Brihadaranyaka Upanishad

I have met thee where the night touches the edge of day;
where the light startles the darkness into dawn,
and the waves carry the kiss of the one shore to the other.
From the heart of the fathomless blue comes one golden call,
and across the dusk of tears I try to gaze at thy face
and know not for certain if thou art seen.

Rabindranath Tagore

And I have felt
A presence that disturbs me with the joy
Of elevated thoughts; a sense sublime
Of something far more deeply interfused,
Whose dwelling is the light of setting suns,
And the round ocean and the living air,
And the blue sky, and in the mind of man:
A motion and a spirit, that impels
All thinking things, all objects of all thought,
And rolls through all things.

William Wordsworth

Disinterestedness is a state of mind, and such a state can never
be cultivated without self-control. One whose left hand
does not know what his right hand does, such a one
knows what it is to be equal-minded. Our yardstick
is the ability to see others as ourselves. We should
think whether we should be happy if others
did to us what we do to them.
Disinterestedness can never
be cultivated without a
spirit of renunciation.

Mahatma Gandhi

We create our own truth of existence in our own
action of mind and life, which is another
way of saying that we create
our own selves, are our
own makers.

Aurobindo

The unmanifest wholeness, the isness of Life, expresses its splendour
and glory and wealth in every expression, be it in a tiny blade of grass,
its deep green colour, its tenderness and freshness. The wholeness
of Life smiles at us through the blade of grass, through the
flow of water, through the rain drops, through the
frightening lightning, the depth of the ocean,
the expanse of space; we are embraced by
that wholeness of Life, that isness of life.

Vimala Thakar

To look at one's habits and yet to be separate from them;
to see one's activities and yet to regard oneself as
not the actor of those activities; to perceive
one's virtues and accomplishments and yet
to lay no claim over them – this is the
characteristic of one who has
freed himself from all
conditioning.

Rohit Mehta

Go to the absolute ultimate Reality, and all levels of relativity
will cease to be a burden. Be illumined, and life
will ever be in freedom and fullness,
away from the darkness
of ignorance.

Maharishi Mahesh Yogi

Introduction

To view the *Bhagavad Gita* (or simply *Gita*, as it is known) in isolation from its Hindu background would be to do it a disservice for such a course would certainly inhibit true understanding of it. The religion we call "Hinduism" is a *pot pourri* of many ideas grafted onto ancient and traditional roots. It has ideas gathered from many periods of time and from many quarters, resulting in a melding of ancient and contemporary beliefs. Thus, we find polytheism, monotheism, pantheism, panentheism, dualism, non-dualism and pluralism all existing side-by-side in the many strands that make up Hinduism – a term that can at best mean rather little in its singular form. The philosophy and metaphysics that accompanied such diversity were essentially a search for Truth, for Reality that is ultimate, for the true nature of the self, and for the kind of knowledge that makes the experience of Truth and ultimate Reality possible. Answers were needed for such questions as: What is the purpose of life? Who am I, and what is my *real* self? What is real in a world of change? Why do human beings suffer? Why does evil exist? What kinds of things can we *really* know? From what or whom did the universe arise? And so on. Hindu philosophical inquiry has usually been characterized by a search for Reality, Truth and Knowledge that transcends both space and time; for space and time impose on life the transience, impermanence and changeability that challenge the reality of the world in which we live. The *Bhagavad Gita* sits in the post-*Vedic* era, a time when devotion to a personal God emerged but, at the same time, the earlier *Vedic* religion maintained by a priestly elite continued to be ritually influential. It is important, therefore, to have some understanding of this *Vedic* backdrop against which the *Gita* is set.

Veda: knowledge

The word *Veda* means "knowledge" or "wisdom" and refers to a broad spectrum of Hindu religious literature, generally referred to as *shruti*, "heard" or "revealed" sacred truth, which was composed over a long stretch of time lasting over a millennium. While this literature is traditionally one composite "wisdom", it is usually divided into two groups of writings, roughly *Vedas* and *Upanishads*. This is because the former are concerned primarily with ritual, and the latter, with more philosophical and metaphysically speculative material. And since the *Upanishads* are relatively later than the *Vedas*, occurring at the end of them, the term *Vedanta* ("end of the *Veda*") distinguishes this more philosophical material from the earlier ritualistic literature. Because the *Vedas* are ritualistic they are concerned with correct ritual action, *karman*; they are thus the *karma-kanda* "ritual action portion" of the *shruti* literature. The *Vedanta*, on the other hand, is concerned with knowledge, *jnana*. This is knowledge of the deep and intuitive type and is the medium for revealed wisdom and knowledge. The *Vedanta* is, thus, the *jnana-kanda*, the "knowledge portion" of *shruti* literature. Nevertheless, it is important to bear in mind that the knowledge that both impart belongs to the same *shruti* tradition. The transition between the two is not abrupt for other *shruti* literature overlaps and integrates with both. *Shruti* literature was considered so sacred that it was eventually committed to written form very reluctantly, and reflects, therefore, a long period of oral transmission during which it was meticulously handed down to successive generations of priests.

Shruti literature was experientially received by the ancient seers or *rishis* and was, and is still, accepted as revealed from the divine. There was, thus, a direct perception of wisdom, of knowledge, though it was wisdom certainly not available to all, but only to those of heightened consciousness. Later Hindu sacred scripture is differentiated from this kind of revealed scripture by the designation *smriti*. This latter is interpretative material – material that develops the earlier *shruti* but does not "receive" it in the same way. While the more popular *smriti* scriptures dictate the religious genre of past and much present Hindu practice, it is *shruti* tradition on which it is based, and from which it claims authority.

So far *shruti* literature has been divided into *Vedas* and *Upanishads*, but other literature is also included. The *Vedas* themselves are divided into four: the *Rig*, which is the "Royal" knowledge and is the most important of the four (indeed, much of the material that comprises the other three *Vedas* is taken from the *Rig*); the *Sama Veda*, which is knowledge of chants, the sacred melodies to which the hymns of the *Rig Veda* were set; the *Yajur Veda*, which deals with sacrificial ritual; and the *Atharva Veda*, which contains magical formulas, incantations and spells. The *Atharva Veda* is the latest of the *Vedas*, though it contains many primitive ideas that must have originated in popular beliefs and praxis including animism and magic. The material of each of the *Vedas* is also given the term *Samhita*, "Collection". All subsequent *shruti* literature is based on these four *Vedas*, so each has its commentary or *Brahmana* that deals with the rites and ceremonies of the respective *Samhita*. Each, too, has its *Aranyakas* or "forest writings", as well as specific *Upanishads*. The *Samhitas* and the *Brahmanas* form the *karma-kanda* (ritual portion) and the *Aranyakas* and the *Upanishads* the *jnana-kanda* (knowledge portion). The *Samhitas* in their written form are in a very old Sanskrit, and are sometimes difficult to understand. Since the chief concern was with ritual, the hymns contained in the *Samhitas* were not systematically but selectively committed to written form; many hymns were probably omitted as not wholly relevant to ritualistic purpose.

In the *Rig Veda* the hymns are arranged in relation to the deities who are worshipped, such as Indra or Agni; the whole of the ninth *mandala*, for example, is devoted to Soma, at once a deity and also a powerful consumable liquid that heightened consciousness. Much of the material of the *Rig Veda* is repeated in the other three *Vedas* and so it is generally regarded as the most important and the earliest of the four. The hymns of the *Rig Veda* are variously dated, some being very old, perhaps earlier than the Aryan migration to northern India,[1] others being composed many centuries later. While Hindus regard the *Vedas* as timeless, the long spell of oral transmission that preceded their written form means that they date from at least 1200 BCE down to about 500 BCE. They are, therefore, the result of many authors. Apart from their religious and cultural value, the hymns reflect the many stages in the growth of Aryan society. Coming from the plains of Central Asia East of the Caspian Sea, the Aryans were one group of many Indo-Europeans who filtered out from this area from about 2000 BCE. They settled in northern India, bringing with them their specific *Vedic* religion and their orally transmitted *Vedas*. To those hymns they brought with them were added others as the centuries passed, and so we are left with a remarkable insight into Aryan or *Vedic* culture.

Vedic religion

The Aryans brought with them the nature religion of their forebears, which developed into worship of deities as the impersonal powers, the forces, or essences, that underpinned the *Vedic* universe of Earth, atmosphere and Heaven. Generally, then, *Vedic* deities were symbols and allowed Aryans to make sense of the world around and beyond them. This profound connection with the less tangible aspects of the universe often tends to make *Vedic* deities somewhat elusive in character rather than overtly anthropomorphic. A somewhat shifting nature of deity is evident in *Vedic* religion as a result, and, if at one time pivotal to human existence, the deities came to be secondary to the whole complex process of ritual celebration. Then, too, the forces that the *Vedic* gods symbolized were sometimes very similar: the function of Agni as fire, for example could be similar to that of Surya as the sun, or Indra as lightning. Thus the characters of *Vedic* deities were often blurred and only rarely distinctive: close to nature they may have been, but they were normally characterized by too much symbolic intangibility to be completely personalized and wholly anthropomorphized. This will be a very important point when we come to examine the nature of God in the *Bhagavad Gita*.

Nevertheless, the gods, at least in the early stages of Aryan religion as we know it from the *Vedas*, were certainly propitiated for what, to the Aryan mind, were the essentials of existence – the necessary results of wealth, particularly in cattle, longevity, success in battle, pleasure and progeny. Demands were made to the gods through the medium of sacrificial ritual which became more and more exclusive and elaborate at the hands of the priests. Yet at the popular level it is likely that the simpler folk continued to propitiate the gods for their basic needs in life, and to overcome their fears of evil forces. The *Atharva Veda*, especially, bears witness to such popular religious thought and practice with its spells and incantations for everything from a reluctant lover to gambling success. Beyond popular religion, great reverence for *Vedic* authority developed and belief in the power of the sacrificial ritual of the *Vedic* religion is the key to understanding the religion of the Aryans in the early centuries of their settlement in India: it was ritual action engaged in for specific results.

The whole complex *Vedic* ritual was called *yajna*, sacrificial ritual, which assumed increasing importance to the point that it was felt to regulate and maintain all aspects of creation. Without it the sun would not rise and the patterns and rhythms of the natural world would no longer obtain. The tiniest mistake in any aspect of the ritual – an incorrect tone in the chants, a mispronounced word, a careless action, a misplaced item, the wrong amount of a material – it was believed, could have the most disastrous effects on the Aryan environment; indeed, on the cosmos itself. It is easy to see how the priests, who were solely responsible for the meticulous conducting of ritual – some of which was elaborate enough to continue for many months – rose to considerable power and prestige. It is also easy to see that, providing the sacrifices were carried out perfectly, the gods became almost superfluous: *Vedic* ritual itself would bring about the necessary effects. It suggested to the Aryan mind that there was some kind of potent magical force that transformed the sacrifice into the desired effects – a belief about which the *Gita* will have much to say.

The sacrificial ritual was considered to be correct action, *karman* or *kriya*, a concept that is partly responsible for the idea of *karma* as the law of cause and effect by which a good action is rewarded by a good result and the converse action by adverse results. Indeed, the efficacy of the cause–result process in *yajna* became a fixed principle that would need only the extension to those actions outside religious ritual to make it a more universal law. And the fact that sacrifice was an action that was an established *duty* is also a link with later ideas of religious duty – in all kinds of prescribed and non-prescribed forms – as a means to good fruitive *karma*. The goal of life for the *Vedic* Indian was, indeed, both correct ritual worship and a righteous existence, presupposing the established doctrines of *karma* and *dharma* that are characteristic of later thought, and that feature extensively in the *Gita*.

So *shruti* literature is mainly priestly, *Brahmin*,[2] focused; that is to say, it pertains almost entirely to priestly study, transmission, practice, knowledge and expertise. Many priestly schools developed, being concerned with specific scriptures and the production of additional texts. Each school would be responsible for transmitting its traditions orally.[3] There was certainly scope for considerable interpretation of the *Samhitas* in the commentaries of the *Brahmanas*, and the complexities of ritual, therefore, led, also, to complexities of scripture. The control of the priests in every area of the complex ritual made Aryan religion wholly elitist, and it should be borne in mind that it is exactly this elitist tradition of the time that has been handed down to us now in written form. For the religious practice of many others in Indian life – the ordinary village folk, for example – we can know relatively little. Such a lacuna in the religious praxis and beliefs of common life is very relevant to the phenomenon of the *Bhagavad Gita* and to its widespread acceptance and popularity.

Thus, *Vedic* religion was an exclusive praxis that centred in the control of the priests and was accessed only by Aryan twice-born classes – priests, kings and warriors, and artisans. Life in the villages is not reflected at all in the Aryan tradition. But if we look back to the pre-Aryan, Bronze Age culture of the Indus Valley civilizations, which date at least to 2500–1800 or 1500 BCE, there is plenty of evidence of nature worship, animal worship, and of female deities. Local areas must have had their own religious practices, and it is likely that many of these older customs survived in various forms at the village level, never to be recorded, since they were outside the elitist *Vedic* culture. This will be an important point in the acceptance of Krishna, the hero-deity of the *Bhagavad Gita*. Krishna was a ruler and the *Gita* was distinctly a text that sprang from the ruling, warrior class and was originally extraneous to the priestly milieu. Its very context in a war puts it outside priestly practice, albeit that its author is at pains to ally the content to orthodox teachings.

But I would not wish to leave the reader with the impression that *Vedic* religion is so ritualistic that it has little spirituality or feeling. The *Samhitas* are poetic hymns that speak of the beauty of the dawn, personified in the beautiful goddess Ushas, the wonder of the setting sun, the marvel of the cow that produces milk. Because deities were assigned to the three parts of the universe – Heaven, sky or intermediate region, and Earth – the writers of the hymns, or *mantras*, had plenty of scope with storm, wind, rain, lightning, stars, sun, moon, and so on, in order to express their ideas. The view of life and death was a linear one, not cyclical. One life was all that was allotted to human beings who, if they had lived it well, could hope for reward in a physical Heaven, a realm of light where they would experience physical pleasures in the company of the gods. But for those who had not the moral fibre, a realm of darkness and punishment awaited them. A similar, linear, perspective of the universe is evident, at least in the sense that it had a beginning and a distinct creation, even if less is evident about the end. There was no belief in transmigration of souls or of cyclical evolving and involving of the universe in the *Rig Veda* but the connection between action and its appropriate good or bad result was established quite clearly, and this is a factor that paved the way for the later belief in *karma* as we have come to know it, and with that belief, rebirth. Essentially, however, *Vedic* religious praxis was completely result orientated.

The Aryan view of the world was a common sense one of a plurality of things and of beings, the reality of which was never questioned. Yet, given the fact that ritualistic practice was believed to have its effects on the immediate and cosmic environment, a certain interconnectedness of all things has to be presupposed. The divine and human worlds were believed to coalesce to some extent but one was not thought to be more real than the other. So there is nothing in the *Rig Veda* to suggest that the world is unreal as in some later philosophical thought. Despite the transience and changeability obvious in the nature of the self, it remained real, though the personality was believed to be separate from the soul, the latter being that part of the self that continued eternally. In no way, however, was the soul linked with the divine; it was, rather, considered to be the vital breath (*asu*) of a being that separated from the body at death and was associated with the thought and emotions of a person (*manas*). It is not until the *Brahmanas* and *Aranyakas* that the word *atman* can be found to hint at a more unifying world Self.[4]

Early *Vedic* hymns certainly show an overt polytheism but not the kind of polytheism to set up the rigid distinctions of polytheistic pantheons, and its more fluid perception of divinity never developed into anything more concrete. Later *Vedic* hymns more clearly express a search for one ultimate Source of the gods, a Supreme Being that is the generator of all things. This was variously conceived of as Sun, Desire, Time, Water, Air, and so on. Coupled with this was the tendency, noted above, for the *Vedic* deities to become more closely identified with each other, fusing their respective characters and their respective roles – an extremely important development that prefigured much that was to emerge in later thought. And just as the earlier period had a distinct kind of polytheism, so the move to a more monotheistic conception of the divine also has its own special features. It could be argued that it was the very lack of a well-defined polytheistic pantheon of deities in the earlier stage that paved the way for the kind of fusion of divine status that made the search for one ultimate Source viable.

If there is a move to monotheism in the *Vedas* it is a move at times to a metaphysical monotheism, that is to say, to belief in a more intangible and transcendent Reality from which all proceeds but which is elusive: it is a One behind the many. And no particular deity is associated with this One as supreme; it is more a fusion of them all. Thus, one hymn states that what is "One" can be called by the names of many deities – Indra, Mitra, Varuna, Agni, Garutman, Yama, Matarishvan.[5] Some of the deities lend themselves well to an all-pervasiveness. Such is Surya the Sun, and Agni, Fire. For if the sun gives its light and warmth it does so pervasively and not selectively. And to the *Vedic* mind Agni, Fire, was One, not many. This more speculative thought did not counteract the ritualism of the *Vedic* period, but was accommodated alongside it, and the polytheism underpinning sacrifice still obtained. But the search for a Source of the deities was moving in a direction of a search for the Source that caused all to *emanate* from it, a unifying link between Source and the world – divine or other – that would develop into panentheistic and monistic ideas. *Vedic* religion witnesses a thread of thought that searches not for the causes behind the natural phenomena of the universe, but for a First Cause that is the ultimate Source.

At times, *Vedic* thought suggests a personal ultimate Source and at others an impersonal one, both being facets of the concept of God in the *Gita*. The move towards focus on One as opposed to many deities is a move to a more monotheistic religious outlook. But just as the polytheism of the *Vedas* is somewhat different to other polytheistic systems, the monotheism of the *Vedic* period is equally so, for there is no effort to make one of the deities supreme, and no evolution of a deity to ultimate status. Instead, totally new concepts are searched for, and this may be one reason why the status of *Vedic* gods – even a god like Indra – diminished at a later date. When we look at the content of the *Gita*, we shall find just the opposite with the projection of Krishna as the supreme deity. There, Krishna is presented as a unifying deity, a trend that was courted in the *Vedas* in the search for a unifying principle *behind* all other deities and the Source of the universe. But in the *Vedas* we find a range of supreme deities: Prajapati, "Lord of Creatures" is one, depicted as laying his seed in the waters of chaos in which he becomes a golden egg or embryo called Hiranyagarbha, from whom emanates the whole universe, though the fact that he is called by different names exemplifies well the rather anomalous nature of such deities.

At one point in the *Rig Veda* (10:129) we find an unnamed and abstract Reality behind the phenomenal universe, an indescribable Source that can only be termed "That" or "That One", *Tat Ekam*. It is neuter in the old Sanskrit and so transcends the dualities of male and female and does not invite speculation about its nature. The One that breathes windlessly or breathlessly and self-sustaining obviously exists here before all other manifestations in the cosmos. So the manifest cosmos does not equate with it, for "That" is a limitless, indescribable, absolute principle that can exist independently of existence – otherwise it cannot be the Source of it. I doubt, then, whether this can be termed a "superpersonal monism"[6] or, even stronger, "the quintessence of monistic thought".[7] It is more expressive of a panentheistic, totally transcendent entity that can become manifest by its own power, and that is exactly the concept of deity we shall find in the *Gita*. It exists in itself, unmanifest, but with the potential for all manifestations of the cosmos. But the fact that it precedes creation as neither this nor that, yet not *nothing*, places "The One" transcendent to the manifest universe. This one hymn of the *Rig Veda*, however, is probably the closest the *Vedas* come to great heights of philosophical speculation. The hymn certainly expresses the fundamental principle of manifest existence emanating from an unmanifest Source, and therefore all existence as a unity. It is heat, *tapas*, that is the latent power in the Unmanifest and that is depicted as the initial medium for creation to take place. But unity with that unmanifest Source is partial and panentheistic, for the Source, though constituting what it creates as the creative Cause, also transcends what it creates. We shall meet these ideas again in the text of the *Bhagavad Gita*.

Another mysterious force that operated in existence was the power and efficacy behind the multitude of sacrificial actions. What was it that ensured a certain result from a particular ritualistic cause? One of the reasons why the *Vedas* were accepted as being testimony of ultimate Truth was that the rituals they prescribed were believed to actually produce the appropriate effects. Two factors are important here: one is the unquestionable belief in *Vedic* testimony, and the other, the belief in the power or force operative between action and its result. We are left with a highly entrenched belief in actions undertaken for results in *Vedic* praxis and this will be a key aspect in the understanding of the *Gita*.

Vedanta

The latest of the *shruti* literature comes at the end of the *Vedas* and is called just that, *Vedanta*, *Veda* and *anta* "end". The particularly philosophical and mystical nature and content of the literature that comprises the *Vedanta*, the *Upanishads*,[8] tend to separate it from the rest of *shruti* literature. The search for an ultimate Reality and essence that underpins all existence is the specific quest of *Upanishadic* thought, and we see in it the ways in which the sages wrestled with the search. Some of the most ancient *Upanishads* represent the oldest attempt of humankind to provide a philosophical explanation of the universe, of ultimate Reality, of the nature of the self and the purpose of humankind. The *Brihad-aranyaka Upanishad* expresses this quest in the words: "From the unreal lead me to the real, from darkness lead me to light, from death lead me to immortality."[9] *Vedanta* also means "end of the *Vedas*" in the sense of fulfilment of the *Vedas*, that is to say, the *Upanishads* brought out what was considered the real meaning behind *Vedic* ritual through the pursuit of true knowledge. Since the *Upanishads* are the major scriptures pertaining to the *Vedanta* the two terms are synonymous.

The importance of *Upanishadic* thought in the development of Hinduism is enormous, for it contains most of the developing concepts that we associate with Hinduism today; belief in the Absolute of Brahman, *karma* and its association with *samsara* (rebirth), *moksha* (liberation from rebirth), *dharma* (what is right), *atman* (the true Self) in relation to Brahman are just some of the most fundamental, and all these are traditional concepts accepted by the *Bhagavad Gita* and will be discussed under separate headings below. The *Gita* relies heavily on the teachings of the *Upanishads*, so reflecting *shruti* tradition, but like *smriti* literature, it reinterprets or synthesizes some of the ideas found there. Yet it is clearly concerned with the deepest *Vedantic* issues of the nature of God, the self and the world. The author of the *Gita*, therefore, included the words of a number of *Upanishads* very frequently.

The style of the *Upanishads* is often a dialogue between a teacher, a *guru*, and his disciple, his *chela*. This usually took place in the quiet of a forest, or at the bank of a river: the scene is calm, quiet and tranquil. The nature of the teaching is dependent on the level of consciousness of the pupil so there is no systematic approach, and what is taught rather depends on the questions and responses of the pupil. The *Bhagavad Gita* is very similar: there is a dialogue between Arjuna and Krishna, but it takes place on a battlefield at a scene wholly engaged with life; it is not tranquil at all, and exemplifies the *Gita's* teaching of involvement in, not renunciation of, the world.

Knowledge is critical to the *Upanishads*, particularly those that posit monistic, non-dual identity of the soul with an Absolute, which was termed Brahman. This deep, intuitive knowledge is tantamount to *being*: to know Brahman is to *be* Brahman. With the emphasis on such knowledge came an antipathy to any action, hence the separation of *jnana-yoga* from ritual *karma-yoga*. As we shall see, the *Gita* will have much to say about both these approaches, and we shall return to some of the important concepts of the *Vedanta* below, in relation to themes in the *Gita*.

The *Bhagavad Gita*

The *Bhagavad-Gita*, "The Song of the Lord" (*Bhagavad* "Lord" and *Gita* "Song"), is a superlative text. The "Lord", here, is Krishna, traditionally the incarnation of one of Hinduism's greatest deities, Vishnu. While some of its passages are pertinent only to the time in which it was written, others transcend that time and are applicable to all ages. It is a delightful text that is at the heart of Hinduism and has been adopted in the present as a very popular text in the West and the wider world. It is likely, however, that its popularity in India did not occur until the last two or three centuries. The *Mahabharata* "Great Bharata" – the great tale of the descendants of Bharata – in which the *Gita* is placed is concerned with the enmity between the Kauravas, led by their eldest brother, Duryodhana, son of Dhritarashtra, and their cousins, the Pandavas. In a game of dice, Yudhishthira, the eldest of the Pandava brothers, lost his kingdom for thirteen years, during which he and his other four brothers had to remain in exile. At the end of this time, the five brothers returned, but Duryodhana did not keep his side of the bargain and hand back the kingdom. All attempts at reconciliation failed and the end result was the war between the two sides, a fratricidal war in which Arjuna, one of the Pandavas, found it difficult to engage. Thus, the *Mahabharata* has every twist and turn of a modern-day drama – intrigue, love, betrayal, sorrow, joy and dynamic characters. It is at this point in the *Mahabharata* that the content of the *Gita* intervenes when Krishna offers his advice to the warrior Arjuna after the latter declines to take part in the war.

Nature of the text

The *Bhagavad-Gita* was written in Sanskrit. It has seven hundred verses in total, and these are divided into eighteen chapters of unequal length, CHAPTERS TWO and EIGHTEEN being by far the longest. As the *Song of the Lord*, it was meant to be sung or recited, and parts, or the whole, learned by heart. The *Gita* is the third section of the sixth of the eighteen Major Books, or *Parvas*, in the *Mahabharata*, forming chapters 23–40 of the 117 chapters of the *Book of Bhishma* or *Bhishmaparvan* – "a little shrine in a vast temple", as one author described it[10] – but in all, just a tiny portion of the *Mahabharata*. Bhishma is an important figure in the *Mahabharata*. This old grandfather of the court was hailed as wise, just and devout, though his pledge to support the kingdom resulted in his being in the army opposed to the Pandavas, with whom his sympathies really lay. He himself had renounced all claims to the throne and had taken a vow of celibacy. However, the placement of the *Gita* in the *Book of Bhishma* is not without its oddities of context, since the death of Bhishma in the battle actually precedes the *Gita* in which the war has hardly begun, and in which he is very much alive: indeed, the *Gita* will have some work to do in justifying the killing of so noble a soul.

So, immediately before our text of the *Bhagavad Gita*, Dhritarashtra's counsellor, Sanjaya, has returned from the battlefield to announce that the armies' Commander-in-Chief, the great Bhishma, has been killed by Shikhandin after a valiant ten days of battle, "breathing his last on earth like a tree snapped by a gale, undeserving of his death in your misbegotten plan, Bharata!",[11] Sanjaya tells Dhritarashtra. He recounts the details of preparations and formations of the armies and not without hints that only the true and just could win, especially if the divine Krishna is on their side. It is then that Sanjaya begins at the beginning, giving the content we know as the *Bhagavad Gita*, when Bhishma has not yet been slain, for the battle has not yet begun. Even after the end of the *Gita*, in the *Book of the Slaying of Bhishma*, Sanjaya recounts events that precede the war, describing how Yudhishthira, the eldest of the Pandavas, walked through the enemy lines in order to ask the permission of each of Bhishma, Drona, Kripa and Shalya in turn to fight against them in battle – a great mark of respect for those who taught him – and from whom Yudhishthira was granted victory. We do not have, then, a strictly chronological setting for the *Bhagavad Gita*, and it is highly likely that it was inserted into the *Mahabharata* like so many other parts of that long epic. Nevertheless, the great war that is the context of the *Gita* places the text at a crucial culminating point in the whole *Mahabharata*.[12]

The *Gita* is, however, not quite like the rest of the *Mahabharata*. It is not a mystical text that is only for the initiate, but it does stand out as a part of the *Mahabharata* that has profound depth, yet not such that precludes its reading by the ordinary individual. Perhaps it is indicative of a more reflective period of time, in that it speaks to a more introspective philosophy than the warmongering of the *Mahabharata* as a whole, though the *Mahabharata*, too, has a good deal of teaching. Many have attempted to weave a course through the pages of the *Gita* in order to claim it as relevant to their own sectarian views, and there are certainly many ways in which it can be understood, but the *Gita* is essentially non-sectarian. Alexandre Piatigorsky, in his introduction to van Buitenen's translation of the *Gita*, claims it as a *"general and universal"* text with wide teaching,[13] and I think this comes close to the nature of the text. The *Gita* deals with the nature of God and matter, with reality, with morality, with the self, and with the means by which the individual can approach God and become liberated from the endless cycle of rebirths. To find a definitive path in it exclusive of all others is to do the *Gita* a disservice. However, since the dialogue between Arjuna, the Pandava hero, and Krishna the God is a dynamic one, there is no continuous thread throughout. Rather, themes are repeated in order to be developed, interrupted in order for explanation of a point, or dropped abruptly for a new dimension to be examined. Such characteristics make it easy for an interpreter to accept or discard what suits or does not a particular bias. Such is not the aim of the present text or commentary by any means. What also makes it possible to travel the *Gita's* pages on a predetermined route are its inconsistencies, for example its occasional criticism juxtaposed with its upholding of *Vedic* ritual. A case could certainly be made for eschewing ritual obligation as much as for the perils of not abiding by it.

At the close of each chapter of the *Gita* is a colophon that describes it as an *Upanishad*, indicating that the *Gita* remains entrenched in, and not divorced from, the *Vedanta*. As was seen earlier, it is in the *Upanishads* of the *Vedanta* that all the profound theories of God and reality and the nature of the self are to be found. Much of this material *is* mystical and the *Gita* reflects a good deal of the *Vedantic* spirituality and conceptual philosophy. In short, it remains orthodox and has always been accepted as such. Yet, at the same time, it synthesizes ideas of its time, converging all on the supreme Absolute, Brahman, and on Krishna as the embodiment of Brahman, melding devotional religion with *Vedantic* tradition, but not without criticism where it sees that fit. The colophons at the end of each chapter describe the contents as *brahma-vidya*, "knowledge of Brahman" or the "science of Brahman", thus placing the material in the *Vedantic* framework. Indeed, on many occasions, the text uses material directly taken from the *Upanishads* or closely reflects many *Upanishadic* passages. Nevertheless, despite a number of inconsistencies, the *Gita* does not have the same level of contradictory thought as the *Upanishads*, where mystical ideas are presented such as they are experienced without any attempt at systematic revelation. But perhaps because the *Gita* is more philosophical than the rest of the *Mahabharata* it is regarded as a key *Vedantic* text. Indeed, "*Vedanta*" came to signify portions of the *Vedas* along with the *Upanishads*, Badarayana's *Brahma Sutras* (a text that attempted to create a systematic *Vedantic* philosophy from the *Upanishads*), and the *Gita*.

The *Gita* seems to be astride both *shruti* and *smriti* literature. It is accorded the nature of *shruti* since it is described as an *Upanishad* at the end of each chapter, yet is of the nature of *smriti* like the *Mahabharata* in which it is set. The great commentators, Shankara, Ramanuja and Madhva saw the text as *shruti* and not *smriti*. Both types of scripture are steeped in oral tradition as the favoured means of transmitting the sacred word, but the *Gita* is not restricted in its readership, unlike the *Vedic* material that is open only to twice-born Hindus. Indeed, the *Gita* has become a widely popular text throughout India and is readily available to all who are able to read it. Such readability is enhanced by the fact that, unlike *shruti* scriptures, the *Gita*, as other epic texts like the *Mahabharata*, and the *Ramayana*, has a less structured style of language that is closer to the populace of the day than the *Vedic* material, and more suited to narrative content. If the author wished to make a longer point, he carried it over into a number of verses to make a long sentence. Then, too, the text accords well with the trend of devotional Hinduism that gained ground during the last few centuries BCE. This was *bhakti*, "loving devotion", to a particular deity, that of the *Gita* being Krishna.

The elitist ritualism of the priests and the aristocracy was far removed from the ordinary person and the lofty speculation of the *Upanishads* even more so. Although we have only glimpses of popular religion from early literature, it is not difficult to imagine how receptive the populace would have been to a *personal* God. And this was not a god that was confined to a locality, but one that was cosmic, supreme and yet whose descent to Earth in mortal form made him close, able to be praised, visualized and to whom tangible devotion could be offered. In short, at local levels there was ample space for the development of overt theism to a God such as Krishna. By the time of the *Gita*, *Vedic* ritualism had begun to decline, but religious praxis continued to thrive at the popular level. The advent of the devotional popular literature originated not in Brahmanical circles but in the higher echelons of the *Kshatriya* ruling class of kings, administrators and warriors[14] but its appeal was to encompass the wider populace and its nature was indicative of a rising devotional theism. The *Upanishads* are Brahman focused and mainly transcend the world, but the *Gita*, though steeped in *Vedanta*, is very much world involved – as, indeed, is Krishna as a character throughout the *Mahabharata*.

Acceptance of a deity like Krishna made manifest a new impetus in religious belief with which the priests must have felt the necessity to accord. Since the *Gita* accepts so much that is orthodox, especially in its conception of the Absolute, Brahman, it is not so far removed from *Vedantic* beliefs to necessitate its rejection by orthodox circles. But at the same time, its theism embodied in Krishna as God on Earth must have had immense appeal in the wider society. There is, then, something of a synthesis of ideas in the *Gita*, but not one that is necessarily an attempt by the author to systematize the material: indeed, contradictions in the text speak only too readily of a lack of systematization throughout. The overall picture is of a harmony of ideas that permits multiple pathways, but which, unfortunately, also permits multiple choices in interpretation and the possibilities of over-emphasizing one pathway and giving lip-service to others.

Date and historicity

Theories as to the dating of the *Gita* vary considerably. It is certainly later than the main classical body of the *Upanishads* and seems also to predate most of the early major orthodox schools of Hindu philosophy.[15] A date of the fifth century BCE is accepted by some,[16] with a later demarcation of the second century BCE, which I think is the more probable. It is a certain looseness and flexibility of terminology in the *Gita* that suggests it is much earlier than most of the philosophical systems as well as an absence of developed ideas of the *avatara* concept, the "descents" of the deity, or even explicit identification of Krishna with Vishnu and Narayana, as was later the case. Some parts seem to reflect Buddhist ideas, which certainly suggest a date no earlier than the late fifth century BCE. Other so-called *gitas* were influenced by the *Bhagavad Gita*, and the *Puranas* also suggest an earlier date, given that the *Gita* would have needed a long time to acquire a high status.[17]

Krishna may have been a real person. He is sometimes identified as the son of Devaki and Vasudeva and there is a Krishna who was a pupil of Ghora Angirisa, mentioned in the *Chandogya Upanishad* (3:17:6). As a pupil, the Krishna mentioned here would not have been a deity or perhaps not even a tribal chief; if this is the Krishna of the *Gita*, it must have been later that he became a divinized god. There seems to have been a cult of Vasudeva, the name of Krishna's father, possibly around the fourth century BCE and this was a cult of the sun. Gavin Flood notes that worship of Vasudeva was noted by the grammarian Panini and that such worship dates back to the fifth or sixth centuries BCE. This, together with other occasional references,[18] seems to suggest some authenticity and historicity for a devotional, sectarian religion devoted to Vasudeva. Vasudeva was the chief deity of the Vrishnis, a tribe that amalgamated with that of Krishna's, the Yadavas,[19] of which Krishna was chief and a descendant of Yadu. It may have been out of such circumstances that a tribal chief, Krishna, became identified with the deity Vasudeva. In any event, he became known as Krishna Vasudeva and chief of the Vrishnis.

In the *Mahabharata* as a whole, excluding the *Gita*, we only have glimpses of Krishna's divinity; his nature as clan leader comes mainly to the fore, but never really to the extent of his being a major figure in the epic. He was certainly one who favoured war, emerging more as a chief than a god. It is with the *Gita* that we are presented with the full flowering of a Bhagavata devotional cult, possibly of the Vasudeva tradition, that was eventually to become the central component of Vaishnavism.[20] The Vasudeva religion was a cult of the sun. Vishnu, a minor god in the Vedic period, is also connected with the sun, and it is he that rises to prominence in later Hinduism and of whom Krishna is said to be an incarnation, an *avatara*, according to Vaishnava tradition. But Vishnu does not feature in a major way in the *Gita*, despite the theophany which we shall see in CHAPTER ELEVEN, and the *Gita* certainly precedes the developed Vaishnava traditions. The origins of the *Gita* are obscure, but it is relevant to ask: Was the *Gita* originally a text devoted to a particular sect? Krishna's name means "Dark",[21] which suggests that he may have been indigenous to India and not a descendant of the Aryan invaders of India who were fairer skinned. Such popularization of a local cult figure is exactly the sort of religious practice that must have been evident at village level, far removed from the lofty ritualism of the court and the elite *Brahmins*. And just as these cult figures were anthropomorphic manifestations of deity, Krishna, too, is exactly that, which brings divinity into an approachable character to which the populace can so much more easily relate. Krishna, then, more readily reflects the older strands of popular religion than the *Vedic* ritual of orthodox circles. But it is in the *Gita* that Krishna the man or cult deity becomes for the first time the supreme Brahman. In all, it is impossible to be certain about the origins of Krishna, and as Douglas Hill aptly warned "in truth the problems raised by the somewhat scanty evidence before us are so difficult of solution that it is only with the utmost diffidence that they can be approached".[22] While his origins may have been as a cultic hero, what is clear is that it is in the *Gita* that Krishna is raised to divine status that far surpasses any local cultic significance.

The dating of the *Gita* is dependent, too, on whether it is accepted as a valid part of the *Mahabharata* or a later insertion into the text. Those who take it as an addition may date it as late as the first century CE.[23] Given that the *Mahabharata* is the longest poem of all world literature, its composition took place over several hundred years, perhaps somewhere between 400 BCE or a little earlier, and the second century CE, though some claim there are parts that can be put as late as 400 CE.[24] Thus, the *Gita* was part of, or added to, the *Mahabharata* before the latter was completed. Certainly, the *Mahabharata* as a whole has emerged from a vast number of sources and contexts and the sequence of events reported by Sanjaya, as we saw above in the context of the setting of the *Gita*, does not provide a continuous narrative, especially with the death of Bhishma preceding the *Gita* and events preceding Bhishma's death placed after the *Gita*. While the *Gita* does not mention the doctrine of *avataras*, "descents" of the deity Vishnu to Earth, *per se*, Krishna is clearly portrayed as an "incarnation", God on Earth, and that might suggest it was inserted into the *Mahabharata* before the close of the second century BCE,[25] or perhaps earlier, somewhere in the third century BCE. Will Johnson makes the very pertinent point concerning the *Mahabharata*: "Like a snowball, the epic picked up and incorporated all the important religious, philosophical, and social changes through which it passed, often juxtaposing layers with little or no attempt at reconciliation."[26] The inclusion of the *Bhagavad Gita* was probably part of this complex process and it would have to be admitted that a long, virtual monologue, from Krishna when battle has commenced or is about to commence, is a most inappropriate inclusion. Even the teaching of Krishna in the *Gita* is contradicted in other parts of the *Mahabharata*. Its dating, then, and the identity and origins of Krishna Vasudeva must remain elusive.

Authorship

The author of the *Gita* is completely unknown, though legend has it that it was the sage Vyasa who wrote it along with the *Mahabharata*. There have been attempts, particularly by German scholars, to impose a documentary analysis on the text that seeks to identify different strands, an original text, and extraneous grafts on it, but that is not in any way my purpose in presenting this text. In the absence of any conclusive evidence as to authorship, it seems to me best to treat the *Gita* as it stands, letting the text speak for itself, bearing in mind that for some it is a composite rather than unitary text. Such has been the approach of a number of past scholars of the *Gita* such as Franklin Edgerton[27] and I see no reason to depart from it. However, the oral traditions that preceded some of it must have stretched back many centuries before its compilation.

Translators and commentators

Since the first translation of the *Gita* into English in 1785 by Charles Wilkins,[28] a senior merchant in the East India Company, there have been a plethora of others, some very academic, some mystical, some poetic, some with distinctive biases, and the reader would do well to bear in mind the words of Eric Sharpe when he says: "Any scripture may fall into anyone's hands and be read not in the light of its 'original' religious, liturgical, philosophical or social setting but against the background of entirely different sets of presuppositions."[29] The oldest extant text and commentary is that of Shankara's and, though he was a non-dualist who interpreted the *Gita* entirely from a point of view of the inner Self being totally identifiable with Brahman and the world and everything else as illusion, his work is sufficiently important for all commentators to refer to him, as will be the case in the commentary of this present work. His dates are 788–820 CE. The Sanskrit text that Shankara used for his commentary is that still used today. It has become the standard text and was edited by S. K. Belvalkar as volume 7 of the *Mahabharata*.[30] While Shankara's commentary is the earliest extant one, it clearly points to the fact that there were earlier commentaries than his.[31]

Later, other famous thinkers from various schools of philosophy interpreted the *Gita* in the light of their own theories. Ramanuja in the eleventh century CE brought a devotional reality to the *Gita* in his *Vishishtadvaita Vedanta*, qualified non-dualism, by which the divine was not devoid of attributes or conscious will and this permitted worship of a *personal* God. Still later, Madhva (1199–1276) went further in being more wholly dualist with his *Dvaita Vedanta*. Madhva's dualist school is so called because he posited a totally dual and separate nature between souls and Brahman and between the world and God. While space does not permit inclusion of Madhva's interpretation of the *Gita* alongside those of Shankara and Ramanuja, it is easy to see here in his total separating of God and soul how different his commentary on the *Gita* would be. Like Ramanuja, however, the path of devotion was deemed by Madhva to be the means to liberation. Suffice it to say that these often radically different interpretations of the *Gita* are not only confined to the past but exist in recent and ongoing translations and commentaries. I have travelled the pages of the *Gita* with an open mind, but of one thing I am certain: those who find the *Gita* favours one or another path to liberation will too readily find that favoured path contradicted by another in the text.

The early commentators belonged to specific schools of philosophical thought, and it depended on their concept of God, the way in which the self and the world could be related to God, and the nature of the self and the world, as to how the *Gita* was interpreted. Both Shankara and Ramanuja, themselves indebted to previous proponents, were staunch supporters of the *Vedanta*, but while both of them were engaged with orthodox beliefs and relied on the *Vedanta* to support those beliefs and the way in which they interpreted the *Gita*, they drew on different *Vedantic* texts or interpreted those texts in their own way. It was the concept of God, in particular, that informed their views. Since both their views will be incorporated into the commentary on the *Gita* that follows this introduction, it is worth pausing here to note, briefly, their different fundamental views.

Shankara was the founder of the school of Advaita Vedanta, interpreting the *Vedanta* as *advaita*, non-dual, and therefore one: everything is totally unified in identity. His concept of God was of a totally transcendent Absolute about which nothing could be said. Brahman, for the Shankara schools is without attributes, *nirguna*. Brahman was the only possible Reality in Shankara's view, so the world and the empirical self are but illusions, like mirages: only Brahman and the inner true Self, the *atman* that is identical with Brahman, can be real. The only way such a transcendent Absolute can be known is through intuitive knowledge by an inner Self that *is*, also, Brahman. Thus, the concept of God informed the nature of liberation from the endless cycle of rebirths, too. For Shankara, the illusory world is lost, and one *becomes* Brahman. To him, knowledge of the true Self is the key to identity with Brahman, and the path of knowledge, *jnana-marga*, is the means, totally devoid of any action. Shankara believed that *all* actions produced results and results meant fruitive *karma* that necessitated rebirth. The only possible way to overcome this was to abandon *all* action. Many of the *Upanishads* emphasized this same identity of the *atman* with Brahman,[32] and the importance of knowledge as a means to realize it.

Ramanuja's concept of Brahman, on the contrary, was of a God with attributes, *saguna*, and there are many times in his commentary on the *Gita* when he indulged in lengthy extolling of the wonderful attributes of such a God. Indeed, the *nirguna* Brahman is absent from his work. While he wrote many works on the *Vedanta*, and accepted the unity of Brahman and the Self, that unity was a qualified one – similarity and likeness, but not identity. Importantly, souls and the world are totally dependent on God. The same qualified unity existed for Ramanuja between the world and God, so he accepted nothing of the illusory nature of the world as did Shankara. The problem of involving God too closely with the world is all too obvious with the question of evil and suffering. But Ramanuja placed evil in the hands of humanity and its boundless *karma* from previous lives. Ramanuja's qualified monism is really qualified unity. That is to say, there is unity between God and selves and between God and the world, but God is greater than both. Ramanuja saw selves and the world as the *body* of God, and just as the body and the world are usually deemed to be inferior to the soul, so souls and the world as the body of God are inferior to God, though united with him like the ordinary body is with the human soul. Such qualified monism enables the ordinary self and even the liberated Self to experience blissful communion with God as a loving and glorious Supreme Person who can be praised and glorified.

Since Ramanuja's view of God was a theistic one, it is the path of devotion, *bhakti-marga*, as well as actions without seeking rewards, *karma-yoga*, that are the means to God. While devotion to God is the paramount means to attain union with the divine, Ramanuja believed that activity could not be abandoned, whether this is for simple maintenance of the body or for adhering to the prescribed rituals of the *Vedas*. Such *karma-yoga*, Ramanuja believed, would bring its own knowledge of the true Self as dependent on God and as the body of God without the practice of *jnana-yoga*, the path of knowledge *per se*. Shankara saw all Selves as identical and as identical with Brahman, whereas Ramanuja believed in a plurality of Selves each with the attributes of knowledge and consciousness and each a part, or *amsha*, of God and absolutely dependent on God. Such dependence on God is the key relationship between the Self and the divine and all are his parts, even the *Shudras*, the lowest class of servants, and women: Ramanuja's comments on the *Gita* suggest that he believed the path of devotion to be inclusive of all. Shankara saw the world as illusion and only the Self as real. Ramanuja did not by any means deny the reality of the world, and though it was a changeable and transient entity, in understanding it to be the "body" of God, it was real, in the same way that the body is the changeable and intransient aspect of the unchangeable and permanent human Self. So Shankara focused on the *nirguna*, indescribable Brahman and Ramanuja on the *saguna* Brahman with qualities. Their translations of, and commentaries on, the *Gita* will reflect these distinct views. But as to the *Gita* itself, it has both views of Brahman as *nirguna* and *saguna* but leans, if anything, towards the theism of Ramanuja rather than the monism of Shankara. However, the *Gita's* theism is fluid and not exclusive of other pathways. Ramanuja's theism is a closed, exclusive one, and pertinent to a specific philosophical school of thought to which he has to force the *Gita* to conform.

One important doctrine of Vishishtadvaita is the notion of surrender, *prapatti*, to God. However, Ramanuja does not use the term because it was mainly a development of later proponents of his school. Nevertheless, we shall find it implicit in many of his comments and it seems as if he understood *bhakti*, loving-devotion, as including it. Such surrender is concomitant with the grace of God, the idea that the individual has, ultimately, to rely on God for final salvation.

Apart from the great commentators like Shankara, Ramanuja and Madhva well back in time, there are many translations from the past and from modern times that have informed this present work. In the main, I have used the traditional commentators, but I have also added occasionally the comments of the more esoteric interpreters, most of whom derive from a particular school of thought and interpret the text in the light of that school. Thus, occasionally, I have included remarks of commentators like Sri Krishna Prem (1889–1965), a devout Vaishnava, as well as the late Maharishi Mahesh Yogi, the founder of Transcendental Meditation in the West. Prem's interpretation of the *Gita* is thoroughly symbolic and the interested reader would do well to read his "Prolegomena: The General Setting", which introduces his commentary,[33] though a symbolic interpretation is not generally an aim of my own commentary. Maharishi is a good example of an individual who was steeped in the non-dual tradition of *Vedanta*, but who could relate that to western existentialism. Trevor Leggett's *Realization of the Supreme Self*[34] is an example of the use of the *Gita* as a text for *yoga* praxis, while Alan Jacobs' *The Bhagavad Gita* is what he calls a "transcreation" rather than a translation, which makes use of, in his words, "contemporary free verse" and "expansion of metaphors".[35] The result here is a very poetic rendering with parts of great beauty (though Jacobs admits "over the top"[36]), with commentary following in the tradition of Ramana Maharshi.

It is no surprise, then, that the interpretations of the *Gita* can be legion. Mohandas Gandhi (1869–1948), for example, influenced by the Theosophists who praised and supported Indian culture and nationalism, first read the *Gita* in English translation in 1898,[37] and emphasized the doctrine of non-violence in his commentary and the transcendence of each individual over anger, passion and hatred. The only way in which he could reconcile the context of the text being at the cusp of a fratricidal war was to interpret it symbolically, as a battle within the self, as did the Theosophists. And there is some measure in seeing the text in this light in CHAPTER THIRTEEN, for example. Eknath Easwaran took a similar symbolic view of the text. While Gandhi was a political activist, his methods were wholly non-violent unlike the activism advocated by Bal Gangadhar Tilak (1856–1920), who saw the text – his "spiritual dictionary" as he called it – as a support for aggressive political activism and its concomitant militant nationalism. He wrote a commentary on the *Gita* during a six-year imprisonment in Burma, taking up the stance of action, *karma-yoga*, in the *Gita* to support his political aims.

Indeed, many political activists were keen to interpret the *Gita* in the same way, seeing selfless actions as the means by which India could rise against political domination by the British on the one hand and solve many of India's social problems on the other. The key word from the *Gita* in this context is *loka-sangraha*, "welfare of (or involvement in) the world". Nevertheless, it is a word that only occurs twice in the *Gita* (3:20, 25). Satya Agarwal has devoted a generally sound work that analyses the way in which some of India's well-known nineteenth- and twentieth-century political figures interpreted and worked for *loka-sangraha*. Agarwal considers it to be the social ideal of the *Gita*, and it is the *karma-yoga* path – the path of egoless actions – that he and the political proponents before him consider the true meaning of the *Gita*.[38] Many of these earlier activists and their causes are now well known – Rammohun Roy's campaign for the abolition of *suttee*, by which a widow was burned on her husband's funeral pyre, and for education; Swami Vivekananda's call for education and lessening of the divide between rich and poor and the abolition of class distinction; Bal Gangadhar Tilak's work in the later nineteenth century for Indian nationalism and his unselfish work for society – these were protagonists that used the message of the *Gita* essentially as a *yoga* of action, *karma-yoga*. An expression not found in the *Gita*, *nishkama-karma*, "selfless action", is with some justification one key to understanding the *Gita*, and all these activists combined the concept with *loka-sangraha*. Linking the *Gita* with Indian political struggle and social reform did much to popularize it throughout India and, indeed, the term *loka-sangraha* was innovative in the thought of the *Gita*, the concept not being evident in the *Vedanta*.

Commentaries came forth, too, from the *advaitist* Swami Sivananda Sarasvati (1887–1963), who set up an *ashram* in Rishikesh at the foot of the Himalayas, and Swami A. C. Bhaktivedanta's (1896–1977) translation and commentary on the *Gita*, *Bhagavadgita As It Is*, is well known in the West, along with the International Society for Krishna Consciousness that he established. Aurobindo Ghose (1872–1950) was also the instigator of an *ashram* in southeast India at Pondicherry. He, too, wrote a commentary on the *Gita* and interpreted the text from a much more spiritual and devotional viewpoint, as we shall see, though at the same time, his earlier views were not separated from Indian nationalism and extremist political activism. Aurobindo internalized the *Yoga* of the *Gita*, emphasizing that once reaching the highest spiritual plane, the *yogin* should return to worldly life for selfless activity in society – a thought not unlike the Mahayana Buddhist *bodhisattva* ideal. For Aurobindo, there was a universalist teaching in the *Gita*. He wrote: "The language of the Gita, the structure of thought, the combination and balancing of ideas belong neither to the temper of a sectarian teacher nor to the spirit of a rigorous analytical dialectics cutting off one angle of truth to exclude all the others; but rather there is a wide, undulating, encircling mind and a rich synthetic experience."[39] Aurobindo interpreted the *Gita* as divine action, lifting the text away from *loka-sangraha* to action done not for society, but for God. Aurobindo's commentary on the *Gita* is a valuable one for its theistic spirituality and lofty thought.

Such, too, is the nature of Sarvepalli Radhakrishnan's (1988–1975) translation and commentary. Although somewhat "Christianized" at times, and certainly apologetic as well as idealistic, his commentary supplies a symbolic interpretation of the *Gita* and an openness of interpretation that does not specify a particular pathway in the text. His belief that different religious paths resulted in the same goal informs much of his commentary, but his perception is mainly *advaitist* in line with much of the *Vedanta*. He accepted higher and lower levels of reality which, at times, the *Gita* certainly supports. Douglas Hill's translation and commentary, originally published in 1928, is a good example of a more balanced commentary to which I shall refer from time to time. Edwin Arnold's poetical translation of the *Bhagavad Gita* at the end of the nineteenth century has been much praised by scholars for its beauty and because it captures the spirit of the text so well in translation. It was this translation that was read by Gandhi. Franklin Edgerton felt it sufficiently important to include Arnold's entire translation alongside his own, and Radhakrishnan also used it as the text for his own commentary. Full bibliographical details of these sources, where relevant, will be found in the *Further Reading* section at the end of this book.

Many translators, commentators and interpreters of the *Gita* have found within its script a central message, a "great saying", "great statement" or *maha-vakya*. Gandhi's, for example, was the whole section of the last twenty verses in CHAPTER TWO. Others chose individual verses as their key to the text and wrote their interpretation around it. Or, they selected a theme, like Tilak's *karma-yoga* on which to pin their thoughts.[40] But there is no one *maha-vakya* in the *Gita* as far as I can discover, and it might be said that there are many. Thus, I have no central concept around which to spin a thesis: I travel with an open mind. My doctoral research many years ago was in the field of Semitic languages and I was fortunate to have an eminent Assyriologist, Alan Millard, as my tutor. He encouraged me to work solely from the primary texts and inscriptions and only after lengthy study, and letting the textual evidence speak for itself, was I advised to peruse other sources. The same approach is mostly undertaken here and I have attempted to present and comment on the *Gita* with an open mind, though with many years of experience of teaching and writing about Hinduism, especially concerning its philosophy and metaphysics. It is hoped that no bias is to be found in the pages that follow.

The present text is an attempt to create a balance between strict academic rendering and a readable (and enjoyable) text. The primary aim of this work is to present aspects of Hinduism through the exploration of the *Gita*. Too often, students who are not Sanskritists are exposed to the historical, philosophical, anthropological, philosophical, social and religious aspects of the diversity of Hinduism without really getting to grips with the beauty of texts. It was for this reason that I introduced a purely textual course to my students long ago. However, finding an appropriate text and commentary on the *Gita* that was not over academic, riddled with Sanskrit grammar, or at the other extreme, not esoteric (if attractive, poetic and beautiful) and pertaining to a particular school of thought, proved difficult, and it was this fact that prompted me to write a text and commentary that suited the student of Hinduism. Nevertheless, the great works of Shankara, Ramanuja and the older translations of such as Franklin Edgerton, Robert Charles Zaehner, Kees W. Bolle, J. A. B. van Buitenen and W. Douglas P. Hill, have been invaluable help for preparation of both text and commentary. Again, details of these and more recent translations and commentaries are given in the *Further Reading* at the end of this book.

The complexities of translating the Sanskrit text of the *Bhagavad Gita* are numerous, not least because a single Sanskrit word can bear many different meanings with far wider meaning than can possibly be conveyed by an English translation. A word like *dharma*, for example, can mean much more than "duty", "law" or "righteousness". Bearing this in mind, I have retained Sanskrit terms that I think are seminal wherever possible, though hopefully not burdensomely so. Terms like *karma* have passed into modern usage, but it is hoped that the reader will become accustomed to many others and appreciate the depth of the meaning that cannot always be encapsulated in translation. While one Sanskrit word can have many meanings, I have tried to keep translations of Sanskrit terms as homogeneous as possible. To aid the reader, and for clarity, I have hyphenated Sanskrit compound words as much as possible; thus, *jnana-kanda* rather than *jnanakanda*, though not for names like *Mahabharata* (which seems odd when divided). I thought long and hard about whether to use diacritical marks in the Romanization of the Sanskrit, the advantages being that their use is so much more academic and so much more indicative of correct pronunciation. But for the ordinary reader, or the student who is studying Hinduism without knowledge of Sanskrit, they can be burdensome and have no meaning at all, and students these days rarely wish to plough through introductory notes on the equivalents in English transliteration. While it is with some regret that I have excluded diacritical marks for the present text, I have, nevertheless, added the diacritical marks where relevant after each entry in the *Glossary and Index of Sanskrit Terms* at the end of the book. My aim has been to favour simplicity for the reader and not to expect too much prior knowledge of the complexities of Hindu thought or Sanskrit phonetics.

I have tried to keep the text as close to the Sanskrit as possible, but not so much as to leave it obscure and unintelligible. While the Sanskrit itself is mostly written in *shlokas*, four lines, each of eight syllables, a simple form of poetic verse known as the *anushtubh shloka*, and occasionally in a longer metre (the *trishtubh*) of four lines each with eleven syllables to emphasize important teaching, it is difficult to present the text in such a form, and I have not done so, though there are translators who have.[41] Both Krishna and Arjuna are given many different names throughout the *Gita*. I have decided to retain these, commenting on each at the first citation but not thereafter: a quick glance at the *Glossary and Index of Sanskrit Terms* will serve as a reminder for subsequent citations. Any attempt to avoid sex-

ism and include feminine pronouns does a disservice to the text. The *Gita* is gen-
derized and speaks only of the male: the *yogin* is never female. I have used such
words as "humanity" in the commentary simply to make the text more applicable
to present-day norms, but it would be perverse to alter the Sanskrit text, so that
retains the male emphasis.

Themes in the *Gita*

The nature of God

The ultimate Reality, the Source from which all emanates, the unchanging
Absolute, is termed *Brahman*. The word was originally associated with "prayer" or
"devotional utterance" in the *Vedas*, and the related word *Brahmanas* denotes the
commentaries that pertain to the sacred prayers and devotions of the priests in relation to Brahman. The word "Brahman" is a kind of philosophical shift in emphasis
from prayer or holy utterance, an internalizing of it, a reflection of the *power* behind
the efficacy of prayer and sacrificial devotion. Although it is a difficult word to pin
down, many suggest a derivation from the root *brh* "to burst forth", or "to grow,
increase",[42] reflecting, perhaps, the emanation of Brahman into the universe as the
Ground of all Being, and the unlimited nature of Brahman. Some suggest a meaning
"to be strong".[43] But whatever Brahman was or was not, the *Vedantic* view was that
It was mainly beyond the conceptions of human imagination. It was a Reality that
was indescribable, though able to be experienced in the deepest part of the self:
something in the depths of the ancient *Upanishadic* sages *knew* that it was the
highest expression of Reality. As the Cause and Source of the universe, Brahman is
both the active generator of all things and yet is also the passive and unmoved
Absolute. Pervading all, Brahman is yet unaffected by all and though the Source of
space and time, and of cause and effect, Brahman is beyond them. Such *Vedantic*
understanding of the indescribable *nirguna* Brahman is also accepted by the author
of the *Gita*. Being beyond the limitations of human conception, Brahman is a neuter
principle, an "It" or "That" rather than a "he" or "she". The term "God" is therefore inapplicable to Brahman in its *nirguna* formlessness. Brahman also transcends
the dualities and differentiation of existence. It is not this as opposed to that, light
as opposed to dark, good as opposed to evil, and so on. Brahman is *neti neti* "not
this, not this". The *Bhagavad Gita* will take up the full force of this *Vedantic* concept
of deity and in many places will use only negative terms to depict Brahman –
unmanifest, unborn, incomprehensible and so on.

But the *Upanishads* were not solely concerned with a totally transcendent
Absolute, for as a creative power, Brahman is often depicted as *Ishvara*, "Lord", a
more personalized Brahman, leaving space for theistic devotion, devotion to a
personal God as the controller and sustainer of the universe. The *Gita* also focuses
on this *saguna* aspect of Brahman – Brahman with qualities that is also a feature of
later *Upanishads* such as the *Katha*, the *Isha*, the *Shvetashvatara* and the *Mundaka*,

which particularly incorporate concepts of a personal, omnipotent and omniscient God. While synthesizing these two aspects of deity, the *Gita* projects Brahman without attributes as greater than all, as the ultimate Cause that exists when everything else does not. It is a distinctly panentheistic conception of deity, whereby aspects of an Absolute pervade the world so permitting theistic devotion, but that Absolute always remains greater than the entire cosmos. Everything is contained in God but God is greater than all things. Nevertheless, the *Gita* blurs the distinction between the impersonal and personal so that the term Brahman can occasionally refer to either. Such a characteristic has a tendency to amalgamate the two *Vedantic* conceptions of God, combining both – Krishna as supreme God in a totally manifest form with Brahman as the supreme Unmanifest. Even so, we never find Krishna saying "I am Brahman", though he does assign to himself the *Vedantic* negative expressions of the *nirguna* and positive qualities of the *saguna* Brahman on many occasions, synthesizing both.

Thus, typical of a synthesizing nature of the *Gita*, the nature of God is seen as the totally transcendent Absolute of the more mystical parts of the *Upanishads* – an Absolute to which nothing can be ascribed and of which nothing can be said – as well as being the deity that is manifest as the world and in the world, and also manifest in human form as Krishna. Many times, the *Gita* will focus on all three, seeing no contradiction whatever in there being different aspects of the One or THAT which is beyond the One. Since Krishna is a "descent", an incarnation, then it stands to reason that it is the personal God that is the main focus. But the God that pervades the *Gita* is at least threefold. First, at its ultimate, it is Brahman that is without any attributes, that is no-thing, inconceivable and indescribable. Secondly, that absolute Brahman is also present in the manifest world that is the expression of Brahman, its creation and manifestation. In later tradition, there is a further manifestation as Vishnu, a deity with visible attributes as far as the divine world is concerned, attributes that the main character of the *Gita*, Arjuna, is permitted to see – though overt identity of Krishna and Vishnu is not yet fully developed in the *Gita*. It is by Vishnu that the universe is pervaded and controlled. And, last, there is Krishna, the manifestation of Brahman on Earth, descending in mortal form in order to correct the imbalance of evil over good. Importantly, all four aspects exist *at one and the same time*. Krishna is at once Vishnu, the Brahman with qualities (*saguna*) and the Brahman without any qualities at all (*nirguna*) and this he will make clear to Arjuna in the text, though, as previously noted, it would have to be said that the distinction between the *nirguna* and *saguna* aspects are often blurred. But if there is one aspect that perhaps transcends others, it is the concept of the *personal* God, the God to whom devotion can be offered, the God who loves his devotee. In the personal God, the *Gita* unites the indescribable with the devotional and the cosmic with the personal, but at the same time, does not deny pathways that incorporate different conceptions of God.

In the *Gita*, Brahman is referred to by a number of different names, *Param-Atman*, "Supreme Self", *Purushottama*, "Supreme Purusha", and *Ishvara*, "Lord", all generally attributable to the *saguna* Brahman that is Krishna, the manifest

Brahman. It is in the concept of *avataras*, literally, "descents" of the divine, that theism and devotionalism can find their most potent expression. While some *avataras* are non-human, Krishna is one of them in human form. However, the *Gita* does not mention the term *avatara* at all, and it is likely that we are witnessing only the beginnings of the concept in the text. Even in general, the idea does not feature prominently at all in the *Gita*, which would be surprising had it been a well-accepted doctrine at the time the *Gita* was written.[44] While the *Mahabharata* does mention some of the non-human descents, their identification with Vishnu, the deity that descends, is not a feature, and the term *avatara* is not used there either. In the *Gita*, we are witnessing the embryonic form of the full Vaishnava doctrine, with a rationale for it in 4:5–8, but no tangible link with Vishnu, mainly because the final identification of Krishna and Vishnu had not yet been forged.

As God in human form, Krishna has a full earthly history and character to which to relate. In later, devotional Vaishnavism, some worship Krishna as a baby, others as the young lover that calls the soul to him, yet others as the supreme Lord, but it is only in this last nature that he is found in the *Gita*. The major reason for such descents of the divine is the imbalance of good and evil in the world – such an imbalance being thoroughly overt in the *Mahabharata*. In later Vaishnavism, it is the deity Vishnu, the Great Preserver, who is the one deity that descends to Earth, along with his feminine counterpart, his feminine power or *shakti*. This feminine aspect does not feature in the *Gita* at all, which pre-dates, for example, later tales of Krishna and his association with the cowherdess, Radha. These descents of the divine are the immanence of God *par excellence*. In the descent, we have an overt synthesis of God and human, of divine eternity with manifest time, of God as subject and humanity and the world as object, and of spirit with material existence. That union is always present; it is just made more explicit through the concept of God in human form.

Since the *Gita* stresses devotion as a means to God and a means to final release from the confines of a perpetual round of births and deaths, God must always remain *personal* for the emancipated one but I do not think we have to project such a personal God beyond the totally transcendent Brahman: the two aspects of deity, the personal and the transcendent, are not mutually exclusive and without total identity with Brahman – which, it seems to me, the *Gita* does not suggest – there must be aspects of divinity that are beyond the devotee even at liberation. What is clear is that the *Gita's* concept of God is a lofty one. The Krishna of the *Gita* is a personal God of immense depth and metaphysical heights, quite the opposite of the portrayal of Krishna's character in the *Mahabharata*. The highest metaphysical concept of deity in the Hindu tradition up to the time of the *Gita* had been the *nirguna*, incomprehensible Brahman, the THAT, about which nothing could be explained, except to posit it as the unmanifest Source of all that is manifest, even of the dissolved unmanifest phases of the universe. There are some commentators, however, who do see the personal God, Krishna, as beyond even this *nirguna* Brahman. I do not want to presuppose what the text might want to say or not say on this point, or to what extent, and will leave further discussion of it until the relevant verses of the text – in the main, 10:12, 14:27 and 15:8. Here, it is important to understand how Brahman, whether *nirguna* or *saguna* relates to the self.

The nature of the self: *atman*

Atman, initially, is the word for "self". It is likely to be derived from the root *an* "to breathe" and, by extension therefore, suggestive of the breath of life that animates human beings.[45] But apart from being the general animated self, the *atman* is also the soul, what Radhakrishnan depicted as "what remains when everything that is not the self is eliminated",[46] and we begin to see it used thus in the *Atharva Veda*. Since breath is the essential element of life – the *essence* of life without which human beings cannot exist – there came about in *Upanishadic* thought the concept of *atman* as the *essence* of the self, the fundamental and *real* part of the self that underpinned the personality. Thus a transfer from breath to essence took place in the usage of the word. And the *atman* in this sense of the true essence of the individual was believed to be separate in some way from the personality self. It is the latter that becomes egoistically bound to the dualities of existence – this as opposed to that, happiness as opposed to sorrow, wealth as opposed to poverty, and so on. The *atman* is the *still* part of the self, the deepest part of the self that transcends the phenomenal world, and is the eternal soul of each person. Concomitant with this conception of the *atman* as the fundamental real essence of the self was for some the comparative unreality of the transient world in which we live, an unreality that, much later, was sometimes pressed as far as sheer illusion as in the *advaita* of Shankara.

Thus the *atman*, while interpreted differently in the various philosophical schools, came to be thought of as the permanent aspect of the self, a concept thoroughly accepted by the author of the *Gita*. To realize this ultimate Self, to experience the reality of it, became the goal. And this experience would transform the egoistic self into one devoid of the usual conceptions of "I" and "mine", for the *atman* is pure and unconnected with the transient processes of life. It is the *atman* that became conceived of as the substratum of all real knowledge about the world and, as the ultimate real aspect of the self, needed no validation for its existence.

Brahman-*atman*

The particular brilliancy of the *Upanishads* was the synthesis of Brahman and *atman*. It was a fairly logical conception in that, if Brahman is the unchanging and permanent but indescribable absolute Reality that underpins all existence, and the *atman* is the fundamental, real and permanent part of the self, then they are conjoined by their particular reality and permanence. Since all in the universe was believed to have emanated from Brahman, then at least the fundamental essence of all things must be equated either wholly or partially with Brahman. Once *atman* had shifted its meaning to "essence" then not only human beings, but also all things in existence, animate and inanimate, were believed to contain this same essence that is Brahman. And, since all things have the same Source, the *same* essence that is

Brahman informs all things, so at the deepest levels of life there is a fundamental and permanent Reality that runs through all things – *atman*, which is Brahman. This, indeed, is the monism so typical of *Upanishadic* thought, by which all is one and each entity in the universe is identical to Brahman.

It is this equation of *atman* = Brahman which was the gem at the heart of *Upanishadic* thought, and which really provided the answer to so many of the philosophical questions that a search for Reality and Truth had engendered. The sages had at last emerged from the unreal to the real, from darkness to light and from death to immortality. Two different concepts had become synthesized in a unique way that would provide a basis for much philosophical thought in the centuries to follow, and provided, with some modifications, the core of much Hindu religious belief and certainly of the beliefs contained in the *Gita*. The microcosmic world of humankind had become intimately equated with the whole of the macrocosm because of the presence of the *atman* in all things. In the *Vedanta*, the inner self became projected out into cosmic identity and unity with all things as the permanent substratum of Reality equated with its divine Source. Each human being is thus identical to another, identical to the cosmos and identical to Brahman. The *Gita* accepts such unity of the *atman* on the microcosmic level, but does not support identity with Brahman. Because its God is personal, identity with God would remove any possible devotional relationship. In any case, as Edgerton rather pointedly stated, the *Upanishads* might be able to claim "I am Brahman", where Brahman is a neuter principle, but "I am God" is a more difficult statement that the author of the *Gita* does not court.[47]

Just as the *nirguna* Brahman is indescribable and beyond human conception so the *atman* is also beyond any empirical analysis: it, too, is indescribable and can only be experienced by the kind of deep, intuitive knowledge that penetrates to the hidden Reality in the depths of the self. Of the many parts of the *Upanishads* that express this identity of *atman* and Brahman it is the expression *Tat tvam asi*, "That you are", of the *Chandogya Upanishad* that epitomizes identity. Indeed, Halbfass refers to this specific text as "one of the most seminal texts in the history of Indian thought".[48] But the *Gita* does not posit a monistic viewpoint. Its perspective of deity is a tiered one with the different dimensions of the divine noted above, one of which totally transcends the *atman* and the created universe. However, it *does* accept the *Vedantic* view that the dualities of existence are inimical to experience of the true Self, and at many points expresses how important it is to go beyond the pairs of opposites. But while steeped in *Vedantic* tradition of a totally transcendent Brahman, it is also on the dualistic and theistic teachings of the *Vedanta* that the *Gita* relies. The Self is a manifestation of God but is not ultimately God.

The empirical self

The self that we know in life is not the *atman*. The self that we know is the egoistic personality that operates in the world from the self-consciousness of individual psyche. Our view of the world is based on our likes and dislikes, our positive and negative responses to our environment, our aims, drives, genetic make-up and inter-action with others and the world at large. The sum total of our personality to date is termed the *jivatman* or simply *jiva*. "that which breathes", from the root *jiv* "to breathe".[49] At its basic, the *jiva* is simply the living being that is an individual, but it becomes the biological, psychological and social self that enjoys, suffers, acts, thinks, breathes, makes choices between this and that, and is subject to the expe-riences mediated by the five senses – all in contrast to the pure *atman* that is the still, non-active, subtle and real Self. It is this *jivatman* that is subject to reincarna-tion, a concept accepted by most Indian thought. Richard Gotshalk, rather aptly, terms the *jiva* the "shadow" of the *atman*.[50] Reincarnation, or *samsara*, occurs because the *jivatman* accumulates both positive and negative *karma* as a result of its actions in mind, speech and body, but it is capable of being free of both and of becoming just the *atman*.[51]

Each individual then is, as Sharma puts it, "a mixture of the real and the unreal, a knot of the existent and the non-existent, a coupling of the true and the false".[52] And it is mainly to the false and unreal world that the *jivatman* leans, and not to the subtle, eternal, real Self within. The only way that the *atman* in life can be expe-rienced is by transcending the "other" egoistic self, and by transcending the dualities of life to experience the unity behind it. The inimical inhibitors of this are desire and aversion – our negative and positive responses to the multitude of stimuli in life – and the egoistic self that they create. The *Brihadaranyaka Upanishad* emphasized desire as the indicator of a being's resolve, action and resulting fate (4:4:5), as well as the need to overcome desire (4. 4. 6 and 4. 3. 22). It is a theme that the *Gita* develops time and time again. What causes the *atman* to be obscured like layers of dust on a mirror is the ego. And what creates ego are the responses we make to all the stimuli in life, desiring one thing and rejecting another, whether that be physical objects or mental thoughts. It is a search for rewards of actions through an egoistic response to stimuli that creates the kind of personal *karma* that must bear fruit in the future – hence the necessity for reincarnation. So if the ego can be lost, all that is left is the pure Self, *atman*. For this to happen, the individual has to be less involved with the dualities of the phenomenal world, and overcome desires, as well as the wish for the end product of those desires.

So there are two aspects of the self, the *jiva* that is caught up in matter and that itself is the combination of a changeable and transient material body with an equally changeable and transient material mind, ego and intellect. The other is the *atman*, the permanent and unchanging pure spirit. Combined, they make up the *jivatman*, the individual being; neither *jiva* nor *atman* can ever exist without Brahman. The understanding of all aspects of body and mind as matter and *atman* as spirit and both as aspects of Brahman, is what the *Gita* teaches. The real Self is still and passive, of the nature of consciousness, and is pure spirit: the closest material component to it is the intellect, the *buddhi*. Purification of the intellect will allow the real Self to be revealed, but the natural path for the intellect is in the opposite direction, towards the data that fill the mind from the senses and to responses to that data. Thus, the true Self is lost, overshadowed by matter.

The true Self is consciousness and lends its consciousness to the actions of the psychosomatic self. The *Gita* does not say that actions should be avoided, only that they should be based in that consciousness of the Self. Only then will there be the separation of matter and spirit that allows engagement in the former without losing sight of the latter. Action is Self-based, not self-based. This is what the *Yoga* of the *Gita* is all about and is a very important point. Because the still, passive *atman* and matter are united in Brahman, the *atman* need never be dissociated from action. And this is a key message of the *Gita*. Action in the world is legitimized; it just has to be devoid of egoistic involvement in the outcomes of personal goals. Throughout the text I have used *Self* to refer to the *atman* as the still, passive, true, inner essence that is identified with the divine, and *self* to refer to the ordinary, empirical self in the usual sense of the word. Strictly speaking, *atman* can also be used of the ordinary self, but to avoid confusion I have retained it throughout as the spiritual Self.

The nature of the world

The fundamental quest of the *Upanishads* was for what is real in a world of change, transience and finitude. There is no doubt that Brahman as the Ground of all Being is ultimate Reality, but does this, then, negate the world itself as having any reality? I have touched on this idea above in that, if Brahman *is* the Ground of all Being, then what emanates forth from it – namely the universe – should have a degree of reality itself, like its Source. The concept of *atman* answers the question to some extent in that it is the subtle *essence* of all in existence, and this might lend to the unified essence of the universe a reality that is not necessarily as evident in the grosser aspects of all existence. But this is in danger of suggesting that the world is a partial emanation (as the subtle essence) of Brahman, while there is a whole aspect of the universe (the gross and physical) that is unconnected with Brahman. The *Upanishads*, however, would support this line of reasoning, so we have to suggest either that all physical phenomena *are* real, or, that they are illusionary, or, that they are a lesser reality. The last two propositions tend to compromise the monistic identity of all things favoured by many *Upanishads*, but it is that belief that is accepted by the *Gita*.

The relative reality of the world is answered in the *Gita* by the *nirguna* and *saguna* aspects of Brahman, the former being the unchanging, indescribable Reality, and the latter being the cause–effect process of the manifested Absolute. The world itself, then, becomes a blend of what is unmanifest (the *atman*) and what is manifest (the phenomenal world), a mixture of Being (Brahman) and non-being (the manifested world of Brahman that is subject to change). Individual egos, in this case, would reflect this same blend and could be said to be real, though the *atman* would be "super real". Thus, Radhakrishnan neatly stated that "the ego is a changing formation on the background of the Eternal Being",[53] which rather suggests a degree of reality for the changing, finite self as much as the changing finite world. So the incessant change and perpetual motion of the universe is the nature of matter that emanates from Brahman. This view of the many things in the world as real (pluralism) coupled with the idea that matter is real (realism) tended not to be prominent in the *Upanishads*, but is present in the *Gita*. Unity not pluralism in the cosmos was the main message of the *Upanishads*, and the contradiction that this poses in the face of the common sense view of the diversity of the world was not articulated to a sound conclusion in the *Vedanta*. The sages of the *Upanishads* were generally content to accept the world as real because it was an emanation of the divine, with its diversity underpinned by a more ultimate kind of reality. This tends to be the view taken by the author of the *Gita*.

So the world, indeed, the cosmos, is also the manifestation of the divine. It is matter, nature or *prakriti*, sometimes termed *maya*. This last term is variously translated, depending on the school of thought. Essentially, *maya*, from the Sanskrit root *ma*, "to form" or "to build", is the whole of matter with its interplay of causes and effects that stem from the manifest aspect of Brahman. It is the power of Brahman manifest in the cosmos and in the *Gita* it is real, manifest reality, but a lower reality than the higher pure spirit that is also Brahman in the world. Thus the world of the *Gita* is composed of the two interrelated realities of spirit and matter, and spirit is that which is permanent and beyond all the changes and transience of matter. Getting involved with matter and ignoring the spirit is what causes the disharmony of existence, the ignorance and misconceptions about the true nature of reality. Such ignorance, as far as the *Gita* is concerned, is delusion, *moha*, but not illusion as *advaitists* like Shankara believed. So the world as matter is not independent of God; it is his creation and is described in the *Gita* as Krishna's "lower" nature, indicative of its being a part of God, though his "higher" nature is beyond it (7:5).

Means to God

The *Gita* is replete with the message that there is a possibility for the individual self to rise to full communion with the divine, and nowhere is this more obvious than in the fact that the divine descends to the human level to make that ascent of the soul possible. Although the *Gita* hardly makes mention of the ego, it is the assertive self that is involved in every aspect of living with choices of action, thought and speech – all dictated by ego – that has to be transcended. The means of transcending the ego are threefold in the *Gita* – the path of knowledge, *jnana-marga*, the path of loving devotion, *bhakti-marga*, and the path of egoless action, *karma-marga*. However, it does not raise any one of these to a status that excludes the others, though the common denominator is always non-attachment to the results of actions. Each involves discipline and constant practice, *yoga*.

Jnana-marga

The *jnana-marga* is the path of knowledge, of wisdom and of a direct experience of Brahman as ultimate Reality. This path traditionally renounces both desires and actions since, as Radhakrishnan so aptly commented: "We cannot cure desires by fresh desires; we cannot cure action by more action".[54] The path is one of strict *yoga* and the *Gita* certainly extols its practitioner, the *jnanin*, as "exceedingly dear" to Krishna (7:17). But the *Gita* depicts it as a path that is only for the few, being steep and very difficult. *Jnana* is the path extolled by Sankhya Yoga, a developing system of beliefs that will inform much of the *Gita's* analysis of the world and, partially, of the inner Self, though at the same time with radical differences. The Sankhya view of knowledge as the means to liberation taught renunciation of *all* actions, and when the *Gita* refers to Sankhya it more than likely refers to this approach to gaining exclusive knowledge. But if the author of the *Gita* is tolerant of the path of pure knowledge, it is clear that *yoga* in the sense of disciplined *activity* is a superior path, even if they both achieve the same end, and that is because the *Yoga* of the *Gita* is active and not inactive and passive. Generally, *jnana-marga* is also particularly associated with the *Vedantic* non-dualist belief of the identity of the Self, the *atman*, with Brahman, and the means to Brahman are concentration and meditation with suspension of the senses to all except the inner *atman*. For those on the path of *jnana*, knowledge is the key to liberation because it is equated with Truth, with ultimate Reality, and so is the exclusive means of realizing the *atman* that is Brahman. The *Upanishads* certainly upheld knowledge as the means to perfection: to realize Brahman, one has to *know* Brahman, according to the *Mundaka Upanishad* (3:2:9) and the *Kaushitaki Upanishad* (1:4). Such knowledge is pure, true and beyond opposites like good and evil. Such a perception of knowledge is upheld by the author of the *Gita* and there are verses that iterate the point, particularly in CHAPTER FOUR (4:36, 37, 40, 41, 42).

Those who attach themselves to *gurus* for the purpose of acquiring knowledge search for a spiritual path of intuitive knowledge rather than knowledge of anything in the material world. It is the realization of wisdom that is the goal, that is to say, the inner, meditative and experiential cognition of the *atman* that is all important. Thus, Robert Zaehner described *jnana* as "the intuitive apperception of ultimate Reality beyond space and time".[55] Considering the intuitive nature of the knowledge that has to be acquired, it is meditation or *yoga* that provides the means. When the mind is pulled away from its attractions to the sense stimuli of the environment then it can become calm and still and receptive to the inner experience of direct knowledge that is independent of the senses. *Yoga* provides the techniques by which the mind and intellect can be stilled and made more receptive to the deeper kind of knowledge that is ultimate. Renunciation (*nyasa*) was particularly important and was (and still is) epitomized in the fourth stage of life, *sannyasa*. This stage stood in contrast to the path of ritual action of the earlier *Vedas* but did not necessarily mean a total world denial and cessation of activity. Chatterjee and Datta, among others, point out that the discipline of *yoga* and the principle of renunciation often encouraged the acquisition of positive traits that were in many ways world-affirming, for example the development of compassion and generosity.[56] The *Gita* certainly endorses such engaged *yoga* rather than total renunciation and its practice of austerities, *tapas*, as an exclusive means of developing the spiritual at the expense of the physical. Non-attachment of the ego to the stimuli of the world is the aim; this is denial of the self and not necessarily the denial of the world *per se*. It is detachment of the self as opposed to attachment of the self. Control of the self is easier when it is withdrawn from the world than when it is bombarded by the sense stimuli of daily existence. But the insistence on the observation of the four *ashramas*, the four stages of life – student, householder, recluse and *sannyasin* – suggests a general well-balanced view of both worldly and spiritual pursuits, and this is the *Gita*'s view, providing that *results* of actions are abandoned. The *Gita* has some antipathy to the path of *jnana* if it involves total withdrawal from, and renunciation of, the world, resulting in inactivity (*nivritti*). Instead, it teaches *jnana* that endorses renunciation of desires, of the fruits of actions, but advocates *activity* (*pravritti*), the opposite of renunciation of actions.

Bhakti-marga

The word *bhakti* comes from the Sanskrit root *bhaj*, "to serve" or "to worship" and means "loving-devotion". The *bhakti-marga* is very prominent in the *Gita*. It has wide appeal because it is not exclusive and is open to women and to all classes regardless of birth, providing the devotee takes refuge in Krishna (9:32). It must surely have gained ground in the local cults of popular religion where devotion to gods was felt to be appropriate to the needs of ordinary individuals. There is the crucial element in the *Gita* of God's *grace* being an aid on this devotional path providing here that the devotee offers to Krishna "single-minded *bhakti*" (11:54). CHAPTER TWELVE of the *Gita* is devoted to such *bhakti*, but notably, it does not state that the path of *jnana* is inferior; it simply states that it is more difficult (12:5). The devotion that is the feature of *bhakti* is of the nature of supreme love, of longing, surrender, trust and adoration; it involves the whole being and is not devoid of effort on the part of the devotee, so that it is always assisted by right knowledge. Essentially, there is a dual relationship between the devotee and the divine that is always retained, even when liberation is achieved. Indeed, for devotion to God to obtain, there can be no question of identity with God. Devotion implies an unequal status between devotee and God, the former as a part of God, sharing some of the nature of God but never wholly God. Faith, *shraddha*, is an important aspect of *bhakti* and a prerequisite of it, with total surrender of the self to God. Both *bhakti* and *shraddha* suggest a chosen object, an *ishta-devata*, a chosen God, with whom the devotee shares a close relationship of love and to whom that devotee is totally loyal. Such, indeed, is the relationship between Arjuna and Krishna.

Before the advent of the *Gita* there is little scriptural evidence of any powerful devotion to one God – a monotheism based on loving-devotion of the *bhakta* and a reciprocal love of God for his devotee. There must surely have been chosen deities at the popular level, and the *Gita* and Krishna may have reflected the growth of a popular devotional cult that, despite hints of devotional religion in some *Upanishads*, was quite different from the arid metaphysics of the bulk of the *Upanishads* and the nebulous, often non-personal nature of official *Vedic* deities. The

Gita, however, takes popular religion to great metaphysical heights, while retaining its popular and very visual God. This was a unique facet that spawned a powerful devotionalism, especially since it was a pathway open to all in society.

The theme of *bhakti* develops with increasing momentum as the *Gita* proceeds, especially from 6:30 on. Here was a doctrine of salvation and a salvific God, faith in whom could give hope for an end to the cycle of continued births and deaths. And this was not a God that was distant and remote but one that descended to live among humankind, one that offered hope to the lower classes and women; one to whom praise and offerings could be given and one who was believed to *respond* with love to his devotee. Whichever path is chosen in the goal of liberation, devotion facilitates that path, for Krishna enhances the attempt, providing the devotee is drawn wholly to him: there is a closer relationship between God and devotee in *bhakti*, one that does not obtain on the other paths. The teaching on *bhakti* in the *Bhagavad Gita* has been an inspiration to devotional Vaishnava Hinduism that hails Vishnu as the major deity and his *avatara*, his descent, as Krishna as the supreme God on whatever stage of that descent the devotee may wish to focus – Krishna as a baby, a youth, a lord, a lover that calls the soul to him, or a great, majestic God.

Karma-marga

The notion of cause and effect is an important one in Indian philosophical thought and it will be necessary to return to it continually. The law of cause and effect known as *karma* suggests that a person has to be reincarnated in order to reap the results – negative and positive – of the accumulation of all his or her actions in life. And since physical and mental actions are taking place in every waking moment of life, the effects that have to bear fruit necessitate countless lifetimes. So at death it is only the body that ceases to exist, while the subtle accumulated *karma* of one's existence in the present and past lives continues into the next. Each *jivatman*, then, creates for itself its specific personality in the next existence and the sorrows and joys that are the fruits of its actions in past existence(s).

Karman is "action", in the *Vedas*, the ritual action that propitiated the gods, from whom tangible results would obtain – wealth, fertility of the land, happiness, success in battle, progeny. The priestly class developed this basic conception of *karman* to a more cosmic level whereby precise and specialist sacrificial ritual offered to the Brahman, the great cosmic principle, ensured the continuation of creation and of the cosmos. Such ritual action will be mentioned many times in the *Gita*. However, *karma* is used in a number of senses in the *Gita* in addition to ritual action. It may simply denote action or activity, work or duty. But it also means action *and reaction*, cause and effect, that is to say action that is connected to a result, to a desire for a result, to a consequence of action, and it is in this sense that the results of actions accrue to an individual immediately, in the future or in future lives.

The path of *karma* in the *Gita* thoroughly upholds the necessity for action. But this action is not that of simply following scriptural injunctions. Rather, it is action that is undertaken without initial desire and, importantly, without a desire for results. This, the *Gita* terms "inaction in action and action in inaction" (4:18) and the whole concept of sacrifice, *yajna*, is widened to include all action that is undertaken with focus on God, what Radhakrishnan called "a making sacred to the Divine".[57] But like the *bhakti-marga*, the path of devotion, the *karma-marga*, too, involves wisdom, knowledge, in order to acquire the right perspective of what action should be. *Karma-yoga* takes the common-sense view that it is impossible to avoid acting in some way or another, simply because we are living beings. The *karma-yoga* of the *Gita* has two dimensions: *action should be done without a view to results* and *one should not be attached to the work*.

The *karma-yoga* of the *Gita* is not against knowledge, *jnana*, but is opposed to the path of knowledge that absolves the *yogin* from any action. Aurobindo believed that the path of *action* in the *Gita* harmonized action and complete inaction: "The Karma-yoga verses of the Gita create a ground for the reconciliation between the two extremes; the secret is not inaction as soon as one turns towards the higher truth, but desireless action both before and after it is reached."[58] *Karma-yoga* certainly has such an expanded view in the *Gita*, but its purpose, as *yoga* in general in the *Gita*, is always the transcendence of nature as matter, and the realization of spirit. It seems to me that it would be perverse to attempt to lessen the importance of *karma-yoga* in the *Gita*. No solution can occur for Arjuna, the warrior about to go to war, that does not include action: it is simply how the *Gita* presents such action and how it synthesizes it with *jnana*, knowledge, and *bhakti*, loving devotion, that is the issue to note throughout the text. Essentially, it is the concept of *nishkama-karma* – a term not used in the *Gita* – that we must watch for underlying the text. It is *desireless action* and of paramount importance for Arjuna. To desire is to want a result, an end, a goal, and it is abandoning this that is the true *Yoga* of the *Gita*.

The principle of *karma-yoga* as desireless action was taken up by many social reformers in nineteenth- and twentieth-century India. Renunciation that eschewed actions came to be regarded as inferior. Vivekananda is one pertinent example of a reformer "who hoped to mobilize the religious resources of Hinduism for the development of a new spirituality and the progress of Indian society", explains Ursula King. What happened, as King explains, was that: "The new interpretation of Vedanta as a religion of work and action, a 'practical Vedanta' praised the necessity and spiritual usefulness of work."[59] This is one of many examples of how *karma-yoga* has been taken forward into modern times, but as a "practical Vedanta", it has its roots firmly in the past.

Yoga

The word *yoga* is derived from the Sanskrit root *yuj*, "to bind together", "yoke", "harness". It has an *active* and *dynamic* sense, not a passive one. That is to say, one yokes or binds oneself to a task, a process, a goal. Such "yoking" in the *Gita* is a yoking to, or unifying with, the divine, and that can be meant in the ultimate sense of accomplishing liberation or in the disciplined process that would bring that goal about. In the *Gita*, the use of the term *yoga* is not confined to the systematic processes leading to the higher meditative stages of the later fully-developed system refined by Patanjali. Yet the *Gita* does include reference to some refined processes that pre-dated Patanjali. *Yoga* is a very ancient and possibly pre-Hindu practice judging by archaeological evidence from the Indus Valley.[60] While it is used in a variety of senses in the *Gita*, the *Yoga* of the *Gita* is crucial to the understanding of the text: indeed, as the colophons ending each chapter state, it is concerned with *Yoga Shastra*, the "Science" or "Knowledge of *Yoga*". The essential message is the *yoga* of the renunciation of the fruits of action, that is to say, of desire for results, goals, rewards – indeed, even if such results of actions are good. Whether *yoga* is the *yoga* of *jnana*, of *karma* or of *bhakti*, the same principle of abandoning the fruits of actions applies. While it is difficult to attain, *yoga* in this sense, is open to all, irrespective of class, caste or gender, but is particularly applicable to *bhakti* where action can be devoted to and through God and not for the self, though the *Gita* does not suggest that *bhakti* is the only path to liberation: action, *karma-yoga* is essential, but it needs to be complemented by knowledge, *jnana-yoga*. What is important is that *yoga* is consistently meant in an active sense. It is less withdrawal from the world as disciplined engagement within it.

While the *Yoga* of the *Gita* is certainly the *yoga* of action that is not attached to results, the term is diversified to encompass the *yoga* of knowledge, of action and of devotion. Each is capable of being a discipline in itself and is an independent pathway to liberation. It is here, more than anywhere, that sectarian bias adopts one path to the detriment of the others. But the *Gita* does not support a definitive preference throughout: it rather extols one *yoga* and then another, or complementary combinations. Perhaps that is why the *Gita-mahatmayas*, the verses glorifying the *Gita*, particularly in the *Puranas*, do not single out any one *yoga* or any sectarian ethos.[61] Aurobindo made the rather relevant point that "the yoga of the Gita is a large, flexible and many-sided system with various elements, which are all successfully harmonized by a sort of natural and living assimilation".[62] And at another point, Aurobindo said: "All Yoga is a seeking after the Divine, a turn towards union with the Eternal. According to the adequacy of our perception of the Divine and the Eternal will be the way of the seeking, the depth and fullness of the union and the integrality of the realisation."[63]

Moksha

To lose the egoistic perceptions of the world, the dualities which that perception engenders, and the desires that create the ego, were the goals of *Upanishadic* thought. It is a *liberation*, a *release*, from all that restricts, binds, and holds humans in ignorance. The term for such liberation is *moksha*. The early *Vedic* idea of liberation was that, at the end of one existence, the soul of the good would be recompensed in Heaven and the soul of the evil punished in a dark abode, a somewhat undeveloped Hell. The later *Upanishadic* idea of reincarnation is sometimes combined with this concept, so that an individual is believed to go on experiencing the results of *karmic* action accumulated in life in the context of some heavenly or hellish abode, only then to be reborn in order to reap the fruits of other positive and negative *karma*. The *Gita* accepts a similar idea in that good *karma* results in rebirth in the heavenly realms of the gods. But this is not liberation even for the gods; for when the good *karma* is exhausted, rebirth in the land of mortals ensues. It is no fruitive *karma* at all that brings release.

Liberation or *moksha* for much *Vedantic* thought was not something that can be "reached" or "acquired". Since the *atman* is already there as the fundamental essence of the self it is merely there to be experienced. But a certain amount of knowledge is necessary to reveal it, not, as we have seen, empirical knowledge, but deep, intuitive knowledge that is, like the *atman* itself, indescribable. The term *mukta* is used of one who has realized the *atman*, has become liberated and enlightened, but who is still contained by the physical body, still living. Such a person is egoless, does not act from the level of the "I", perceives the unity of all things, and does not differentiate between this and that to feed any egoistic desire. The *jivan-mukta*, then, is one liberated while alive; one freed from personality, freed from fruitive *karma*, freed from rebirth, *samsara*. The ignorance that characterized all the past lives is removed and its opposite of wisdom is experienced. But liberation does not mean that a *jivan-mukta* has to be divorced from the world. It simply means operating in the world in an egoless way. As the point at the centre of a circle is equidistant from all points on the circumference, so the *jivan-mukta* is equally poised between all dualities of life, observing all, actively engaged in all, but not from the level of desire of one thing more than another, or preference for this as opposed to that. Such a view of egolessly engaging in the world is what the *Gita* has to teach, for it is entirely against renunciation of all action *per se*.

While the perspective of *moksha* in the *Upanishads* was mainly of monistic identity with Brahman, there are times when the more dual and theistic perspectives of *moksha* are to be found, and it is a perspective with which the *Gita* again resonates with *Vedanta*. Here, there is a more intimate and personal relationship with the divine at *moksha*. Where a personal Brahman is accepted in the *Upanishads*, then monism is lost for a panentheistic view of the relationship of the world, and the individuals in it, to the divine. Despite the fact that Shankara interpreted the whole of the *Gita* as extolling the path of knowledge as the best means to *moksha*, and a total identity of the *atman* with Brahman, the *Gita* is overwhelmingly dualistic in its view of the relationship between the Self and God, though there are always hints at the impersonal Brahman also being the goal. The very fact that God has descended in human form is a catalyst for theistic, personal devotion that is not eroded at the point of liberation. The author of the *Gita* relies heavily on those *Upanishads* like the *Katha* and *Shvetashvatara* that depict the personal God, the *saguna* Brahman.

The *Gita* implies that liberation from the endless round of rebirths and of suffering in the world is brought about not by one path in particular but by their complementary, or even independent, nature. Knowledge is needed, desireless actions are also needed, and devotion to God. The overall message, however, is that it is essential to give up attachment to the fruits of actions, but not actions *per se*. But we should never lose sight of the pragmatic context of the *Gita*, and that is the dilemma of a warrior who is despondent at having to engage in a fratricidal war that is not of his own choosing. Knowledge will help to answer his dilemma, but ultimately he must *act*. Arvind Sharma makes this point when he says of apparent contradictions in the *Gita*: "They arise because Krsna uses as many points of view as he can to convince Arjuna to fight, and in such a situation these points of view may be contradictory. What is required is that they should all converge (on the issue at hand), not that they should merge."[64] Of course, such a view would depend on whether the focus of the author was on Krishna's teaching pegged onto Arjuna's dilemma, or *vice versa*. But as Sharma later states, the *Gita* not only presents one of the paths of *karma*, *jnana*, or *bhakti* as pre-eminent at different points, but may synthesize two at one point and another two elsewhere, or treat different ones as ancillary to a third only for the third to be itself ancillary at another part of the text.[65]

The colophons at the end of each chapter describe the *Gita* as a *shastra*, a teaching or science about *Yoga*: we cannot pin it down to one precise aspect of *yoga*, only accept that the *Gita* deals with many dimensions of it and leaves the individual to choose the best path. For Arjuna, that will surely be an active one that does not concentrate on the results of that action, through sacrificing action to Krishna. So there is no need for Arjuna to deny the world, but just to have the right knowledge about it, not to be attached to its transience or to what one wishes to gain from it. Focus on God assists any pathway, but this is by no means emphasized in the earlier chapters of the *Gita* and we find now knowledge, *jnana*, now action without desire for results, *karma-yoga*, coming to the fore. Then, too, we could argue for liberation encompassing oneness with the *nirguna* Brahman without attributes or encompassing the more personal, *saguna*, Brahman who is describable. Nevertheless, the emancipated Self is at one with the universe but not obliterated by it. That Self has an expansion of knowledge that encompasses the universe and all other Selves and the nature of God as the Source of all matter and spirit. Such is "having become Brahman" or "attaining Brahma *nirvana*" in the *Gita*. Becoming Brahman is suggestive of unity or identification with Brahman, and the *Gita* does not shy away from such an idea, though its overall theology only suggests partial unity and identity, never full monistic fusion.

Sprinkled throughout the *Gita* are to be found descriptors of the liberated state as an eternal abode of bliss, perfection and peace. There is no sense of an obliteration of experience that prevents such supreme states being realizable, again, pointing to a dual relationship between God and human. To be liberated is to come to Krishna as Brahman, to enter his being, reaching the highest realm where all is calm, all is peace. "The marks of such a man are balance and steadfastness of judgement, clearness of vision, independence of external things, and utter satisfaction in the Self."[66] The liberated Self rises beyond nature, knowing that Self as separate from it. Pleasure and pain and all such pairs of opposites are experienced with equanimity; all things are the same and the liberated one acts in the world without thought of gain or reward, in total equilibrium.

The genealogical backdrop

Before turning to the text a word is necessary on the complicated genealogy that led to the war against which the *Bhagavad Gita* is set. Commentary on the text will bring out the necessary background information to the content, but the following points are placed here in order to clarify the scene.

The kingdom over which there is a dispute is that of Bharata, or Kurukshetra, in northern India close to the Himalayas. Its capital was Hastinapura. Bharata is the ancient name for India and the name of its ancient ruler. The ruler of the kingdom of Santanu was a descendant of Bharata and father of Bhishma, a great character in the *Mahabharata*. Bhishma should have inherited his father's kingdom, but gave up the right so that his father could marry Satyavati. Her father would not let her marry unless it was her sons and not Bhishma who inherited Kurukshetra. The royal line, however, was later at the point of dying out, when Satyavati asked her only son Vyasa – he who is said to be the author of the *Gita* – to produce heirs by two sisters. One produced Dhritarashtra who was born blind, and the other the pale Pandu. Both were Kurus, or Kauravas, descendants of Kuru, the grandson of Bharata. Because he was blind, Dhritarashtra could not rule, so Pandu took the throne.

Pandu was cursed so that he could not live if he had intercourse with his two wives. He renounced the throne, handing it to blind Dhritarashtra, and retired to the forest. His first wife, Kunti, conceived four sons by different gods, though she abandoned Karna, one of these sons. Three – Yudhishthira, Bhima and Arjuna – became the Pandus or Pandavas, the sons of Pandu. Pandu's second wife, Madri, bore him the twins Nakula and Sahadeva, again with the help of the gods. Thus, all the Pandava brothers had divine fathers. The hundred sons of Dhritarashtra and the five sons of Pandu are the two sets of cousins involved in the war.

Intercourse with Madri brought about the death of Pandu, and Madri committed ritual suicide on her husband's funeral pyre. Kunti took the five sons back to the royal court at Hastinapura. Dhritarashtra's intention was to take care of the kingdom until Pandu's sons grew up, the eldest of the Pandavas, Yudhishthira being the rightful heir to his father's kingdom. He and his brothers were brought up at the court of Dhritarashtra, taught by Bhishma their great-uncle and by Drona the priest and master archer, among others. The five Pandava brothers excelled at everything. It was during this time that they became friendly with a neighbouring clan, the Vrishnis, of whom Krishna was chief.

Duryodhana, the eldest of Dhritarashtra's hundred sons, became jealous of the Pandavas and sought to acquire their inheritance, even conniving to murder his cousins. Dhritarashtra tried to conciliate the two sets of cousins by dividing the kingdom into two. Duryodhana, to whom Dhritarashtra gave his throne, took the

North with Hastinapura as capital, and Yudhishthira the South, from Indraprasta, but tensions remained. Attempts at reconciliation were thwarted by Duryodhana and, finally, he engineered a game of dice with Yudhishthira at which the latter lost all – kingdom, wealth, possessions, himself and his brothers and their common wife – because his opponent cheated. As a result, Yudhishthira had to take his brothers into exile in the forest for twelve years followed by another year during which, if their identities were discovered, they were to submit to a further twelve years of exile. If not discovered, then they could reclaim their share of the kingdom.

When the Pandavas returned to claim their kingdom, Duryodhana refused to grant them even as much soil that could be held on the point of a needle. The result was the war that is the setting of the *Bhagavad Gita*. It is Arjuna, the third youngest of the Pandavas, who is the master warrior and the character with whom Krishna is in dialogue throughout the *Gita*, albeit that Arjuna says very little. In the *Mahabharata*, Krishna and Arjuna are shown to be the best of friends, two warriors who participate in joint adventures. Here, in the *Gita*, however, Arjuna is about to realize the true identity of his friend as God.

Arjuna's journey in the *Gita* reflects a *process* of understanding, a gradual process in which the mind disengages with external aims, fears and goals and interiorizes thought to concentrate on what is within, devoid of ego. But at the same time there is an exterior object that is Krishna, the means by which the inner Self can be integrated. Krishna begins as the friend and advisor and ends as the friend and God. Turning now to the text of the *Gita*, many of the themes inherent in the "Hinduism" of the *Gita* will unfold further in the commentary.

CHAPTER ONE

Arjuna Vishada

Arjuna's Despondency

This first chapter of the *Bhagavad Gita* sets the scene for the whole of the teaching that is to follow. The scene is Kurukshetra, the great plain or field where the battle between the Pandavas and the Kauravas is about to take place. Arjuna is one of the five Pandava, or Pandu, brothers and is a brave and immensely talented warrior as his exploits in the *Mahabharata* show only too well. Here, however, the first chapter of the *Gita* culminates in Arjuna's despair and total despondency in having to fight a fratricidal war. Some, like Gandhi, saw this first chapter as depicting not just an impending physical war but, also, the psychological battles that take place within the human mind – battles between good and evil. While it sets the scene for the teaching of Krishna in subsequent chapters, this first chapter is not to be taken lightly. The *Yoga* of the *Gita* begins with its hero, Arjuna, slipping into a state of utter despair and despondency (*vishada*), that state from which there can only be one direction and that is upwards. Perhaps Krishna needs Arjuna to be in such despair in order to be better placed for his teaching.

VERSE 1   Dhritarashtra said:
On the Field of *Dharma* at Kurukshetra, my people and the sons of Pandu assembled together desirous to fight. What did they do, Sanjaya?
    Blind Dhritarashtra undertook the rule of the kingdom of the Kauravas when Pandu, his younger brother, renounced the throne and retired to the forest, where he eventually died. The five *sons of Pandu*, the Pandus or Pandavas, are Yudhishthira, Bhima, Arjuna, Nakula and Sahadeva. It is the question of the succession of the Kurus or the Pandus that is the issue running through the *Mahabharata*. Dhritarashtra's eldest son, Duryodhana, as the fierce enemy of the Pandus, is the individual responsible for bringing events to the point of battle. *Sanjaya* is Dhritarashtra's charioteer and counsellor. He is also the eyes of the King, advising and consoling him. The earlier verses that precede our text in Book 16 tell us that Sanjaya has divine insight: "I have vision beyond the range of the senses and hearing from afar, King, and knowledge of the thoughts of others, of past and present, and awareness of portentous happenings, and power to move through the sky."[1] Thus, in this first verse, Dhritarashtra is asking Sanjaya to use his skill to report on the events that take place at the beginning of the battle between the Kurus and Pandus. His function is to report things exactly as they are with integrity and without prejudice. Tradition has it that Vyasa, the reputed

author of the *Mahabharata*, had offered to restore Dhritarashtra's sight, so that he could see from a distance the events of the battle. But Dhritarashtra did not wish to witness the carnage, so instead, it was Sanjaya who was granted the ability to visualize and hear all the events of war from a distance.

The Field of the Kurus, *Kurukshetra*, is a large plain owned by the Kurus. It is a place of pilgrimage today situated North of Delhi and symbolizes the struggle of good over evil. It is mentioned in the *Vedas* as a place of worship and is, therefore, sacred ground. Dhritarashtra calls it the *Field of Dharma*, the Field of Righteousness or Truth. *Dharma* is a prominent feature of the *Mahabharata* as a whole and has a number of meanings. Fundamentally, it means "what is right". Coming from the root *dhri* "to support", it has the idea of inner sustaining of something as its basic essence; that which sustains, holds, keeps something right. Thus, *dharma* can extend to the essence of duty, law, class, social norms, ritual, and to the cosmos itself. *Dharma* represents the way things should be in all these different dimensions. It is fundamental to the evolution not only of the individual and society, but to every part of life. Here, *dharma* is probably being used as the *sanatana dharma*. Indeed, there is much in the *Gita* that relates to the eternal *dharma*. Sanatana-*dharma* is what Hindus understand as their religion, for it is a term that encompasses wide aspects of religious and traditional thought and is more readily used for "religion". While there are different kinds of *dharma*, the eternal *dharma*, as its name suggests, is that which pervades the whole cosmos, that which is *ultimately* true and right.

Thus, Dhritarashtra probably knows that only the righteous can win in the ensuing battle, that the five Pandu brothers are virtuous and righteous, and that the eternal *dharma* will favour them against his hundred sons. The Field of *Dharma* is also what Aurobindo called the "field of human action" in a "period of transition and crisis as humanity periodically experiences in its history, in which great forces clash together for a huge destruction and reconstruction, intellectual, social, moral, religious, political, and these in the actual psychological and social stage of human evolution culminate usually through a violent physical convulsion of strife, war or revolution."[2] Sarvepalli Radhakrishnan, too, saw the Field of *Dharma* as the world, "the battleground for a moral struggle".[3] Moreover, *dharma* – particularly *sanatana-dharma* – is that which promotes evolution, so when it is radically upset by *adharma*, the opposite of *dharma*, there is a danger of involution, with evil overwhelming good. It is for this reason that a "destruction and reconstruction", to use Aurobindo's words above, has to take place in order to restore proper balance. Thus, for some, the battlefield has relevance for the moral and spiritual evolution of humankind well beyond the time of the *Gita*.

VERSE 2   Sanjaya said:

Then Duryodhana, the King, seeing the Pandava army in battle array, approached the Teacher and said these words:

Duryodhana is responsible for leading the Kurus into battle against the Pandus. In an attempt to reconcile the two sides, Dhritarashtra had divided the kingom between the Kurus and the Pandus and had abdicated in favour of Duryodhana, his eldest son. Before the battle commences, Duryodhana approaches Drona, the great *Teacher* or Master, an *acharya*, who is primarily a teacher of the scriptures but, also, the commander-in-chief of the armies. Drona is certainly a master in the art of warfare and, as teacher, has taught the art of war to both the Pandus and the Kurus. *Karmic* fate has placed him on the side of the Kurus against the Pandus. Perhaps Sanjaya is trying to keep up Duryodhana's spirits here, for having Drona on one's side was a great advantage. And yet, on the adverse side, Duryodhana must surely realize that the armies of the Pandus are mighty and that the battle will take place on the Field of Righteousness, the Field of *Dharma*. These are factors that Duryodhana cannot take lightly and the need for Drona's support and blessing are exigent.

VERSE 3

Behold, Teacher, this great army of the sons of Pandu, drawn up by the son of Drupada, your talented pupil.

Drupada is a monarch and father of Draupadi the wife of all five Pandu brothers and so he is their father-in-law. His *son*, Dhrishtadyumna, had also been taught by the great Teacher and Master, Drona, with care and affection. Indeed, Drupada and Drona were once friends but they quarrelled and, at the Battle of Kurukshetra, they find themselves on opposite sides. After his quarrel with Drona, Drupada performed a great sacrifice as a result of which he was granted a son, Dhrishtadyumna – a son capable of killing Drona. Later, in the battle itself, Drona will kill Drupada only to meet his own death on the following day at the hands of Dhrishtadyumna, commander of the Pandu armies. Duryodhana is perhaps implying here that his armies have the mighty Drona, whereas that of the Pandus has only Drona's pupil. There is the added point, too, that Drona himself has to stand against the pupils that he taught and loved. *Pupil*, here, is *shishya*, a word that can also mean "disciple" and expresses a particularly strong relationship between teacher and pupil.

VERSE 4

Here are brave men, mighty archers equal to Bhima and Arjuna in battle; Yuyudhana, Virata, and Drupada the great warrior . . .

The chapter contains a plethora of names, many of which will not feature again in the text. The author of the *Gita* would have wanted to lend his account historical authenticity and to mention renowned heroes as was the custom for epics.[4] Duryodhana continues to analyse the force of the armies against whom he is to fight. *Bhima* is the second eldest of the Pandus and second only to Dhrishtadyumna in control of the Pandu armies, but here he is commander-in-chief. He is an immensely powerful warrior, the greatest in the whole army, and a huge man with immense strength. Duryodhana had always despised Bhima for such attributes and because of his skill as a warrior. *Arjuna* is the third youngest of the Pandu brothers and the greatest of all archers. *Yuyudhana*, sometimes called Satyaki, is usually Krishna's famous charioteer, though in this battle, Krishna will act as the charioteer for Arjuna. *Virata* is a prince in whose territory the Pandus had stayed when they had been forced into exile by the Kurus. *Drupada* we have already met. Here, he is described as a *great warrior*, a *maharatha*, which not only signifies a highly skilled warrior that could fight ten-thousand archers single-handedly, but also a great charioteer: yet he will meet his death at the hands of Drona on the fourteenth day of the battle.

VERSE 5

. . . Dhrishtaketu, Chekitana the valiant King of Kashi, and Purujit, Kuntibhoja, and Shaibya the bull among men . . .

The name *Dhrishtaketu* means "Audacious Leader". He is the brother-in-law of Nakula, one of the youngest of the Pandavas. His father was King of the Chedis, who had always opposed Krishna, leading Krishna eventually to kill the father and place the son as King in his stead. Despite the fact that Krishna had killed his father, Dhrishtaketu fights on the same side as Krishna in the battle to come. *Chekitana* is a famous warrior and friend of the Pandavas. The *Kashi* kings and their families feature considerably in the *Mahabharata*. Their capital was Varanasi, modern-day Benares. *Purujit* and *Kuntibhoja*[5] are brothers and *Shaibya* is King of the Shibi tribe. This last warrior is described as a *bull among men*, meaning foremost or greatest among warriors.

VERSE 6

. . . courageous Yudhamanyu, and brave Uttamaujas, the son of Subhadra, and the sons of Draupadi, all of them great warriors.

Yudhamanyu and *Uttamaujas* are famous charioteers and powerful warriors. *Subhadra* is one of Arjuna's wives. Her son spoken of here is Abhimanyu, also called by the matronymic Saubhadra. He will be slain on the thirteenth day of the battle. The five Pandus also have one wife common to them all, and that is Draupadi, daughter of Drupada, whom Arjuna won in a contest. She bore each of the Pandu brothers one son, and all five sons will be killed in their sleep during the ensuing war.

Verse 7

Know, best among the twice-born, those distinguished ones who are ours, the leaders of my army. For your information, I shall relate their names to you.

In all these verses, Duryodhana seems to want to draw Drona's attention to the importance of using all his energy in the forthcoming battle. He has pointed out the strength of the opposite side and now he turns Drona's attention to their own side. Duryodhana addresses Drona as *best* or noblest of the *twice-born*. The twice-born classes have undergone the sacred thread or *upanayama* ceremony and are known as *dvija*, "twice born". At this ceremony, a boy of around eight years of age undergoes purification, a rebirth, after which he is able to study the *Vedas* under the tutelage of a master. Three classes are twice-born: the *Brahmins*, the *Kshatriyas* and the *Vaishyas*, though these days, it is usually only *Brahmins* who undertake the *upanayama* ceremony. The lowest class of *Shudras* cannot go through such a cere-mony and so do not have access to the *Vedas*, neither do women. Since Duryodhana refers to Drona as noblest or best of the twice born, he is addressing him as a great or noble *Brahmin*, one from the highest of the four classes,[6] even though he is a teacher of military arts.

VERSE 8

Yourself, Bhishma, and Karna, and Kripa, victorious in war, Ashvatthaman, Vikarna, and the son of Somadatta also . . .

Bhishma, despite the meaning of his name as "Awesome", "Terrible", is a great and well-respected man. He is the son of the river goddess, Ganga. He is an old sage, loyal, full of honour and chivalry and deeply upset by the strife between the Pandus and Kurus. Both Dhritarashtra and Pandu had been brought up by him, and he is Dhritarashtra's paternal uncle who has cared for him since the death of his father. Of all the warriors in both armies, Bhishma is the most experienced, hence his position of commander-in-chief of the Kuru armies. During the battle, he will sustain many injuries from arrows on which he will lie as if on a bed of spikes for many days. Tradition has it that this is the origin of *sadhus* lying on beds of nails.[7] *Karna* is Arjuna's half brother, though neither of them will be aware of the fact until, in the ensuing battle, Arjuna kills Karna and then learns who he is from his mother. Karna comes from a low class and his mother, Kunti, who later married Pandu, abandoned him to be brought up by low-class parents. The enmity between Karna and Arjuna arose when the former was denied the right to compete for the hand of Draupadi at her *swayambara*. At this, suitors contested for the right to marry a maiden, and both Karna and Arjuna were brilliant archers. However, since Karna was forbidden to compete because of his class, Arjuna was the successful contestant and incurred the hatred of Karna. *Kripa* is Drona's brother-in-law and was teacher to the Pandavas before Drona. *Ashvatthama* means "Horse-voiced", and he was so-called because the first sound he made after birth seemed like that of a celestial horse. He is Drona's son and an outstanding warrior. He will last until the end of the battle and it will be he who will kill the five sons of Draupadi while they sleep in the Pandu camp. Yet he will survive the battle since Arjuna and Krishna will spare him. *Vikarna* is the third of Dhritarashtra's hundred sons. *Somadatta* is King of the Bahikas.

VERSE 9

. . . and many other heroes armed with various weapons and all well-skilled in battle, will give up their lives for my sake.

Duryodhana emphasises the might of his armies.

VERSE 10

Unlimited is that army of ours headed by Bhishma, but limited is their army headed by Bhima.

There are difficulties with this verse in the Sanskrit and so it is variously interpreted. The verse could read as Parrinder had it: "Our force is insufficient yet Bhishma is our guard, but theirs is more efficient and Bhima is their guard".[8] This would not really reflect the truth of the matter if referring to sheer numbers since the five Pandu brothers are clearly outnumbered by the hundred sons of Dhritarashtra, symbolically reflecting the disproportionate levels of good and evil respectively – one of the points of the *Gita*. van Buitenen's translation suggests this: "Their army, protected by Bhima, is no match for us, but this army, protected by Bhishma, is a match for them."[9] The fact that the Kurus have the greatest of all warriors, Bhishma, on their side is clear. Yet it hardly suits the boastful character of Duryodhana to admit the Pandus have a greater army. Since the Sanskrit can suggest *unlimited* (*aparyapta*) and *limited* (*paryapta*), many commentators transpose Bhima and Bhishma to make sense of the verse.[10] In this case, as reflected in the text above, Duryodhana is saying that *his* army is the larger and has the better warrior, Bhishma, while that of the Pandus is limited and has only Bhima. Yet the Sanskrit has to be borne in mind as, for example, in Hill's more loyal translation: "Guarded by Bhishma, this force is all too weak; and all too strong that force of theirs by Bhima guarded."[11]

VERSE 11
So all of you be stationed according to your divisions in the army. Above all, protect Bhishma.
Duryodhana is shrewd here. He is not a likeable individual and support for him is not likely to be deep. Bhishma, however, is the opposite: by telling everyone to protect and support Bhishma, for whom there is the deepest respect and love, he could rally all to his cause. He is also iterating the point made in the last verse that Bhishma, the greatest of all warriors, is on *his* side. Further, in the *Book of Bhishma* preceding the *Gita*, Dhritarashtra had made it clear that he wanted Bhishma protected at all costs.

VERSE 12
In order to encourage him, the oldest of the Kurus, the mighty grandsire, made a sound like a lion's roar and blew his conch.
Bhishma is the *mighty grandsire* referred to here, and in response to Duryodhana's words roars like a lion and blows his conch shell in order to encourage him, and to give the signal for the battle to begin. Notably, it is the aggressors who begin the battle. The *conch* shell, the *shankha*, is still used in worship today.

VERSE 13
Then quite suddenly, conches, kettledrums, tabors, drums and cow-horns burst into sound: it was a tremendous noise.
The uproar that comes from the Kuru army is a massive burst of energy as if all the previous years of aggression had their outcome in this tremendous sound. It is the point at which the years of evil and the threats to creative evolution are about to be destroyed.

VERSE 14

Then, standing in the great chariot yoked with white horses, Madhava and also Pandava, the son of Pandu, blew their conches.

Attention is now turned to the defending side, the Pandus. They have not caused the war and are not the aggressors, but they are obliged to respond. *Madhava*, here, is the God Krishna, the name perhaps connected with Madhusudana, "Slayer of the Demon Madhu" or meaning descendant of Madhu.[12] Arjuna is referred to as *Pandava*, his family name. He and Krishna are close friends and relatives. Arjuna had taken Krishna's sister, Subhadra, as a wife and so is Krishna's brother-in-law. Both Krishna and Arjuna have divine conch shells, a hint that they are on the side of righteousness. Such righteousness is reflected, too, in the *white horses*, white being the symbol of truth. Whatever the limitations of the Pandu army, the God Krishna as Arjuna's charioteer, is the most powerful hint of purity and justice in the war.

VERSE 15

Panchajanya was blown by Hrishikesha, and Devadatta by Dhananjaya. Vrikodara, terrible in action, blew his great conch, Paundra.

Krishna is referred to here as *Hrishikesha*. The name probably means "Lord of the Senses" (*hrishika* "senses" and *isha*, "lord"), though some prefer "One With Long/Strong Hair" (*hrish*, "strong" and *kesh*, "hair"). Cutting the hair in much Indian tradition prevents control of the senses so the latter meaning might amount to the same as the former. Such control of the senses means that the mind is not swayed by external stimuli and Krishna's role in the battle is a neutral one. He had given both sides a choice of either his armies or himself in the battle. Duryodhana had first choice and chose Krishna's armies, so Arjuna had Krishna to drive his chariot. While neutral, however, the reason for Krishna being incarnate on Earth is to restore the balance of good and evil.[13] Krishna's conch, *Panchajanya*, is so called because it is made from the bone of a demon of the same name. *Devadatta* means "God-given" for it was given to Arjuna by his divine father, Indra. In this verse, Arjuna is called *Dhananjaya*, which means "Conqueror of Wealth". The name refers to a time when Arjuna helped his older brother to acquire the necessary expenditure for royal sacrifices. *Vrikodara* here, meaning "Having the Belly of a Wolf", is the name given to Bhima, a reference, perhaps, to his legendary voracious appetite, or even to his temper.

VERSE 16

The King Yudhishthira, the son of Kunti, [blew] Anantavijaya, and Nakula and Sahadeva [blew] Sughosha and Manipushpaka.

Yudhishthira, a wise and just man, is the eldest of the five Pandavas. Yudhishthira should have succeeded his father, but Dhritarashtra handed the throne to his son Duryodhana rather than Yudhishthira. Kunti, the mother of the eldest three of the five Pandavas, we have already met in verse 8. She gave birth to Yudhishthira, Bhima and Arjuna by the deities Dharma, Vayu and Indra, respectively. *Anantavijaya* is the name of Yudhishthira's conch shell: it means

"Eternal Victory". *Nakula* is the fourth of the Pandava sons and an expert in training horses. His conch is called *Sughosha*, meaning "Sweet-toned". *Sahadeva* is the youngest of the Pandavas and Nakula's twin. His conch, called *Manipushpaka*, means "Gem-flowered".

VERSE 17

The supreme archer King of Kashi, Shikhandin the great warrior, Dhrishtadyumna, Virata, and the unconquered Satyaki . . .

The rest of the powerful warriors and charioteers of the Pandus also blow their conches. *Shikhandin* is Drupada's son and brother-in-law to the Pandavas. As a eunuch, he has no beard and no moustache. Bhishma had taken a vow that he would not fight a woman or a eunuch, so Shikhandin will be the means of his death. *Dhrishtadyumna*, the son of Drupada, we met in verse 3. His name means "He Who Cannot be Successfully Encountered". Virata and Satyaki/Yuyudhana we met in verse 4.

VERSE 18

. . . Drupada, the sons of Draupadi, O Lord of Earth, and the mighty-armed son of Subhadra all blew their respective conches.

Sanjaya addresses Dhritarashtra here as *Lord of Earth* because Dhritarashtra is still capable of preventing the battle that is about to start.

VERSE 19

The tumultuous roar sounded in the sky and the earth and rent the hearts of Dhritarashtra's men.

When Bhishma and the Kurus gave the sign for the beginning of the battle by sounding their conches, we are not told of any reaction amongst the Pandu army. Here, however, when Krishna and the Pandus blow theirs, the effect on the opposing side is to create fear. At this moment, we have an electrifying suspense as the battle is about to begin.

VERSE 20

Then, O Lord of Earth, seeing Dhritarashtra's men standing arrayed, about to begin the battle, Pandava, whose ensign is a monkey, raised his bow and spoke these words to Hrishikesha.

The *monkey ensign* may refer to Hanuman, one of the heroes of the *Ramayana*. Hanuman was utterly devoted to Lord Rama. In battle, Hanuman was victorious, so the little detail here is probably indicative of the success awaiting the Pandus. But the reference, if to Hanuman, is odd in that little, if anything is said in the *Gita* of Rama of the *Ramayana*, who was also later said to be a descent of Vishnu just like Krishna. The *Ramayana*, however, does not hint in any way that Rama is a descent of any deity: there, he is simply a righteous hero, so there is no reason to link him with Krishna here. Some commentators suggest that the battle actually begins here,[14] though it makes more sense if it is *about* to begin. Subsequent verses,

I think, indicate that it is imminent, though not yet begun. However, Arjuna is about to commence battle by raising his bow.

VERSE 21   Arjuna said:
Place my chariot, Achyuta, between the two armies . . .
Arjuna addresses Krishna as *Achyuta*, meaning "Immortal", "Immovable", "Unshakeable" or "One Who Has Not Fallen", another of Krishna's many names. Krishna is neutral and his senses are in perfect equilibrium, so there is a sense here of the necessity for Arjuna to be so too. He will place himself *physically* between good and evil, but, as we shall see, he has a long way to go before he is *mentally* in such a state. The *Gita* sees no problem with the engagement of the divine in the ensuing battle, albeit only as a neutral charioteer. As a chariot driver, Krishna, here, represents the Vrishni tribe, and as a ruler-warrior would be a *Kshatriya*. Arjuna, on the other hand, is expected to engage in a much more physical way. We have the spiritual and physical, knowledge and action juxtaposed in the characters in the chariot: it is the uniting of these dual aspects in Arjuna that will be all important in the events that follow. The chariot and chariot driver here are reminiscent of a parable in the *Katha Upanishad* (1:3:3–11), and also in the *Shvetashvatara Upanishad* (2:9). The relevant aspects of the parable are as follows:

- The horses are the senses that need to be controlled.
- The charioteer is the Self, the *atman*.
- The chariot is the body.
- The reins are the mind.

The point is that the expert charioteer controls the horses and thus the chariot through the reins, just as the *yogin* controls the senses that entrap the body through the mind.

VERSE 22
. . . that I may survey closely those standing there desirous to fight, with whom, in the great battle, I must fight.
The Pandavas are not the aggressors and do not want the war. We are not sure here what is in Arjuna's mind. Is he hesitating here for the first time? Is the text cleverly showing us his mental state? Whatever the reason for his action, it will be the reason for the whole teaching of the *Gita*.

VERSE 23
I wish to observe carefully those who are assembled here about to do battle wishing to please the evil-minded son of Dhritarashtra in waging war.
Such is Arjuna's contempt for Duryodhana that he refrains from mentioning him by name. This must surely sting Dhritarashtra very hard, for Arjuna lays at his feet the blame for not restraining the evil in his son. However, the evils perpetrated by

the Kurus have now reached a cumulative point and the catastrophe of war cannot be averted. *Evil-minded* here is more expressive of a deep hardening of the intellect, the *buddhi*.

VERSE 24   Sanjaya said:
Thus addressed by Gudakesha, O Bharata, Hrishikesha stationed the great chariot between both armies . . .
Here, Krishna is again referred to as *Hrishikesha*, perhaps indicative that, just as the chariot is now to be poised mid-way between the two armies and between good and evil, so are Krishna's mind and senses in perfect equilibrium. Arjuna is called *Gudakesha* meaning "Lord of Sleep" (*gudaka*, "sleep" and *isha*, "lord"). Sanjaya may be using the term here to suggest that Arjuna will control his mind in the same way as he has control over sleep and will be victorious. As an expert archer, Arjuna already has great strength and concentration of mind. Less probable is a meaning "Thick-haired" or "Bluish-black-haired" as van Buitenen suggested,[15] or "with hair twisted into balls" (*guda*, "balls" and *kesha*, "hair"), with Hill.[16] Sanjaya calls Dhritarashtra *Bharata*, meaning King of Bharata, the old name for India. Bharata was the grandfather of Kuru, the ancestor of the Kauravas and Pandavas.

VERSE 25
. . . in front of Bhishma and Drona and all the rulers of Earth, and said: "Behold, Partha, all those Kurus assembled together."
These are the first words of Krishna in the text. Krishna does not feature promi-nently in the *Mahabharata*, though there are accounts of his interaction with the Pandavas, and clear accounts of his close friendship with Arjuna. Krishna here is the chariot driver, the *suta*, who will sing Arjuna's praises after the battle; thus, *suta* can also mean "bard". The closeness between them in such battle exploits means that Krishna's function is to advise his warrior passenger. These first words of Krishna are interesting. Does he see some weakness in Arjuna? Arjuna is not expected to falter and Krishna may be encouraging him to become alert to the situ-ation. But Krishna calls Arjuna *Partha*, another name for Kunti, mother of the three eldest Pandavas. Kunti is the sister of Krishna's earthly father, Vasudeva. Perhaps Krishna wants to create a conscious awareness of Arjuna's family ties, in order to encourage him to fight. Yet Krishna must see the hesitation in Arjuna that will need more than pull-yourself-together tactics to get the battle going. On the other hand, perhaps the reference to Arjuna's mother is the catalyst for opening up the familial love and compassion in Arjuna that will now ensue. Could it be a delib-erate act on the part of Krishna to render Arjuna open to his teaching?

VERSE 26
Partha saw standing there fathers, grandfathers, teachers, maternal uncles, brothers, sons, grandsons, also friends . . .
Certainly, it seems here that the term *Partha* used in the previous verse has stim-ulated familial thoughts in Arjuna's mind, for he sees the enemy ranks not as

opponents but as family. If his aim in the war is to uphold the eternal (*sanatana*) *dharma*, it is his own (*sva*) *dharma* that now begins to sway his thoughts.

VERSE 27

. . . fathers-in-law and also friends in both armies. He, Kaunteya, seeing all these relatives standing there was filled by deep compassion, and sorrowfully said:

Arjuna's strength dissipates into love, compassion and soft-heartedness: his mind is aware of his duty and his heart is full of compassion. There is no equilibrium between the two, so again, he is in the middle physically, but not mentally. There is no unity between mind and body or between mind and heart. Sanjaya, appropriately, calls Arjuna *Kaunteya* here, meaning "Son of Kunti", similar to Krishna's use of Partha in verse 25. The term emphasizes the familial ties that are hindering Arjuna's focus, though it may also hint that Arjuna's manliness is becoming too soft-hearted and womanly.

VERSE 28

Seeing these relatives, Krishna, arrayed eager to fight . . .
The crux of Arjuna's dilemma is now about to unfold.

VERSE 29

. . . my limbs fail me and my mouth is dry. My body trembles and my hair stands on end . . .

Arjuna's strength has waned because his sense of duty has been overcome by his sense of compassion. He has no mental equilibrium and his thoughts have become trapped in the idea of the suffering caused by the war and his own suffering and unhappiness in engaging in a fratricidal war. Here, it is his own ego, his own feelings, which are too strong for him to gain the equilibrium needed to fight. Although his compassion is noble, it is, in this instance, divorced from duty. His body is reacting to the dichotomy of being compassionate and allowing evil to persist on the one hand, and of following his duty and turning away from compassion on the other. Imbalance on the inner levels of his being is causing an imbalance – and so weakness – in his physical being.

VERSE 30

Gandiva slips from my hand and my skin burns all over. I am not able to stand and my mind seems to be whirling.

Gandiva is the extraordinary bow that no weapon can damage. It was given to Arjuna by Agni the god of Fire. It has the power of a thousand bows and two inexhaustible quivers. Arjuna has never before lost his grip on Gandiva; he does so now because his sense of duty is weakened. The physical changes in his being are, again, reflecting the inner imbalance – loss of control, self-interest, desertion of the cause of righteousness. His *mind* (*manas*) whirls because the sense of duty is trying to re-establish itself.

VERSE 31
I see adverse omens, Keshava, and I can foresee no good in killing our own people in battle.

Arjuna calls Krishna *Keshava*, a name with two possible meanings: "One Who Has Destroyed the Demon Keshin", or "Hairy", indicative of one who has a fine head of hair. The dilemma in Arjuna's mind is clear from his words: the idea of *killing* comes from his sense of duty, but *our own people* from his compassionate heart. He can only foresee terrible consequences to a fratricidal war. His mental state is weakened and his physical body follows suit. We should remember that, in the chapters preceding the *Gita*, Bhishma has been the first great general to be slain, so at this point of the *Gita* some sympathy with Arjuna's plight would need to be recognized if we already know of the death of Bhishma.

VERSE 32
I do not desire victory, kingship or pleasures Krishna. What is kingship to us, Govinda; what are enjoyments or even life?

Arjuna sees no glory, pleasure or victory in destroying his kinsmen, but he is thinking subjectively and not focusing on the wider scheme of things. *Govinda* is one of the names for Krishna: *Go* means "living being" and *vinda* "the knower of"; thus, the name means "Knower of Living Beings". This suggests that Krishna knows all that is going on in Arjuna's mind. The name Govinda may also mean "Master of the Senses" – quite the opposite to Arjuna's state at this time. It was also the name given to Krishna to refer to him as the object of pleasures for cows and the senses and, thus, can simply mean "Cowherd" or "Cattle-finder". Krishna's links with bestowing pleasure (*sukha*) and enjoyment (*bhoga*) through the name Govinda may be juxtaposed here with Arjuna's lack of desire for them if he goes to war.

VERSE 33
Those for whose sake we desire kingship, enjoyment and pleasures stand here drawn up for battle, giving up their lives and wealth.

Still subjectively, but altruistically, Arjuna says he only wants victory for others, yet those others are the very ones he has to slay. It is impossible for him to overcome evil without killing those who perpetrate it and who are determined on war. Some translators consider Arjuna here to be referring to the enemy as those for whom kingship is wanted.[17] The following verse, it seems to me, suggests there may be some merit in interpreting the verse in this way, since Arjuna's focus is on the opposing armies.

VERSE 34
Teachers, fathers, sons as also grandfathers, maternal uncles, fathers-in-law, grandsons, brothers-in-law, as well as kinsmen . . .

The reasoning for avoiding a fratricidal war is now grounded by seeing such familiar faces on the opposite side. One side of the argument against war is being presented. Notably, Arjuna is attached to many of these family members and it is attachment that later he will be advised to overcome.

VERSE 35

. . . I wish not to kill these, Madhusudana, even if I am killed, even for the sake of dominion over the three worlds, let alone for the sake of the earth.

Arjuna addresses Krishna as *Madhusudana* here, a name meaning "Slayer of (the demon) Madhu". Perhaps he is suggesting that Krishna is able to destroy the evil rather than for himself to be the slayer of kith and kin. *The three worlds* (*trailokya*) are Heaven, Earth and the lower regions like hells, though this last may be the intermediate region where semi-divine beings were thought to exist. The phrase *even if I am killed* makes sense in the light of the later verse 46, where Arjuna says he is prepared to die, but some translators prefer "I do not wish to kill these, who themselves are killers."[18]

VERSE 36

What pleasure would there be for us having slain the sons of Dhritarashtra, Janardana? Evil alone would take hold of us having killed these wicked people.

Again, the argument against war and against killing is presented. Arjuna is saying that it is always wrong and that whoever kills must reap the results of that action. To kill is *evil* (*papa*) and can only result in evil: it is a negative act that can only produce negative effects. The Sanskrit term for *wicked people* is *atatayin* and literally means "felons". The crimes committed by the Kauravas are described in detail in the *Mahabharata*. They had frequently tried to kill the Pandava brothers and there is no doubt of their inherently evil natures. They had set fire to the house where the Pandavas were thought to be sleeping, they had attacked them with weapons, stolen their land, wealth, and even their wife – all aggressive acts that were punishable by death according to *Vedic* injunctions. Thus, the text is implying the legality of destroying them, despite Arjuna's reluctance. However, not all the opposing side are, evil: men like Bhishma and Drona are wise and noble. *Karmic* fate and *dharma* have placed men like this on the wrong side. Arjuna is probably thinking here not only of personal *dharma*, *sva-dharma*, that dictates how one should live one's life, but of eternal *dharma*, *sanatana-dharma*. It may be the Kauravas' personal *dharma* to die in the battle, but Arjuna believes he cannot go against the higher, eternal *dharma*. Arjuna calls Krishna here by another of his many names, *Janardana*, which is variously translated – "One Worshipped to Gain Prosperity and Freedom", "He Who Slays Evil", "Liberator of Beings", "Exciter of Men", though the name may simply mean "Slayer of (the demon) Jana".

VERSE 37

Therefore, we are not justified in killing our relatives, the sons of Dhritarashtra. Indeed, having killed our kinsmen, how could we be happy, Madhava?

Arjuna takes his argument to a further level. Whereas before he said he does not *wish* to kill, now he is saying that he has no *right* to kill. However, as far as being *justified* is concerned, Arjuna is paying no attention here to his own (*sva*) *dharma* or his class (*varna*) *dharma* as a *Kshatriya*, a warrior/ruler – both of which dictate that he should uphold *dharma* through battle if necessary. He is also at the second of the four stages of life (*ashramas*), the householder stage. He is married and has to protect society as a warrior, though he wants to protect society without acting.

VERSE 38

Though they, through reason overpowered by greed see no evil in the destruction of families, no sin in hostility to friends . . .

Arjuna's mind is still aware of the evil nature of the Kauravas. The Sanskrit for *evil* here is *dosha* and, while usually translated as "evil", can also mean "defect", which would not be as strong a meaning: but *papa*, "evil", occurs in the next verse so endorses the same sense of *dosha* here. *Reason, chetas,* refers to the whole thought process and consciousness.

VERSE 39

. . . why should we not learn to turn away from this evil, Janardana, clearly seeing evil in the destruction of a family?

The Sanskrit has the sense "should we not know" or "should we not be wise enough" to refrain. Arjuna is virtually saying "we know that this is wrong, but they are blind to the fact". In ruining a family, no one would be left to continue the religious traditions – no males, no firstborn sons, no one to perform death rites, no one to ensure spiritual growth in the family. Despite Arjuna's possible earlier appeal to eternal *dharma* as a reason not to kill, now he is moving towards class *dharma, varna-dharma,* as an argument. Hill noted that the use of family, *kula,* in these verses is probably meant in the wider sense of castes.[19] This seems to be the way in which Arjuna's mind is working, judging by the content of the following verses.

VERSE 40

In the destruction of a family, ancient family *dharmas* perish. With the destruction of these *dharmas* the whole family is overcome by *adharma*.

Destroying a whole family, or most of it, means that there is no tradition of *dharma* that can be handed on. The result is *adharma,* unrighteousness. Family *dharmas* is in the plural in order to reflect the special nature of the many family rites. When everything is in balance, evolution is guaranteed. Family *dharmas* or religious traditions are imperative for the evolution of individuals and society and for the normal rhythms of social life. All this would be lost, Arjuna thinks.

VERSE 41

From the growth of *adharma*, the women of the family become corrupt and from corruption in women, Varshneya, arises confusion of *varna*.

Arjuna is saying here that the *status quo* in society would be overthrown if the Kaurava men are killed. Women would marry outside their *varna*, their class, and not only would the socio-religious system collapse but the progeny would be of mixed class. Without a clear religious and spiritual role for each individual, society would break down: a huge *confusion (sankara)* of societal norms would occur. In Hinduism, changing class (*varna*) or caste (*jati*) is tantamount to changing *dharma*, which, in itself, would cause suffering. Each individual has his or her *own dharma*, *sva-dharma*, to follow and that personal *dharma* is tied into both class and caste. The mother of a family is responsible for carrying out religious practices and traditions and some Hindus believe this keeps her chaste: without the religious practices, women may be prone to degradation. Marriage outside one's class is regarded as impurity though there were certainly important anomalies to the rule even in royal lineages. Krishna is called *Varshneya*, which is a patronym meaning a descendant of Vrishni.

VERSE 42

Such confusion leads the family, also the slayers of the family, to Hell, and the ancestors, deprived of rites for the dead, also fail.

When someone dies, the eldest son in the family or the nearest kinsman performs certain *Vedic rites* called *pindodaka*. In this ceremony, food and water are offered as *prasada*, "grace", first to the deity, and then to the ancestors. Ancestors, just as humans, are believed to be caught up in the processes of cause and effect, *karma*. They may be suffering the results of past actions, in a hellish situation or not able to acquire a physical body and reincarnate. The offering of *pindodaka* from direct blood relations – usually the eldest son, as noted above – brings these ancestors goodwill and peace, aiding them on their evolutionary paths. However, the *Vedas* are prohibited to any but males of the three highest classes. If *varna*, class, breaks down, as suggested in the previous verse, rites for ancestors will fail through polluted ritual. *Hell* (Naraka) is referred to in the verse not as a permanent place of eternal punishment but either a specific plane of existence where one must work off negative *karma* or perhaps, in the context of the verse, any hellish situation as the result of evil *karma*.

VERSE 43

Because of the evil deeds of those who destroy families causing the confusion of *varnas*, the eternal *dharmas* of caste and family are destroyed.

The verse refers to the *confusion* or intermingling of *varnas* or classes, but it also refers to the *dharmas* of birth, and the reference here is to *jati*, which is both birth and *caste*. While there are only four classes, there is a plethora of castes subsumed within each class. *Jati* perhaps more so than *varna* dictates social norms, so here Arjuna is saying that extreme social disorder would follow his actions. He sees himself now as reaping the most *evil* (*dosha*) of *karma* by acting as the destroyer of the Kauravas. In verse 40, Arjuna was thinking of the *dharma* of the family: here, he is thinking about the interrelated *dharmas* of the whole of society and the devastating results if the ancient traditions that uphold the societal system were to be lost.

VERSE 44

We have heard of the men whose family *dharma* is destroyed inevitably dwelling for an unknown period in Hell, Janardana.

The individual *dharmas* in any family are interrelated as well as being independent. Each member of a family will have a personal *dharma*, his or her *sva-dharma*, but that personal *dharma* will be linked to those of other family members simply because they are *karmically* related. If each member of the family carries out his or her *dharma* well, the whole family will evolve. Thus, traditions help to maintain the functioning of family *dharmas*. When individual *dharmas* in a family become *adharmic*, against *dharma*, the result is involution, wretchedness and a living hell. If, Arjuna thinks, he destroys the Kurus, then the family *dharmas* will cease to function in the right way and *adharma* will result for all. *Hell* here is, again, probably a specific place called Naraka.

VERSE 45

Alas, we are intending to do a great evil. Through greed for pleasures of a kingdom, we are prepared to kill our kinsmen.

Against the loss of family class and caste *dharmas*, the gain of a kingdom is small and insignificant to Arjuna. Killing his kinsmen will be a *great evil* to Arjuna, a *mahat papa* in the Sanskrit, because it will mean the destruction of righteousness. *Greed*, *lobha*, indicates that Arjuna is losing any sense of the righteousness of the war.

VERSE 46

If the sons of Dhritarashtra, weapons in hand, should slay me, unresisting and unarmed in the battle, that would be better.

As a member of the second of the four classes, the *Kshatriya* class, Arjuna cannot really refuse to fight, nor can he flee from the battlefield, for his own *dharma* is to fight for justice and maintain righteousness. His only recourse is to unarm himself and be attacked and killed without attempting to defend himself. Only then could he be sure of not committing the *great evil* of which he spoke in the previous verse. His thoughts are noble here: out of love for his kinsmen and friends, out of compassion for the society he is meant to protect, he would rather die than sin. Love and compassion are by no means out of place as essential characteristics of many Hindu devotees. Perhaps Krishna wishes Arjuna to experience such emotions to the full before embarking on his duty as a warrior. Nevertheless, at this point the *Gita* raises the perennial question: "Is it ever right to kill?"

VERSE 47   Sanjaya said:
Having said thus on the battlefield, with a mind distressed with sorrow,
Arjuna sat down on the seat of the chariot and cast down his bow and
arrow.

Arjuna has put forward all his thoughts and his resolve not to fight is epitomized by dropping his bow and arrow. However, his decision not to fight has not
brought him peace of mind. On the contrary, his despondency and dilemma have
now reached their climax. We await the response of Krishna who, perhaps, has soft-
ened Arjuna's heart in preparation for the teaching that follows.

In the *Upanishad* of the *Bhagavad Gita*, the knowledge of Brahman,
the teaching of *Yoga* and the dialogue between Shri Krishna
and Arjuna, this is the first chapter called
Arjuna Vishada.

Sankhya-Yoga
The *Yoga* of Knowledge

CHAPTER TWO deals with knowledge of Brahman and the true Self. The subsequent chapters take up, and elaborate on, the seeds sown here, so the chapter is an important one in the context of the whole text. Throughout the chapter, knowledge of what is real and unreal is the essential foundation of Krishna's teaching. Such knowledge is presented as the wisdom of Sankhya.

The Sankhya-Yoga of the *Gita* needs some explanation at the outset, since it differs from the classical Sankhya of the famous school of thought propounded by Ishvarakrishna in his *Sankhyakarika* and linked also to a sage, Kapila, of whom little is known. What is clear is that the atheist classical school is a later phenomenon than the *Gita* and it is to its pre-classical stage that the *Gita* most probably refers, some strains of which may well have been theistic. Such earlier Sankhya concepts are not so widely different from orthodox *Vedanta* in that there was no denial of an absolute Brahman or *Purusha*. Sankhya, indeed, even in its full classical expression, was always considered as orthodox. The term *sankhya* is usually taken to mean "enumeration", an apt meaning in that Sankhya enumerates all phenomenal existence, including an unmanifest state of matter, into twenty-four categories, with one completely separate category that is pure spirit. However, *sankhya* can also mean "summing up of" in the sense of calculating, analysing and discriminating in a more reflective sense,[1] and it is in this sense of discriminating knowledge that it is used in the *Gita*.

Although the *Gita* predates the classical school of Sankhya, the division between spirit and matter is clearly accepted by the text, and the *Gita* has knowledge of the twenty-four evolutes that compose all nature in Sankhya. The phenomenal world called *prakriti* has both unmanifest and manifest phases and separate, non-material souls called *purushas*. Classical Sankhya will make these souls multiple and independent of each other, but the *Gita* will unite them by the presence of a supreme Purusha, Brahman, the *Param-Atman* that dwells in each being at the same time as it transcends them all. This *Param-Atman* is Lord of all *prakriti*. The classical school of Sankhya has no concept of an Absolute, of Brahman, and the liberation of each *purusha* from its entrapment in the world of matter was into a state of total isolation in its own essence and in no way linked with any divine principle. The Sankhya of the *Gita*, on the other hand, does not stray far from the teachings of the *Vedanta* about Brahman as the Source and Supporter of the whole universe that is present in all things from deities to a blade of grass and, importantly, is the unchanging

Self deep within all beings. The *Gita* is very theistic and it is possible that early
Sankhya may have been, too. There is, thus, a synthesis between developing
Sankhya and *Vedanta* in the pages of the *Gita*. A third strand is also part of that
synthesis and that is Yoga, which will be dealt with in its context later in this
chapter. Suffice it to say here, that we should watch for this particular synthesis of
the three in the pages that follow, though the *Gita* is at no great pains to differentiate between Sankhya and Yoga and tends to see them as complementary pathways.

VERSE 1

**Then Madhusudana spoke these words to him who was overcome with
pity, agitated, eyes filled with tears and despondent.**

Arjuna is full of compassion for his kinsmen whom he came to destroy but now
he himself is the object of compassion. However, Arjuna's compassion is tied up
with his ego, with emotional thinking; it is a compassion that renders him no longer
in control of the situation and that is causing a state of total suspension and the
inability to find any solution. Emotion is controlling Arjuna because he cannot kill
and love, do his duty and follow the compassion in his heart, at the same time.

VERSE 2   The Lord said:[2]

**From where, at this perilous time, comes this un-Aryan-like weakness
that does not lead to Heaven, Arjuna?**

Krishna's words must be an immense shock to Arjuna for they are certainly
forceful. He dismisses all Arjuna's arguments as *weakness*. Here, Krishna does not
attempt to deal with Arjuna's arguments one by one; he will soon get to the root
of the problem, though he addresses generally those put forward by Arjuna in verses
29–46 of CHAPTER ONE. His words must surely bring Arjuna out of a state of
suspension to a state of attention – a jolt, as it were. Alan Jacobs describes Arjuna's
depression rather aptly as "Hamlet's disease", the kind of mind oppression that para-
lyzes action. Krishna's response is, therefore, a "pull yourself together one".[3]
Krishna describes Arjuna's weakness as *un-Aryan-like*, that is to say, totally
unworthy of noble self-control and indicative of failing to follow his *dharma* as a
true Aryan should. The Aryans, or nobles, were the race of people that brought to
India the *Vedic* religion with its scriptures, the *Vedas*, its class system and *Vedic* gods.
They came through the northern regions and saw the indigenous people they
conquered as barbarian and non-Aryan. As an Aryan, and from the high class of
Kshatriyas, Arjuna is expected to uphold every religious and social duty. Krishna is
speaking here as the charioteer of Arjuna, Krishna the man, whose function it is to
counsel the warrior. Therefore, we should not be surprised that his words are man
to man and not God to man at this point.

VERSE 3

**Do not become impotent, Partha, for this is ill-fitting in you. Abandon
weakness of heart and get up, Parantapa.**

Here, Krishna jolts Arjuna even more by the term *impotent*, the Sanskrit actually supporting a translation "eunuch". Krishna is using good psychological tactics here, on the one hand condemning Arjuna's weakness and on the other praising his strength in the name *Parantapa*, "Scorcher/Chastiser" or "Harrasser of Enemies". *Ill-fitting* is appropriate in the light of the last verse, where Krishna tells Arjuna he is not behaving like a true Aryan and a true *Kshatriya*.

VERSE 4   Arjuna said:
How shall I fight Bhishma and Drona with arrows in battle, Madhusudana, who are worthy of veneration, Arisudana?

We can sympathize with Arjuna's feelings here. He is citing the two most honourable men in the enemy's ranks. Both are renowned for their wisdom and greatness. His objection seems apt; they *are* men worthy of reverence (*puja*). Arjuna addresses Krishna as Madhusudana, referring to Krishna's slaying of the evil demon Madhu, perhaps, as in 1:35, making the point that, whereas Krishna slew those that were evil, *he* would be slaying ones worthy of veneration! Arjuna also calls Krishna Arisudana, "Destroyer of Enemies", which subtly stresses the same point. Gandhi believed that Arjuna is making a distinction between his own kinsmen and outsiders, not being concerned about killing outsiders, but desperately anxious not to kill his own kith and kin.[4] Clearly, Arjuna is showing attachment, a sense of belonging; he is thinking of connection between "me and them".

VERSE 5
Instead of slaying these most noble teachers, it is better to beg here in the world. Having slain the teachers, enjoyment of wealth and pleasures would be stained with blood.

Arjuna has no thought of personal desire other than not to kill those he loves, those who are his noble superiors and *teachers*, *gurus*. He would rather forego his *Kshatriya* high-born status as a prince and live life as a beggar than destroy the like of Bhishma and Drona. He is not so much totally confused as not evolved enough to see the bigger picture. He is attached to his family, his teachers, his former friends, but he is sufficiently detached from worldly acquisitions to consider begging. Should he kill these great men, Arjuna feels that even in this world, he would really be in Hell.

Arjuna's reference to *wealth* and success (*artha*) and sensual *pleasures* (*kama*) are to two of the proximate goals of Aryan life. Egoistic as they may seem, they are appropriate in the stages of life suited to the growth of family and society, but they are tempered by the remaining two, *dharma*, what is right, and *moksha*, liberation. These last two restrict wealth and pleasures to ethical means and ends. *Dharma*, in particular, is an active, dynamic concept that sustains what is right for an individual, society, class, caste, religion and the universe. The four together are known as the *purusharthas*. *Moksha*, however, was probably a later addition to the first three. Gavin Flood makes the point that the four goals of wealth and pleasure on the one hand, and *dharma* and *moksha* on the other, reflect "a synthesis of two distinct value systems" one world-affirming and one world-transcending.[5] As Flood later writes, the list of four goals "does not necessarily express a common vision concerning the human subject, but hides, rather, a tension and divergent views concerning, on the one hand, the nature of the self as a social actor embedded within a social world, and, on the other, the self as a transcendent entity beyond the social world".[6] This is a very interesting point and, by extension, reflects rather well the problem Arjuna has in being both involved in the world and yet wishing to be separate from it. The four goals reflect the accommodation of varied traditions through a fusion of what appear to be opposing elements that is rather typical of Hinduism.

While the *enjoyment* (*bhoga*) mentioned in the verse is widely accepted as referring to that of a victory for Arjuna and the Pandavas, others transfer the subject of the enjoyment as the enemy. Thus, Douglas Hill's translation, which admittedly remains close to the Sanskrit is, "were I to slay my masters, greedy though they be for wealth",[7] though the word *bhoga*, "enjoyment", seems to suit Arjuna better, with his vision of the lack of it: the following verse rather depicts this sense of the present one.

VERSE 6
We do not know which is better for us, that we should conquer them, or they should conquer us. By slaying those very sons of Dhritarashtra standing before us, we should not wish to live.

Victory for Arjuna would be useless if he could not share it with those he has to kill. There must surely be a conflict in Arjuna's mind, too, between the fundamental principle of non-violence (*ahimsa*), so important in Hindu religion, and the duty of battle.

VERSE 7
With my nature afflicted with the taint of pity, with my thoughts in confusion about *dharma*, tell me decisively what is best. I am your disciple, teach me, who has surrendered to you.

Here we have the deep spiritual anguish not only of Arjuna but of all those who experience suffering. Arjuna's whole being – psychological and physical, innate and subconscious – is expressed in the word *nature* (*bhava*). The verse also expresses the answer to those in a state of spiritual anguish: it is the turning to or turning around to Krishna for guidance that provides the solution. Such a step is taken when all seems lost, and surrender to, and trust in, someone else is the only way forward. Arjuna cannot think what is right to do. He has the added burden that, at the householder stage of life he should be protecting his family not destroying it, yet the same stage of life expects him to protect society, too.[8] Aurobindo commented on this verse: "For the whole point of the teaching, that from which it arises, that which compels the disciple to seek the Teacher, is an inextricable clash of the various related conceptions of duty ending in the collapse of the whole useful intellect and moral edifice erected by the human mind."[9] *Confusion about dharma* could also be confusion about the *Vedic* scriptures that teach it, and Krishna will have something to say about this in later verses. But confusion here, *sammudha*, is a profound disturbance of normal reasoning.

Notably, Arjuna sees pity (*kripa*) as a *taint*, a fault, a *dosha*. In his dark night of the soul, Arjuna now surrenders himself and perhaps it is here that the *Gita* really begins for there is now a change in Arjuna. The Sanskrit uses the emotive word *prapanna* "surrender", or "refuge", a term essential in devotional Hinduism, which this verse epitomizes so well. The term can also be indicative of the capacity for the realization of truth. No longer is Arjuna reasoning so much with himself; he reaches out to Krishna. *Disciple* here is *shishya* and Arjuna is clearly placing himself in a position to be taught. Gotshalk makes the interesting comment that *shishya*, like *shadhi*, "teach", comes from the root *shas*, which also means to chastise or correct. He writes: "That initial meaning should be kept in mind here, as also a particularization of that meaning in regard to adult and child. There is a 'childish' element to Arjuna's response, enacted in his behaviour as well as in his words."[10] And, like the law of cause and effect itself, Krishna also changes to match Arjuna's need. Serious teaching by Krishna is not possible until his disciple is ready for it. Arjuna refers to himself as a *kripana*, a term usually connoting a miser, but not in the usual sense here. A *kripana* is so locked in worldly affairs and grieves so much about them that it is impossible to evolve towards any spiritual goals. Despite Arjuna's surrender to Krishna, however, the following verses show that his turning around is not yet total.

VERSE 8

I do not see what would remove the grief that dries up my senses, though I were to obtain unrivalled, prosperous dominion on Earth, and even lordship over the gods.

Arjuna may realize that only Krishna can help him in his state of deepest despair, but he is not yet totally receptive and silent. *Gods* here are probably a reference to the demi-gods or celestial beings that dwell in the heavenly spheres.

VERSE 9　　　　Sanjaya said:

Having spoken thus to Hrishikesha, Gudakesha, destroyer of foes, said to Govinda, "I will not fight", and became silent.

Arjuna is called *Gudakesha*, "Conqueror of Sleep", which suggests that Sanjaya is not hinting at any dulling of Arjuna's senses. Although still at a point of indecision, it seems he is still alert. But, when he says that he will not fight, Arjuna shows that his surrender to Krishna is not total, yet it is enough. Krishna will lead him to a higher level of consciousness relative to Arjuna's altering states of mind. Up to now, Krishna's response has been man to man; now it will become God to man, and the serious teaching of the *Gita* will shortly begin. Importantly, Arjuna *became silent*, silence being the medium necessary for Krishna's teaching, the medium in which great things happen.

Sanjaya again refers to Krishna as Hrishikesha, "Lord of the Senses" and Govinda, which, as was seen in CHAPTER ONE, refers to Krishna as the object of pleasure for cows and the senses and also master of the senses. Sanjaya is perhaps using these names to let Dhritarashtra know in a subtle way that it would be unwise to be elated at Arjuna's refusal to fight. Arjuna is alert and, in the presence of Krishna, Lord of the senses, all ignorance must eventually be dispelled.

VERSE 10
Then, Bharata, between the two armies, Hrishikesha, with a faint smile, spoke these words to the despondent man.

Krishna responds with a smile. Will Johnson has captured the nuance of meaning well with his "with the shadow of a smile".[11] The smile suggests encouragement and the easiness of the task of releasing Arjuna from his present state. The smile is also the forecast of the liberation that is to come to Arjuna. There is a great contrast here between the states of the two, and of the gap that will begin to close until union is reached. Yet, it seems to me that Krishna's smile is tantalizing. Has he been aware all along of guiding Arjuna to this point? When he told Arjuna in CHAPTER ONE to survey the opposing army – the only words spoken by him in that chapter – is it possible he wished to bring Arjuna to this point of surrender? Indeed, we are reminded of that very moment by the mention again in this verse of the physical position of the chariot *between the two armies*, symbolic of Arjuna's suspension between compassion and duty, heart and mind. Whatever Krishna's aims, it is from this verse on, that serious teaching begins – with a faint smile.

VERSE 11   The Lord said:
You speak words of wisdom yet grieve for those who should not be grieved for. The wise grieve neither for the living nor the dead.

Krishna is not saying that the enemies are so evil that no one should grieve for them. What he means is that the truly wise do not grieve at all; the wise do not grieve over death any more than the disappearance of the sun at the end of the day. Arjuna's wisdom, here *prajna*, is apparent and not real. Robert Zaehner suggested here that the Sanskrit can mean partly wise, which suits the tone of the verse well.[12] Then, too, Krishna is indicating Arjuna's faulty wisdom because of his grief. And, as Gotshalk points out, Arjuna's *buddhi*, his discriminating intellect, is not sufficiently fully evolved to include the depths of reality and wisdom; it contains, as yet, an element of negativity.[13] Both Bhishma and Drona are highly evolved men and both of them can meet death with equanimity because of their true wisdom: they speak, think and act from the equilibrium of that wisdom. Arjuna, on the other hand, has no such harmony at this moment and he clearly has no idea of the distinction between the perishable body and the imperishable *atman* that is within and that is the true Self. Krishna's teaching on this has yet to come.

This verse begins Krishna's teaching about the relative and absolute aspects of existence in terms of the Sankhya and *Yoga* of the *Gita*. The same separation of the world of *prakriti* from the pure self as *purusha* is accepted as in the later classical schools of Sankhya and Yoga. Arjuna's problem is that his mind is drawn to *prakriti*, which includes intellect, ego, mind functioning and responses to sense stimuli. If he can transcend *prakriti* and function from his true Self, the *purusha* or *atman* within, his problems will be overcome.

VERSE 12

There was never a time when I did not exist, nor you, nor any of these rulers of men; nor will we ever cease to be hereafter.

Krishna points out that Arjuna is grieving for those who, in any case, have eternal existence. This is why the wise do not grieve about death for they know that the essence of everything is everlasting. The inner soul of a being is permanent; it is part of an ultimate Reality. It is the unchanging *atman*, the deepest essence of every entity. The *Gita* is generally accepted as expounding a theistic religion in which the soul, the *atman*, is dualistically related to absolute divinity, so that individuality is retained at liberation, though without any vestiges of egoism. The divine essence is unchanging in each being, but there is a differentiation between beings and the divine. The Vishishtadvaita or qualified non-dualism approach of Ramanuja is probably near the mark here, certainly nearer than Shankara's monism. In commenting on this verse, Ramanuja maintained that God and the individual souls are not the same, nor are the individual souls, and that these differences are real and not illusory.[14] It is from this verse that Ramanuja found evidence of a plurality of selves: "Thus it is seen that the Lord Himself declares that the distinction of the souls from the Lord as well as from one another, is the highest truth"[15] – a view strengthened, he believed, by the use of "I", "these", "you" and "we".

When the body ceases to be, the Self continues, so Krishna is saying that each individual on the battlefield existed in the past and will continue to exist in the future. Though their deaths should occur in the present, they will not cease to be, so there is no need to lament over something that does not really die. The verse may also hint at the perpetual cycle of births and deaths, reincarnation or *samsara*, which the following verse takes up.

VERSE 13

Just as in this body the embodied Self (passes through) childhood, youth and old age so, too, it transfers to another body. The wise are not distressed by this.

There is no reason why Arjuna should grieve if each individual at death merely changes its body but not its real Self. Those who understand this and the nature of the unchanging embodied Self are called *dhiras*, very *wise*, firm or sober individuals. However, the verse also refers to the cycle of rebirths brought about by the principles of cause and effect, the *samsaric* cycle of reincarnation. Even so, the true Self does not change in youth or old age, nor from one life to the next; it is only the body that undergoes change. The Sanskrit word for *embodied Self* in the verse is *dehin*. We have two words for "self" here; the *deha*, which is the body, and the *dehin*, which is the true Self within. The total separation of the two is the key point Arjuna needs to understand.

VERSE 14

Contacts of the senses with objects, Kaunteya, produce cold and heat, pleasure and pain. They come and go and are impermanent. Bear with them, Bharata.

Impermanent, anitya, reminiscent of Buddhist philosophy, is applied to the phenomenal world of sense objects.[16] It is reaction to sense stimuli that blinds the individual to true Reality. Opposites like heat and cold, and particularly pleasure (*sukha*) and pain (*duhkha*), are transient. The dualities of life are what motivate us, and the pendulum swings between all kinds of opposites to create a multitude of likes and dislikes, fears, anxieties and responses to the environment and all life. Implicit in the verse is the idea that, though sense perceptions and the body are constantly changing, the Self within is the only permanent, unchanging entity. The more one can experience this, the less one is affected by the changing world of the senses and the disagreeable aspects of life. After all, what gives pleasure one moment can give pain the next. So Arjuna is advised to put up with them or bear them bravely, a practice of *titiksha* or forbearance.

Arjuna is called by Krishna both *Kaunteya*, "Son of Kunti", and *Bharata*, "Descendant of Bharat", perhaps implying that he is being asked to transcend both maternal and paternal ties, yet to fulfil his duty to both by fighting.

VERSE 15

The person whom these cannot afflict, chief among men, who is the same in pleasure and pain, wise, he is fit for immortality.

A clear distinction is being drawn in these verses between the impermanent and the permanent. Once the permanent Self is realized, the impermanent senses of the worldly level have no effect on such a state: the individual rises beyond them. This clear distinction between the ever-changing and the never-changing is the wisdom of Sankhya, since both the Sankhya of the *Gita* and classical Sankhya separate soul and matter, *purusha* and *prakriti*. To realize the former is to be released from the dualities of the latter, including the duality of life and death. Then, the individual becomes immortal, rising above the ever-changing phenomenal world and is the same in all situations. *Same* here, *sama*, is indicative of perfect and permanent equilibrium, a state of *neti neti* "neither this nor that". Thus, the human being is composed of two parts, the inner changeless Self and the outer, changeable self. *Pleasure* (*sukha*) and *pain* (*duhkha*) are felt because of identification with the outer self: identification with the inner Self ensures that the individual is unruffled by such dualities. *Immortality* is *amrita*, literally "nectar", the nectar of the gods being that which grants immortality. Here, its use is synonymous with *moksha*, liberation from rebirth and being in unison with God.

VERSE 16

The unreal has no being, the real never ceases to be. The final truth about both of these is seen by seers of the essence of things.

The first part of the verse is difficult and translations vary considerably.[17] The problem arises with the opposites of *real* (*sat*) and *unreal* (*asat*) and, similarly, what has being (*bhava*), and what has *no being* (*abhava*). If the verse is linked to the next one, then what is real is THAT by which all this is pervaded, that is to say, Brahman and the permanent essence of Brahman in all things. But what is *the unreal*? Is it, as in Sankhya, unmanifest *prakriti*, the potential for manifestation that has not yet happened? Or does it mean nothing at all, *absolute* nothing, as accepted by Zaehner?[18] The view I have taken here is that it is *prakriti*, the material world, that is in many ways unreal in the sense of being a lesser or partial reality because it is changeable and impermanent, unlike the Self that is real, unaffected by time, causation and space. So, continuing the context of the previous verses, we have an unreal, impermanent body and mind, but a real, permanent Self embodied within it. Similarly, Shankara saw *asat* as anything linked to the process of cause and effect and so unreal. *Sat* is what is not caused and is, thus, the reality of the *atman* that is Brahman, which is the only reality.[19] Hill's comment seems sensible, "the phrase is intended to present a strong contrast between the Self, which is the *svabhava* [essential nature] of Brahman (cf. 8:3) and not-Self, which is Brahman veiled by *maya* [divine power]".[20] Thus, *seers of the essence of things*, (*tattva-darshana*), is suggestive of knowledge of the true relationship between *atman* and matter, between ultimate Reality and the phenomenal world.

VERSE 17
Know THAT by which all this is pervaded to be indestructible. No one can bring about the destruction of the Imperishable.

Despite the unreality of the phenomenal world, and despite its impermanence, its very *essence* is indestructible (*avinashi*) and real. Those who know the reality, the essence, thusness, or underlying nature of things, the *tattva-darshana* of the previous verse, are not affected by the dualities of the changing, transient world. Ultimate Reality pervades everything, and since it is ultimate it is indescribable and presented here as simply THAT, like the *tat tvam asi*, "That you are", of the *Chandogya Upanishad*. The word *pervaded* in the verse is literally "spun", with the inherent analogy of the world issuing forth from Brahman in the same way as thread from a spider. Brahman is clearly the Creator of the world which, unlike Shankara's view, gives the world a degree of reality. But it is only the *essence* of Brahman that is the everlasting, indestructible and immeasurable part of all things. *Imperishable* is Sanskrit *avyaya*, a term that will occur many times as a descriptor of Brahman throughout the *Gita*.

VERSE 18
The bodies of the everlasting, indestructible, immeasurable, embodied Self are said to have an end. Therefore, fight Bharata.

From the moment of birth, each body, here, *deha*, is in the process of approaching death: death is inevitable, so it is pointless to lament over it. But while the body is subject to change and to death, the inner essence, the embodied Self that pervades it, is eternal and therefore deathless: it is only the body that dies. The term used for *embodied Self* here is *sharirin*, which has exactly the same meaning as *dehin* in verse 18, and is, like *dehin*, a synonym of *atman*. Krishna tells Arjuna to *fight*. Arjuna is not a sage, a mendicant, a recluse or a philosopher, he is a man of action, a warrior. His actions must be wise and right for society, but all the same, he must *act*.

VERSE 19
Anyone who believes this (embodied Self) is the slayer or who thinks this is the slain, both do not know. It slays not, nor is slain.

The inner Self that is the real Self is neither slain nor slays, and so is neither the subject nor the object of any action. As the clouds in the sky constantly form and disappear while the sky around them remains changeless, so experiences of life and death come and go while the true Self remains constant. To say "I slay" or "he is slain" is to think at the level of the egoistic self not from the real, eternal Self. All that happens in death is that the permanent *atman* is separated from the imperma- nent body so there is no point in grieving for the *atman*. The real Self is *purusha* or *atman*, the ordinary egoistic self is matter, *prakriti*. In this and many of the verses that follow, we find the embodied Self referred to less directly – it, he, this, that.

VERSE 20
It is never born and never dies. Not at any time having come to be will it come to be again. Unborn, eternal, permanent, ageless, it is not slain when the body is slain.

The verse is a difficult one, though it seems to continue the thought of an embodied Self that is eternal, in line, as also the last verse, with the *Katha Upanishad* (1:2:18–19), which has the identical thought. The embodied Self is totally unaf- fected by anything that takes place in the relative world, so it remains the same when the body (*sharira*) changes or ceases to be. It cannot come to be or pass out of existence; it simply for ever is. However, commentators are divided on whether the verse is referring to the embodied Self or to the ultimate Absolute, Brahman. Indeed, the terms used in the verse – *unborn* (*aja*), *eternal* (*nitya*), *eternal* (*shashvata*), *ageless* (*purana*) – are all used of Brahman, but are also applicable to the *atman*. The former, that is to say, the embodied Self, I think, seems to suit the context better in the light of the preceding and following verses, especially verse 22 and in the light of the phrase *not slain when the body is slain*. It is the empirical self that comes into being in each wave of the transmigratory cycle and that ceases to exist for a time at the close of each life. Only the true Self is always the same and is not subject to birth or death. A monist like Shankara would find the verse refers to both Brahman and *atman*, since they would be identical.

VERSE 21
He who knows this indestructible, eternal, unborn, imperishable, Partha, whom does he cause to be slain? Whom does he slay?

This in the first line probably refers to the embodied Self, the *atman*, which can never be destroyed. To be established in the consciousness of the inner Self is to be beyond the influence of actions and to become a non-agent. Because the inner Self is actionless and free from ego, it is, therefore, beyond *karma*. Acting from the level of the embodied Self, from non-ego, then, ensures no *karmic* results whatever. While all action is of the ever-changing world of *prakriti*, undertaking it while rooted in *atman* absolves the individual from the effects of it. The terms used to describe the *atman*, the embodied Self, are, again, also applied to Brahman – *indestructible* (*avinashi*), eternal (*nitya*), unborn (*aja*) and imperishable (*avyaya*).

VERSE 22

As a man casting away worn-out clothes takes other new ones, so the embodied (Self), casting away worn-out bodies, enters new ones.

The verse is a clear reference to the chain of reincarnation, *samsara*, and to the *karmic* self that passes from life to life, as well as the unchanging embodied Self (*dehin*) that passes, always the same, from each body to the next. The self that trans-migrates is the *jivatman*, the self that carries the personality and *karmic* potentiality engendered by all the innate tendencies and dispositions built up by the last and previous lives. So it is this *jiva* that is reincarnated in order to reap the results of its own causes. It is the atomic, individual self that is composed of ever-changing atoms, and the self that is too absorbed in the world of the senses to become aware of the true Self within. In the *Mundaka* (3:1:1–2) and *Shvetashvatara* (4:6–7) *Upanishads* these two aspects are described as two birds in a tree. One bird is eating fruit oblivious of the other, absorbed in its actions. The other silently sits and watches the anxieties and pleasures of the one destined to go from tree to tree in search of yet more fruit. The silent bird needs no fruit at all. In the context of the *Gita*, the silent bird is Krishna and the busy one, Arjuna. When the latter realizes his true state and real nature as united with Krishna, he will be able to fight.

Mentally, the *jivatman* creates its new body before it leaves its old one. The *Brihad-aranyaka Upanishad* (4:4:1–6) likens such passage to a caterpillar that stretches out onto a new leaf before finally releasing its grip on the last one, and a goldsmith making a new and more beautiful form from an old object. Just so, the mental personality leaves its old body at death and passes to a new one taking with it its past characteristics and causes. As the *Katha Upanishad* (1:6) puts it: "Like grain a mortal ripens and like grain he is born again." The true Self, the *atman* changes only the body, like a cast-off garment, in each new life.

VERSE 23

Weapons do not cut this (Self), fire does not burn it, waters do not wet it and winds do not dry it.

The true Self is immortal, unchanging, has no parts and so is indivisible. Weapons like Arjuna's arrows cannot really slay people, only the outward body. The five elements, earth, *fire, waters*, air – the *winds* of the text – and ether (this last, *akasha*, is not mentioned in the text since it is formless and inactive), Krishna says, are unable to destroy the Self since it is beyond any of the dualities of the relative world. The Self is not any element in particular, but is all of them and none of them. The element earth is not mentioned explicitly, but is represented in the idea of *weapons* – instruments made from the earth.

VERSE 24

This Self cannot be cut, cannot be burnt, cannot be made wet, cannot be dried up. It is eternal, all-pervading, stable, immovable and primeval.

Krishna is directing Arjuna's mind to the level of absolute divinity, to Brahman, which is the nature of Arjuna's own, real Self. He will then be able to understand that his despondency is only part of his unreal self. Again, the descriptors of the true Self are also applicable to Brahman – *eternal* (*nitya*), *all-pervading* (*sarva-gata*), *stable* (*sthanu*), *immovable* (*achala*) and *primeval*, ancient, eternal (*sanatana*).

VERSE 25

This (Self) is said to be unmanifest, inconceivable, unchangeable. Therefore, knowing it thus, you ought not to grieve.

The words *unmanifest, inconceivable* and *unchangeable, avyakta, achintya,* and *avikarya* respectively, are epithets of Brahman but, here, are certainly being used to describe the embodied Self, and serve also to push the mind of Arjuna beyond all phenomena and thought, beyond anything that can be conceptualized. Yet it is exactly THAT, which each person is, as a part of the absolute Reality that is Brahman. If Brahman and this embodied Self are beyond the senses, are inaccessible by the senses, then despondency about the world of the senses – all of which belong to the bodily self not to the true Self – is completely unnecessary. *Unmanifest, avyakta,* is also the term given to the unmanifest state of *prakriti* in the Sankhya scheme of things, which will be examined in detail in CHAPTER THREE. It is more reminiscent here, however, of the immaterial *atman* and of the eternal, incomprehensible Source that is the Creator of all things and known simply as THAT. There seems to be a subtle link between the inner Self and the universal Self as Brahman, aided by the descriptors in this and the previous verse that are so readily applicable to Brahman.

VERSE 26

Even if you think of this (Self) as eternally born and eternally dying, Mahabaho, you ought not to grieve.

Thus far, Krishna has explained to Arjuna that the Self embodied in each individual is immortal and continues eternally even when the body is slain. Krishna now argues from the opposite point of view. He says that even if the true Self were subject to the cycle of births and deaths, to *samsara*, there is still no cause to grieve for what is born will die and what dies will be reborn. The materialists of the time and the Vaibhashika and Lokayatika schools of philosophers argued that the soul cannot exist beyond the body: Krishna will have more to say about them in 16:8. Arjuna is called *Mahabaho*, "Mighty-Armed" or "Strong-Armed", a reminder of his warrior strength.

VERSE 27

Death is certain for those who are born: birth is certain for those who are dead. Therefore, you ought not to grieve over a thing that is inevitable.

Just as the only inevitable thing about birth is death, so the only inevitable thing about death is birth. Birth and death are part of the process of change in all life and are not something about which to grieve. They are processes of evolution to the state of perfection, part of the cosmic purpose and of the law of cause and effect. It is necessary to "go with" such a process and not react against it for it is inevitable. The battle at Kurukshetra is part of the evolutionary path, a facet of cause and effect, and so it, too, is inevitable. Arjuna, as everyone, cannot avoid what is inevitable: he can only make a right or wrong choice about it.

VERSE 28

Beings are unmanifest in the beginning, manifest in their interim state and unmanifest again in the end, Bharata. So why lament?

Continuing the context of the previous verse, this one probably suggests that beings begin in an unmanifest state (*avyakta*), that is to say, before birth. Their interim state is manifest (*vyakta*), then their end state is once again unmanifest (*avyakta*) after death. Krishna is putting forward another argument so that Arjuna can see the human *samsaric* cycle as the rather unimportant part between the two identical conditions of a non-manifest state that is a natural "home" and an origin. All the relatives that Arjuna sees in the opposing army are simply in their interim, manifest state before returning to their natural, unmanifest origin. Nevertheless, a more cosmic interpretation is possible here. The *Gita* certainly accepts the Sankhya view of the division of spirit and matter, *purusha* and *prakriti*. The universe, too, stems from, and returns to, an unmanifest potential, also termed *avyakta*, with interim stages of manifest evolution, *vyakta*. Whether on a cosmic scale or in cycles of life and death, however, life continues, but it is only in its *interim state* that it can be known.

VERSE 29

Someone sees this (Self) as a wonder and another also speaks of it as a wonder: yet another hears of it as a wonder, yet having heard of this, none really knows it.

This is not an easy verse and several translations and interpretations are possible. It also seems out of place with the previous and following verses. The thought is perhaps similar to Jesus' teaching in the *New Testament* of those who see but do not perceive and hear but do not understand (*Mark* 4:12) and there are similarities with the *Katha Upanishad* (1:2:7), which depicts how difficult it is to have full understanding of the divine. Since previous verses emphasize the inscrutability of the real Self, it is possible that this verse is also saying that those who think they know the real Self or the supreme Self are wrong, because the Self and Brahman are inconceivable and indescribable, *neti neti*, not this, not that. Or is the verse referring to those who are unable to understand because of their continued involvement with the senses? In other words, it is not possible to understand the embodied Self or, indeed, Brahman, through any of the senses since, as matter, they can have no means of understanding pure spirit. Given that the verse mentions many of the senses, it seems to me that it is this last interpretation that is more appropriate, its tenor indicating that sense perceptions are not viable means of knowledge of Brahman.

VERSE 30

This embodied Self in every body is eternally indestructible, Bharata. Therefore, you should not grieve for any living being.

The body (*deha*) is impermanent, a mere container for the Self (*dehin*) within that is the real and immortal essence and which is *indestructible*. So one can not really slay another and no one should, therefore, grieve for another.

VERSE 31

And considering your *sva-dharma* also, you ought not to waver. For there is nothing better to a *Kshatriya* than a righteous war.

Hitherto, Krishna has been arguing from a spiritual point of view. He now turns to an argument on the level of *sva-dharma*, "one's own *dharma*", what is right on a personal level. Such personal duty is consonant, too, with class duty (*varna-dharma*). A *Kshatriya* is in many ways an instrument of the divine. In the same way that a *Brahmin* is responsible for maintaining the religious laws, so the *Kshatriya* maintains justice, righteousness and moral order in society. It is his personal *dharma* to do so and to fulfil the important role of being the instrument by which the appropriate balance of positive forces in the cosmos is maintained. Here, Arjuna is the instrument by which the negative forces have to be checked at the battle of Kurukshetra. Krishna needs to make Arjuna aware that it is his personal *dharma* to protect the eternal *dharma*, the *sanatana-dharma*, as much as promoting what is right for society. It is that universal righteousness that is superior to any life and must be maintained at any cost. To obey his *sva-dharma* – what is *better* or good (*shreya*) for Arjuna – would not be acting for sense or self-gratification, but for righteousness itself. Since it is a war of *dharma*, a *righteous war*, Arjuna must fight or turn his back on righteousness. Krishna is also, here, putting forward the traditional views that meld religious and social duty. At the householder stage of life, married, with a family to protect and support, it is not appropriate for Arjuna to renounce action.

VERSE 32

And the gate of Heaven opens itself to happy *Kshatriyas* who obtain such a battle, Partha.

Following one's *dharma* is a way to Heaven and Arjuna's way to Heaven (*svarga*) is, therefore, to fight. According to traditional laws on battles, a *Kshatriya* in battle gains whether he is victorious or not, simply because he is following his duty, what is right for him. Even Duryodhana eventually enters Heaven after his death on the battlefield despite his evil intent. It will be something that

Yudhishthira, the eldest of the Pandavas, will object to most strongly! But the time is right for Arjuna to exercise his personal (*sva*) and class (*varna*) *dharmas*; it is not the time for despondency.

VERSE 33

But if you will not wage this righteous warfare, then having abandoned your *sva-dharma* and honour, you will incur evil.

Dharma is the instrument by which individual evolution takes place. Following *dharma*, however difficult this may be at times, enhances each personal path. But to go against *dharma* is to go against evolution, and it is *this* that is *evil* (*papa*) and which causes suffering. Again, in the *Gita*, *righteous warfare* is a war of *dharma* and, therefore, one that is just.[21]

VERSE 34

And beings will forever tell of your dishonour. To the once honoured, dishonour is worse than death.

Krishna now turns to a very personal argument – cowardice and losing face and fame. Arjuna has always been a defender of justice and righteousness. As such, he had been the object of goodwill, fame, honour and esteem. By refusing to act now according to his *dharma*, it would be better if he died, for shame and dishonour would be harder to bear. Honour and fame are attributes that help to inspire others to the same levels of right and honourable living; dishonour would have a converse effect. Nevertheless, at later points of the *Gita*, Arjuna will be told to be the same in praise or blame; in other words, to maintain equanimity. Krishna appears to be reverting to a man-to-man talk here.

VERSE 35

The great warriors will think you have withdrawn from the battle from fear. You who have been much thought of will be held lightly.

Here, the accusation is one of cowardice and must have touched Arjuna deeply – another jolt from Krishna. His enemies would not understand his compassionate reluctance to fight, they would ridicule him as a coward who ran from the battlefield in fear. Those who once held him in awe will despise him. Arjuna is greatly renowned. He had even fought against the deity Shiva, who had disguised himself as a mountaineer. Such was Arjuna's bravery and subsequent reverence when he discovered the true identity of his assailant that Shiva gave him the celestial weapon Pasupata. Indeed, Arjuna is, himself, a *great warrior*, a *maharatha*, and it is others of the same status who will judge him harshly.

VERSE 36

Your enemies will vilify your power and many will say words unfit to be spoken. What could be more painful than that?

Arjuna had argued that the consequences of his fighting would be immense suffering, but Krishna tells him that the actual consequences of *not* fighting will be worse. Tradition has it that he *must* engage in the war; that is his correct role in society, and if he does not, then negative results will follow. Arjuna will not be able to bear the pain – here, *duhkha*, which also means "suffering" – of contempt. Some commentators find this verse out of character with the main body of teaching in the *Gita* as a whole.[22] Indeed, Krishna will argue for total equilibrium in verse 38 so that praise or blame should mean nothing. Here, and in the following verse, he seems to be stating what must have been obvious to Arjuna. Krishna knows Arjuna's nature as a *Kshatriya*, knows that the war must take place, but also knows exactly *how* Arjuna should act, though for the moment, he is offering man-to-man, warrior-to-warrior advice.

VERSE 37

Slain, you will obtain Heaven or, having conquered you will enjoy Earth.
Therefore, stand up, resolved to fight, Kaunteya.

Arjuna's *dharma*, both personal and class, is to fight. As long as he follows his *dharma*, he cannot lose even if he dies in battle, as we saw in verse 32. What is happening is that his ego is dictating how he thinks: *dharma* may appear prescriptive and straightforward, but the ego is powerful and will divert attention away from *dharma* all too easily.

VERSE 38

Making pleasure and pain, gain and loss, victory and defeat the same,
engage yourself for battle: then you will not incur evil.

Since from the point of view of Brahman all things are the *same*, (*sama*, a word that also means "equanimity") and there are no dualities, *pleasure* (*sukha*) and *pain* (*duhkha*), gain or loss are ultimately one and the same thing. Arjuna is thinking in terms of opposites, of pleasure or pain, of ill-gained victory in a fratricidal war or not fighting at all, of life and death. What he needs to do is abandon such dualities and gain the perfect equilibrium that will allow him to fight. Then, too, Krishna is asking Arjuna to fight not from the viewpoint of gain or loss, but because if he does not fight it will be an *evil* act, *papa*. Action is important as long as it is the right action and the necessary action. And as long as Arjuna has no desire for gain or loss, but has total equanimity, no negative *karma* can ensue from such action, for it will be undertaken without desire for any particular result. Arjuna simply needs to fulfil his religious obligation to fight. He is told to *engage*, or "get ready", "brace himself" for the battle – an expression encompassed by the more secular use of the verb *yuj* from which *yoga* is derived. Nevertheless, there is some incongruity here with the proposal of equanimity in contrast with the pleasure of Heaven or Earth of the previous verse. In fact, as a *Kshatriya* and a householder, the pursuit of pleasure and wealth with success would be legitimate desires for Arjuna and well within the realms of *dharma*. Satya Agarwal suggests that *sva-dharma* and equanimity (*samatva*) in all activity are harmonized in this verse, and this is perhaps the case. Agarwal goes as far as to say that "this can be considered as a basic, new teaching of the *Gita*", the previous verses simply stating traditional views.[23] Indeed, the verse gives us a core teaching of the *Gita* – right action without desire for results.

VERSE 39

This declared to you is the Yoga of the wisdom of Sankhya. Hear, now, of the integrated wisdom with which, Partha, you will cast off the bonds of *karma*.

Sankhya, as was seen at the beginning of this chapter, can mean "enumeration", as it probably does in classical Sankhya. However, it can also convey the idea of reflection, understanding, or the knowledge that brings about understanding. It is this last meaning that suits the context here,[24] with the important word *buddhi*, "wisdom" or "intellect". *Buddhi* is the intellect, the discriminating factor in mental processes that brings wisdom. It determines how we think, our knowledge, understanding, volition, intuitive intelligence, insight and reason, though with Arvind Sharma we need to note that it is "a floater which can be set to any use".[25] The system of matter devised by Sankhya will be examined in detail in CHAPTER THREE, but it is important to recognize at this point that the *buddhi* and also the mind and ego are *matter* in the Sankhya scheme of things. The state of the *buddhi* will dictate the character of the being, so if it is subject to desires and aversions and the results of actions, it will accumulate *karma* and necessitate rebirth. If, however, it can be purified so as to be pure wisdom, pure intellect, it will be *detached* from desires, aversion, goals, egoism and *karmic* results. The *buddhi* here is *integrated*, *yukta*, which is the whole point of *yoga*. In translating *buddhi* as "wisdom" or "intellect", then, neither is meant here in the sense of intellectual capacity, even though *buddhi*, generally, might include such a sense. *Buddhi* is the highest principle of each individual self and it is also the highest aspect of cosmic matter, close – very close – to pure spirit and so the means to pure *atman*.

Krishna turns from the knowledge or *wisdom of Sankhya*, to Yoga, the practice of that knowledge. Important to remember, however, is that wisdom, knowledge, underpins practice. *Buddhi* is the foundation for praxis in the sense of being the kind of intuitive wisdom that recognizes and has insight into the essence of things so that praxis takes place from the depth of that knowledge. Thus, the word is often conjoined with *yoga* to indicate the *yoga* of intellect/wisdom/knowledge, *buddhi-yoga*; indeed, the concept of yoking or uniting suggests the conjoining of two entities. In the Sankhya system of matter or *prakriti*, *buddhi* was that part of matter that could reflect the spirit, the *purusha*, more than any other matter. Its refinement, therefore, was essential for the final separation of the *purusha* from all matter – and in classical Sankhya that meant even from the *buddhi* itself, though this is not the case in the Sankhya of the *Gita*. The present verse conveys the idea that by acting through the practice of *yoga* there can be no *karma* that accrues to an individual. Thus far, the reasoning has been intellectual peppered with pragmatism, but now Krishna will teach how the practice of *yoga* helps to make one established in the Self.

The word *yoga* is derived from the root *yuj*, which has a variety of meanings –

"unite", "join", "yoke" – but its meanings are many and, in the *Gita*, its derivatives are used in many senses, both religiously and secularly. When associated with the word *buddhi*, as it is in the *Gita*, it suggests "integrated in wisdom or intellect" or even "practised in wisdom". Essentially, however, *yoga* usually supports an active and dynamic nuance of meaning. The school of Yoga was systematized by Patanjali whose dating could be anywhere from the second to the fourth centuries CE. However, *yoga* is a very varied phenomenon not only pertinent to Hinduism but also to Buddhism and Jainism. The *Gita* exemplifies this well, dealing with the *yoga* of action, the *yoga* of devotion and the *yoga* of knowledge, showing how practice can be deployed in different religious dimensions. Underpinning such different expressions is usually the idea of yoking the senses, of disciplining the mind. The diversity of *yoga* means that it has had a long history even with some evidence on the ancient Indus Valley seals.[26] Wherever and whenever there is an attempt to transcend human desires and aversions and to control the mind then some form of *yoga* is usually involved as the means. The *Gita* will develop its own theory of it as skill in renunciation of the fruits of actions.

The school of classical Yoga is a later phenomenon than the *Gita*, representing a time when, though accepting the philosophy of Sankhya, it had separated into an independent school of thought. The *Gita* is probably witnessing the rise of these two schools, but its own point of view is a synthesis of Sankhya and Yoga and a theistic interpretation of both with a good deal of the philosophy of the *Vedanta*. While both schools came to be recognized as complementary and brought together as Sankhya-Yoga, classical Yoga accepted a supreme Lord, Ishvara, who could aid the *yogin* on the path to liberation but with whom there would be no relationship whatsoever when the goal was attained. The *Gita* probably reflects earlier trends of both Sankhya and Yoga when both were more in line with traditional ideas, especially those of the *Upanishads* that accepted a supreme Self, Brahman, as both the Source and Sustainer of all things and with whom, as some *Upanishads* suggested, the human soul is identical. Other *Upanishads* and the *Gita*, accept the human soul is a part of Brahman. *Karma* in the verse is meant in the sense of action and reaction, action that brings results because it is undertaken with a view to results and egoistically. It thus creates bondage because an individual has to be reborn in order to reap the results of such motivated actions.

VERSE 40

In this there is no loss of effort or adverse results. Even a very little of this *dharma* protects one from great fear.

The sense of this verse is that even a little *dharma* practised through *yoga* is enough to deliver a person from fear. *Dharma*, here, is used more in the sense of right practice, that is to say, of *yoga*. It is a very optimistic verse since it suggests that as soon as one steps out on this path, then there is no slipping back; the beginning of the path of evolution to liberation takes place. The *great fear* mentioned in the verse is thought by most commentators to refer to the endless cycle of reincarnation.

VERSE 41

Here is one-pointed, single-minded intellect, Kuru-Nandana, but many-branched and endless are the thoughts of the irresolute.

The *buddhi* or intellect of the *yogin* is bent on the *single-minded* pursuit of his goal, unlike the irresolute individual who is lost in the world of the senses with the intellect pulled in all kinds of directions. Concentration on the goal with single-minded intent is the path that will bring results. If Arjuna had been resolute in any way before the battle, that resolution is not deep enough to see him through his current crisis. He needs the *one-pointed* resolution that springs from the inner Self. Until then, his *buddhi*, his intellect, will remain *many-branched* with multiple *thoughts*. The school of Yoga emphasized single-pointed concentration, *ekagra*, as the mainstay of its practice. In the experienced *yogin*, *ekagra* becomes "a motionless meditation, a silent collecting of the mind's powers".[27] Arjuna here is called Kuru-Nandana which means "Joy of the Kurus" or "Descendant of the Kurus". Both Arjuna and the sons of Dhritarashtra are descendants in the Kuru line.

VERSE 42

The unwise who utter flowery speech and take pleasure in praising the words of the *Vedas*, Partha, say that there is nothing other than this.

The verse seems to be critical of the *Vedas* and since it refers to speech and vocalized worship, suggests the criticism is directed to the *karma-kanda* section of the *Vedas*, the ritual part, and to the ritualists who upheld the *Vedas* to the letter. It is probably these ritualists, rather than the *Vedas* as a whole, who are criticized at this point, especially those who use the teachings to gratify the senses with material rewards, those who endorse certain actions that they believe will bring resultant fruits of good births, wealth, power and so on. As we shall see, the *Gita* demonstrates somewhat ambivalent attitudes to the *Vedas* throughout. Perhaps the answer to this is, as Arvind Sharma says: "The attitude of the *Gita* to the Vedas is like that of a wayfarer towards a raft – which is to be used while crossing but is to be abandoned after the crossing has been made. For one who has had self-realization the Vedas are not binding, but for one like Arjuna who is not a realised soul they are."[28]

VERSE 43

Minds full of desires, Heaven is the highest goal, and rebirth through the fruits of *karma*. They pontificate about specific rituals for sense enjoyment and lordship.

The *yogin* does not have Heaven as his goal but total liberation. Paradise simply represents a place where those who have good *karma* may go after death. Ultimately, however, that good *karma* will be used up and they will have to return to earthly existence. Those who use the *Vedas* to achieve such short-sighted aims are still trapped by their own egos, and by the *desires, kama*, that ensure there must be *fruits* of their actions, *karma-phala*. Again, the *Gita* is pointing out that even religious activity if result orientated is fallacious.

VERSE 44

Those deeply attached to sense enjoyment and lordship, whose thoughts are drawn away from a one-pointed intellect, are not established in *samadhi*.

Those dependent on *Vedic* injunctions do not have their *buddhi*, their *intellect* or reason, established or fixed in *samadhi*. *Samadhi* is absorption in the consciousness of Brahman through deep meditation, intense concentration and a still mind, in which no response to sense stimuli takes place; no *thoughts* ripple the placid lake of the mind. This is the goal and that which is missed by those who wish for *enjoyment* through the senses. The context of the verse suggests that it is still the ritualists who are its subject. For such ritualists, for whom the necessity of good results is supplied by highly specific and meticulous observances, *samadhi* would be impossible. The verse, thus, continues its criticism of those devoted to the *karma-kanda* portion of the *Vedas*, which is, after all, bound up with the manifest world of *prakriti*.

VERSE 45

The *Vedas* deal with the three *gunas*. Be without these three attributes, Arjuna, without the pairs of opposites, ever remaining in *sattva*, free from acquisition and preservation, established in the Self.

Vedic activity that is result geared is, again, criticized. *Prakriti*, matter, is made up of three modes, forces or qualities. While in later Sankhya philosophy the *gunas* are physical properties, substances, it is likely that in the *Gita* there is a blurring of their nature as both physical matter and qualities or attributes.[29] *Guna* means "strand" and the three are depicted as combined like the strands that make up a rope. They are *sattva*, *rajas*, and *tamas*. All things are a blend of these three qualities. *Sattva*, the white strand, represents light, evolution, purity and goodness. *Rajas*, the red strand, represents energy, restlessness, passion, motion, activity and creativity, and *tamas*, the black strand, inertia, heaviness, stupidity, darkness and involution. A fuller discussion of them will be undertaken when they occur again in CHAPTER THREE. Important here, however, is the point that they are quiescent in their unmanifest state – whether that is the unmanifest state of *prakriti* in Sankhya-Yoga or in the Unmanifest that is Brahman in the *Gita*. It is the transcending of the *gunas* that Krishna is placing before Arjuna as the goal to which he needs to aspire. He is asking Arjuna to go beyond the dualities that the *gunas* create and be *nirguna*, no *gunas*, for it is reaction in the world of *gunas* that ensures fruitive *karma*. Nevertheless, there is an inconsistency in the verse in that, on the one hand Krishna is telling Arjuna to go beyond the *gunas* and, on the other, he asks him to *ever remain in sattva*. Thus, many commentators answer the problem by translating the word *sattva* as "truth" or "purity", indicative of purity in equilibrium or purity in mastering the self. In the Sankhya-Yoga schemes of matter, *sattva* is the *guna* that is closest to *dharma*, to positive evolution and to liberation. It is also the best quality of the *buddhi* to enable it to realize the *purusha*. To have a *sattvic buddhi*, then, is to be touching liberation in both Sankhya and the *Gita*.

Arjuna's problem is that he cannot reconcile the dualities of what is good and evil. Krishna points out that these dualities cannot be reconciled from the point of view of matter, but they can be reconciled from the point where all dualities dissolve and are harmonized. Dualities, *pairs of opposites*, are manifestations of time and space. If they can be transcended, then the true Self that is beyond time and space can be experienced, concomitant with Brahman and Krishna. Then, Arjuna will be free from the relative field of opposites and, in being free, whatever he gains or possesses will be of no consequence to him. Aurobindo called this state "spiritual impersonality".[30] Arjuna's decision not to fight is made from the standpoint of dualities and attachment to the results of his actions: he must go beyond dualities and operate on the level of the non-dual. The Sanskrit for the pairs of opposites, *dvandva*, also carries the nuance of meaning "doubt", indicative of their changeability. They are the dimension by which we make sense of all life, knowing *x* because of its opposite *y* and all the names and shades in between. Almost every opinion, attitude, spoken word, piece of knowledge, behavioural pattern we have is dictated by the relation between two opposing ideas. Transcending these opposites lifts the mind to total freedom of inner intellect, and the individual becomes *established in the Self, atmavan*. Thus, it is necessary to be *without the pairs of opposites*, in Sanskrit, *nir-dvandva*.

VERSE 46

For the *Brahmin* who knows all, the *Vedas* are as much use as a water tank when everywhere around is flooded.

The subject of the verse is an enlightened *Brahmin*, one who, because of his state of consciousness has no need of *Vedic* rituals and guidance, just as one has no need of a tank of water when there are floods everywhere. On the other hand, *Brahmins* are also those responsible for the excessive ritualism of some of the *Vedas*, so presumably here Krishna is talking of the sage of the *Vedanta*. Such an enlightened being has transcended all ritualism. The verse is, however, a difficult one. Placing the comma after *Brahmin who knows all, the Vedas . . .* is in line with previous criticism of the ritualists. But a translation *For the Brahmin who knows, all the Vedas . . .* is also possible and this would provide a very different perspective as critical of *all* the *Vedas*, presumably of the more mystical portions of *Vedanta* as much as the ritualistic. Many sages had turned away from ritual sacrifice, dwelt in the forests and became seers. It is their experiences from which the *Upanishads*, the more mystical literature of the *Vedanta* came. Given that the *Gita* synthesizes Sankhya, Yoga *and* Vedanta, it might be justifiable to translate the verse, I think, with that important comma linked to the *Brahmin* – *the Brahmin who knows all*. We must remember, however, that Arjuna is a *Kshatriya*, not a *Brahmin*; it is his duty to follow an active path and not a meditative one. The following verse seems to clarify this point, though it will be action rooted in inner equilibrium that will be right for Arjuna.

VERSE 47

In action only you are right not at any time in its fruits. Let not the fruits of action be the motive nor attachment to inaction.

Here begins what is the central tenet of the Gita, that action should be undertaken without thought of gain from the results. It is action without desire, without ego. The rationale behind it is the law of action and reaction. The word *karma*, "action" occurs twice in the verse. Whatever action, *karma*, a person undertakes, the *fruits of action*, *karma-phala*, must occur, but it is only the *action* over which one has control, not the result. Trying to work out the result of a specific action is not possible – albeit that this is exactly what the ritualists purported to do. So energies need to be concentrated on actions *per se*. This is not to say that possible results should be entirely dismissed, but actions are nearly always undertaken entirely for the results desired, and it is *desire* that brings about fruitive *karma* – a corresponding negative or positive result. Some of the ritualists like those of the Mimamsa school believed that desire was absolutely necessary in ritual sacrifice, that is to say, the *result* had to be firmly in mind before the ritual action to bring it about took place. But in the *Gita*, concentrating only on the action and not on the fruits of action frees one from desires and, therefore, from the *karma* incurred by the action.

Krishna also maintains that inactivity is wrong; we have to be active, active for the right reasons, but not for their results. Arjuna is attached to *inaction, akarma*, refusing to fight and is going against his *dharma*, the actions already laid down for him. He is experiencing attachment to the results of inaction. J. A. B. van Buitenen suggested that in the use of the term *akarmani*, "to avoid acting", Krishna is steering a middle course between over-zealous *Vedic* ritualistic activity and the necessary maintenance of general traditional laws.[31] Indeed, such a view would be consonant with Krishna's earlier emphasis on obeying personal and class *dharma* on the one hand, and his criticism of the ritualists on the other.

VERSE 48

Act steadfast in *yoga*, Dhananjaya, having abandoned attachment, being the same in success and failure: this equanimity is called Yoga.

The term *steadfast in yoga* (*yoga-stha*) or "fixed in *yoga*" refers to the enlightened state of consciousness. *Yoga* is discipline, the discipline and yoking of the mind and senses so that no *attachment* is formed. It is natural to be pleased with success and unhappy at failure but to be unmoved by either causes a shift in emphasis from results to actions themselves, while, at the same time, the mind remains placid and calm. When the mind is poised in a state of perfect equilibrium, *yoga* is taking place. Such *equanimity* in the verse was translated by Zaehner as "sameness-and-indifference",[32] indicating a wider nuance of the expression that encompasses all that the verse is stating. Nevertheless, *yoga* remains a practice. While it means being established in equilibrium, it also means *acting* from that level. The *Gita* will have much to say later about renunciation or abandonment, *tyaga*.

VERSE 49

Action alone is by far inferior to the *yoga* of wisdom, Dhananjaya: seek refuge in wisdom. Wretched are the seekers after fruits of action.

This is a difficult verse in that much of its sense has to be assumed. *Action alone* is presented as inferior to wisdom and it is this that presents the problem. Does this action refer to the carrying out of *Vedic* rituals? If so, this would make sense of the verse, since *Vedic* ritual was conducted with a view to specific results, and this is exactly what the second part of the verse is against. Or does action alone mean action carried out for the purpose of results, the *alone* referring to an absence of wisdom? This would also suit the context and the verse, and I am inclined to favour it. It would imply that action, that is to say, the path of *karma-yoga*, needs to be combined with knowledge/wisdom, *jnana-yoga* to be efficacious. To be fully integrated, the *yogin* needs the fully developed wisdom of the *buddhi*, the *buddhi* that is the cosmic *buddhi* closest to pure spirit. Thus, the verse implies that *jnana-yoga* is superior to actions based on desire, but, by implication, not necessarily to actions where the fruits have been abandoned. The last part of the verse makes this clear and seems to suggest that any action done in a state of equilibrium is a better action than one in which there is attachment to results, the *fruits, phala*, of action, thus continuing the sense of the last verse. If an action is done in order to achieve a result, there is grasping at something and concentration on results is involved. Action with all the attention on the action is giving one-pointed attention rather than grasping, with no sense of desire involved. For *yoga of wisdom, buddhi-yoga*, Zaehner preferred "spiritual exercise", so incorporating the sense of activity that *yoga* always has.[33] Such *yoga* is action without seeking rewards – action done in the controlled state of *buddhi-yoga*. The *buddhi*, especially the completely *sattvic buddhi*, provides the means for the *yogic* practice of disinterest in the fruits of action and in turn the constant *yogic* practice maintains and enhances the *sattva* of the *buddhi*: such is *buddhi-yoga*.

VERSE 50

One integrated in intellect casts off in this life both good and evil. Therefore, devote yourself to *yoga*, skill in actions.

Good or bad actions produce results that ensure the continuity of the *samsaric* cycle. *Yoga* is still action, but it has no results for its perpetrator: it becomes *karmaless* action. The character of *yoga* as a practice is emphasized with the word *skill, kaushala*, suggestive of discipline in the process of *yoga*. One must be a *karma-yogin*, one acting in the wisdom of *yoga*. The beginning of the verse refers to one *integrated in intellect*, a *buddhi-yukta*, one who has no personal motive for action or its results. Such is a mental equilibrium that will allow the best possible action.

VERSE 51

The wise, integrated in intellect, having abandoned the fruits of action, are certainly liberated from the fetters of rebirth and go to the abode beyond all ill.

Those who are *integrated in intellect, buddhi-yukta*, are united with the Self or "controlled-and-integrated" by the soul, as Zaehner put it.[34] They have the skill of acting without producing *fruits of action*, *karma-phala*, and are freed from the cycle of *samsara*. Krishna is telling Arjuna here that this is the kind of wisdom he needs in order to act in the right way. Once integrated in his inner Self – which is what *yoga* seeks to achieve – Arjuna will be able to engage himself in the field of action from a totally different viewpoint. Such is the Sankhya-Yoga of the *Gita*, being established in the Self (Sankhya) and being disciplined and egoless in action (Yoga). The twin characteristics of being *integrated in intellect* and abandoning the *fruits of action* effectively combine the two paths of *jnana* and *karma*, knowledge and action, as the means to liberation. The *abode* (*pada*) *beyond ill* is, thus, the integrated Self from which actions can be undertaken that cannot result in any ill or negative *karma*.

VERSE 52
When your intellect transcends the mire of delusion, then you will attain to disgust of what has been heard and what is yet to be heard.

Arjuna is conditioned about what he believes to be right and wrong. He is looking at things from the perspective of *prakriti* and not *purusha*. *Heard* is *shruti* in the Sanskrit and, therefore, highly likely to refer to the *Vedas*, but there is no indication in the verse as to whether it is merely the ritualistic parts of the *Veda* that are the object here. The *mire of delusion*, delusion being *moha*, refers to the condition of identifying the Self with the ego, with the non-self or false self and with the *prakritic* world of matter. Perhaps, rather than being critical of the *Vedas per se*, the verse suggests that the enlightened *yogin* transcends the scriptures to become integrated in intellect or wisdom (*buddhi*). The same point seems to have been made previously in verse 46.

VERSE 53
When, perplexed by what you have heard, you stand immovable in *samadhi*, with steady intellect, then you will attain *yoga*.

Again, *heard* in the verse is *shruti*, and may refer to the *Vedas*, possibly even *all Vedic* scriptures, including the *Vedanta*. The *Vedas* put forward a variety of theories, but the enlightened person can draw on the inner nature, the true Self, to establish the correct norms of life. *Samadhi* is the highest state of consciousness that featured in verse 44, a state tantamount to liberation for a *yogin*, providing it is maintained. It is the *steady intellect* of the *buddhi* fixed in *atman*, from where it does not stray; true *buddhi-yoga*.

VERSE 54　　　Arjuna said:
What is the description of the sage of steady wisdom, Keshava, of one immersed in *samadhi*. What does the steady one say? How does he sit? How does he walk?

Arjuna is clearly reacting to Krishna's words. Perhaps he wonders how someone in an immovable inner state of *samadhi* can act at all, since his questions, at present, seem a long way from the internalized knowledge of the Self. In the remainder of the chapter, Krishna will proceed to describe the *Brahma-jnanin*, one who has knowledge of Brahman. This is the *sage of steady wisdom*, the *sthita-prajna*, the *one immersed in samadhi* (*samadhi-stha*). Wisdom here is not *buddhi* as previously, but *prajna*, a word with similar meaning, suggestive of being fully focused in the Self, in the pure *sattva* state of *buddhi*. Gandhi believed that this verse to the end of the chapter were the most important in the whole of the *Gita* – the "essence of *dharma*", he said of them. "They embody the highest knowledge. The principles enunciated in them are immutable. The intellect, too, is active in them in the highest degree, but it is intellect, disciplined to high purpose. The knowledge which they contain is the fruit of experience."[35]

VERSE 55   The Lord said:
When a man casts off all the desires of the mind, Partha, satisfied in the *atman*, within the self, then he is said to be one of steady wisdom.

The *Brahma-jnanin*, the *one of steady wisdom*, or *sthita-prajna*, also of the previous verse, realizes that happiness is not to be found in the *desires* (*kama*) or pleasures external to the self, but in the Self. Happiness comes from within, not from without. Concentrating energies on the pursuit of happiness in the external environment makes it difficult to become aware of the depth of happiness that is within, in the Self, the *atman*. This is the first time that the term *atman* occurs in the *Gita*, though it is implied many times previously in this chapter. Until now, the expression used has been "embodied Self" (Skt. *dehin* and *sharirin*). The Sanskrit *atmany ev'atmana*, "in the Self within the self", then, refers both to the composite self and to the true Self, and to the necessity of operating from the level of the true *atman* within, transcending the pairs of opposites that dictate knowledge to the unenlightened, remaining at the level of the *atman*, equipoised, balanced and integrated. The *sthita-prajna* is the liberated Self, one who is desireless, having no *desires of the mind* – a key aspect of the *Yoga* of the *Gita*.

The state of being *steady in wisdom*, or steady in intellect, is the state of *samadhi*, when all desires have been transcended: the mind, once preoccupied with desires, is now rooted in the *atman*. To act well, knowledge of the Self is necessary, so that action will be without attachment, without desires or aversions. Krishna's comments here have not answered Arjuna's question directly. Arjuna asked for *outward* signs of the man of steady wisdom – what is he like, how does he speak, sit and walk? The sage actually does these things no differently to others; what characterizes him is an *internalized* condition.

VERSE 56
Of unshaken mind in suffering, without longing for happiness, free from attachment, fear and anger – he is called a sage of steady thought.

The *sage* here is the *muni*, he whom neither sorrow nor pleasure can affect, who is rooted in *atman*. The state depicted here is the liberated one of perfect equilibrium throughout all life's ups and downs. Again, Krishna does not refer to aspects that can be seen; they are *internal* attitudes of being. The sage is free from any desires, aversions, fears, anger or emotion: he is spiritually free. The important word *sthita-dhi*, *steady thought*, in the verse depicts such spiritual freedom of the sage, described by Gandhi as "one whose intellect remains steadfast and is never caught in a whirlpool".[36]

VERSE 57

He who everywhere is without attachment, who does not rejoice at having obtained what is good nor hates the evil; he is established in intuitive wisdom.

The *atman* is separated from activity because it is not part of material *prakriti*. This does not mean that separation from activity is the goal but that activities should not have any effect on the state of equilibrium. Remaining *without attachment* in all activity is essential. Life is full of things that are judged good and bad bringing joy and sorrow respectively. Attachment or aversion to such things traps the self in the dualities of their influences, and it is only the sage that is free from them. Arjuna asked what the sage might say, and Krishna's answer is that his words will be neither of praise nor blame and will not reflect choices between good or evil. Radhakrishnan poignantly commented on this verse: "Flowers bloom and they fade. There is no need to praise the former and condemn the latter. We must receive whatever comes without excitement, pain or revolt."[37] *Established in intuitive wisdom* (*prajna pratishthita*), is the state of being settled in the *buddhi*, and centred in the *atman*.

VERSE 58

When he entirely withdraws his senses from sense objects, like a tortoise withdraws its limbs, he is established in intuitive wisdom.

Just as the tortoise can withdraw easily and spontaneously into its self, so the sage, the *muni*, is able to withdraw into the *atman* and remain unaffected by sense stimuli: his *senses* (*indriyas*) are inward, not outward looking. It is unlikely that Krishna is suggesting that the wise person withdraws from the world: this would hardly solve Arjuna's problem. Rather, the wise experience sense stimuli but do not allow them to make any impression; stimuli reach the mind, but the mind does nothing with them. Arjuna will still need to act, but with a non-attached state of mind. The senses will still be operating but without attraction or aversion to their stimuli; they will have to be tamed. Such bringing back of the mind from sense reaction is called *pratyahara* in the school of Yoga.

VERSE 59

The objects of the senses of the abstinent Self fall away, though the taste of them remains: but even this taste falls away with a vision of the Supreme.

It may well be possible to restrain the body and the senses on the grosser levels, but at the subtle levels of the mind, the finer levels of the senses still have a tendency to recognize dualities such as pleasure and pain. Consider, for example, the very real sensations often conjured by dreams. The *objects of the senses* in the Sanskrit is an expression gleaned from the word *ahara*, "food". Just as flavour remains after food is eaten, so recollections remain after the senses have been stimulated. In early Buddhism, *ahara* referred to food for the senses, not just bodily food[38] and this is likely to be its meaning here. The message, then, is not to feed on objects of the senses. Franklin Edgerton likened the words to a fasting man who, though he continues to fast, cannot refrain from longing for food until he reaches a point where he is no longer hungry.[39] The Sanskrit word *rasa*, "flavour" or *taste* in the verse endorses the analogy of food. *Rasa*, according to van Buitenen, is "an abstract quality of things enjoyable", abstract because the quality remains as a subtle perception.[40]

Such subtle "flavours" or "tastes" resemble the latent residues in the dark, unknown world of the subconscious which, in Hindu terms, is stocked full of the residues of past experiences of countless lives and is constantly being replenished by present consciousness. These subtle, dynamic, but latent, impressions in the self are called *samskaras*, and they inform the whole personality of each individual during each new life. So not only is an individual *predisposed* to behave in a certain way because of these subtle impressions from past lives, but those impressions cause repetitive actions in the present existence and so reinforce the same kind of behavioural personality, because they combine to make habit patterns called *vasanas*. So subtle are these tendencies, these "flavours" and "tastes" from past existences that the mind cannot become free without immense discipline. The whole point of the school of Yoga was to train the *yogin* to overcome these difficult restraints in the inner being.[41] The present verse of the *Gita*, however, seems to suggest that the only way to overcome these subtle inclinations is for the soul to be united with Brahman *before* the senses are completely controlled rather than the senses being under control *so that* Brahman is experienced. The *Self* in the verse is *dehin* which, in every other instance in the *Gita* is used as the embodied Self, the inner *atman*, and I am inclined to see it as such here, also. This would suggest that subtle inclinations of the *yogin* are only controlled when focus is on God.

VERSE 60

The turbulent senses, Kaunteya, forcibly carry away the mind of even the man who strives.

The *senses* (*indriyas*) are the media by which life is lived and the subtle tendencies spoken of in the last verse make it difficult to avoid subtle reaction to the senses. Beings are conditioned from birth to avoid what hurts and seek what is pleasurable. To try to overcome and conquer this natural inclination of the *mind*, the *manas*, is a mammoth task. It is the breaking of the mind's habit of reacting to stimuli – whether from the outer world or the subconscious – that is the secret of quelling desire and the ego. It is the connecting thread between stimulus and response to stimulus, which carries away the mind of even the wisest person.

VERSE 61

Having restrained them all, integrated, he should sit intent on me.
Indeed, his wisdom is settled whose senses are firm.

To sit *intent on* Krishna is to sit with the self united with the Self. Here, for the
first time, the focus of attention is internalized on devotion to Krishna, where the
senses are at rest. *Intent on me* hints at what is to come in later chapters – the intensity of concentration on the divine that permits transcendence of the egoistic self
to reveal the *atman* within. This is true restraint, *samyama*. Simply to control the
senses is unlikely to work: but by focusing on Krishna they can be controlled. The
person who can do this is *yukta*, *integrated*, or "in union", his *wisdom (prajna) is settled*.
Classical Yoga has the same view that concentrating on a divine figure, Ishvara,
"Lord", aids the *yogin* to final liberation.[42] However, in classical Yoga, Ishvara ceases
to exist for the *yogin* at *moksha*, whereas in the *Yoga* of the *Gita*, liberation will bring
permanent union with the divine. Before the classical school of Yoga, however,
formative Yoga was theistic, drawing its inspiration from the *Vedanta*. The verse
answers Arjuna's question: "How does he sit?" but, again, internalizing the
response.

VERSE 62

When a man thinks of objects of the senses, attachment to them arises.
From attachment is born desire; from desire, anger is born.

The thought in this verse is akin to Buddhist ideas. Paying too much attention
to pleasurable sense stimuli causes one to react to them. It is such reaction that
engenders *desire*, *kama*, and, if that desire is frustrated, *anger*, *krodha*. Like
Buddhism, Hinduism believes that the way out of this is to check the level of attention paid to stimuli.

VERSE 63

From anger comes delusion, from delusion loss of memory, from loss of
memory destruction of the intellect, from destruction of the intellect,
ruination.

Anger, (again, *krodha*) caused by the frustration of not getting what is desired
leads to the mind suffering from *delusion (sammoha)* about reality, so that the whole
intellect and reasoning (*buddhi*) gradually becomes distorted. Perspectives are lost
as a result of no control over the mind. It is often those subtle stimuli that come
very quietly and softly to the mind that are the most dangerous, for they attract the
mind's attention and cause growing desires which, if not gratified, can lead to frustrated anger. But Radhakrishnan's comment on this verse is most pertinent here:
"To hate the senses is as wrong as to love them. The horses of the senses are not to
be unyoked from the chariot but controlled by the reins of the mind."[43]

Verse 64

But, free from attraction and aversion while moving among sense objects, with senses self-restrained, the self-controlled attains peace.

So the answer is to avoid reaction to the subtle stimuli, thus to move and operate in the world of matter without being affected by pleasurable or undesirable stimuli – free from *attraction* (*raga*) and *aversion* (*dvesha*). To do this, one has to be established in the Self. Krishna shows Arjuna the fate of those subject to desires and the senses in the previous verse and here, in this one, he shows him the fate of those who are desireless. That fate is *prasada*, "*peace*", "serenity", "grace", "quietness", "tranquillity", or even "grace". The verse is perhaps the answer to Arjuna's question in verse 55: "How does he walk?" The answer is that he moves in the world rooted in the calm serenity of the Self, where sense stimuli cannot affect him. The peace attained is *samadhi*, what Aurobindo described as "this calm, desireless, griefless fixity of the buddhi in self-poise and self-knowledge".[44]

Verse 65

In peace, all pains are destroyed, because the intellect of him of serene thoughts soon becomes steady.

Once in the state of calm serenity, sorrow, pain, suffering (*duhkha*) is destroyed. Because the intellect, the *buddhi*, that is the discerning, reasoning, volitional part of the self becomes calm, the outer world becomes the same: all is *peace* (*prasada*).

Verse 66

There is no wisdom in one not integrated and one not integrated has no steady thought. How can one without a steady thought and not peaceful be happy and at peace?

Unless the self is rooted in the Self and is *integrated* and in harmony, there can be no steadiness, no peace, no happiness. The *one not integrated* or unsteady is *ayukta*, the opposite of *yukta* "integrated". *Steady thought* is *bhavana* in the Sanskrit and could mean "contemplation", "meditation" or "steady intelligence".[45] Without steady thought, the *buddhi* is focused on *prakriti*, on the world of the senses. *Peace* in this verse has a different word than the previous verse; here, it is *shanti*.

Verse 67

For the mind that follows the wandering senses has its wisdom carried away like the wind carries away a boat on the water.

The *mind*, *manas*, in Sankhya and Yoga is a sense, the sixth one, part of *prakriti* and, therefore, material as opposed to spiritual. Its nature is to search for happiness and enjoyment, so it is drawn outward to the material world of which it is a part. It is, therefore, diffused, spreading its attention ever wider rather than focusing on one thing, even in the space of a very short time. Senses are attracted to sense stimuli involuntarily and they carry the mind with them like the wind blows a ship without a rudder. The *senses* (*indriyas*) have mastered the mind and the mind loses its wisdom, here *prajna*, having no control over itself like a ship far from shore.

VERSE 68

Therefore, Mahabaho, his wisdom is steady whose senses are completely restrained from sense objects.

The verse iterates the idea of restraining the *senses* (*indriyas*) similar to verse 58, and is a conclusion to the last six verses. It is necessary to lose desire and aversion, and the only way to do this is to prevent reaction to sense stimuli. We cannot prevent the stimuli but we can restrain the senses so that they do not react to them in any positive or negative way. The tie between senses and objects is then broken. While it would be impossible to prevent the senses from operating, it is *reaction* that should be prevented and controlled at will.

VERSE 69

That which is night to all beings is being awake to the self-controlled: that to which all beings are awake is night to the sage who sees.

Here, the state of the enlightened sage, the *muni*, is compared to that of the ignorant. Bibek Debroy's interpretation of the verse is rather neat. He writes: "ordinary beings are awake to sensual objects, but asleep on matters of wisdom", which captures the meaning of the verse very well.[46] The sage, the *muni* always exists in the light, the ignorant in the dark. Shankara's interpretation of this verse is particularly apt, too. He said that to all people, the Absolute is night; they are unable to perceive and knowledge remains inaccessible to them. The *muni*, by contrast, is always awake; he has lost the night of ignorance.[47] He is the one who is *self-controlled* (*samyama*).

VERSE 70

Just as waters from all sides enter the ocean settled in stillness, so do all desires enter he who attains peace, but not the desirer of desires.

This is not an easy verse and commentators vary considerably in how they interpret it. There is a suggestion that the sage has desires which, despite all that has been said previously, would indicate a response to sense stimuli. If the analogy of streams joining the changeless ocean could be applied to sense stimuli invading the mind of the *muni*, the verse would make sense, but it is desires, pleasures (*kama*) that are said to invade the mind of the sage. It seems to me that the key to the verse lies in the streams that enter into the ocean, since Sanskrit *pravisanti* can mean "merge". If, on the same analogy, all desires merge into one in the liberated sage then we are back to the concept of all dualities becoming one. All desires then would merge into the stillness of the enlightened, and would be *settled in stillness, achala-pratishtha*. Thus, most commentators interpret desires in the verse as sense stimuli, a strategy that instantly overcomes the problem. The *muni*, then, is not affected by desires that enter his mind, for they are dissipated without reacting to them, just as streams enter the ocean without disturbing its depths. The opposite is the *kamakami*, the *desirer of desires* who is totally trapped in matter and lacking any permanent peace (*shanti*).

VERSE 71

That man attains peace who, abandoning all desires, moves about free from longing, without ownership, without ego.

Forsaking *desires* is more clearly iterated here. Desires must be abandoned along with any sense of *I* or *mine*. Then, activity can be engaged in without any sense of ego. Suppression of desire and ego is consonant with Buddhist philosophy and many commentators find much that is Buddhist in these last two verses of the second chapter of the *Gita*. Zaehner is one such commentator, contesting that here is evidence of Buddhist terminology that has "made its way into Hinduism for the first time in the Bhagavad-Gita".[48] But we should, I think, remember that there is a good deal of consonance, too, with *Vedantic* teaching and the loss of the egoistic self in merging with Brahman. Then, too, the goal of both Sankhya and Yoga is the loss of ego (*nir-ahankara*), mind (*manas*) and even intellect (*buddhi*), all of which belong to the material world, which will leave the pure spirit devoid of any *I* and of any material self. Maybe the verses are borrowed terminology but not borrowed concepts. *Peace* is, as in the previous verse, *shanti*, a perfect state of liberation.

VERSE 72

This, Partha, is the state of Brahman. Having obtained this, one is not deluded. Being established in this even at the end of life one attains Brahma-*nirvana*.

The ultimate liberated state is one of *Brahma-nirvana*. Again, Zaehner pointed out, as do many commentators, that *nirvana* is a Buddhist term rather than a Hindu one. He also noted that *Brahma-* is a Buddhist prefix (compare, for example the *Brahma-viharas*), and concluded that the verse has strong Buddhist overtones. Yet he admitted that the term *Brahma-nirvana* is not found in Buddhism at all, only in separate compounds.[49] Johnson thinks the use of *nirvana* here is borrowed from Buddhism deliberately to "upstage the Buddhist renouncers by linking that state of liberation with the supreme or absolute principle of the Upanishadic (and hence Vedic) tradition, Brahman".[50] *Nirvana* is certainly not a Hindu term prior to its use in the *Gita*.

On the other hand, van Buitenen suggested that, at the time the *Gita* was written, the term *nirvana* was not confined to Buddhist usage.[51] The message to the Buddhists here, if there is one, may well be that enlightenment is the stilling of the mind, the cessation of desires and the fruits of thoughts but *not* inaction. Prefacing the Buddhist term *nirvana* with the Hindu Brahman might also be an attempt to claim that Brahman is greater than *nirvana*. *Brahma-nirvana* is not the extinction or emptiness (*shunyata*) of the Buddhists, but the fullness of experience of the divine and action without thought of its fruits. *Nirvana* means "to blow" (*va*) "out" (*nir*) in the sense of extinguish, the object of the extinguishing being the egoistic self. Joined with Brahman, the true Self attains its natural state as in unity with (though not necessarily identical to) Brahman. Brahman is derived from a root with an opposite thought, "to burst forth", "to grow great", "to increase" and so has the nuance of meaning of evolution, of expansion of the individual's inner being as *atman.* Notably, too, in the early part of the verse *state of Brahman, Brahmi-sthiti,* is also a synonym of Brahma-*nirvana*, the Brahman state of liberation, and has no suggestive Buddhist overtones.

In the *Upanishad* of the *Bhagavad Gita*, the knowledge of Brahman,
the teaching of Yoga and the dialogue between Shri Krishna
and Arjuna, this is the second chapter called
Sankhya-Yoga.

CHAPTER THREE

Karma-Yoga

The *Yoga* of Action

CHAPTER TWO was concerned with Sankhya-Yoga and many see that chapter as mainly advocating *jnana-yoga*, the *yoga* of knowledge. The teachings of the *Gita* about both Sankhya and Yoga are different from their classical expressions. While Sankhya is the theory, the knowledge, or *jnana*, and Yoga is the practice, this present chapter is very much concerned with their *complementary* nature, theory *and* practice, that is to say, knowledge *and* action. Indeed, the former in isolation from action would not solve Arjuna's immediate problem, and his question in the opening verse of CHAPTER THREE – If knowledge (*jnana*) is superior to action (*karma*) is there any need for him to act at all? – sets the scene for a chapter dealing mainly with desireless, egoless action. Nevertheless, non-dualists such as Shankara upheld the supremacy of *jnana* as the only way to liberation, eschewing any suggestion of knowledge and action as complementary. Shankara believed that the path of knowledge and the path of action were independent, that the latter was much inferior, and that both were pertinent to separate groups of people. Ramanuja, on the other hand, upheld *karma-yoga* as superior, as we shall see in this chapter.

The important difference between the Sankhya of the philosophers and the Sankhya of the *Gita* is exactly the latter's emphasis on action. Rohit Mehta commented that: "The uniqueness in the teaching of the *Bhagavad Gita* lies in the fact that it asks the spiritual aspirant not to leave the world and retire into a forest for the practice of spiritual life but to live it where one is, even in the midst of one's mundane duties. In fact, the *Gita* says that to live is to act, because, not even for one moment can man exist without action."[1] The main emphasis of CHAPTER THREE is the necessity of acting while established in *yoga*, in the embodied Self, the *atman*. But, while action without ego and desire for results is the key, knowledge of the true nature of the Self is the *raison d'être* of it. Such knowledge is the basis for actions that do not bind the Self, whereas, without that knowedge, individuals are locked into *karmic* activity.

VERSE I   Arjuna said:
If knowledge is thought by you to be superior to action, Janardana, then why do you engage me in this terrible action, Keshava?

Arjuna is making a distinction between the paths of knowledge and action and suggests that Krishna favours the former. While non-dualists such as Shankara would endorse this distinction, others see Arjuna's question as posing the classic question that if one is established in *atman*, does one need to act, in order for Krishna to answer it. Arjuna's state of mind has not yet altered; he is still not ready to fight, and puts this question forward as a further argument against going into battle. Perhaps he thinks that if he could obtain *ultimate* knowledge, it could outweigh human activity in life and so there would be no need to fight. Arjuna could be forgiven for thinking that Krishna favours the path of knowledge since *buddhi*, "wisdom", "knowledge", "intellect", "understanding", has been stressed so much in CHAPTER TWO, whereas *karma-yoga* as a path has not, though *yoga* as a practice, conjoined with knowledge has. In 2:49, Krishna said: *"Action alone is by far inferior to the yoga of wisdom, Dhananjaya: seek refuge in wisdom. Wretched are the seekers after fruits of action."* Such words may be in Arjuna's mind, but he will have to learn that what is inferior is *action alone*, that is to say ordinary action that seeks rewards, rather than desireless action. And yet, to act without accruing *karma* necessitates knowledge of the difference between the self of *prakriti*, the material self, and the true Self that is pure spirit. A different kind of knowledge than ordinary knowledge has to underpin Arjuna's actions: he will not be able to fight until his perception of reality changes. He makes a distinction between knowledge and action whereas Krishna reconciles the two, though Krishna does, indeed, see knowledge as superior to any actions that are result orientated.

VERSE 2
With seemingly perplexing words you confuse my understanding as it were. Tell me for certain of that by which I may attain the best.

Since Arjuna admits that Krishna's words have confused him, his question in verse 1 cannot be taken as evidence that knowledge is superior to action. Arjuna is asking for more specific teaching on both. The message of CHAPTER TWO is clearly not one of inaction but of action based on knowledge of the Self, the *atman*, and of Brahman. Should Arjuna choose just knowledge, he thinks he may not need to act, and this is perhaps what he is hoping for: he is asking whether knowledge can take precedence over his *dharma*. Then, too, in denying any reality to the material self, Sankhya philosophers did not accept the necessity for action, and this may also have confused Arjuna. The followers of Sankhya stressed that knowledge was the key to liberation of the true Self from matter, contrasting with the *karma-yogins* who favoured the path of prescribed ritual action. Arjuna is asking what is best, what is good, *shreya*. He is deeply confused, the term *moha* also meaning "delusion".

VERSE 3 The Lord said:
In this world, the twofold path previously told by me, sinless one, was the *jnana-yoga* of the Sankhyas and the *karma-yoga* of the *yogins*.

Both *jnana-yoga* and *karma-yoga* have the idea of *yoga* as common to both. Thus, for both, the discipline and integration of the Self is the common denominator and, hence, the complementary factor of the two paths. Some commentators believe that Krishna is differentiating between two separate groups of people here, the theorists with the path of knowledge and the activists with the path of action.[2] Ramanuja's position here was that *karma-yoga* is the path for those not yet able to fix the *buddhi* in the *atman*, and *jnana-yoga* is for those who can,[3] yet he also saw *karma-yoga* as superior to *jnana*. In a way, Arjuna has a blend of both knowledge and action in his character. As a *Kshatriya*, his predominant quality, or *guna*, is the active *rajas*, but his secondary one is that of *sattva*, the more reflective, evolutionary and contemplative, though less dominant *guna*. His question in verse 1 indicates that he is aware of both. Then, too, in the four stages of life – student, householder, forest dweller and mendicant – the *Brahmins*, *Kshatriyas* and *Vaishyas*, those who were the twice-born classes of Hinduism, would have found *karma-yoga*, the path of action in its non-ritualistic sense particularly applicable to the householder, second stage. Arjuna himself is at this second stage and would, therefore, be expected to *actively* support family and society. We must remember that Krishna himself is a *Kshatriya*, so his teaching to Arjuna will sometimes be *Kshatriya* to *Kshatriya*. Krishna is not differentiating between the efficacy of the two paths; he will simply qualify the best praxis of both.

VERSE 4
Man does not attain actionlessness through non-performance of actions, and does not attain perfection only through renunciation.

Krishna, here, is referring to the traditional view of *sannyasa* as *renunciation* of *all* activity: he does not accept that such a path is a valid one. Renunciation as *sannyasa* means total abandoning, discarding of, or casting away (*sam* "total", *ni*, "down", *as*, "to cast") of all actions. As the last of the four stages of life, it meant casting off all social and religious intercourse and living the life of a wandering ascetic devoted to God and to liberation from rebirth. Here, Krishna is clearly critical of this kind of renunciation that avoids the world. The Sanskrit *naishkarmya*, "actionlessness" or "non-activity", is an important word, for in the *Gita* it means freedom from *karma* gained by non-attachment to action and the fruits of that action. That is true non-activity, desireless, *karma*-less, activity. Simply not acting, *akarma*, "inactivity", is sheer idleness and is not true freedom from action because it is *karma* producing. It is *prakriti* that is involved in activity – the busy bird that flies from tree to tree in search of food. The *purusha* of the *Gita* acts but is not affected by the actions – like the bird that passively watches. Thus, Aurobindo referred to *naishkarmya* as "a calm voidness from works . . . for it is Prakriti which does the work and the soul has to rise above involution in the activities of the being and attain to a free serenity and poise watching over the operations of Prakriti, but not affected by them. That, and not cessation of the work of Prakriti, is what is really meant by the soul's *naishkarmya*".[4] *Naishkarmya*, then, is indicative of liberation from fruitive *karma*, from the results of all one's actions, whether those are of deed, word or thought.

The ideas here are reminiscent of Buddhism but this section of the *Gita* is perhaps not so heavily influenced by Buddhism as some suggest.[5] Shankara considered *actions* in this verse to refer to sacrifice, *yajna*, in the sense of ritual actions, so that *renunciation* referred to *Vedic* rituals. This would give the sense that abandoning ritual actions does not help one become liberated. Shankara contended that ritual worship in past and present lives prepare an individual for the path of knowledge and only *then*, with knowledge, can preparatory ritual be renounced.[6] The general sense of the chapter as a whole, however, suggests that *actions* here refer to general actions rather than ritually performed ones. *Perfection*, *siddhi*, and *naishkarmya* are really synonymous, so that one is unlikely to occur without the other.

VERSE 5

No one remains even for a moment without performing action, for all are helplessly made to act by the *gunas* born of *prakriti*.

Life means activity and no individual can exist without it. It is the *gunas born of prakriti* that ensure this. In all life, the three *gunas* – *sattva*, *rajas* and *tamas* – are represented in some combination: it is only when an individual is rooted in the Self, has become liberated, that these *gunas* are stilled: such is true non-activity. An individual cannot possibly be free of the *gunas* simply by inactivity; this is not *naishkarmya*, actionlessness. Action, change and flux is the nature of *prakriti*; we eat, breathe, sleep, and all is action. Again, Shankara considered that it is the ritualist *karma-yogins* who are bound by actions and *prakriti* and that only the *jnana-yogin* could be truly free. Indeed, Shankara saw *karma-yoga* as "for the ignorant only".[7] The *Gita's* view thus far, however, is that knowledge of the Self and being established in that Self are the means to overcoming fruitive *karma* but *in activity*.

VERSE 6

He who sits restraining the organs of action but remembers sense objects in the mind is self-deluded and is called a hypocrite.

The organs of action in Sankhya-Yoga are speaking, grasping, walking, excreting and generating; they are called *karmendriyas*. Even if one were to avoid them, thought is also *karma*-producing, so physical inactivity cannot possibly be a path to perfection. Gandhi said it is rather like a person who fasts all day but cannot stop *thinking* about food at the same time.[8] So even when individuals restrain (*samyama*) their sense organs, their minds are active. They may seem to be on the right path but they are really hypocrites because their renunciation of action is only outward; their minds remain impure. In the Sankhya scheme of matter, the mind, though still matter, is a higher entity than the physical environment of the senses and the organs of action, and it is the *mind* (*manas*) that is more important to control.

Ramakrishna told a story of two men who happened to pass a group listening to the words of a holy man while they were on their way to a good night out. One stopped to listen; the other went on to a brothel. The man at the holy meeting couldn't stop thinking of the pleasures he was missing, while the other couldn't stop thinking about the possibilities of divine bliss that he might have passed by. It is the latter who is the better man for the mind is the superior part of *prakriti*. A similar story finds a holy man living at a temple with the house of a whore nearby. He was so annoyed at the number of men visiting her that he told her of her evil ways. She was very repentive and prayed a great deal, but continued in her ways.

The enraged holy man decided to put a pebble outside her house for each visitor she had and built a rather large pyramid! Then he summoned the woman and showed her the visible sign of her evil. She was full of remorse and prayed fervently. That night both died, the holy man having an honourable funeral, the whore's body being thrown to the vultures. Their fate thereafter was somewhat different! The holy man whose mind was always on unholy things was enraged to find himself in Hell: the whore, whose body was polluted but whose mind was always on God, went to Heaven.

VERSE 7

But whoever controls the senses by the mind, Arjuna, unattached, engages by the organs of action on *karma-yoga*, he excels.

Translations of this verse by commentators vary considerably but the thought is mainly that detached action is the right kind of action – an action in which the *senses* (*indriyas*) are not only controlled on the physical level but also by the *mind* (*manas*). *Karma-yoga*, then, is the skill of action without attachment (*asakta*); it is utilizing all the abilities that the body has to act; it is registering experiences through the senses, but it is controlling desires and ego-involvement. The senses experience objects but do not react to them, a concept also akin to Buddhism. Commenting on this verse, Ramanuja believed disinterested *karma-yoga*, which he interpreted as ritual praxis, to be superior to *jnana-yoga*, providing the mind remained focused on the *atman*.[9] Sacrificial action, he believed, should not be abandoned but should be performed without emphasis on results. With the self focused on the *atman*, knowledge of it would occur naturally, as well as knowledge, rather than ignorance, of the *prakritic* world. Thus, Ramanuja believed that *karma-yoga* would bring about knowledge without the need of *jnana-yoga*.

VERSE 8

Therefore perform your prescribed action, for action is superior to inaction: even maintenance of the body would not be possible with inaction.

Krishna reiterates the point that it is impossible to live without action, but here he also stresses that individuals should do those actions that are prescribed and necessary for them, *niyata*. Thus, ordinary activity like eating and sleeping are necessities even on the spiritual path and are better than *inaction* (*akarma*). Actions must be undertaken to keep the body in good physical condition, but they also need to be undertaken in order for an individual to evolve, and for life to progress. Aurobindo commented here: "For knowledge does not mean renunciation of works, it means equality and non-attachment to desire and the objects of the sense; and it means the poise of the intelligent will in the Soul free and high-uplifted above the lower instrumentation of Prakriti and controlling the works of the mind and the senses and body in the power of self-knowledge and the pure objectless self-delight of spiritual realisation, *niyatam karma*". Aurobindo thought that *niyata* should be linked with the *niyamya* of the last verse suggesting the meaning "desireless works controlled by the liberated *buddhi*".[10]

VERSE 9

This world is bound by action other than for the sake of *yajna*. Therefore perform action free from attachment, Kaunteya.

The verse is difficult and interpretations will depend on whether it is linked with the previous verse or those verses that follow. The emphasis, again, is on action that is free from attachment and desire. The difficulty arises because *yajna* can refer to the sacrificial ceremonies of *Vedic* ritual and Ramanuja was one who certainly understood *yajna* here as such. *Karma* for Ramanuja was the inimical force of bondage of embodied Selves. In particular, it is the *vasanas*, the "subtle impressions" left after action that build up *karmic* personality. But Ramanuja believed that God could play a part in eradication of this *karma* for those who performed prescribed actions free from attachment, so that "the Supreme Person (Paramapurusa), pleased by sacrifices and such other works, bestows on him the undisturbed vision of the Self [my capital], after eradicating the subtle impressions of *karma* of that person which have continued from time immemorial."[11] The grace of God is implicit in Ramanuja's comments here. A more modern interpreter like Douglas Hill thought, too, that the *yajna* here is "literal sacrifice".[12] *Yajna* as referring to *Vedic* sacrificial ritual is supported in the light of the following verses. Verse 11 particularly seems to endorse sacrificial ritual to the gods. *Bound by action* might indicate the importance of *yajna* beyond just *Vedic* sacrificial ritual, that is to say, ordinary activity, continuing the sense of the last verse, which says that we cannot avoid action. But it could also mean that *except* for sacrificial ritual laid down in the *Vedas*, all other actions are *karma*-producing. Verses 11 and 12 might just endorse such an interpretation.

However, we must not lose sight of Arjuna's needs here. Since it is egoless performance of action for the purpose of sacrifice that seems to be the sense of the verse, it suggests that Arjuna's actions in fighting are the equivalent of sacrificial duty, that is to say, for the sake of *yajna*. The whole of sacrificial ritual was controlled by the priests, but we shall see a shift in the interpretation of *yajna* throughout the *Gita*. It is a shift that will emphasize sacrifice *for* God, which will widen the context of it beyond prescriptive ritual, and will lift it out of any involvement with results – all contrary to *Brahmin* praxis. It may be this sense of *yajna* that is implied here. *Bound by action* might, then, convey the idea of being *karmically* bound, that is to say, having to reap the results of actions, though the sense may be that it is impossible not to act in some way or other. *Yajna* as duty and egoless action avoids one being bound by one's actions. Lars Martin Fosse captures this well in his interpretation of the verse: "With the exception of action done for the sake of sacrifice, this world is bound by the consequences of action. Therefore, Son of Kunti, perform actions free from attachment."[13] The world, being *prakriti*, is in the bonds of action unless, through *yajna* that is focused on Brahman, the intellect transcends the material world for spiritual reality. Only then can detached action take place in a desireless, egoless and non-attached way. In this case, *yajna* is a wider concept than religious ritual, encompassing the pouring back of one's essence to the divine, what Vimala Thakar described as "the pouring of the contents of one's own being into every movement, at every moment".[14] Indeed, Gandhi saw spinning and weaving and even cleaning the latrines as *yajna*.[15]

VERSE 10

Having created humankind in the beginning, together with *yajna*, Prajapati said "By this you shall propagate: let this be your milch cow of desires".

Yajna is described as the *milch cow*, the cow yielding milk, and in Aryan terms this was tantamount to the fulfilment of all one's desires. The milch cow was Kamadhuk, a mythological cow owned by the sage Vashishtha. It had a woman's head and a bird's wings, and was believed to grant its owner anything desired. Prajapati means "Lord of Creatures". He was the instigator of creation in one of the older creation myths of the *Vedas*. As a *Vedic* deity and creator of all creatures, he was often identified with the later god Brahma – an obvious correlation of two creator gods. It was the voluntary sacrifice of Prajapati's own body that was the source of all creation, so the reference to sacrificial *yajna* is particularly apt in the verse. Since *yajna* is created alongside beings, it is suggestive that it is an appropriate path to Brahman. Krishna has been critical of *Vedic* ritual in earlier sections, accusing the ritualists of sacrifice *for results*, so many consider it unlikely that *yajna* in this verse refers to ritual sacrifice. Easwaran, thus, translated *yajna* as "selfless work", "selfless service" or "self-sacrifice",[16] which would suit the tenor of the verse well. Again, however, the following verses seem to refer to *Vedic* sacrificial ritual to the gods, and it cannot be ruled out that this is to what the *yajna* of the verse refers. Ramanuja believed that God created beings in order to redeem them aided by his creation, too, of the sacrificial system as a means to worship him.[17] He believed that the reference to Prajapati was not to Brahma, but to Narayana, the favoured name for Vishnu in Vishishtadvaita Vedanta.

VERSE 11

Nourish the gods with this and may those gods nourish you: nourishing one another you shall attain the highest good.

The *yajna* mentioned in the difficult verse 9 is possibly being made more specific here as ritual offered to the gods. We know from CHAPTER TWO that Krishna finds *Vedic* ritual unnecessary for the enlightened. Here, he appears to be saying the very opposite in that *yajna* to the gods is necessary. The use of the term *bhavayata* suggests "nourish", "sustain" or "cherish" in a mutual sense. For *gods* the Sanskrit term is *devas*, "shining ones", which can refer not only to gods but to highly evolved souls or even cosmic forces symbolized by the gods, "powers governing different impulses of intelligence and energy", as Maharishi Mahesh Yogi described them.[18] Being in line with these forces is pouring energies towards divinity so that divinity will pour back blessings in return. The Sanskrit *shreya param*, *the highest good*, is usually thought to be liberation, though this would be out of line with much of the other teaching in the *Gita*, which claims that worship of the gods cannot lead to release. Interpreting the verse symbolically overcomes such a problem, the gods being symbolic forces pointing beyond themselves to a reality that is more ultimate, but it is likely that the highest good is Heaven, the abode of the gods, to which those who worship them well can go after death.

VERSE 12

So, nourished by *yajna* the gods will give to you the objects you desire. Who enjoys what is given by them without offering to them is truly a thief.

The verse certainly appears to endorse the sacrificial ritual that is the root of reciprocal aid between human and divine and, it would seem, propitiatory sacrifice at that. Nourishment is explicit in that food was burned to the deities, who savoured the smoke and essence of it, as in Hinduism today. Only then could the offering be partaken of by the givers. *Yajna* in the form of food offerings is not only offered to the gods but to enlightened seers and ancestors. It would be difficult to shift the meaning here from anything other than *Vedic* sacrifice, but Krishna is not suggesting liberation from *karmic* rebirth is gained from such sacrifice, only that good service to the gods provides appropriate rewards.

VERSE 13

The righteous who eat the remnants of the *yajna* are freed from all sins but those evil ones who cook for their own sake, eat evil.

Food is prepared for the gods, is offered to gods, and only *then* is it returned to the individual to partake of it. The actions of an individual who does this are good. Conversely, there is the individual who prepares food only to gratify personal hunger, with no thought of the gods. Here, all is taken and nothing is given. The former are ego-free, the latter ego-bound, and with the latter, their actions belong to them and not to the divine. It is in this way that they commit *evil* (*papa*) and, as the previous verse states, steal from the universe, satisfying only themselves.

VERSE 14

From food beings come forth, from rain food is produced, from *yajna* comes forth rain, and *yajna* is born of *karma*.

In the context of the previous verses, we should perhaps interpret this one literally, seeing the sacrifice as purely ritualistic – sacrificial action or *karma*, as it is in the verse, and a biological cycle. Human beings need food, to have food they must have rain, sacrificial ritual brings the rain and sacrificial ritual comes from ritual action. This seems to be the fundamental level at which Ramanuja understood the verse.[19] He was always keen to stress obedience to the *Shastras* and to sacrificial ritual providing it was conducted without thought for the end results. Propitiatory ritual to the gods for the continuance of such worldly benefits was a major facet of *Vedic* sacrifice. Nevertheless, we might here, as well as in the previous verse, widen the concept of *yajna* as the *essence* of creation sacrificed back to the divine so that it can be replenished. John Koller thinks that this is the whole *raison d'être* of *Vedic* sacrifice.[20] Thus, through *yajna*, the created order can continue, the cycle of life proceed, the rains fall. There is, thus, a harmony in existence as a result of *yajna*. But *yajna* itself stems from *action*, action that is performed correctly and in the right frame of mind. When action is performed, a subtle energy takes place, which is the important link between the action and its effect. It is known as *apurva*. Just as the sun changes water to mist or material waste is converted to carbon dioxide by fire, so the action of *yajna* converts gross into subtle energies that bring human beings in line with the divine and maintains the continuous flow of creation. *Apurva* is the unperceived potency between cause and effect. The Mimamsa school upheld the importance of ritual action claiming that without *apurva* sacrifice would have no value whatsoever. Looking at this verse from the macrocosmic perspective, then, we could say that it is not the sacrifice itself that is referred to but the subtle energy into which it is converted, and the following verse certainly lifts *yajna* out of the mundane. But, at the microcosmic level of propitiation of the gods for the rains, for wealth, fertility and the reward of Heaven after death, *Vedic yajna* was the means.

VERSE 15

Know action to have arisen from Brahman and Brahman to have arisen from the Imperishable. Therefore all-pervading Brahman is eternally established in *yajna*.

The verse has two direct references to Brahman and one indirect one. This last is to *the Imperishable*, *akshara*, of which the syllable *Om* is a synonym. Brahman is frequently synonymous with *Veda* and could be meant as such for the first and second reference to Brahman in the present verse. In this case, *Veda* would be the source of ritual action, and would itself have emanated from the Source as Brahman, linking, inextricably, *Vedic yajna* to Brahman as eternally present in ritual sacrifice. However, the first Brahman, the Brahman that arises from the Imperishable, could well refer to *manifest* Brahman, *saguna* Brahman, as nature or *prakriti*, which gives rise to ritual action, but itself stems from the unmanifest, *nirguna* Brahman. Ramanuja believed that the first two citations of Brahman here are to Brahman as *prakriti* as his "body", his material manifestation. Then, the *all-pervading* (*sarvagata*) Brahman is Brahman as the supreme Soul, the Source of all action who is present in all that is his body.[21] Again, we are left uncertain as to whether Krishna is referring to *Vedic yajna per se*, or to broader *yajna* as *dharmic* living from an egoless self.

A few, such as Gandhi,[22] see Brahman here as Brahma, one member of the *Trimurti*, the three deities of Vishnu, Shiva and Brahma. Brahma is the creator of the universe, the active and dynamic force, *rajasic* in nature, and responsible for the birth and evolution of all nature. The sequence in the verse would be logical in that activity of any kind stems from the Creator God Brahma who, himself, has Brahman as his Source, Brahman then being the essence within all creation. The problem with such a theory lies in the dating of the *Gita*, which may be precedent to the doctrine of the *Trimurti*.

VERSE 16

Thus the wheel is set revolving and who does not follow it here lives in sin, rejoicing in the senses: in vain he lives, Partha.

The wheel here perhaps refers to human evolutionary progress caught up in *prakritic* existence of cause and effect. Only through reaching higher states of consciousness, can harmony with Brahman be attained. Those who prefer a life filled with the pleasures of the *senses* (*indriyas*) cannot evolve in such a way. The *Shvetashvatara Upanishad* (1:4–6) refers to the wheel of Brahman and captures the meaning of the present verse very well. For example in verse 6 of the *Upanishad*: "In this vast brahma-wheel, which enlivens all things, in which all rest, the soul flutters about thinking that the self in him and the Mover (the Lord) are different. Then, when blessed by him, he gains life eternal."[23] Thus, there is some justification in seeing the image of the wheel as denoting Brahman as the Source and means of human pathways to liberation. van Buitenen described it as a "symbol of universal dynamism, of the cosmic power of change and transformation".[24]

VERSE 17

But he who rejoices only in the *atman*, who is satisfied in the *atman*, the man contented only in his *atman* does not have anything to do.

Atman is the obvious emphasis in this verse, which refers to the liberated state of one who is detached from everything except it. Then, there is no *karma* to be reaped, so if one acts while rooted in *atman* it is possible to move through the world of *prakriti* without attached action and in complete freedom. Chidbhavananda wrote: "The river is active until it reaches the ocean. On merging in it, its functioning is over. Likewise the functioning of the mind is over in its being resolved in Atman. Bliss is the characteristic of Atman. The mind which is set in the Self is therefore ever satisfied, pacified and blissful. The finale of all activities is for the mind to rest in Atman."[25] The end of the verse, however, may suggest freedom from obligatory duty, freedom from the necessity to perform ritual, in line with Krishna's words in CHAPTER TWO. The verse does not, however, mean that nothing should be done, endorsing inactivity: such a view would be inconsistent with the rest of the chapter. One rooted in *atman* does not *have* or *need* to do something; actions are simply done naturally without attachment to them or their results. *Rejoices in* or *delights in* is *rati* in the Sanskrit, denoting immense satisfaction, bliss and complete contentment of the one centred in *atman*. For Ramanuja, not having *anything to do* referred only to one who is completely released being absolved from *Vedic* ritual, so leaving his high opinion of *Vedic* ordinances intact.[26]

VERSE 18

There is not even concern in him for actions done or not done here: and this man is not dependent on any being for any object.

Detached action is the key to life, so that acts are not undertaken *for* this or *for* that; they are simply undertaken.

VERSE 19

Therefore, always perform the action which should be done without attachment because the man performing action without attachment attains the Supreme.

The verse summarizes this major tenet of the *Gita* here of unattached (*asakta*) action. Just as we pay no attention to the action of our heart beating, so we should pay no attention to the other actions we do. Actions should be those that *should be done*, which suggests that they are pure, correct actions.

VERSE 20

Truly by action only Janaka and others attained perfection: you should perform only having in view the welfare of the world.

Janaka may be a reference to the King of Videha and Sita's father in the epic tale the *Ramayana* and, therefore, father-in-law of Rama, the hero of that epic.[27] This Janaka was born a *Kshatriya* but, because of his austerities along with his insistence on performing religious ritual himself as opposed to accepting *Brahminic* dominance over ritual procedures, he was eventually granted the status of *Brahmin*. However, he still held his position as King of Videha and, therefore, had to fulfil his duty as a *Kshatriya* through action. As a king, Janaka had to consider the welfare of his subjects; action and setting a good example were necessary in order to do this, even though he had attained perfection. Like Arjuna, Janaka was initially a *Kshatriya* and his qualities were *rajas-sattva*, He could fulfil his *sattvic* side but not neglect activity dictated by his dominant *rajasic* nature. Ramanuja took such an emphasis on activity as endorsing the superiority of *karma-yoga* over *jnana-yoga*, especially since, while known for their knowledge, these perfected beings had attained *atman* through *karma-yoga*.[28] *Welfare of the world*, *loka-sangraha*, is suggestive of involvement in worldly affairs rather than dissociation from the world. It is verses such as this present one that are emphasized by those who see *karma-yoga* as the main message of the *Gita* and by the Indian activists of the past, who sought to use political activism against British domination. Certainly, this verse and those that follow are firm advocates of involvement in the world and not withdrawal from it. *Welfare* would imply not only moral guidance but also maintenance of societal norms, a "holding together" of society, thus addressing Arjuna's fears of societal breakdown through his actions in fighting. In Radhakrishnan's view, such world welfare carries with it the concept of the unity of the world and an interconnectedness of society.[29]

VERSE 21

Whatever the best of men does only that will the other people do. Whatever standard he sets the world follows.

People have a tendency to venerate evolved or enlightened individuals. Here, Krishna is hinting to Arjuna that *he* should be an example to the people – a highly responsible position.

VERSE 22

There is nothing to be done in the three worlds by me, Partha, nor anything unattained to be attained: yet I engage in action.

Even Krishna himself is here on the battlefield as an example that action must be undertaken in order to uphold righteousness. The two aspects of the divine are the indescribable, unmanifest, *nirguna* Brahman, *nirguna* signifying having no qualities, no *gunas*. The other aspect *is* manifest, with true, real qualities and is *saguna*. Krishna is the *saguna* aspect of Brahman, manifest here on the battlefield of Kurukshetra, as a descent into the world. The relationship between the two was attractively conveyed by Vimala Thakar: "The inter-locked nature of the manifest with the unmanifest cannot be separated. The very existence of the manifest and the unmanifest depend upon each other. The manifest declares the unmanifest as its essence, and the unmanifest declares that the variety of the manifest world, the diversity, is contained in emptiness. The one declares the existence of the other. Diversity decorates unity, and unity breathes into the expression of diversity."[30] Being both *nirguna* and *saguna*, Krishna has nothing to achieve, nothing to gain, no duty to perform: and yet he acts, he is here on the battlefield. Clearly, Krishna presents Brahman as the creator and sustainer of all *prakriti*, as the unchanging Source of the ever-changing, transient universe.

VERSE 23

Certainly, if ever I did not engage in unwearied action, Partha, humanity would follow my path in every way.

This verse continues the thought of the previous verses, particularly the idea of an individual being an example to others as in verse 21. Without Krishna's ceaseless activity in the world – his ceaseless activity in the whole of the created order – there would be inertia, nothing. Krishna is, indeed, the *Karma-Yogin par excellence*. All creation is the manifestation of the Unmanifest, but while remaining unmanifest, *nirguna*, Brahman is also *saguna*, manifest, and it is this manifestation that is creation. The process of manifesting or making manifest is action, and manifest existence itself is all activity. Then, too, Krishna acts in the world in the physical descents, with *direct* action to restore the balance of right over wrong. Even so, he is neutral in the battle; he does not need to act in the sense of physical fighting. This verse, and the following one, are clear indicators of Krishna's role as the Source of *prakriti* and of the clear differentiation between classical Sankhya's non-theistic stance and the powerful theism of the *Gita* that places Brahman as the Source of manifest existence.

VERSE 24

These worlds would perish if I did not perform action. I should be the cause of social confusion and I should destroy these creatures.

In CHAPTER ONE, Arjuna had made the point that if he refrained from fighting, from action, society would not be harmed. In the present verse, Krishna seems to answer that point by saying that if he, Krishna, were inclined to the same attitude of inaction there would be *social confusion*, the overthrow of the class system by the mixture of classes and castes. The Sanskrit *samkarasya* in the text refers to the confusion of castes, to hybrid castes and so to the breakdown of social norms. Arjuna has already pointed out in CHAPTER ONE that this would lead to disaster. On a more cosmic scale, since Krishna mentions the *worlds* (Heaven, Earth and the intermediate world of spirits and lesser deities, or perhaps the Underworld – the three worlds of verse 22), he is probably also referring to his role in creating and sustaining the whole universe. Without such a role, the universe would be destroyed, and lapse into non-existence.

VERSE 25

As the ignorant act attached to action, Bharata, so the wise should act unattached, wishing the welfare of the world.

The ignorant that are *attached to* their *actions* are those who act selfishly for their own ends, in which case, the results of those actions will also be attached to the doers of the actions. In contrast, the wise act without attachment (*asakta*) to their actions so that no results can be attached to what they do. The unwise act for themselves alone: the wise act for the *welfare of the world* through selfless action. *Welfare of the world* is, again, *loka-sangraha*, an important concept for those who interpreted the *Gita* as essentially a scripture with a social message, as was seen in verse 20. Combined with *nishkama-karma*, "selfless activity", it is a concept that many have lifted from the past of the *Gita* to the pertinent context of the modern and postmodern world. Operating from the level of *atman* ensures that actions will be in line with what is cosmically, universally, worldly, socially and individually right. Even the same action performed by the ignorant and the wise has different personal results – fruitive *karma* for the former, but not for the latter. All actions are the result of the *gunas* of *prakriti*, but it is only the wise who realize such and act without attachment to the *prakritic* world. Acting *unattached*, yet *wishing* world welfare is, however, somewhat incongruous!

VERSE 26

Let not the wise produce unsettlement in the understanding of the ignorant persons attached to actions. The wise should engage in all actions, acting integrated.

Produce unsettlement in the understanding in the Sanskrit is *buddhi-bhedam*, "split the intellect". Krishna is saying that the ignorant have a split mind, not the unity of mind of the wise, for they are torn this way and that between choices, desires and aversions. The wise act as an example to the unwise, showing them how an integrated individual acts and that is really all that can be done. The verse, however, is difficult and several interpretations are possible. It could suggest that it is better to let the unwise get on with result-geared actions rather than confuse them with teachings about detached actions that divide their minds between activity and inactivity. It could also suggest that the level of consciousness of the unwise is insufficient to understand anything other than actions for the purpose of results.

The following verse suggests that people's natures are already dictated by the *gunas* and that cannot be changed. Or perhaps it is a reference to lower castes and the encouragement of them to carry out their appropriate class/caste duties. Robert Minor certainly takes this last view, suggesting that this verse and verse 29 are against truth being taught to those who might, as a result, neglect their class duties.[31] We have to remember, also, that, pragmatically, Arjuna is on the battlefield, with thousands in his armies ready to fight. How would they understand his reasoning not to fight? Confusing them would be an ill-timed action.

Radhakrishnan took a completely different view, believing that the *ignorant persons attached to actions* are those who simply have lower forms of religious devotion but which are necessary for them and that it would be wrong to impose "absolute and final forms of human thought" on such people.[32] Ramanuja understood *ignorant persons* to be "those who do not know the entire truth about the self". He believed they are "unavoidably connected with work" For him, the development of a *sattvic buddhi* that could contemplate the *atman* was all important. Thus, *unsettlement* for Ramanuja meant the confusing of the *buddhi* by introducing *jnana-yoga* to those who were not ready for it, especially since he saw *karma-yoga* as an autonomous means to liberation.[33] The ignorant persons are subject to the kind of *karma* that is inimical to their knowledge of the Self, but to Ramanuja, "*karma-yoga* alone, independently of *jnana-yoga*, is the means for seeing the Self (my capital), and should stimulate love for all kinds of work among these who do not know the entire truth about the self."[34] Shankara would have wholeheartedly disagreed with Ramanuja's elevation of *karma-yoga* here.

Despite such biased views, the verse can be interpreted quite straightforwardly. It seems to me that a distinction is being made between those whose *buddhi* is involved in reaction to sense perceptions, those who have desires, aversions, and who act for results, and those whose *buddhi* is *integrated* (*yukta*), steady, anchored in itself, not swayed by reaction to sense stimuli, and is free from attachment to results of actions. This would differentiate between those who have knowledge and the ignorance (*ajnana*) of those who do not.

VERSE 27

In all cases, actions are performed by the *gunas* of *prakriti*. One whose mind is deluded by egoism thus thinks, "I am the doer".

All life, or *prakriti*, is composed of the three *gunas*, *sattva*, *rajas* and *tamas* in various combinations. The whole of nature and the entire phenomenal world is an interplay between these forces. It is the *gunas*, however, that create all experience, not the egoistic *I*. We say: "I am hungry", but, in fact, it is the particular combination of *gunas* in the body that causes hunger, not an *I*. The ego (*ahankara*), or personality self, assumes authorship, ownership and causation of all that takes place, and becomes in bondage to the results of actions. Such egoism mistakes *prakriti* for *purusha*, when in reality they are both separate. So the ego thinks it is reality when all it is, is a blend of constantly changing *gunas*. True reality is *purusha*, *atman*, a state where the *gunas* in the self are balanced. The underlying idea put forward in this verse, then, is Sankhya philosophy of a dualism between spirit and matter, *purusha* and *prakriti*.

VERSE 28

But the knower of truth of the division of the *gunas* and *karma*, knowing that *gunas* [as senses] operate on *gunas* [as objects], remains unattached, Mahabaho.

The verse refers to the three *gunas* working as the constituent elements of *prakriti*. The whole scheme of matter outlined by Sankhya philosophy might be appropriate at this point. So we have:

2 *Unmanifest prakriti*
/
3 *buddhi**
(intellect)
/
4 *ahankara**
(ego)
/

From the ego, *ahankara*, evolve "horizontally" and simultaneously the mind or *manas,* five capacities for sense, the *buddhindriyas*, five capacities for action, the *karmendriyas* and five subtle elements, the *tanmatras*. These, then, are as follows:

5 manas	6–10 buddhindriyas	11–15 karmendriyas	16–20 tanmatras
(mind)	(senses)	(organs of senses)	(subtle elements)
	hearing	*speaking (mouth)*	*sound**
	feeling	*grasping (hands)*	*touch**
	seeing	*walking (feet)*	*form**
	tasting	*excreting (anus)*	*taste**
	smelling	*generating (genitals)*	*smell**

Five gross elements, the *mahabhutas*, evolve directly from the *tanmatras*:

21–24 *mahabhutas*
ether (akasha) associated with sound
air or wind associated with touch
fire associated with form
water associated with taste
earth associated with smell

* = created and creative in nature.

Every single aspect in this entire scheme of things is informed by the *gunas*, except for the very first category, which is completely separate and is *purusha*. Once it is known that all life is composed of the ever-changing interaction of the *gunas* with these twenty-four constituents in various combinations, it is difficult to see how belief in an ego-self controlling them all can be maintained. Only the liberated *purusha* sees all this matter as it really is; others will always be in bondage to actions and results that they think they own. The real Self, the *purusha*, is not involved in any of the *prakritic* phenomena at all. Thus, to return to the verse in question, the *gunas* are subject and object, as well as the interplay between subject and object: they are all life. To the ignorant, the *gunas* are operated by them: the wise, however, act, but are merely spectators of their own actions, so separating *gunic* activity from their true selves. Important to remember is that *buddhi*, intellect, *ahankara*, ego and *manas*, mind – all the thinking and reasoning aspects of the self – are, in fact, matter.

VERSE 29

Persons deluded by the *gunas* of *prakriti* are attached to the actions of the *gunas*. The man of perfect knowledge should not unsettle the imperfect knowledge of the foolish.

The thought here is similar to that in verse 26. Whoever knows the Self, reality, *purusha*, *atman*, sees actions and their results at the surface of life and not at the depth of it, and knows the Self as separate from existence. Those who do not know this are attached to the actions of the *gunas* and the verse seems, once again, to suggest that it is better that they are left unenlightened about the real state of things, lest they become confused, or think that simple inactivity is the right path. Again, Ramanuja took the word *unsettle* as meaning confusing someone attempting *karma-yoga* by introducing them to *jnana-yoga*.[35] The word *foolish* (*manda*) is a strong one, indicative of stupidity, dullness and slowness of mind and contrasts with *perfect knowledge*. The only way to overcome the interplay of the *gunas* is to transcend them and root oneself in their Source that is Brahman and the *atman* within. Aurobindo put this point well when he wrote: "Here there is the clear distinction between two levels of consciousness, two standpoints of action, that of the soul caught in the web of its egoistic nature and doing works with the idea, but not the reality of free will, under the impulsion of Nature, and that of the soul delivered from its identification with the ego, observing, sanctioning and governing the works of Nature from above her."[36]

VERSE 30

Renouncing all actions in me, with the consciousness centred in the intrinsic *atman*, free from hope, free from ownership, having become free from fever, fight!

Zaehner described this verse as "one of the most obscure in the *Gita*",[37] though it seems quite simply to suggest the complementary nature of focus on the divine at the same time as being centred in the Self. The school of Yoga offered a theistic means to liberation, with focus on Ishvara, "Lord", a divine being, a supreme *Yogin*, who disappeared after liberation. Perhaps this verse says more. We have seen nothing up to now of the theism of classical Hindu *bhakti*, "loving devotion", to

God, but here we have Krishna virtually identifying himself with the *atman*, the Self. Renunciation here is *sannyasa*, the term normally associated with the complete renunciation of all activity, ritual and social interchange, particularly so in the final, fourth stage of life. Here, it is clear that Krishna is not endorsing such inactivity. "*Fight!*" he says, but by focusing the activity on him, not on the self.[38] The verse endorses suppression of the ego, the *I*, until it ceases to think it is the author and owner of actions, in which case it ceases to be the owner of the results of actions. When the attention is entirely focused on Brahman, what Mehta termed the "immutable centre of endless mobility",[39] it is focused beyond the *gunas*; then, all actions are surrendered to God. Ultimately, God is the true owner of all things, not the individual, who needs to become like a tube through which the divine energy pours. That tube should not be blocked with ego and desire, so that the individual centres on its *intrinsic* Self, the *atman* (*adhyatma*). Thus, Ramanuja took *renouncing all actions in me* to mean allowing God to be the performer of acts through the *atman*, which is what the verse probably means, though Ramanuja meant it more intensely since, for him, the *atman* is God's body: so "God himself causes his own acts to be performed by his own atman".[40] The *fever* mentioned in the verse probably refers to the mental fever or agitation Arjuna experienced in CHAPTER ONE when, in verse 30, his skin burned all over, he was not able to stand, and his mind was whirling.

VERSE 31
Those who constantly practise this teaching of mine, full of *shraddha*, not contentious, they also are freed from actions.

Again, we should note the theistic element in this verse. The idea of *shraddha*, "faith", follows on from that in the previous verse of *renouncing all actions in me*. Krishna has already said that those who are unwise are better left as they are, for they cannot understand the ultimate truths of the universe. This new element of faith, *shraddha*, that is introduced here, may be the bridge between the two states, since faith in itself is often the agent that aids focus on the divine, whatever the level of consciousness of a devotee. *Shraddha*, however, has a wider connotation than just faith, since it is more of a mental attitude of sincere reverence and sincerity of purpose so that it can be directed not only to a deity, but also to a teacher, to scriptural teachings and so on, even if, in the case of the latter, those teachings are not fully understood. Thus, faith without contention or fault-finding is endorsed. *Freed from actions* means being capable of detached action and, therefore, freed from fruitive *karma*.

VERSE 32
But those who, contending this my teaching, do not practise it, know them to be deluded in all knowledge, ruined, devoid of discrimination.

Those who are wise and who understand the nature of existence and the Self reap the reward of freedom without even trying to. Those who are totally unwise, who turn away from such wisdom and knowledge, or criticize it, reap results of their lack of wisdom, and these results condemn them to being lost.

VERSE 33

Even a wise man acts in accordance with his own nature. Beings follow nature. What can restraint do?

In the light of the foregoing, this is a strange verse, since it suggests that even the wise follow their own nature, that is to say, their *prakritic* make-up – what Zaehner termed "that parcel of the whole material cosmos which has attached itself to his individual self".[41] Presumably, two beings that are liberated will not be the same; there will still be variations in mental temperament for no two people can ever be the same, enlightened or not. The physical variations of *prakriti* in the form of the *gunas* have bestowed on each individual a distinct pattern of being. As Chidbhavananda put it: "Attaining perfection is their thread of unity in the midst of mental variations."[42] Each nature is the appropriate measure of *prakriti* that has come about through past actions. Until all *karma* has been worked out, even the wise will be subject to their own *prakritic* make-up, what Ramanuja termed "their beginningless *vasana*",[43] *vasana* being the *karmic* habits that have built up in past lives. As to the *restraint* mentioned in the verse, most take the reference to mean prohibitions laid down by scriptures, and how futile these are in the face of each person's innate nature. But what the verse seems to be saying is that restraint or repression of actions or the senses are not going to achieve anything; detached action will not be gained by inactivity. It is thus in the nature of all beings to undertake activity however wise or unwise they may be.

VERSE 34

Attachment and aversion of the senses adhere to the [objects of the] senses. None should come under the sway of these two; truly they are his foes.

It is *attachment* or attraction (*raga*) and *aversion* (*dvesha*) that are the two dualities of reaction to sense experience. Occasionally, we are neutral, but mostly we are attracted or repelled by what stimulates the *senses* (*indriyas*) and we act on such reaction either mentally or physically, moving towards or craving what we desire and avoiding or fearing what we dislike. This is what causes the building up of *karma*. Aversion is really nothing more than restraint, so we can see how the current verse enlarges on the idea of the last. It is these two entities of aversion and desire that Krishna calls the greatest enemies, "like thieves on the road", according to Shankara.[44] Attachment and aversion are the passion and anger in the three roots of evil in Buddhism, the third being *moha*, "delusion". Attachment and aversion arise *karmically* from the intricate likes and dislikes of countless previous lives and the habits, *vasanas*, that one acquires as a result of previous existences.

VERSE 35

Better one's own *dharma* devoid of merit, than the well-discharged *dharma* of another. Death in one's own *dharma* is better; the *dharma* of another is fraught with danger.

This verse is a very well-known and frequently quoted one. It upholds the individual *dharma, sva-dharma*, of each person. *Dharma* is evolutionary in essence and, as Hinduism evolved, it was felt that one cannot miss stages on the evolutionary ladder. It may seem as if someone else's *dharma* is better, but one's own is better for it reflects a level of consciousness pertinent to personal evolution and the best position to work out *karmic* inheritances. Therefore, its merit at its own level is just as great as what seems to be a higher *dharma* of another. *Death* doing one's own *dharma* is evolutionary; death trying to follow someone else's is involutionary and *adharma*. In CHAPTER ONE, Arjuna said he would rather beg for food, in other words, become a recluse – tantamount to changing his *dharma*. But Arjuna as a *Kshatriya* cannot abandon his *sva-dharma* and become a recluse. He *desires* such a course of action and he has an *aversion* to fighting, so he is operating in *prakriti*, on the level of the senses, and wants a *dharma* that is not his. Such a change can only lead to *adharma*. In an ideal Golden Age, mentioned, for example, at the beginning of the *Ramayana*, the four classes represented the perfect and complementary balance of all individuals in society. None was hierarchized above or below another, each individual played a vital part in the harmony of a perfect whole. Such is the Hindu ideal in following personal *dharma*. Since *dharma* involves acting, and disinterested action is *karma-yoga*, Ramanuja, again, saw this verse as a reason for the superiority of *karma-yoga* to *jnana-yoga*.[45]

VERSE 36   Arjuna said:
What impels a man to do this evil even when reluctant, Varshneya, constrained, as it were, by force?

Arjuna wishes to know what the force is in life that causes the Kauravas to commit *evil* (*papa*) and causes him to engage in a fratricidal war. He addresses Krishna as Varshneya, one from the Vrishni race.

VERSE 37   The Lord said:
This is desire, this is anger, born of the *rajas guna*, greatly consuming, greatly evil: know that as the enemy here.

Desire, passion or attachment (*kama*), and anger (*krodha*) are the enemies of one on the spiritual path and are engendered by the *rajas guna*. *Rajas* is the *guna* that causes motion, energy and activity. All the constructive and destructive forces in nature are dictated by *rajas*. *Rajas* is what causes the vibration of the conscious mind in order to produce thought, and thought arises most frequently as a reaction to stimuli from the environment, to sense experience. It is when reaction to stimuli from the environment is blocked that anger occurs. Desire keeps a person anchored in the world of sensory perception, while anger operates against evolution, and occurs if desire is inhibited or challenged. Again, desires are dictated by deep-rooted *karmic* tendencies accumulated in past lives. The level of the anger of the opposing Kauravas is implicit here, and said to be *greatly evil*.

VERSE 38

As fire is enveloped by smoke, as a mirror by dust and as an embryo by the womb, so is this enveloped by it.

Desires cover the true Self like smoke envelopes fire and so on. Desire is like illusion, *maya*, it hides reality. Dust on a mirror is a frequent metaphor for the illusions that obscure the true Self. The *this* in the verse is clarified in the next verse as wisdom.

VERSE 39

Wisdom is enveloped by this constant enemy of the wise, Kaunteya, whose insatiable fire is the form of desire.

Desire in the verse is *kama* meaning pleasure in a variety of dimensions that are conducive to happiness. Desire is like the fire which, continuously fed, burns higher and higher: if not checked it reaches further and further afield to consume all in its path. So desire continually fed with sense stimuli and encouraged by thoughts becomes unchecked and damaging. It is through desire that an individual is perpetually involved with the material world of the *gunas*. Here, then, *kama* as desire runs very close to *rajas*, the *guna* of energetic involvement and passion in response to the world, both of which inhibit *wisdom* or knowledge (*jnana*).

VERSE 40

The senses, the mind and the intellect are called its seat. By these it deludes wisdom, enveloping the embodied.

Desire overwhelms the *senses* (*indriyas*), *mind* (*manas*) and *intellect* or reason, the *buddhi*. In doing so, the true nature of the Self is overwhelmed also; the Self – here, the embodied (*dehin*) – is overshadowed, again like the dust that covers the mirror. Instead of the *buddhi*, the intellect, being pervaded by *sattva*, it is dominated by *rajas* so forcing activity, energy, result-orientated acts and desires. *Wisdom*, knowledge or understanding (*jnana*) is deluded (*moha*). Ramanuja summarized the verse: "The meaning is that it [desire] deludes (the self) in various ways, makes (the embodied self) disinclined for knowledge of the self, but intent upon the enjoyment of sense-objects."[46] Krishna, to use an analogy of Chibhavananda's, is like a general who identifies a fort belonging to an enemy that needs to be attacked:[47] he identifies the cause of all problems – desire. Aurobindo wrote that "you must uplift yourself beyond this lower nature to that which is above the three gunas, that which is founded in the highest principle, in the soul. Only when you have attained to peace of the soul, can you become capable of a free and divine action".[48]

VERSE 41

Therefore you, best of Bharatas, having controlled the senses first, will surely strike down this evil, the destroyer of wisdom and realization.

The Sanskrit *niyamya*, which has something of the sense of "controlled" or "restrained", can also mean bringing into orderly function. Since earlier, in verse

33, it was stated that it is impossible for anyone to exercise total restraint of the senses, control, or bringing to order, may be preferable. If, then, an individual can bring the *senses* (*indriyas*) into orderly function, this suggests that the senses are not repressed, but effectively controlled and can eradicate *this evil*, desire. *Wisdom and realization* are, respectively, *jnana* and *vijnana*. *Jnana* may be meant as knowledge of the scriptures and *vijnana*, the personal experience of that knowledge in life. However, *vijnana* can have a deeper meaning of intuitive realization – a point that will be the subject of CHAPTER THIRTEEN. Shankara interpreted the two terms in a similar way – *jnana* being the knowledge acquired from the *Shastras* and from a teacher concerning the true nature of the Self, and *vijnana* being the internalized, personal experience of that knowledge.[49]

VERSE 42

They say the senses are superior, the mind is superior to the senses, but the intellect is superior to the mind, but what is superior to the intellect is He.

If we return to the Sankhya-Yoga scheme of matter as outlined in verse 28, the *senses* (*indriyas*) are superior to the physical world and to the connecting means between them and the world. They involve both the capacities of hearing, feeling and so on and the functions and organs by which these take place – speaking, grasping, etc. Superior to these senses, however, is the internal organ, the *antahkarana*, which encompasses the *mind* (*manas*), the ego (*ahankara*) and the *intellect* (*buddhi*), here in reverse order of superiority. Intellect, *buddhi*, then, is the highest form of manifest matter, but what transcends it is the non-material *purusha*, which in the *Gita* equates with *atman*, the embodied Self and the indwelling divinity that is both unmanifest potential and the manifestation of that potential as the world and cosmos. Maharishi Mahesh Yogi commented on this verse: "Go to the absolute ultimate Reality, and all levels of relativity will cease to be a burden. Be illumined, and life will ever be in freedom and fullness, away from the darkness of ignorance."[50] Thus, *He* is usually taken to be the *atman* or Brahman in line with the thought of the final verse that follows. Nevertheless, the context of the previous verses is concerned with desire, *kama*, and Ramanuja believed the pronoun *He* in the verse to refer to this. The problem then would be how *kama* could be superior to *buddhi*, unless that is meant in the sense of all higher aspects of the self being overcome by desire as an inimical force.[51] The *Katha Upanishad* (3:10) sheds some light on the options and, it seems to me, endorse taking *He* as either *atman* or Brahman:

Higher than the senses are their objects;
Higher than sense objects is the mind;
Higher than the mind is the intellect;
Higher than the intellect is the immense self;[52]

VERSE 43

Thus, knowing Him as superior to the intellect, restraining the self by the *atman*, slay the enemy in the form of desire, hard to conquer, Mahabaho.

Him in the verse is normally accepted as the embodied Self, the *atman*, but that which is superior to the *buddhi*, the intellect, is also the Supreme, the *Akshara*, the Imperishable and *Om*, which we met in verse 15. *Knowing him . . .* is instructing Arjuna to root his whole being in the *atman* beyond intellect, otherwise desire will be difficult to subdue. The chapter thus ends pointing to the solution to all Arjuna's problems that lies within his own self.

In the *Upanishad* of the *Bhagavad Gita*, the knowledge of Brahman,
the teaching of *Yoga* and the dialogue between Shri Krishna
and Arjuna, this is the third chapter called
Karma-Yoga.

CHAPTER FOUR

Jnana-Yoga
The *Yoga* of Knowledge

Although this chapter is entitled *Jnana-Yoga*, and would be expected to deal solely with the path of knowledge, *jnana-marga*, it does, in fact, suggest that there are diverse paths to liberation. It diverges to discuss worship of minor deities, the four classes and sacrifices, but it also retains an emphasis on the fundamental teaching concerning detached action. Clearly, knowledge *per se* without such action is not advocated, so the *yoga* that will be taught is knowledge that underpins and is concomitant with *karma-yoga*, the discipline of desireless action that is devoid of concentration on its results. Such linking of Sankhya and *karma-yoga* as paths to liberation will depart from their separate beliefs – Sankhya's that action should be abandoned to free the soul, and traditional *karma-yoga*'s that correct ritual praxis is the key to life. What the *Gita* will endorse in this chapter is knowledge or wisdom of both ultimate and manifest reality *combined* with *karma-yoga* as sacrificial action in the widest sense of every action in life being a sacrifice, a *yajna*, to Brahman. Aurobindo thus believed that this *Yoga* of the *Gita* is "a highest Yoga synthetic and integral directing Godward all the powers of our being".[1]

VERSE 1   The Lord said:
This imperishable *Yoga* I proclaimed to Vivaswat, Vivaswat told it to Manu and Manu taught it to Ikshvaku.
Krishna begins this section of the *Gita* by describing the beginnings of the *imperishable (avyaya)* tradition of *Yoga* that he has taught so far in the previous chapters. He describes this *Yoga* tradition as imperishable, everlasting and refers to the combined Sankhya and *karma-Yoga* that he has taught earlier. He tells of the early history of the teaching of *Yoga* in this age. *Vivasvat*, the "Brilliant One", was a sun deity, one of twelve *Adityas*, and the son of the sage Kashyapa and his wife Aditi. Manifested from Surya, the sun deity, his whole line is connected with the sun. As was seen in the main *Introduction*, there seems to have been some connection of Krishna's ancestry with a cult of the sun. *Manu*, the son of Vivasvat, is the progenitor of the human races in the present age, being the seventh of fourteen, each one appearing in a new age.[2] The same seventh Manu is also known for his *Laws of Manu (Manu Samhita)*, a code of conduct for all kinds of communal praxis in *Vedic* society, including rules about class and caste. *Ikshvaku* was the son[3] of the seventh Manu and the real head of the solar dynasty as the first King of Ayodhya. Notably, in the ancient past, it was to kings, not priests, that knowledge was revealed.

VERSE 2

Thus handed down in succession, the royal seers knew this. Through a long lapse of time, this *Yoga* was destroyed here, Parantapa.

India has always accepted that religious tradition should be handed down from *guru*/master to *chela*/pupil and in ancient times it was the ruler of a race that was responsible for maintaining and passing on such knowledge. Thus, such rulers were expected to be saints or *rishis* as much as kings, *rajas*: they were therefore called *raja-rishis*, "royal sages, seers", and were philosopher kings. It is an interesting point considering the *Brahmins* of Aryan society were later those who were expected to know, maintain and hand on scriptural teachings and practices amongst their own class. Here, in this verse, the importance of *Kshatriyas* in religious, and thereby social traditions, is emphasized. It will be up to Arjuna to restore the balance of *dharma* that will allow the correct knowledge and praxis to be restored.

VERSE 3

That same ancient *Yoga* has been taught to you by me today, for you are my devotee and friend; and this is the supreme secret.

Despite the disappearance of the knowledge in practice, it is eternal and imperishable by nature and so Krishna tells Arjuna that he is imparting it to him. Such knowledge, then, is not new; Krishna is merely restoring an age-old, eternal, established tradition, one that is revealed at the beginning of each cycle of manifestation of the world. Arjuna is chosen to receive this knowledge because he is Krishna's friend and devotee. *Devotee* is *bhakta*, and here it occurs for the first time in the *Gita*. It comes from the root *bhaj*, like the important word *bhakti*, "loving-devotion" or, with Robert Zaehner, "to participate in something or someone through affection",[4] though it can have other meanings in the epic literature. The Sanskrit word for *friend* is *sakha*, which has a much stronger meaning than just an ordinary friend; thus, Bibek Debroy aptly annotates "kindred soul".[5] *Supreme secret* are the words that Krishna uses to depict the knowledge he reveals, and this suggests Arjuna's worthiness to receive it.

VERSE 4   Arjuna said:

Your birth was later, the birth of Vivasvat earlier, so how am I to understand this, that you taught in the beginning?

Arjuna, at this point, does not understand Krishna's true nature or, if he does, he wishes it to be clarified.

VERSE 5   The Lord said:

Many are the births I and you have passed through, Arjuna. I know them all, you do not, Parantapa.

Several interpretations are possible here. Krishna could be saying that he has been born many times as the eternal *atman* in all entities, the multiple births of each and every one of which he knows. Thus, Krishna knows every entity that has ever been or ever will be in existence. Arjuna, in contrast, has no memory of even his own previous births. Those who are not liberated would not remember past lives. On the other hand, Krishna may be referring to his descents, full or partial incarnations in many places and many forms, though, as noted in earlier chapters, the doctrine of *avataras* is not fully developed in the *Gita*. Then, again, Krishna may be referring to the whole of *prakritic* creation, to "the playground of the time which he creates", as Maharishi Mahesh Yogi put it, and continued to say: "he is the ocean of life, while time rises and falls as the tide on the surface of the ocean. Though the tidal waves draw on the depths they can never fathom the unfathomable abyss . . . The life of man is like a wave which rises up to see – it can see so far and no more."[6] The following verse might endorse this last interpretation related to *prakriti*. Shankara looked on Krishna's birth here as only apparent, as his comment on the following verse 6 shows: "I appear to be born and embodied, through my own Maya, but not in reality, unlike others."[7] For Ramanuja, the birth of God as Krishna was real, just as his numerous previous births, which he mentions in the verse, though Krishna always retains his supreme and absolute nature.[8]

VERSE 6

Being unborn, also an imperishable *Atman*, and being Lord of all beings, controlling my own *prakriti*, I come into being by my own *maya*.

Here, Krishna talks of his *prakriti*, manifest creation, linking himself with manifest existence in important ways. There is a suggestion of the manifest world emerging from the Unmanifest; yet the Unmanifest ever remains itself, ever remains unborn (*aja*). And here in this verse, too, Krishna really puts forward to Arjuna the true nature of himself as supreme Being and *imperishable* (*avyaya*), who has total control over, governs, or directs, the whole of manifest existence. Krishna is *Lord*, *Ishvara*, a descriptor particularly associated with devotional worship. The complete separation of *purusha/atman* and matter, as believed by the Sankhyas, is not present in this verse. Krishna has ownership of *prakriti*, which, though ever-changing because of the nature of the *gunas*, is bestowed a certain degree of empirical reality as an emanation of the divine, and a reality in which Krishna becomes tangible, *atmamayaya*, "by my own *maya*", he says. *Maya* usually means "illusion" or "magical power" but, here, it means the divine power of empirical existence in comparison to ultimate Reality, and is synonymous with *prakriti*. It implies the delusion of *prakritic* involvement as opposed to knowledge of the true Self and Brahman. The unique relationship between the *prakritic* world that is *maya* and the ultimate Reality of Brahman was depicted well by Maharishi Mahesh Yogi when he wrote: "That transcendental unmanifested absolute eternal Being is full, and this manifested relative ever-changing world of phenomenal existence is full. The Absolute is eternal in its never-changing nature, and the relative is eternal in its ever-changing nature."[9] There is no sense here in the *Gita* of *maya* being non-reality that is complete illusion as in the non-dualist philosophy of the later school of thought of Shankara. The *Gita* is more truly *Vedantist* in tone, unifying both manifest and unmanifest reality. *Maya* is, thus, more of a "power of projection", as Rohit Mehta put it,[10] or, with Srinivasa Murthy, "supernatural power".[11] Nevertheless, its effect on the unenlightened is one of delusion as to what is real, that is to say, as to the *atman*.

VERSE 7

Whenever there is a decline of *dharma*, Bharata, and a rise of *adharma*, then I manifest myself.

This verse and the following one are frequently quoted as the whole reason behind the concept of the *avataras* of Vishnu in Hinduism. Many commentators see the verse as referring to the decay of the class system, *varna-dharma*, and the system of stages of life, *ashrama-dharma*. Others, however, interpret the verse more generally. Viewing *dharma* on a wider level, it is the force that upholds all life and that is necessary for human evolution in all sorts of ways – indeed, the word *dharma*, coming from the root *dhri*, means "what holds together". The natural patterns of existence are upheld by this powerful force, but if *adharma* occurs in an exaggerated extent, the path of evolution is distorted and society declines. The collapse of the *varna-* and *ashrama-dharmas* is only part of this *adharma* rather than constituting it wholly. When evolution can no longer progress, then God descends, and becomes anthropomorphically manifest.

Important in the concept of the descent is the identical nature of the descent with Brahman as ultimate Reality at the same time. Mehta thus depicted an *avatara* as "a living touch with Reality": Krishna becomes the bond with Brahman. But, as Mehta pointed out, there is no diminution of Brahman, just as the sun is in no way diminished by its rays: the descent is like a tiny particle of divinity in the manifest world.[12] Here in the *Gita*, we have the embryonic stages of the full doctrine of *avataras*. The verse gives us the rationale for the doctrine but does not make mention of any of the other descents. One must perhaps assume, too, that Krishna is not yet totally identified with Vishnu who was to be the immediate source of *avataras* in later developments.[13]

VERSE 8

For the protection of the good and for the destruction of the wicked, for the firm establishment of *dharma* I am born in every epoch.

The righteous are protected and the wicked destroyed because this is the only way in which evolution can continue: without *dharma*, evolution is not possible, so the positive forces in the universe have to be preserved and the negative ones destroyed. The preservation of the force of *dharma* is the boosting of the *sattva guna* to balance out *rajas* and *tamas*; *adharma* occurs when there is too much of these last two. *Sattva* is the *guna* that is responsible for spiritual evolution. God descends *in every epoch*, in the Sanskrit, *yuga* to *yuga*. There are four *yugas* – *Kritya* or *Satya*, *Treta*, *Dvapara* and *Kali*, this last being the present age. Their unequal time-spans total over four million years, equal to one *maha-yuga*, one "great epoch", a *maha-kalpa* that accounts for just one day and one night in the life of Brahma, the creator god. It was Manu who is purported to have introduced this theory. In the Vaishnava tradition, it is believed that the descents of God in human form not only have the purpose of restoring the balance of *dharma* over *adharma*, but also provide a support to devotees. Thus, Ramanuja's comments on this verse encompass the rescuing of leading Vaishnavas through the visible form, words and actions of Krishna.[14] "As they will become weak and unnerved in every limb (on account of separation from Me) I am born from age to age in the form of gods, men etc., for protecting them by giving them opportunities of seeing, talking about and doing similar things in regard to My body and My activities."[15]

VERSE 9

Thus, whoever knows of my divine birth and action as they really are, having abandoned the body, is not born again: he comes to me, Arjuna.

When God descends, he remains divine, even though his form appears human. To understand the nature of these descents, and his actions in manifest form, the verse says that the human being has to rise to the level of the divine. If this can be done, then liberation from perpetual birth and death, *samsara*, takes place. There is a parallel between the manifest aspects of Brahman that are active in the world while remaining rooted in passive, unmanifest Being, and human activity in the world, which should be rooted in the passive *atman*. Brahman as pure Purusha is not, however, divorced totally from *prakriti*, but is active within it, just as the embodied *atman* should be inwardly still in activity, while still engaging in the manifest world. Thus, *abandoned the body* is probably meant in the sense of abandoning bodily reactions to sense stimuli, since *tyaga*, "abandonment" is frequently used as renunciation of the fruits of action in the *Gita*.

The words *he comes to me* at the end of the verse are very important, for they express the classical Hindu notion of liberation as a dualism between human and God, the drop merging into the ocean, but not becoming the whole ocean itself. There is a hint here of *bhakti*, loving-devotion between human and divine and *vice versa*, but it is not explicit.

VERSE 10

Freed from attachment, fear and anger, absorbed in me, taking refuge in me, purified by the austerity of knowledge, many have attained my being.

Attachment (*raga*) and *anger* (*krodha*) are reminiscent of the previous teachings of the *Gita* against desire. Shankara interpreted this verse as endorsing the supremacy of *knowledge*, *jnana*, over all other paths to Brahman, because of the expression *jnana tapas*, the *austerity of knowledge*, by which one is freed from passion, fear and anger. *Tapas* is typically "austerity", and comes from the root *tap*, "to be hot". *Tapas* involves the severe penances and practices undertaken by those on the ascetic path to Brahman, especially those who uphold *jnana* and the path of knowledge as the supreme route to Brahman. For Shankara, the path of *jnana-yoga* was the *only* one to *moksha*, liberation. He translated *absorbed in me* as "knowing Brahman, i.e., seeing their identity with Isvara".[16] Yet there seems no suggestion here that the *many* are fused as one, are at one, or identical, with Brahman. It seems to me that the thought here is as in verse 9, one of dualism, not monism. Further, since Krishna speaks earlier of his *maya*, presumably his reference to *my being*, *mad-bhava*, is to his change-less, eternal state. Later, in verse 24, we find a more explicit statement of unity, though not identity, with Brahman. However, *attained my being* is synonymous with total liberation.

VERSE 11

In whatever way men approach me, so do I reward them. Men follow my path in all ways, Partha.

Here in this verse we have what appears to be a hint of *bhakti*, loving-devotion of human to God and God to human. The word that portrays this is *bhajami* and, like *bhakti*, it comes from the root *bhaj* noted in verse 3. Most translate *bhajami* as "reward", "favour", "fulfil", "carry out", though Zaehner is one commentator that maintained a stronger link with *bhakti*. His preference for a devotional interpreta-tion stemmed from the use of *prapad*, which, he said, "means not only to approach but also to be utterly devoted to somebody".[17] Richard Gotshalk points out the idea of apportioning, sharing with or participation in, indicated also by the root *bhaj*, suggestive of a "participation in the divine which, in its fullest and transparent form, involves clear-sighted mutuality of loyal devotion and love (from the human side) and of care and love (from the divine side)". He notes, too, the connection with *prapad*, with its nuance of meanings of "go forward to take refuge with" and "fall down (at a person's feet)".[18] There is some justification, then, for seeing this verse as pregnant with *bhakti*, reciprocal loving-devotion between human and divine.

In whatever way and to what extent God is approached, so he will respond in the same way: if with love, God will respond with love. Commenting on this verse, Gandhi wrote: "In other words, people reap as they sow. As the quality of your *bhakti*, so is its reward. If there is motive behind your *bhakti*, if you seek anything through it, you will get what the quality of your *bhakti* entitles you to."[19] Ultimately, however, though the paths and ways are different, they all lead to the same source, like different fingers pointing to the same moon, each individual's path being different because of varied levels of consciousness. Inherent in the verse is the idea that whatever ultimate goal human beings desire – Heaven, absorption into the Absolute, personal relationship with God or a god, oblivion – so, also, this will be granted. It is suggestive that the ultimate goal can be different for each indi-vidual, and the verse is a good example of the universality of the *Gita*.

VERSE 12

Longing for success of action in this world they sacrifice to the gods, because in the human world success born of action is quickly obtained.

The verse may refer to *Vedic* ritual, *yajna*, and to correct ritual and sacrificial cere-monies to the gods by which immediate success is gained. The fruits of action, that is to say of ritual action, are, therefore, more easily and quickly achieved. The idea implied is that this is an easier path than Self-knowledge. On the other hand, the verse may refer to actions of ordinary people who worship gods in order to seek certain rewards and who do not have the level of consciousness to seek the higher goal of total liberation, or who cannot follow the more difficult path of *karma-yoga*, action without attachment to results.

VERSE 13

The fourfold class system has been created by me according to the differentiation of *guna* and *karma*. Though I am the doer thereof, know me also as the imperishable non-doer.

All nature, or *prakriti*, consists of the three *gunas* in varying combinations and the *fourfold class system* (*chatur-varna*) is no exception. *Sattva* and *tamas* are opposites, the dualities, while *rajas* is complementary to both and is, therefore the possible equilibrium between the two or the antagonist that unbalances them. *Sattva* is necessary for creation, and *tamas* for dissolution, but it is *rajas* that brings about creation after dissolution and dissolution after creation. There are four possible combinations of the *gunas* and these inform the class system – *the differentiation of guna* – as well as all existence.

Dominant	Secondary	Class
sattva	*rajas*	*Brahmin*
rajas	*sattva*	*Kshatriya*
rajas	*tamas*	*Vaishya*
tamas	*rajas*	*Shudra*

The combinations *sattva-tamas* or *tamas-sattva* are impossible because they cancel each other out. Thus, all life reflects just four *gunic* patterns. Each member of the class system has a specific nature, "that nature assigning him his line and scope in life according to his inborn quality and his self-expressive function", as Aurobindo put it.[20] *Brahmins* are mainly *sattvic*, for they are the leaders in spiritual life, memorizing the scriptures, upholding them and passing them on within their class. *Kshatriyas*, like Arjuna, are predominantly *rajasic*, needing the active energy to rule, to defend in times of war, and to uphold righteousness. They also need to do this in the right way, which the wisdom of *sattva* as their secondary *guna* supplies. *Vaishyas*, being the artisans, agriculturalists, merchants and craftspeople are predominantly *rajasic*, active, their secondary *guna* of *tamas* indicating that it is others who direct their path in the best evolutionary ways. It is the fourth class, the *Shudras*, who serve the rest of society and do not need to think actively for themselves. They are mainly *tamasic* and are believed not to have the capabilities of understanding the *Vedas*, which are barred to them. Importantly, this division of *gunas* makes it impossible for someone in one class to take on the nature of another in a different class. Arjuna could not be a *Brahmin* since his main *rajasic guna* would prevent it. But it is not just the class system that is so composed, for all creation and every species will be divided in a variety of ways.[21]

The whole of creation, the multitude of phenomena, has its source in the *imperishable* (*avyaya*) Unmanifest that causes all to be, yet does not act. Krishna identifies this Source as himself. Again, there is an interconnection between manifest existence and unmanifest, ultimate Reality in this verse. Zaehner put this succinctly when he wrote: "The Samkhya system sought neatly to divide time from eternity, the phenomenal from the Absolute: what the Gita sets out to do is to bring the two together again in a more or less coherent whole – to bring religion back to the spirit of the Upanishads for which the supreme Principle is not a static monad but a dynamic reality which is at the same time eternally at rest."[22] It is only the *saguna* (with qualities), manifest aspect of Brahman that appears to act in creation: at the same time, the unmanifest, *nirguna* (without qualities) aspect remains passive and inactive. Either way, while the Creator of the *gunas* and of the cause–effect processes of *karma*, the verse is explicit that Krishna remains passive and so does not actively predetermine or predestine causes and their results.

VERSE 14
Actions do not taint me: nor have I desire in the fruit of action. He who knows me thus is not bound by actions.

CHAPTER THREE, verse 28, spoke of the action of *gunas* on *gunas* that make up *prakriti*. The present verse really reiterates that idea. If an individual does not act from the level of the *gunas* but acts from the level of the *atman*, focused on Brahman, there can be no *fruit of action* (*karma-phala*), no *karma* to reap. Divine action is also beyond the *gunas*, totally free of *prakriti* and yet totally in control of it, and totally free of desire. Krishna thus acts as Creator and Source but is separate from activity. Those who can also act in the same way are free from fruitive *karma*. The verse is important because it emphasizes the association between Sankhya and Yoga, knowledge and action, and how knowledge underpins *karma-yoga* in its proper sense of egoless action. Concomitantly, the passivity of the divine, while active in creation, is the fundamental knowledge that informs true wisdom. Past *karma* accumulates to inform the present life and the degree to which and the ways in which the *atman* will be involved in *prakriti*. *Actions do not taint* God in the way they taint the *prakritic* bound *atmans* ever involved in the results of actions. In short, God creates nature but does not interfere in its operation and does not affect the cause–effect processes of *karma*.

VERSE 15
Having known thus, even the ancient seekers of liberation performed action. Therefore you perform action as did the ancients in olden times.

Krishna is saying here, again, that he is not teaching anything new: the truth of what he says has been found by others in ancient times. But *liberation* (*moksha*) is not to be found in inertia and inactivity; the ancient sages who sought liberation were never inactive, but engaged in action that was egoless and free from desire.

VERSE 16
Even sages are deluded as to what is action and what inaction. I shall teach to you that action which, knowing it, you will be liberated from evil.

The path of *karma*, ritual *action*, and *akarma*, *inaction*, non-action, practised by some who withdraw from life in the latter case, are both incorrect. Krishna has been critical of the ritualists and, implicit here, of those who see passive inactivity and total sense withdrawal as the only path to liberation: activity without desire for its fruits is the real key. Conversely the *action* and *inaction* in the verse may refer to the egoless action that is grounded in inaction – the stillness of the *atman* – consonant with so much that has gone before, and leading up to a more explicit statement of both in verse 18. Liberation in the verse is *moksha*, while *evil* probably refers to reincarnation, *samsara*.

VERSE 17

For action should be understood, also forbidden action should be, and inaction should be. Deep is the path of *karma*.

The verse has two possible interpretations. Krishna indicates three types of action, *karma, action, vikarma, forbidden action,* and *akarma, inaction*. If, in the previous verse he is referring to ritual action and sense withdrawal then *karma* could be auspicious ritual action, *vikarma*, wrong or prohibited action by the scriptures, and inaction, *akarma*, total sense withdrawal. If, however, action and inaction are the desireless actions of the one rooted in *atman* – and the following verse suggests this is the better interpretation – then *vikarma*, wrong action, is that full of action for results. Mehta depicted *vikarma*, wrong action, as "reaction". He wrote: "Most often, in response to the challenges and the impacts of life, we do not act, we only react. Be it remembered that action never binds, it is only the reaction that binds. Man is caught up in a chain of reactions. He mistakenly thinks that it is action which binds, and therefore seeks freedom from action. There can never be freedom from action, for, to live is to act. There can, however, be freedom from reaction."[23] *Action and inaction* in the verse I take to be meant positively. Either acting for results or trying not to act at all are erroneous ways to freedom. When reaction or wrong action because it is result geared is abandoned for truly egoless action then *inaction, akarma*, action without concern for results occurs. It is only acting while focused inwardly on the *atman* that will bring freedom. *Deep* has two possible meanings. It may be meant in the sense of mysterious because the reverberations of actions cannot be fully understood outside divinity. Or it may refer to the depth of *karma* that each individual carries from one life to the next. Thus, Aurobindo translated deep as "thick and tangled". He wrote:

> Action in the world is like a deep forest, *gahana*, through which man goes stumbling as best he can, by the light of the ideas of his time, the standards of his personality, his environment, or rather of many times, many personalities, layers of thought and ethics from many social stages all inextricably confused together, temporal and conventional amidst all their claim to absoluteness and immutable truth, empirical and irrational in spite of their aping of right reason.[24]

Given such a tangled web of influences on the self, finding the path of egoless action is bound to be elusive even for the sages of the previous verse.

VERSE 18

Who would see inaction in action and action in inaction, he is wise among men. He is integrated, the performer of all actions.

Seeing *inaction in action* is to be involved in activity without allowing the ego to be involved. The physical self is active, but the ego is still, inactive, because it is established in *atman*. Action is the characteristic of all *prakriti*, while inaction is the characteristic of *atman*. Action is fluid, perishable, always in the state of becoming, while *atman* is static, is being rather than becoming and is permanent and imperishable. The knower of this does not see *prakriti* as ultimate reality. Any living entity has to engage in action, but to experience action in inaction, wisdom and understanding, the right kind of *buddhi*, is necessary, bringing deep intuitive knowledge of the nature of the *atman*, but in the *Gita*, the ability to operate from this level in the field of activity. This is the one who is *integrated, yukta*.

Seeing *action in inaction*, it seems to me, amounts to the same as inaction in action; one sees the *atman*, inaction, as the source of action rather than the ego. There is no *I*, there is no personal agent present and the action is rooted in inaction, "anchored to the silence of the inner Being", as Maharishi Mahesh Yogi put it.[25] Actions performed at this level produce no future *karmic* results, for there is no *I* to which they can be attached. The opposite, which is how Shankara understood inaction, are those who are simply inactive, who withdraw from sense activity but are still agents of their own thoughts and will still be creating binding *karma*; their very inactivity is *karmic* for, Shankara said "inaction is but a cessation of bodily and mental activities, and like *action* it is falsely attributed to the Self and causes the feeling of egoism as expressed in the words "quiet and doing nothing, I sit happy".[26] But the tenor of the verse needs to be suited to the predicament of Arjuna. Krishna, as his chariot driver epitomizes inaction in action – the still, calm divine equanimity that is maintained in all activity – and action in inaction – the same ability to act with a still, non-egoistic equipoise. Arjuna is, actually, *inactive* in the negative sense, at the same time, having very active thoughts; he is mentally active without a still and inactive ego.

VERSE 19

He whose undertakings are all devoid of desire and intention, whose actions have been burnt up by the fire of knowledge, the wise call a sage.

This verse, and those that follow, develop the foregoing ideas, stressing desireless action, inaction in action. *Intention* is Sanskrit *sankalpa* suggesting also "will" and "determination". Before beginning religious ritual, its intention was declared by the person conducting it. In the present verse, however, the intention has to be abandoned in order to act without attachment to the action or its results. Thus, in the wider sense, for any action to be desireless and egoless, it has to be free from motive or intention; it simply has to be carried out. Any action that has *desire* (*kama*) or intention as its motivating factors is one undertaken for a result and the result becomes more important than the action. So the wise act without purpose. They act without thinking of the beginning, the process, or the end result of the action.

In Mehta's words: "The flower of Wisdom can bloom only in a mind that is utterly silent, and it is only the wise that know what Right Action is."[27] The pure actions of one who is a *sage*, a *pandit*, are not personal actions but the actions of the *gunas*. The sage remains unattached, disciplined, beyond dualities and liberated because his actions are purified in the *fire of knowledge (jnana)*.

VERSE 20

Having abandoned attachment to the fruits of action, ever content, depending on nothing, even engaged in action, he does not do anything.

By *engaged in action, he does not do anything*, the verse is, again, referring to inaction during action. At the deepest level of *atman*, the state of the wise person is still – "outwardly engaged in activity, inwardly established in eternal silence".[28] For a more modern simili, Chidbhavananda likened such action to that of a postman who delivers letters but is not affected by the happy or sad news they contain.[29] Abandonment *(tyaga)* of the *fruits of action (karma-phala)* is tantamount to the loss of desires, but specifically the goals that inform them.

VERSE 21

Without hope, with consciousness and self controlled, having abandoned all possessions, doing merely bodily action, he incurs no sin.

Doing merely bodily action is really performing action by the body alone, that is to say the body undertakes action but the consciousness is rooted in *atman* so actions produce no fruits and one is separate from the three *gunas* and their combinations in relative existence. To be free from sin it is necessary to be free from desire, and the idea of abandonment *(tyaga)*, again, appears in this verse. Shankara, however, saw this section of the *Gita* as endorsing the ascetic way of life, the mendicant stage of the *ashrama-dharma*, the stages of life.[30] As a strict non-dualist, who divorced material existence from the spiritual Brahman by positing the former as illusion, renunciation of the world and activities in it were for him the right path. Ascetics kept bodily functions to a minimum on their path of knowledge, but the *Gita* does not support this. It is unattached and desireless *activity* that is the solution to Arjuna's problems. Commenting on this verse, Ramanuja believed that it is solely concerned with *karma-yoga* without any knowledge, *jnana-yoga*, at all.[31] For Ramanuja, the *atman* itself has the form of knowledge, so *karma-yoga* and knowledge that is *atman* are closely correlated.

VERSE 22

Content with what comes to him by chance, free from dualities, free from envy, even-minded in success and in failure and though acting, not bound.

Dualities here is *dvandva* "the pairs of opposites", which refer to the dualities in life like happiness and sadness, success and failure, and so on. It is by relation to opposites that we make sense of life and operate in it. The verse says it is necessary to be without these dualities, *nir-dvandva*, remaining *even-minded (sama)* in all the events of life.

VERSE 23

One who is devoid of attachment, liberated, whose consciousness is established in knowledge, acting for *yajna*, his whole *karma* melts away.

The verse depicts one who is *liberated, mukta*. Although Shankara saw this verse as advocating the renunciation of all works, even all *dharma* as well as *adharma* – in short, the complete denial of the world, the true *sannyasa* state,[32] *acting for yajna* suggests that actions/works *should* be performed, again, from the stillness of the *atman*. These are works sacrificed to God. Such is true action, true *karma-yoga*, not ritual action with ritual intention, but disciplined, egoless action that is based on knowledge of Brahman and knowledge of the Self. In Aurobindo's words, "such are the actions of the accomplished *Karmayogin*. They rise from a free spirit and disappear without modifying it, like waves that rise and disappear on the surface of the conscious, immutable depths."[33] For such enlightened souls, there can be no results of past or present actions to reap. One who acts *for yajna* is one whose every action is a sacrifice to Brahman. *Established in knowledge* (*jnana*), *acting for yajna* amalgamates the two paths of *jnana-yoga* and *karma-yoga* particularly well in this verse.

VERSE 24

The offering is Brahman, the oblation is Brahman, offered by Brahman in the fire of Brahman. Brahman will be attained only by him who is absorbed in action that is Brahman.

The verse is suggestive of the interconnectedness of all existence in the unmanifest Absolute that is Brahman. All things are ultimately Brahman, so all sacrifice, *yajna*, is Brahman. Again, we find the immanence of the unchanging Brahman as manifest in all *pakriti* and, thus, in every part of sacrificial ritual, but it is only those who are so *absorbed* (*samadhi*) in Brahman while engaged in sacrifice, who will attain him. To be absorbed in Brahman is to be liberated and the means to that is loss of the *I*, the ego, and selfish desire so that there is no separation between the worshipper and the worshipped. The entire life of someone at this level of consciousness is one whole *yajna* that is Brahman. Shankara commented on this verse at length, given that it is so easily representative of total non-dualism and true *jnana-yoga*. He explained that once everything is realized as Brahman, *yajna* becomes no action at all, for Brahman takes all sense of duality out of the sacrifice. It is *knowledge, jnana*, that is seen by Shankara as the sacrifice of he who has abandoned rites and all action. That is to say, the *yajna* is an inward one of total renunciation of the ordinary self and all its activities.[34] But, solidly against Shankara's view, *action that is Brahman* takes up the ideas of actions without thought of the results, the *nishkama-karma*, "desireless actions", that is the context of all these verses. The message is *yajna* that is desireless activity in a wide sense of involvement in the world. Ramanuja's view was quite different to Shankara's: he believed that one who knows the *atman* and acts from its realization has no need of *jnana-yoga* at all.[35]

VERSE 25

Some *yogins* perform *yajna* only to the gods; others perform *yajnas* as *yajnas* in the fire of Brahman.

Beginning with this verse, Krishna now outlines different types of *yajna* here, and in the verses that follow. All the approaches to God outlined in these verses were considered by Ramanuja to be aspects of *karma-yoga*. The *yogins* here are likely to be the *karma-yogins* who perform ritual sacrifices to *Vedic* deities. All deities are manifested aspects of Brahman according to the previous verse, so it is possible to perform *yajna* to these with great devotion and sincerity, yet it is also possible to transcend this type of worship and become established in Brahman where all actions are *in the fire of Brahman*. Such proponents are perhaps the philosophical Vedantists of the *Upanishads*, those who rejected ritual for more mystical, meditative pathways. Shankara preferred to see the renunciation of actions as the sacrifice of the self *in the fire of Brahman.*[36] Such an interpretation may be close in that gods, *devas*, are sometimes regarded as the senses, and the following verse takes up the idea of the role of the senses in sacrifice.

VERSE 26

Others offer hearing and other senses in the fire of restraint; others sacrifice sense objects like sound in the fire of the senses.

The verse is a difficult one. According to some commentators, two types of person are mentioned here: the one who restrains the *senses* (*indriyas*), and the one who uses the senses in more overt worship. The former would advocate self-control, self-restraint, *atma-samyama*, probably referring to ascetics, and the latter are perhaps those who use the senses for devotion to God. In the former the senses are denied and in the latter the whole realm of the senses is seen as manifestations of the divine and used for righteous action. Chidbhavananda was one translator and commentator who preferred such an interpretation. He wrote: Two diametrically opposite types of *Yajna* are enunciated here. The function of the one is to make the senses ineffective and that of the other to make them super-effective."[37] *Fire* is a destroyer, an annihilator, so in either case presented here, the senses are annihilated in the sacrificial action. The *restraint* (*samyama*) of the senses suits the path of knowledge, as it is favoured by Shankara, for example. The *use* of the senses favours the path of devotion. On the other hand, many commentators prefer to see the verse as referring to the annihilation of all senses. Debroy, for example, thinks both senses and sense objects are sacrificed, implying control of the senses and non-attachment to the senses.[38] The function of fire is to eradicate, so whether senses like hearing or sense objects are eradicated from the mind, the result is non-attachment to all senses.[39]

VERSE 27

Others offer all the actions of the senses and the actions of the breath in the sacrifice of the fire of the *yoga* of self-restraint kindled by knowledge.

Offering up *all actions* probably refers to the proponents of Sankhya who eschewed every action in order to realize the *purusha* alone. The *yoga of self-restraint* (*atma-samyama-yoga*) is, again, control of the senses (*indriyas*) by being rooted in *atman*. But knowledge, *jnana*, is clearly the means here, thus endorsing the view that it is the Sankhyan view that is referred to. *Breath, prana*, is the life-energy, the vitality of life. While concentrating on the *atman*, senses and all but essential breathing are suspended.

VERSE 28

Again, there are others who offer wealth as *yajna*, those who offer austerity as *yajna*, those who offer *yoga* as *yajna*, and those who offer study and knowledge as *yajna* – ascetics of rigid vows.

Other types of *yajna* are outlined here. Giving away wealth perhaps refers to the maintenance and building of temples, but the tone of the verse is one of ascetic praxis, so giving up wealth may mean the abandonment of all possessions. Thus, *austerity* (*tapas*), *yoga*, study and knowledge (*jnana*) may all refer to the more stringent pathways of *ascetics of rigid vows*.

VERSE 29

Others sacrifice the outgoing breath in the incoming breath and the incoming in the outgoing, restraining the course of outgoing and incoming breath, solely absorbed in *pranayama*.

Those who practise *pranayama*, breath control – one of the eight *angas* or "limbs" of classical Yoga – aim to still the breathing to the extent that the mind also becomes still and raised in consciousness. This, too, is portrayed as a *yajna*. In daily life, there is a close correlation between the mind and breathing patterns, for example in fear, stress, contentment and so on. The *yogin* aims at transcending such emotional influences while practising *pranayama* and in general living.

VERSE 30

Other people, who regulate their food, sacrifice breaths in breaths. These also are knowers of *yajna*, whose sins are destroyed by *yajna*.

Restricting food normally reduces oxygen use because the metabolism of the body is slowed down and breathing, therefore, becomes shallower: this, too, is a *yajna*. van Buitenen suggested *breaths in breaths* means to "reduce the functioning of their vital faculties (*pranas*) to the mere maintenance of life (*pranas*),[40] which was, and still is, an ascetic practice in *yoga*. Breath is life, so Shankara saw *breaths in breaths* as all life breaths being merged into, or sacrificed in, the one Life-breath while on the ascetic path.[41] The picture is of the *yogins* who practise *pranayama*, "breath control", which is believed to lead to the state of *samadhi*. The *knowers of yajna* suggests that knowledge has to underpin praxis.

VERSE 31

Eaters of the nectar remnant of the *yajna* go to the eternal Brahman. This world is not for the non-sacrificer, how, then, the other world, best of Kurus.

Yajna can take many forms, but what they have in common is that they are processes of purification. What remains of the *yajna*, the sacrifice, is described as *nectar* or ambrosia (*amrita*); it is the sweetness that remains when true *yajna* takes place. Those who perform no *yajna* at all will fail not only in this life but the next one, too, and would certainly not attain the other world that is liberation to the *eternal Brahman*. The thought is also rather reminiscent of 3:13, where the selfish sacrifice rather than that offered to God was criticized.

VERSE 32

Thus, manifold are the *yajnas* spread out in the mouth of Brahman. Know them all to be born of action and, knowing thus, you will be liberated.

So there are many kinds of *yajna*, all of which are described as stemming from action: *yajna* is, therefore, an expression of *activity*. The previous seven verses have described a number of different paths to Brahman and, it seems, without prejudice to any one of them as a legitimate way to Brahman. In the context of the chapter as a whole, however, it is surely the *way* in which such *yajnas* are performed that will aid the path to liberation. Ordinary action will result in fruitive *karma*; *yajna* focused wholly on the divine will not. The expression *in the mouth of Brahman* is an interesting one. Debroy points out that ritual *yajnas* generally include Agni, the *Vedic* god of fire, who is the mediator between human and divine and the means by which food offerings are conveyed to the gods. Debroy, therefore, thinks that the reference to the *mouth of Brahman* is to Agni.[42] Gotshalk understands the expression to mean "spread out at the gate of Brahman" or "door of Brahman".[43] In the context of the previous verses, such a meaning would suggest that in whatever ways people approach Brahman, they will all enter his gate. Either way, however, the ultimate receiver of the *yajna* is Brahman and *mouth* of Brahman is a figurative way of indicating attaining the divine.

VERSE 33

Yajna of knowledge is superior to *yajna* of wealth, Parantapa. All action in its entirety culminates in knowledge, Partha.

Wealth (*dravya*) is also "material objects" as in verse 28, but the verse is obscure. *Yajna of knowledge*, *jnana*, suggests that any *yajna* performed with the knowledge of the *atman* is bound to be superior to *yajna* involving material wealth and is elevating *jnana*, knowledge, as the superior path – an interpretation obviously accepted by Shankara. And yet, Arjuna is called Scorcher of Foes, *Parantapa,* in this verse, which suggests that, while *jnana* is the means by which liberation is reached, it is also the means by which detached action in a very dynamic sense can be undertaken. Thus, knowledge needs to underpin action but is not necessarily the right path on its own.

Yajna of knowledge is likely to mean that conducted with understanding. All paths need knowledge of Brahman, which is the filter for any *yajna*, but the fact that *all action culminates in knowledge* rather combines *karma-yoga* with *jnana-yoga*.

VERSE 34

Know that by prostration, by question, by service, the wise, those who have realized the Truth, will instruct you in this knowledge.

Wisdom, *knowledge (jnana)* can be attained through the help of the wise. Prostration, or humble reverence implies a lessening of the ego, a surrendering of the self. As a *chela*, a disciple, of an enlightened *guru*, the path to freedom is easier than trying to attain it alone. The idea of *service* is notable in the verse and, again, is an emphasis on activity not passivity. The wise, here *jnanins*, are revered as spiritual masters who impart the Truth, the knowledge of Brahman. Arjuna is not actually told to seek out a teacher in the verse, but the concept of learning from others is clear: it is not, however, iterated anywhere else in the *Gita*. Arjuna has actually professed himself to be the disciple of Krishna and has asked Krishna to advise him (2:7). But what he wants is advice about his immediate problem. He is not asking for that which he is about to get – teaching about the deeper nature of reality. So, as yet, he is not a true devotee. As in all life, "the Teacher is there, but we are so used to listening only to the trumpet tones of desire that the still small voice in the heart passes unheeded".[44] Arjuna is still lacking the true knowledge that is concomitant with deep understanding: his knowledge is still bound. Mehta commented on what it *should* be: "It is like a mirror which reflects every image that comes within its range but does not hold on to it. If the mirror were to retain the images that are cast upon it then it would cease to be a mirror. The sensitive mind acts like a mirror – it reflects but does not gather dust. The mind freed from the dust of knowledge is like a quiet lake into which is reflected the Wisdom of the Ages."[45]

VERSE 35

Which, having known, you will never again become deluded. By this, Pandava, you will see all beings in your *atman* and also in me.

The verse has a theistic flavour, but also emphasizes *jnana*, knowledge, explicitly as the pinnacle of *atman* realization. It is through knowledge that delusion (*moha*) is overcome. Krishna has been teaching Arjuna about the nature of true knowledge, *jnana*, and now he tells him that he can be free from dualities of conflicting forces, free from delusion, by the realization of the interconnection of all existence that the *atman* provides. Once consciousness of such unity is experienced, the dualities of life disappear: all beings will be seen in the *atman* and that *atman* as united in Krishna. The unity is pertinent to both the relative and absolute and is a removal of the veil of *prakriti*. Linking the present verse to the last one, it would be the wise, sages and *gurus*, who would be the medium for such knowledge. Given the different routes to Brahman outlined in previous verses, Veeraswamy Krishnaraj comments on such knowledge: "Truth has many sides, many depths, and many views, and is neither all right nor all wrong. It is a journey from one truth to another truth and is from a lower to higher truth. The proof of the highest Truth is absorption into the Absolute or Brahman. The Truth is the hub and the spokes of the wheel are the paths leading to the Truth. How far away you are from the hub tells you as to how far away you are from the Truth.[46] The *Gita* will, however, in its later chapters differentiate between Brahman and all creation. While Shankara interpreted this verse to say that every entity in existence from the creator deity Brahma down to a blade of grass *is* Brahman,[47] the *Gita*, as we shall see, tends to speak of the drop being absorbed in the ocean, not becoming it, the soul at one with, but not identical to, Brahman.

Verse 36

Even if you are the most evil of all evil people, by the raft of knowledge alone you shall cross over all sin.

The previous verse stated that *knowledge, jnana*, could overcome delusion or confusion, and this one states that it can overcome *evil (papa)*. Notably, it is *the raft of knowledge alone* that rescues one from sin, intimating that knowledge is the prerequisite for obtaining release from fruitive *karma* or sin. Action is normally done with good or evil intent, producing appropriate resulting *karma*. Through knowledge, this can be understood, so that ego activity can be avoided. Typically, Ramanuja took *jnana* here to be knowledge of the *atman* and not *jnana-yoga*. Such knowledge in this verse and the following two he considered to be that acquired through *karma-yoga* and nothing to do with *jnana-yoga*.[48]

Verse 37

As the blazing fire reduces fuel to ashes, so, Arjuna, the fire of knowledge reduces all *karma* to ashes.

Since knowledge, *jnana*, results in being established in *atman* and stillness, activity ceases in the inner Self; there is *akarma*, inaction, and so no fruits of action. Thus, it is a state that cancels out *karma* in the same way as fire *reduces things to ashes*. The real Self, the *atman*, cannot be associated with action so, similarly, the fruits of action cannot be associated with *atman*. Cause and effect in action cease and so, then, does the need for another birth in which to experience the fruits of past actions. Nevertheless, some *karma*, cannot be avoided. There are three basic kinds of *karma*. *Prarabdha-karma* has already been accumulated and is beginning to take effect, or is waiting to come into function, in the present life. It will already have determined the nature of the physical and mental person. It cannot usually be changed, only used up. *Sanchita-karma* is that which is beginning to mature from past or present life. Since it is in the process of being formed, it has not yet produced any effects, nor will it in the present existence. *Agami-karma* is that being formed in this life and still has to mature.[49] While some *karma*, then, is on its way, like the unavoidable arrow that has left the bow, that which is in the process of being formed can be burnt in *the fire of knowledge*. Thus, even the enlightened sage will experience adverse *karma*. However, the enlightened individual pays no attention to the results of past actions that happen in life. Remaining focused in *atman*, no reaction to the environment occurs so that all thoughts, words and deeds remain fixed in the divine. *Karma* is being burned up, but not replaced.[50]

VERSE 38

Truly, there is nothing here as pure as knowledge. In time, he who is perfected in *yoga* finds that in his own *atman*.

There is nothing *as pure as knowledge*, *jnana*, this verse says. It is *jnana* – the *that* in the verse – which can separate the pure from the gross, the *atman* from *prakriti*. Thus, Maharishi Mahesh Yogi wrote: "Knowledge is the purifier of life. It purifies life in the sense that it analyses the different aspects of existence and distinguishes and separates the eternal aspects from the transient. It acts like a filter to clear the mud from muddy water."[51] But knowledge is not separated from *yoga*; for these are, as Aurobindo put it, "the two wings of the soul's ascent".[52] Whoever is *perfected in yoga* (*yoga-samsiddha*) has discovered the state of absolute knowledge, perfect knowledge, knowledge of *atman*. No impurity can be attached to the one perfected in yoga because the world of *prakriti* no longer has any effect. The verse also says that such knowledge is found *in time* (*kaleni*), so it cannot be quickly attained. There is a sense of a purification process leading to Self-realization, rather like the truths that Krishnaraj described in relation to verse 35, and also like the evolving disciple demanded by the later school of classical Yoga. And yet, later parts of the *Gita* seem to suggest that liberation is a prerequisite to the ability to see the separation of *purusha* and *prakriti*. Arjuna is, after all, being brought to that state of liberation by Krishna. If we were left with this verse, then the path of knowledge, *jnana-marga*, would be the supreme path to liberation, echoing verse 36.

VERSE 39

The man of *shraddha*, devoted, having restrained the senses, obtains knowledge. Having obtained knowledge he goes rapidly to supreme peace.

There is a definite process depicted in this verse: faith is the overriding thought underpinning sense restraint that leads to *jnana*, and *jnana* to the end goal of supreme *peace* (*shanti*), rather in line with the *Mundaka Upanishad* 3:1:5 and the *Prashna Upanishad* 1:2. There is no suggestion here that knowledge is needed to restrain the ego. Faith, *shraddha*, occurred in 3:31 in connection with Krishna. Faith is needed in oneself, one's teacher, but essentially here, in God, and is one of the aspects needed to attain true knowledge, so it precedes knowledge. Faith, said Radhakrishnan "is the aspiration of the soul to gain wisdom. It is the reflection in the empirical self of the wisdom that dwells in the deepest levels of our being".[53] Devotion reflects the teaching in verse 34 and so may refer to teachers, sages and *gurus* as well as God.

VERSE 40

The ignorant, faithless and doubting self goes to destruction. The doubting self has not this world, nor the next, nor happiness.

The sequence in the verse is lack of knowledge (*ajnana*), lack of faith (*ashraddha*), doubt and destruction. The one who is ignorant has no knowledge, *jnana*, of the Self/*atman*. Whoever doubts cannot see things as they are, is discontented with the world around and will be the same in the next life to come, for doubt "creeps in like a dark fog over the sea, blotting out the guiding stars and filling the soul with despair".[54] Then, there can be no *happiness* (*sukha*).

VERSE 41

One who renounces actions through *yoga*, whose doubts are rent asunder by knowledge, who possesses the *atman*, *karma* does not bind, Dhananjaya.

The first part of the verse referring to one who *renounces action* (*sannyasa-karma*) by *yoga* is reminiscent of action in inaction, desireless action and non-attachment to the results of action. The *yogin* is involved in activity but is not tainted with it. Whoever is established in *atman* cannot doubt because there are no dualities to be perceived. Earlier verses have extolled the *jnanin* and this verse is likely to be an acceptance by Krishna that the completely non-active ascetic path with true knowledge can bring liberation, even if it is not a path that he favours.

VERSE 42

Therefore, having cut with the sword of knowledge of the *atman* this doubt born out of ignorance dwelling in the heart, take refuge in *yoga*. Stand up, Bharata!

The doubts that have been referred to in the last few verses are now assigned to Arjuna in this final verse. He is told to slay his doubts with the sword of knowledge, *jnana*. Here, clearly, it is *ignorance* (*ajnana*) that is held to be the source of doubt. Arjuna's doubts, Krishna tells him, have stemmed from the heart; they are, therefore, emotional ones. Thus, the chapter ends, and the advice to Arjuna is to combine *buddhi-yoga* the discipline of knowledge with *karma-yoga*, the discipline of acting from the stillness of the *atman* within, so that all activity becomes a *yajna*, a sacrifice to Brahman. The last words, *Stand up*, suggest that *karma-yoga*, disinterested action, is the outcome of knowledge of *atman*, illustrating the complementary nature of *jnana-yoga* and *karma-yoga*.

In the **Upanishad** of the **Bhagavad Gita**, the knowledge of Brahman, the teaching of **Yoga** and the dialogue between Shri Krishna and Arjuna, this is the fourth chapter called **Jnana-Yoga**.

CHAPTER FIVE

Sannyasa-Yoga
The *Yoga* of Renunciation

So far, Krishna has presented Sankhya, which is renunciation of action through knowledge – *jnana-yoga* – and the *Yoga* of the *Gita*, which is action without desire for its results – *karma-yoga*. This present chapter will combine both renunciation and action so that they are complementary, though the various sects and philosophical schools tend to prefer either renunciation or action depending on their religious and philosophical perspectives. The separation rather than complementary nature of the two arises through Arjuna's clear separation of them at the beginning of the chapter. *Sannyasa*, "renunciation", is normally accepted as renunciation of action in line with Sankhya thought, but from CHAPTER FOUR the *Gita's* stance is clear that it is action in inaction that is recommended and not inactivity, and thus, renunciation *in* action. The renunciation of action in this chapter will be by the inner *atman*, the inactive and passive stillness of the Self that remains unattached to action by the outer self. It is this kind of renunciation that is important for true *karma-yoga*. Thus, the theme of this chapter is integration of *sannyasa* and *karma-yoga* culminating in the integrated *yoga-yukta*, the one integrated in *yoga*, reminiscent of the last eighteen verses of CHAPTER TWO.

VERSE I   Arjuna said:
You praise renunciation of actions, Krishna, and also *yoga*. Of the two, which one is better? Tell me that conclusively.

While the word *sannyasa*, "renunciation",[1] has hardly been used in the *Gita* so far, it is very closely linked to Sankhya as knowledge, though it also carries with it the concept of ascetic praxis and withdrawal, something that Sankhya, with its emphasis on knowledge and renunciation of all action also accepted. Thus, in its association with Sankhya, renunciation of action has been treated extensively in CHAPTER FOUR, but what was not advocated at all by Krishna was the abandonment of all action. Clearly, CHAPTER FOUR emphasized action that is conducted from an inactive inner state. It is, thus, renunciation of action motivated by desire for results that is essential: Arjuna has never been told to abandon action, but at this point he does not appear to understand this. He differentiates between renunciation and praxis incorrectly, between Sankhya and *yoga*, whereas Krishna sees them as complementary.

Robert Zaehner pertinently pointed out here that Arjuna "thinks in 'either/or' categories: he has not yet realized that Krishna's categories and those of the religion he inherits and further develops are not 'either/or' but 'both/and'. Opposites do not exclude each other but complement each other."[2] Arjuna, however, continues to raise the same question but, to give him credit, from different perspectives. Then, too, as Rohit Mehta pointed out: "One of the unique features of the *Gita* is that it indicates the irrelevance of conclusions of thought and shows the importance of the process of thinking."[3] Arjuna's initial question, therefore, is a further exploration of the dimensions of his enquiry, as much as Krishna's responses are applied from different aspects. Arjuna is distinguishing between relinquishing all actions and practising disciplined action.

Sannyasins were devoted, as today, to the monastic and austere ascetic life. They renounced the world; class and caste duties were obviated; they had no social duties to perform or even prescribed religious duties. The fourth stage of life, the fourth *ashrama*, was the ideal mendicant stage of total focus on the divine and not on the body. The *Gita*, however, does not view *sannyasa* from the same, strictly ascetic, viewpoint. Thus, the *yoga* referred to in the verse is likely to be the discipline of desireless action. Really, then, Arjuna has to learn that *sannyasa-yoga* and *karma-yoga* can mean the same; that is to say, both have to renounce actions based on desire and its fruits. Then, too, knowledge, *jnana*, which Krishna has praised so highly in Chapter Four, is a key aspect of *sannyasa* and Krishna has made it clear that such knowledge needs to underpin action. While *sannyasa-yoga* is normally associated with *jnana-yoga*, which was certainly so for the *advaitist*, Shankara, Ramanuja clearly saw Arjuna's question as enquiring which is the better, *jnana-yoga* or *karma-yoga*, and he was in no doubt that it was the latter,[4] and that *jnana-yoga* cannot occur without *karma-yoga*. For Ramanuja, *karma-yoga* was superior because it is easier to practise and quicker.[5] Krishna would have agreed on this point. Shankara, on the other hand, who extolled *sannyasa* as *complete* renunciation, understood the *sannyasa* of this chapter as a kind of lesser, partial approach of the non-liberated.[6]

VERSE 2   The Lord said:
Both renunciation and *karma-yoga* lead to the highest good but of these two, the *karma-yoga* is superior to renunciation of action.

Here, Krishna states that both renunciation, *sannyasa* and *karma-yoga* lead to liberation but makes the latter superior. Krishna is responding to Arjuna's understanding of renunciation of action as the ascetic path and avoidance of any action, in which case, the path of egoless action would certainly be superior. Indeed, the following verse explicitly mentions the ascetic, *sannyasin*. The reason for the superiority is the action in inaction aspect of *karma-yoga*, which Krishna has already praised, as well as the point that *yogic* action is better than no action at all. Shankara saw *sannyasa* here as renunciation without knowledge, so had no difficulty in seeing *karma-yoga* as preferable with this provision. For Shankara. *karma-sannyasa*, that is to say *karma* with knowledge, is superior to *karma-yoga* without knowledge.[7]

VERSE 3

He is known as a permanent *sannyasin* who does not hate, does not desire, is without dualities. Truly, Mahabaho, he is easily set free from bondage.

Krishna describes to Arjuna the real *sannyasin*, the *permanent* (*nitya*) man of renunciation as opposed, perhaps, to Arjuna's understanding of a *sannyasin* who is totally inactive. The true *sannyasin* is free from desire and aversion and is *without dualities*, *nir-dvandva*, free from the pairs of opposites like happiness and sadness, but can act in the world from the inactive *atman* within. *Bondage* is likely to be that ensuing from actions that reap *karma*, thus enslaving the individual in the cycle of births and deaths, *samsara*. The path of knowledge of the *sannyasin* is, therefore, combined with renunciation not of all action in typical *sannyasin* tradition, but of the *fruits* of action, permitting *karma-yoga*. It is to be renunciation while action takes place.

VERSE 4

Sankhya and Yoga are considered different by children, not the wise: he established in one really obtains the fruits of both.

Sankhya believed that freedom of the *purusha* could be obtained by total dissociation from the *gunic* world of activity. Yoga provided the discipline for this. The *Gita*, however, has the different view of Sankhya as knowledge of Brahman and of *atman*, the true Self, while the *Yoga* of the *Gita* is the disciplined, desireless action that liberates the Self. Sankhya becomes synonymous with renunciation, *sannyasa*, in this chapter. The uniting of the microcosm of the *atman* with the macrocosm that is Brahman is what *yoga* and liberation is all about in the *Gita* and is brought about by knowledge and renunciation of ego-filled action. Krishna says that providing one is truly established in *one* of these paths, the same point, the same goal, is reached, so it does not matter which path is taken. Perhaps this answers a question often posed in the earlier chapters – Is knowledge, *jnana*, necessary for unattached action or *vice versa*? The answer here is that both in themselves are independent paths, but the wise will see them as complementary and leading to the same goal; right knowledge brings right action and right action brings right knowledge. Thus, there is harmony between Sankhya and Yoga, as presented in CHAPTER TWO. The word *bala*, "children", probably refers to those who are simpletons.

VERSE 5

That state reached by the Sankhyas is reached also by the Yogins. He sees who sees Sankhya and Yoga as one.

The state attained through both Sankhya (knowledge) and Yoga (disciplined action) is exactly the same. The verse, then, depicts the unity of Sankhya and Yoga yet the efficacy of their independent routes to liberation. The paths of *jnana* and of *yoga*, that is to say of *karma-yoga*, are complementary. In the Sankhya of the *Gita*, one has to experience the reality of *purusha*, *atman* and Brahman as permanent and the relative level of *prakriti* as transient. In the *Yoga* of the *Gita* one has to be unattached to the transient world of *prakriti*, while being engaged in the world through unattached action, all the time knowing that the *atman* is the still, passive and permanent Reality that is Brahman. As a *Kshatriya* and one at the householder, socially active, stage of life, Arjuna does not, then, need to abandon action for knowledge; he just needs to abandon the either/or choice he thought appropriate in verse 1.

Verse 6

But renunciation is hard to attain without *yoga*, Mahabaho; a sage integrated in *yoga* quickly goes to Brahman.

Any doubts about the superiority of *yoga* appear to be resolved in this verse, but there are difficulties with the text because of the possible different uses of *yoga*. In the second part of the verse, we have a reference to the *yoga-yukta*, one *integrated in yoga*, which could refer to one who has reached the goal of liberation, one integrated in the *atman*, or it could refer to one intent on integration, though the *sage*, the *muni*, is usually a highly evolved, if not liberated, being. It could also refer to the *karma-yogin*, the one engaged in detached action, which seems to me by far the better option. What is likely is that both uses of *yoga* refer to *karma-yoga* as the ability to act while *integrated*, being established in *atman*, making *karma-yoga* and *sannyasa*, again, complementary. Thus, the verse probably demonstrates the complementary nature of renunciation and disciplined, egoless action, though it hints that the latter is the easier and certainly the quicker pathway. Indeed, *hard* is actually *duhkha*, synonymous with pain and suffering. Here, then, there is a shift from discussing Sankhya and Yoga to *sannyasa* and *yoga*. It is unlikely, therefore, that *yoga* in the verse is a reference to the *karma-yoga* that is performance of *Vedic* ritual, as suggested by Shankara.[8]

Verse 7

Integrated in *yoga*, one of purified self, whose self is conquered, whose senses are subdued, who realizes his Self as the *atman* in all beings, though acting is not tainted.

The use of *yoga* in this verse may suggest that, in the last verse, it refers to the liberated soul for here, in this verse, the sense is very much about one whose Self has become the Self of *all beings*, Brahman, in somewhat pantheistic tones. *Yoga-yukta*, *integrated in yoga*, is again mentioned, and the *purified* Self is an obvious reference to the liberated state. Here, the Self, the *atman*, is separated from *prakriti* so there is no taint from the phenomenal world that can affect the enlightened soul. He who has *conquered* the self is he who has fully mastered the lower self to discover the higher Self that is the *atman*. To do this the individuality of the egoistic self needs to be mastered, for it is that lower self that is subject to causative *karma*, to time, and to space. Once the higher Self is realized, it is possible to act in the world of *prakriti* in a totally free way, without any kind of bondage. The liberated one is not affected by sense stimuli, has complete control over the mind and is not tainted by action: no fruitive *karma* ensues. *Realizes his Self as the atman in all beings* is indicative of the fusion of the *atman* within with everything in the whole cosmos: everything is interrelated and in unison.

VERSES 8–9

The integrated one, the knower of truth thinks "I do not even do anything". Thus, seeing, hearing, touching, smelling, eating, going, sleeping, breathing, speaking, evacuating, seizing, opening and closing [the eyes], he is firmly aware that it is only the senses that move amongst the sense objects.

These two verses are normally linked together since verse 9 really continues directly on from verse 8 in mid-sentence, and both verses expand on the description of the *yogin* in verse 7. The *integrated one* is, again, the *yukta*, the *muni* or sage. This is one whose Self (*atman*) is independent of activity or *prakriti*, one whose senses engage in activity in a detached manner. *The knower of truth* is one who understands such separation of *atman* from the *prakritic* domain of the three *gunas*. This integrated one has no *I* that is involved in any activity in the world of the *gunas* regardless of how basic that activity may be: he is non-attached, fixed in *atman* and can incur no causative *karma*. Thus, the *senses* (*indriyas*) can experience stimuli while leaving the sage free; all activities are undertaken from the still and inactive *atman*. Action is related to the world of the *gunas* of *prakriti* so all the actions listed in the verses are products of *prakriti*. Thus, as Vimala Thakar described it, "it is the Cosmic movement and the Cosmic energies that are the doer".[9] The *atman* as the microcosm of Brahman is always passive and still. The senses alone are involved with the objects of the senses, not the inner *atman*. So, as Thakar further commented on a later verse: "Out of the divine, the Cosmos has emerged. In the Cosmos I am born, organically related to the wholeness. There is no myth of separation between me and the divine, so how can I attribute anything to myself? As I am not the doer, I do not want the fruit for myself."[10]

VERSE 10

Having rooted his actions in Brahman, having abandoned attachment, he who acts is not tainted by evil, like the lotus leaf [is not] by water.

Rooted his actions in Brahman is likely to mean dedication of actions to Brahman,[11] but not Franklin Edgerton's "casting all actions on Brahman",[12] which is too suggestive that the all-powerful Brahman is the source of all actions since he/it is, after all, the source of *prakriti*. Indeed, as Edgerton pointed out, this is "despite the fact that elsewhere we are told often and clearly enough that all actions are done by Prakriti".[13] Verse 14 later in this chapter certainly separates Brahman from action and its consequences. So, then, continuing on from the last verse, there is the idea of being rooted in the *atman* that is Brahman so that attachment to anything in the world of *prakriti* does not exist: there is no *I* that acts, so *evil* (*papa*) acts cannot take place. There can, thus, be no *karma* to be reaped, for it has been neutralized. The *Gita*'s use of Brahman is fairly flexible and can refer to the impersonal or personal. But there is no sense here that actions are to be abandoned, as was accepted by those focused on the impersonal Brahman, so the message to the *jnana-yogin* is that *karma-yoga* is essential too. The *Gita* will have more to say about abandonment, *tyaga*, the renunciation of the fruits of actions, in the verses that follow.

Zaehner considered the metaphor about the lotus to have been taken over from Buddhism.[14] It is, however, a widespread image and the whole verse is very similar to one in the *Chandogya Upanishad* (4:14:3). The lotus leaf does not hold water on it despite its watery environment, similar to water on an oily surface. Nor is the lotus flower soiled by the muddy water in which it grows. Just so, the one who is *rooted in Brahman* does not become affected by evil, despite the *prakritic* environment – evil, here, probably referring to *karmic* fruits. As Radhakrishnan put it: "Such a renouncer acts not for his fleeting self but for the Self which is in us all."[15]

VERSE I I
Yogins perform action by the body, by the mind, by the intellect, also merely by the senses, having abandoned attachment, for the purification of the Self.

This verse makes it clear that renunciation or abandonment (*tyaga*) of *attachment* in action is the goal, rather than renunciation of action *per se*. The subject of the verse is *yogins* or the true *karma-yogin*, the adept of detached action. The word *merely*, or "only", is noteworthy, indicating that the *senses* (*indriyas*) engage in activity with no reaction to that engagement taking place because the true Self is established in Brahman. Richard Gotshalk conveys the sense with his translation of being active by way of "bare senses",[16] annotating that "bare" means "without egoistic distortion in terms of passion and the like."[17] In the Sankhya scheme of matter, the *intellect* (*buddhi*), *mind* (*manas*), body and *senses* are all part of *prakriti* and in both Sankhya and the *Gita* they have to be transcended for the permanent reality of the non-material *atman* within.

VERSE I 2
The integrated one, having abandoned the fruit of *karma* attains final peace. The non-integrated one compelled by desire, attached to fruit, is bound.

Again, the subject of this verse is the *yukta*, the *integrated one*. Several commentators see this expression as meaning one having gained unity with Brahman. When a *yukta* can act in the world in such a way that he accrues no *fruit of karma, karma-phala*, then, *karma*-less, some kind of unity with Brahman would be expected. Indeed, this chapter deals very much with the ultimate goal and, therefore, there is some justification for viewing the *yukta* as united with, or established in, Brahman. *Having abandoned the fruit of karma* not only refers to *karma*-less action in the sense of acquiring no positive or negative future *karma*, but also to unattached action in activity and the state of peace (*shanti*). The opposite of the *yukta* is the *ayukta*, the one who is bound by *desires* (*kama*), whose activity in the world is ego-bound and whose *karma* is therefore of the fruitive type. This is the one who cannot separate the *atman* or *purusha* from *prakriti*. *Attains final peace* is the attainment of *moksha*, liberation, and really justifies seeing a *yukta* as liberated. Shankara did not accept that the *karma-yogin* could reach *moksha* simply by this path, He saw this as one stage only in a path of purification, which he outlined as: "First, purity of mind; then, attainment of knowledge; then renunciation of all actions; and, lastly, devotion to knowledge."[18] However, while Shankara emphasized knowledge, the tone of these verses has more to do with *karma-yoga per se* as a valid path to liberation.

VERSE 13
Having renounced all actions of the mind, the self-controlled, embodied one rests happily in the city of the nine gates, neither acting nor causing to act.

The *self-controlled* here refers to the *yukta* of the previous verses and *renounced* is *sannyasa*, the more formal and traditional term for renunciation. The *city of the nine gates* is the material body, the nine gates being the eyes, nostrils, ears, mouth, anus and genitals. The point being made here is that even though the Self (in this verse, *dehin*) is *embodied* in the material body, to the *yukta*, there is freedom even while having to perform bodily actions. It is the *mind* (*manas*) and intellect that do not engage in the actions. Bibek Debroy thus translates the first line of the verse as: "Discarding all action *through* his mind"[19] annotating: "Recognizing that action is performed by the senses and the organs. That is, action is mentally discarded, not physically."[20] Debroy's translation captures the meaning admirably. In Gandhi's words, too: "This life is a play proceeding before us. If we devote ourselves to our work without taking an interest in the play or letting our mind be distracted by it would be *karmasannyasis*",[21] that is to say egoless, disinterested, renouncing of action for results while never leaving the stillness of the Self within.

VERSE 14
The Lord does not create agency or actions for this world: he does not create union with the fruits of actions. One's nature leads to action.

The word for *Lord* in the verse is *prabhu*, which could refer to Krishna as the supreme Lord, the ultimate Brahman that is *nirguna*. As total stillness and passivity and separate from activity the *nirguna* Brahman does not dictate the actions of human beings nor the results of actions, just as the still and passive *atman* of the body. On the other hand, *prabhu* can be the common noun "lord", suggesting, in this verse, the *lord* of the body, that is to say, the *jivatman* or *atman*. This latter interpretation is the way in which many commentators translate it,[22] and such a translation would certainly suit the sense of the verse. Each individual is lord of his or her own self in that actions and the results of them are totally dependent on that individual. The true lord, however, is the *atman*, completely separate from the world of action, from *prakriti*, and from the three *gunas*. Because each individual is ignorant, he or she assumes ownership of actions and their consequences linking the inner *atman* to the *prakritic* world. Thus, every individual is entirely responsible for his or her own suffering. It is *sva-bhava, one's nature*, which dictates activity and its results. To be lord of this nature is to control it, otherwise, the doer, the actions, and the results of the actions belong solely to *prakriti* and are connected to the doer purely by ignorance as verse 27 of CHAPTER TWO explained. What is clearer, however, is that it is individual nature, *sva-bhava*, that is responsible for actions and for the *karmic* results of them: the cause–effect processes in this verse are separated from divine involvement; nor can they ultimately taint the *atman*.[23]

VERSE 15
The Lord takes no note of evil or even merit of any one. Knowledge is enveloped by ignorance; by this, beings are deluded.

Again, we have *the Lord* as subject in the verse, but this time the Sanskrit has *vibhu*. Zaehner took this to mean "all-pervading lord", and considered that, like *prabhu* in the previous verse, it refers to the individual Self as *atman*.[24] In making *lord* the individual Self in this verse, Zaehner claimed that works and their consequences must be ascribed not to the individual self, but "to Brahman seen as the nodal point and 'womb' from which the multiplicity of Nature arises".[25] Such an interpretation hardly suits the general trend of the "inaction in action" thesis of the *Gita* thus far, and Shankara, for one, accepted the term as referring to God:[26] it is the *gunas* that create actions and their consequences, from which the *atman*, along with Brahman as *Param-Atman* are separate, even if all *prakriti* emanates from Brahman. Some commentators, therefore, see *Lord* in this verse as Brahman,[27] and I am inclined to do so also, given that *prabhu* means "all-pervading" or "omnipresent". The evil or good one does and the results that ensue from such actions belong to the individual *gunic* self. The *atman* or *purusha* is the silent witness of all life: it observes the world of *prakriti* but is not responsible for the actions that are part of this *prakritic* existence. In the ordinary world, *knowledge (jnana)* of the *atman* and the understanding of it as the true Self, is overlaid with *ignorance (ajnana)*. It is this ignorance that causes one to identify with *prakriti* rather than *purusha*. Ultimately, the *atman* is lord of the reality of the Self, just as Brahman is the Supreme *Atman* and Lord. That *Supreme* is depicted clearly in the next verse, and has to remain, like the *atman* of the body, separate from *gunic* activity and its consequences. Verse 20 will repeat this point, just as the previous verse states that the embodied one neither acts nor causes to act. Activity, however, cannot be avoided in life, and any action rooted in *atman* is regarded as a *yajna* to Brahman, as the previous chapter so often stated. So, at this level, as Thakar commented: "Whatever you do becomes the flowers that you offer to the divine."[28] Nevertheless, the divine passes no judgement, and gives no praise or blame, but remains passive and still. Ramanuja would have concurred.

Evil (papa) or *merit*, as well as *ignorance (ajnana)* and being *deluded* all come about through the accumulated *karma* that overlays the *atman* with desire-filled motivation and involvement in *prakriti*. Ramanuja was keen to emphasize the effect of *vasanas*, the habits one inherits from past actions and the preferences and aversions that are a major part of *prakritic* involvement.[29] Thus, said Ramanuja:

His knowledge is enveloped, that is, contracted by a series of previous *karmas* which are opposed to knowledge – contracted so that he might become fit to experience their own results. By this *karma*, which is in the form of a veil over knowledge, union with the bodies of the gods etc., and the delusion which is in the form of mistaking such bodies for the self are produced. In consequence there will arise the unconscious subtle impression of such misapprehensions of the self and the unconscious subtle impression in favour of activities suitable thereto.[30]

Importantly, the verse distances Krishna from involvement with good or evil, that is to say, with the actions undertaken by *any one*. There is no hint of determinism or divine predestination here, though, as Ramanuja rightly pointed out, present life conforms to accumulated past impressions and behavioural patterns.

VERSE 16

But those whose ignorance is destroyed by knowledge of the *atman*, their knowledge, like the sun, reveals THAT Supreme.

The idea here is of *ignorance* being destroyed by *knowledge*, that is, *ajnana* by *jnana*. So *jnana* is like the sun that removes darkness and spreads light, revealing the Supreme, Brahman. In Aurobindo's words, "it is a luminous growth into the highest state of being by the outshining of the light of the divine sun of Truth".[31] According to Ramanuja, *karma* is the enemy of knowledge, and knowledge is identified with the Selves: this knowledge, which "belongs to their essential nature, which is unlimited and uncontracted, illuminates everything as it is in itself". Commenting on the same verse, Ramanuja also said: "Knowledge is taught to be an attribute inseparable from the essential nature of the Self" and "Therefore, indeed, the contraction of knowledge by *karma* in the state of *samsara* and (its) expansion in the state of *moksa* is proper and appropriate." [32] For Ramanuja, then, knowledge *is atman*. THAT *Supreme, tatparam*, Radhakrishnan translated as "ultimate reality",[33] and it seems justifiable to translate THAT Supreme in the light of the following verse.

VERSE 17

With their intellect in THAT, their *atman* THAT, established in THAT, with THAT for their supreme goal, those whose sins have been dispelled by knowledge go, not again returning.

The Sanskrit *Tat*, "That", is a word often used for the indescribable Absolute, Brahman (hence the upper case) particularly in the *Upanishads*. The classic statement of unity – indeed, in this case identity – with Brahman is to be found in the *Chandogya Upanishad* (6:13) where Shvetaketu is taught by his father that the essence of his very self is Brahman. "*Tat tvam asi*", he tells his son, "You are That". The whole tone of this verse in the *Gita* seems to be depicting the liberated state, *moksha*, total integration in Brahman when one's whole being, intellect, soul and mind are focused on and absorbed in Brahman. The individual is no longer trapped in *prakriti*, no longer enslaved by the cycle of births and deaths, and therefore never returns. Only the liberated have such an enduring experience. There is, then, a great deal in the context of this verse suggestive that the *THAT* is Brahman, as some commentators suggest.[34] There are commentators, however, who believe the *that* (in the lower case) of this verse is referring to the *knowledge of the atman* in the previous verse. Such commentators are those who, likewise, interpret the *Lord* of verses 14 and 15 as the controlled self, the *atman*.[35] The reference to *THAT Supreme* in the previous verse, however, and the words *their atman THAT* in the present one, really endorse the whole tone of the verse as Brahman being the *supreme goal*.

VERSE 18

The wise see the same in a learned and humble **Brahmin, a cow, an elephant, a dog and even an outcaste.**

This verse states that one must be impartial in everything one sees, *see the same*, *sama-darshina*, thus, not making distinctions between this and that even though one thing or person (like a *Brahmin*) may seem superior to something or someone else (like a dog or an outcaste). Once liberated, everything is seen as united. Seeing everything the same means that the *gunas* are still; neither one nor another is predominant. It is, as in verse 7 of this chapter, seeing the Self, the *atman*, in all beings. Each being and each entity has Brahman as its essence, and to know and recognize such is to make no distinctions and engage in no dualities. In Gandhi's words: "Ganga water in separate vessels is Ganga water after all",[36] or, as Veeraswamy Krishnaraj more philosophically puts it, "there is a metaphysical unity in empirical diversity".[37] Ultimate Reality underlies all existence. The *Brahmin*, the cow, the elephant, the dog and the outcaste are composed of combinations of the *gunas*. The liberated being, however, is *guna*-less and so makes no distinctions. Just as the sun shines on everything without distinction, so the enlightened one sees everything in the same light, leaving the ignorant to continue to operate in divisional dualities. Inequality can only exist because of *prakriti*; it disappears at the level of the *atman*. Sameness or even-mindedness is often thought of as the characteristic of the *jnanin*, the *sannyasin*, who remains in a state of equilibrium of mind, while divorced from the world. Here, it is clear that in contrast, the wise are involved *in* the world.

Pragmatically, of course, class is a difficult social Hindu concept given the inequalities of the class and caste systems even if, in a legendary Golden Age, equality was thought to exist between all classes. The differentiation of duties according to individual and class natures was not believed to do any injustice to an ideal society in which each member was valued though different. In the light of *prakriti* and its composition of active *gunas*, it is *purusha*, the *atman*, that is the equalizing factor, the *gunas* and *prakriti* being the forces that create inequality. The word for *outcaste* is *shvapaka*, which is often translated as "dog-eater", or perhaps is indicative of one who prepares food for dogs, but is often used as a term for an outcaste. To eat dog meat is a sign of utter degradation. The outcaste is also sometimes the child born of a *Kshatriya* father and a mother who is an *Ugra*, and will be considered to be of the lowest class, like *Chandalas*.

VERSE 19

Here, the created world is conquered by those whose minds are based on equanimity. Brahman is flawless and always the same. Therefore, they are established in Brahman.

It is *equanimity* and stillness that conquers the *gunas* of the *created world* and permit transcendence of the dualities of *prakriti*. The reference is, again, reminiscent of verse 7 with the realization that the *atman* within is the same in all things, *a fortiori*, Brahman too, is the same, *sama brahma*, in all things. It is to this knowledge and state of living that the *yogin* aspires. The *created world* is *prakriti*, the round of births and deaths, *samsara*, and the sensory stimuli that bind the self. Being *established in Brahman* (*brahmani-sthita*), suggests that the goal of liberation is attainable in life, *jivan-mukti*.

VERSE 20

One with steady intellect, not deluded, knowing Brahman, established in Brahman, should not rejoice having obtained the pleasant nor be troubled having obtained the unpleasant.

When established in Brahman the delusion of *prakriti* is gone and the *intellect* (*buddhi*) is steady. There is total equilibrium in which neither great joys nor sorrows can affect the Self. There are neither desires nor aversions and no deep impressions that can be made on the liberated individual. Stillness of intellect and *gunas*, stillness of desires and aversions and stillness in Brahman is attained. *Established in Brahman* again, depicts the ultimate aim of the *yogin*.

VERSE 21

One whose Self is unattached in external contacts finds in the *atman* that which is happiness. With the *atman* integrated in the *Yoga* of Brahman he enjoys endless happiness.

Here, again, we have the idea of the Self that is unaffected by, and unattached (*asakta*) to, external stimuli of any kind. The Self is established in its own, true essence, the *atman* that is Brahman. The thought is reminiscent of the second verse of CHAPTER TWO, *satisfied in the Self, within the self*. Thus, the soul is one with or yoked to, Brahman, *brahma-yoga-yuktatman*, with the Self *integrated in the Yoga of Brahman*. True happiness, then, is not to be obtained from outward pleasures but from the inward realization of *atman*.

VERSE 22

Truly, enjoyments which are born of contact are generators of pain only: they have a beginning and an end, Kaunteya, the wise one does not rejoice in them.

The first part of this verse refers to enjoyments or pleasures (*bhoga*) that are born of contact with the world, that is to say, through the senses. Whereas the previous verse depicted the unattached Self, this verse depicts the opposite, the attached self, the one bound to the world of senses, who searches in the sense world for happiness. The verse is akin to some Buddhist thought, which teaches the impermanence and transience of all life and, therefore, the folly of trying to obtain happiness from something that cannot last and that has a beginning and end like all things in phenomenal existence. In any momentary happiness, therefore, there is always the *pain*, suffering (*duhkha*) of loss of it. Happiness and real pleasure can only come from deep within, from the *atman*: since only the *atman* and Brahman are permanent, permanent happiness can come from no other source. The idea of pleasures *born of contact* stresses, again, the importance of non-attachment to sense stimuli – again, reminiscent of Buddhist thought.

VERSE 23

He who is able to withstand the impulse born of desire and anger here, before liberation from the body, he is a *yogin*, he is a happy man.

There is a clear suggestion in this verse also that *liberation, moksha*, can be obtained *here*, in this world and before death, provided the *yogin* does not become subject to desire or anger, that is, positive or negative attachment to sense stimuli. Such a person is a *jivan-mukti*, one who has attained liberation while still in the body, a *yukta*, a *yogin*, or integrated person. Mehta's words here are particularly poignant: "When one touches the Intangible in the tangible, when one sees the Infinite in the finite, when one is established in the Eternal even while living in time – then does one know happiness that is exempt from decay."[38] *Desire* (*kama*) and *anger* (*krodha*) Krishna has already depicted as the deadliest of enemies (3:37–41). These can take no hold of the one who "is anchored to eternal silence as a ship is anchored to the sea-bed".[39]

VERSE 24

One who has happiness within, who rejoices within also, one who is illuminated within, that *yogin* attains Brahman-*nirvana* and is Brahman become.

Maharishi Mahesh Yogi described this verse as "the crest of the teaching of this chapter on renunciation".[40] Indeed, the verse contains some very important ideas. The subject of the verse is the *yogin* who has happiness (*sukha*), contentment and inner light within himself, in the Self. Such a *yogin* attains the *nirvana* of Brahman (*brahma-nirvana*) and becomes one with Brahman (*brahma-bhuta*). The expression *Brahman-nirvana*, we have already met in 2:72 and the comments made there are relevant here, too. Buddhist influence, as suggested by Zaehner,[41] is possible, even though the use of the term *nirvana* with that of Brahman makes the emphasis a Hindu one. The expression *brahma-bhuta* is an interesting one. Zaehner, again, considered the expression to be a thoroughly Buddhist one because it occurs often in the Buddhist Pali canon but rarely in other Hindu literature. He wrote: "The phrase *brahma-bhuta* seems to have been taken on in the Gita in its Buddhist sense of entering a form of existence which is unconditioned by space, time and causation, the very 'flavour' of Nirvana."[42] In the Buddhist sense *brahma-bhuta* means one who has reached enlightenment and, therefore, *nirvana*, and the Buddha himself is said to have become Brahman.[43] Zaehner further commented "The Gita starts by taking the Buddhist conception of liberation fully into account: it adopts much of its terminology and accepts its conclusions and ultimate goal (Nirvana), but it goes further than this in that it seeks to adopt the Buddhist ideal into its own essentially theistic framework."[44] It seems to me, however, that it is exactly the theistic stance of the *Gita* that renders any borrowing from Buddhism, particularly early Buddhism incompatible in its outcome. While the term only occurs three times in the *Gita*, it is to be found in the *Mahabharata* itself.

Generally, major commentators other than Shankara do not suggest that any union with Brahman in this verse is pressed as far as total identity. Rather, becoming Brahman is more of a synonym for the liberated, enlightened being. But the expression does point to a purely Hindu conception of an Ultimate, an Absolute, the Brahman, with which one is in unison at *moksha* though, in the *Gita*'s view, dualistically. Aurobindo, though not certain about the ultimate state of liberation attained in *Brahma-nirvana*, said of it: "The Yogin ceases to be the ego, the little person limited by the mind and the body; he becomes the Brahman: he is unified in consciousness with the immutable divinity of the eternal Self which is immanent in his natural being."[45] But Aurobindo certainly eschewed any hints of monism when he pointed to the enlightened perspective of seeing Brahman in all existence, not just in one's own self.[46] His words are more suggestive of a unity of interconnectedness than of outright monism. Thus, he wrote: "By living in that self we live in all, and no longer in our egoistic being alone; by oneness with that self a steadfast oneness with all in the universe becomes the very nature of our being and the root status of our active consciousness and root motive of all our actions."[47] The tone of the whole verse is one suggestive of immense happiness, joy and inner light.

VERSE 25

The *rishis* obtain Brahman-*nirvana*, those whose sins are destroyed, whose doubts are dispelled, those who are self-controlled, rejoicing in the welfare of all beings.

Rishis are holy men, the enlightened seers. *Self-controlled* (*yatatma*) means that the whole world of reaction to sense perception is contained. *Rejoicing in the welfare of all beings* is an important expression. It suggests a more active participation in the world than the path of total renunciation of works; again, the emphasis is on detached action not non-action. Comparable is 3:20, where Arjuna is told to act for the welfare of others.

VERSE 26

For those ascetics who are free from desire and anger, for those who have controlled their thoughts, Brahman-*nirvana* exists on all sides for those who have realized the *atman*.

The subject of this verse are *yatina*, *yatis*, or *sannyasins*, disciplined, holy, self-controlled men whose *desire* (*kama*) and *anger* (*krodha*) are under control. The term *yatina* can also mean "ascetics" and, thus, could refer either to those who renounce actions, or, and more likely, to the disciplined *yogins*, who have controlled their senses. Such individuals have disciplined their *thoughts* (*chetas*): they are established in the Self. Notably, they are liberated while still in the body, *jivan-mukti*. *Brahma-nirvana exists on all sides* because the *atman* is the essence in all things. Again, the point is reminiscent of verse 7, which spoke of the one who *realizes his self as the Self in all beings*: once liberated, one sees Brahman everywhere.

VERSES 27–8

Excluding all external contacts and [fixing] the gaze between the eyebrows, making equal the outgoing and incoming breaths moving within the nostrils,

with senses, mind and intellect controlled, the sage, having liberation as his supreme goal, who is free from desire, fear and anger, he truly is liberated for ever

These two verses combined are concerned with the meditative process of *dhyana* to which the following chapter of the *Gita* will be devoted. The subject of the verse is the *sage*, the *muni*, whose *senses* (*indriyas*), *mind* (*manas*) and *intellect* (*buddhi*) have turned inward to the Self and totally away from any reaction to the world with the *goal* of liberation, *moksha*. We seem to have the more structured processes of Raja Yoga, "Royal Yoga", here; the processes that were to be systematized in Patanjali's *Yoga Sutras* at a later date. Vision comes *between the eyebrows*, an action that blocks sense impressions and rests the eyes. The inbreath (*prana*) and outbreath (*apana*) are regular and harmonious, flowing evenly and completely balanced in the process of *pranayama*. *Desire, fear* and *anger* are stilled through this rhythmic breathing. *Truly liberated* (*mukta*) *for ever* is the epitome of renunciation of action for results and renunciation of any action that is not Brahman focused. Such more structured praxis will be taken up again in CHAPTER SIX, verses 10–15.

VERSE 29

Knowing me as the enjoyer of *yajna* and *tapas* the Great Lord of all the worlds, friend of all beings, he attains peace.

The verse is overtly theistic: Krishna is saying that he is the whole object and focus of sacrificial actions, probably in the broadest sense of any egoless action that is sacrificed to Brahman, which is the *Yoga* of the *Gita*, and renunciation of action in ascetic practice as *tapas*. He refers to himself as *enjoyer* of *yajna* "sacrifice", and *tapas*, "austerities", reminiscent of 4:24, where he says he is every part of sacrificial offering. Here in this verse Krishna is manifest as *Lord of all the worlds*, *Loka-Maheshvara*, and friend of all. In Aurobindo's powerful comments on this final verse of the chapter: "We get back to the great idea of the Gita, the idea of the Purushottama – though that name is not given until close upon the end, it is always that which Krishna means by his "I" and "me", the Divine who is there as the one self in our timeless and immutable being, who is present too in the world, in all existences, in all activities, the master of the silence and the peace, the master of the power and the action, who is here incarnate as the divine charioteer of the stupendous conflict, the Transcendent, the Self, the All, the master of every individual being."[48]

In the *Upanishad* of the *Bhagavad Gita*, the knowledge of Brahman, the teaching of *Yoga* and the dialogue between Shri Krishna and Arjuna, this is the fifth chapter called *Sannyasa-Yoga*.

CHAPTER SIX

Dhyana-Yoga
The *Yoga* of Meditation

This section of the *Gita* is called *Dhyana-Yoga*, the *Yoga* of Meditation, and has a good part of its contents devoted to *yogic* practice similar in content to that in Patanjali's *Yoga Sutras*, which later systematized it. The chapter describes the character of the *yogin*, his meditative practice, both physically and mentally, and the *yogic* state, taking up the meditative praxis mentioned in the closing verses of CHAPTER FIVE. Yet, the chapter is also an elaboration of the previous one in that it continues to stress the complementary nature of the paths of renunciation and action and it also, like the *Gita* as a whole, never strays far from its explicit or implicit tenets of avoiding the dualities of life that are fuelled by the world of *prakriti*. Non-attachment to the fruits of action will remain a key concern in this chapter.

VERSE I
He who performs action to be done not depending on the fruit of action is a *sannyasin* and a *yogin*, not he who is without fire and without action.

CHAPTER SIX begins with the familiar theme of detached action and the non-dependence on the fruits of actions, *karma-phala*, which are core teachings of the *Gita*. The paths of *sannyasa* (renunciation) and *yoga* (disciplined action) are presented here as complementary, since both are dependent on these core concepts, and Krishna has, hitherto, even presented them as equal (5:4). Thus, we find a neat synthesis of both *jnana-yoga* and *karma-yoga*. Arjuna has said earlier that he wishes to tread the *sannyasa* path of knowledge; refraining from action. But Krishna has here combined the path of knowledge of the *sannyasin* with the desireless actions of the *karma-yogin*. *Action to be done* is probably prescribed ritual action, and has the sense of duty, since *fire* is *agni* the sacrificial ritual fire. Some commentators, therefore, see all references to action in this verse as ritual action.[1] The verse does not use the term *niyata-karma*, obligatory *Vedic* duties, like the daily fire sacrifice, but the reference to *agni* naturally draws the mind that way. Strictly speaking, *sannyasins* were absolved from ritual praxis and would need no sacrificial fire. Having renounced bodily needs, they were not expected to cook their food either – a point that might suggest a purely non-ritualistic meaning by the reference to fire here. If the reference is to ritual action, then it would seem that the *sannyasin* should not renounce it and is expected to continue it. In the general sense, duty is upheld, not inactivity, so Arjuna cannot escape action by wishing to be a *sannyasin*: his prescribed duties would have to be fulfilled as a *Kshatriya* and a householder.

All in all, it seems to me Krishna is saying that whereas the ritualists perform sacrificial actions for a result, and the *sannyasins* none at all, the true *sannyasin* and the true *yogin* are superior to both because they continue to perform all actions but without desire for their results, bringing us back to the core concept of non-dependence on the fruits of actions. Non-attachment is the common denominator of the true *sannyasin* and *yogin*. A very liberal translation of the verse by Alan Jacobs captures the sense well: "He is a true renunciate who performs his duty regardless of expectation, profit, or result. It is not enough merely to renounce the fire ceremony and business of the average householder."[2] This would certainly be sound advice to Arjuna, given that he wanted to abandon his *Kshatriya* and householder status for the renouncing mendicant. Those, then, who see the *sannyasin* as one who renounces all action, even ritual *yajna*, have an incorrect view: the *Gita*'s *sannyasin* is one who undertakes action for action's sake, who undertakes detached, non-fruitive action, and this is what Arjuna is expected to do. Such a view would have been a problem for Shankara, who believed that a true *sannyasin* could never be a *karma-yogin* for he had to abandon all sacrificial ritual and all action.

VERSE 2

Know that which is called *yoga*, Pandava, as *sannyasa*. Truly, no one becomes a *yogin* who has not renounced *sankalpa*.

The verse expands on the thought of the previous one concerning detached action. *Sankalpa* is an important word that is indicative of the egoistic thought or intention behind an action. It is "determination", "will", "intention" or "purpose" – all indicative of emphasis on results of actions; the planning, imagining, forming, idealizing of actions and their results before they take place. At the level of sacrificial ritual, it was the *intention* that informed a specific ritual as well as the expectation of specific results of the ritual action. Here, Krishna seems to be saying that such intention for results must be abandoned. *Vedic* ritual action was engaged in with the precision and specification the *Brahmins* brought to it. Concentration on the action would have been all important and the results would then naturally occur, but these results were the *raison d'être* of the rituals. In the *Gita*'s view, both the *sannyasin* and the *yogin* have to achieve the cessation of *sankalpa* because *sankalpa* involves an ego-bound process and it is only when this process is controlled that action can be undertaken for action's sake and not for results. *Sankalpa* is the cause of the thoughts that create desires and crave results. Rohit Mehta aptly commented here: "Yoga is concerned with Action, not with reaction nor with mere activity. Action in terms of *Yoga* arises from the Ground of Inaction, a negative state where all mentation has come to an end."[3] It is renunciation of *sankalpa* that brings this about. Thus, true *yoga* is desireless action rather than no action.

VERSE 3

Action is said to be the cause of a sage wishing to attain to *yoga*, but of one who has attained [it], quiescence is said to be the cause.

The word *cause*, or "means", "path", "way", suggests that both *sages* in the verse are still on the path to final liberation. *Action, karma*, may be meant as ritual action, or perhaps selfless action as the means for the first one, and *quiescence* or serenity (*shama*), presumably detached action or inaction in action, for the second. It is the latter who appears as superior. While the word *muni, sage*, used for both adepts might suggest a degree of synonymy between the two, the silence that comes with renunciation of desire, which is the *Yoga* of the *Gita*, is clearly the higher attainment. Mehta captured the difference between the two *munis* when he translated: "For a sage who is seeking *Yoga*, activity is called the means; when he is enthroned in *Yoga*, serenity is called the means",[4] and Aurobindo wrote of the sage "who is ascending the hill" and the one who "has got to the top".[5] Of the two *munis*, the first is probably the sage who is steeped in knowledge, who is in the process of practising action without seeking its results and who is still dependent on ritual action and *yogic* action in the world: he has yet to experience the peace of more permanent realization of the *atman* within. For the time being, his focus needs to be external – *Veda*, ritual, knowledge – until *real*, internalized experience of Brahman occurs. First, he needs to acquire restraint and control of the ego while engaged in action. Then, when this is achieved, quiescence and quietude are the means to complete integration of the *yogin* in the Self. In a way, the verse pre-empts the concept of knowledge and realization that is the subject of the next chapter, CHAPTER SEVEN. However, given the emphasis in the *Gita* on the necessity of detached action by any *muni* or *yogin*, it is unlikely that the *one who has attained yoga* is to rest on the laurels of peace: engagement in the world through detached *action* is the message of the *Gita*.

VERSE 4

Truly, when one is not attached to sense objects or actions, a renouncer of *sankalpa*, then one is said to have attained to *yoga*.

This sums up much earlier teaching for the *renouncer*, the *sannyasin* – loss of *sankalpa*, detached and non-fruitive action. The process of *dhyana*, meditation, brings the *yogin* to *samadhi*, the state in which there is no desire, no dualities, and in which the ego is still. The attainment mentioned here is perhaps a reference to the more advanced of the two *munis* of the previous verse.

VERSE 5

Let the self be lifted by the *atman* not the *atman* lowered by the self. Truly, the *atman* can be the friend of the self or the self can be the enemy of the *atman*.

The word for *self* in this verse is consistently *atman*, which can refer simply to the ordinary self or to the passive, true Self. Where I think it is indicative of the true Self, I have retained *atman*, but *atman* eight times in the verse causes some problems. Indeed, Douglas Hill called it the "riddle of the *atmans*".[6] Taking the ordinary self throughout, the sense of the verse would mean that individuals are responsible for their own pathways through life whether that is evolutionary – the self being lifted by the self – or involutionary – the self being the enemy of the self.[7] On the other hand, the ordinary self here may be juxtaposed with the true Self, the passive, inner *atman* that is Brahman,[8] and such, I think, is the tenor of the verse. Arjuna is then being told to raise his self by his true Self, to free himself by being established in *atman*; this inner Self is his true friend and can aid the ordinary self, otherwise the ordinary egoistic self will be inimical to the discovery of the real Self. Thus, the lower self has to be influenced by the higher Self in the sense that if the lower one is enticed by *prakriti*, the higher Self cannot be open to it. Verse 26 later in this chapter will repeat the same idea. However, whether the translation should be *the self can be the friend of the Self* or *the Self can be the friend of the self* is difficult to say: both would provide valid meanings. On balance, I am inclined to favour the latter, the *atman* as the true Self, the inner teacher influencing, though passively, the way the outer self perceives and reacts to sense stimuli.

Krishna is clearly saying that the lower self needs to be *lifted*, elevated, raised, and presumably this could only be done by the higher Self, which, then, would be the only true friend of the lower self. In whichever way the verse is interpreted, unless focused on the inner *atman* that is Brahman, the self and the Self are estranged, the one engaged in the sensory world, the other still and passive, "opposed to each other in their essential natures" as Maharishi Mahesh Yogi put it.[9] Either way, as Mahesh Yogi also commented: "Conquest of the self by the Self and conquest of the Self by the self amounts to the same thing. It can be understood in either way so long as the conquest denotes the Union of the two, or merger of the one into the other."[10] Indeed, this is exactly what integration in *yoga* is all about.

VERSE 6

The *atman* is the friend of the self in whom the self is conquered by the *atman*, but he of unconquered self would remain in the place of an enemy, the self being just like an enemy.

As in the previous verse, the word *atman* occurs several times and, likewise, is accepted by some as referring to the ordinary self on each occasion. In this case, the verse would be stressing the need for control of the self with the discipline that underpins detached action. On the other hand, the possibility that the verse refers to the higher Self conquering the lower seems to me better and, again, I have retained *atman* to indicate this. When the individual is rooted in the inner *atman* there are no problems with the egoistic, personality and individual self, for it is simply not there; but when the inner Self is lost, the egoistic self is the worst enemy. Thus, the self rooted in *atman* is a very different one from that without knowledge of the *atman*. As in the previous verse, there is a sense of harmonizing of self and Self that is essential but there can only be such harmony when the egoistic self is still. Here again, then, conquering of *sankalpa* and the desire that it brings allows the *atman* to be a friend. Moreover, since the next verse picks up the supreme *atman of the controlled self*, we may be justified in finding some reference to it in verses 5 and 6. Nevertheless, the problem lies in which self to identify as lower or higher. Can the ordinary self be the friend of the inner Self,[11] or should it be the other way around as I have presented them here for both verses 5 and 6? Zaehner's view was that only the self can *act* as a friend or enemy, since the true Self does not act at all.[12] But the sense may be more in the line of association between the self and Self and it is that which dictates friendship or enmity, closeness and evolution or distance and involution. The *yogin* who is rooted in *atman* will have found the harmony between his lower self and higher Self.

VERSE 7

The *param-atman* of the controlled and peaceful self is balanced in cold and heat, pleasure and pain as, also, in honour and dishonour.

What is described is that state in which dualities no longer exist, the state of equanimity, "enstasis", as Zaehner called it.[13] The important word in this verse is *param-atman*, "supreme Self", or highest Self. Usually, it refers to Brahman or *Atman* as Brahman, though here the emphasis is on the *atman* of the individual self that has realized Brahman, the higher Self, and has gained peace (*shanti*). *Balanced*, that is to say being the same (*sama*) in all dualities – especially *pleasure* or happiness (*sukha*) and *pain* or sorrow (*duhkha*) – is the hallmark of the true *yogin*.

VERSE 8

A *yogin* is said to be one who is satisfied with knowledge and wisdom, unshaken, who has conquered the senses, integrated, one to whom a lump of earth, a stone and gold are the same.

Knowledge here is *jnana* and *wisdom* is *vijnana*. There is a subtle difference between the two. *Jnana* is knowledge itself and *vijnana* is intuitive realization or insight. Such a distinction suggests a twofold conception of truth, intuitively intellectual on the one hand and intuitively experiential on the other. Both bring about a balanced view in responding to the world of *prakriti*, the world of the *senses* (*indriyas*). We are reminded here of the two *munis* of verse 3, the first gaining knowledge, the second the realization of *atman*. In this present verse, the *yogin* is satisfied with knowledge; it is complete, and he has, too, the culminating realization. Once the mind is established in Brahman, it is possible to view all things equally: the word used to depict this is, again, *yukta, integrated.* The verse also contains the word *kuta-shta*, "unshaken", "unmoved", "changeless", if somewhat difficult and variable in translation. It refers to the real Self that is "superior to all appearances and mutations", as Aurobindo described it.[14] Literally, it can mean something like "set on a high place".[15]

VERSE 9

He excels whose intellect is the same to the good-hearted, companions, friends, enemies, neutrals, arbiters, the hateful, relatives, the righteous and also the evil.

The first part of this verse *he excels* could be translated "stands supreme", "is distinguished", "is outstanding" or "is esteemed". We have seen in earlier verses that the ideal state of mind is one unaffected by sense stimuli. Here, the same principle is applied to relationships with people – perhaps the area in which the assertive self, the ego, is so involved. We naturally make distinctions between parents, friends, acquaintances, colleagues, and people we do not like very much. But just as inert, inanimate objects, as in the previous verse, are to be viewed from a perspective of equanimity, so also should humans be for, ultimately, they are all parts of the same reality. There is no sense here of the equanimity and even-mindedness or sameness of intellect (*sama-buddhi*) of the *jnanin* and *sannyasin* who withdraws from the world, but clear engagement of the even-minded *buddhi within* the world. This may be timely advice for Arjuna, who, in CHAPTER ONE, made clear divisions between friends, relatives, enemies, and his own and the opposing armies.

VERSE 10

Let the *yogin* constantly keep the mind and self steady, remain alone in solitude, with thoughts and self controlled, without expectations, without greed.

Here we have the picture of the *yogin* living in seclusion, deep in meditation, owning nothing, expecting nothing. *Without expectations* is synonymous for being without desire for results, as is *without greed*. And yet, the instructive tone of the verse suggests that this is a *yogin* who is still on the path, not having reached the final goal. Hinduism has generally accepted that those on the spiritual path should renounce life and live in seclusion, and what is recommended here is a more stringent renunciation than we have seen hitherto from the *Gita* – again, suggestive of someone still on the *yogic* path. These are vague and not systematized instructions for the *yogin* and reflect the *Shvetashvatara Upanishad* 2:10. Such instructions predate the formalized *Yoga Sutras* of Patanjali, but illustrate that much formal *yogic* praxis already existed.

VERSE 11

Having established for himself a firm seat in a clean spot not too high, not too low, [placing] a cloth, a skin and *kusha* grass one on top of the other.

Krishna now deals with formal *dhyana*, the meditative practice of the *yogin*. Arjuna had asked Krishna earlier (2:54) how a *yogin* sits. The place and position in which *yoga* is undertaken are deemed to be very important for there is a close correlation between mind and environment – quiet natural places like a hilltop or a river bank are, therefore, favoured. Normally, a slightly raised platform is used and the sacred grass that is spread on it is *kusha grass*, which has been used in religious ritual since ancient times. Usually, a deer skin is then placed over the grass, with a cloth on top, thus in reverse order to that in the verse. The *firm* or steady (*sthira*) seat is *asana*, which has the additional meaning of "posture", *yogic* postures being a fundamental aspect of *yoga*. *Clean* can also mean "pure"; perhaps meant in the sense of an area that is not going to distract the meditation. *Yoga* is, therefore, both a physical and psychological process where body and mind are harmonized during meditation.

VERSE 12

Seated there on the seat, having made the mind one-pointed, having controlled the thoughts and the senses, let him practise *yoga* for the purification of the self.

The true state of the self is one of purity but the mind loses this when it becomes involved with sense objects. Being *one-pointed, ekagra*, prevents this impurity so that the *mind*, the *manas*, and the intellect, the *buddhi*, transcend to a pure level. One-pointedness is usually directed to a single object like the tip of the nose or the middle of the forehead, or it could be more subtle like light within the head. *Ekagra* is a *sattvic* activity but a highly concentrated stage of consciousness. Nevertheless, it still involves a process of thought as opposed to total cessation of the fluctuations of the mind when all actions of the mind, all *thoughts* (*chitta*) disappear. In classical Yoga, there is no ultimate divine being, only a temporary one to aid the *yogin*. However, *ekagra* in the *Gita*, as verse 14 will state, has Krishna as the point of focus. The *yoga* of the verse is meant in the sense of meditation, *dhyana*.

VERSE 13

Holding body, head and neck erect, still, steady, gazing at the tip of the nose, not looking round about him.

The verse deals with the *yogin's* posture during meditation. It is important that the spinal column is vertical because this aids smooth, unrestricted breathing. The tip of the nose is said to be the point at which the breath and the line of vision coincide: the one-pointedness of this is obvious. Actually, the eyes only seem to be directed towards the tip of the nose; really they are not directed on anything outward but are concentrating inwardly and there is more of a one-pointedness of mind than of vision. The eyes are simply staring vaguely ahead, partly closed and not concentrating on anything in particular. The words *still* or steady (*achala*) and *steady* or firm (*sthira*) describe every aspect of the praxis.

VERSE 14

With the self serene, fearless, firm in the vow of **Brahma-charya**, having restrained mind, thinking on me, integrated, let him sit supremely [intent on] me.

With the self serene is the self stilled, the whole being in deep peace. In such a state, stimuli of the senses cannot disturb the mind for the mind is no longer in the world of sensory stimuli but established in *atman*. Since there is no duality in this state, there can be no fear, any more than there can be any other polarity. The Sanskrit refers to the vow of *Brahma-charya*, the one devoted to the spiritual path, devoted to Brahman. The emphasis here is not on what one should vow *not* to do, but on the path one vows to tread. *Brahma-charya* is the first of the four stages of life (*ashramas*) in Hinduism. It is a time of studentship, celibacy and dedication to one's teacher and to God. Containing the word *Brahman*, it is obvious where the focus of that discipleship should be. Vimala Thakar described this well: "When your creative energies are not utilized for outward activities, but focused, along with the physical and psychological on the Cosmic reality, on Brahman, then such a Brahmacharya is fresh, vibrant and vigorous."[16] The first and fourth, final, stages of life, *Brahma-charya* and *sannyasin*, respectively, are both characterized by celibacy and dedication to the spiritual life rather than the physical. *Restrained* (*samyama*) *the mind* (*manas*) means the senses are subdued, that is to say, the senses are controlled through being under the control of the inner Self. In the last part of the verse, Krishna presents himself as the focus of the spiritual path, being the divine essence that is the inner *atman*. We have a hint here of the theistic devotionalism that is to come, despite the context of set practice of *yoga*. The word *yukta* appears in this verse again, referring to one who is *integrated*, "balanced" or "united".

VERSE 15

Thus, always balancing the self, the *yogin* of controlled mind attains to the peace abiding in me that culminates in *nirvana*.

The *yogin's* practice culminates or has the end product of peaceful *nirvana*. *Shanti*, *peace*, is a term virtually synonymous with *moksha* here because it is the kind of permanent peace found only in liberation. Again, we should note the use of the term *nirvana*, since it is normally a Buddhist one. This *nirvana* is seen to subsist in Krishna in the verse, making him truly the Brahman in which all is contained. Thus, here, he asserts his true nature to Arjuna and that nature is in a dualistic relationship to the world that abides within him.

Zaehner's view that this chapter presents the personal God Krishna as superior to Buddhist *nirvana and* the Brahman of the *Upanishads*[17] is not really supported by the text but does have support amongst a few translators and commentators.[18] The words *abiding in me* are likely to refer to the *nirvana* that abides in Krishna, though the expression might refer to the *yogin* that abides in him. Either way, thus far in the *Gita*, Krishna has revealed himself only as the Absolute, Brahman, not as superior to Brahman as put forward by Zaehner. Some, however, translate *culminates in nirvana* as "beyond *nirvana*": van Buitenen, for example, suggested that Krishna/Brahman is being portrayed as superior to the Buddhist *nirvana*.[19] Far more plausible is his claim that the expression is indicative of "not pure extinction [as Buddhist *nirvana* would be], but a positive union of the persisting *atman* with the personal God".[20] Elsewhere, too, van Buitenen says that beyond *nirvana* is "that which cannot be described or thought of as any state of religious enlightenment, however high, or ultimate aim of religious (or yogic) experience – an unfathomable absolute".[21] Whether Krishna as Brahman is beyond *nirvana* or *nirvana* culminates in him, this last idea aptly fits both possibilities.

VERSE 16

Truly, *yoga* is not at all for one who eats too much, or for one who does not eat or for one who sleeps or is awake too much, Arjuna.

Harmony and balance are the key ideas here, suggesting balance and not excess in needing or avoiding the necessities of life. There may be inferences to other religions here. Bibek Debroy thinks that the reference to *one who does not eat* is an allusion to the Jains.[22] Then, too, one is reminded of the Middle Way of early Buddhism, which advocated neither extreme asceticism nor extreme indulgence; rather, as the Buddha himself experienced, it is moderation that aids the spiritual path. In the *Gita*, *all* desires are subdued in the state of harmony that is equipoised between extremes, "like a steady flame which while it gives warmth is for ever unmoved and unmodified", as Mehta put it[23] – a point that will be echoed in Verse 19.

VERSE 17

For one who is balanced in eating and recreation, who is balanced in carrying out actions, who is balanced in sleep and wakefulness, *yoga* becomes the destroyer of pain.

The word for *balanced* is the familiar *yukta*, which suggests that a certain element of discipline is needed to achieve balance and that the *yogin* remains integrated in all activity. Again, the emphasis is on harmony. Harmony, balance and integration suggest that it is wrong to place too much importance on any one aspect of life as opposed to any other: thus it is necessary to overcome the dualities of life. Pain, here, is *duhkha*, perhaps, given the context, another hint of the first of the *Four Noble Truths* of Buddhism, that all life is *duhkha*, though the term has already occurred many times in the *Gita*, especially in relation to its opposite of happiness (*sukha*) and the need to be the same regardless of either. Thus, for the integrated *yogin*, pain cannot be experienced because it is one aspect of a duality and the *yogin* is beyond dualities.

VERSE 18

When the perfectly controlled consciousness rests only in the *atman*, without longing, without desires, then is one said to be *yukta*.

He whose *consciousness*, actions of the mind, or thought (*chitta*) is disciplined and rests in the Self, the *atman*, is *yukta*, that is to say, he is "integrated" or "united", "established" in *yoga*. Then, *desires* (*kama*) cannot affect the *yogin*.

VERSE 19

"As a lamp put in a windless place does not flicker" – this simile is used of the *yogin* of controlled thought practising the *yoga* of the *atman*.

When the mind is influenced by sensory stimuli it is like a flickering flame, but once the mind's reactions to stimuli are steadied, then the mind is like a flame that is still. Gandhi said that: "If we are unsteady in mind, the storm of the cravings of the senses blows out the atman as a breeze blows out the lamp. As the latter gets its food from the air, so the atman gets the food it needs through the senses and the mind. The lamp gets its food from air which is motionless; likewise the atman gets its nourishing food from the mind if we keep the air of its impulses still."[24] Veeraswamy Krishnaraj also comments attractively on this verse: "There are no thoughts wafting in and out; the wind has died down; the thoughts have died down; there is that little steady flame of the Self; there is oneness, stillness, absolute freedom."[25] *Thought* in this and the next verse is *chitta* and when stilled it renders the mind as a rippleless, calm lake, facilitating the goal of *moksha*, an integrated, purified Self, pure *atman*, devoid of *gunas* and dualities.

VERSE 20

When thought attains quietness, restrained by the practice of *yoga*, and when seeing the *atman* by the self, is satisfied in the *atman* ...

The inner essence of *atman* is experienced by the disciplined self. Two important and related words occur in the verse, *chitta* and *nirodha*. *Chitta*, as seen in the previous verse, is "thought" – that part of the mind that is almost impossible to control. *Nirodha* is "cessation", "negation", and it is exactly the cessation of thought that is the aim of *yoga*.[26] Verses 20–23 form a very long sentence and thus, make more sense when taken together.

VERSE 21

... when infinite happiness can be grasped by intellect, transcending the senses, when this is known, established, one never moves from the Reality ...

Zaehner translated *intellect, buddhi*, here as "soul", which is probably nearer the true sense of the verse, for, in fact, the intellect has ultimately to surrender itself to the *atman*. In the Sankhya scheme of things it is the *buddhi* that is the *sattvic* matter that can best illuminate the *atman*. *Happiness* (*sukha*) is described as *infinite* and is the state that is possible when the *senses* (*indriyas*) are transcended. It is a state that is infinite and eternal because it is associated with the permanent and infinite *atman*. Only the soul can experience this, though *buddhi* as pure intellect is the ultimate means to it. *The Reality, tattvata* in the Sanskrit, is suggestive of Brahman, though it is sometimes translated in a more secular sense such as "one never really moves from it" or, with Gandhi, "he swerves not from the Truth".[27]

VERSE 22

... and having obtained which, he thinks there is no other gain greater than that in which he is established; he is not moved by the greatest sorrow.

Having gained the infinite happiness spoken of in verse 21, there can be no higher gain, for this is the supreme state. Because in such bliss there are no dualities, there can be no *sorrow*, suffering (*duhkha*); the body becomes like its shadow, something that affects the *yogin's* real Self in no way at all. Zaehner's translation: "He wins a prize beyond all others – *or so he thinks*"[28] shifts the emphasis rather unnecessarily to suggest some goal beyond the *Reality* of the previous verse, a Reality that is surely the ultimate rather than the penultimate goal, given the contextual sense of these verses.

VERSE 23

Be it known that a state of separation from union with pain is called *yoga*. That *yoga* should be practised with determination and with an undismayed consciousness.

The *union* (*samyoga*) or integraton of *yoga* serves to disunite one from sorrow or pain and suffering (*duhkha*). It is an "unlinking of the link" between them, as Zaehner described it.[29] Zaehner saw this as a Buddhist idea, suggesting the necessity of refraining from linking the senses and objects of the senses with desire or aversion. There have been hints at Buddhist belief in a number of the verses in this section of the *Gita* so he may well have been right. The separation is brought about by an avoidance of positive or negative thought about points on the continuum between two opposites as opposed to the perfect centre between them that is completely balanced. Hill commented here that "the word *yoga*, originally meaning 'union', was later used for any method of 'control' or 'restraint' by which union with *isvara* might be attained".[30] Its use in this verse is probably meant in such a wider sense.

VERSE 24

Having abandoned without reserve all desires born of *sankalpa* and by the mind completely restraining all the senses on every side . . .

The verse defines *yoga* rather well with its depiction of disciplining, restraining and yoking (*niyamya*) – here, the senses being the object. *Sankalpa* has been met earlier; it is will, determination, intention, purpose and the formative thought that creates *desires* as its oft used synonym of *kama*, "desire", shows. *The senses on every side* is literally "the village of the senses", the mind (*manas*) with its many inhabitants being the thoughts and stimuli that invade it. Abandonment, *tyaga*, again, will feature considerable throughout the *Gita*.

VERSE 25

. . . little by little let him gain quietude by the intellect held firm. Having made the mind fixed in the *atman* let him not think of anything.

The more the *mind* (*manas*) becomes fixed in the Self, the *atman*, the more it is able to control *sankalpa*, so that little by little desires are stilled until total quietude – no *sankalpa*, no desires, no thoughts – is reached. The mind becomes *fixed* or merged in the Self within, but it is the *intellect*, the *buddhi*, that is the means for the mind to become calm.

VERSE 26

From whatever cause the restless and unsteady mind wanders away from that, having restrained it, let him bring it under control only of the *atman*.

This verse, as well as 25 and 27, suggest that the mind, the *manas*, must control the senses and, in turn, the *atman* should absorb the mind, so that the whole being is established in *atman*. Control of the mind is very difficult for it all too soon becomes absorbed in the world of the senses which is its normal state. Krishnaraj graphically describes this state of the mind when he writes:

> The mind is fuzzy and woozy, wild and woolly, agitated and avaricious, and narrow and shallow. Mundane thoughts come easy. It is anchored in pleasure. And the mind knows not what it thinks it knows. It blinks and flickers. Thoughts rush in and thoughts rush out; they are erotic and erratic. The thoughts are light and fluffy one time, and at another slap like waves. There is no end to this onslaught. The mind wanders near and far like the wings on the wind. Mind jumps between unrelated thoughts. What a mind, what a bind![31]

When the mind leaves the distraction of the senses and is *restrained* (*niyamya*) it is no longer swayed by dualities and remains balanced in all situations.

VERSE 27

Truly, supreme happiness comes to this *yogin* of peaceful mind, one whose passion is quieted, Brahman-become, one who is free from blemish.

Passion in this verse is *rajas*, the impulse to activity aspect of the three *gunas*. The *mind*, the *manas*, must be *guna*-less in order to experience Brahman. When in this state, blemishes, stains, sins are impossible because fruitive *karma* is obviated when dualities and desire are absent. *Brahman-become, Brahma-bhuta*, is translated by some commentators as realization that all is Brahman, but the Sanskrit seems more expressive than this. Shankara naturally saw the expression as indicative of total identity with Brahman and the expression admittedly seems non-dual, but few press the identity of the Self with Brahman, preferring "at one with Brahman", suiting the tone of the *Gita* thus far. Indeed, the following verse speaks of the same *yogin* as having *contact* with Brahman, not identity.

VERSE 28

Thus the *yogin*, always practising the *yoga* of the *atman*, freed from blemish, easily enjoys the infinite happiness by contact with Brahman.

Always practising the yoga of the atman is variously translated: "constantly engaging the mind this way",[32] "keeping the self steadfast",[33] "continually disciplining himself".[34] The Sanskrit is *yunjan*. *Contact with Brahman* is sometimes translated as "the touch of Brahman".[35] The phrase is indicative of the total harmony of the inner and outer Self with Brahman, but not, it seems to me, with any thought of identity.

VERSE 29

One whose self is integrated by *yoga* sees the *atman* as dwelling in all beings and all beings in the *atman*. One sees the same everywhere.

Despite the comment at the end of the last verse, it would have to be admitted here that those who wished to find monism in the *Gita* could find a classic statement of it here. Indeed, Shankara wrote: "he sees all beings – from Brahman, the Creator, down to a clump of grass – as one with the Self; and all the different beings – from Brahman, the Creator, down to inanimate objects – he sees the same; i.e. he sees that the Self and Brahman (the Absolute) are one."[36] Often cited as the basis of this verse, the words of the *Isha Upanishad* certainly seem to uphold a monistic view:

> When a man sees all beings
>   within his very self,
>   and his self within all beings,
> It will not seek to hide from him.

> When in the self of a discerning man,
>   his very self has become all beings,
> What bewilderment, what sorrow can there be,
>   regarding that self of him who sees this oneness.[37]

The *Gita*, however, normally accepts a duality between Brahman and the created world. Its spirit is a panentheistic[38] unity rather than a monistic one. It will be in the light of the later, more theistic, verses of the *Gita* – so far only touched on – that we may need to interpret this verse. Indeed, in the light and context of the following verse, which is highly theistic and dualistic, monism is unlikely. But this present verse is certainly pantheistic. The *atman* may be the same in all beings, and there have been statements of such already in the *Gita*, but that fact does not necessarily exclude the *Param-Atman* as greater than all, especially since, in the Sankhya of the *Gita*, human beings, as all *prakriti*, are manifestations of the divine.

Ramanuja's qualified non-duality clearly separated Brahman and *atman*, the latter being the body of God. Ramanuja believed that all *atmans* have the same form, and that is knowledge: when focused on *atman* alone, through *karma-yoga*, this sameness in all beings is experienced.[39] It is not identity but more like similarity:

> Because there is similarity between his self and other beings (i.e., selves), when they are in a state of separation from the *prakrti*, on account of (all of them) having only the nature of knowledge, and because the inequality among them rests on the *prakrti*, one whose mind is engaged in *yoga* has equality of vision everywhere, in respect of all selves as separated from the *prakrti*, on account of their having the nature only of knowledge: he sees his self as existing in all beings (or selves) and all beings (or selves) in his self.[40]

Ramanuja was adamant that this is not identity, "he sees his self as similar in form to every being (or self) and all beings (or selves) as similar in form to his self".[41] Mention of the *integrated self, yuktatma*, occurs here again (cf. 5:21) and is tantamount to liberation.

VERSE 30

He who sees me everywhere and sees all in me does not become lost to me and I do not become lost to him.

The concept of God in all things and all things in God, and yet a dualism between God and beings, suggests a pantheistic belief system. Everything in the cosmos is an expression of Brahman, the Source of all manifested existence: the One manifests itself as the many. The general trend of the *Gita*, however, is panentheistic, where God is greater than all he creates, not just the sum total of what is created. This verse is important because it is a clear expression of theism. It emphasizes a *personal* relationship between God and humanity even when one becomes a *jivan-mukti*, one liberated while in the body, or at final *moksha*. Thus, even though the individual self is transcended to reveal pure *atman*, identical to all others in essence, the *atman* is only part of God, not the whole of God. That famous statement of the *Chandogya Upanishad*, "That you are", *tat tvam asi*, does not obtain here. God is not lost, or does not vanish at *moksha*, he continues to be experienced. Classical Sankhya taught the suspension of the liberated *atman* in its own timeless essence, so that it was totally alone at liberation: but there is none of this here. There is not only a unity of all in *moksha*, as opposed to an "innumeration" of souls as in Sankhya but a dual relation between *each* of those souls and divinity. *Atman* does not equal Brahman here, yet unites all. This is at least pantheism or, more probably, as far as I can see, panentheism, but not monism. Zaehner believed that *lost to* in the verse means "merged in to or swallowed up in the Infinite",[42] influenced, perhaps, by his idea that Krishna transcends the infinite Brahman. At this stage, in my view, the text does not support such a conclusion. The implicit reference to the unity and diversity of the divine in the manifested world suggests that it is the manifest Brahman that is represented by the *me* in the verse.

VERSE 31

Whoever worships me as abiding in all beings, remaining established in unity, whatever his mode of life, that *yogin* abides in me also.

The verse continues the tone of the former verse. Zaehner described the verse as "the climax of the chapter",[43] and, indeed, the powerful word *worships, bhajati*, is pregnant with ideas of surrendering of the self, of devotion and dedication to the object of worship. Again, such devotion to God emphasizes the personal relationship and harmony between devotee and divine but, at the same time, the essence *abiding in all beings* directs that devotee to the passive stillness of the Unmanifest Brahman. The verse is one that seems to harmonize the three paths of *bhakti* (*worships me*), *jnana* (*established in unity*) and *karma* (*whatever mode of life*). *Whatever his mode of life* is variously interpreted. It perhaps suggests whatever one is doing in life, whatever level of consciousness one is at on the pathway to Brahman, or at whatever stage of life one is at, or class one is in. It could be translated as "in every way", or even "in everything". Debroy has the useful "wherever he happens to find himself".[44] However it is interpreted, one who sees the divine in all, *and* is *established in unity* is well-integrated in *yoga*.

VERSE 32

Whoever sees things everywhere as the same as his Self, Arjuna, whether pleasure or pain, he is regarded as the highest *yogin*.

Here, again, the unity of the cosmos is emphasized and, thus, the identification of the inner Self with everything in it. All dualities like *pleasure*, happiness (*sukha*) and *pain*, sorrow (*duhkha*) disappear for the *highest yogin* who is a particle of the divine in the same way as all others. Further, by extension, the respective pleasure or suffering of others is seen by the highest *yogin* as if his own.

VERSE 33   Arjuna said:

This *yoga* of equanimity, which is taught by you, Madhusudana, I cannot see its steady constancy because of restlessness.

Arjuna recognizes how difficult it is for the mind to remain totally stilled and in *equanimity* particularly when activity has to be undertaken. Thus, the *restlessness* spoken of in the verse refers to that of the mind. That restlessness is like the waves of the ocean: to try to still them so that they are as flat as a millpond is an impossible task. So the *steady constancy* of which Arjuna speaks is of a mind that never changes and stays constant through the whirlwind of life. Such a fixed, still state of the *atman* is the enlightened state that Arjuna has not yet reached. It is difficult for him as yet to realize what that higher state is like.

VERSE 34

Truly, Krishna, the mind is restless, turbulent, strong and unyielding. I think of it as just as difficult to control as the wind.

Arjuna considers it as difficult to master the *mind* (*manas*) as to catch the wind. Indeed, Krishna himself endorsed this in 2:60 and 67, when he described the senses in the same way. It is probably the senses and their impact on the mind that Arjuna is referring to here. Only when the mind is controlled by the *atman* can it cease to be swayed by the senses. In Thakar's rather apt words: "The body is a biological material structure, containing innumerable conditioned energies of impulses, of ideas, concepts, defence mechanisms, patterns of reactions, value structures, order of priorities and so on. There is a vast ocean of conditioning contained in the human body. We are the product of the total human evolution that has taken place through untold centuries.[45] It is no wonder that Arjuna finds the idea of controlling the restlessness of the mind like trying to control the wind.

VERSE 35   The Lord said:
Undoubtedly, Mahabaho, the mind is difficult to control and restless, but
by constant practice, Kaunteya, and by non-attachment, it is restrained.
We are products of our own minds, so if the *mind*, the *manas*, can be changed so
can the personality. But this takes practice, though the very fact that Krishna says
it needs practice shows that it can be done. *Constant practice* is *abhyasa*, and it is
continuous, involves sustained effort, intense endeavour and constant repetition:
this, indeed, is what *yoga* is all about. *Non-attachment*, *vairagya*, that is to say desireless action, has already been treated a great deal in the previous chapters and it is
through *yoga* that it is achieved. It is a condition of non-response to sense stimuli,
of witnessing events without reacting to them, though *vairagya* is also associated
with withdrawal from the world in ascetic practice.

VERSE 36
For a man of uncontrolled self, *yoga* is hard to attain, I hold, but by one
who is self-controlled, who strives through [proper] means, it is possible
to obtain.
The last verse stated that practice and non-attachment to the results of actions
are the tools of the *yogin*. This verse adds self-control, once again, stressing that
control of the mind and the senses is essential for *yoga*.

VERSE 37   Arjuna said:
If one possessed of *shraddha* does not have control, one whose mind
wanders away from *yoga* not having attained perfection in *yoga*, with what
end does he meet, Krishna?
This is an important question. Arjuna obviously sees that what Krishna teaches
is like the ultimate goal of life, but it is very difficult to achieve and many must
fail in the attempt. What then of the person who has faith, *shraddha*, in the goal
but fails on the path to it? The question is really linked with the words of the
previous two verses in that Arjuna wants to know what happens when the three
criteria of verses 35 and 36 cannot be met, even when someone still has faith. Then,
too, perhaps Arjuna thinks that faith in itself may be a viable path without the
discipline of *yoga*.

VERSE 38
Fallen from both, does he not perish like a rent cloud, supportless,
Mahabaho, deluded in the path of Brahman?
The term *fallen from both* may refer to Earth and Heaven since, in Krishna's
answer beginning in verse 40, he refers to this world and the world to come. But
it is also possible that *both* refers to the two paths, the way of renunciation and the
way of *yoga* or, with Shankara, the way of action and the way of *yoga*.[46] On the other
hand, it could refer to the higher level of consciousness of *yoga* and even the lower
level of ordinary faith-consciousness. So one falls between two stools, or perishes
like a rent cloud, a cloud that disperses in the sky.

VERSE 39
Could you dispel this doubt of mine completely, Krishna, for truly there is none other than you who is really fit to dispel this doubt?
Again, Arjuna raises a question knowing that Krishna as teacher is able to provide a definitive answer.

VERSE 40   The Lord said:
Partha, truly there is no destruction of him here or in the next world. Truly, he who does good never comes to grief, my son.
My son here expresses very deep affection and a *guru–chela*, teacher–pupil, relationship. *Son* is actually *tata*, which means "father" but is used affectionately in the sense of my son, like a son. It is an expression of grace from teacher to pupil, or Lord to disciple. The word seems to possess not only affection for Arjuna himself, but also great compassion for the one who has faith but falls from the path. Thus, such a fall is not tantamount to destruction; it is not punishable by life in the hells, for good has been attempted and can only reap good, a birth lower than the present one is not the fate of such a person.

VERSE 41
Having attained the worlds of the righteous and having dwelt there countless years, one fallen from *yoga* is born in the home of the pure and wealthy.
The *worlds of the righteous* are the heavens to which those with good merit go after death, but only until their good *karma* is used up. So the fate of one who strays from *yoga* is still good for it will bring rebirth in these good planes of existence and eventual rebirth in good circumstances on Earth, perhaps meaning one of the higher classes. It is only in human form that one can attain liberation, so good *karma* can only bring temporary happiness in one of these worlds, just as bad *karma* brings only temporary suffering in the lower planes of existence as hells. For the lapsed *yogin*, rebirth in favourable circumstances on Earth is the eventual fate. Clearly, successive lives are meant to be evolutionary, with death nothing but a momentary pause on the path. Shankara took this verse to refer to those who perform correct ritual and the like[47] but this does not really relate well to Arjuna's question.

VERSE 42
Or, he is born in the family of wise *yogins*. Truly, a birth which is like this is very rare in the world.
Advantageous as it may be to be born in the home of the righteous and wealthy, to be born into a family of *yogins* is infinitely more advantageous because of its spiritual atmosphere and its dedication to the spiritual path. However, this is rarer. Shankara believed that birth in a wise *yogin* family necessarily excluded any wealth.[48]

VERSE 43

There he obtains that union of intellect which he acquired in his former body and strives more than before for perfection, son of the Kurus.

There, here, refers to the home of the family of wise *yogins*. The spiritual path is an evolutionary one; there is not really any slipping back but a taking up of where one left off. All the progress of earlier lives is not lost because of death or failure. The *union of intellect*, *buddhi samyoga*, accumulated through past lives continues to reap its rewards. *Samyoga* here has the idea of conjoining and connecting. *Perfection*, *siddhi*, is tantamount to final liberation.

VERSE 44

Truly, by that former constant practice he is, indeed, borne along helpless. Even he who wishes not to know of *yoga* goes beyond *shabda* Brahman.

The strength of desire to be on such a spiritual path in *former* lives is sufficient to ensure that one does not regress: even if there is initially only vague interest, the lapsed *yogin* will be drawn to *yogic* praxis, *constant practice* (*abhyasa*), in spite of himself, that is to say, involuntarily. It will be one's *dharma* to continue on that path. It is even possible to transcend the *Vedas*, the "word Brahman" or *shabda Brahman*, the words about Brahman. Hence, many commentators prefer to translate *shabda Brahman* as something like "transcends performance of *Vedic* rites". Krishna has already been critical of mere performance of *Vedic* ritual in 2:42–6 and 52–53. Shankara said of this verse that even if *adharma* occurred resulting in bad *karma*, when the negative *karma* associated with the evil is exhausted, the spiritual path will again become clear and will again be pursued.[49] The previous verses, however, particularly verse 40, seem to suggest nothing but evolutionary fortunes.

VERSE 45

The *yogin* striving with assiduity, purified from sins, perfected through many births, then reaches the supreme path.

Path here, *gati* in the Sanskrit, can also mean "goal", so the verse may be referring to the supreme goal of liberation; indeed, this is likely. Notable, is the constant endeavour over many lifetimes.

VERSE 46

The *yogin* is thought superior to those who practise *tapas*, even to men of knowledge; and superior to the men of action. Therefore, be a *yogin*, Arjuna!

The *yogin*, according to this verse, has transcended all paths whether of *jnana*, knowledge, or *karma*, here, ritual action or result-geared action. Both knowledge and action, *karma*, in the verse probably refer to the *Vedas*, to those who learn and study them and to those who carry out their rituals. *Tapas* is austerity, ascetic praxis, undertaken by those, especially *sannyasins* and the Sankhya ascetics who renounce the world and even religious ritual. The *yogin* undertakes action devoid of emphasis on results, unlike austerities *for* results, knowledge gained through inactivity or ritually-based activity. He is the true *karma-yogin*. It is the following, last verse of this chapter, however, that tells us the best possible path. Hill's comment on this verse and the following one is important. He criticized commentators who misinterpret these verses: "They do not realize that the superiority of the true *yogin* consists in the combination in himself of all those elements which up to the time of the Bhagavadgita had been too severely separated; and especially in the addition of devotion, *bhakti*, as the most essential element of all."[50]

VERSE 47

Of all *yogins*, whoever worships me endued with *shraddha*, with the inner *atman* merged in me, he is deemed by me to be integrated in the Self.

CHAPTER SIX ends with this very significant and important theistic verse. Of all *yogins*, Krishna says, those who worship (*bhajate*) him with faith (*shraddha*) are held in the highest regard. *Bhajate* is an important term. It means "to worship", "devote oneself to", and derives from the root *bhaj*, as does that other very important word *bhakti*, "loving devotion". Ramanuja took the opportunity in this verse to extol the attributes of Krishna as Vishnu somewhat extensively:

> . . . who am the refuge of all beings without exception, the distinctions among them remaining unconsidered: who am the remover of the afflictions of those who bow down (to Me): who am the great ocean solely of motherly affection for all who take refuge with Me: who have made Myself capable of being seen by the eyes of all men: who (still) have not given up My essential nature: . . . [51]

The true *yogin* who is *integrated in the Self*, *yuktatma*, is also totally committed to Krishna. It is important to be integrated in the Self, to be unattached to sense objects, to be able to act while anchored in the Self, but one must also enter into relationship with God. This chapter, then, ends on a totally theistic note. Even though the enlightened being experiences the unity of the whole of the cosmos, total equanimity and non-duality, devotion to God is the essential ingredient. The verse is an explicit statement of theism, of the dualism, between God and human. *Merged in me* is indicative of that duality; the drop is merged in the ocean but does not become it. Devotion *with faith*, Maharishi Mahesh Yogi described as "the glory of Union with the Lord. The Lord embraces the devotee and makes him one with Himself, and the devotee holds fast to the Lord in worship. This is the state of oneness where each upholds the other. This is the duality and the Unity in the Great Union."[52]

It is, indeed, an important closing verse, which Aurobindo believed "contains in itself the seed of the rest".[53] Ending with the dualism of worship of the divine and having outlined the nature of the *yogin* as the worshipper, the following chapter, CHAPTER SEVEN, will focus on the nature of the divine itself. The *Gita* is poised here, not with the cold philosophy of Sankhya that had as its goal the isolation (*kaivalya*) of the liberated Self, but with the portals open to an eternal devotional relationship with divinity.

In the *Upnishad* of the *Bhagavad Gita*, the knowledge of Brahman, the teaching of *Yoga* and the dialogue between Shri Krishna and Arjuna, this is the sixth chapter called *Dhyana-Yoga*.

CHAPTER SEVEN

Jnana Vijnana Yoga

The *Yoga* of Knowledge and Realization

The first six chapters of the *Gita* are mainly concerned with the realization of *atman* as the level of reality from which the self operates in the world, whether in action, meditation, knowledge – indeed in anything. The next six chapters concentrate on the nature of God, God as Krishna and as Brahman. This chapter, then, is called *The Yoga of Knowledge and Realization*, and the object of such is God. *Jnana*, "knowledge", of God refers to the understanding of the nature of God, but *vijnana* goes much further; it is realization and experience of the very *essence* of God in all things. However, both terms come from the same Sanskrit root, *jna*, "to know", and though *vijnana* carries the more intense meaning, *jnana*, too, can sometimes be used of intense experience of God and certainly of intuitive knowledge. Rohit Mehta made the point that knowledge is normally a *process*, "a collection of parts to which the Mind sometimes gives a framework of synthesis through the process of abstraction". He saw *jnana* as quantitative and *vijnana* as qualitative, the quantitative being a gradual process and the qualitative a sudden awakening, which seems to me a useful differentiation. Mehta further differentiated between the two by describing the quantitative as knowledge of the parts and the qualitative perception of the whole.[1] Such ideas relate well to what we know about the *Yoga* of the *Gita* from the previous chapters: *yoga* is a practical path supported by knowledge, but the goal is qualitative realization of Brahman.

This is a chapter much suited to Shankara's view of the path of knowledge as the means to liberation. Quite different, knowledge for Ramanuja was essentially devotional worship to a God who would choose his devotee. Both sought to interpret this chapter in the light of their own respective beliefs. Krishna has shifted his response to Arjuna from the mundane level of tradition and man-to-man advice, to increasingly deepened awareness of the nature of himself as God and how he is to be known. Increasingly now, we shall find Krishna as the focus of devotion and the means, as such, to true knowledge and *yoga*. The chapter begins by portraying the kind of theism we associate so much with classical Hinduism and the path of *bhakti*.

VERSE I
Listen, Partha, how, with your mind attached to me, practising *yoga*, taking refuge in me, you will know me fully without doubt.

The words *taking refuge in me* are more forceful in the Sanskrit because they suggest turning away from all else – worldly wealth, fame, attachments and the results of action. Indeed, the Sanskrit *ashraya*, "refuge", according to Aurobindo, encompasses "the whole basis, lodgement, point of resort of the conscious being and action".[2] Robert Zaehner considered that the words *with your mind attached to me* contradict the teaching of the previous chapters which, he claimed, teach non-attachment to *anything*.[3] But the previous chapters have done much to stress that one should be rooted or integrated in the *atman*, and this is *Atman* or Brahman. Being focused on, or attached to, Krishna as the manifestation of Brahman is surely the same thing as being focused on the *atman* within. We should note in the expression under question the dualism between worshipper and God reflected in the verse, which suggests that individuality, even when liberated, is retained. For *know me fully*, Richard Gotshalk translates "gain insight into me fully",[4] which perhaps lessens the *all*-knowing nature suggested by *know me fully* but, in doing so, accords better with a pantheistic but especially panentheistic perception of deity that the *Gita* tends to put forward. So, Krishna's advice is to focus the mind on him in the same way as others focus on the world, always practising the *Yoga* of the *Gita*, that is to say, action without desire for results. But the crucial point here, too, is the refuge in Krishna, with the whole being rooted in the divine and nothing else.

VERSE 2

I will declare in full to you this knowledge combined with realization, having known which, nothing else here remains that ought to be known.

Although *knowledge*, *jnana*, is often used in the sense of intuitive knowledge, it usually refers to knowledge that is acquired through tuition, through the scriptures and the senses. In comparison, *realization*, *vijnana*, is total intuition, total realization. Both are necessary for *moksha*, liberation, as the word *combined* in this verse demonstrates, but *vijnana* involves internalized insight and is not acquired through the medium of ordinary knowledge, though that might be preparatory to it. Nevertheless, knowledge here is indicative of the path of knowledge, *jnana-marga*. Krishna does not deny its efficacy as a means to liberation and full realization of Brahman, but he presents himself as a focus and aid even for the *jnana-yogin* who undertakes this most difficult path.

VERSE 3

Among thousands of men scarcely one strives for perfection; even of the successful ones of those who strive, scarcely one knows me in essence.

The word for *perfection* in this verse is *siddhi*. It is a word that is difficult to translate because it has so many different meanings – fulfilment, completeness, accomplishment, success, maturity, perfection, bliss, final freedom and so on; the list is considerably long. Here, *siddhi*, is all-embracing perfection, and Krishna says those who strive for it are rare. But, of all those who strive for perfection even rarer is the one who understands the ultimate Truth of the divine nature, the divine *essence*, *tattva*, "truth", "reality", and the "thusness" of something. Presumably, if successful perfection is liberation, then it does not necessarily mean that God is fully known. Perhaps Krishna is referring to the path of knowledge that is non-theistic for, in the context of devotion in verse 1, he says he can be *fully* known. Ramanuja certainly believed that no-one at all is capable of knowing God.[5]

VERSE 4

Earth, water, fire, air, ether, mind, intellect and also egoism – this is thus my *prakriti* divided eightfold.

The complexity of the twenty-three evolutes in the philosophical system of Sankhya is here simplified to just eight, the five elements of the verse incorporating the capacities for sense (*buddhindriyas*), the capacities for action (*karmendriyas*) and the subtle elements of sound, touch, form, taste and smell (*tanmatras*). *Buddhi*, the *intellect*, *ahankara*, *egoism*, and *manas*, *mind*, are the remaining three, though in the verse they are not presented in the usual Sankhyan order. These three make up personality, while the five elements are responsible for the world of the senses. Thus

- *Ether* is connected with the ear, being the medium through which sound travels.
- *Air* is connected with the skin, the medium responsible for touch and the air around makes that possible.
- *Fire* is connected with the eye and is the medium by which light is produced to make sight possible.
- *Water* is connected with the tongue and is responsible for the functioning of taste.
- *Earth* is connected with the nose and with the sense of smell produced by earth.

This, much simpler, eightfold elemental system of the *Gita* constitutes perhaps an earlier idea of *prakriti*. The elements mentioned here, along with *buddhi*, *manas* and *ahankara*, intellect, mind and ego respectively, are the properties in Sankhya philosophy that enable response to sense stimuli. In the previous verse, Krishna mentioned his *essence*, the truth or reality about himself but, here in this verse, he indicates that *prakritic* elements are also part of that reality: his manifest reality and *prakriti*, "nature", are one and the same. It is a radical departure from Sankhyan thought. Indeed, Aurobindo commented that: "Here is the first new metaphysical idea of the Gita which helps it to start from the notions of the Sankhya philosophy and yet exceed them and give to their terms, which it keeps and extends, a Vedantic significance".[6] His point rather neatly shows, I think, the *Gita's* position between the philosophical schools proper and the *Vedanta* of the *Upanishads*. Thus, it would be justifiable to take *my prakriti* as being meant in a cosmic sense – certainly in relation to *buddhi* – rather than the elements being compounds of individuals.[7]

VERSE 5

This is the lower, but different from this, know my higher *prakriti*, the very life-element, Mahabaho, by which this universe is upheld.

The first word, *this*, here refers to the lower *prakriti*, lower nature, of the previous verse and is the world of matter. The *higher prakriti* is the *life-element* of the whole universe, the *jiva-bhuta* in the Sanskrit, or "what develops into life". It is rather like the spark that causes fire and is the potentiality for life and matter that is the divine essence, the "beingness of Life" as Vimala Thakar called it.[8] This verse is an important one in that it expresses the idea of two natures in the divine, but is, therefore, subject to various interpretations. In my view the cosmic *Param-Atman* (higher Self) is evident as essence in all existence and the lower nature represents the world of matter. We really have here a closer binding of the individual with the supreme Self because all is a part of the lower nature of Brahman. There is nothing here, then, of the separation of *purusha* and *prakriti* that Sankhya philosophy accepted, but it would depend on how the word *jiva-bhuta* is interpreted.

It seems to me that, given two complementary natures of Krishna, lower as the manifest world and higher as the life-element of the universe, the higher is surely the Unmanifest Brahman as the Source of manifestation. All that is manifest is likely to be a *part* of the nature of the Unmanifest, including the self – a minute particle of the manifested divine energy and nature, a wave on an infinite ocean. And yet Krishna has said in verses 1 and 3 that it is possible to know *all* dimensions of his nature – and that must include his higher nature – in full. Having mentioned the components of *prakriti* in the previous verse, he is pulling Arjuna's thought away from gross manifestation, through mind and egoism to pure intellect and beyond, to the Unmanifest. Is *jiva-bhuta* then to be equated with the manifestation of Brahman in the cosmos in the form of his essence, the life-element, which exists in all phenomena and without which, nothing could be? Or is *jiva-bhuta* the potentiality for all existence that subsists in the *nirguna*, Unmanifest Brahman? I rather think the answer may be both. The higher nature as *jiva-bhuta* is both the potentiality for all existing as the essence of the Unmanifest, the *nirguna* Brahman *and* that same essence existent in all manifestation, so that all are sparks or parts of Brahman. In Aurobindo's words: "The unity is the greater truth, the multiplicity is the lesser truth, though both are a truth and neither is an illusion."[9] The lower and higher *prakriti*, in my view, might be linked also to the two aspects of knowledge, *jnana* and *vijnana*, *jnana* being that which comprehends the world of *prakriti* and the necessity of egoless action in it, and *vijnana* the realization of the Unmanifest beyond it and underpinning it. Mehta depicted the two *prakritis* rather well with the analogy of white light: "Manifestation is thus the spectrum in which the white light of the Unmanifest is split up into its variegated colours. But the spectrum has a derived existence, and not an intrinsic one. It has a dependent origination. It lives, moves and has its being in that White Light which is imperceptible to the eyes. In other words, the Manifest derives its existence from the Unmanifest, and so while the former is partial, the latter is whole."[10] The unity of the *atman* as Brahman in all is part of the higher nature that is unchanging and permanent, while the changing world of *prakriti* is the lower nature.

VERSE 6

Know that this is the womb of all beings. Thus, I am also the Source and dissolution of the whole universe.

The *this* here probably refers to the lower and higher *prakritis*, the lower as material, manifest *prakriti*, matter and *saguna* Brahman, and the higher, the immaterial, Unmanifest and *nirguna* Brahman. This last is the *Source, the womb* (*yoni*), as the verse has it, of all that is manifest, including its *dissolution, pralaya*, when all is absorbed back into the unmanifest. Such dissolution is only temporary for there is no escape from rebirth for the non-liberated. In Aurobindo's words:

> The souls that do not arrive at liberation, live through the returning aeons; all exist involved or secret in the Brahman during the dissolution of the manifest worlds and are born again in the appearance of a new cycle. Pralaya, the end of a cycle of aeons, is the temporary disintegration of a universal form of existence and of all individual forms which move in its rounds, but that is only a momentary pause, a silent interval followed by an outburst of new creation, reintegration and reconstruction in which they reappear and recover the impetus of their progression.[11]

Little sense can be made of the verse if *this* is taken to mean the lower *prakriti*, but the possibility that it refers solely to the higher *prakriti* needs consideration given the content of the following verse. In the last resort, everything originates from the *prakriti* of Krishna and, ultimately, from Brahman as Supreme. There can be nothing beyond this Ultimate. The verse does, in fact, rather blur the distinction between the personal and impersonal aspects of deity, rather amalgamating the Absolutist with the theistic *Vedantic* views of God.

VERSE 7

Nothing is higher than me, Dhananjaya, in me all this is strung like clusters of pearls on a thread.

Notably, this verse, like the previous one, blurs the distinction between the personal Brahman as Krishna and the impersonal *nirguna* Brahman. *Nothing is higher than me*, Krishna says, so there can be no entity whatever beyond *nirguna* Brahman. "It is the supreme nature of Spirit", said Aurobindo, "the infinite conscious power of its being, self-conscient, all-conscient, all-wise, which maintains these phenomenal existences in relation to each other, penetrates them, abides in and supports them and weaves them into the system of its manifestation."[12] Krishna has presented himself as the sustainer and dissolver of the universe in the previous verse and relates all that is manifest to his own being with the imagery of a string of pearls. The pearls may be different sizes and different colours but Brahman is the connecting thread that is the same throughout and that makes manifestation possible. This verse, then, presents Krishna as the cause of all and the uniting factor in the cosmos. The analogy of thread is also applicable to the *gunas* of *prakriti*, which are "strands" like the filaments of a rope. Trevor Leggett turns the simili of the strand of pearls into an attractive analogy: "One of the points is, that the string is invisible, being hidden by the pearls strung on it. But a second point is that the string is known to be there; otherwise the pearls would not remain in order but would be scattered. In the same way, the order in the world shows that there is an underlying intelligence which holds it together, which integrates it."[13]

VERSE 8

I am the taste in water, Kaunteya, I am light in the moon and sun, the primeval sound in all the *Vedas*, sound in ether and manliness in man.

Here, Krishna is seen as the essence, the innate nature of all things. Every object of the senses is pervaded by this essence. *Manliness* could be interpreted as "humanity". Shankara thus said: "I am humanity in men, i.e., I am that in a person which makes that person regarded as a human being."[14] But "prowess" or "virility" are also possible, and may be an indirect reference to Arjuna's loss of fighting power, of which, Krishna has already reproved him. The *primeval sound* is *pranava*, from the verb *pranu*, "to praise", and is *Om* or *Aum*, the sacred syllable that represents Brahman, the vastness of the cosmos and its oneness and unity. It is pronounced at the beginning and end of every *Vedic* reading. *Aum* is made up of three Sanskrit letters, *aa*, *au*, and *ma* which, when combined together, make what was believed to be the basic sound (*shabda*) of the cosmos and to contain all other sounds. The symbol represents both the unmanifest (*nirguna*) and manifest (*saguna*) Brahman. Eknath Easwaran made the point that this essence of Brahman "may be what is meant by the *vijnana* of our title – the mystic's vision of the divine as present here and now is perhaps the real meaning of the term".[15] Such a view is, I think, likely; it is knowledge of God transformed to indescribable experience of the essence of God in all. I have kept as closely as possible to the Sanskrit text in translation, but a liberal though rather beautiful rendering of verses 8 and 9 by Alan Jacobs is worth adding here for its poetic value.

> I am the primal blue water lily
> Floating in clear lustrous waters,
> The shining silvery Grace
> Of the radiant moon,
> The burnished gold of
> The blazing sun.
> The sacred chant of Aum in
> The revealed Rig Veda,
> The electric current that
> Throbs through the ether,
> And the strength
> Inherent in Man's seed.
>
> The healthy sweet smell of
> The damp Earth

And the red, crackling blaze of fire,
The transparent vital air
Moving all that moves,
The holiness of hallowed souls,
The undying root, Brahman,
From which all has sprung,
All that Is.[16]

VERSE 9

I am the sweet fragrance in earth, am the vigour in fire, the life in all beings and am the *tapas* in ascetics.

The thought here continues that of the previous verse and the subsequent verses will also express the idea of Brahman as the essence of all things. It is easy to see from these verses how monists, non-dualists, like Shankara, have evidence for their views. Yet, it seems to me that these verses are probably to be interpreted in a panentheistic rather than in a non-dual sense: Brahman is, ultimately, over and above all manifested existence. *Vigour (tejas) in fire* is meant in the sense of its brilliance or burning power; the same word occurs in the following verse as a descriptor of the brave. It can also mean "splendour". *Tapas*, "austerity", is the practice of those associated with the path of knowledge.

VERSE 10

Know me, Partha, as the eternal seed of all beings, the intellect of the intelligent, and I am the bravery of the brave.

Not only is Brahman the essence of all tangible entities as the *eternal seed (bija) of all beings*, but also the abstract essence of abstract entities. Since Brahman is eternal, the *eternal seed, bijam-sanatam*, implicit in the verse is the thought that the constant varieties of manifestations coming forth from Brahman will do so eternally, though each comes and goes. *Tejas*, here translated as *bravery*, is variously interpreted – vigour, brilliance, splendour, glory are also possible.

VERSE 11

Of the strong, I am the strength devoid of desire and passion. In beings I am desire unopposed to *dharma*, lord of the Bharatas.

Verse 11 is interesting. It depicts the power and strength of Krishna and, *a priori*, the *atman*, the true Self, in comparison to the self that is subject to passions and desires. *Passion* is *raga*, clinging to things we want or have; it is attachment that dissipates strength. *Desire* is *kama*, the longing for things to which we become attached and it is interesting to see it stated here that it is not always wrong provided it is directed to the right end and is in line with *dharma*. Thus, *unopposed to dharma* means not contrary to *dharma*. Arjuna is a *Kshatriya* with certain duties to perform involving the conscious will to desire the protection of society. Similarly, his householder stage of life does not negate the pursuit of pleasure and social wealth. *Dharma*, too, does not exclude the basic fulfilment of desires like hunger and the general maintenance of the body. However, having any desire seems to contradict the idea of action undertaken without it – the important teaching of the *Gita* – and it would have to be accepted that there is some inconsistency here. But on the path to *moksha*, the obliteration of desire is impossible: thus, *desire* to reach *moksha* may be necessary, as *desire* to have faith in God, *desire* to follow *dharma*. Desire channelled in the right direction seems to be acceptable. Similarly, Aurobindo made the distinction between desire that springs from the lower nature of the *gunas* and desire that springs from the essence within one, from "the pure quality of the spirit in its inherent power of conscious will and its characteristic force of action. The desire meant here is therefore the purposeful will of the Divine in us."[17] Krishna's words here may be another implicit response to Arjuna's state – his reluctance to fight, and his pleas that *dharma* would be destroyed if he does fight. Here, Krishna depicts the right kinds of strength, desire and *dharma* for him.

VERSE 12

And whatever natures are *sattvic*, *rajasic*, or *tamasic*, truly, know them as from me, but I am not in them; they are in me.

Nothing can exist that does not emanate from Brahman: everything exists in the Being of Brahman, has Brahman's essence, and cannot come into being without that essence. All matter is completely dependent on Brahman, on pure spirit, and is not separated from it totally as in Sankhya philosophy. Brahman creates the world and the *gunas* of *prakriti* that combine to make all phenomena and the causes and effects that produce active life, growth and decay, birth and death. However, it is these activities of the *gunas* in which Brahman as Creator is not active, remaining, like the *atman* within that is his essence, the passive observer. Brahman, the creator of *gunas*, is *nirguna*, without *gunas*, and so is *not in them*, not in the interplay of human desires and aversions dictated by *gunic natures* (*bhava*) and activity – the *they* of *they are in me* referring back to the *gunic* natures in the first part of the verse. Thakar described this beautifully: "Whatever is in a form, be it an animal, a bird, a tree or a human being, there will be *sattva*, *rajas*, *tamas*, in varying degrees in each. But that is only the outer crust of the being. It is not the essence. It is like the skin of a fruit, not its substance."[18]

Thus, there is a difference between the workings of the world and the *ultimate* Reality, and those over-involved with the former cannot experience the latter, as the following verse will point out. Ultimate Reality remains passively aloof. Mehta put this very well when he wrote: "And so while Reality is immanent, it is at the same time transcendent. The Formless cannot be caught in the Form, the Transcendent cannot be imprisoned in the Immanent. The Creator is more than His Creation; He is immanent in his creation only as the musician is immanent in his music. The music, however beautiful it may be cannot contain the musician. While the music resides in the musician, the musician does not reside in his music."[19]

VERSE 13

By these three natures composed of *gunas* all this world is deluded; it does not know me who is higher than them (the *gunas*) and imperishable.

Since Brahman is beyond all intellect and comprehension, beyond dualities and knowledge gained through the senses, nothing in the world of *prakriti* can describe Brahman, which is independent of all the modifications and manifestations of the *gunas*. Brahman is, thus, the substratum of all. These last two verses make Brahman the essence of all things but over and above them, especially since *prakriti*, in which all things exist, is a lower level of reality. This is surely panentheism. Brahman is *para*, *higher*, than the world and higher than *them*, the *gunas* of *prakriti*. *Imperishable* is *avyaya*, which can also mean changeless or indestructible, pointing to the *nirguna* Brahman that is over and above the manifest universe and that absorbs it in its stages of dissolution. Because beings have no knowledge of what is beyond matter, they are trapped in delusion (*moha*).

VERSE 14

Truly, this divine *maya* of mine, made of *gunas* is difficult to transcend: only they who take refuge in me transcend this illusion.

Maya, here, is "power", the power of the divine Reality that is in the guise of *prakriti*. For those who take refuge in Krishna, the world of *maya* disappears and Reality is known. *Maya* comes from the root *ma*, "to form", or "to measure out" and is a synonym of *prakriti*. As such, it can mean "creative power" as much as "illusion", or even "magic". The created world of *prakriti* emanates from Brahman and has a kaleidoscope of changing patterns of existence that come and go like waves on the ocean, but which captivate the senses, masking the creative Reality that is the Source behind the whole myriad *gunic* possibilities. It is in this sense that the world is *maya*, a "play" of God, a marvellous creation but, all the same a lesser reality than the Source from which it comes, which itself is not subject to the same kind of change. In earlier texts, *maya* carried the nuance of meaning *magical* power, indicative of divine creative power that could make a world and yet conceal the creator behind and within it. Such a thought is not out of place, I think, in the context of this verse. *Maya* is certainly not the total illusion and unreality that Shankara much later took it to be. Ramanuja considered *maya* to be real, unlike Shankara: for Ramanuja it is that which obscures God[20] or, more appropriately, veils God, that is to say, the more one is involved in the world, the thicker the veil, the *maya*, becomes. So *maya* for Ramanuja was certainly not an illusional non-reality. God's *maya* is real, is made up of the *gunas* and is *prakriti*.[21] It is what produces marvellous effects. To *take refuge in* (*prapadi*) is, again, implicitly of the nature of *prapatti*, "surrender", to God.

VERSE 15

Evil doers, the deluded, the lowest of men, do not seek me. Deprived of knowledge by *maya* they belong to the nature of *Asuras*.

Those who do evil and are *deluded* (*mudha*) are classed as having the *nature* (*bhava*) of *Asuras*. *Asuras* are "demons", who perpetrate all kinds of evil. The verse denotes demonic states being the conditions of those who do not seek God and who are sufficiently evil to be unable to discern between what is divine and what is evil. Richard Gotshalk has the useful translation of these lowest of men as those "who have fallen subject to what is demonic in nature",[22] which picks up their state and condition rather than assigning them to the class of *Asuras per se*. Those in this state lack sufficient discriminating *knowledge* (*jnana*) to lift themselves out of their malevolence. It is worth pointing out that since all manifest existence stems from Brahman, even *Asuras*, it would have to be said, are part of that creation too. However, evil as such is simply that part of existence that is estranged or separated from knowledge of God in varying degrees, but the *Gita* will have more to say about such evil, demonic individuals in CHAPTER SIXTEEN.

VERSE 16

Four kinds of virtuous people worship me, Arjuna, the distressed, the seeker of knowledge, the seeker of wealth, and the *jnanin*, lord of Bharatas.

The Sanskrit for *worship* here is *bhajante* and carries the nuance of meaning of complete devotion, of turning towards God, like the word *bhakti*, "loving devotion", which comes from the same root. In some ways the ideas portrayed in the verse seem to clash with those already put forward in the *Gita*. People in distress or sorrow need not necessarily be good or virtuous, but it seems they become good when they approach God with sincerity. The seeker of knowledge is the seeker of spiritual knowledge – a more obvious "good" person. It is the third kind of virtuous individual – the seeker of wealth – who seems problematic, particularly after all that has been said about the necessity of actions being undertaken without desire for results. The Sanskrit refers to *artha*, which is normally taken to be physical wealth, though it can mean purpose or goal, but it is difficult to avoid a materialistic sense completely even if such pursuit is in line with *dharma*. Thakar defined *artha* as: "That which makes your life meaningful",[23] which might imply pursuit of God as the goal. Sri Krishna Prem had a very interesting interpretation of *artharti* as "he who seeks the Real", "he who seeks the true Wealth, the *Paramartha*, which is *mukti* or liberation."[24] It was his belief that the four *virtuous people* in the verse are graded – the sufferer, the knowledge seeker, the liberation seeker and the *jnanin*, the one who has achieved true knowledge of God. The idea is an attractive one that easily overrides the difficulties of the verse. Gotshalk, too, translates *artharti* as "the seeker of purpose", with a similar nuance of meaning.[25] Perhaps the reference to wealth here is pointing to the ritualistic intentions of those who carried out *Vedic* sacrifice for the purpose of acquiring material rewards, but Krishna has not spoken too kindly of these, so they are hardly likely to be virtuous. The verse does not seem to be about actions, but about states of mind, so maybe we should see these paths with the exception of the fourth as representing psychological motivating factors for reaching out to God.

Verse 17

Of these, the *jnanin*, ever integrated, devoted to the One, excels. Truly, I am exceedingly dear to the *jnanin* and he is dear to me.

The combination of *jnana* and *bhakti* here is clear, but it is the path of *jnana* that is hailed as supreme in this and the next two verses. The *jnanin*, the "wise one", the verse says, is *nitya-yukta*, "ever integrated". Zaehner considered that this expression does not mean union with the divine, though it is difficult to see how it could be interpreted otherwise.[26] van Buitenen has the helpful "and is always yoked" for *nitya-yukta*, which is rather expressive of the whole concept of the unity between devotee and divine.[27] The *jnanin* is he whose devotion to God asks for no results, whose actions are non-fruitive and whose love and devotion are directed entirely to God. Such devotion is rewarded by devotion from God to man. Ultimately, of course, the *jnanin* recognizes Brahman as the very essence of his own self. Thakar summed up the *jnanin* rather well when she said: "So, the wise one does not feel at all attached to the whole drama of duality. He walks through the corridors of duality, in the majesty of inner renunciation and his goal is focussed only on the ultimate reality of Life, on the ground of existence."[28] Devotion here is *bhakti*, not just devotion but *loving-devotion* in which the whole being is focused on *the One* (*eka*). We have another firm departure from Sankhya, here, not the Sankhyan emphasis on the path of knowledge *per se* as the means to *moksha*, but knowledge *combined with* devotion.

Bhakti incorporates elements of reciprocity of relationship, of closeness, but essentially of dual relationship rather than total fusion or identity. Ramanuja understood the verse much in this way. He linked the *jnanin* of the verse to the *bhakta*, one devoted only to God as opposed to others whose devotion is for selfish aims. Given that Ramanuja accepted *jnana* as concomitant with true *karma-yoga*, there is no way in which he would have accepted the *jnanin* of the verse as a *jnana-yogin*.[29]

Verse 18

All these are surely noble, but the *jnanin*, in my opinion, is my very *Atman*. He is integrated in the *Atman* and is truly established in me, the supreme goal.

This verse supplies very good evidence against Zaehner's contention in the previous verse that the *jnanin* is not one in union with God. In the *jnanin*, *atman* and Brahman are united, not in a monistic sense in the *Gita* but panentheistically, the drop, the *atman*, in the ocean, Brahman. Shankara, of course, interpreted the verse monistically,[30] but Zaehner goes to the other extreme suggesting that *is my very Self* "probably means no more than 'he is the apple of my eye'"[31] This is quite out of character with the chapter. While Zaehner diminished the meaning of *my very Atman*, it is unlikely that it is to be taken as identity, and is expressive more of unity or being in unison with. Such is the way Ramanuja interpreted the verse, notably, with God's dependence on the devotee as much as *vice versa*: "I regard Myself as depending on him for My support and sustenance", he says of God, "Why is it so? Because this man holds Me to be the highest goal, finding it impossible to support himself without Me." However, Ramanuja added, "therefore it is not possible for Me also to maintain Myself without him. Thus he is indeed Myself."[32] The dependency of the self on God is acceptable in the *Gita* but God's dependency on his worshippers is totally adverse to its message. Ramanuja certainly overstretched the evidence here to suit his tenets. *Integrated in the Self* is the important *yuktatma* in the Sanskrit.

VERSE 19

At the end of many births, the wise come to me, Vasudeva, the All: such a *mahatma* is very hard to find.

Krishna refers to himself as Vasudeva. It is the name he is given in his manifest form since it was the name of his father. Some translate here "Vasudeva is everything", or "is all" though this demands a prior verb.[33] The statement is important for its suggestion of the immanence of God in all things – if somewhat pantheistic – Vasudeva is the all and in all. Really speaking, a *jnanin*, one of *the wise*, may *know* that Brahman is the essence of all but does not realize it in a complete experiential sense. This is the stage of *jnana*. It may take many births before total realization, *vijnana*, occurs, when Brahman is actually *experienced* as the same in all. Ramanuja used the term *shesha* to refer to each individual as a "dependent" of God, a subordinate of God, and believed that it would take many births before that could be known.[34] The fruit of these many births, he said, would be the acquisition of knowledge of the real nature of the Self as dependent on, and taking refuge solely in, God.[35] A person who finally reaches Brahman is a *mahatma*, a "great soul". Needless to say, such individuals are rare.

VERSE 20

Those whose knowledge has been torn away by desires and by this or that, approach other gods, having followed this or that rite, restricted by their own *prakriti*.

This is an interesting verse in that it seems, on the surface, to be critical of devotional practices to other *gods* (*devas*). Hinduism has a multiplicity of deities representative of aspects of Brahman and it is perhaps this idea that is behind the words of the verse. The key word here is *desires* (*kama*), which provide the motivations for religious praxis: people are attracted to a deity by their own natures, their *gunic* make-up, their levels of consciousness, or their needs in a particular situation. In reality, then, it is ego, personality, which attracts people to a deity. Krishna has been critical of *Vedic* rituals – here, *this or that rite* which is result geared – directed to *Vedic* gods for the purpose of gaining results – desire for wealth, happiness, cattle, Heaven, progeny – all of which feature widely in *Vedic* hymns. Individuals also create their own *prakritic* natures by the *karma* of their previous lives. It is this *karma* that will dictate to which deities each will be attracted. When ultimate Reality is experienced, the existence of other gods and goddesses independently of it is no longer relevant. Without such realization, however, the lesser goals arising from worship of the many manifestations of

Brahman seem all important and true *knowledge* (*jnana*), is *torn away*. Krishna is quite different from *Vedic* gods, being totally equated with Brahman in the *Gita* and not even one aspect of Brahman.

VERSE 21

Whatever form any devotee wishes to worship with *shraddha*, truly, I make that *shraddha* of his firm.

Form here refers to the variety of deities that can be approached. Ramanuja claimed that all of them are also God's body, so even if the worshipper is ignorant of the true nature of the divine and prefers to offer devotion to one such as Indra, God would reward the devotee:[36] whether god, ghost or ancestor, these objects of worship are, ultimately, *prakritic* manifestations of Brahman. Nevertheless, individuals are allowed to worship according to their levels of consciousness, according to their natures. So Krishna is saying here that he provides the means for *shraddha*, "faith", at these levels: he provides the stepping stones for an individual's personal spiritual evolution. Such worship, then, is not wrong, for it is appropriate at certain levels. So the *All* that Krishna is in verse 19 also extends to individual worship and the gods worshipped. Nevertheless, *shraddha* is a strong word suggestive of total devotion to the object in question, and it is Krishna who directs that level of faith. *Shraddha* has to come from deep within, from the heart, so it is the inner state of someone, what someone is, and will therefore dictate how one behaves, acts, interacts and thinks. Only then is that faith *firm* (*achala*).

VERSE 22

He, steadfast in that *shraddha*, engages in worship of it and truly obtains from that those desires really ordained by me.

The object in the verse is the *form* worshipped in the previous verse. Krishna as Brahman is the Source of all manifest existence as well as the essence of it. Gods to whom worship is offered are parts of manifest Brahman. If those deities are solicited for help in the fulfilment of *desires* (*kama*), it is ultimately Krishna as Brahman that is the Source of that fulfilment, though being *steadfast*, here *yukta*, in that faith is a pre-requisite, just as it is for the higher paths. Krishna knows exactly the level of devotion of each individual and is the provider of appropriate results of it. However, while devotion may be directed to a manifest deity it is always Brahman that is the real Source of anything manifest and, thus, of any worship and its results.

VERSE 23

But the fruit of those of low intelligence is really finite: the worshippers of the *devas* go also to the *devas*; my devotees go to me.

Those that worship minor deities, *devas*, are at a lower level of consciousness according to their *karma*. Accordingly, the results, the *fruit* (*phala*) they reap, the subsequent lives they live, will be at a lower level. If Heaven is their goal, then Heaven they will eventually reach, for Heaven is the result of their level of consciousness. Those whose consciousness is higher will have higher goals: if they aspire to Brahman as *devotees*, *bhaktas*, of Krishna, they will attain him. Lower gods are subject to ultimate rebirth when their good *karma* is used up; just so, worshippers' happiness will also be *finite*: the results they reap are all material and, therefore, transient. The *Gita's* message is always to avoid concentration on results of actions in order to lessen entrapment in matter.

VERSE 24

The foolish come to think of me, the Unmanifest, as manifest, not knowing my highest nature – immutable and unsurpassed.

Although Krishna appears on Earth in manifest form, his supreme state as the Unmanifest remains unknown to those of poor understanding. Zaehner's translation of this verse is typical of that of a number of commentators: "Fools think of Me as one unmanifest [before] who has reached the stage of manifestation",[37] indicating that fools regard Krishna as being human with a human birth, unmanifest before his life and one who will naturally disappear at death.[38] It seems to me a very narrow and unnecessary translation given the context of the lower and higher natures of Krishna that have been the subject of the chapter and in the light of the following two verses. Indeed, Gotshalk points out that the use of *avyakta*, "unmanifest", and *vyakta*, "manifest", in the verse, as well as the content of verses 5 and 13 in this chapter, are more likely to suggest that the verse is referring to *prakriti*, with the higher nature as its Source and the lower its manifestation. This seems to me the most sensible conclusion. The contrast in this verse is really a continuation of that in the previous verses – the idea of manifest deities as opposed to the ultimate Unmanifest that is Brahman. Thus, the foolish have no understanding of the absolute Brahman, only of tangible deities that they worship and believe to be all there is to divinity. Krishna points beyond his own manifestation to the *nirguna* Brahman that is the true Reality, "the immutable (*avyaya*) centre of endless mobility", as Radhakrishnan termed it.[39]

VERSE 25

I am not manifest to all, veiled by *yoga-maya*. This deluded world knows not me, the Unborn, the Imperishable.

I am not manifest is sometimes translated as: "I do not shine forth",[40] with the same sense as "am not revealed", for the Sanskrit *prakasha*, "shining, luminous, effulgence". *Yoga-maya* is *prakriti* made up of the three *gunas*, and *prakriti* cannot exist apart from Brahman, but Brahman is separate from it. Few see through *maya* to the true ultimate Reality, and so the world is *deluded* (*mudha*). Brahman here is the *nirguna*, Unborn (*aja*) and Imperishable (*avyaya*). As Aurobindo put it: "He is self-enveloped in this immense cloak of Maya, that Maya of his Yoga, by which he is one with the world and yet beyond it, immanent but hidden, seated in all hearts but not revealed to any and every being. Man in Nature thinks that these manifestations in Nature are all the Divine, when they are only his works and his powers and his veils."[41]

VERSE 26

I know the past, present and future, Arjuna, but truly, no beings know me.

The total omniscience of Krishna is depicted here.[42] *Truly, no beings know me,* Krishna says, because the unmanifest, ultimate Reality is beyond any definition, beyond the limitations of the mind. Nevertheless, this rather contradicts other parts of the *Gita* that suggest the possibility, albeit rare, of knowing Krishna fully, as in verses 1 and 3 of this chapter. But if the enlightened Self is but part of Brahman – again, the drop merging into the ocean and not becoming the ocean – then ultimate Reality, Brahman, always remains panentheistically over and above the world. So despite hints that Krishna can be *fully* known earlier in this chapter, Zaehner pointed out – and most appropriately here, I think – that Brahman is *atattva,* "beyond all essences", according to the *Shvetashvatara Upanishad* (2:15), "and what has no essence", Zaehner stated, "cannot be defined"[43] or, I might add, known. Here, in this verse, we have a continuation of the thought of the previous verses, which describe the unwise individual who is bound up in *prakriti* and *maya.* The following verse also continues this trend.

VERSE 27

By the delusion of pairs of opposites arising from desire and aversion, all beings, Bharata, are subject to delusion at birth, Parantapa.

Pairs of opposites we have met before with the word *dvandva,* which refers to the dualities in all life – life and death, pleasure and pain and the innumerable opposites expressed in *desire (kama)* and *aversion (dvesha)* in every aspect and every level of life. But this is, of course, all *prakriti,* all *maya,* and involves the self in dualities. *Delusion (moha)* is the reality of worldly exixtence, which blocks the true knowledge, the true realization, of the non-dual nature of things, and of Brahman as the ultimate Reality.

VERSE 28

But for men of virtuous actions, whose evil is at an end, they are liberated from the delusion of the pairs of opposites, worship me, steadfast in vows.

The theism of this verse is prominent. Those whose *evil (papa)* has come to an end are those who have worked off past *karma* and who gain no new *karma* because they are desireless. In being beyond dualities, the *pairs of opposites, dvanvdva,* their *virtuous actions* are undertaken without desire for, or aversion to, specific results: their actions are, thus, pure and their *delusion (moha)* eradicated. While the verse, again, advocates action that is done without desire for its fruits, *karma-yoga,* it is worship of Krishna by the steadfast devotee, *bhakti-yoga,* that is the concomitant pathway that makes one *liberated (mukta).*

VERSE 29
Those who strive for liberation from old age and death, having taken
refuge in me, know completely that Brahman, the intrinsic *atman* and all
action.

Whereas the unenlightened concentrate on the dualities of life, particularly aversion to death as the antithesis of life, those who know Brahman – and this verse
clearly states that Brahman can be *completely* known, in contrast to verse 26 – those
who know *atman*, the Self that is Brahman, and engage in *action* (*karma*) that is non-
attached and non-fruitive, understand ultimate Truth. Implicit in the verse is the
idea that Krishna aids those who take refuge in him, those who strive for Truth,
and those who seek *liberation* (*moksha*). He has already said in verses 21–3 that he is
the force behind all worship. The *intrinsic atman* is *adhyatma*, the very depth of the
self as *atman*.

VERSE 30
Those who realize me in the *adhibuta*, *adhidaiva* and *adhiyajna*, they of
integrated consciousness realize me even at the time of death.

The following chapter, which deals with the nature of Brahman, will analyse
adhibuta, *adhyatma*, *adhidaiva* and *adhiyajna* in its opening verses. For those whose
consciousness (*chetas*) is *integrated* (*yukta*), their realization, contact and knowledge of
Brahman are not even obliterated at death.

In the *Upanishad* of the *Bhagavad Gita*, the knowledge of Brahman,
the teaching of *Yoga* and the dialogue between Shri Krishna
and Arjuna, this is the seventh chapter called
Jnana Vijnana Yoga.

CHAPTER EIGHT

Akshara Brahma-Yoga
The *Yoga* of the Imperishable Brahman

At the close of the previous chapter, Krishna used three words – *adhyatma*, *adhibuta* and *adhidaiva*. These three technical *Upanishadic* terms recur as the introduction to this chapter which, as a whole, is a continued analysis of the nature of Brahman. At the heart of the chapter is the relationship between what is manifested – in both its creation and dissolution – and the true Unmanifest that is Brahman. It is this that is *Brahma-Yoga*, the *Yoga* of Brahman. To introduce these concepts, in the first two verses, Arjuna takes up Krishna's words and asks for an explanation of them.

Arjuna said:

VERSE 1
What is that Brahman? What is *adhyatma*? What, Purushottama, is *karma*? What is said to be *adhibuta* and what is called *adhidaiva*?
Krishna is addressed as *Purushottama* in this verse. It is a name indicative of a supreme person, "Supreme Purusha".

VERSE 2
Who and how is *adhiyajna* here in this body, Madhusudana? And how, at the time of death, can you be known by the self-controlled?
Seven questions are raised in these two verses and Krishna now answers each in turn.

The Lord said:

VERSE 3
Brahman is the Imperishable, the Supreme. The self's intrinsic nature is called *adhyatma*. The creative force that causes the origin of beings is called *karma*.
Krishna answers the first three questions here. *That Brahman, tat Brahma* of verse 1, is the Supreme (*Para*) and imperishable (*Akshara*). The universe is subject to time, space and causation, continual flux and impermanence. Brahman is not subject to any of these, is not subject to anything at all and cannot be known through the senses or intellectually. This is why Brahman is called the Supreme, ever Itself and, importantly for what comes hereafter, Imperishable, *Akshara*. *Akshara* refers to what is unmanifest and also to the syllable *Om*, the subtle sound that is said to contain all others, to have originated at the beginning of time, and

that is representative of Brahman as *Akshara*. Thus, Brahman is established unequivocally as the Absolute that is beyond the senses and empirical reality: "beyond all and alone stands the Supreme Eternal, the Imperishable *Brahman*, dark in utter mystery, the Root of all that is, was, or shall ever be," as Sri Krishna Prem put it.[1]

Thus far, the interpretation is straightforward. Hereafter, there are more possibilities. It seems to me, however, that Arjuna's questions relate to Brahman. That is to say that all the terms raised by the seven questions are directly related to the nature of the divine which, after all, is what the chapter is about. The term *adhyatma* refers to the intrinsic essence of something, and I am taking the term here to refer to the intrinsic essence of Brahman as the *atman* in all things. Every entity has an *intrinsic nature* or property, which is called its *sva-bhava*, its "own being", like the light in the sun. It is Brahman that is the *sva-bhava*, the essence in all things as the *adhyatma* and the reality of all. Radhakrishnan's understanding of *adhyatma* was to the point:

> The Immutable which is above all dualities of subject and object, becomes, from the cosmic end, the eternal subject, *adhyatma*, facing the eternal object which is mutable in nature, prakrti, the receptacle of all forms, while karma is the creative force, the principle of movement. All these are not independent but are the manifestations of the One Supreme. The subject–object interaction which is the central pattern of the cosmos is the expression of Brahman, the Absolute Spirit which is above the distinctions of subject and object.[2]

Radhakrishnan's interpretation suits the tenor of this chapter very well, but other commentators are inclined to see the *adhyatma* as the *jivatman*, the *individual* nature and essence, though perhaps that devoid of selfish ego. Here, it is the nature that is unique to each individual and to that individual's "I" identity. Ramanuja, too, identified *adhyatma* as *sva-bhava*, the "own being" that is *prakritic*, not the *atman* alone, but the body joined with the *atman* to form the individual being, along with the *karmic* effects from past lives that make up the whole person.[3] This, however, seems to be encompassed by *adhibhuta*, where *bhuta* is the transitory human being. Such interpretations would obtain if we accept *sva-bhava*, "own being" in a wider sense, though my inclination is to accept *adhyatma* as referring to Brahman being the "higher nature" of each individual, that which is the deepest Self, the *atman*. This was how Shankara understood it,[4] as also, Douglas Hill, who defined it as "the manifestation of Brahman in its proper form as Self in individuals"[5].

Karma, here, is again, I suggest, referring to the action of Brahman as the creative force that causes the origin of beings, the action that takes place in order for creation to occur; in Sankhya terms, the original vibration of the *gunas* that causes manifestation. It is the word *visarga* that makes an alternative view possible here for, though it can mean *creative force* suggestive of a cosmic force that causes all creation, it can also mean "offering", which would refer to sacrificial and ritualistic offerings. Such ritual is inherent in human cause and effect in manifest existence which is how Franklin Edgerton interpreted *karma* in this verse.[6]

VERSE 4

Adhibhuta is perishable nature and *adhidaiva* is Purusha. I alone am the *adhiyajna* here in the body, best of the embodied.

The complexities of interpretation in verse 3 are evident in this verse, too. Indeed, it is well to note Edgerton's advice that: "All the terms used here are somewhat loose and vague; the language is grandiloquent."[7] *Adhibhuta* is the opposite of *akshara*; it is *kshara*, what *is* perishable, and is usually considered as the five elements which, in varying combinations, constitute all manifest existence. Since they are ever-changing, they render things impermanent in contrast to the *Akshara* that is Brahman. *Adhibhuta*, then is that which makes possible the whole of manifest material existence, all of which is perishable, but still pervaded by Brahman.

Adhidaiva is Purusha, the Universal Self, the divine, as the centre from which everything is filled, the word *purusha* being derived from Sanskrit *pri*, "to fill". It is the centre from which all derives being and senses. As such, it can be equated with the *atman*. *Adhidaiva* is the term often given for Hiranyagarbha, the creator deity of the *Vedas* and so may also be that which underpins all deities. Hiranyagarbha was amalgamated with the Primeval Being, Purusha, whose self-sacrifice in the *Vedas* provided the materials out of which the universe came into being. His head, for example, became the class of *Brahmins*, his arms the *Kshatriyas*, his thighs the *Vaishyas* and his feet the *Shudras*.

Adhiyajna is the presence of the deity at *yajna*. *Yajna*, as we saw in earlier chapters is not always sacrificial ritual, for the height of *yajna* is the loss of ego and individuality in total focus on the divine. This is probably what *I . . . am the adhiyajna . . . in the body* means, though it could also mean that all gods are ultimately expressions of Brahman, so whatever deity is the object of sacrifice, ultimately Brahman is the recipient – a point made in chapters 5:29 and in 7:21. The phrase is, however, difficult and Shankara commented: "As an act of sacrifice (*yajna*) has to be performed by the body, it is said to be inherent in it, and as such it may be said to rest *in the body*."[8]

How then do we interpret these responses of Krishna? Bibek Debroy usefully paraphrases all these terms thus: "The *brahman* is without qualities. But the *brahman* is manifested in a form with qualities for purposes of creating the universe and the elements and that is *adhyatma*. However, the universe and all action are temporary, they are *adhibhuta*. Nevertheless, the universe and all action retain a permanent quality that is *adhidaiva*."[9] Thus, there is always a subtle relationship between what is manifest, *adhibhuta*, and what is divine, *adhidaiva*, for the latter pervades all of the former. There is certainly measure in seeing Brahman as the object of each of Arjuna's questions. Richard Gotshalk brings this out explicitly in his translation of the first two verses: "1. "What is that holy power? What is *it* in its very self? What is *its* action (*karman*), Supreme Spirit? What is *it* declared to be in relation to beings and to the manifest world at large? 2. How and what is *it* in this body in relation to sacrifice, Slayer-of-Madhu? And how are you to be cognized by those with restrained selves at the time of their departure?"[10] My italics here serve to highlight the point. In verses 3 and 4, the responses to the questions would, thus, all relate to Krishna. Again, Gotshalk draws out such an interpretation in his translation of verses 3 and 4. I have not italicized at points here, since the sense is clear: "3. The holy power is the imperishable and supreme and it is its ownmost (creational) nature-and-being (*sva-bhava*) that is its very self; that creating which initiates the existence-and-nature of beings, is its action (*karman*). 4. In relation to beings, it is perishable existence, and in relation to the manifest world at large, it is spirit. And in relation to sacrifice, it is none other than I, O Best-of-Embodied beings, here in the body."[11] Such a clear expression of questions and responses, having Brahman as their focus, is, I think, the best interpretation.

One further important point needs some discussion here before moving on and that is the interesting subtle difference between the Brahman of verse 3 and the Purusha of verse 4. In verse 1, Arjuna addresses Krishna as Purushottama, "Supreme Self" and the very name is indicative of manifest divinity, of the highest Soul. Brahman, the Imperishable of verse 3, is clearly the indescribable Unmanifest, without *gunas* that transcends the universe in all its stages. Purusha, on the other hand, is identified with *adhyatma*, essential nature, or *Atman*, within all manifestation. It is a point worth remembering as we proceed. Brahman is beyond all subject–object descriptors, but Purusha is clearly that with attributes, *saguna*. Krishna is the divine manifestation, the human form who, himself, is the manifestation of Brahman. Really speaking, then, in the *Gita* Krishna is both form and non-form.

VERSE 5

And whoever goes forth at the time of death, leaves the body remembering only me, he attains my state of being, there is, here, no doubt.

The state of the self at death is believed to dictate the birth conditions and environment of the next existence. If one is concentrating entirely on God, devoid of all other thoughts, then *my being* (*mad-bhava*), Krishna says, the supreme *state of being* or, with Gotshalk, "nature-and-being",[12] can be attained. But to achieve this at the last moment is impossible unless one's whole life has been directed to such thoughts and their associative actions. This is because it is also believed that the thought that fills the mind at death is the one that has been most prominent during the whole of the present existence: it thus represents the most prominent aspect of the personality. Since the mind is usually unclear at death and incapable of directing its own thoughts, little control of the last moments is inevitable. If God is not at the centre of thought during life, he is unlikely to be in death. Notably, *time of death*, is *antakale* which, more literally is "end of time", but even then souls are merely suspended until the universe is recreated.

VERSE 6

Or, whatever state is remembered in the end when leaving the body, thinking constantly of that state, to that only he goes, Kaunteya.

State in the verse is *bhava*, which also means "being" or "nature". While it could mean a person or being such as a deity of some sort, it can also mean a condition of being, a state of being. Krishna has already said that however life after death is thought of, to that one will go (7:23). As long as *karma* is present, however, rebirth is inevitable, whether on Earth or a higher plane of existence. The Sanskrit contains the idea of "growing into" what one most believes in, which makes sense *karmically*. So, if the overriding thoughts are of God, there is a concomitant growing into God.[13] Radhakrishnan put this point graphically: "The soul goes to that on which its mind is set during the last moments. What we think we become. Our past thoughts determine our present birth and our present ones will determine the future."[14] Notably, then, it is thoughts as much as actions that create the individual. Essentially, there is no total destruction at death, only dissolution. In Aurobindo's words: "If birth is a becoming, death also is a becoming not by any means a cessation. The body is abandoned, but the soul goes on its way."[15]

VERSE 7

Therefore, at all times, remember me and fight. With mind and intellect fixed on me alone, you will without doubt come to me.

It is Arjuna's individual, personal duty, his *sva-dharma*, to fight, and Krishna takes this opportunity to remind him thus. Embarking on the spiritual path or concentrating one's thoughts on Krishna does not mean abandoning *sva-dharma* but acting with the mind focused on Krishna. This is, in effect, using Krishna as a focus to enable egoless action. *Mind* and *intellect* here are *manas* and *buddhi* respectively, indicative of the whole self. The three paths of *karma-yoga*, *bhakti-yoga* and *jnana-yoga* seem to be harmonized in this verse.

VERSE 8

With thought integrated by the constant practice of *yoga*, meditating on the Supreme Resplendent Purusha not wandering towards any other thing, he goes [to him], Partha.

Several expressions are notable in the Sanskrit of this verse. *Abhyasa-yoga-yuktena*, *integrated by the constant practice of yoga*, is life-long meditation on *parama Purusha*, the highest or supreme Purusha. Purusha is *divya*, *Resplendent*, like the essence of the sun and rather like the *adhidaiva* of verse 4.

VERSE 9

Whoever remembers the Seer, the Ancient, the Ruler, minuter than the atom, Supporter of all, in form inconceivable, radiant like the sun beyond all darkness . . .

VERSE 10

. . . with steady mind, with devotion, integrated by the power of *yoga*, placing life-breath between the eyebrows fixedly, at the time of death reaches that Resplendent, Supreme Purusha.

It is constant practice of *yoga*, *abhyasa-yoga*, throughout life that brings the *yogin* to the state at the time of death that this verse describes. The *mind* is *steady* (*achala*) as is the *life-breath* (*prana*) All is *integrated, yukta*. Eight terms are used as focus for meditation and as descriptors of the divine in these last two verses:

- *Kavi*   *Kavi* is literally a *seer* or poet-seer, the poet indicative of creative imagination, and the seer of omniscience. Here it is the cosmic intelligence that is the source of creation.
- *Purana*   *Ancient*, that is to say, pre-existing temporal time, and the source of all that is.
- *Anushasita*   *Ruler*, the controller of the universe.
- *Dhatara*   *Supporter* or Ordainer, Establisher, Creator: Brahman is that which creates and sustains the entire cosmos.
- *Achintya*   *Inconceivable*; this term projects to that which is unthinkable in form and beyond all logic.
- *Adityavarna*   Radiance or effulgence of the sun. Brahma, the creator deity, is said to be a reddish-coloured seer in the *Shvetashvatara Upanishad* 5:2.
- *Tamasah parastat*   That which is above the darkness of ignorance and untouched by *prakriti* is the *Param-Atman*.

In addition to these eight terms, three means of approach to the divine are added:

- *Achala-manas*   An unwavering, steady mind.
- *Bhakti*   Devotion.
- *Yoga-bala*   The power or strength of *yoga*.

Yoga tradition has it that when an enlightened person dies, the breath is not expelled normally but is concentrated in the area between the eyebrows. Fixing the whole of *prana*, the "life-breath" or "life-energy", on this point means concentrating the whole will and consciousness in one place. The constant practice of *samadhi* allows this state to be reached. The verses depict partly the inconceivable and inscrutable deity as Brahman and yet also mentioned is *devotion, bhakti*, which seems to link the *nirguna* Brahman with the *bhakta*. These two verses have a tendency to blur the distinction between the *saguna* and *nirguna* aspects of Brahman, which is a trait occasionally to be found in the *Gita*.

VERSE 11

I shall declare briefly to you that goal which the knowers of the *Veda* call Imperishable, into which the self-controlled, freed from attachment, enter, desiring which they practise celibacy.

Goal here could also be "way", "place" or "path". The path that Krishna is about to reveal is that which leads to *Akshara*, the *Imperishable*. Those who know the *Veda* know that Brahman is the Imperishable in contrast to the world that is perishable. Those who are *freed from attachment* or passion (*raga*) are, in the Sanskrit, *yataya* the *self-controlled*. This is perhaps a reference to the *sannyasins*, traditionally those who reject worldly desires and lead a celibate life. *Celibacy*, *brahma-charya* in the Sanskrit, strictly translated is a celibate student. Chastity helps the physical energy, particularly sexual energy, to be transformed into spiritual energy. There is a link here with the beginning of verse 9, *Whoever remembers . . .* and to the syllable *Om*, for all the descriptors of Brahman in these verses are believed to be incorporated into the syllable, and Brahman and *Om* are synonymously portrayed by the word Imperishable, *Akshara*. Shankara, however, considered *Om* to be for "persons of dull and middling intellect".[16]

VERSE 12

Having controlled all the gates [of the body], having confined the mind in the heart, and having placed the life-breath of the self in the head, established in *yoga* concentration . . .

This verse lists the necessary conditions for the *yogin* at death. *The gates* are the apertures of the body and these nine – the two eyes, ears and nostrils, the mouth, anus and genitals – are closed. In short, the physical and sensory bodily functions are ceased. The *mind* (*manas*) is confined within the heart, the heart in Hindu thought being the seat of contemplation, the "lotus of the heart" as it is frequently termed. It is the mind that engages through the senses with the outside world, the heart being the more spiritual. Thus, when the mind is in the heart, it is controlled by focus on the divine, the divine being held in the heart. *Prana*, the *life-breath*, is fixed in the head and does not escape through the apertures of the body, so the head can retain its warmth and focus. *Yoga concentration* (*dharana*) was a specific end-stage in the eight stages of classical Yoga. Indeed, in the classical Yoga of Patanjali's *Yoga Sutras*, it is accepted that the *yogin* is able to have total control of the process of his own death.[17] Such *control*, *samyama*, is essential for every aspect of *yogic* praxis.

VERSE 13

. . . thus uttering *Om*, the one-syllabled Brahman, remembering me, he who departs, leaving the body, attains the supreme goal.

Since the breath of life, *prana*, is fixed in the head, the enlightened *yogin* is able to concentrate on Brahman until the very last moment. So the sound vibration of *Om* persists and since it *is* Brahman, this is the dying thought enabling the *yogin* to achieve the supreme goal and merge with Brahman. *Om* is the object of the *concen-*

tration of the previous verse. There is a clear link between Brahman and Krishna in the verse and since *Om* symbolizes the *nirguna* Brahman, too, the identity of Krishna with the *nirguna* Brahman is also clear.

VERSE 14

I am easily attainable, Partha, by him who thinks of nothing else, an ever-integrated *yogin* always constantly remembering me.

Krishna says that he is easily obtainable by the one who remembers him continually and thinks of nothing else. Ramakrishna is reputed to have said that when we take one stride towards God he takes ten strides towards us.[18] The aim is to be *an ever-integrated* (*nitya-yukta*), *yogin*, whose thought (*chetas*) is exclusively on God.

VERSE 15

Having attained to me, the *mahatmas*, having reached to the supreme perfection, are not reborn in this transitory place of suffering.

Once liberated, the great souls, the *mahatmas*, are no longer subject to the suffering (*duhkha*) of *samsara*. They have reached the highest perfection (*samsiddhi parama*). Others are reborn. Thus, death is never final; it is but "a moment of discontinuity".[19]

VERSE 16

The worlds as far as the world of Brahma are subject to return, Arjuna, but having attained to me, Kaunteya, there is no rebirth.

The *Gita* accepts that there are other planes of existence than the one in which we live. There are higher ones to which those with extremely good *karma* go, and lower ones for those with bad *karma*. There are six *lokas* or planes above Earth to which go those whose exceptionally good causes made on Earth enable them to reap positive rewards. But when those good rewards have been experienced – the good *karma* used up – rebirth then occurs back on Earth. Even the highest plane, the *Brahma-loka*, the plane of Brahma, is subject to *karma* and even to dissolution. However, those who reach this plane have the chance to move on to liberation after the dissolution of the universe. Others are reborn on Earth.

VERSE 17

Knowers of day and night are people who know a day of Brahma lasts a thousand *yugas* and a night lasts a thousand *yugas*.

The *yugas* are vast periods of time of interminable length, each being a whole era or eon. One day of Brahma, the creator deity, is a thousand *yugas* and one night another thousand *yugas*. So, though the universe exists over an incalculable time, it is, in fact, finite and lasts only as long as a day of Brahma, when it is withdrawn into an albeit temporary, unmanifest state. However, Brahma is also finite for he, too, has days and nights, months and years and so a beginning and an end. In later mythology, it is Vishnu who brings him into being in order to create manifested existence and when Brahma ceases to be manifest at the end of a century of days and nights he is liberated at *moksha* and after an unthinkable amount of time Vishnu creates a new Brahma who brings about the process of manifestation once more. Each day of a Brahma is divided into a thousand cycles of four *yugas* of unequal length – the *krita* or *satya*, the *treta*, the *dvapara* and the *kali*, just one such cycle amounting to one *maha-yuga*, "great age", which is 4,320,000 human years. A thousand such cycles amounts to 4,320,000,000 human years. The night lasts the same length of time.[20]

VERSE 18

At the coming of the day, all that is manifest proceeds from the unmanifest. At the coming of the night, indeed, it is dissolved in that which is called the unmanifest.

At the break of day of Brahma, manifested existence emerges from an unmanifest state and during the night of Brahma it is drawn back into the unmanifest. Just as on the microcosmic level beings have their waking and sleeping times, so has the universe. The word for unmanifest in the Sanskrit, *avyakta*, this time has no intimation of Brahman. Rather, it simply suggests a night of Brahma and the non-manifestation of the universe, which reverts to its dissolved state. Brahman is over and above this system. That is why, in the Sankhya system, *avyakta* as "unmanifest" is seen on the side of *prakriti* and separated from *purusha*. Nevertheless, Brahman is frequently referred to as the Unmanifest, that is to say, the *nirguna* Brahman, the *Avyakta* in a totally different sense. Brahma, while subject to *karma*, is the creator deity with whom creation, preservation and dissolution of the universe are involved. And yet, in the dissolved, unmanifested state, the *potential* for all manifestation is present. Importantly, there is no sense of destruction here, only *dissolution*. Vimala Thakar put this well when she said "it is only the drastic way of changing the form, the cohesion of various principles. That cohesion is dismantled, so that it can be recreated, that is how the dance between the unchanging imperishable principle, Purusa and this whole manifestation goes on by *prakriti*."[21] Whatever is dissolved – the body, the world, the universe – is absorbed into an unmanifest state, with its essences nothing but seed-like potentiality, latencies for newly creative energies; seeds in the darkness of an unmanifested reality.

VERSE 19

This multitude of beings that are being born again and again, dissolves, helpless, at the coming of night, Partha, and comes forth at the coming of day.

Samsara, the cycles of birth and death, for most individuals continues through a number of manifestations of the universe, latent *karmas* being dormant in the long period of quiescence between one manifested universe and the next. Individuals are *helpless* because they are bound by their own *karma*; only when non-fruitive *karma* is permanently undertaken can they hope for liberation. Even inanimate objects are subject to the same process of suspension between manifestations of the universe.

But all are helpless, too, by being drawn into the unmanifested state of the universe from which, after an infinite period of time, they cannot prevent their renewed manifestation.

VERSE 20

But beyond this unmanifest there is another Eternal Unmanifest Existent, who is not destroyed even when all other beings are destroyed.

Over and above the cycles of manifest and *unmanifest*, *avyakta*, existence is another *Unmanifest*, *Avyakta*, that is different, an *Existent* that is *eternal* (*sanatana*) and indestructible. It is the THAT, which is Para-Brahman. Zaehner considered that the Unmanifest beyond the unmanifest is a *personal* Krishna beyond Unmanifest Brahman, that is to say, Brahman becomes the penultimate not the ultimate goal[22] There are already hints in verses 9–10 and 13 that the *nirguna* Brahman and the *saguna* Krishna are coalesced to make devotion a viable pathway. Thus, I see no reason to accept a personal deity beyond the *nirguna* Brahman from the evidence of the *Gita* so far, and certainly not a "being beyond that being".[23] The context here in these verses of a manifest and unmanifest universe is how we should be viewing the term *avyakta*, with THAT as the ever-present Unmanifest that is the uncaused cause and underpinning factor of the cycles of manifestation and dissolution. Yet, this present verse refers to what is beyond *avyakta* as the unmanifest state of *prakriti* as another Unmanifest *bhava*, *Existent*, Existence, Being, or perhaps, with Gotshalk, "nature-and-being".[24]

While verse 22 will mention a supreme Purusha, we have no clear reason to project this beyond the Unmanifest Brahman or to isolate it from its context. Indeed, Zaehner himself found a certain "deliberate ambiguity" at this point of the *Gita*, though he believed verse 22 resolves this with the exhortation to *bhakti*.[25] The exhortation in verse 22, as far as I can see, is to be focused on devotion to Krishna as a means to, and as, the ultimate Unmanifest as Brahman. The fact that verse 22 mentions a *supreme Purusha* that is attainable through *bhakti* is suggestive of a manifestation of Brahman as Krishna, who is not *beyond* Brahman but Brahman manifest. And in the present verse 20, a translation *he is not destroyed* is possible, meaning *he*, Krishna, as the Unmanifest, *nirguna* Brahman is not destroyed.

What is important is that there is a causative link between what is manifest existence and the Unmanifest Brahman as its ultimate cause. While the universe has its phases of creation and dissolution, this very process is itself contained in Unmanifest Brahman: the *avyakta* of *prakriti* is linked to the *Avyakta* that is the Unmanifest Brahman by the potentiality that each holds for phenomenal existence, and by the hidden presence of the Unmanifest Brahman in all that is manifest. Each contains the other. How different this is from the Sankhya school, which has no possible link between unmanifest *purusha* and manifest existence.

VERSE 21

What is called the Unmanifest and Imperishable, [they] say it is that highest goal, having reached which, they do not return. That is my supreme abode.

This is another important verse that deals with the *Unmanifest, Avyakta,* beyond the unmanifest; the *Akshara,* the *Imperishable* that is Brahman. This is Unmanifested Reality, that which is totally beyond the mind and the intellect and that cannot be modified in any way. The term *Akshara* is important here because it is the idea of imperishability that differentiates the Unmanifest Brahman from the non-manifest state of *prakriti.* When *prakriti* is manifest, it could not be said that it also exists in the unmanifest state, just as when Brahma is awake he cannot be asleep. Only Brahman can be both manifest and unmanifest, *saguna* and *nirguna,* at the same time. So the unmanifest state of *prakriti,* called *pralaya* or "dissolution", is only temporary and perishable. Thus, involvement in *prakriti,* whether manifest or unmanifest, is impermanence. Those who attain Brahman, however, reach the supreme goal, the supreme abode and imperishability. Here in this verse Krishna unequivocally identifies himself as Brahman. Abode *(dhama)* is not used in any physical sense but more in that of "ambience", or "timeless bliss", as Zaehner suggested.[26] Ramanuja noted three spheres here, the first as *prakriti,* the second as spiritual *prakriti,* that is to say the co-created *atman* within the body, and the third, the released *atman* separated from *prakriti.*[27] It is the third sphere that, for Ramanuja was the *supreme abode.* Nevertheless, it is not possible to separate Brahman and *prakriti* entirely because of the presence of the *Atman* in all things. This is perhaps the point at which the *Gita's Sankhya* philosophy is at its most elusive as, also, Sankhya philosophy in general. The following verse anticipates this criticism.

VERSE 22

That supreme Purusha, Partha, within whom all beings dwell, by whom all this is pervaded, is truly attainable by exclusive *bhakti.*

This verse, unlike the strict Sankhya dualist view of matter and spirit, depicts the non-separation of Purusha and *prakriti,* for Purusha pervades all, is the thread by which all is strung, or the ocean that makes possible the surface waves. Thus, manifest or latent, unmanifest *prakriti* cannot exist without the underlying Brahman as its cause. Shankara made the point that: "All the created beings abide within the Purusha; for every effect rests within its cause",[28] which suits the sense of this verse admirably. Brahman and Purusha are identical, but it is in the form of Krishna, in all probability, that this verse suggests *ananya-bhakti, exclusive* loving-devotion, should be directed. There is a strong sense of panentheism in the verse, with the concept that all beings are part of Brahman or Purusha and Purusha indwells all things. The verse is not without its difficulties if *bhakti* is to be directed to an Unmanifest Imperishable of the previous verse. However, *bhakti,* here, is directed to the *supreme Purusha,* which, from what we have seen before, is likely to be the *saguna,* manifested aspect of Brahman, here as Krishna. If Krishna is identifying himself as Brahman, and it seems to me that he is, then the verse is without difficulty.

VERSE 23

I shall tell you, chief of Bharatas, that time in which the *yogins* depart, never to return, and also the time in which they return.

Two types of *yogins* are described here, those who depart from life and are not reborn and those destined for rebirth. Thus, what is to be described in the following verses is the fate of the *yogins* who become liberated and of those who do not.

VERSE 24

Fire, light, the bright fortnight of the moon, the six months of the northern path of the sun, departing then, people who know Brahman go to Brahman.

The two paths of the deceased outlined here and in the following verse are not peculiar to the *Gita* but reflect a very ancient tradition indeed. The *Brihad-aranyaka Upanishad* (6:2:15–16), for example, describes both paths in detail as does the *Chandogya Upanishad* (5:10:1–2).[29] The path of light in this present verse is known as *deva-yana*, the way of the gods, and was believed to lead the soul to higher regions. Thus, fire and light are symbolic of the evolution of the soul. The idea is a primitive one for all the attempts at allegory. Those dying in the daytime, during the light fortnight of the moon and during the six months of the northern solstice were destined to reach Brahman. It is the path of the gods that will either lead to Brahman or to the highest plane of *karmic* existence, that of the creator deity, Brahma, from where access to Brahman is possible.

VERSE 25

Smoke, night, also the dark fortnight of the moon and the six months of the southern path of the sun, then, the *yogin* having attained the lunar light returns.

Smoke, night, the dark fortnight of the moon and the six months of the southern passage of the sun are the inauspicious times to die, for the soul will be reborn. This is the way of the fathers, *pitri-yana*. In the *Chandogya Upanishad* (5:10:1–2), the path for such souls is smoke > night > the latter half of the month > the moon > the food of the gods > space > wind > smoke > mist > cloud > rain > vegetation > food > semen. Those who wish to provide allegorical meanings for the verse see the dark path as one involved with ignorance and engagement in the world, though Shankara reminded us that verse 23 says these are both paths of *yogins* not of ordinary mortals.[30] Reduced to their basic sense, these two verses can at best be said to reflect the fates of the godly and the worldly.

VERSE 26

The bright and dark paths are, indeed, thought to be the world's eternal paths: one leads to no return, the other to returning again.

The paths are *eternal* because they have always existed as the positive and negative possibilities for individuals, as have the choices between the divine and the sensory world. Shankara saw the bright path as that for the *yogin* of knowledge and the dark one for the *karma-yogin*, the *yogin* engaged in ritual action. All other beings he believed to be beyond both paths.[31] The beliefs outlined here are certainly old, older perhaps than the *Upanishads* and representing ancient and primitive ideas.

VERSE 27

Knowing these two paths, Partha, no *yogin* is deluded. Therefore, be integrated in *yoga* at all times, Arjuna.

The *yogin* who knows these two paths is he who knows there *is* a path to *moksha* and devotes himself to that path. Presumably, however, in knowing *both* paths, the *yogin* will choose the better one, the one that does not lead to *samsara*. Arjuna is told to be *integrated in yoga*, *yoga-yukta*, the message Krishna has been giving him thus far in the *Gita*.

VERSE 28

Whatever is declared the fruit of merit of the *Vedas*, of *yajna*, of *tapas* and also of gifts, the *yogin*, knowing this, transcends all that and attains to the supreme primeval abode.

By following the scriptures, performing religious ritual (*yajna*), practising austerities (*tapas*) and by giving gifts (*dana*), it is maintained that one will achieve good *karma*, good *fruit* (*phala*) of one's actions. Nevertheless, it is still *karma* and the result of causes from which results must accrue. The *karma* may be very good, resulting in birth on a higher plane of existence, but when used up, rebirth occurs on the earthly plane. Knowing *Akshara* Brahman brings the *yogin* beyond such more immediate goals to the ultimate goal that ends rebirth.

Krishna has now answered the seven questions posed by Arjuna in the first two verses of CHAPTER EIGHT.

In the *Upanishad* of the *Bhagavad Gita*, the knowledge of Brahman, the teaching of *Yoga* and the dialogue between Shri Krishna and Arjuna, this is the eighth chapter called *Akshara Brahma-Yoga*.

CHAPTER NINE

Raja-Vidya Raja-Guhya Yoga

The *Yoga* of Royal Knowledge and Royal Mystery

This chapter deals with the nature of *saguna* and *nirguna* Brahman, Brahman with and without qualities respectively. The *saguna* nature as *prakriti* and manifest God are important in the chapter but Krishna goes well beyond that aspect and presents himself as the Supreme Brahman, the Ground of all Being of the universe. All manifest existence is his lower nature as *prakriti*, though he is not affected by it in any way, because, at the same time, he is the *nirguna* Brahman that exists when all *prakriti* disappears and is in no way limited in, defined in, or dependent on, manifest existence. Yet it is Krishna as the *saguna* Brahman who is the personal God, the object of devotion. *Bhakti*, "loving devotion", to Krishna along with knowledge of his true nature are the culminating themes of the chapter. Notably, the knowledge (*vidya*) and the mystery (*guhya*) are divulged by Krishna as a *Kshatriya* and warrior, where normally such religious teaching is the domain of *Brahmins*.

The Lord said:

VERSE I

I shall indeed declare to you, who is not frivolous, this most profound mystery, knowledge combined with realization which, having known, you will be liberated from evil.

Not frivolous is indicative of not being given to dispute or cavil, not fault-finding or censorious. The remark shows that Krishna considers Arjuna to be ready to receive what he has to say. *Knowledge* here is *jnana*, which Robert Zaehner believed meant "wisdom based on holy writ",[1] thus following both Shankara and Ramanuja's commentaries. This may well be justified given the way knowledge was defined in CHAPTER SEVEN. But *jnana* as intellectual or even intuitive knowledge is not sufficient for *moksha*: there must be a profound intuitive *realization, vijnana,* of Brahman. It is this sudden realization, a direct intuition of Reality, which is both the Royal Knowledge and the Royal Mystery or Secret. Rohit Mehta commented here:

This experience is not to be arrived at through the cogitations of the mind. The mind sees everything through its veil of interpretation. It never sees a thing directly, but always through the glass, darkly. The direct experience is possible only when the veil of mind's interpretation is rent asunder. But to remove mind's veil of interpretation is to render mind, mindless. It is indeed true that only when the mind becomes mindless that man can come to that direct experience where alone the Secret of Life is communicated to him.[2]

And as Mehta went on to say: "The understanding of the Formless is an intuitive experience – it comes to the mind, the mind cannot go to it."[3] Such is the nature of realization.

Evil in the verse probably means that which binds the individual to fruitive *karma*, and hence to rebirth, in so far as it is the functioning of the ego in ignorance that prevents liberation. Again, as Mehta put it: "There is nothing good or evil *per se*. It is the mind with its projected grades of significance that brings the element of good and evil into existence."[4] Thus, the *profound mystery* is going to be about ultimate Truth, what Aurobindo termed "the wisdom of all wisdoms, the secret of all secrets."[5] It is going to lift realization far beyond any other kind of knowledge to make the *yogin* liberated (*mukta*). Nevertheless, Ramanuja brought such mystery down to basic levels. For him, the profound mystery was *bhakti*, devotion to God,[6] and he took knowledge, *jnana*, to be *bhakti* and realization, *vijnana* to be worship!

VERSE 2

Royal knowledge, royal mystery, highest purifier is this: realizable by direct intuition, conforming to *dharma*, very easy to practise, imperishable.

At first sight, this seems to be saying that knowledge of Brahman is easy to obtain through practice, but Krishna has already said in 7:3 that those who are liberated are very rare. Perhaps the verse is saying that final realization is that which requires no effort at all, no striving. It has to be full realization of Brahman that brings *moksha* and that is the *purifier*, but it would be futile to think that realization can just happen without any prior effort. Purification here means the final burning up of all prior *karma* so that there are no seeds of action remaining that would cause rebirth. For most, the *karmic* burden is massive. So *easy to practise* may refer to the *yogin* who is adept at practice. On the other hand, *moksha* is really humankind's natural state to which all are travelling whether they know it or not, and in that sense it may be *easy*. Shankara's understanding of the *knowledge* of the verse was as knowledge of Brahman, *Brahma-jnana*,[7] (using *jnana* for knowledge, rather than the *vidya* of the text), though this is not at all very *easy to practise*. *Direct intuition* is *pratyaksha*, immediate, direct perception of the truth – here, of Brahman. *Imperishable, avyaya*, means that the result is not an impermanent one like the results of ordinary actions. An ordinary action is a cause that has to have a result, but when the result, the effect, occurs, then the cause no longer needs to exist. The Royal Knowledge and Mystery is neither cause nor effect and so is permanent.

Dharma in the verse Ramanuja saw as "virtue",[8] and the "means for final beatitude".[9] In short, the verse for Ramanuja was advocating *bhakti-yoga* as the means to God. Additionally, in commenting on Krishna's words here, Ramanuja said that "with reference to one who carries out this kind of worship, even though the giving away of Myself (to him) is done, it appears to Me that nothing has been done by Me at all to him".[10]

VERSE 3

Men without *shraddha* for this law of *dharma*, Parantapa, return in the path of this world of *samsara* without attaining me.

The thought returns to *shraddha*, "faith", and speaks of those who are without it. Having no faith means being ignorant that there *is* a path to total freedom. It is this absence of *shraddha* in the sense of ignorance that causes individuals to be trapped in the *samsaric* cycle, so they are destined for rebirth because they operate from the level of cause and result, *karma*. *Dharma* is mentioned in this and the previous verse. Clearly, following *dharma* in all its relevant dimensions in an individual's life is important, but here, in this verse, it is specified that it is *shraddha for this law of dharma* that is essential, that is to say, faith in the path of knowledge and in the *vijnana*, the realization, that brings about liberation. The verse does not hint at *bhakti*, but such is the way Ramanuja understood *this law of dharma*, that is to say, worship "which is of the form of being surpassingly dear on account of its having for its object Myself who am surprisingly dear, which is the means for the attainment of Myself constituting final beatitude and which is inexhaustible".[11]

VERSE 4

All this world is pervaded by me in my unmanifest form. All beings exist in me but I do not exist in them.

It is not clear in the verse whether the unmanifest (*avyakta*) refers to the unmanifest state of *prakriti*, as in the Sankhya system, or to the Unmanifest (*Avyakta*) that is *nirguna* Brahman. I am inclined to think it is probably the latter that is referred to, for Krishna identifies himself with this indestructible Brahman on numerous occasions, most recently, in 8:20. Thus, *I do not exist in them* would mean that the *nirguna* Brahman is not dependent on beings for continued existence, but they are dependent on Brahman. Manifest existence is but the manifested energies of Brahman that stem from the *nirguna* form, but the converse cannot be said to be the case. Ultimately, as Shankara stated, Brahman is the essence of everything but cannot be contained by anything.[12] *Nirguna* Brahman is the Unmanifest Source, the ultimate causeless Cause from which everything must spring and into which everything must dissolve at the end of a life of Brahma. Anything other than Brahman is finite and dependent, which is what Brahman can never be. *Pervaded* is, thus, the important word in the verse. Such pervasion is manifestation of the *nirguna* Brahman in *nirguna* form as the *Atman* in all existence. Thus, as Shankara put it, beings "are what they are in virtue of Me, the Self, underlying them all".[13]

The verse was important to Ramanuja who saw God as the *antaryamin* or "Inner Ruler" of selves and the world. This is how he understood *pervaded by me*, and the concept constituted one of the major tenets of Vishishtadvaita. Some, like Zaehner, translate "spun" for pervaded[14], which captures the sense of a transcendent Cause admirably. Aurobindo described such a Royal Mystery thus: "The supreme secret is the mystery of the transcendent Godhead who is all and everywhere, yet so much greater and other than the universe and all its forms that nothing here contains him, nothing expresses him really, and no language which is borrowed from the appearances of things in space and time and their relations can suggest the truth of his unimaginable being."[15]

VERSE 5

Nor do beings exist in me; behold my divine *Yoga* – my Self bringing forth and supporting beings but not existing in beings.

And here we have a paradox! Verse 4 has already included the statement *all beings exist in me*, and here in verse 5 we have the contradictory statement: *Nor do beings exist in me*. When we get to verse 6, we will again find *all beings exist in me*. Presumably, it is the *divine Yoga*, the massive power in *bringing forth and supporting beings* that goes some way to clarify the anomaly in that what is being created and supported cannot take part in its own creation. Then, too, Krishna refers to his *Self*, *Atman*, in the verse, and this must surely be the *nirguna* Brahman that exists when the universe does not and from which the *saguna* aspect of Brahman becomes manifest and brings forth creation. Verses 7 and 8 will make this clear. Some translators highlight the paradox by translating "and yet", instead of *nor*.

Ramanuja explained the paradox by saying that it is God's will, his *Yoga*, by which he causes beings to exist as his body, which he maintains, but has no need of.[16] For Ramanuja, God was the "Inner Ruler" "whose *murti* (lit. form) is not manifest, that is, whose essential nature is not made known. The meaning is that all this is pervaded by Me as the proprietor in order to sustain and rule this universe".[17] Ramanuja went to some length here to demonstrate that the idea of God as the Inner Ruler has foundation in the *Vedanta*. *Nor do beings exist in me* Ramanuja explained as meaning God is not dependent on beings for his own existence. His *divine Yoga* is his innate qualities that are the manifestation of his will, and it is this will by which beings exist and by which he sustains the world.

In my view, verses 4, 5 and 6 can only be understood in relation to the *nirguna* and *saguna* Brahman. J. A. B. van Buitenen said something similar in relation to the word *exist* or "subsist" in verse 4: "Krsna works here with two meanings of *avyakta* he has just described: as the *avyakta = prakriti*, he is the domain of phenomenal life, in which all creatures have their being, so that 'they exist in me', *matsthani*. But even as the lower *avyakta* he is not summed up by these creatures." And for the expression "do not exist in me" he said "as the *Avyakta* beyond the lower *avyakta* God represents an order of being completely transcendent to the creatures".[18] Lars Martin Fosse offers the following, equally possible rendition: "And yet, the beings do not exist in me – behold my divine magic power! My self is the source of beings. It sustains them, but does not exist in them."[19] Here, it is the divine *Yoga* brought forth from the Self of Brahman that does not ultimately *exist* in beings. The use of "and yet" at the beginning of verse 5 is particularly appropriate in linking verses 4, 5 and 6. However, there is always the problem with Self, *Atman*, in that it actually *does* exist in beings. Brahman *pervades* all manifest existence from Brahma down to a blade of grass as the essence or *Atman* within all, but only while manifestation exists. Beyond manifestation, the *nirguna* Brahman ever remains.

In short, everything emanates from Brahman, the Ground of all Being, yet Brahman is beyond and unaffected by the whole of the manifest cosmos. The thought is rather like 7:12, where the whole of *prakritic* existence is said to be dependent on Brahman, but Brahman is in no way dependent on *prakriti*. The following verse will help to make sense of the present one in that it refers to the wind that is transient as, likewise, is all manifest existence: Brahman is beyond this transience. So Brahman is the Source of and sustains all things but is not attached to them, does not "appropriate" them, as Vimala Thakar put it,[20] or is not "contained"[21] by them, and exists when the finite universe does not. Douglas Hill's comment was most accurate, "all beings dwell in Krsna (or Brahman) inasmuch as *prakriti* is his, but as his proper, or higher, nature is *atman*, which is in reality quite unconnected with the work of *prakriti*, it is equally true that beings do not dwell in him, nor he in them."[22] The point is that *ultimately*, the Unmanifest is beyond person, personality, divinity: it is absolute and ulimate and no-thing. It is in this sense, I think, that beings cannot exist in Brahman. It is the panentheism of the *Gita* that helps to clarify the verses.

Verse 6

As the great wind moving everywhere always exists in the *akasha*, so know thus, all beings exist in me.

Akasha is usually referred to as "ether". It is the source of the elements of fire, air, water and earth. But though *akasha* is the source of the other elements, it is unaffected by them and remains just the same. Just so, Brahman as the Source of all things is unaffected by them. *Akasha* is all-pervading as, also, is Brahman. Verses 4, 5 and 6 are indicative of a thorough panentheism in the *Gita*; God in all things but over and above all things.

The difficulty of verses 4, 5 and 6 is, according to Zaehner, resolved in *bhakti*, as we shall see later in verse 29. Zaehner wrote: "The philosophical puzzle of whether it is proper to say that contingent beings subsist in God or do not subsist in Him, is here transcended because *bhakti* introduces a new dimension. Love means giving, sharing, participation, total self-giving, and total interpenetration, and so God abides in his lovers and they in Him."[23]

Verse 7

All beings, Kaunteya, go into my *prakriti* at the end of the *kalpa*. At the beginning of a *kalpa*, I send them forth again.

These words, indeed, suggest why Brahman is not dependent on *prakritic* existence in any way, for Brahman continues to exist when the universe is in its unmanifest state, and it is Brahman that causes it to become manifest again at the beginning of a new eon, a new *kalpa*. Thus, *prakriti* here is the unmanifest, *avyakta*, which is why Krishna refers to it as *my prakriti*; he controls it as the true *Avyakta*, the Unmanifest Brahman. All the same, both the manifest and unmanifest aspects of *prakriti* are part of the *saguna*, manifest Brahman. The enormous time-span of the life of Brahma and the concomitant cycles of manifestation and dissolution are all caused by Brahman, but when all those cycles are over, at the end of a life of Brahma, what remains is *nirguna* Brahman, the *ultimate* Cause, and even that is Krishna.

VERSE 8

Having animated my own *prakriti*, I send forth again and again this multitude of beings, all helpless by the force of *prakriti*.

The Unmanifest Brahman causes the unmanifest state of *prakriti* to become manifest; Brahman *animates* unmanifest *prakriti*, *my own prakriti*, he says. There is a distinct difference between the Sankhya of the *Gita* in which Brahman controls *prakriti* and classical Sankhya in which what is spirit has no connection whatever with *prakriti*. *Having animated* is glossed as "resorting to" by Shankara[24] and this was followed by Zaehner, who saw it in the sense of "consorting with" *prakriti* in a sexual sense in order to create manifest existence, *purusha* being regarded as male, and *prakriti* as female.[25] *Animated*, I think, is the better term, however, with a hint of effortlessness and non-dependency and it is sometimes translated as "leaned on" or "rested on", which highlights the independence of Brahman in the creative process. Shankara believed that it is ignorance (*avidya*) that renders all beings helplessly trapped in *prakriti*[26] and, while the verse does not indicate the thought, it is obviously the *karmic* destinies of *multitudes of beings* caught up in *samsara* that make *prakriti* necessary.

VERSE 9

And these actions do not bind me, Dhananjaya; like one sitting indifferent, unattached in those actions.

So much of the earlier sections of the *Gita* are reflected in this verse, particularly that in 3:22, where Krishna says he engages in action and yet does nothing. And we are reminded of the times when the *Gita* stresses that stillness of the inner Self, the *atman*, is the root from which egoless action without desire for results needs to come. Brahman, *Purusha*, *Atman* is always still and actionless; it is *prakriti* that is active and in which the *gunas* and the system of cause and effect operates. Yet, despite the indifference and unattached nature of Brahman, it is from Brahman that *prakriti* receives the power of manifestation and action. The aim of beings from the *Gita*'s message so far is to achieve the same kind of indifferent and *unattached* (*asakta*) action as that of the *saguna* Brahman. That will not eschew devotion, for the *Gita*'s teaching on Sankhya is not an impersonal one; it leaves room for theism whereas later classical Sankhya did not. The *actions* (*karma*) in the verse refer back to the cycles of manifest and unmanifest *prakriti*. Since Krishna is separate from the cause–effect processes that he has created within the workings of *prakriti*, the law of *karma* operates while he remains *indifferent* and *unattached*. He does not predetermine the effects that arise from individual causes any more than he creates the causes himself.

VERSE 10

By me as supervisor, *prakriti* produces the moving and the unmoving; by this cause, Kaunteya, the world revolves.

Chidbhavananda used the useful analogy of the sun to explain this verse. Just like sunbeams exist and have an effect on the world only because they gain their potential from the sun, so *prakriti* can only operate because it gains potential from Brahman. Brahman does not do anything and is not dependent in any way on the effects that are emanated.[27] Verses 7–10 may reflect a method of argument known as *Arundhati-Nyaya* promulgated by the *Nyaya* school of philosophers and is the idea of reaching a subtle conclusion through progressive steps.[28] When a bride is first taken to her husband's home he is expected to point out to her the *Arundhati* star. It is very tiny and he can only point it out by directing her attention to something larger on the immediate horizon, then a large star, and so he proceeds until the tiny star is found. Argument that is *Arundhati-Nyaya* proceeds in the same way. Krishna first says that he causes unmanifest *prakriti* to become manifest, then he says that this action has no effect on him; he remains neutral and unattached. The final important point, the *Arundhati*, is that he does nothing; *prakriti* is the producer of everything, animated effortlessly by Brahman. *Supervisor*, then, is *adhyaksha*, one who presides over or supervises and is simply a witness to proceedings. *The world revolves* is a reference to the *samsara* of the world, its perpetual cycles that go "round and round"; the "wheel of the world" as Gandhi described it.[29]

VERSE 11

The deluded disregard me assumed in human form, not knowing my higher nature as the Great Lord of Beings.

This verse could be interpreted in two ways. First, it could mean that *the deluded* (*mudha*) do not regard Krishna as divine at all; that is to say, they do not recognize him as a divine descent, let alone have any knowledge of his *higher nature*. The second possibility is that the deluded *do* recognize his divinity in human form but do not have any knowledge of his higher nature as that which is the uncaused Cause as Brahman. The latter possibility would continue the thought of the previous verse. Most commentators prefer the former interpretation and the following verse perhaps supports this, but the content of the previous verses is focused on the Unmanifest, Brahman, and this I think is likely to be the underlying concept of the whole chapter and, therefore, the point being made here. Verse 13, indeed, takes up this point after describing the deluded.

Krishna has a human body but is not bound by that body, being not just the *Param-Atman* but the *Atman* in all, pervading all as the connecting thread between manifestation and his supreme nature as Brahman. The example of *akasha*, "ether", here, is again relevant, for no element can exist without ether as that which makes possible all existence and yet existence cannot change or affect ether. However, this verse brings Brahman into *saguna* form as Lord, *Ishvara*, and it is this *saguna* form that is able to be the object of devotion as the *Great Lord* (*Maheshvara*) *of Beings*.

VERSE 12

Of vain hopes, of vain actions, of vain knowledge, senseless, truly possessed of the delusive nature of *Rakshasas* and *Asuras*.

The thought of the previous verse is continued here with those who are deluded as the subject. Delusion (*moha*) causes people to see bodily existence as the only reality, sense indulgence as important, and the search for permanence in a transitory world a necessary goal. The deluded are called *Rakshasas*, "devils", "fiends", and *Asuras*, "demons", "anti-gods". The former are darkly *rajasic* and the latter *tamasic*.[30] The terms serve to describe the states of mind of the deluded. Nevertheless, these deluded beings are still part of *prakriti* and, as such, are dependent on Brahman as much as anything else in existence. *Prakriti* is the divine *maya*, the divine delusion that causes beings to be trapped in egoistic desires and aversions resulting from their interaction with the *gunic* world. Does this, then, suggest that evil ultimately stems from the divine? Certainly it would have to be said that the *potential* for it within *prakritic* existence and the *gunic* make-up of these deluded beings must come from Brahman. But Brahman is the witness of them, the passive observer; they exist in Brahman, but Brahman is not *in* their actions, as verse 4 made clear.

VERSE 13

But the *mahatmas*, Partha, depending on the divine *prakriti*, worship me with a mind devoted to nothing else, knowing me as the imperishable Source of beings.

The *divine prakriti* is that which is pervaded mostly by the *sattvic guna,* the spiritual, enlightening, evolving aspect in creation. The "great souls", *mahatmas*, who are devoted to the path of reaching the *imperishable* (*avyaya*) Brahman, are also highly characterized by *sattva*. Such people worship Krishna in his human form with loving-devotion, but also understand his higher nature. In contrast, the deluded of verse 11 are drawn only to the non-divine, non-*sattvic* aspects of life. *Bhakti* is neatly underpinned by *jnana* in the verse, *jnana* being epitomized in the expression *with a mind devoted to nothing else, ananya-manasa*.

VERSE 14

Always glorifying me, striving and firm in vows, and bowing before me, they worship with devotion, always steadfast.

Devotion here is *bhakti*, "loving-devotion", and the verse is replete with it, with Krishna as the object of devotion. In concentrating on God, the *sattvic* quality is increased, so divine qualities also increase. When the whole being is devoted to God, this is the highest devotion. The more a devotee concentrates on God, the nearer that devotee comes to him. *Always steadfast* is *nitya-yukta* which, for the *yogin* would be "ever-integrated". There is, thus, a blend of devotion, knowledge and *yogic* praxis in this verse.

VERSE 15

Others also sacrifice with *jnana-yajna*, and worship me as One, different and various, the all-facing.

Jnana-yajna is the "sacrifice of knowledge", the path of knowledge, so the first phrase is straightforward. However, the second part of the verse is difficult. The problematic phrases are:

ekatvena	*prithaktvena*	*bahudha*	*vishvato mukham*
as One	as different	in various ways	the all-facing or all-faced

How are these expressions related to each other, for they are variously interpreted? Attractive is the non-dual, dual and qualified dualism that may be alluded to. Thus, some worship Krishna as the *One* – a monist, strictly non-dual, *advaitist*, view where all is one as Shankara believed and as professed by the thinkers of Advaita Vedanta. Others may worship Krishna as *different*, separate and distinct from the self and the world – a dualist view where divinity remains separate from the world in every way, as the later Dvaita thinkers professed. *Various* is suggestive of a plurality of divine forms – the later Vishishadvaita view of qualified non-dualism by which the world is considered to be the body of Brahman and so many divine forms are possible as foci for devotees. The last phrase is the most difficult. It seems to suggest something like "facing in every direction",[31] "I who face in all directions",[32] "universal manifestations"[33] which, allied to the previous *various*, is what is suggestive of the many forms of God in Vishishtadvaita. Thus, Ramanuja understood the verse to mean God is worshipped as the One underlying the multiplicity of forms – God as one and his body as plurality:[34] "They worship Me who, by being marked by diversity in various ways, in the form of the world, am multiform, that is, having all things as modes."[35] To Ramanuja, the whole world was the body of God.

On the other hand, the context of the verse in the chapter as a whole and, in particular, in relation to the following verses, may simply reflect the pervasiveness of Brahman in all things; the One Source behind the plurality of manifestation and worshipped as such. Krishna has already said that beings are in him, but he is not in them, so perhaps the meaning here is that he is one in all existence as the essence of all, yet separate as the Unmanifest Brahman. The same phrase occurs in 10:33 where it certainly refers to the presence of God in all manifestations.

VERSE 16

I am the *kratu*, I am *yajna*, I am *svadha*, I am the medicinal herb, I am the *mantra*, I am also the clarified butter, I am the fire, I am the offering.

Verses 16–19 list the characteristics of the divine Krishna encompassing his manifest as well as unmanifest states. His presence in ritual, already stated in 4:24, is detailed here in a variety of ritualistic terminology:

- *kratu*   *Vedic* prescribed sacrificial ritual

- *yajna*   sacrifice
- *svadha*   sacrifice of food offered to ancestors
- *aushadha*   medicinal herbs and plants or perhaps *soma*, the intoxicating drink used by priests in sacrificial ritual.
- *mantra*   the sacred chant with which the oblation is offered
- *ajya*   ghee, the clarified butter
- *agni*   the fire
- *huta*   the offering, oblation

VERSE 17

I am the Father of this world, Mother, Ordainer, Grandfather, the Thing to be known, the Purifier, the syllable *Om, Rik, Sama* and also *Yajus*.

As the Source of all, Brahman is father, mother and grandfather of all beings and entities in the universe. *Ordainer* (*dhata*) or perhaps Dispenser, Maintainer, Supporter, has as object the cause–effect processes of the universe. To know Brahman is to have true knowledge and a purified self. The *Rik, Sama* and *Yajus* are the three major *Vedas* – the *Rig Veda*, the *Sama Veda* and the *Yajur Veda*. The *Rig Veda* is concerned with the nature of Brahman, *Sama* with chants and *Yajur* with ritual. All three in ritual praxis are essential to creating and sustaining the universe. The fourth *Veda*, not mentioned in the verse, is the *Atharva Veda*, which is different in tone, being mainly concerned with incantations. While it contains some very ancient material, it may have been compiled later than the other three *Vedas*. For *Purifier*, van Buitenen has "strainer", referring to the implement that strained the *soma* of the previous verse[36] though given the shift of thought in this verse, "strainer" would have been better placed in the last one. Sound is the entity said to have been used as the seed to create the universe and Brahman is identified in this sound source of *Om*. Since *Om* is the symbol for the indescribable, impersonal Brahman, and yet these are describable elements of divinity in the verse, we have another example of the blurred distinction between both that the *Gita* often displays (cf. 7:6, 7).

VERSE 18

I am the Goal, the Supporter, the Lord, the Witness, the Abode, the Shelter, the Friend, the Origin, the Dissolution, the Foundation, the Treasure-house and the Imperishable Seed.

Brahman is the *goal* (or path, *gati*) to which the devotee should aspire, but also, as the previous verse stated, that which ordains and so creates the cause–effect processes by which the universe operates. *Witness* is important, however, for while being the sole causeless Cause, Brahman is merely the passive witness of the process of cause and effect not the active perpetrator. *Abode* is reminiscent of verse 4, which stated that all beings exist in Brahman. *Treasure-house* is suggestive of the rewards for those who realize Brahman, when Brahman is *Shelter* and *Friend* to devotees, or it may be the unmanifest state of *avyakta* when all is stored awaiting future manifestation.

VERSE 19

I give heat, I withhold and send forth rain: I am immortality and also death and I am existence and non-existence, Arjuna.

In saying that he is *immortality and also death*, Krishna is pointing to his nature as the Source of all cause and effect – of the immortality, *amrita*, (though temporary) of the gods and of the deaths in individual lives as results of past causes. *Existence and non-existence* are *sat* and *asat* respectively, or "being and non-being." Zaehner thus translated "what IS and what is not."[37] Krishna, then, is the Being of the cosmos in his manifested state and the Non-Being as Unmanifest Brahman. Zaehner, however, considered that *sat* and *asat* refer to immortality and death,[38] though there seems no reason why Krishna should repeat the same idea in the verse, given that verses 16–19 form a composite list. Shankara saw *sat* as what is manifest, the effect, and *asat* as cause, the unmanifest,[39] presumably the *vyakta* that is *prakriti* and the *avyakta* of its unmanifest state.

VERSE 20

Those who know the three *dharmas*, the *soma*-drinkers, purified from evil, worshipping by *yajna*, pray for a way to Heaven. Having reached the holy world of the lord of gods they enjoy the divine pleasures of the gods.

The *three dharmas* are the three major *Vedas* noted in verse 17 and the verse suggests that the rituals of these suffice only to result in Heaven and nothing more, even though they are *purified from evil* (*papa*). We need to remember that even the highest Heaven of Brahma is temporary. The Heaven referred to here is that of Indra, the *lord of gods*. This title was conferred on him because he had performed a hundred *yajnas* that gave him an enormous amount of merit, of good *karma*. When such merit is exhausted, Indra will be born again in the realm of humankind; so will all who reach his realm as the following verse says. *Soma* was both a deity and a potent, possibly hallucinogenic drink partaken of by the priests during the sacrificial rituals. It was believed to bring immortality. Its origin and the substance from which it was made are long lost despite vivid descriptions of how it is made in the ninth book of the *Rig Veda*, which is wholly devoted to it. The verse makes it clear that *Vedic* ritual cannot bring about liberation. Ramanuja saw those mentioned here as those who followed the *Vedas* but not the *Vedanta*, without knowledge of which, as the following verse will show, they will continue to be reborn.[40]

VERSE 21

Having enjoyed that vast world of Heaven, they enter the world of mortals at the exhaustion of merit. Thus, abiding by the three *dharmas* they, desiring desires, attain the state of going and returning.

These words are again critical of the *Vedas*, the *three dharmas*, and of those who desire to achieve good *karma* (rather than no *karma* at all) and reach Heaven, *svarga*, as the previous verse suggests. The ritual portion of the *Vedas* was thoroughly result orientated, exactly what the *Gita* will not advocate. Those who practise such ritual fail to appreciate that creation comes from Krishna or Brahman; so, ultimately, all the gods are creations of Brahman. *Desiring desires* is *kama kama*, while *going and returning* refers to the cycles of birth and death, *samsara*.

VERSE 22

To those men who worship me thinking of no others, who are ever-integrated, I bring what is not already, and preserve what is already, possessed.

What is called for here is singular devotion to Krishna, depicted by the term *ananya*, literally, "without others", and so "exclusively" and with the addition of *cintayanta*, *thinking of no others*. The phrase is, however, variously interpreted – "with undivided heart",[41] for example, which captures the sense of the phrase rather well. The verse also mentions the *ever-integrated* (*nitya athiyuktana*), "always steadfast", "ever-united" or "ever-devout". *What is already possessed* is probably what is already attained on the evolutionary path of *yoga*. Thus, *what is not already possessed* is further progress. Those who desire Heaven may well attain it, but the genuine worshipper who is totally absorbed in, and dedicated to, God will be free of *karma* and will not need to be born again. There will be no sense of "I" or "mine" and this is why the verse stresses the idea of security and gain on the path: through the grace of Krishna, the devotee will receive what is not asked for and will retain progress already possessed. Such grace is indicative of the protection of the devotee.

VERSE 23

Even devotees who worship other gods in full *shraddha* they also worship me alone, Kaunteya, by the wrong method.

It is *shraddha*, "faith", which unites all devotees – still *bhaktas* here – of different gods: they will have different ways of worship, different ways of practising their faith but, ultimately, Krishna says, it is to him that their faith is directed. The thought is reminiscent of 7:21, where Krishna says it is he who encourages such faith. *The wrong method* is variously translated: Zaehner had "though the rite may differ from the norm"[42] and van Buitenen also translated "without proper rite", explaining "not by a rite devoted to Krsna himself".[43] Murthy, too considers the phrase to mean "though not according to the law",[44] and Shankara interpreted it as "in ignorance".[45] Will Johnson is very specific, "not according to the prescribed rules".[46] All these meanings have some merit, though given the restricting results of following *Vedic* ritual mentioned in verses 20 and 21, ritual law is less likely to be a correct means and the right method. I do not think we should read into this verse the idea that Krishna is referring to the gods of other religions: the context, particularly in the light of the verses that follow, suggests that he is referring to devotees of minor gods. The thought is similar to 7:23, so *wrong method* perhaps means worshipping gods for gain, for reaching Heaven, for good rewards, but not for true knowledge and liberation. Ramanuja clearly saw those who worshipped others as those worshipping *Vedic* gods, again, devoid of knowledge of the *Vedanta*.[47] But, given that he accepted any god, ghost or ancestor as the body of God, any such worship is, ultimately, to the one God though, as verse 25 will show, the fate of each worshipper is different.

VERSE 24

Truly, I alone am the Enjoyer and Lord of all *yajnas*. But they do not know me in reality, hence they fall.

The thought here is similar to that in 8:4, where Krishna says: "I alone am the *adhiyajna* here in the body." Worshipping the minor gods means that people will worship in an inferior way simply because their view of the divine is inferior: the level of consciousness of the devotees is such that they are unable to see the higher truth. However, since all the minor gods exist in Brahman, it is to Brahman as *Lord* (*prabhu*) of all religious praxis that, ultimately, all the *yajnas* are performed. But because the sights of the devotees of the minor gods – the *they* of the verse – are set rather low, and are *karmic* in nature, rebirth is inevitable; thus they *fall*, or fail. Even so, we should remember that, as in 7:21, Krishna encourages such devotion because it develops *shraddha* in the devotee. So having faith in a god who will aid the journey to Heaven is encouraged because such faith is a sound quality even though it falls short of the kind of faith necessary for liberation.

VERSE 25

Worshippers of the *devas* go to the *devas*; worshippers of the ancestors go to the ancestors; also worshippers of the *bhutas* go to the *bhutas*; my worshippers come to me.

One reaps what one sows; if worship is directed to a specific goal, that goal will eventually be achieved, but the goal itself is relative to the level of consciousness within and, in particular, relative to the balance of *gunas* in the devotee. Those who set their goal on ultimate Reality will have the necessary predisposition and level of consciousness to strive towards it and reach it. *Devas* are the gods. Their life-span is very long because of their good *karma*; but eventually they will be reborn in the world of mortals. They also have supernatural powers because of their high evolutionary state, so those who worship them have the goal of gaining such power and an immensely long existence like the gods. They do not realize that when their good *karma* is exhausted in the realm of the *devas*, they will return to mortal state. A similar fate meets those who worship the *pitris* or *manes*, the ancestors or fathers; the goal is limited, especially since ancestors are not remembered or even linked after one is reborn. *Bhutas* are beings or spirits somewhere between humans and gods in their evolutionary development. They may also be ghosts who have not been sent on their way by traditional rites. Again, they are still subject to *karma*. None of these paths, then, can lead to *moksha*: the only real path is the worship of Krishna, Brahman. So not only does *karma* ensure that we reap what we sow, it also operates so that our ultimate goal is also related to what we sow, that is, what we want the result to be.

VERSE 26

Whoever offers to me with devotion, a leaf, a flower, fruit, water, that I accept, offered with *bhakti* by the pure-minded.

This is a beautiful and well-known verse. It is not what is offered that is important but the degree of love and devotion – *bhakti* – with which it is offered. Similarly, no other qualifications of wealth, position, intelligence, knowledge or ritual are necessary. *Accept* here is literally "eat" in the Sanskrit. Zaehner described these verses as the "lower stages of loving-devotion"[48] but to take such a view is, I think, to strip the power of the word devotion, *bhakti*, which is a profound *loving*-devotion. Given the elaborate rituals normally associated with worship, the *Gita* is lifting the sense of worship to a whole new level. Complete surrender in devotion seems to be part of the secret mystery Krishna is divulging.

VERSE 27

Whatever you do, whatever you eat, whatever you offer in sacrifice, whatever you give, whatever *tapas* you practise, Kaunteya, do that as an offering to me.

As Chidbhavananda said here: "The panacea for all evils of earthly life is presented here. To change the secular into the sacred is the only way to metamorphose the human into the divine."[49] If all actions are undertaken while being totally focused on God then the ego will be lost. Any action undertaken for a result is *karmic*: even if it is a very good action geared to a very good result, the self is still thoroughly involved. Here, Krishna implies that it is selfless action that is needed, disinterested action that is *karma*-less because it is totally devoted to God. What is called for is a process of religionizing of the secular; penetrating through all the layers of *prakriti* to the ultimate Source. The same was said in 4:24: "Brahman will be attained only by him who is absorbed in action that is Brahman." Even *tapas*, "austerities", which are usually associated with *sannyasins* who devote themselves entirely to knowledge of ultimate Reality, are asked to practise their austerities with focus on Krishna. Devotion to a *nirguna* Brahman is difficult: devotion of the entire self – in every dimension of that self – to Brahman manifest as Krishna is a more realizable path and one that has more obvious, yet unsought for, rewards. In Eknath Easwaran's words: "If Arjuna can live in complete union with Krishna's will, doing everything for Krishna alone, then by that purity of will he will be free from selfish motives and thus released from *karma*. His spirit will be free, and he will attain his goal of mystic union with Krishna."[50] It is mark worthy that action, *karma*, is combined here with *bhakti*, a neat harmonizing of the paths of *karma-yoga* and *bhakti-yoga*.

VERSE 28

Thus you shall be liberated from good and evil fruits of the bonds of *karma*: with the self integrated in the *yoga* of renunciation you shall come to me, liberated.

When every action is offered to Krishna there is no thought of ego, of personal gain. *Karma* then becomes non-fruitive and the individual becomes free. Even good *karma* is lost, though it stems from the highest of the *gunas*, *sattva*. In the end, the *gunas* must be stilled for liberation, *moksha*, to occur: offering everything to Krishna purifies the self and stills these *gunas*. Renunciation of ego-orientated action, action for results, brings freedom, and this is what is meant by the *yoga of renunciation*, *sannyasa-yoga*. *Integrated* is *yukta* and the whole phrase *sannyasa-yoga-yukt'atma* sums up much of the qualitative teaching of the *Gita* – "the self integrated in the *yoga* of renunciation", and liberated (*mukta*).

VERSE 29

I am the same to all beings; none is hateful to me, none is dear. But whoever worships me with *bhakti* they are in me and also I am in them.

Brahman is in all things equally as the *Atman* and relates to all equally passively as the witness as verse 9 expressed, permitting the *karmic* laws of cause and effect to operate without partiality. His devotees, however, *feel* that presence because they are focused on, and devoted to, God. What Krishna is saying here is that he is uninvolved with all, unattached, and that is what the *yogin* should be. But there is already a strong contradictory hint in the verse that the devotee is especially dear to Krishna and later in the *Gita* we shall find this thought developed. The essential concepts of complete devotion of theism and a dualistic *relationship* between devotee and the divine are beginning to emerge but only those close to God will appreciate the reciprocal relation. The *same* (*sama*) *to all beings* also suggests no direct involvement of the divine in the cause–effect processes of *karma*. Again, there is no hint here that Krishna predetermines one life as different from another.

VERSE 30

Even if a really evil person worships me with exclusive devotion to none else, truly he should be regarded as righteous; indeed, he is rightly resolved.

This verse should be interpreted in the context of the last one and in the idea of God being the same in and to all things, like the sun that shines equally on the evil and the good. However evil something may appear, its innate element is divine and its source is divine. In its turn, contact with the divine serves to purify the nature, weaning individuals away from evil onto the right path. They become *righteous*, *sadhu*, a word that can mean "good" or "spiritually right". It is the right resolve that is necessary to change evil into good. The verse reiterates the need for devotion to Krishna and no other – exclusive devotion, *ananya-bhakti*, which was expressed in verse 22. There is a possibility that this verse and the next relate to those of "inferior birth" in verse 32, those in sinful birth because of past evil deeds. I do not think the verse implies impending *karmic* results can be overcome, only that devotion to Krishna sets up new and better causes for future, improved *karma*, but the verse shows the power of the path of devotion and, indeed, that it is the easiest path.

VERSE 31

Soon he becomes righteous and attains to eternal peace, Kaunteya: know that my devotee does not perish.

Following on from the previous verse, the *devotee*, the *bhakta*, loses wicked ways and becomes righteous. The word *soon* is optimistic and differs from the *Gita's* teachings elsewhere in 7:3, where it is claimed that even for the best of *yogins* few attain the goal. Verse 2 in the present chapter also spoke of the royal knowledge and mystery being "easy" to attain. We would expect the journey to be far greater for one who is evil, but Krishna seems to be saying here that once on the path of devotion, the goal of peace (*shanti*) for some can be realized quickly. This is perhaps one of the important messages of the *Gita*, that while other paths are certainly viable, alongside desireless actions, the path of devotion, *bhakti-marga*, to Krishna is easiest and is open to all.

VERSE 32

Indeed, Partha, those who take refuge in me, even those of an inferior birth – women, *Vaishyas* and also *Shudras* – they also attain the supreme goal.

Inferior birth here, *papa-yoni*, is actually quite strong, more like evil birth. The suggestion is that members of the two lowest classes and women have been so placed because of their sinful pasts.[51] Their *gunic* make-up lacking any *sattvic* component means that they are thought not to have the capacity to read the *Vedas*, so they are disqualified from such and from much religious ritual. It is clear from this verse of the *Gita*, however, that no one is barred from either the path to liberation or to liberation itself. Aurobindo commented here: "In the spiritual life all the external distinctions of which men make so much because they appeal with an oppressive force to the outward mind, cease before the equality of the divine Light and the wide omnipotence of an impartial Power."[52] Krishna, in fact, was a cowherd as a boy, in other words, was involved in the *Vaishya* profession of agriculture.

VERSE 33

How much more then holy *Brahmins* also devoted royal seers! Having obtained this impermanent, unhappy world, worship me.

If women, *Vaishyas* and *Shudras* can obtain the goal through *bhakti*, then how much more so can *Brahmins* and sage-kings. Both *Brahmins* and *Kshatriyas* like Arjuna are considered to be highly evolved and devoted to God, the *Brahmin* in a more passive lifestyle with *sattva–rajas gunas* and the *Kshatriya* in a more active sense with *rajas–sattva gunas*. These two classes are expected to transcend the impermanence of the world with its relative joys and sorrows. *Royal seers* are *raja-rishis*, enlightened rulers – the very best of *Kshatriyas*.

VERSE 34

Fill your mind with me, be devoted to me, sacrifice to me, bow down to me alone. Thus, having integrated the self, with me as the supreme goal, you shall come to me.

Integrated the self is the powerful expression denoting total integration of the self, *yukt'atma*, when the self is united and integrated with the inner Self that is the divine *Atman* that is Krishna and Brahman. For Ramanuja, this kind of total focus on the divine arises from the utter dependence of the devotee on God. His comments on this verse were extensive in describing the *saguna* God – "who am omniscient, whose will is unfailingly true, who am the only cause of the entire universe, who am the Supreme Brahman, who am the Supreme Person . . . who have long, shining eyes like a lotus petal; who am like a transparent blue cloud; whose dazzling lustre is like that of a thousand suns risen at the same time, who am the great ocean of the nectar of beauty . . ." and so on.[53] Such descriptors are far removed from Shankara's totally indescribable and *nirguna* Brahman.

So what is the *Royal Knowledge* and *Royal Mystery*. There are not two concepts here but one, two ways of saying the same thing – that Brahman at once exists in and does not exist in manifestation as verses 4–6 mysteriously explained, leaving us with the *saguna* and *nirguna* aspects of Brahman to explain the anomaly. But there is another aspect of the knowledge and mystery which is surely the heart of the chapter, and that is the direct pathway to God through total loving-devotion of the soul. There is certainly a coalescing of knowledge and devotion as a unitary path to God. Aurobindo described it thus: "This is the Gita's teaching of divine love and devotion, in which knowledge, works and the heart's longing become one in a supreme unification, a merging of all their divergences, an intertwining of all their threads, a high fusion, a wide identifying movement."[54] In other attractive words much in the spirit of the *Gita*, Sri Krishna Prem wrote: "No pen can ever write down this Secret, nor can any lips reveal it, but it is written in the inmost heart of man and has lain there through countless ages, awaiting the day when the disciple, tearing aside the veils of ignorance, perceives its blazing letters in his heart. There is no man, however mean or sinful, in whose heart it is not written, but few there are who read its life-giving words."[55]

In the *Upanishad* of the *Bhagavad Gita*, the knowledge of Brahman, the teaching of *Yoga* and the dialogue between Shri Krishna and Arjuna, this is the ninth chapter called
Raja-Vidya Raja-Guhya Yoga.

CHAPTER TEN

Vibhuti-Yoga
The Yoga of Manifestation

As the title of the chapter suggests, its content is concerned with the *vibhutis*, the divine glories or divine powers that are the manifestations of Brahman in all existence, especially in the sense of Brahman being the essence that underpins everything. Almost the whole of the chapter is devoted to this theme. Right from the beginning, Krishna is presented as the Source of all, the supreme Being, the highest Brahman, the merest fraction of which maintains the whole universe. The presence of the supreme Brahman as the essence that pervades the cosmos is reminiscent of Ramanuja's Vishishtadvaita, qualified non-dualism, especially his theory that the universe is the body of Brahman which makes devotion to a personal God and a thorough theism possible.

The Sanskrit term *vibhuti* has been variously translated and described. Putting it simply, Vimala Thakar said it "is the capacity, the faculty, the energy to permeate something which emanates out of you, though you retain your uniqueness and individuality at the same time. To be immanent and transcendent at the same time is called *vibhuti* in this chapter. It is a beautiful word."[1] It is, indeed, a beautiful and powerful word in that it encapsulates the ability of divinity to permeate all creation and yet transcend it, not be bound by it in any way, and remain inexplicably and indescribably greater than it. *Vibhuti*, then, has connotations of all-pervading power, what J. A. B. van Buitenen termed "ubiquity".[2] The *Yoga* of the title is not the general *Yoga* of the *Gita*. It is the *divine power*, that which makes the *vibhutis* possible. And yet, it is the practice of *yoga* in its general sense that permits some experience of the *Yoga* that is divine Power.

VERSE 1 The Lord said:
Once again, Mahabaho, listen to my supreme word, which I will declare to you who is delighted, wishing your well-being.

What Krishna is about to impart has been touched on in the seventh and ninth chapters. Arjuna is deemed ready to receive this teaching, this *supreme word*, for he has been delighted with all he has heard up until now and has clearly responded well. The theism in the verse is evident in the dual, personal relationship between devotee and God, between pupil and teacher. For *you who is delighted*, Robert Zaehner gave the alternative "you are beloved [to Me]"[3] and some turn this last around to "you who loves me".[4]

VERSE 2

Neither the hosts of *devas* nor the *maha-rishis* know my origin: I am in every way the Source of the *devas* and of the *maha-rishis*.

The divine Source can only ever be partially revealed, even to those who are completely enlightened. While 7:1 and 3 seemed to suggest that Krishna can be fully known, the ultimate Cause of all can never be known since it is still extant when the universe is not, so has no origin (*prabhava*), which is probably behind the thought of 7:26, which states the opposite. The verse, then, provides sound reasoning against the monism of such as Shankara and certainly a pantheistic view. And yet, this panentheistic relationship does not push the ultimate *nirguna* Brahman into total remoteness. In Aurobindo's words: "But at the same time the divine Transcendence is not a negation, nor is it an Absolute empty of all relation to the universe. All cosmic relations derive from this Supreme; all cosmic existences return to it and find in it alone their true and immeasurable existence."[5] Thus, *prabhava* is preferably read as *origin* in this verse, though with slight amendment it can mean "strength" or "Lordly power", as Shankara pointed out:[6] since the content of the chapter as a whole deals with the power of the divine to produce limitless manifestations, Lordly power is perhaps plausible. Yet the following verse expands on the idea of Krishna as the Source. Of the *maha-rishis*, "great seers", there are seven, though the seven are variously named. Bhrigu usually heads them, and the seven of them form the seven main stars of the astronomical Great Bear.

VERSE 3

Who knows me as unborn, beginningless and Great Lord of the Worlds, he among mortals is undeluded; he is liberated from all evils.

Only the liberated can know Brahman as *unborn* (*aja*) and as *beginningless* for this is something that can be "known" only at a deep intuitive level through realization, *vijnana*, and to one who is free from all *evil* (*papa*). It is such knowledge that puts *prakriti* in its true perspective and ends delusion. Yet again, *Great Lord of the Worlds* (*Loka-Maheshvara*) emphasizes the engagement of what is beginningless and the Source of all in what is created. Utterly transcending creation, the expression *Lord* nevertheless epitomizes the ongoing divine support. But since *everything* that comes into being will cease to be, the emphasis on *unborn* and *beginningless* seeks to demonstrate how different Krishna is from anything else.

VERSE 4

Intellect, knowledge, non-delusion, patience, truth, self-restraint, calmness, happiness, pain, becoming, non-being, fear and fearlessness as well . . .

Intellect is *buddhi* and *knowledge* or wisdom is *jnana*, two qualities we have heard much of earlier in describing the *yogin* or one who is *yukta*. Shankara explained *self-restraint* (*dama*) as outward control, and calmness (*shama*) as "the tranquillity of the inner sense".[7] *Becoming* (*bhava*) or being, and *non-being* (*abhava*) are arising and passing away, birth and death. It is worth noting that Krishna is the Source of dual possibilities like *happiness* (*sukha*) and *pain* or suffering (*duhkha*), which are *prakritic* qualities, but he is not involved in them.

VERSE 5

. . . non-injury, equanimity, contentment, austerity, beneficence, fame, ill-fame – these different kinds of natures of beings arise from me alone.

Non-injury is *ahimsa* and *austerity, tapas*. While *tapas* is mentioned widely in the *Gita*, *ahimsa* is not. Indeed, it could hardly be a major doctrine of the text considering the carnage about to take place on the battlefield. All the dispositions mentioned here are only a fraction of the manifestations of *karma*. But all these qualities emerge from Brahman as the Source. These *different kinds of natures* are here given as examples indicative that every possible quality or condition – whether that is positive or negative, good or evil, happy or sad – are all *vibhutis*, essences and potentials of reality. The divine essence is the energy that pervades all things, even if it is that which is evil. The energy itself, however, is neutral; it is not the energy that is good or evil.

Is this verse suggestive of all characteristics of humanity being predetermined? Is it suggesting there is no free will? In my view, the characteristics listed are *gunic* qualities, modes of being, all part of Brahman's lower *prakriti*. But we must, I think, hold firm to the earlier statements of the *Gita* in which Krishna says he has no part in agency, actions, cause and effect or evil and merit (5:14–15).

VERSE 6

The seven *maha-rishis* and the four ancient Manus also are of my natures, born from my mind; and from them all these creatures in the world.

Much of this chapter cites Krishna's *vibhutis* as characters that are mythological creatures and beings from legends, some of which hint at indigenous tribes and Indo-Aryan ancient lore. The names of the *seven maha-rishis* "great seers", tend to vary but, according to the *Mahabharata* are Marichi, Atri, Angiras, Pulaha, Kratu, Pulastya, and Vashishtha. Other texts furnish some of these and different others. They were the great teachers who were responsible for passing on the teaching of the *Veda* and were all great *Brahmins*. The word *rishi* is derived from the Sanskrit root *drs* "to see" and so the *rishis* were believed to "see" or cognize truth. Since they issue from the *mind* (*manas*) of Brahman, they are originators of divine knowledge. *Born from my mind* may mean their origin is Brahman or, since they are believed to be sons of the creator god Brahma and mind-born of him, Krishna may be referring to himself as the origin of both *rishis* and Brahma.

The reference to *four ancient Manus* is problematic in that there are really fourteen of them, not four. Gandhi got over the problem by translating: "The seven great seers, the ancient four, and the Manus too . . ."[8] Aurobindo saw the four as representing "the active nature of Godhead" as fourfold – "Knowledge, Power, Harmony and Work".[9] Franklin Edgerton suggested that the greater number of Manus is a later idea and, at the time of the *Gita*, only four were known, one for each of the world ages or *yugas*,[10] and this seems to me the most sensible view. The four are a *Vedic* concept of the original law-givers, those who, at the beginning of an age, carried the laws of the previous one for humanity, establishing the religious and sacrificial duties. As such, they were the progenitors of the human race and, like the *maha-rishis*, had their Source as Brahman and so were the link between humanity and the divine at the dawn of each *maha-yuga*, a period of 4,320,000 human years. Indeed, the name Manu means "man" and is connected with Sanskrit *man*, "to think", and *manas*, "mind". The seventh Manu, Vaivasnata, is the ruler of the present age and is reputed to be the author of the *Manu-Samhita*, the ancient *Laws of Manu*. It is the later *Puranas*, the books extolling the gods in which we find fourteen Manus as rulers of celestial planes.

VERSE 7

He who knows in truth these *vibhutis* and my *yogic* power truly becomes established in unshakeable *yoga*; there is no doubt.

This verse has to be linked with the preceding verses, which underline the fact that Brahman is the Source of all. He who sees all entities as miraculous manifestations, *vibhutis*, of Brahman can only be one *established in yoga*, one totally integrated within and therefore able to recognize the integrated unity of the cosmos with Brahman as its Source. These *vibhutis* are also divine attributes. Zaehner called such manifestations "far-flung power"[11] and van Buitenen preferred a translation "ubiquity". He wrote: "I find this rendering of *vibhuti* more helpful than 'power manifestation', etc. The root *bhu-* with preverb *vi* indicates a pervasive, ubiquitous display of appearances."[12] *My yogic power* refers to the divine power of manifestation as in the title of this chapter. *Unshakeable yoga* probably refers to the supreme state of human *yogic* practice and to the *yogin* who is integrated in the self, of whom we have already heard so much. Thus, the verse suggests that there is a link between the *yogic* power of Krishna and the *practice* of *yoga* by the *yogin* by which the divine is experienced. Further, *established, yujyate*, might also be "united", and the word is suggestive of such integrated unity between what is manifest and its Source as Brahman.

VERSE 8

I am the Source of all, from me everything evolves. Understanding this, the wise worship me full of affection.

The verse hints that devotion follows knowledge. Nothing can come into being that does not emanate from the divine Origin or Source (*prabhava*). Aurobindo's words are particularly apt here: "God does not create out of a void, out of a Nihil or out of an unsubstantial matrix of a dream. Out of himself he creates, in himself he becomes; all are in his being and all is of his being."[13] *Full of affection* expresses an intensity of focus on the divine and it is variously translated – "full-filled with warm affection",[14] "immersed in devotion",[15] "endowed with faith",[16] "filled full with love".[17]

VERSE 9

With their thoughts on me, with life-breath absorbed in me, enlightening each other and always speaking of me, they are satisfied and delighted.

The true worshipper is utterly devoted to God with the whole being, as *life-breath* (*prana*) suggests, and invites others to participate in this devotion. Thus, there is mutual communion about God, the kind of environment in which it is possible to evolve spiritually.

VERSE 10

To them, ever integrated, worshipping with love, I give the *yoga* of intellect, that by which they come to me.

Yoga of intellect or discipline of wisdom, *yoga* of understanding, is *buddhi-yoga*, the gift to those who are *integrated* (*yukta*). Zaehner translated it as "integration of the soul",[18] Shankara as "devotion of knowledge",[19] and Chidbhavananda as "Yoga of discrimination".[20] Those who are devoted to God will be granted that *buddhi-yoga* that draws them closer and closer to God in every way, until they reach the goal. But what is noticeable here is the harmonizing of *bhakti* with *jnana-yoga*, quite different from the harmonizing of *karma-yoga* and *jnana* in, say, 2:49. And if anything, the verse is suggestive that knowledge, the *yoga of intellect*, follows devotion. Ramanuja naturally understood the verse as indicative of *bhakti-yoga*: "To those who are constantly united (with Me), that is, who desire constant union with Me, and who are worshipping Me, I give with love that same mental condition (of *bhakti*) which has reached a ripened stage of development and by which they attain to Me."[21]

VERSE 11

Only out of compassion for them, existing within their selves, I destroy the darkness born of ignorance by the luminous lamp of knowledge.

Compassion, here, is pure compassion beyond human experience. Krishna says it is this divine compassion that causes him to exist within the self as the *atman*. A literal translation of the Sanskrit for *existing in the self* is probably something like "standing within my own nature", suggestive of Brahman being unchanged while the *vibhutis*, including the *atman*, are present. Many, however, translate, as I have in the verse, to suggest the divine presence in each self making the potential to dispel the *darkness born of ignorance* possible, such darkness being *tamas*, the inertia and stagnation of the *tamas guna*. But the choice between interpretations of *existing within their selves* (*selves* being singular in the Sanskrit) remains. Thus, Zaehner translated "[ever] in my own [true] nature / in the state of being peculiar to the self".[22] The *lamp* has caused many commentators to draw analogies with its components – the oil container with discrimination, the oil with pure *bhakti*, a pure flame with meditation, the wick with knowledge and the lamp niche with a free mind and heart. Shankara, for example, referred to this last as the "wind-sheltered enclosure of the mind which is withdrawn from the sense objects and untainted by attachment and aversion, and shining with the light of right knowledge generated by incessant practice of concentration and meditation".[23] *Knowledge* (*jnana*) refers to knowledge of God, and is juxtaposed with its lack in *ignorance* (*ajnana*). Ramanuja took such ignorance to be *karma* and addiction to objects of the senses,[24] which is probably an accurate interpretation.

VERSE 12   Arjuna said:
You are the supreme Brahman, the supreme Abode, the supreme Purifier, the eternal divine Purusha, the primeval God, the Unborn, the Omnipresent.
Supreme Brahman, *Para-Brahman*, here, is *nirguna* Brahman, unlike *apara-Brahman*, which is *saguna* Brahman or Ishvara, "Lord". By *supreme Abode* (*dhama*) is meant the Ground of all Being, the substratum of all that is manifest, and of the unmanifest phases of the cosmos. Arjuna, clearly, accepts Krishna not just as a divine descent, but as the *nirguna* Brahman. However, there is still a slight blurring of the distinction between the *saguna* and *nirguna* Brahman.

VERSE 13
All the *rishis* acclaimed you, also the *deva-rishi* Narada, Asita-Devala, Vyasa and even you yourself say it to me.
The *rishis*, "seers", having attained liberation, have the knowledge of ultimate Reality that comes through contemplative spiritual living. Less concerned with ritual, they cognized or perceived intuitively the truths of the universe. *Narada* is called a divine *rishi*, a *deva-rishi*, "divine seer", said to have been born from the creator god Brahma. He was known for his music since he was lord of the celestial musicians, the *Gandharvas*, and invented the lute.[25] He has close connections with Krishna in the *Mahabharata* and it is in this sense that he is included here, for he is an outstanding devotee. He is sufficiently great for several hymns of the *Rig Veda* to be ascribed to him and there are many stories about him in the *Puranas*. He is also featured in the *Atharva Veda*. *Asita-Devala* is likely to be one person though a number of commentators separate the names as indicative of two different people. Bibek Debroy seems to be clear that it is the name of one individual: "The same sage, who lived on the banks of the Saraswati river, is sometimes called Asita, sometimes Devala and sometimes Asita-Devala."[26] Hill, on the other hand, found Asita mentioned in the *Lalita Vistara* and Devala, son of Vishvamitra, in the *Vishnu Purana*.[27] *Vyasa* is the legendary author of the four *Vedas* and is therefore sometimes known as Vedavyasa. The *Vishnu Purana* mentions twenty-eight Vedavyasas who were said to be responsible for the arrangement of the *Vedas*: indeed, the name Vyasa means "Arranger" or "Editor". Vyasa is also popularly believed to be the author of the *Mahabharata* and of many *Puranas*, the books extolling the gods.

VERSE 14
I believe all this that you say to me is true, Keshava. Neither the *devas* nor the *Danavas* really know your manifestation, Lord.
Devas are gods and *Danavas* are the *Asuras* or anti-gods, sometimes translated as

"demons". *Lord, bhagavan*, is a title that contains six divine qualities – omnipotence (*bala*), righteousness (*dharma*), lordship (*aishvarya*), wealth (*sri*), wisdom and knowledge (*jnana*) and dispassion (*vairagya*). *Manifestation* is *vyakta* and could refer to Brahman as a descent, though given the content of the previous verses it could also refer to the manifest world.

VERSE 15

You alone know yourself by yourself, Purushottama, Source of beings, Lord of beings, God of gods, Ruler of the world.

The first part of the verse is difficult and variously translated but the sense is that Krishna is so inscrutable that only he himself is able to understand his ultimate own nature; no one else can. Again, this would contradict what was said in 7:1 and 3. Brahman is *Purushottama*, Supreme Purusha, because he is the Source and Lord of all *prakriti*. As such, when all the manifest world is drawn into the unmanifest state, only the supreme Purusha remains, so only the supreme Purusha can know Brahman as Self.

VERSE 16

Indeed, you should relate without reserve your divine Self-*vibhutis*, by which *vibhutis* you remain pervading these worlds.

The last phrase of the verse, *you remain pervading these worlds* is difficult, since the word translated here as *remain* (*tishthasi*) could equally well mean "exist in" or "subsist in". Murthy, for example, has "abide in".[28]

VERSE 17

How, by constant meditation shall I know you, Yogin? And in what aspects are you to be thought of by me, Lord?

Since it is difficult for the mind to contemplate ultimate divinity, Arjuna asks by what means, *aspects*, states of being or manifestations of the divine he can continue to understand Brahman. Arjuna calls Krishna *Yogin* because Krishna is the supreme *Yogin*, the one that can act with dispassion as the supreme observer who acts without involvement. And yet, despite the passive observance of Brahman, the whole of manifest existence owes its origin and continuation to Brahman. As this chapter unfolds, then, we shall see that the whole of existence represents the various aspects or states of being of the divine.

VERSE 18

Tell me again in detail of your power and your *vibhutis*, Janardana, for I am not yet contented in hearing such nectar.

Arjuna feels the pull, the magnetism of the divine presence here: the more he concentrates on God, the more he experiences the evolutionary drive to liberation. The title *Janardana* is, according to Shankara, a compound of *janas*, "people" (the *Asuras* or anti-gods) and *ardayati*, the verb "to go".[29] The name is, then, indicative of one who gets rid of, or causes to go, with the object being the forces in opposition to *moksha*. Thus, it may mean "Liberator of Men" as was seen in CHAPTER ONE. *Nectar* here is *amrita*, literally "not dead", *a* being the negative and *mar* the root "to die", and so *amrita* is the nectar of immortality. According to Hindu religious legend, the gods and demons churned the ocean in order to bring up such nectar of immortality. It was through one of the earliest *avataras* of Vishnu that this was made possible. In the process of churning, other things also emerged, some of which are mentioned later in this chapter. Many of the legendary figures and beings in the chapter became exclusively associated with Vishnu.

VERSE 19   The Lord said:
Very well, now, indeed, I shall declare to you my divine *vibhutis* according to their prominence, best of Kurus; of such details there is no end.

Since the divine is manifest in all things, there is no end to the manifestations of it: Krishna, here, says he will only give a sample of the main ones. In what follows, then, we have a list of his divine attributes, manifestations, glories – his *vibhutis*. "The world", wrote Radhakrishnan, "is a living whole, a vast interconnectedness, a cosmic harmony inspired and sustained by the One Supreme."[30] The following verse endorses such a view.

VERSE 20
I am the *Atman*, Gudakesha, existing in the hearts of all beings: I am also the beginning, the middle and the end of all beings.

One of the jewels in the *Gita*, this verse epitomizes the essence of much Hindu thought. Krishna begins to outline the manifestations of himself, his *vibhutis*, and the *atman* is pre-eminent. He is the essence, the Self, the vitalizing energy, of every being. The whole universe, in fact, is but the appearance or manifestation of Brahman. Brahman causes *prakriti*, sustains it and dissolves it, along with all the beings involved in it. Ramanuja lost no opportunity here to comment that the *atmans* in all beings constitute the body of God, which he can create, maintain and dissolve in the same way as the individual *atmans* are the rulers of their bodies.[31] It was an important verse for Ramanuja, who saw God as the Soul of all, and the Inner Ruler of each individual.

VERSE 21
Among the *Adityas*, I am Vishnu; among the luminaries, the radiant sun; I am Marichi of the *Maruts* and of the constellations, I am the moon.

The *Adityas*, the sons of the goddess Aditi (*a* "not" *diti* "limited"), are a group of *Vedic* celestial deities all owing their immediate existence to the sun: thus, they are golden. Their importance here is subtle because they are believed to personify all that is manifest. Originally about six in number, they later became twelve, one for each of the twelve months. Later, in verse 30, we have a reference to the *Daityas*. Aditi and Diti were two sisters who gave birth to the *Adityas* and *Daityas* respectively. The *Adityas* were devotees of God, but not the *Daityas*. Three of the *Adityas*, Indra, Surya and Vishnu, are the most prominent. Vishnu, of whom Krishna came to be accepted as an incarnation or descent, is the *Aditya* for January, being the *Aditya* that begins the path to the summer solstice and is thus a major one.

Surprisingly, this is the only occasion that Krishna actually says he is Vishnu, though CHAPTER ELEVEN implies the association throughout, and explicitly states it twice (11:24, 30). In addition, some of the names given to Vishnu are given to Krishna throughout the text. As was pointed out earlier, the *avatara* doctrine had not been fully developed when the *Gita* was composed, and other "descents" get no mention, not even Rama, the central character of the epic *Ramayana*, and who became an important *avatara*. The reference to Vishnu here is to a chief among the *Adityas* and not to Vishnu as supreme deity. In the *Gita*, we get the impression that Krishna is a direct descent of Brahman, not Vishnu. The *Maruts* are the sons of Rudra and are the gods of the storms and winds, the chief and most beneficial of whom is said to be Marichi, a word that means a particle of light. Rudra was a fierce old *Vedic* god; hence the *Maruts* were associated with storms and with Indra the god of thunder and rain. They, like Indra, were warriors, all brothers of identical age. The *constellations* are, more literally, the "lights of the night".

VERSE 22

Among the *Vedas*, I am the *Sama-Veda*; I am Vasava of the gods; among the senses, I am the mind; I am consciousness of living beings.

Sama Veda is the *Veda* of the chants that accompany religious ritual and known for their musical charm. These chants are the important sound in ritual and the means by which the priests reach the gods. One would have thought, however, that it would have been the *Rig Veda* that would have been prioritized here, given its focus on the Absolute. Debroy suggests that perhaps the chants are more relevant to *bhakti* than the *mantras* of the *Rig*.[32] However, at the beginning of the *Chandogya Upanishad*, the *Sama Veda* is described as the very essence of the *Rig Veda*. *Vasava* is one of the names of Indra, the lord of the gods. *The mind (manas)* is the sixth sense in much Indian thought and is that which synthesizes responses to stimuli, but has nothing to do with the *atman*. While *buddhi*, intellect, is superior to the mind, it is still matter, though it is not a sense (*indriya*). *Consciousness*, thought, is *chetana*, and a function of the mind. Consciousness is stimulated by sense perceptions unless it is absolutely still, like a rippleless lake, which is perhaps what Krishna is referring to here.

VERSE 23

And among the *Rudras*, I am Shankara; among the *Yakshas* and *Rakshasas*, I am Vittesha; among *Vasus*, I am Pavaka, and of mountains, I am Meru.

The *Rudras* are identified with the *Maruts*. Their name means "Red Ones" or "Howling Ones", and they were, like the *Maruts*, connected with storms, though they were later reduced to eleven and represented the eleven vital life-energies in each individual. In the early *Vedic* material, their chief was Rudra, who was depicted as a ruddy, swarthy man with a wild temper and the murderous temperament of a wild beast. He was the lord of thieves and shot arrows of death and disease at gods, men and cattle. He thus personified the dangerous and destructive elements of nature. While relatively unimportant in *Vedic* texts, he later became identified with the great God Shiva. *Shankara*, "Auspicious", here, is another name for Shiva; thus, Krishna is saying that he is also Shiva. *Vittesha* is Kubera, the god of wealth and a very old *Vedic* god. He is the leader of the demi-gods, the *Yakshas* and *Rakshasas*, who guard his wealth. Vittesha/Kubera is the deformed half-brother of the villain of the epic tale the *Ramayana*, who was the many-headed monster called Ravana. It was Ravana who abducted Sita, the wife of Rama, the seventh *avatara* of Vishnu. Krishna's *vibhutis*, then, extend to all aspects of the universe even to anti-gods and evil demons. The *Vasus*, whose name means "Bountiful" or "Good", were gods of the atmosphere, so they symbolized luminaries and elements. They were associated with the god Indra and were led by Agni, the god of fire. In the *Vedic* hymns, we find them being propitiated for good things. *Pavaka* is the *Vasu* mostly associated with fire. *Mount Meru* is the most sacred of mythical mountains. It is believed to stand in the middle of the world so that the heavenly bodies revolve around it. The gods, too, are thought to assemble and dwell there from time to time. The Ganges is said to fall from its summit before dividing into four.

VERSE 24
And of the household priests, Partha, know me as the chief Brihaspati; among generals, I am Skanda and among waters, I am the ocean.

Priests are mediators between God and humanity and so their role in religion is a crucial one. *Brihaspati*, "Lord of Prayer", is Indra's chief priest and so that of all the gods themselves. In the *Rig Veda*, he is called Brahmanaspati. He is also lord of Jupiter. The God Shiva had two sons, Ganesha and *Skanda* or Kartikeya, the latter being leader of the armies of the gods and the god of war, who led Shiva's heavenly armies to victory against demon forces. His mount is a peacock and he carries a bow and arrows.

VERSE 25
Among the *maha-rishis*, I am Bhrigu; of words, I am the one syllable. Among *yajnas*, I am the *yajna* of silent repetition; among unmoving things, the Himalayas.

At the beginning of the world system, Brahma, the creator god, created seven sons from his mind. These were the seven *rishis*, of whom *Bhrigu* was reputed to be the greatest. It is the *Vishnu Purana* that includes or adds Bhrigu to the seven given in the *Mahabharata*. The *one syllable*, *eka akshara*, is *Om*, the most sacred of all sounds that represents Brahman. The *yajna of silent repetition* is the *japa-yajna*, which is continuous silent repetition of the divine name. It is thus the simplest of all forms of *yajna* and one that can be carried out at any time and in any place. Mehta believed it requires a silent mind – "a totality of attention in the midst of repetition".[33] *Unmoving things* are not inanimate: vegetation, hills and mountains are considered to be living but unmoving.

VERSE 26

Among all trees, I am the *ashvattha* and among the divine *rishis*, I am Narada; of *Gandharvas*, I am Chitraratha and among *siddhas*, I am the sage Kapila.

The *ashvattha* is a wild tree of the fig family, sometimes equated with the *pipal* tree and the *bodhi* tree of Buddhism. It is considered to be very sacred, despite its bitter fruit. It is often included in morning worship in India and, indeed, is tall, beautiful and inspiring. *Rishis* are enlightened seers, as we have seen. There were different kinds of *rishis*. Some were royal *rishis*, some were priestly *rishis* like Bhrigu mentioned in the previous verse. Some were accorded the title *maha*, "great", some were *divine rishis* like *Narada*. He, too, is sometimes listed as one of the seven great *rishis*, and Arjuna has already noted him as outstanding in verse 13. The *Gandharvas* were the celestial musicians of the gods and could fly. Here, it is *Chitraratha* who is said to be their king and best singer that is mentioned. Chitraratha was also king of the *Apsaras*, the nymph-like creatures who were the mistresses of the *Gandharvas* and very much associated with water, mists and clouds. The *Gandharvas* themselves were often associated with water, too, having some connection with rain and with the intoxicating ritual drink, *soma*. They could take human form but were often conceived of as part animal or part bird and were rather feared. *Siddhas* are "perfected ones", those who have reached a high level of consciousness. *Kapila* was the foremost of these *sages* or *munis*. He is reputed to have founded the Sankhya system of philosophy and is sometimes thought to have been an incarnation of Vishnu.

VERSE 27

Among horses, know me as Ucchaihshravas, born of nectar; among princely elephants, Airavata; of men, the king.

In the story of the second *avatara* of Vishnu as a tortoise, the ocean of milk is churned by the *devas* and *Asuras* who form an alliance in order to obtain the *nectar*, the *amrita*, of immortality. But, apart from the nectar, all sorts of things also emerged during the churning of the ocean. One of these was *Ucchaihshravas*, "Long-eared" or "Loud-neighing", Indra's white horse, except for his black tail, and another, *Airavata*, Indra's four-tusked elephant. Both were the very best of their species. Monarchs were expected to be seers. While their *gunic* make-up was *rajas-sattva*, they were expected to have developed their *sattvic* natures to the point that they could be enlightened rulers. But it is interesting, again, that Krishna sees the king, the *Kshatriya*, not the priest, the *Brahmin*, as pre-eminent.

VERSE 28

Among weapons, I am the thunderbolt; of cows I am Kamadhuk and I am Kandarpa the progenitor. Among serpents, I am Vasuki.

The *thunderbolt* is the *vajra* owned by Indra. When Indra found it impossible to defeat an enemy it was necessary to create a weapon from the bones of a pure and perfect sage in order to do so. Indra found such a person in the sage Dadhichi, who willingly gave his life for such a righteous purpose. Allegorically, then, the *vajra* is a symbol of self-sacrifice for the purpose of righteousness. *Kamadhuk*, which we have already met in 3:10, is Surabhi, the heavenly cow and the first thing to appear from the churning of the ocean. She is the "Cow of Plenty" or "Cow of Desire", because she fulfils all desires in life: the first part of the name, *kama-* is the word for desire. *Kandarpa* is the beautiful and boy-like god of love, the Hindu Cupid, also known as Kamadev, a name that uses *kama-* to describe his nature. He is often accompanied by celestial nymphs while he rides on a parrot as his mount. He carries arrows whose tips are blossoms and have the function of affecting the senses. *Vasuki*, king of the serpents, was massive and poisonous. Nevertheless, he was used as a rope to churn the ocean of milk by rotating Mount Meru.

VERSE 29

Among the *Nagas*, I am Ananta; of water-dwellers, I am Varuna; of ancestors, I am Aryaman, and among governors, I am Yama.

The *Nagas* are snakes or serpents. They are associated with water and rain and are occasionally portrayed as human, at other times, half human and half snake, and sometimes wholly snake. *Ananta*, usually called Shesha, is many-headed, and is the favourite serpent of Vishnu who sleeps on Ananta at the close of a cosmic eon while the universe remains dissolved and unmanifest. Ananta was a brother of Vasuki in the previous verse, and their mother, Kadru, has a clear connection with the *Naga* tradition. Any attempt to divide Vasuki and Ananta into separate species, therefore, is not going to work. I fail to see any reason why the terms "snake" and "serpent" cannot be synonymous in these two verses. What is perhaps possible here is that the *Nagas*, of whom Ananta/Shesha is clearly one, became something of a separate legendary group, especially given their ability to take on human form. However, the legends surrounding snakes in Indian and Hindu thought are so intricate as to defy clear conclusions.

Varuna was a very important *Vedic* deity who was responsible for cosmic order. In time, he became known as lord of the water deities, sea monsters and sea dwellers. *Aryaman* was the first of the *ancestors*, fathers (*pitris* or *manes*), to die and so was king and god of the ancestors. *Yama*, "Controller", "Restrainer", is responsible for those who die and so is the lord of death. Legend has it that Yama and his sister Yami were the first humans. Since Yama was the first to go to the realm of the dead, he is pre-eminent amongst those who control, judge and govern that realm. His name is derived from *yam*, "to curb", hence the use of *yama*, "self-control", in *yoga*.

VERSE 30

Among the *Daityas*, I am Prahlada and among reckoners, I am time; of beasts, I am the lord of beasts and among birds, I am Vainateya.

The *Daityas* are descendants of Diti and are the demons and enemies of the gods. They are Titans, Giants, synonymous with *Asuras*. When the ocean was churned, they seized the cup of nectar of immortality from the gods and it was only through the intervention of Vishnu that the gods were able to retrieve it. *Prahlada* was the son of Hiranyakashipu, who was King of the *Daityas*. Although being born a

Daitya, Prahlada was a devotee of Vishnu, much to his father's great anger. When his father tried to have him killed, Prahlada's faith was sufficient to save his life. He became the epitome of a *bhakta*, a devotee. It was another of Vishnu's *avataras* in the form of half man and half lion that slew Prahlada's father. *Time (kala)* is the great reckoner that cannot fail, while *the lord of beasts* is the lion or the tiger. The divine Mother is usually depicted on a lion as her vehicle. *Vainateya* is the son of Vinata, the King of birds, and is also called Garuda or Garutmat. He is the eagle that is the vehicle of Vishnu, though is half man and half bird.

VERSE 31

Among purifiers, I am the wind; of wielders of weapons, I am Rama; among fish, I am Makara and of rivers, I am Jahnavi.

Although it would be true to say that all the elements purify, air, or *wind, pavana*, is perhaps that element that reaches everything. The god of the wind is known as Pavana or Vayu. *Wielders of weapons* are warriors, *Kshatriyas*, and Rama is singled out as the pre-eminent of these. The reference could be to Vishnu's seventh incarnation as the hero Rama in the *Ramayana* or it could be to his sixth incarnation as Parashu-Rama, Rama-with-the-axe. Given the stress on weapons in the verse, the latter is more likely to be the case. If the reference is to Rama the hero of the *Ramayana*, who was a major *avatara* of Vishnu, we might expect more emphasis here and elsewhere. Then, too, this is the only occasion when Rama is mentioned in the *Gita*, which rather suggests the *Ramayana* is unknown here,[34] though Hill thought it was Rama of the *Ramayana* to which the verse referred.[35] Many commentators translate *makara* as "shark", though "crocodile" is a respectable translation. As a mythical creature, it could probably be either. *Jahnavi* is the Ganga, the River Ganges, the most sacred of rivers. According to legend, the name Jahnavi, "Jahnu's daughter", is derived from that of a sage, Jahnu, who drank the Ganges dry after his devotions on its banks were interrupted. He later let the Ganges flow once more from his ear.

VERSE 32

Among creations, I am the beginning and the end and also the middle, Arjuna; among sciences, I am the knowledge of intrinsic *atman*, and among those who discuss, I am the reason.

Whatever exists is subject to time and transcience. Krishna says here, as he did in verse 20, that he is the beginning and end of all that comes to be as well as constituting what exists between those two states. The sense is that Krishna is also outside time. The science or *knowledge (vidya)* of the Self we have met before in the form of *Brahma-vidya*, knowledge of Brahman or *Atman* (9:2); it is the knowledge that brings liberation. Whether we translate science or knowledge here, Self-knowledge *(adhyatma-vidya)* is clearly the very best kind of knowledge. *Reason* is *vada*, which could mean reason or logic but is essentially that which determines what is true. Shankara saw *vada* as the main method of disputation in established kinds of argument.[36] There are three of these, supplying different ways of winning an argument, but since *vada* is the most objective approach it is deemed superior here. On the other hand, this is considered to be a modern translation and some commentators insist that the possessive cannot be abandoned here; thus, "the speech *of* those that speak" is possible.[37]

VERSE 33

Of syllables, I am the *A*; I am the *dvandva* among all compounds. Truly, I am everlasting time: I am the Dispenser, the all-facing.

The Sanskrit alphabet begins with the letter *A* and each consonant carries that letter unless indicated otherwise. Thus, *a* is the most frequently used vowel. The letter *A* is also the first sound of the *mantra Om*, sometimes, indeed, written as *Aum*. The universe is said to have begun by this sound manifestation emanating from *nirguna* Brahman. The *dvandva among all compounds* refers to the grammatical rule of *dvandva* in Sanskrit when two nouns of equal importance are brought together as a compound, like Rama and Krishna, Ramakrishna. It can, thus, refer to two things at the same time. *Dvandva* can also refer to opposites like light and dark, good and evil, happiness and sorrow, illustrating the nature of the term meaning "pair" or "the two". It is in this last sense that we have encountered it before in the *Gita*.[38] Brahman is equated with the eternity of all time in the verse that is to say, absolute time, *everlasting time (akshaya kala)* that is without beginning and without end. Brahman is also the supreme *Dispenser* in the sense of being Creator, Ordainer or Supporter of his manifestations into all the phenomena of the universe – thus he is the *all-facing*. The all-facing is an expression also used in 9:15, where its problems there may well be explained by its context here and the general content of this chapter describing the ubiquitous and omnipresent nature of the divine.

VERSE 34

And I am all-devouring death and the origin of all that is yet to be. And among the feminine, I am fame, fortune, speech, memory, intelligence, steadfastness and forbearance.

Once something is manifest, it is subject to *death*, and that which is responsible for its creation is also responsible for its destruction. But while the first part of the verse says that Krishna is responsible for death, all things yet to come owe their origin to him. *Feminine* refers to feminine nouns, all those listed in the verse being in the feminine gender in Sanskrit, though they are also feminine in their qualities, exemplifying the *shakti*, feminine force, and are the seven wives of Dharma.

VERSE 35

Also, of the *Samans*, I am Brihatsaman; of metres, I am the *Gayatri*; among months, I am Margashirsha and of seasons, the flowery season.

The *Samans* refer to the hymns of the *Sama Veda*, the ritual chants, some in the *brihati* metre, that were such an important part of *Vedic yajna*. All the *Vedic* hymns were composed according to certain metres, the most important of these being the *Gayatri* metre of twenty-four syllables. Different deities have their respective

Gayatri, such as the *Rudra Gayatri*, the *Brahma Gayatri*, and so on. There is also a sacred *Gayatri* verse in the *Rig Veda* (3:62:10), which is thought to be the heart of the *Vedas* and is chanted by twice-born Hindus at morning and evening worship. *Margashirsha*, an auspicious month, is the first month of the ancient Hindu calendar, according to Murthy.[39] Others make it the ninth month of the Indian lunar calendar, though all agree it is November/December (January).[40] It is harvest time and worship is specially significant at this time. The *flowery season*, *Kusumakara* in the Sanskrit, is Vasanta, the spring.

VERSE 36

I am the gambling of the fraudulent; I am the splendour of the splendid; I am victory; I am effort; I am the courage of the courageous.

Gambling was a favourite pastime in ancient India. Indeed, the Pandava brothers had lost their kingdom to the Kauravas through dice. But, since everything in existence has the essence of manifest Brahman, the skills and intelligence of the gambler have to be included as well. Brahman is the essence of what is intangible as well as the tangible. It does, however, seem odd that, since Krishna is listing the *best* of everything in the preceding verses, he chooses this particular example. For *courage of the courageous*, a meaning *sattva* of the good, or *sattva* of the *sattvic* is also possible, but the former is more in keeping with the content and tone of the rest of the verse and the way in which the word *sattva* is used in the Sanskrit (*sattvam sattvavatam*).[41]

VERSE 37

Among the Vrishnis, I am Vasudeva; of the Pandavas, Dhananjaya; also of the sages, I am Vyasa; of the poets, I am the poet Ushanas.

Krishna belonged to the *Vrishni* race or clan, one branch descending from Yadu and the Yadava clan. Krishna's father's name was Vasudeva, so he himself is sometimes called Vasudeva also. *Dhananjaya*, "Conqueror of Wealth", "Treasure-winning", is another name for Arjuna, given to him because he used the stored up treasures of many kings for good purposes, and has occurred a number of times already in the text. Arjuna and Krishna are close friends – indeed, so close that they were often referred to as the two Krishnas. This would be why Krishna does not refer to Yudhishthira here, the eldest of the Pandava brothers. Of the *sages*, *munis*, mentioned many times in the *Gita*, Vyasa stands out as the alleged author of the *Mahabharata*, much other literature, and even of the *Gita*. *Poets* or seers were *kavis*, wise ones, who were experienced in intuitive knowledge. *Ushanas Kavya* was a famous *rishi* who is mentioned a good deal in the *Rig Veda*. He is said to have made or bestowed power on Indra's *vajra*, his thunderbolt. Later, he was associated with the *Asuras* and the *Daityas*.

VERSE 38

Of punishers, I am the rod; I am the statesmanship of those who seek victory; and I am the silence of secrets; and among the knowers, I am the knowledge.

Again, we have the portrayal of Krishna as the essence of what is intangible. His *vibhutis* extend to the subtle aspects of the world, too. *Rod*, *danda*, can also be interpreted as "sceptre" as well as "stick" or "staff", but is likely to be the punishment meted out by a ruler; the sceptre would stand as a symbol of justice, the rod for punishment. The *silence of secrets* (*guhya*) and *of knowers, the knowledge* (*jnana*) may refer to knowledge of Brahman who, alone, is both ultimate silence and ultimate knowledge. On the other hand the knowledge referred to here may be simply the wisdom of those who really know. The whole of CHAPTER NINE dealt with the royal knowledge and royal mystery or secret, both of which amounted to the same thing, that Brahman is both manifest in all and yet transcends all.

VERSE 39

And whatever is the seed of all beings, Arjuna, that also I am: there is no being, moving or unmoving, that can exist without me.

Following on from the previous verse, and concluding this description of his *vibhutis*, Krishna says that he is the essence, the *seed* (*bija*) of all. Without this essence of Brahman, nothing can exist. As Shankara put it, "anything into which I have not entered would be without Self (could not exist) and would be void (*sunya*). Wherefore, everything is of my nature, i.e., I am the essence of everything."[42] This verse really encapsulates the message of the entire chapter that everything that exists has Krishna, Brahman, as its essence: God can be found anywhere and everywhere.

VERSE 40

There is no end to my divine *vibhutis*, Parantapa; indeed, this brief statement has been given by me of the range of my manifestation.

To know God, then, is to see God in all things but at the same time, the infinitude suggested by the verse suggests that no one can know entirely this ultimate infinitude. It is, then, a verse that has strong panentheistic overtones. *Range of* means examples of, extent of, illustrations of, instances of. Sri Krishna Prem wrote magnificently of this verse: "But all the spendours of the cosmic depths, their mind-annihilating magnitudes of time and space, symbol to all men of Eternal Law and Beauty, are but a moment of the *Mighty Atman*; infinities ranged on the shoulders of infinities; a wondrous hierarchy of living spiritual Powers where each is each and each is All and all dance forth in ecstasy the Cosmic Harmony. Vast beyond thought as is this spiritual realm, this flaming Cosmos of Divine Ideas, yet still beyond lies That, the One Eternal, the *Parabrahman*, Rootless Root of all."[43]

VERSE 41

Also, whatever being is manifest, prosperous or powerful, know that to be a *vibhuti* of only a fragment of my splendour.

Again, this is panentheistic: humankind, or, indeed, anything in existence, can only be a part (*amsha*) of God. The individual remains dualistically related to God and God is always greater, irrespective of how beautiful, powerful, glorious or god-like an entity may appear.

VERSE 42

But what need is there, Arjuna, to know all this? I exist, supporting all this world with a single fragment of myself.

The *Gita* ends on a thoroughly panentheistic note. Although everything is part of Brahman, the sum total of all those parts does not constitute Brahman, but merely a *single fragment* (*eka amsha*). Brahman is always beyond all that is manifest, and yet touches all that exists. The *Rig Veda* had a similar idea of a cosmic man, Purusha, the sacrifice of whom constituted just one quarter of the whole universe (*Rig Veda* 10:90:3, 4).

Thus ends the chapter with its illustrations of the *vibhutis*, the ways in which Krishna, Brahman, is manifest in the world. Nothing can exist without the divine essence, the infinitesimal spark that is but a fragment of total divinity. In Prem's excellent description: "From that *Eternal Brahman* issue forth the *Mighty Atman*, great beyond all thought, and all the countless starry worlds that fill the wide immensities of space. Yet so vast is Its spaceless, timeless grandeur that all these wondrous emanated worlds are as a drop taken from out the ocean, leaving Its shores being ever full."[44]

In the *Upanishad* of the *Bhagavad Gita*, the knowledge
of Brahman, the teaching of *Yoga* and the
dialogue between Shri Krishna and Arjuna,
this is the tenth chapter called
Vibhuti-Yoga.

CHAPTER ELEVEN

Vishva-Rupa Darshana Yoga

The *Yoga* of the Vision of the Universal Form

This chapter is always hailed as a very important one; it is regarded as the climax of the *Gita*, for in it, Arjuna is permitted to have a vision of the Universal or Cosmic Form of Krishna. The Universal Form, *vishva-rupa*, is a manifest, *saguna*, form that is twice (verses 24 and 30) referred to by Arjuna as Vishnu, of whom Krishna came to be accepted as an *avatara*. Krishna will show Arjuna that, while he may be manifest in human form, he has also, at the same time, a Cosmic Form that no one sees. Then, of course, as earlier chapters have stated, he is also the Unmanifest, *nirguna* Brahman. In this tremendous vision, all the multiplicity of forms in the universe converge into the one Universal Form. Through this experience, Arjuna realizes Krishna's true nature. He also comes to understand that the fate of the participants in the battle is already divinely ordained. Arjuna will see two forms of Krishna; first, as Lord, *Ishvara*, and then as the terrible universal aspect.

Nevertheless, Krishna's identification with Vishnu in this chapter, though made explicit twice, is not prominent in the *Gita*, and neither is the fully developed *avatara* doctrine. Indeed, the mention of Vishnu might be regarded as something of an anomaly in the context of the whole text.[1] Krishna does not refer to himself as Vishnu in this chapter, even if Arjuna does. Are these rare instances of additions, or are they early stages of identification of Krishna with Vishnu? Decisive answers are not possible. If Krishna were to be totally identified with Vishnu, we should expect it to be stated very explicitly here, not incidentally or implied. My inclination is to accept the text refers to Krishna as the Universal Form, with features associated with Vishnu, but with the total amalgamation of the features of the two yet to come. The abrupt change of tone and anti-climax that follows in CHAPTER TWELVE lead some to suggest that CHAPTER ELEVEN is a later insertion.[2] The change to a longer metre at times is more noticeable in this chapter, also suggesting to some that it is an addition to the text, though given its powerful nature and content, the change of metre may well have been deliberate.

In the previous chapter, Arjuna was presented with the extensions of the divine *vibhutis* out into the universe. In this chapter, he will witness the terrifying image of them all rushing into the divine, all returning to one. Rather aptly, then, Aurobindo called this chapter: "Time the Destroyer".[3] Much of the chapter is poetic, almost hymnal in character. Indeed, Gandhi said: "If we wish to learn true *bhakti*, we should know this chapter by heart. If we do so, we shall feel, when reciting it, that we are bathing in a sea of *bhakti*."[4] And yet, despite its fifty-five verses, commentary on the chapter is sparse in most volumes. In coming away from the *nirguna* Brahman, which is indescribable, I would have to say that much *less* can be said of the *saguna* Universal Form that Arjuna is about to see. Against what is usually said about this chapter, it seems to me remarkable that Arjuna should depart from the concept of Krishna as supreme Brahman to expression of Brahman in the *saguna* form of Vishnu. Be that as it may, Arjuna says in the opening verse that he has had all his delusion expelled and, therefore, one is left wondering why he might want to see the Universal Form and, even more so, why Krishna should fulfil his desire.

VERSE 1   Arjuna said:
Out of compassion for me, you have spoken of the highest secret, which is called *adhyatma*, and by that word my delusion has gone.

Arjuna says he is now free from *delusion* (*moha*). As a result of Krishna's words, his *secret* (*guhya*), Arjuna has come to know the intrinsic nature of his own self, *adhyatma*, the nature of the world as the manifestations of Brahman, the nature of *dharma* and the nature of the divine. Krishna has, hitherto, presented himself as the ultimate Source of all, which goes far beyond the concept of a manifest God, for he is, in fact, the ultimate Unmanifest as Brahman. *Adhyatma* we met at the end of CHAPTER SEVEN and the beginning of CHAPTER EIGHT, where it depicted the true Self as *atman*, the intrinsic essence of the self.

VERSE 2
Indeed, Lotus-Eyed, from you the origin and dissolution of beings have been heard in detail by me and also your imperishable greatness.

Origin and dissolution, referring to the creation and dissolution of the universe, could be read as "coming to be and passing away" in the narrower sense of life and death of contingent beings. I am taking it here as the former.

VERSE 3
As you have declared yourself to be, Parameshvara, thus it is: I desire to see your sovereign form, Purushottama.

Arjuna requests a vision of the form beyond the human one that he knows. This *sovereign* form is that of Krishna as *Ishvara*, "Lord", the omnipotent, omnipresent, infinite, omniscient form of God. *Parameshvara* is, therefore, the supreme Ishvara, the supreme Lord, and *Purushottama*, is the supreme Purusha. It is a *saguna* form that Arjuna is requesting to see: since the *nirguna* Brahman is beyond form and comprehension, it is Krishna as manifest God that Arjuna is asking to see.

VERSE 4
If, Lord, you think that it is possible for me to see this, then show me, Lord of *Yoga*, your imperishable Self.

Lord of Yoga is the title *Yogeshvara*, which Robert Zaehner translated as "Lord of creative power",[5] creative power defining the divine *Yoga* that is totally different from the general use of the term in the *Gita*. *Imperishable* here is *avyaya*, a term that has been used many times previously as a descriptor of Brahman, and Arjuna addresses Krishna as *Lord (prabhu)*, indicative of his awareness that Krishna's powers extend well beyond his human form.

VERSE 5   The Lord said:
Behold my forms, Partha, by hundreds and by thousands, of various kinds, divine, and of various colours and shapes.
Since all phenomena are manifestations of Brahman, there is no end to the diversity contained by the cosmic Brahman; yet all this is but a fraction of Brahman. Humankind only sees the microcosmic universe; Arjuna is about to perceive the macrocosmic one.

VERSE 6
Behold the *Adityas*, the *Vasus*, the *Rudras*, the *Ashvins* and also the *Maruts*. See many wonders never seen before, Bharata.
The *Adityas* and *Maruts* we have met in 10:21 and the *Rudras* in 10:23. The *Ashvins* are twin sons of the sun god, Vivasvat. Their name means "Horsemen" or "Horse Possessing" and they are a symbol of duality that acts in unity. They personified the first light of dawn, the transition between darkness and light, appearing in the sky as a golden carriage just before dawn. Their mother was in the form of a horse when she conceived the twins so they have horses' heads. They are eternally young with gifts of healing and restoring youth. Thus, they are divine physicians. They are ancient gods and feature in early *Vedic* hymns.

VERSE 7
Behold now, Gudakesha, this whole universe existing in one, with the moving and unmoving in my body, and whatever else you desire to see.
Existing in one and *in my body* suggest that all phenomena in the universe are united in the being of Ishvara and that whatever happens in life is also held in that being. Aurobindo saw this as "the keynote, the central significance. It is the vision of the One in the Many and the Many in the One."[6] It is, therefore, unnecessary and fruitless for Arjuna to be anxious about the outcome of the war, which is probably what is meant by *whatever else you desire to see*, for Arjuna will be able to see the outcome of the battle.

VERSE 8
But you cannot see me with these your own eyes: I give you the divine eye. Behold my sovereign *Yoga*.
Arjuna is granted the *divine eye* by Krishna, by which he will have the super-sensory spiritual vision that will give him knowledge of the immanent Ishvara. The same visionary ability was also given to Vyasa, the legendary author of the *Gita*, as well as to Sanjaya, who is narrating these events. As such, however, it is knowledge

of the manifested aspects of Ishvara that will be gained by Arjuna, not knowledge of the totally transcendent Reality that leads to liberation in unison with Brahman. Thus, the chapter is concerned with *vision*; it is involved with what is manifest, with *prakriti*.

VERSE 9   Sanjaya said:
Having thus spoken, O King, Hari, the Great Lord of *Yoga* then showed to Partha his supreme sovereign form.
We must remember that all this time, Sanjaya, himself having the gift of the divine eye that Arjuna is about to receive, is reporting events on the battlefield to Dhritarashtra. *Hari* means "red-yellow", "yellow", "reddish brown" or "tawny", the colours of the sun. Hari normally refers to Krishna as Vishnu, *Ishvara*, "Lord", and particularly, to Narayana, the personification of solar or cosmic energy. Narayana represents the divine essence in humans, God in humanity. It was particularly associated with Vishnu since he is the deity that takes human form. So, the form that Arjuna is about to see is that of the Lord, of Ishvara, termed here *Great Lord of Yoga* (*Maha-Yogeshvara*).

VERSE 10
With many mouths and eyes, with many wonderful sights, with many divine ornaments, with many divine weapons.
The verse begins the description of Krishna's divine Form, though *many wonderful sights* might extend the vision to the wider scene. However, the following verse suggests the description pertains only to Krishna. The *many mouths and eyes* are suggestive of being all-devouring and all-seeing.

VERSE 11
Wearing heavenly garlands and robes, anointed with divine perfumes, the all-wonderful, resplendent, endless, with faces on all sides.
With faces on all sides is reminiscent of 9:15 and 10:33, where Krishna describes himself as "the all-facing", in relation to his ubiquitous manifestations and omnipresence, literally, having faces turned in every direction, and so seeing and knowing everything.

VERSE 12
If a thousand suns were at once arisen in the sky, that splendour would be like the splendour of that Mahatma.
Mahatma, "Great Soul" (*maha* "great", *atman* "soul") refers to the Universal Form, the splendour of which is so great that nothing can compare with it, "Greater than an atomic explosion", as Parrinder described it.[7]

VERSE 13

There, in the body of the God of Gods, Pandava saw the whole universe, divided in many groups, existing as one.

The whole multiplicity of the universe, with all its diversity and variance, is ultimately one (*eka*); everything is an expression of Brahman. *Many groups* probably refers, as Shankara stated, to gods, ancestors, humans and other classes[8] such as animals, birds, vegetation and so on. Thus, Lars Martin Fosse translates as "united in its infinite diversity"[9] and van Buitenen as "in its infinite differentiation",[10] both of which capture the sense of the phrase with considerable credence.

VERSE 14

Then, filled with wonder, with hair standing on end, Dhananjaya, with joined palms, bowing his head, spoke to the God.

Sanjaya is able to see the same vision as Arjuna, here called *Dhananjaya*. Arjuna is seeing the Universal Form of Krishna, for the time being, splendid beyond comprehension. Arjuna adopts the hand gesture known as *anjali*, indicative of greeting and respect.

VERSE 15   Arjuna said:

O God, I see all the gods in your body, also all the hosts of various classes of beings; Brahma, the lord, seated on the lotus and all the *rishis* and divine serpents.

Parrinder described what follows in verses 15–20 as "the most tremendous vision in religious literature".[11] The style of the chapter changes at this point to a poetic long metre. Arjuna sees *Brahma*, the creator god, sitting on the *lotus* that traditionally rises out of Vishnu's navel – the event that marks the beginning of creation in each eon. In this scene, the whole of manifest existence is symbolized as coming forth from Brahma. The *various classes of beings* are as those in verse 13. Shankara understood *the lotus* to be "the centre of the Earth-Lotus" on Mount Meru.[12] *Rishis*, "seers", have already occurred a number of times. It is noticeable that Krishna is referred to as God by Arjuna in these last three verses, not as Vishnu.

VERSE 16

I see you on every side, of endless form, with manifold arms, stomachs, mouths and eyes. But I see no end, nor middle, nor beginning, Lord of the Universe, O Universal Form.

The myriads of variety in manifested existence are ultimately all manifestations of the *Lord of the Universe* (*Vishveshvara*), of which there is no origin, or end. Krishna is the Universal Form, the *vishva-rupa* of the title of this chapter. The *manifold arms* are indicative of power and Douglas Hill thought the stomachs were representative of "the storehouse of creatures at their dissolution".[13]

VERSE 17

I see you with crown, mace and discus, a mass of radiance shining everywhere, hard to look at, all around blazing like burning fire and sun,
immeasurable.

The scene is one of immense brilliance and is so dazzling that it is difficult to
see. This is divine light, and so magnified that it is as brilliant as a thousand suns,
according to verse 12. Vishnu normally carries in his four hands a mace, a discus, a
conch shell and a lotus, and so is implicitly mentioned in the verse.

VERSE 18

You are the Imperishable, the Supreme One to be known. You are the
great Abode of this universe, the imperishable protector of eternal
dharma; you are, I believe, the eternal Purusha.

Arjuna now understands the nature of Krishna in relation to the universe.
Zaehner took such understanding further, believing that *akshara, imperishable,*
refers to the highest Brahman, the Unmanifest beyond the Unmanifest,[14] but this
is highly unlikely given that we are dealing with the Universal *Form*, not the
formless. *Akshara* and *avyaya*, both meaning *imperishable*, are used to depict the
divine. *Abode* is in the sense of a resting place. The recognition of Ishvara as total
protector of eternal dharma is important for Arjuna, since it was questions about
dharma that he originally raised and that have been an important part of Krishna's
teaching.

VERSE 19

I see you without beginning, middle or end, infinite in power, of endless
arms; your eyes the sun and moon, your mouth flaming fire, with your
radiance heating this universe.

Since Ishvara is beyond time, he has no beginning, middle or end and creates
and dissolves the universe that *is* subject to time. *Mouth* is sometimes translated as
"face", though the many-mouthed form has already been witnessed in verse 10.
Heating is sometimes translated as scorching, burning up, since the vision that
Arjuna has is both of the marvellous and the terrible form of the divine. So, as
Aurobindo commented: "This Godhead embraces the worlds with His numberless
arms and destroys with His million hands."[15]

VERSE 20

Indeed, this interspace between Heaven and Earth and all the quarters
are filled by you alone. Having seen this your marvellous and terrible
form, the three worlds are trembling with fear, Mahatma.

In his Universal Form, Krishna is all-pervading, omnipresent in Heaven, in
the four points of the compass (*quarters*) on Earth, and in the middle space *between
Heaven and Earth* – a separate world in Hindu cosmogony. Ishvara has terrible
forms as much as wonderful. His terrible forms probably serve to put Arjuna's
anxieties about the impending battle more into perspective since they would be

instruments for overcoming evil. The *three worlds trembling with fear* is relevant only to the vision, not to events beyond it, in the same way that the deaths of the warriors will be portrayed in verses 26–7, whereas, in reality, they are lined up on the battlefield.

VERSE 21

Behold, these hosts of *suras* enter you; some in fear extol you with joined palms. Bands of *maha-rishis* and *siddhas* having said "May it be well", praise you with abundant hymns.

May it be well is Sanskrit *svasti*, which could also be Hail! or Homage! The word suggests that the "great *rishis*", the *maha-rishis*, and *siddhas*, "perfected ones", are those that respect Ishvara, regardless of how terrible his form: they understand that what takes place is for the good of the universe. Men such as Bhishma and Drona, though fighting for the other side, for the Kurus, will have entered the battle with such rationale in their minds. What will happen is part of the divine purpose; it cannot but be ultimately good. *Suras* is usually taken to mean "gods", *devas*. Shankara commented that they are divine beings "who have incarnated on Earth as human beings for lightening the earth's burdens".[16] It is as such that they will take part in the battle, but they, too, enter the Universal Form.

VERSE 22

The *Rudras* and *Adityas, Vasus, Sadhyas, Vishvas, Ashvins, Maruts, Ushmapas,* hosts of *Gandharvas, Yakshas, Asuras* and *siddhas* – all are looking at you astonished.

Most of these groups we have met before. *Sadhyas* are semi-divine ascetics and of a somewhat inferior nature to heavenly deities. They dwell in the world between Earth and Heaven and are connected with certain sacrificial rituals. *Vishvas* are *Vishvadevas*, the general term for a group of gods and the energies they personify. Sometimes called "All-gods", there are ten of them and they are said to be sons of Brahma. *Ushmapas* are a class of *pitris* or ancestors. The name means "steam-drinkers", or "heat drinkers", because they drink up the steam from hot offerings. *Yakshas* tend to pertain to specific localities since they are local spirits and inferior to the gods. *Asuras*, we have already met a number of times. They are anti-gods and demons, and the highest class of those who are not deities. They seem not to pester humankind so their role is mainly as antagonists to the gods. At one time, the term referred to prominent *Vedic* deities like Indra but, over time, took on a more negative meaning.

VERSE 23

Having seen your great form, with many mouths and eyes, Mahabaho, with many arms, thighs and feet, with many stomachs, fearful with many tusks, the worlds are terrified, and I also!

Arjuna is finding the vision frightening. He seems to imagine that the whole universe can see what he can at this moment when he says *the worlds are terrified,* though he could be speaking of the three worlds mentioned in verse 21. Here, it is Krishna not Arjuna who is called *Mahabaho*.

VERSE 24

Seeing you touching the sky, blazing in many colours, with mouths wide open, with large fiery eyes, truly, my inmost self is terrified and I find no courage, no peace, Vishnu.

Inmost self is difficult, since *antaratman* is really the inner Self that is the *atman* that is Brahman. Such, indeed, is how Zaehner understood the term,[17] but the true Self can hardly experience terror and lack of courage. "In my heart" would seem to me the sense of the term in this verse, for Arjuna's terror is so great that he is losing any bravery he has, and any possible sense of *peace* (*shanti*). One of the rare occasions in the *Gita* when Krishna is addressed as Vishnu occurs here, in this verse and later in this chapter in verse 30: the other is only 10:21, where it is less likely to be the deity from whom Krishna traditionally descends. When Arjuna addresses Krishna in this chapter, he more often uses the term Lord, Ishvara.

VERSE 25

Having seen your mouths fearful with tusks, blazing like *pralaya* fires, I know not the quarters, nor do I find refuge. Have mercy, Lord of gods, Abode of the universe.

Pralaya fires refer to the all-devouring fires that consume everything at the dissolution of the universe, fires at the end of time, though can also signify death. The *quarters* are East, West etc., and Arjuna is saying that he is so frightened that he is disorientated; he doesn't know his East from his West. Thus, Zaehner translated: "I cannot find my bearings,"[18] and Srinivasa Murthy, "I lose my sense of direction".[19] *Mercy*, here, is grace, *prasada*, which occurs again in verses 31 and 45.

VERSES 26–7

All these sons of Dhritarashtra, as well as the hosts of the kings of the Earth, Bhishma, Drona, also Sutaputra with our warrior chiefs, enter hurrying into your terrible-tusked mouths, fearful to look at. Some are found sticking in the gaps between the teeth, with their heads crushed to powder.

This terrifying image shows the result of the impending war. *Sutaputra* means "Son of a Charioteer", and refers to Arjuna's great enemy, the general Karna in the Kuru army. The fact that Arjuna speaks of Karna without giving his name, may well smack of a little contempt. Karna and Arjuna had the same mother, Kunti, to whom Karna was born before she married Pandu. Kunti abandoned Karna at a river, leaving him to be brought up by a charioteer and his wife; hence, Karna's name, Sutaputra. Since Pandu could not bring children into the world on pain of death, all the Pandavas, and Karna, were conceived by different divine fathers, and were all equally illegitimate, though all except Karna were accepted as sons of Pandu.

Arjuna sees the fate of the sons of Dhritarashtra in the mouth of the divine Form and the fate of great men like Bhishma and Drona: death awaits them.

VERSE 28

Truly, as many torrents of rivers flow faster towards the ocean, so these heroes in the world of men enter your flaming mouths.

Just as rivers cannot stop their flow towards the ocean, so all the participants in the battle to come cannot alter their own fate or the outcome of the battle, for all their plans and desires.

VERSE 29

As moths enter a blazing fire to destruction with quickened speed, so also worlds with quickened speed enter your mouths to destruction.

The image is more severe than the previous one: the rivers merged into the ocean, but the moths are utterly destroyed. The similes of the rivers and moths was beautifully translated by Rohit Mehta in a rendering that brings out very well the inevitability of the results of causes that are, in the end, human originated:

As river-floods impetuously rush,
Hurling their waters into ocean's lap,
So fling themselves into Thy flaming mouths,
In haste, these mighty men, these lords of earth.
As moths with quickened speed do headlong fly
Into a flaming light, to fall destroyed,
So also these, in haste precipitate,
Enter within Thy mouths destroyed to fall.[20]

The blind directions taken in life are so well brought out here by the choice of words – impetuously rush, hurling, fling themselves, in haste, with quickened speed, headlong fly, in haste precipitate. Such words, though not all in the Sanskrit, bring out the full nuances of meaning in the text. Sri Krishna Prem, too, wrote: "These selves of ours to which we cling so fiercely, are streams of psychic states linked each to each by changeless causal law; and all these streams wind through the fields of Time like rivers flowing swiftly to the sea."[21] Again, the inevitability of the results of causes quickens the speed to a temporary end. Thus, all the warriors lined up for battle are rushing to destruction as a result of their own natures.

VERSE 30

You lick on every side devouring all the worlds with flaming mouths. Your fierce rays are burning, filling the whole world with radiance, Vishnu.

Vishnu is the preserver who pervades the universe, holding it together as the centripetal force. It is usually the deity Shiva that is the centrifugal, dissolving force of the universe, but here Vishnu appears as the destroyer to Arjuna. *You lick on every side* probably means "you lick your lips", given that everything is disappearing into

Vishnu's mouths. *Filling the whole world with radiance*, may be meant in a destructive sense of burning up, causing a massive blaze, as in verse 19, though *tejas* is normally positively meant in the sense of splendour or even vigour. "God's radiance is both a light and a burning fire", wrote Eknath Easwaran.[22] Again, as in verse 24, Krishna is addressed as Vishnu, though Arjuna usually uses Ishvara or, as in the following verse, God.

VERSE 31

Tell me who you are, so fierce in form? I bow to you, Supreme God; have mercy. I wish to know you, the original Being; indeed, I do not know what you are doing.

Arjuna has had a vision of the divine Krishna in all his manifestations, the beautiful and the terrible and, despite his fear of the latter, he is asking about Krishna's purpose – *what you are doing* (literally, your "activity", *pravritti*) – as this terrifying being, Arjuna shows how terrifying he finds the experience by the statement *have mercy* (*prasada*), but he still wants to know the purpose behind the terrifying form. The fact that he really does want to know, despite his terror, is shown by Krishna's response in the next verse.

The problem of evil and pain in the world that arises from the idea of such beautiful and terrible forms prompted Aurobindo to lay the presence of evil a little too squarely at the feet of God:

> We have to look courageously in the face of the reality and see that it is God and none else who has made this world in his being and that so he has made it. The torment of the couch of pain and evil on which we are racked is his touch as much as happiness and sweetness and pleasure. The discords of the worlds are God's discords and it is only by accepting and proceeding through them that we can arrive at the greater concords of his supreme harmony, the summits and thrilled vastnesses of his transcendent and his cosmic Ananda.[23]

The *Gita* never suggests such a premise! Evil is removed from God by the cause–effect process that operates independently of divine intervention. The similes of the rivers and moths seem to suggest that it is the individual psyche that dictates what that individual's fate would be. And the complex processes of *dharma* are human orientated, not divinely manipulated. To reiterate what was said in the comments on 9:1, evil is that which binds the individual to fruitive *karma* in so far as it is the functioning of the ego in ignorance that prevents liberation. Verse 4 of the same chapter also finds Krishna saying that *all beings exist in me but I do not exist in them*, which is suggestive of the meaning of the present verse – everything is dependent on God, owes its existence to God, is a manifestation of God, but God is not *in* the *way* that manifestation in human form behaves: though he *is* the essence and provides the potential for evil as much as good – *the gambling of the fraudulent* in 10:36, for example. God is not the perpetrator of evil as far as I can see from the text of the *Gita*.

VERSE 32   The Lord said:
I am world-destroying time grown full, acting here to destroy the world. Even without you, all these warriors arrayed in hostile armies shall not live.

Krishna is *maha-kala*, great *time*, which swallows up all things, and to which all manifest existence past, present and future, is subject. Just as everything is seen as being swallowed by the terrible form, so time swallows every action, every thought, every era, and all things. Here, in this verse, however, *time* is death, and may not refer to the end of an eon and the total dissolution of the universe, but rather a concentrated, intensive destruction in terms of war, though the end of an eon, a *yuga* is accepted by most. "The time has come" might be an apt way of conveying the sense of the first sentence. The fate of warriors like Bhishma, Drona and Karna is already sealed; Arjuna's involvement in the war is immaterial. This is not in the sense of some predestined plan of Krishna's as much as the result first, of the complicated network of causes and effects, of *karma*, both individual and collective and, secondly, of the imbalance between *dharma* and *adharma*. The causes that have brought about these particular conditions in time have all been made; the results are inevitable and the warriors already dead. So *time grown full* is the fullness of time, time grown old, and the time is ripe to put an end to the imbalance between evil and good. The sons of Dhritarashtra can no longer be allowed to continue against *dharma*.

I do not think that this verse and the two that follow should be extended to be indicative of a total absence of freewill for each individual human. The will of God here is that which comes into play, for example, at the end of time, at the end of an age, and at this point, for the specific reason that evil has outweighed good. No, these are special times, and while Krishna has prescience of what is to happen and is cognizant of the events, to accept that humanity has no real choice at all and is simply an instrument of Krishna as some suggest[24] is to make the laws of cause and effect redundant, and evil to be wholly the responsibility of God.

VERSE 33
Therefore, stand up, obtain fame, conquer your enemies and enjoy the unrivalled kingdom. Truly, these have been slain by me already. Be a mere instrument, Savyasachin.

To be totally at one with the divine, it is necessary to become transparent to the divine will, a total implement or tool, rather like a tube through which the divine shines and operates. This, indeed, is what Krishna asks Arjuna to be, *a mere instrument*. But even should Arjuna refuse, the same events will take place. And if he *does* refuse, Arjuna also refuses to be the willing instrument of God: that is why he must follow his *dharma*. The *fame* mentioned in the verse is the fame of one who can stand against evil and uphold eternal *dharma*. Krishna calls Arjuna *Savyasachin*, which means one who can use his bow with the left hand as well as the right or, according to Ramanuja, it is one who can bring arrow *and* bow together with the left hand.[25] The word is used to remind Arjuna of his invincibility in war and the fame he already possesses. Such fame will be enhanced immensely when Arjuna conquers Bhishma and Drona in battle, two warriors whom even the gods, the *devas*, could not conquer. However, there is no real fame since it is Krishna, not Arjuna, who brings about defeat because *karmic* events have brought things to this point, and their consequences cannot be avoided.

VERSE 34

You kill Drona and Bhishma, Jayadratha and Karna and also other brave warriors, slain by me. Do not be distressed with fear, fight! You will conquer the enemies in battle.

Drona and *Bhishma* – great warriors and men that they are – are still subject to *dharma* and it is their *dharma* to die in the battle. Indeed, as Krishna says, they are already dead. Yet they are seemingly invincible. Drona, Arjuna's archery teacher, has divine weapons; Bhishma also has divine weapons and can only die by his own consent. *Jayadratha*, Dhritarashtra's son-in-law, the King of Sindhu, cannot be slain unless his slayer has lost his head, while Karna has a deadly weapon called *Sakti*, given to him by Indra. Despite all this invincibility, Krishna has shown Arjuna that they must die and that Arjuna merely functions as the implement in the process. Ramanuja believed that these men mentioned in the verse are to be slain, and are doomed by Krishna, because of their sins, though this is not the picture we normally have of Drona and Bhishma.[26] It is possible that they may have been criticized here because they failed to restrain Duryodhana.[27] *Do not be distressed with fear* is probably meant literally, given the reference to the great warriors, though it may refer to Arjuna's fears to kill close relatives and teachers, given his immense reputation for bravery.

VERSE 35   Sanjaya said:

Having heard that speech of Keshava, with joined palms, trembling, the crowned one, bowing down, again addressed Krishna in a choked voice, prostrating, overwhelmed with fear.

Here, Arjuna is called Kiriti, *the crowned one*, a name he bore because Indra had given him a crown. Though kingly, however, Arjuna bows down before God in all humility. Sanjaya is still witness to the contents of Arjuna's vision. He must hope that Dhritarashtra will change his mind while he is reporting the great theophany and the fate of his sons that it reveals. But the war is destined to take place and nothing can prevent it. *Choked voice* is sometimes translated as "stammering", but both are indicative of an immense shock following his vision.

VERSE 36   Arjuna said:

It is right, Hrishikesha, that the world is delighted and rejoices in your praise. The *Rakshasas* fly in fear to all quarters and all the hosts of *siddhas* bow [to you].

Although, ultimately, all entities are manifestations of God, those of high levels of consciousness – here, the *siddhas* as perfected beings – are devoted to him and less fearful than those of unevolved consciousness who, like the *Rakshasas*, flee in terror. Thus, we have the opposites of on the one hand those like the *Rakshasas* opposed to God – the evil and harsher aspects of life that move away from God – contrasted with, on the other hand, the good, epitomized by the *siddhas* who move towards him. The terms *fly* and *bow* in the verse are, therefore, neatly juxtaposed. Vimala Thakar's comment was most apt here: "The evil is in moving away from the source in awareness, and the good is homecoming, being aware of the unity, the wholeness."[28]

VERSE 37

And why should they not bow to you, Mahatma, the Primal Cause, greater even than Brahma; Infinite Being, Lord of gods, Abode of the universe, the Imperishable, the Being and the Non-Being, that which is supreme.

Zaehner took Brahma here to refer to Brahman, simply because Brahma has only been mentioned once before and Brahman increasingly frequently. He suggested at great length that Krishna is being portrayed here as the *Primal Cause* of Brahman and he went to considerable lengths to justify the idea of a highest Brahman beyond Brahman in this verse.[29] The usual acceptance is, however, the creator god Brahma – the masculine noun rather than the neuter Brahman. Yet the word *greater* is not without difficulty. A translation something like "greater than the primal cause, even Brahma", is possible, taking primal cause as the material cause that is Brahma (or Vishnu).[30] Arjuna continues by citing the supreme Non-Being, that is to say, the *nirguna* Brahman, and there is a sort of increasingly powerful portrayal of divinity in the verse. *Primal cause* may, then, be relative to Brahma or may stand alone as I have put it in the verse.[31] *Being* and *Non-Being* are *sat* and *asat* respectively, and refer to *saguna* and *nirguna* Brahman, also respectively. Thus, it seems that the verse is referring to the Unmanifest *Param-Atman*, the *Imperishable* (*Akshara*), behind the manifest not, as Zaehner preferred, an Unmanifest beyond the Unmanifest. The final expression *tat param yat*, then, I have translated *that which is supreme* rather than "what surpasses" both (*sat* and *asat*), as Zaehner, though many besides Zaehner prefer a translation as that which is beyond or higher than *sat* and *asat*. Shankara certainly suggested such,[32] as did Edgerton, who had: "Thou the imperishable existent and non-existent, and beyond both!"[33] Richard Gotshalk, too, understands the verse as indicative of Krishna "as the imperishable which is beyond being and not-being".[34] Such a translation would not do violence to the Sanskrit. However, I do not think we should take this any further than a reference to a *nirguna* Brahman as the Unmanifest that is beyond the manifest and unmanifest phases of the universe. Krishna is not beyond Brahman; he *is* Brahman.

VERSE 38

You are the primal God, the ancient Purusha. You are the supreme Abode of the universe. You are knower and that to be known, and the supreme Abode. The universe is pervaded by you, O Being of infinite forms.

The words *primal God, ancient Purusha* and *supreme Abode*, refer to the ultimate

Brahman that is the Source of all and that is the supreme Abode of all manifest existence when it is drawn into its unmanifest state during *pralaya* at the end of an eon. The Sanskrit *param nidhana*, "supreme Abode" has the sense of a resting place. As the cause of all, God knows all, but since everything is his manifestation, then all that is knowable is also God. The second reference to the *supreme Abode* is not quite the same as the first in Sanskrit. It is *param dhama* rather than *param nidhana* and Shankara suggested that it refers to the abode of Vishnu.[35] Zaehner translated the second reference as "highest home", comparable with highest Brahman.[36]

VERSE 39

You are Vayu, Yama, Agni, Varuna, the Moon, Prajapati and the Great-grandfather. Hail, hail to you a thousand times and again and again hail, hail to you!

Most of the names in this verse we have already met. *Vayu* is the god of the wind and is often found in the *Vedas* with Indra. Whereas he inhabits the air, *Agni*, the god of fire, belongs to the earth. *The Moon* is Shashanka ("hare-marked") in the Sanskrit, which also implies the moon god. *Prajapati* is the "Lord of Creatures", the progenitor of all beings and is sometimes synonymous with Brahma. However, the title "lord of creatures" is also used in the *Vedas* for Indra, certainly for Hiranyagarbha, who is also equated with Brahma, and for others. More specifically, the early concept of the sacrifice of a primal man, Purusha, out of which the world was created, was merged with the creator Hiranyagarbha and then with the creator god Brahma. All in all it is perhaps Brahma who is being referred to here as Prajapati, since Brahma has been referred to recently in Verse 37. It is Krishna himself who is the *Great-grandfather* in this verse, and Vishnu is traditionally the "father" of Brahma, the first living entity of the universe. *Hail* is *nama* as in the greeting *namaste*, "I bow to you" and thus means homage or salutations.

VERSE 40

Hail to you before, also to you behind, hail to you on every side even. O All! Infinite in power, infinite in strength, you pervade all and therefore are all.

Before, behind, and *on every side* refer to the omnipresence of God in the four quarters of the world. *O All!* is very significant here. Arjuna now recognizes the *vibhutis*, the manifestations of Krishna, as Brahman, that which is responsible for the whole universe. At the same time, Arjuna expresses and worships Krishna as in the previous verse with that word *hail* and cannot repeat it enough in order to show he understands who Krishna is. The Sanskrit *samapnosi* is usually translated in this verse as *pervade,* though Zaehner preferred "bring to their consummation",[37] since the word can also mean "to complete". In the view of Vishishtadvaita, *pervade all and therefore are all* would be an excellent statement of the manifest world and all selves being the body of God. *Power* and *strength* are almost synonymous in the Sanskrit. Thus, words like might, daring and valour, could also be used for either.

VERSES 41–42

Whatever was said by me rashly, from carelessness or even through love, regarding you as a friend – Hey Krishna! Hey Yadava! Hey friend! – thus not knowing your greatness . . .

And whatever way I have been irreverent for fun, while at play, resting, sitting or at meals, alone, Achyuta, or in company, that, Immeasurable One, I implore you to forgive.

Even if Arjuna knew Krishna to be divine in nature earlier, he now has come to understand the immensity of this *Immeasurable* (*aprameya*) *One* in all its manifest forms. Small wonder it is, then, that he thinks of all the moments in which he has laughed and joked with Krishna in what now seems to him a disrespectful and over-friendly way. *Yadava* refers to the ancient lineage of Krishna and means a descendant of Yadu.

VERSE 43

You are the Father of the world, of the moving and unmoving. You are to be revered by this [world], the greatest *Guru*, none is equal to you: whence in the three worlds is there another superior to you, O Being of unequalled greatness.

Arjuna now understands the manifest nature of divinity that is embodied in Krishna, the *greatest Guru*, that is to say, the Source of all knowledge.

VERSE 44

Therefore, I bow to you, prostrating my body, I implore your forgiveness, adorable Lord. Bear with me, O God, as father with son, as friend with friend, as lover to loved one.

The verse is full of devotional theism and adoration of the divine, the *Lord*, Ishvara, as well as the ability to relate to God. In later Vaishnavism, Krishna is, indeed, worshipped as father, friend and lover and, though not mentioned here, as a child. The Sanskrit *prasada*, usually translated "grace" is here, with most others, *forgiveness*, for the idea of forgiveness suits the statement *Bear with me*, literally "you should bear with me," rather well, just as a father's, friend's, lover's forgiveness is more apt than grace.

VERSE 45

I am delighted having seen what was never seen before but my mind is distressed with fear. Show me only that form, O God; have mercy Lord of gods, O Abode of the universe.

The reference to *that form* here is to the quieter form, the regal one that now stands in sharp contrast to the terrifying aspect. It was necessary for Arjuna to see that terrifying aspect so that he can engage in the war with the knowledge that *dharma* would run its course, for Krishna has determined that it should be so. But his mind (*manas*) cannot cope with any more.

VERSE 46

I desire to see you as before, crowned, bearing a mace, with a discus in the hand. Be that same form, having four arms, O Thousand-Armed, O Universal Form.

In the *Bhagavata Purana* we are told that Krishna occasionally revealed himself in the form of Vishnu to close devotees, though this text is much later than the *Gita*. However, the reference to the four-armed form is closely linked with Vishnu and in his four hands, Vishnu is normally depicted as holding a lotus, a crown, a mace and a discus. The reference to many arms symbolizes the might and power of such a divine form. Arjuna's request suggests that he is not yet wishing to see Krishna in his ordinary human form. However, it is the ordinary human form that Krishna will now proceed to adopt, though perhaps by way of himself first as the four-armed image that is normally associated with Vishnu.

VERSE 47   The Lord said:

By me, gracious to you, this supreme form has been shown, Arjuna, by my Self's *Yogic* power, full of splendour, universal, endless, primeval, which no other but you has ever seen before.

It is through having experience of this kind described in the verse that Arjuna is able to put his own problems in perspective. *My Self's Yogic power* is *atma-yoga*. *No other but you* is odd, given that Sanjaya is having the same vision since he is reporting it to Dhritarashtra.

VERSE 48

Neither by study of the *Vedas* nor by *yajna*, not by gifts, not by rituals, not by severe *tapas*, in such a form can I be seen in the world of men by anyone but you, great hero of the Kurus.

Shankara considered that study of the *Vedas* referred to the learning of the *Vedas* by rote as opposed to the acquisition of the inherent knowledge they provide,[38] though it is unlikely that the verse implies this, and there has been criticism earlier in the *Gita* of using the *Vedas* for results (2:45, 53). It is, again, surprising that there is intimation that the vision of the Universal Form is exclusive to Arjuna. Perhaps the solution lies in the lack of a divine eye *in the world of men*, but we still have to remember that Sanjaya, too, continues to have this divine eye. *Yajna*, "sacrifice", *dana*, "giving", and *tapas*, "austerity" will be taken up by Krishna in detail in the last chapter.

VERSE 49

Do not be afraid or in a state of bewilderment having seen this terrible form of mine. With fear dispelled, with gladdened heart, behold again this my form.

No qualification is placed on the word *form* in the Sanskrit, so Zaehner added [same, familiar] in parenthesis.[39] Shankara, like many, inserted "former" form, and adds that this would be Krishna four-armed, with conch, discus and mace,[40] just as

Arjuna had requested. However, subsequent verses suggest that Krishna reverts to his human, two-armed form.

VERSE 50   Sanjaya said:
So having spoken thus to Arjuna, Vasudeva showed his own form again and the *Mahatma*, having become of gentle form again, consoled him who was terrified.
Of gentle form suggests a very beautiful form.

VERSE 51   Arjuna said:
Having seen this human, gentle form of yours, Janardana, I am now composed and my consciousness restored to its own nature.
This verse and the remainder of the chapter continue in short metre, indicative that the vision is over.

VERSE 52   The Lord said:
It is very hard to see this form of mine which you have seen. The gods also are always desiring to see this form.
The *gods*, *devas*, are still subject to *karma* that is fruitive. They are where they are because of excessily good *karma* but, all the same, *karma*. Eventually, they must be reborn in human form if they wish to lose all *karma* and achieve liberation. Though regarded as superior to human beings, it is not inconceivable that a mortal can be superior to the gods as, here, Arjuna is presented as being.

VERSE 53
Not by the *Vedas*, not by *tapas*, not by giving and not by sacrifice can I be seen like this as you have seen me.
Inherent in the verse is the idea that the grace of God is necessary for an experience such as Arjuna has had, and grace is given by him only to those who are his true devotees, as the following verse shows. Again, *tapas*, "austerities", *giving*, *dana*, and *sacrifice*, *yajna* mentioned also in verse 48, will be taken up later in the *Gita*. Clearly, observance of *Vedic* ritual is, again, believed to be insufficient on the true path.

VERSE 54
By single-minded *bhakti*, I am indeed really able to be known and seen in this form, Arjuna, and to be entered into, Parantapa.
This is a powerfully theistic verse that Prem described admirably: "Only the power of love, the Soul's own power, love that for ever seeks to give itself, straining towards Eternity, can bring about the union of the self with the One Self by which alone the Cosmic Form is seen and ultimately entered."[41] *Single-minded* or exclusive, undistracted, unswerving devotion is *ananya-bhakti*. It represents the kind of absolute total devotion that involves surrendering of the ego and surrendering the entire being to God. The verse seems to suggest that such *ananya-bhakti* enables

Krishna to be known in his Ultimate Form, though *entered into* must surely be a later stage, for the Ultimate Form is unlikely to be the final goal as either *saguna* or *nirguna* Brahman. Entering into Krishna is meant in a dualistic sense of an intimate personal relationship: there is no hint of non-dualism. To be noted, however, is the combination of devotion and knowledge in the verse; though it seems, at this point, that devotion is the pre-requisite to knowledge. In commenting on this verse, Ramanuja included observation of the *Shastras* alongside exclusive devotion as the means by which Krishna could be known.[42] But Ramanuja added the words of the *Katha Upanishad* 2:23 and the *Mundaka Upanishad* 3:2.3. that God *chooses* to whom he will reveal his form.[43]

VERSE 55
He who does actions for me, who looks on me as the Supreme, who is devoted to me, is freed from attachment, is without enmity towards all creatures; he comes to me, Pandava.

Even Shankara justifiably described this verse as "the essential teaching of the whole Gita-sastra".[44] It is, indeed, a beautiful verse, profoundly theistic and one that would not be out of place in most religions. The verse sets the tone rather well for the chapter on loving-devotion, *bhakti*, which follows.

In the *Upanishad* of the *Bhagavad Gita*, in the knowledge of
Brahman, the teaching of *Yoga* and the dialogue between
Shri Krishna and Arjuna, this is the eleventh chapter called
Vishva-Rupa Darshana Yoga.

CHAPTER TWELVE

Bhakti-Yoga
The Yoga of Devotion

The great theophany of the last chapter closed on the theme of *bhakti* and this present chapter takes up that same theme. Robert Zaehner described the opening of this chapter as "one of the biggest anti-climaxes in literature".[1] Indeed, it does seem that Arjuna's opening question – whether those devoted to Krishna's personal form or those devoted to the imperishable Unmanifest are better versed in *yoga* – brings us to a more mundane level rather abruptly. It is a differentiation between the *nirguna* and the *saguna* Brahman that is at the heart of Arjuna's question. Both aspects are, in fact, unified in Krishna: as the focus of knowledge, *jnana*, he is the *nirguna* Unmanifest and yet, for the devotee, the *bhakta*, he is the *saguna*, manifest deity. Despite Zaehner's comment, the previous chapter was devoted entirely to the manifest aspect of Brahman and earlier chapters dealt with an Unmanifest, the *nirguna* Brahman. So, in a way, it is Arjuna's request to have sight of the Universal Form in CHAPTER ELEVEN that seems to me the anti-climax. Here, we are veering back to more important aspects of divinity. Since the Universal Form is not the ultimate goal to be reached, Arjuna's question is rather appropriate here. Nevertheless, no really new thought occurs in the chapter and many of the verses have their parallels in earlier chapters. The exception is the powerful emphasis on *bhakti*, devotion, indeed, *loving* and *reciprocal* devotion from devotee to God and God to devotee. *Bhakti* emerges as the major necessity, whatever the chosen pathway to God. Hitherto, the *Gita* has almost synthesized the more mystical teachings of *Vedanta* with its identity of the Self with a *nirguna* Brahman and with the *saguna* Brahman that is Krishna. Here, though both are one, it is the devotional love of Krishna that is preferred, and clear descriptions of the *bhakta* are given.

VERSE 1   Arjuna said:
Which of these are better versed in *yoga*, those ever-steadfast devotees who worship you thus, or those the Imperishable, Unmanifest?
The question asks which is better, to worship *saguna* or *nirguna* Brahman? It is a choice between *bhakti-yoga* and *jnana-yoga*, the paths of devotion and pure knowledge respectively. Zaehner considered that this verse follows on very neatly from 10:10, and that if we take out the theophany of CHAPTER TWELVE, there is better continuity.[2] Shankara, on the other hand, saw the *thus* in the verse as referring back to the final verse of the last chapter.[3] This seems to me the more sensible option.

Indeed, Arjuna's question in this present verse may well be posed as a response to the last two verses of CHAPTER ELEVEN, which speak vividly of *bhakti* in contrast to the emphasis on the Unmanifest in earlier chapters. *Worship* is used in the sense of "draw near to", "approach" or "attend on", so Arjuna's question is surely related to the *yoga* that concentrates on the *nirguna* Brahman or that which focuses on the personal. The *steadfast (yukta)* devotees *(bhaktas)* have a visible form on which to focus, something that is impossible in the case of what is Unmanifest *(Avyakta)*, the *Imperishable (Akshara)* and *nirguna* Brahman.

VERSE 2   The Lord said:
Those who, fixing the mind on me, ever steadfast, worship me, endowed with supreme *shraddha*, these I consider are the most steadfast.
Ever steadfast here is *nitya yukta*, "ever integrated" in the Self, and has been used many times to depict the true *yogin*. Here, it is linked with profound faith, *shraddha*. Krishna has already said earlier that all paths lead to the same goal, and in this verse the emphasis is not on which path is better, but which provides the basis of being more *steadfast (yukta)*: clearly, Krishna sees focus on, and faith in, him as the better method.

VERSE 3
But those who truly worship the Imperishable, the Indefinable, the Unmanifest, the Omnipresent, the Unthinkable, the Unchangeable, the Immovable, the Eternal . . .
This is a clear reference to the *nirguna* Brahman that is beyond *prakriti*. *Imperishable* is, again, *Akshara*, that which *is*, when the universe is not. It is the highest or supreme Brahman, the Unmanifest beyond the manifest or even unmanifest world – beyond all senses, beyond definition and relative to nothing that can be known and so *Unthinkable (achintya)*. *Unmanifest* is *avyakta*, again suggesting what is beyond the senses as *nirguna*, having no qualities as no-thing. *Unchangeable* is *kuta-stha*, a word that has already occurred in 6:8 and will be used again in 15:16. It has the nuance of meaning of being at the peak of a mountain or even of the head, with whatever understanding of such imagery the commentator prefers – "standing on the peak",[4] or "sublime on the mountaintop",[5] with connotations of "the highest". It is often translated as "Immovable" like the following word, *achala* where I have "Unchangeable", and, equally so, *achala* is sometimes translated as "Immovable", so both words are close in meaning. Presumably, by being on a mountain peak, one is not involved with events below, and so is unchanging. The verse contains very powerful descriptors of Brahman that use the negative – saying what Brahman is not, in order to push the mind beyond thought, beyond any possible conception. This is Reality without form in contrast to the Universal Form, the *vishva-rupa* of the previous chapter.

VERSE 4
... having restrained all the senses, even-minded everywhere, rejoicers in the welfare of all beings, they also obtain me.

The verse depicts the one who is *yukta* again, one who has total mastery of the senses (*indriyas*), and is integrated and free from desire and aversion. Thus, the *yukta* is *even-minded*, the Sanskrit referring to evenness (*sama*) of the *buddhi* rather than the mind, so involving the highest part of the inner self. While the one who is *yukta* is the same in sorrow and in joy, he is not passive in that there is concern for the *welfare of all*. Zaehner went to considerable lengths to show that Krishna equates himself with the Imperishable, *nirguna* Brahman in his comments on this verse,[6] though this is a fact that could hardly be disputed. What Zaehner went on to suggest, however, was "the realisation of the identity of the self-in-itself with the Imperishable Brahman *as a mere preliminary* [my italics] to the self's subsequent encounter with the personal God." Thus, Zaehner, as in earlier comments, placed the personal God as higher than the imperishable Brahman.[7] However, it seems to me that *they also obtain me* is not meant in the sense of the personal beyond the *nirguna* Brahman, but the *nirguna* Brahman who is *also* the personal God. It is worth noting that obtaining God with its implicit *jnana-yoga* in the first part of the verse, does not exclude action, *karma-yoga* in attention to *the welfare of all beings*.

VERSE 5
The toil is greater for those whose thoughts are set on the Unmanifest, for the goal of the Unmanifest is hard for the embodied to reach.

It is extremely *hard* (Skt *duhkha*, "pain") for anyone to attempt union with a formless, *nirguna* Brahman simply because one's whole life is involved with the world of forms and worldly *thoughts* (*chetas*) cannot be avoided. Being *embodied*, here meant simply in the sense of having a body (*deha*), places an immediate restraint on the ordinary self with its self-consciousness, its bodily needs, thoughts, emotions, psychological make-up, reactions to the environment, let alone its *karmic* residues from past lives. Even basic self-identification is a hindrance. Thus, it is almost impossible to focus attention entirely and exclusively on the *Unmanifest* (*avyakta*). Worship of a personal deity is inevitably easier for here thought forms are acceptable. Existence in the world of phenomena is necessarily involved with form, with empirical reality, with the physical and mental fact of bodily existence. Focusing on the *nirguna* Brahman necessitates transcending all such form – a difficult path to choose. Nevertheless, the goal is always the same, whatever the path. Krishna has already spoken of the path of knowledge and the path of devotion and faith, but having taken on physical form, Krishna himself is evidence that divinity need not be mystically elusive and totally remote. However, he does not deny that the path of knowledge of the *nirguna* Brahman is an invalid one, he only presents it as a more difficult one.

VERSES 6–7
But whoever worships me, renouncing all actions in me, regarding me as
supreme, meditating on me with single-minded *yoga* . . .
. . . for them whose thoughts are set on me, ere long, Partha, I become
the deliverer from the ocean of mortal *samsara*.

Release, liberation, is to be reached by those who give single-minded (*ananya*)
attention to God in every aspect of their lives. Thus, *renouncing (sannyasa) all actions
in me* involves total focus on, and devotion to, God. "To love God means to be free
from attachment to any work", said Gandhi.[8] The message is of exclusive devotion
to Krishna and the verse is intensely theistic, Krishna presenting himself as the
saviour or *deliverer* of his devotees. The *ocean* is often used as a metaphor of that which
needs to be crossed for liberation – passage from the worldly shore to the divine one
– so *mortal samsara* is the human round of redeath and rebirth that exists until the
other shore is reached. In the beauty of Rabindranath Tagore's words:

> I have met thee where the night touches the edge of the day; where the light star-
> tles the darkness into the dawn, and the waves carry the kiss of the one shore to the
> other. From the heart of the fathomless blue comes one golden call, and across the
> dusk of tears I try to gaze at thy face and know not for certain if thou art seen.[9]

Meditation, *dhyana*, is usually associated with the later stages of formal *yoga* and
the path of knowledge. The pathway to liberation in this verse is the easier one of
devotion to, and meditation on, the personal God, the manifestation of the impersonal Brahman, providing a focus for all internal *thoughts* (*chetas*) that precede
worship and action.

VERSE 8
Fix the mind on me only, place the intellect in me. Without doubt, you
will live in me alone hereafter.

Mind here is *manas* and *intellect* is *buddhi* and the following verse suggests it is
thought (*chitta*) that is meant. As Chidbhavananda pointed out in his commentary on this verse, people are where their minds are.[10] Life can be hell or heaven
depending on the focus of the mind, so if the mind is focused on God, then that
is where one will be. *Manas* and *buddhi*, then, are the whole power of the mind,
its whole purpose, thought, reason, the determining factor, and the very depth
that makes up an individual. The thought in the verse is epitomized by the words
in me. This is absorption of the whole being in God, and a combination of *bhakti*
and *jnana*, but continuing the thought of the previous verse with an emphasis on
bhakti-yoga.

VERSE 9
If you are not able to fix thought steadily in me, Dhananjaya, then seek
to reach me by the *yoga* of constant practice.

Verses 8–11 are usually taken as a kind of sliding scale of praxis – if you cannot do this, then do this – influenced, perhaps, by verse 12, which does impose a hierarchy on praxis. However, it may be that Krishna is simply offering alternative practices in verses 8–11, not suggesting that one is any better than another, but that if this does not suit you, then do this. The present verse, verse 9, therefore, may be advocating *abhyasa-yoga*, the *yoga of constant practice*, more like the path of *jnana*, without the focus on Krishna as in verse 8, but still, ultimately, reaching him. Shankara aptly defined *abhyasa* as "withdrawing thought from all quarters and fixing it again and again on one particular object",[11] and that object would not necessarily have to be God. Nevertheless, many want to suggest a decreasing scale of importance in approaching Krishna. Douglas Hill believed that constant practice is suggestive of intermittent practice – "again and again" rather than the superior "steady concentration" of the previous verse[12] and van Buitenen translated the second part of the verse as "still cherish the desire to reach me by repeated yoga".[13] As far as I can see, however, this verse is indicative of *jnana-yoga* in contrast to the previous one on *bhakti-yoga*.

VERSE 10

If you are not capable of constant practice, be intent on actions for me: by doing actions for me you will also attain perfection.

Since people are rarely able to turn their attention away from the world, the ability to focus attention entirely so that worldly thoughts are lost is limited. If this is the case, Krishna says, then the best course of action is to project God onto the worldly affairs in one's life. Life with all its variety still goes on but with a different perspective – a more God-focused one and *actions for me*, as Krishna puts it. Perhaps this means the maintenance and building of temples and Ramanuja's comments on this verse are another indication that he accepted temple worship as an expression of *bhakti*.[14] There is a vague possibility that *actions for me* refer to ritual actions,[15] but it is much more likely to refer to true *karma-yoga* by which all actions are undertaken not for the self, but for God. Thus, Shankara saw this as only one stage to liberation[16] though the verse actually mentions *perfection* (*siddhi*).

VERSE 11

If even this you are not able to do, then take refuge in my *Yoga*; self-controlled, renounce the fruits of all actions.

My Yoga, here, is surely the *Yoga* of the *Gita*, the *yoga* of renunciation (*tyaga*) of the *fruits of . . . actions* (*karma-phala*). It is such an important teaching in the *Gita* that it could hardly be considered as least important in a descending order of praxis. This is the path of action that does not incur fruitive *karma*, the path that does not renounce actions, but only the results of them, the *karma-yoga* of the *Gita*, with *self-control, yatatmavan*, that comes also with *jnana*. Such thought brings us back to earlier parts of the *Gita* that upheld action in inaction. Action should be undertaken in a state of equanimity for the intrinsic value of the action, not for the result it would give. The text states that this is *taking refuge in my Yoga*, a phrase that many translate as Shankara did, "refuged in devotion to me",[17] though my inclination is to see it more in terms of *karma-yoga* than *bhakti-yoga*, since renouncing all actions in God, would make the sense the same as the previous verse. Are these four means, then, representative of a descending order of capability or are they simply meant to be alternative paths – if this path does not suit you then try this? The complexities of the following verse suggest to me that the latter would be a sensible option, though it would have to be said that the Sanskrit portrays the idea of not being able, not being capable, rather than not being inclined to, but one might not be capable because of one's innate nature (*sva-bhava*), of which much is said in the *Gita*.

VERSE 12

Indeed, knowledge is better than constant practice, meditation is better than knowledge, renunciation of the fruits of action is better than meditation; from renunciation, peace is immediate.

Knowledge here is *jnana*, perhaps knowledge of the scriptures, rather than *vijnana*, the realization that brings liberation. *Constant practice* is *abhyasa* and *meditation* is *dhyana*. It is an odd verse that hardly fits the context logically or the *Gita* itself. It would seem sensible to accept the different practices in the previous four verses as different, acceptable means and here, *karma phala tyaga*, the *renunciation of the fruits of action* is clearly the superior path that leads to peace (*shanti*). Indeed, *karma-yoga* is the important path that Krishna advocated earlier for Arjuna (CHAPTER THREE). Zaehner made sense of the verse by putting God as the object of each action.[18] Thus, practice of *yoga* to God is inferior to knowledge of God, which is inferior to meditation/concentration on God, which is inferior to egoless action. This would accord well with the true *karma-yoga* of egoless action without desire for results that Krishna has hitherto recommended for Arjuna. On the other hand, Richard Gotshalk makes the point that practice, knowledge etc., are here mentioned singularly *lacking* any focus on the divine: devotion is clearly the point of this chapter so really all these paths are inferior without the ingredient of devotion.[19] Aurobindo dealt with the difficulties of the verse in the following way:

> *Abhyasa*, practice of a method, repetition of an effort and experience is a great and powerful thing; but better than this is knowledge, the successful and luminous turning of the thought to the Truth behind things. This thought knowledge too is excelled by a silent complete concentration on the Truth so that the consciousness shall eventually live in it and be always one with it. But more powerful still is the giving up of the fruit of one's works, because that immediately destroys all causes of disturbance and brings and preserves automatically an inner calm and peace, and calm and peace are the foundation on which all else becomes perfect and secure in possession by the tranquil spirit.[20]

This is perhaps a possible explanation of what is an odd verse, the relevance of which at this point is rather problematic. It should be noted, too, that non-fruitive actions are characteristic of the other paths besides *karma-yoga*. A glance at many of the previous verses indicates that Krishna speaks of himself as the focus of the mind (verse 2), as that to be obtained (verse 4), worshipped (verse 6), the object for renunciation of actions (verse 6), seeing him as Supreme (verse 6), meditating on him (verse 6), setting thought on him (verse 7), fixing the mind on him (verse 8), placing the intellect in him (verse 8), living in him (verse 8), reaching him through *yoga* (verse 9), doing actions for him (verse 10) taking refuge in his divine *Yoga* (verse 11) – all these focus on Krishna. This present verse has none of the focus of devotion to Krishna, so that none of these methods is acceptable. This seems to be what Hill was suggesting as a solution to this difficult verse.[21]

VERSE 13

Not hating any creature, friendly and also compassionate, without a sense of "I" and "mine", without egoism, the same in pleasure and pain, forbearing . . .

Compassionate here is *karuna*, one of the pillars of Buddhism, and notable, too, is the stress on loss of ego and of "I-ness" (*nir-ahankara*), a lack of self-centredness that is also typical of Buddhism. However, it is doubtful whether there is a conscious adopting of Buddhist precepts here as Zaehner suggested:[22] the thought in the verse is as much Hindu as Buddhist.[23] Being *the same* (*sama*) and maintaining equilibrium in all the dualities of life such as *pleasure* (*sukha*) and *pain* (*duhkha*) has been a constant message of the *Gita*.

VERSE 14

. . . contented, a *yogin* ever steady, self-controlled, firm in purpose, with mind and intellect dedicated to me. He who is my devotee is dear to me.

The inclusion here of *the yogin ever steady* is more reminiscent of the *jnana-yoga* of renunciation, though the last line retains the flavour of *bhakti* with its mention of *my devotee, mad-bhakta*. The words *dear to me* are expressive of the reciprocal love of God for his devotee and they will be repeated again in the verses that follow, though it must be said somewhat irreconcilably with Krishna's unattached and indifferent nature put forward in 9:9 and 29.

VERSE 15

He is dear to me by whom the world is not agitated and whom the world does not agitate, who is released from joy, envy, fear and anxiety.

The verse is reminiscent of *jnana-yoga* in that it emphasizes being detached from pain or sorrow and from happiness, in other words, it stresses the ability to be unaffected by the world and the dualities of life. However, it is in *karma-yoga* that an individual affects the world in a positive way with activity in the stillness of the inactivity of the *atman*, the latter informing the former. Yet again, the phrase *he is dear to me* retains the element of *bhakti*. *Released* or "liberated" is *mukta*, though here it may simply mean "freed".

VERSE 16

He who is free from wants, pure, skilled, unconcerned, untroubled, renouncing all undertakings, he who is my devotee, is dear to me.

Again, the first part of the verse reiterates earlier teachings of the *Gita* – here, the importance of lack of desire or aversion in order to promote egolessness and to ensure that there are no fruits of actions. Sense stimuli do not produce any reaction that will lead to *karmic* consequences. *Skilled* means "clever", "capable". *Renouncing all undertakings* does not mean total inactivity and inertia, but being selfless in undertakings, renouncing the results of actions and so simply doing what is necessary without thought of gain – non-fruitive *karma*; as Mehta put it: "To act but not to begin anything."[24] As such, the verse would blend *bhakti-yoga* with *karma-yoga*.

VERSE 17

He who does not rejoice, does not hate, does not grieve, does not desire, renouncing good and evil, he who is full of devotion, is dear to me.

The earlier idea of the *yogin* in a state of equilibrium, unaffected by joys or sorrows, desires or aversions is now joined with the loving-*devotion* of *bhakti*. Total devotion to God enables the devotee to maintain equanimity as much in those occasions that may involve grief as those of great happiness.

VERSES 18–19

The same to foe and friend, and also in honour and dishonour, the same in cold and heat, in pleasure and pain, free from attachment . . .
. . . to whom censure and praise are equal, silent, contented with anything, homeless, steady minded, full of devotion – that man is dear to me.

The individual described here is one with total equanimity (*sama*), like one at the centre of a circle, perfectly balanced between any points on its circumference – an individual who is neither this nor that. However, again, rather than stressing any identification with an impersonal Absolute, it is the intensely theistic, dualistic *relationship* between the *bhakta* and the personal God that is so important here. There is much in these last verses that is in common with 2:56–7 and 6:7–9. *Homeless* probably refers to a *sannyasin* and much here describes such an individual, but even the *sannyasin* has to be a *bhakta*.

VERSE 20

Truly, whoever follows this immortal *dharma*, as declared, endued with *shraddha*, regarding me as supreme, devotees – they are exceedingly dear to me.

Shraddha, "faith", we have met many times before and it is inextricably woven with *bhakti*. *Immortal* (*amrita*) *dharma* is the *sanatana-dharma*, the eternal *dharma*, and being in line with it is the goal of life for it is tantamount to giving oneself over entirely to the divine. On the other hand, the *amrita* of the phrase is literally "nectar" – a *dharma* of nectar. Indeed, Arjuna has already described Krishna's teaching as nectar in 10:18.

Whatever path is chosen – whether that is the difficult one of knowledge that leads to the Unmanifest, or focus on manifested divinity – the goal is the same. Those who strive with devotion and with faith are dear to Krishna. Even the great non-dualist, Shankara, accepted a devotional means on the path of knowledge. Rohit Mehta's comments here were particularly apt when he wrote that Shankara "found it necessary to express his deepest experiences in hymns that are surcharged with a devotional spirit of the profoundest nature. He scaled the Everest of Knowledge but stood there speechless with the complete surrender of a devotee."[25] If this were the case for one of the founders of Advaita, how much more so is it for the devoted *bhakta*.

In the *Upanishad* of the *Bhagavad Gita*, in the knowledge
of Brahman, the teaching of *Yoga* and the dialogue
between Shri Krishna and Arjuna, this is
the twelfth chapter called
Bhakti-Yoga.

CHAPTER THIRTEEN

Kshetra Kshetrajna Vibhaga Yoga

The *Yoga* of the Differentiation of the *Kshetra* and *Kshetrajna*

This chapter is perhaps the most difficult in the *Gita*. At the same time, it is a very important one. First, let us look at the Sanskrit terms in the title, terms that will be retained throughout the chapter. *Kshetra* is literally "that which is protected from perishing" but, here, it means "field" as in Kurukshetra, "Field of the Kurus", the place where this great battle is about to take place. *Kshetra* can also be used in the sense of matter, and there are times in the chapter when it refers to the body and times when it means whatever is derived from and constitutes *prakriti*. *Kshetrajna* adds *–jna* to *kshetra* and means "knower of the field". If used in relation to the body, this knower is the *purusha*, the pure consciousness of an individual that is synonymous in most cases with *atman* and so is the very essence of the individual and, as essence, is separate from matter. If used in relation to *prakriti* the *Kshetrajna* is the supreme Purusha, the *Param-Atman* that is Brahman.[1] Thus, the *kshetra* is the created order, the empirical world of unconscious matter: it is all *prakriti* including the human body. *Kshetrajna* is the pure, conscious spirit that is *purusha* and *atman*. Such a view accords well with the scheme of things in classical Sankhya.

Vibhaga means "differentiation", "discrimination", "division", "separation", so the chapter is concerned with the separation of spirit and matter: indeed, this is exactly how many entitle the chapter. Despite the obvious correlation with classical Sankhya, the *prakriti* and *purusha* of the *Gita* are not separate as in the Sankhya system, for both are united in Brahman. In terms of the individual, however, it is the *atman*, the individual *purusha*, which is specifically Brahman and the same as the *essence* that, though *in* all matter is not matter itself. It is in this sense that the spirit and matter, *purusha* and *prakriti*, are separate, whether soul and body or Brahman and the world.

Some manuscripts contain an initial verse that sees Arjuna asking to know the nature of *purusha*, *prakriti*, the *kshetra* and the *kshetrajna*:

> *Prakriti* and *purusha*, also the *kshetra* and *kshetrajna*, knowledge and what ought to be known, I wish to know, Keshava.

Most commentaries leave this verse unnumbered. While it serves to indicate what Krishna is about to speak of, and gives a certain expected structure to the verses that follow, some commentators omit it, as Shankara, for example, and it is highly likely to be a late addition to the text. Perhaps it is partly the expected structure of Krishna's response to this interpolated verse that brings commentators to criticize the structure of what is to come. Be that as it may, it is verse 3 that sets the order of the chapter, but even this verse does not account for the divergence of verses 7–11 that focus instead on the attributes necessary for the true *yogin*. Such is one difficulty in this complex chapter, while on a more philosophical level, it is not always clear whether *purusha* and *prakriti* are to be interpreted microcosmically as soul and body in the human being or macrocosmically as Brahman, the knower, the *Kshetrajna*, and *prakriti* as the manifest universe – all fields. However, the supreme Purusha as *Kshetrajna* is also the true Self that resides in the body that is the *kshetra*, the Self being the pure subject and the body being the object. Important to remember is that any aspects normally equated with the psychological self – intellect (*buddhi*), ego (*ahankara*) and mind (*manas*) – are all *matter* and so constitute the *kshetra* not the *kshetrajna*. And just as a field is sown to produce crops as a result, so we sow seeds by actions through involvement in the *prakritic* world, which must then reap *karmic* results.

The *yoga* of the differentiation between *kshetra* and *kshetrajna* must surely refer to *knowledge* of the difference between them, so knowledge is a key feature of the chapter. Such knowledge is repeatedly *jnana* in the text, and is not knowledge about something or knowledge that something is the case, it is not subjective knowledge. Rather, it is totally objective knowledge by a pure subject, much as Rohit Mehta put it when he said: "Now a true objective perception is that from which all subjective projections have been eliminated."[2] Such objective perception is a neutrality of perception, perception that is not entangled and involved, and to bring this about, one has to have knowledge of the field, the *kshetra* and the knower, the *kshetrajna*. These are not subject–object combined, but subject and object differentiated and separated, *vibhaga*. Thus, Ramanuja defined a *kshetrajna* as one who has knowledge that the body is different from the *atman*, the *kshetrajna* being the subject and the body, the object.[3]

VERSE I   The Lord said:
This body, Kaunteya, is called the *kshetra*, who knows it is called the *kshetrajna*; thus say those who know that.
The first proper verse of the chapter equates *kshetra* with the body. Shankara speculated that the body is called a field "because it is shielded from injury, or because it is destructible, or because it is liable to decay, or because the fruits of actions are reaped in it as in a field".[4] I am inclined to think it is meant in the sense of the endless field of all activity of thought, speech and action in which the embodied Self can become involved. Just as a field can yield good or bad produce according to its condition, so the individual, in the field of the body, reaps what is good or bad through the law of *karma* according to the condition of his or her *jivatman*, the being he or she has become. It is that *jivatman*, that individual self that has the appearance of being the "knower" of the matter, the body, which

serves it. However, the *true* knower, the true *kshetrajna*, is the pure *atman*, that which can differentiate between unchanging pure spirit that is Brahman, and the world of matter that is constantly changing through the *gunas* of *prakriti*. Body, *sharira* in the verse, is clearly the human body,[5] so we begin on the microcosmic level of the human being rather than the metaphysical, macrocosmic level of Brahman. The human body, just like all *prakriti*, is subject to change; it will be born, will develop and will die in these processes of change that characterize all phenomena whether living or inanimate. The *kshetrajna* as the *atman* is the unchanging element that permits consciousness and that is the same in all. In Radhakrishnan's words: "The human being is a union of the universal-infinite and the universal-particular. In his subjective aspects, he is not a part of a whole but is the potential whole."[6]

VERSE 2

And know me also as the **Kshetrajna** in all fields, Bharata. Knowledge of the *kshetra* and of the **Kshetrajna** is considered by me to be [true] knowledge.

Now the text moves to the macrocosmic level with Krishna referring to himself as the true knower, the *Kshetrajna* in all *kshetras*, that is to say, the *Atman* that is the true essence of all, the knower of all knowers and of whatever can be known. Each individual has the choice of identification with matter, *prakriti*, and the non-Self on the one hand, or with *kshetrajna*, the true Self, on the other. The former is a *jivatman* with its own personality, the latter is pure *atman* that exists in all entities and without which nothing can exist. Knowledge of this *atman* is true knowledge, the highest knowledge. The *vibhaga*, "differentiation", found in the title is related to this division of knowledge involved in matter on the one hand, and true knowledge that can see the separation of the Self from all matter on the other. This is not to say that true knowledge separates the knower *entirely* from the world of matter; rather, it puts matter into its correct perspective, permitting non-involved activity in it. But *know me* in the verse also means that Brahman is the supreme Knower, the supreme *Kshetrajna* and it is this fact that is the ultimate in knowledge for any devotee.

Given that *prakriti* is a manifestation of God, Ramanuja was not far off the mark in linking the *Kshetrajna* as God with the *kshetra* as *prakriti*. According to Ramanuja, both are God, both being different particularizations of God, both being the body of God. God is the *antaryamin*, the Inner Ruler of all *kshetrajnas* as their *atman*, so *kshetrajna* and *kshetra* are different but in relation with God because he is the *atman* of both.[7] Such relation, however, does not jeopardize distinction for Ramanuja: *kshetrajna* is the subject, *kshetra* the object and God, Lord of both.[8] God is the material cause of *prakriti*, its cause and its effect, but is greater than both. Ramanuja was at pains to say that while the world is the modifications of Brahman, no "transformation" of Brahman takes place to bring these about; he remains distinct.[9]

VERSE 3
Hear briefly from me what that *kshetra* is and what it is like, what its modifications are, whence is what, who he is and what his powers are.

He and *his* refer to the knower of the field, the *Kshetrajna* which, from the following verse, we can accept as Krishna. Since Krishna has referred to himself as such in the previous verse, also, *he* and *his* are unlikely to be the individual, human subject. *Kshetra* here, is clearly *prakriti*, because *its modifications* (*vikara*) are mentioned, while *powers* are indicative of origins, sources (*prabhava*). *Whence is what* is probably meant in the sense of the causes from which effects occur, as Shankara suggested.[10] It is this verse that should set the pattern for what follows – description of the *kshetra* and then of the *kshetrajna* – albeit that there seems to be an interlude containing the best kinds of knowledge or qualities.

VERSE 4
It has been sung in many ways by *rishis* in various distinctive chants and also in the *sutras* concerning Brahman, full of reasoning and conclusive.

Since the *rishis*, the "seers", are believed to have reached a perfected state, their *sutras* or aphorisms about Brahman are regarded as authoritative and sound. *Chants* here, *chandas*, are hymns or metres, so the reference is perhaps to the more mystical *Vedic* hymns composed by the great seers, though there must have been many loose collections of *sutras* on the nature of Brahman. A collection of such aphorisms known as the *Brahma-sutras* was compiled by Badarayana whose date is uncertain; anything from the last two centuries BCE to the first century CE is possible. He undertook a systematization of the philosophical teachings of the *Upanishads*, and many see this reference to the *sutras* of Brahman in this verse to be to Badarayana's work. Such a view would be rather dependent on the date of the *Gita* and a rather early date for the *Brahma-sutras*. More likely, the *sutras* on Brahman were extracts of sayings about Brahman from the *Vedanta*.[11]

VERSE 5
The great elements, egoism, intellect, the unmanifest, the ten senses and one, and the five objects of senses . . .

This verse picks up the "modifications" (*vikara*) mentioned in verse 3, the modifications in *prakriti* brought about by the three *gunas*. Thus we have the twenty-four evolutes of *prakriti* that have been outlined in the Sankhya system. The great elements, *maha-bhutas*, are the gross elements of air, fire, water, earth and ether. From these elements, the whole universe is composed. *Egoism* is *ahankara*, self-consciousness or I-ness. *Intellect* is *buddhi*, the discriminating and determining factor that gives rise to egoism but without *ego* is pure consciousness sometimes called *mahat-buddhi*. *Unmanifest* is *avyakta*, the state of equilibrium of the *gunas* when no modifications take place and the universe is withdrawn. It is from this unmanifest state of the universe that the first evolute of *prakriti*, *mahat-buddhi*, emerges. Since egoism emerges from intellect in the Sankhya scheme, the verse has reversed the generating order up to this point. The *ten senses* are the *indriyas*, the five sense organs of perception (*buddhindriyas*), hearing, feeling, seeing, tasting and smelling, and the five organs of action (*karmendriyas*), speaking (mouth), grasping (hands), walking (feet), excreting (anus), generating (genitals), and *the one* is the mind, *manas* which, as in Buddhism, is regarded as a sense. The *five objects of senses* are "realms" of the senses, the subtle elements – sound (which makes hearing possible), touch, form or colour (which is necessary for sight), taste and smell.[12] This categorization is clearly more in line with the twenty-four evolutes of classical Sankhya but the mention of the *kshetrajna's powers* in verse 3 may suggest that what we have here is meant in a more divine cosmic sense.

Verse 6
. . . desire, aversion, pleasure, pain, the body aggregate, consciousness, firmness, this *kshetra* with modifications has been briefly described.

Desire and *aversion* and especially *pleasure* (*sukha*) and *pain* (*duhkha*) are the dualities that inform the lives of every living being. They are opposites, pairs of opposites, *dvandva*, which themselves dictate behaviour and *karmic* merit and demerit. They underpin human behaviour in the Sankhya scheme of things, causing the entrapment of consciousness in the *prakritic* world. These dualities presented here are all modifications of *prakriti*, what Ramanuja described as *dharmas*.[13] From this point of the verse on, however, the description of the *kshetra* in terms of the modifications of *gunas* in *prakriti* begins to diverge from the concrete scheme into the manifest qualities necessary to avoid entrapment in the desires and aversions and pleasures and pains of the world. The *aggregate* (*sanghata*) is the composite whole of the body, mentally in terms of responses to sense impressions, as well as physically. On the other hand, Franklin Edgerton believes aggregate to be unlikely since it is not, like the other aspects mentioned in the verse, a quality. He preferred "association",[14] though he gave no indication as to what the association would be of, leaving the word unclear. Douglas Hill also preferred "association", though pointing out that *samghata* normally means "collection", here in this verse, an abstract noun, "the idea of combination, association",[15] which is really very close to aggregate of the body. I take aggregate to mean responses of body and mind to sense impressions, which would fit in with the other qualities in the verse. *Consciousness* or intelligence is *chetana*. It is consciousness and volition, what Chidbhavananda described as "the power to reveal and interpret".[16] *Firmness* (*dhriti*) can also be fortitude, steadfastness or, as Zaehner suggested, constancy or consistence.[17] All such qualities constitute the body, *kshetra*: none of them is permanent and each is an object of knowledge, even consciousness or intelligence, given that intellect, ego and mind are all matter in the Sankhya system.

Verse 7
Humility, unpretentiousness, non-violence, patience, uprightness, service to the teacher, purity, steadfastness, self-control . . .

Zaehner considered verses 7–25 to be an interpolation into the text, since we would expect an explanation of the *kshetrajna* now that the *kshetra* has been described.[18] Instead, we have a description in these verses of the right state of mind needed for knowledge of the *kshetrajna*, and we are back to parts of the *Gita* that depicted the *jnanin*, one who is *yukta* or the *yogin*. Perhaps the qualities depicted in this and the following verses serve as a bridge between the body and the spirit, object of knowledge and knower, *kshetra* and *kshetrajna*. What follows, then, are the means by which one becomes the true *kshetrajna* and the verses depict the right kinds of knowledge. *Non-violence*, *ahimsa*, is doing no harm to any living being. It is an important concept in Hinduism but, surprisingly, is hardly mentioned in the *Gita*, though given the context of the war and Arjuna's misgivings about it in CHAPTER ONE, perhaps stress on non-violence would have been seen as out of place to the author of the *Gita*. *Patience* (*kshanti*) is also close in meaning to forgiveness. *Service to* is devotion to a spiritual teacher, a *guru*, and to one who is already liberated and able to guide the devotee on the path to *moksha*.

VERSE 8

... detachment from sense objects and absence of egoism also, perception of the evils of birth, death, old age, sickness and pain ...

The thought here is similar to the Buddhist *Four Noble Truths* and the nature of all as impermanent, even the self. Attachment to anything that is impermanent can only result in evil and suffering. The verse is also reminiscent of the Buddha's visions of old age, sickness and death in his early search for enlightenment, and his discovery that all life is suffering (*duhkha*). The processes of life mentioned here are also transient and belong to the *kshetra*: the *kshetrajna* will need to transcend them. *Detachment* (*vairagya*) from *objects* of the *senses* (*indriyas*) is essential in order to disengage the self from worldly affairs and disengage that difficult commodity the ego (*ahankara*) from reaction to life's stimuli.

VERSE 9

... non-attachment, non-entanglement with son, wife, home and the like, and constant even-consciousness in the attainment of the desirable and undesirable ...

Non-entanglement is non-clinging to, non-involvement with, non-affection for, *non-attachment* (*asakta*) to family and possessions or, indeed, anything. It is "refusal to be wrapped up in" in Gandhi's words,[19] so that a certain distance from close relations and sense objects is always maintained. When attachment of the self to others occurs, happiness tends to be linked with their happiness and misery with their misery. In many subtle ways, each individual is therefore affected by someone else. Further, there is often a sense of ownership of others – spouse, children, for example – and the ego finds it difficult not to behave in a possessive way. Ultimately, the only thing one owns is personal *karma* and the only permanent aspect of the self is the *atman*. Seeing all things as *atman*, as manifestations of the divine essence, promotes the *even-consciousness* (*sama chitta*), the equanimity, to treat all things equally and dispassionately.

VERSE 10

. . . and unswerving devotion to me by single-minded *yoga*, resorting to solitary places, distaste for crowds . . .

Devotion here is *bhakti*. *Single-minded yoga* (*ananya yoga*) is sometimes translated as "*yoga* of non-separation", or "exclusive *yoga*", but here, it seems to me to be similar in idea to verse 12:6, indicative of *yoga* that is totally focused on God: unswerving *yoga* would also be possible. Taken in the context of the last verse, consciousness would be focused on God as opposed to family members and the home. *Crowds*, society or the company of others may refer to the mundane company of social life, given the tone of the previous two verses, or it may refer to the collective communities of those dedicated to God, but even this has to be abandoned eventually, as with the *sannyasin* in the final stage of life. However, though the typical solitary nature of the path of knowledge and *jnana-yoga* appears here, it is combined with *bhakti*, with loving-*devotion*.

VERSE 11

. . . constancy in knowledge of the intrinsic Self, perception of the end as knowledge of Truth. This is thus declared knowledge; what is opposed to it is ignorance.

Knowledge of the intrinsic Self, adhyatma-jnana, is knowledge of the Self, the *atman* – the *adhyatma* of the end of CHAPTER SEVEN and beginning of CHAPTER EIGHT – as opposed to knowledge of the non-self, the worldly self that is trapped in sensory involvement in the world of matter. It is the former that is necessary for liberation leading to the *end*, the goal of *Truth* – with all that that has meant in the *Gita*. Its opposite is ignorance, *ajnana*.

VERSE 12

I will describe that which has to be known, knowing which one attains immortality. That supreme Brahman, beginningless, is said to be neither *sat* nor *asat*.

Immortality is *amrita*, literally "nectar". *Sat*, as in 11:37 is "being", "existence", "manifestation" and represents the manifested aspects of Brahman – *saguna* Brahman. *Asat* is "non-being", "non-existence", "non-manifestation" and is the unmanifest state when no *gunas* are evident and the whole of *prakriti* is absorbed into an unmanifest potential. Beyond this is the Ultimate, the *nirguna* Brahman. Normally, *asat* would also refer to this ultimate, indescribable, *nirguna* Brahman but here, in this verse, Brahman is said to transcend both *sat* and *asat*. Presumably, then, *asat* refers here to non-being in the sense of the non-manifestation of the universe when latency and potentiality is all there is. Since it is Brahman that causes such latency to become manifest so that the world is created, Brahman is beyond both *sat*, manifestation, and *asat* the unmanifest (*avyakta*). On the other hand, the earlier verses of the chapter deal with objects of knowledge, conditions of the *kshetra*. In this case, *sat* and *asat* here may refer to existence and non-existence of objects of knowledge, like a pot that exists or does not exist. Such was the way

Shankara interpreted the verse.[20] The *Gita* here is faithful to mystical *Vedanta* in seeing Brahman as *neti neti*, "not this, not that" – totally transcending every possible duality including *sat* and *asat*. *Sat* is related to *prakriti* and the three *gunas*, whereas *asat* is non-*prakritic* and *guna*-less. But of the ultimate Brahman, there is nothing that can be said, not even to say that it is *asat*, for it is entirely beyond the mind. *Sat* and *asat* are dualities and at *moksha* all dualities cease to exist.[21] The knowledge of which Krishna speaks is *real* knowledge, knowledge of *Reality*, without which, as Aurobindo lucidly commented, the soul is lost:

> The soul, when it allows itself to be tyrannised over by the appearances of Nature, misses itself and goes whirling about in the cycle of the births and deaths of its bodies. There, passionately following without end the mutations of personality and its interests, it cannot draw back to the possession of its impersonal and unborn self-existence. To be able to do that is to find oneself and get back to one's true being, that which assumes these births but does not perish with the perishing of its forms. To enjoy the eternity to which birth and life are only outward circumstances, is the soul's true immortality and transcendence.[22]

VERSE 13
With hands and feet everywhere, with eyes, heads and mouths everywhere and ears everywhere, It exists in the world enveloping all.

The verse is identical to the *Shvetashvatara Upanishad* 3:16. As in this *Upanishad*, the point is made that not an atom can exist in the cosmos that is not dependent on Brahman. Eknath Easwaran reflected such a thought in his interesting translation here: "It dwells in all, in every mouth and eye and ear in the universe",[23] which is tantamount to what the verse is saying. Yet the verse is reminiscent of the description of the *vibhutis* of Krishna in CHAPTER NINE, as well as Arjuna's vision of Krishna as the Universal Form with many eyes, heads and mouths in CHAPTER ELEVEN.

VERSE 14
Having the appearance of the qualities of all the senses, yet devoid of senses; unattached, yet supporting all; *nirguna*, yet also experiencer of the *gunas*.

Diametrically juxtaposed in the verse is Brahman as the source of all and the supporter of all – the senses and the *gunas* – with Brahman as the passive Experiencer and true *Kshetrajna*, without senses, without attachments and *nirguna*. *All the senses* (*indriyas*) refers not only to the physical organs of sense and action but to the mental senses also. These are all facets of the *kshetra*. But *appearance of the qualities of all the senses*, where *qualities* is *gunas*, is a difficult phrase. Zaehner had: "Devoid of all the senses, It yet sheds light on all their qualities",[24] which is eminently sensible and similar to the thought in the *Shvetashvatara Upanishad* 3:17. I have tried to convey that though Brahman has the appearance of the qualities of the senses, it is really devoid of them. Some translate this difficult phrase as shining on or shedding light on the qualities of the senses. Aurobindo, for example used the idea of reflection:

> All relations of Soul and nature are circumstances in the eternity of Brahman; sense and quality, their reflectors and constituents, are this supreme Soul's devices for the presentation of the workings that his own energy in things constantly liberates into movement. He is himself beyond the limitation of the senses, sees all things but not with the physical eye, hears all things but not with the physical ear, is aware of all things but not with the limiting mind – which represents but cannot truly know.[25]

Brahman makes all possible but is unaffected by all, just as a screen makes possible the images imposed on it but is really separate. *Nirguna* here is indicative of that ultimate separation and Brahman devoid of all qualities – the true Absolute that is *neti neti*, "not this, not that", and so no thing.

VERSE 15

Outside and within beings, the unmoving and also the moving; because of its subtlety, THAT is incomprehensible, and THAT is far and near.

While I prefer to retain *THAT* or It, as indicative of the *Kshetrajna* when it refers to the *nirguna* Brahman, many have "he" and refer to "his subtlety" – usually those who stress worship of the *form* of God, such as Krishna.[26] But *THAT* in the verse is *tat*, as in the well-known *tat tvam asi*, "That art thou" of *Upanishadic* thought.[27] *Outside and within* probably refer to the body and its surroundings (outside) and to the *atman* (within). Similarly, *unmoving and also moving* may refer to the still *atman* contrasting with the world of constant motion as *prakriti*, both of which are informed by Brahman. There is a strong similarity with the *Isha Upanishad* 5, where Brahman is said to move and yet not move, to be far away and yet near (transcendent and yet immanent) to be within this whole world and yet outside it.

VERSE 16

Undivided, yet as if existing divided in beings. It is to be known as supporter of beings, yet devouring and generating.

Whether the cosmos is manifest (generated) or unmanifest (devoured), the *Kshetrajna*, Brahman, always exists. *Undivided* makes Brahman the One that is responsible for all manifested existence through creation, that which pervades and supports and unifies all creation in its manifest state and that brings about its dissolution, holding it latent until creation begins again. Even the still *atman* and the manifest being are in a sense undivided, both being the creation of Brahman. *Devouring* is reminiscent of verse 11:30, where Krishna is seen in the Universal Form, devouring worlds.

VERSE 17

Light of lights, THAT is said [to be] beyond darkness, knowledge, that which is to be known, the goal of knowledge, seated in the heart of all.

Light is not only meant literally but also figuratively as the light of the soul and the light of *sattva*. In the same way, *darkness, tamas*, is inertia, the dissolved universe, and ignorance that is opposite to *sattvic* enlightenment. Krishna is saying here that knowledge, *jnana*, what has to be known, and the goal of knowledge exist in the heart, in the deepest part of the self, the *atman*. It is the inactive *atman* that is the light by which any knowledge can take place and that no darkness can conceal. *Seated in the heart of all* is true knowledge of Brahman that is also the goal and the ultimate objective knowledge: the incomprehensible or unknowable of verse 15 is knowable as *atman*. Since this is pure subject and pure spirit, it is presumably the *kshetrajna* as *atman*. Aurobindo commented here: "This eternal Light is in the heart of every being; it is he who is the secret knower of the field, *ksetrajna*, and presides as the Lord in the heart of things over this province and over all these kingdoms of his manifested becoming and action."[28] The verse has many similarities with some of the *Upanishads*.[29]

VERSE 18
Thus, the *kshetra* as well as knowledge and the knowable have been briefly described. My devotee, knowing this, enters into my being.

While the *kshetra* was dealt with explicitly in the earlier verses, the previous verses have dealt implicitly with the *kshetrajna*, the implicit nature being encompassed here in the words *as well as*. This is suggestive that *the knowable* of verses 12–17 is meant ultimately here, knowledge of Brahman, not knowledge of *prakriti* as the *kshetra*. Entering the being of Krishna is meant in a dualistic, theistic sense, since the expression *mad-bhakta, my devotee*, stresses the dualism of a personal relationship with the divine. *Enters* is meant in the sense of attains to, the important goal being *my being, mad-bhava*.

VERSE 19
Know that *prakriti* as well as Purusha are both beginningless: and know also that modifications and *gunas* are born of *prakriti*.

Here, *kshetra and Kshetrajna* are *prakriti* and Purusha/Brahman respectively. We are not used to *prakriti*, manifest existence, being depicted as beginningless, which has such a strong hint of imperishability about it. What is meant here, however, is probably the inseparability of the two, *prakriti* being the emanation of Purusha. Thus, two apparent dualities are ultimately united as one, but Purusha is considered as superior and *prakriti* as inferior. This is unorthodox Sankhya metaphysics in that the *Gita* does not accept separation of Purusha and *prakriti*, though Purusha always causes the evolution of *prakriti*. In classical Sankhya, there is no First Cause: *prakriti* is an eternally evolving/dissolving entity and so beginningless. The same idea is presented here, but not the totally separate nature of Purusha. *Modifications* (*vikara*) mean change, characteristic of all manifest phenomena but with Purusha and *prakriti* as different aspects of a single ultimate Reality that ever continues. In all such change, all modifications, there can be no permanence; anything subject to change is matter, but while phenomena are subject to birth and death and inherent change, the *prakritic process* of manifestation and dissolution is without beginning or end.

VERSE 20

Prakriti is said to be the cause of generation of cause, effect and agency.
Purusha is said to be the cause in experience of pleasure and pain.

Prakriti is the cause of all processes, production or instrumentality that bring about cause (*hetu*) and effect (*karya*) and all processes of activity. This is certainly the view of Sankhya proper and the Sankhya of the *Gita*. At first, the sense seems to be difficult in that *purusha*, pure spirit, is said to be the experiencer of pleasure and pain. The difficulty, it seems to me, is overcome, providing the verse is interpreted in the light of the more classical views of Sankhya. That *prakriti* is the immediate cause of all manifest existence, and of the body and the senses is clear from both the Sankhya of the *Gita* and classical Sankhya. But what of the statement that *purusha* is the *cause in experience of pleasure and pain*? In classical Sankhya, *purusha* as pure spirit is totally separate from all *prakriti* but it becomes entangled through "proximity" in the functioning of the *buddhi*, intellect, *ahankara*, ego and *manas*, mind, and mistakenly believes that it is the agent in all activity, the instigator of thought and the experiencer of all *prakriti*. Thus, the *purusha* "lends" its spirit to matter and so becomes the "cause" of the experience. Matter, of course, can never experience anything.

In Sankhya terms, this is fairly straightforward except that it is always difficult to see why the separate *purusha* should be in any way involved with *prakriti* in the first place. In the Sankhya of the *Gita*, the same separation is not so evident since Brahman is manifest in all *prakriti* as the *atman*, and the previous verse has already expressed that both *atman/purusha* and *prakriti* are different aspects of the same ultimate Reality. But similar to classical Sankhya, the *atman* is the passive witness, lending functioning to a *buddhi*, ego and mind, and in that sense is the cause of experience: again, matter cannot experience, only spirit. *Prakriti* is the cause of the body as matter and is at the same time an effect: both are *kshetra*, while *purusha* is the *kshetrajna*. Nothing in the verse indicates whether *purusha* is to be accepted as the Purusha that is Brahman or the individual *purusha*: the latter is certainly the better option and is the subject of the following verse, so is contextually supported. Shankara, indeed, took *purusha* here to be the individual *jiva*.[30] We have to remember that the *Gita*'s philosophy is a dualistic and a theistic one. That is to say, there must be some aspect that experiences the divine. The *atman* or *purusha* that makes this possible is at once part of total divinity and the pure *subjective* experiencer of it: alternatively, it can give its attention to the world of pleasures or happiness (*sukha*) and pains or sorrow (*duhkha*) so, as Ramanuja said, pleasure and pain are dependent on the interchange between *atman* and *prakriti*,[31] as the following verse will point out.

VERSE 21

Purusha residing in *prakriti* experiences the *gunas* born of *prakriti*.
Attachment to the *gunas* is the cause of his births in good and evil wombs.

Here, it is certainly the individual self that is referred to by the *purusha seated in prakriti*. Since the *jivatman* is constantly interacting with *prakriti*, it comes to regard the aspects of *prakriti* as its own. Really speaking, it is attachment to the *gunas* of *prakriti* that is the *cause* (*karana*) of a personality existing at all. But it is such attachment that causes rebirth – rebirth in the form that corresponds to the particular blend of *gunas* one had and responded to in a previous life or lives. And so the wheel of *samsara* continues – *births in good and evil wombs* literally "being (*sat*) and not being (*asat*)" in appropriate wombs – until the *purusha*, the *atman*, comes to experience the world of *prakriti* but not react to it, just passively observe it.

VERSE 22

The supreme Purusha in this body is also called the Spectator, the Permitter, the Supporter and the Enjoyer, the Great Lord and also the *Param-Atman*.

The *purusha* or *atman* is always Brahman, but here it is also Purusha as the *Param-Atman*, as supreme Brahman, the supreme subject that is the *Kshetrajna*. At the same time, it is the essence of the individual as *atman*, the expression of Brahman within each person. Like the bird that passively sits watching another bird flitting from branch to branch, tree to tree in the pursuit of fruit, the *Atman* that is Brahman within is the Source that passively witnesses as the *Spectator*. It is this *Atman* that is the *Permitter* of the being of the *jivatman*, allowing it to continue its existence (the *Supporter*), all the time lending conscious experience (the *Enjoyer*) to each individual. *Enjoyer, bhokta*, is not meant in the sense of participation, but as the experiencer of, knower of. The *supreme Purusha* is that which understands and has knowledge of *all prakriti* and of every modification of the *gunas* within it. *Prakriti* cannot operate at all without this supreme Purusha that is Brahman, because *prakriti* is matter. It is only by way of the *purusha* that mental and physical functions of the body (here, *deha*) can be interpreted, though these functions can take any direction – towards ignorance or enlightenment. Supreme Purusha and supreme *Atman, Param-Atman*, are used synonymously in the verse.

VERSE 23

Whoever thus knows Purusha and *prakriti* with the *gunas* is not born again, whatever his state of living.

Whatever his state of living indicates that *karma* in the process of formation is eradicated by knowledge of the differentiation of Brahman or Purusha and *prakriti*. Like an arrow already on the way from a bow, some *karma* cannot be stopped, but *karma* in the making can be changed or obliterated. The verse crystallizes rather well the theme of the whole chapter – the differentiation between pure spirit and the *prakritic* world of the *gunas*, *Kshetrajna* and *kshetra*, respectively, with knowledge as the means.

VERSE 24

By meditation, some behold the *atman* in the self by the self, others by Sankhya-*yoga* and others by *karma-yoga*.

Meditation here is *dhyana*, that process by which the senses are withdrawn and the mental faculties stilled so that the whole being comes to rest in the stillness of the *atman* within. The *atman in the self by the self* is the path of the *sannyasin*, the highly introspective, usually independent and solitary path whereby the Self, the *atman* deep within the ordinary self, is realized through transcending the physical and mental *prakritic* body. *Sankhya-yoga* is the more prescribed path of knowledge and withdrawal from action, *jnana-yoga*. *Karma-yoga* is probably the path of egoless action without desire for results – the *karma-yoga* of the *Gita* – rather than ritual action. The *Gita* does not say here that any path is wrong or right, only that meditation, *jnana-yoga* or *karma-yoga* will all be efficacious. No suggestion that *bhakti*, devotion, is necessary is being made at this point, though Krishna has previously held *bhaktas* with faith, *shraddha*, as exceedingly dear to him (12:20).

Verse 25

Others, not knowing thus, worship having heard from others: they also cross beyond death, with supreme refuge in what they heard.

Not knowing thus suggests that there are some who have no knowledge of the meditative paths and, rather than transcend their own ordinary selves to realize the *atman* within, rely on what others have told them and approach the divine in this way. Many commentators see the previous verse as referring to the three paths of *raja-*, *jnana-* and *karma-yoga* and this one as referring to *bhakti-yoga*, the path of devotion, though there is no clear reference to devotion here. To *cross beyond death* is to bring to an end the cycle of rebirth and re-death, so whatever path is meant here is a valid one for the devotee who learns not by personal exploration but by the influence of others. But Shankara added: "How much more so, then, those who can independently appreciate evidence and discriminate."[32] *What they heard* in the text is *shruti*, which leads some to assume that it refers to the *Vedas*, though given Krishna's antipathy to *Vedic* learning as a sole path to Brahman, it is unlikely that it should be accepted as a valid path here.

Verse 26

Whatever being is born, the unmoving and the moving, know that to be from the union of *kshetra* and *kshetrajna*, best of Bharatas.

In reality the *Kshetrajna* that is Brahman is still, yet produces the *prakritic* existence full of motion, *guna* varieties and manifestations – all illusions as far as Shankara was concerned. Because of the close association of the two, the *Kshetrajna* always seems to be *prakriti* and *vice versa*, but the *kshetrajna* of the body and the *Kshetrajna* that is Brahman are unchangeable and passive. Brahman as *Kshetrajna* is the witness of *all prakriti*.[33] Manifested existence can only come about from its unmanifest cause, whether that is in the classical Sankhya view, or in the Sankhya of the *Gita* where Unmanifest Brahman is the cause of unmanifest *prakriti*. There is, then, when manifestation exists, a union (*samyoga*) between Purusha and *prakriti*,[34] just as there is a union between the two when birth and subsequent life of a being takes place, and it is this union of material body as *kshetra* and *atman* as *kshetrajna* of which the verse speaks. Perpetual birth is brought about by involvement with *prakriti*, but that involvement can only happen because of the presence of *purusha/atman*. Only when *purusha* and *prakriti* are correctly known and differentiated can rebirth cease. The ability to appreciate the relationship between the two is the ability to see the universe as it really is and this is what liberation is all about. While there is unity, however, ignorance equates with confusion of the two – seeing matter, *kshetra*, as sentient and mistaking the *kshetrajna* as matter.

Verse 27

He sees, who sees the Supreme Lord existing the same in all beings, the Imperishable in the perishable.

The idea of God as the same (*sama*) in all has already occurred in 5:18. In this verse the *Supreme Lord*, *Parameshvara*, is described as the *Imperishable* (*avinashi*) what is permanent and undying in all the *perishable* transient matter that comes into being and passes away. Such is another distinction between the imperishable *Kshetrajna* that is the same in all things and the individuated perishable *kshetra*: the latter can never exist without the former.

Verse 28

Seeing Ishvara equally existing the same everywhere, the self is not destroyed by the self, so he reaches the supreme goal.

To see all things equally as *Ishvara*, "Lord", the *saguna* Brahman, is to realize the *atman* within and to be liberated. When this state is not reached, all in existence is seen as separate and the ego remains to the fore in order to make such differentiation possible – especially liking this and disliking that. Thus, there is a *jivatman* subject to death and rebirth, and it is this self, this *jiva*, that destroys itself. The sense of the verse is possibly best maintained by retaining both uses of *self* as referring to the ordinary self, given the context of the verse. Thus, each self is responsible for its own journey through births and repeated deaths, its own destruction – a process that destroys also the revelation of the *true* Self within, which, while actually indestructible, is seemingly also destroyed through being bound in the world of *prakriti*.

Seeing the *kshetrajna* everywhere, in all things, prevents this process. Some commentators make the point that, if all selves are equally Brahman, then by destroying another self, one is really destroying one's own self and destroying one's own self is also destroying the selves of others. Thus, Ramanuja said: "If he sees the self as varied everywhere on account of its being in association with the forms of gods and others, he harms the self, that is, throws it into the middle of the sea of *samsara*.[35] Others prefer the Self is not destroyed by the self,[36] though the statement is awkward given the indestructible nature of the embodied Self, unless *destroyed* is meant in the sense of being thoroughly obscured or the like, and this is possible, rather in line with how I have interpreted 6:5 and 6.

VERSE 29

He sees, who sees all actions are performed by *prakriti* alone, and the *atman* as the non-doer.

This verse takes us back to a familiar theme in the *Gita* of the actionless, desireless state of the still *atman* and the detached action that is the hallmark of the *yogin*. For the unenlightened, it seems that the self is the centre of an action, is responsible for all that happens in its life, and is the controller of events. In fact, it is the operation of the three *gunas* that control all, even the self. Again, the *kshetrajna*, the *atman*, is still passive: all activity belongs to the world of the *kshetra*.

VERSE 30

When he sees the whole variety of beings resting in the One and radiating out from that alone, then he becomes Brahman.

Whatever exists in the cosmos evolves from Brahman, *radiating out*: nothing can exist independently of Brahman. Brahman is like the centre of a circle from which radiates out every possible point on that circle both on its circumference, beyond it and within it. All these seemingly differentiated points emanate from one point and are unified by it. Richard Gotshalk notes in commenting on this verse the synonymy of etymology of the word Brahman with the idea of expansion in the verse.[37] The word *Brahman* is complex but has the idea of "blowing out", rather suggestive of the radiation, expansion and evolution that takes place from *One* (*eka*) in the verse.

VERSE 31

Having no beginning, having no *gunas*, this *Param-Atman*, imperishable, though existing in this body, Kaunteya, neither acts nor is defiled.

Having no beginning, Brahman is not created, so the *Kshetrajna* here is different from the *kshetrajna* that is the *atman*, which only exists when the material body exists. While Brahman has *no gunas*, is *nirguna*, and is beyond them, it is yet creator of them, but is not subject to the changeability and impermanence that characterizes all *prakriti* that is made up of the *gunas*. Brahman is the supreme *Atman*, the *Param-Atman*, and is totally *imperishable* (*avyaya*). Brahman is both actionless and undefiled by action, that is to say is unaffected by *karma*,[38] yet exists in the material body (here, *sharira*).

VERSE 32

As the all-pervading *akasha* is not defiled because of its subtlety, so the *Atman* existing in the body everywhere is not defiled.

Atman of the verse is the *Param-Atman* of the previous verse. *Akasha* is ether, one of the five elements and the most subtle of them, for the other elements cannot affect it. Sometimes, Brahman is depicted as *akasha* for, like it, Brahman is *all-pervading* (*sarva-gata*) yet not affected by what it pervades. *Akasha*, too, is vast, yet also contained in the tiniest space; it is all and nothing, it is neither this, nor that.

Existing everywhere is more specifically "seated in the body (*deha*)" reminiscent of the expression in verse 17 "seated in the heart of all".

VERSE 33

As one sun illumines this whole world, so the Lord of the *kshetra* illumines the whole *kshetra*, Bharata.

Although the sun shines on all alike, it is unaffected by the objects it illuminates. Just so, Brahman – here, the owner or *Lord of the kshetra* – resides in all but remains unaffected by all, whatever the nature of the object. *Illumines* is in the sense of making manifest or revealed (*prakasha*). Ramanuja took *Lord* here to be the individual *atman*,[39] which is a viable alternative: once the individual becomes lord, it acquires the knowledge that *atman* and *prakriti* are different, as the following verse suggests.

VERSE 34

Those who, by the eye of knowledge know the distinction between the *kshetra* and *kshetrajna* and liberation from *prakriti* of being, they go to the Supreme.

Human beings are bound up in the world and cannot see the true nature of things, cannot experience Reality. They are unable to differentiate and separate the *kshetra* from the *kshetrajna*. Knowledge of the *kshetra* and *kshetrajna*, *prakriti* and the Self respectively, disperses all delusions so that disengagement from attachment to, and ego-involvement in, *prakritic* existence can occur. Then, Brahman is realized. Thus, *liberation from the prakriti of being* is liberation from the whole realm of sense experience that humanity builds for itself. Those who can differentiate between *prakriti* as *kshetra* and Purusha as Brahman and as *Kshetrajna* in their very heart, *go to the Supreme*, "become Brahman" (verse 30), "enter into my being" (verse 18). Aurobindo wrote here: "That splendid and lofty change is the last, the divine and infinite becoming, the putting off of mortal nature, the putting on of an immortal existence."[40] The whole point of this chapter is here in the last verse: knowledge – true knowledge – is of the differentiation between *purusha/atman* and the *prakritic* world, and that knowledge releases one from the cycle of births and deaths.

In the *Upanishad* of the *Bhagavad Gita*, the knowledge of Brahman, the teaching of *Yoga* and the dialogue between Shri Krishna and Arjuna, this is the thirteenth chapter called *Kshetra Kshetrajna Vibhaga Yoga*.

CHAPTER FOURTEEN

Guna-traya Vibhaga Yoga

The *Yoga* of the Differentiation
of the Three *Gunas*

The previous chapter dealt with spirit and matter, *kshetrajna* and *kshetra*, *purusha* and *prakriti*. At the microcosmic level of the human being it is the reaction of spirit to matter that results in ignorance, in *karmic* rebirth through involvement in the cause–effect processes of matter and in seeing a false self as egoistically existent. All such ignorance exists because of the Self's entrapment in the *prakritic* world of the *gunas* and it is these constantly changing constituents that are the subject of this chapter: it is a focus on the nature of *prakriti* and the need to transcend it. The importance of correct knowledge (*jnana*) is emphasized at the outset, followed by a kind of creation story that may be replete with symbolism at the macrocosmic level or, microcosmically, is simply a primitive account of creation. The chapter then proceeds to describe the functioning and nature of the three *gunas* – *sattva*, *rajas* and *tamas* – and the nature of the one who is able to transcend them.

VERSE 1   The Lord said:
I shall declare again that supreme knowledge, the best of all knowledge, having known which, all the sages have passed from here to supreme perfection.
Sages here are the *munis* who have achieved knowledge of Brahman, and found *perfection* (*siddhi*), presumably liberation, *moksha*. Therefore, their cycles in *samsara* are at an end. Krishna says that the knowledge he has divulged to Arjuna and will repeat is the best, and a guarantee of *moksha*. *From here* probably means from this world, after this life, or, with Shankara, "from this bondage of the body".[1]

VERSE 2
Who, having resorted to this knowledge, having attained unity in me, are not born at the time of creation and are not disturbed at the time of dissolution.
Again, it is those who have knowledge of Brahman who are referred to here. *Unity in me* is not meant in any non-dual sense; the identity of the individual soul is not lost. Indeed, *unity*, *sadharmya*, could also be translated as "likeness", "similarity". Thus, Aurobindo translated *sadharmya* here as "become of like nature and law of being with Me" or, better, "that putting on of the divine nature".[2] Similarly,

Franklin Edgerton translated: "Come to a state of likeness with Me",[3] and as far as Ramanuja was concerned, the unity here is "attain to the possession of qualities that characterise Me, that is, attain similarity with Me".[4] Shankara, as an *advaitist*, a non-dualist, saw unity here as total identity with Brahman.[5] The unity of the verse means that there is no rebirth, and even at *pralaya*, the *dissolution* of the universe, there are no latent *karmas* remaining that will cause a living form when *creation* and manifest existence occurs again. J. A. B. van Buitenen made the point here that at dissolution "they do not disappear as *persons*, but continue to exist with their unimpaired memory and full awareness of themselves".[6] It is an interesting comment that rather supports the dualism between God and human that seems to be the message of the *Gita*. *Unity in me* is, therefore, not to be taken as a statement of non-dualism.

VERSE 3

My womb is the *Mahat Brahma*. In that I place the germ: thence is the birth of all beings, Bharata.

Mahat Brahma "Great Brahman" is *prakriti*, "Great Nature", the whole of created existence. This great entity, which Krishna says is *my womb* is, thus, equated with Brahman. It is Brahman that gives rise to all existence and is the cause of manifestation. In short, *prakriti* is the womb of Brahman and the material cause of the three *gunas*. Sri Krishna Prem graphically described this *prakriti* as "a dark matrix full of unlimited potentialities".[7] In the dissolved non-state of the universe, the *gunas* are completely still. In classical Sankhya, it is the proximity of *purushas* to the *gunas* in equilibrium that causes material existence, *prakriti*, to occur through imbalances of the *gunas*. In the *Gita*, Brahman is that cause as the supreme Purusha. In classical Sankhya, *purushas* are separate from *prakriti*, but in the *Gita*, *prakriti* belongs to Brahman: it is his *saguna* presence, here described as his *womb* (*yoni*). *Prakriti* alone cannot produce existence; it is the *germ* or seed of Brahman placed within *prakriti* that causes all in it to be. Male and female, Purusha and *prakriti*, respectively, are different expressions of, yet are united in, Brahman. When Brahman is *nirguna* then all is in a state of equilibrium, but when Brahman becomes manifest, *saguna*, he is at once male and female, Indeed, as Hinduism developed, when that *saguna* expression finds itself in a form, then there is always a female counterpart, a *shakti* force, that balances out the male. Thus, the *shakti* force of Vishnu became the Goddess Lakshmi, of the *avatara* Rama, Sita, and of Krishna, Radha. Such *shakti* energy is usually the active side of the deity, the male side being the passive, so in the relationship between Brahman and *prakriti*, it is the former that is the still, passive aspect and the latter, the active principle. But active *prakriti* cannot operate without the seed within it that is the male, passive, Purusha.[8]

The *germ* (*garbha*) or seed mentioned here, then, is the *atman*, the presence of Purusha in the depth of everything that exists, both animate and inanimate. It is in this way that the union between Purusha and *prakriti* is meant. It is a macro-cosmic reflection of the union between man and woman that creates life at the microcosmic level. The whole concept implies the higher Unmanifest Brahman that is the higher nature infusing the lower nature that comes forth from him as creation in its unmanifest potential, and its realized forms. This offers, too, a way back from the lower nature pervaded by the essence of Brahman, if that essence can be experienced.

VERSE 4

Whatever forms are produced in any wombs, Kaunteya, *Mahat Brahma* is their womb, I the seed-giving father.

Again, we have the idea of procreation at the microcosmic level and the combination of Purusha and *prakriti* to create manifest existence at the macrocosmic level. *Prakriti*, then, is the Cosmic Mother, whose evolutes can only become manifest through the *seed* (here, *bija*) or germ of Brahman. *Prakriti* is the *kshetra*, total matter; only the *Kshetrajna* can motivate it to evolve. But whatever exists comes from *prakriti* and is born of *prakriti*. The reference to many *wombs* suggests the infinite variety of possible manifestations such as gods, humans, beasts and so on.

VERSE 5

Sattva, rajas, tamas – these *gunas* arising in *prakriti*, Mahabaho, bind fast the imperishable, the embodied one, in the body.

Prakriti and the *gunas* are one and the same. The *imperishable* (*avyaya*) refers to the *atman* that is seemingly bound up in the *prakritic* body, though in reality it is independent of the *gunas*. It is *purusha*, the *kshetrajna*, which reveals *prakriti*, but when it does not react to it, comes to know itself as separate. The *embodied one* (*dehin*) is the true Self, the *atman* and the *kshetrajna*, contrasted with the material body (*deha*). A detailed analysis of the *gunas* follows. *Guna* means "strand" or "thread" and together they are the strands that make up all of life. They are the whole field, the *kshetra*. As Ramanuja said of God: "I am the agent for uniting the multitude of intelligent selves in accordance with their respective *karmas*, with each of these (types of bodies)."[9]

VERSE 6

Among these, *sattva*, being stainless is luminous and healthy. It binds fast, sinless one, by attachment to happiness and attachment to knowledge.

The *sattvic guna* is associated with the light of joy, happiness and evolutionary knowledge: it is thus *luminous* (*prakasha*) and so enlightening. It is associated with the religious path and a high level of consciousness but this consciousness and knowledge are, in themselves, pleasurable and things to desire. At best, *sattva* represents purity, steadiness and goodness, though attachment to any of these will result in rebirth. *Happiness* (*sukha*) is often as much a problem for the embodied Self as an aversion to suffering. In fact, each *guna*, even *sattva*, will distort perception through conditioning the mind. Rohit Mehta pointed out rather well that happiness is an emotion and knowledge a thought process:

Thus in *Sattva* there is a conditioning arising out of its attachment to a thought-synthesis or an emotional synthesis – its addiction to knowledge or happiness. *Sattva* contains an artificial product of the mind, very attractive to look at but having no fragrance in it. Thus the virtues of the mind are like artificial flowers. *Sattva* may indeed be described as mind's virtuosity. There is a semblance of good in it, but it is a goodness where opposites have been temporarily balanced – they have not been transcended.[10]

The problem with goodness is that its dual opposite of evil is all too often the benchmark for good; evil is that to be averted, disliked, avoided, detested and so it becomes the emotion that conditions behaviour. All such dualities of emotions have, rather, to be transcended. It is also difficult to be egoistically separate from happiness and knowledge; it is so easy to think *I* am happy, *I* am knowledgeable. Such thoughts are *karmic* even if sometimes admirable. Thus, *attachment to knowledge* Shankara understood as attachment to knowledge on the *prakritic* level, not as attachment to knowledge of Brahman.[11] This is likely to be the way in which the phrase is meant here. *Sattvic* knowledge is bound to be *manifest* knowledge, and is an activity of the *buddhi*, the intellect, whereas knowledge of the Unmanifest should be *guna*-less. So what is *bound fast* is the passive *atman* that is obscured by involvement in *prakriti* even though the life of the *sattvic* individual is evolved, happy, and may be lived in pursuit of knowledge of God.

VERSE 7
Know *rajas* as of the nature of passion, the source of thirst and attachment; it binds fast the embodied one, Kaunteya, by attachment to action.
Rajas is an active *guna*. It makes the mind *thirst* with the desire to do this or that with ambition and *passion* (*raga*), and to respond to sense stimuli. It stimulates and encourages attachment to action and emotional responses as well as thirst for what one has not and *attachment* for what one has.

VERSE 8
But know *tamas* to be born of ignorance, deluding all embodied beings, that binds fast by heedlessness, indolence and sleep, Bharata.
Tamas is basically inertia, non-evolutionary inertia. It is heavy, dark, lazy, enshrouding, enveloping and, as such, it is inimical to the *sattvic* energies and causes a barrier to knowledge: thus, the verse mentions *ignorance*, *ajnana*, and delusion, *moha*, as its effects. Notably, however, the verse refers to the *dehin*, of *embodied beings*, the *atman*, which exists even in the darkest of characters.

VERSE 9
***Sattva* attaches one to happiness, *rajas* to action, Bharata, but *tamas*, really shrouding knowledge, attaches one to heedlessness.**
Whatever *guna* is dominant in an individual will cause that person to be

attracted to a lifestyle appropriate to the *guna*. There is little of value in a *tamasic* existence, though even here, the *atman*, deeply enshrouded, has to be present. Attachment is the key thought: even the *sattvic* person is attached to *happiness* (*sukha*), while the passion of the *rajasic* individual forces perpetual *action* (*karma*). The *tamasic* person, having quiescent *sattva* and some *rajas*, is trapped in ignorance.

VERSE 10

Having overcome *rajas* and *tamas*, *sattva* arises, Bharata: and *rajas* over *sattva* and *tamas*, and *tamas* over *sattva* and *rajas*.

Each individual is characterized generally by one particular *guna* but all *gunas* are present in some degree in all beings, and there is a continual interplay between the *gunas* during day-to-day life so that at one moment one *guna* is to the fore and then another. *Brahmins* and *Kshatriyas* are expected to be mainly without *tamas*, while the two lower classes are predominantly without *sattva*.

VERSE 11

When the light of knowledge shines through every gate of the body, then it may be known that *sattva* is indeed predominant.

The gates of the body (body, here, being *deha*)[12] are the sense organs, and when the *sattva guna* predominates in an individual, there is a sensitivity to what is heard, clarity of vision and thought, beauty of speech and so on, the senses reflecting the *sattva guna*. The whole being will function in an evolutionary manner, grounded in goodness, the *sattva* shining or illuminated (*prakasha*) in the individual.

VERSE 12

Greed, activity, the undertaking of actions, restlessness, longing – these arise when *rajas* becomes predominant, best of Bharatas.

The *rajasic* characteristics depicted here are clearly *karmic* producing: they contain the common factor of *longing* or desire. *Activity* is *pravritti*, movement forwards and outwards. *Undertaking of actions*, or beginnings of actions, refers to actions undertaken for their results. *Restlessness* is the result of the desires of the mind yet unfulfilled, as is *greed* (*lobha*).

VERSE 13

Darkness, inertia, heedlessness and delusion – these arise when *tamas* is predominant, Kuru-nandana.

Darkness is *aprakasha*, the opposite of the shining, luminous nature of *sattva* in verse 11 and is tantamount to ignorance. Here, it refers to the darkness of the mind that prevents an individual from evolving in life, from discriminating the correct paths and choices in life. *Inertia* is *apravritti*, that which prevents movement forward and so is stagnation, again, the opposite of *pravritti* in the previous verse. *Heedlessness* is *pramada*, negligence. Lethargy and dullness of mind result from the predominance of the *tamas guna*, so that one becomes inactive and negligent. *Delusion, moha*, is the thorough ignorance that makes it impossible to live life with any perspective of true knowledge.

VERSE 14

If the embodied one meets dissolution when *sattva* is predominant, then, indeed, he attains to the pure worlds of the knowers of the highest.

Dissolution, pralaya, is normally the term used for the dissolution of the universe, when latent *karmas* are suspended in the unmanifest state of the universe until manifestation occurs again and beings are reborn according to their predominant *gunic* make-up. In this verse, however, *pralaya* refers to ordinary death and the dissolution of the body, with *pure worlds* the fate of the *sattvic* individual. Aurobindo combined the two concepts of death and final dissolution admirably:

> Our physical death is also a *pralaya*, the soul bearing the body comes to a pralaya, to a disintegration of that form of matter with which its ignorance identified its being and which now dissolves into the natural elements. But the soul itself persists and after an interval resumes in a new body formed from those elements, its round of births in the cycle, just as after the interval of pause and cessation the universal Being resumes his endless round of the cyclic aeons.[13]

The thoughts at the end of life are believed to determine the birth circumstances of the next existence, so if one's thoughts are wholly *sattvic* at death, it is possible to be born on one of the god-like planes of existence such as the realm of Brahma. Such lands are pure, shining, spotless – in short, thoroughly *sattvic* lands – where only good prevails. Those who reach such lands carry good, *sattvic karma*, which is why they are born there, but when that good *karma* is used up, rebirth in human form again is inevitable. Presumably, *knowers of the highest* are knowers of the highest divine realm, which would be that of the creator god Brahma, himself subject to *karma*.

VERSE 15

Meeting death in *rajas*, [he] is born among those attached to action; dying in *tamas*, [he] is born in the wombs of the deluded.

Death is, again, *pralaya*. When a soul leaves the body while in a state of excitement, desire or aversion, then the new birth situation will be the same. To die inert is likely to cause birth in a low form, perhaps in sub-human or in animal form. For *deluded* (*mudha*), Shankara translated "irrational" and understood the term to refer to "cattle and the like".[14]

VERSE 16

The fruit of good action [they] say, is *sattvic* and pure, while the fruit of *rajas* is pain and the fruit of *tamas* is ignorance.

Ignorance (*ajnana*) is not only a mental state but is an active state in that one *acts* in ignorance and so often does what is wrong. The *karma* that results from such *tamas* is that which makes a being unable to evolve until the negative *karma* is used up. In the meantime, *tamasic* beings are often destined to be involved in *adharma* and sinful action.[15] *Rajas* is the drive to action on the mental side with physical actions the normal outcome. Being bound by desires and aversions, *rajasic* actions are *karmic* and cause *pain*, suffering (*duhkha*) in life. Only *sattvic* actions bring good results, but all three states are depicted as bearing *fruit*, *phala*, that is to say, *karmic* results that necessitate rebirth.

Verse 17

From *sattva* arises knowledge, from *rajas* greed: heedlessness and delusion arise from *tamas*, and also ignorance.

For the kind of knowledge that permits spiritual evolution, *sattva* is a prerequisite characteristic, which is why *Brahmins*, who are *sattva-rajas* in nature, and *Kshatriyas*, who are *rajas-sattva* are most suited to read the *Vedas*. The *knowledge* (*jnana*) mentioned here is, presumably, that which permits knowledge of God as opposed to the *delusion* (*moha*) that is concomitant with being *tamasic*. The *rajasic* individual will always want – here, have *lobha*, *greed* – whether that is for something materialistic, mental, academic, ego-enhancing, or a need such as for praise, love and the like.

Verse 18

Those established in *sattva* go upwards, the *rajasikas* exist in the middle, and the *tamasikas*, abiding in the modes of the lowest *guna*, go downwards.

Rajas is the *guna* that, at the macrocosmic level, is the energy that creates life. It is symbolized in the creator god, Brahma. In humanity it is the hallmark of a middle state so the *rajasic* individual neither evolves nor involves, he or she more or less remains static in a middling position in terms of consciousness from one life to the next. It is the predominance of *sattva* that causes evolution, *go upwards* in the verse. Evolution could mean rebirth as a god or as one destined to be released from *samsara* if the focus of the *sattvic* individual is on the *atman* within. The predominance of *tamas* causes a downward involution, *go downwards* in the verse, towards animal form so that involution could mean birth as an animal or insect, or even lower as a plant, tree or stone. Thus, such involution according to Ramanuja would be – in order of severity it seems – animals, insects, vegetables and immovable matter.[16]

Verse 19

When one who sees beholds no other agent than the *gunas*, and knows [what is] higher than the *gunas*, he attains to my being.

The *gunas* are nothing but *prakriti*. Any thought, activity or manifested object – whether animate or inanimate – is a result of combinations of these *gunas*. It is in this sense that they are *agents*, for all that happens on the material level – even sense experience and egoistic thought – does so through their activity. It is the *gunas*, even pure *sattva*, that are responsible for *karma*. To reach God, or *nirguna* Brahman, one has to transcend even *sattva* and also become *nirguna*. Only then is there no *karma* to be reaped so that *samsara* ends. It is the *gunas*, then, which are the agents in all manifest existence, not the ego, the "*I*". One who recognizes the real Self, the *atman* within, separates that Self from the *gunas* and is liberated, attaining, Krishna says, *my being, mad-bhava*. Such a one is a perceiver of the truth, *one who sees*, described by Mehta as having "unconditioned perception".[17]

VERSE 20
Having crossed beyond these three *gunas* giving rise to the body, the embodied one is liberated from birth, death, decay and pain and attains to immortality.

The mental and physical body is *prakritic* and composed entirely of the three *gunas*. As soon as individuals dissociate themselves from these *gunas* and identify themselves with the *guna*-less *atman*, they are free. *Giving rise to the body* is a problematic approximation of a difficult Sanskrit compound. If literally translated, it would suggest that the *gunas* arise from the body (*deha*), when in fact it is the opposite that is the case. And yet, given that the natural state of the body is the *gunas* in equilibrium, the attraction and aversion to external stimuli are what causes them to arise in the body, thus creating the imbalance that results in the mind–body complexity of each individual. The reference to *birth, death, decay* and suffering or *pain, duhkha* is, once again, similar to the Buddhist *Four Noble Truths*, the first of which is "All life is *duhkha*, suffering". The reference is also reminiscent of the visions of the Buddha on his paths to enlightenment. Importantly, the verse suggests that liberation can be attained *in life*, with the achievement of freedom from *prakriti* and the state of *jivan-mukti*, enlightened while still in the body. The Buddha is certainly recorded as such and Shankara also accepted such enlightenment.[18] *Immortality* in the verse is the now familiar *amrita*, "nectar".

VERSE 21   Arjuna said:
What are the hallmarks, Lord, of him who has crossed beyond these *gunas*? What [is his] conduct and how does he cross beyond these three *gunas*?

Arjuna asks three straightforward questions about the *jivan-mukta*:

• What is he like?
• How does he act?
• How did he become *jivan-mukti*?

He addresses Krishna as *Lord, prabhu*.

VERSE 22   The Lord said:
Light, activity and delusion, Pandava, he does not hate when present, nor longs for when absent.

Light is the illuminated (*prakasha*) nature of one who is *sattvic*, while the *rajasic* individual is characterized by *activity* (*pravritti*), but not the action in inaction of CHAPTER FOUR of the *Gita*. The *tamasic* individual is characterized by *delusion* (*moha*). In total contrast, the *jivan-mukta* is in a state of *guna*-less equilibrium, whether exposed or not to the *gunas*. The *gunas* in one who transcends them are totally balanced: no one of them predominates over the others. The liberated one is not attached to activities associated with any of the *gunas*, and this reiterates the idea of detached action that we met earlier in the *Gita*. Still able to act, there is, nevertheless, total equilibrium that remains irrespective of whether *sattvic*, *rajasic* or *tamasic* sense stimuli present themselves. The liberated Self does not *react*, just observes. Thus we have an answer to Arjuna's first question: What is he like?

VERSE 23
As one indifferent he sits, unmoved by the *gunas*, who moves not, is established, even though the *gunas* operate.

Even for the *jivan-mukta*, the *gunas* operate, but he is unmoved by them. Seated, or *established* in the *atman*, he is a witness to what happens rather than being a motivator of events. Arjuna has asked how he acts and Krishna's reply is that he does not: he remains still within, indifferent to and disinterested in, the necessities of his own actions and those of others. How difficult this is was admirably put by Mehta when he said: "To stand apart and look at the modes functioning within oneself is indeed a supremely spiritual state. To look at one's habits and yet to regard oneself as not the actor of those activities; to perceive one's virtues and accomplishments and yet to lay no claim over them – this is the characteristic of one who has freed himself from all conditioning."[19] The difficulty of achieving such a state even for a few seconds is obvious, and demonstrates how the *gunas* bind fast each individual self in the maze of *prakritic* living.

VERSE 24
The same in pleasure and pain, established in his own being, regarding a clod of earth, a stone or gold the same, the same to the dear and the not dear, firm, the same in blame or praise.

Whoever is rooted or *established* in *his own being* (*sva-bhava*) has the equilibrium that is maintained in all activities and towards all beings at all times. This really reiterates what has already been said in the *Gita*, especially in 7:8.[20] Since Brahman is the essence in all things, all things are seen as the same (*sama*). *Pleasure* (*sukha*) and *pain* (*duhkha*) have been used consistently in the *Gita* to epitomize the mental and physical goals that desire of the former and avoidance of the latter involve.

VERSE 25
The same in honour and dishonour, the same to friend and foe, abandoning all undertakings, he is said to have crossed beyond the *gunas*.

These last two verses endorse the transcending of the dualities of existence, the dualities caused by responding to the *gunas*. *Abandoning all undertakings* refers not to total inactivity but to the relinquishing of activities for the purpose of results they bring, that is to say, fruitive undertakings that reap fruitive *karma*. Eknath Easwaran said of the inactivity of the inner Self: "The Self abides in the inner chamber of the heart, always at peace, whatever forces of prakriti may storm outside. The illumined man or woman maintains a joyful evenness of mind in happiness and sorrow."[21] The outer self, of course, can continue to engage in life without attachment, projects, actions for a purpose and without need for results, having *crossed beyond the gunas*, in other words, having become liberated. These last three verses, then, are in answer to Arjuna's second question related to how a *jivan-mukta* acts. Now we will have the answer to the third question as to the means of becoming *jivan-mukti*.

VERSE 26

And who serves me with unswerving *bhakti-yoga*, and crosses beyond these *gunas*, is fit for becoming Brahman.

Bhakti-yogena, with unswerving devotion, lends a highly theistic tone in this answer to Arjuna's last question. *Becoming Brahman*, then, cannot be meant in a non-dual sense, where the individual is lost in total identity with Brahman. Importantly, then, at the close of this present chapter, it is by *bhakti-yoga* that the devotee attains and becomes Brahman. While the *Gita* does not deny the efficacy of other paths, Ramanuja certainly saw *bhakti-yoga* as the ultimate means.[22]

VERSE 27

For, indeed, I am the abode of Brahman the Immortal, the Imperishable and eternal Dharma and absolute happiness.[23]

The word for *abode* in the text is *pratishtha* and it is variously translated. It certainly could mean "foundation", which is something of a problem for much other content of the *Gita* if Krishna is saying that he is the foundation of Brahman. Some commentators insist that it can not mean "abode". Zaehner certainly is one and is consistent in seeing Krishna as the personal God beyond the impersonal Brahman.[24] Geoffrey Parrinder clearly took the same position in accepting Krishna as the "Ground" of, and beyond, Brahman,[25] and Franklin Edgerton also found the subordination of the impersonal Brahman to God as "unambiguous" in this verse.[26] Aurobindo, too, believed that Krishna is greater than the *nirguna* Brahman.[27] But even if the word *pratishtha* is accepted as meaning "foundation" or support, it is likely to be describing Brahman rather than positing Brahman as being dependent for existence on Krishna – a theory that few commentators accept. Richard Gotshalk believes that the term should be taken to mean Krishna as the incarnation, the *place* (*pratishtha*) "where that power dwells (particularly for the purpose of approaching human beings and receiving worship and devotion from them".[28] "Embodiment", then, might be an appropriate synonym. Indeed, *pratishtha* can mean "gross matter", "earth",[29] suggesting Krishna as materialized Brahman. There is a certain blurring of the impersonal and personal Brahman at times in the *Gita* and Krishna may be referring to himself as the abode/source/foundation of the manifest Brahman that is the higher *prakriti*.

Thus, this chapter ends with the familiar theme of *bhakti-yoga*, after expressing the need to transcend the *gunas* and break free of the overpowering conditioning wrought in the mind and emotion by their incessant interaction.

In the *Upanishad* of the *Bhagavad Gita*, the knowledge of Brahman, the teaching of *Yoga* and the dialogue between Shri Krishna and Arjuna, this is the fourteenth chapter called
Guna-traya Vibhaga Yoga.

CHAPTER FIFTEEN

Purushottama Yoga
The *Yoga* of the Supreme *Purusha*

The *Yoga* of the Supreme Purusha begins with a description of the cosmic tree of life, the tree being the symbol of *prakriti* and of *samsara*, the cycle of births and deaths that have to be overcome in order for liberation to be attained. It then describes the nature of *samsara*, the nature of the *jivatman*, the individual self, ending with the immanence of Brahman in the world and the nature of Brahman as greater than *prakriti* and even as greater than the *atman* within.

VERSE I   The Lord said:
They speak of the imperishable *ashvattha* tree with roots above and branches below, leaves of which are the metres of hymns; he who knows that is a knower of the **Veda**.

The *ashvattha* tree is a member of the fig family that includes, and is sometimes identified with, the *pipal* and, less correct, with the *banyan*, though here it seems to have characteristics of both and may be just an improvized tree with unusual features taken from others.[1] It is featured as being unusual in that its branches reach down into the earth and its roots upward. The sap in the tree also passes down the tree rather than up. The *Vedic* hymns, the rhythms or *metres of hymns* in the verse, are believed to contain all knowledge, all branches of knowledge and so the *leaves* of the tree are equated with every kind of knowledge in the *Veda*: knowledge of the tree of life, then, is a special, intuitive knowledge.

Krishna has previously identified himself with the *ashvattha* tree in 10:26, and a reference to it is to be found in the *Rig Veda* where Varuna sinks its stem deep below and: "Its rays, whose root is high above, stream downward."[2] The *Katha Upanishad* also refers to "its roots above, its branches below" and to its eternal nature: "That alone is called the Immortal! On it all the worlds rest; beyond it no one can ever pass."[3] Traditionally, the *ashvattha* symbolizes the cosmos and the endless cycle of births and deaths, *samsara*. Like the tree, *samsara* is described as *imperishable* (*avyaya*), which is tantamount to saying that *prakriti*, too, is imperishable and eternal, albeit that it is temporarily suspended during the unmanifest stages of the universe. Indeed, there will always be a *process* of birth–death–birth of *prakriti* and while individuals may evolve to the point of liberation from it, the *process* will still continue, though everything in that process is subject to change. It is in this way that the tree and *prakriti* are imperishable. The tree is dependent on the sap that comes down from above, just as *prakriti* is dependent on its Cause that is Brahman. Unlike the *Katha Upanishad*, however, the *Gita* equates the tree with *prakriti* and will project Brahman beyond it. The word *ashvattha* is variously broken down, perhaps *a-* "not", *shva* "tomorrow", *stha-* "standing", "existing", indicative of the inability to last, of transience and impermanence, or even as Douglas Hill suggested, simply *ashva-stha* "the tree under which horses stand".[4] Arvind Sharma, follows Hill's interpretation and describes the tree thus:

> It does not, like its cousin the banyan, drop aerial rootlets to take fresh root in the earth. . . . The formation of the tree is peculiar, in that its roots (which often stand in part above the ground) do not altogether, as in other trees, lose themselves in a central rounded trunk, but to a great extent retaining their separate form, climb up in a cluster, each to spread out into a separate branch. Each root is thus continuous with its own branch, and, therefore, root and branch being inseparably one, it is possible to speak of the branch as descending to the earth, and of the root as rising aloft.[5]

Sap and roots in the tree are both interdependent, just like the supreme Purusha and *prakriti*. The symbolism of the various parts of the tree varies between commentators, but the overall message is that the roots and branches take their life from above, from Brahman; and it is from Brahman that the multitude of varieties of manifestations emanate like the branches of the tree. What is *above* in the verse, then, is an indirect reference to Brahman as the Purusha from which all the evolutes of *prakriti* come forth.

Verse 2

Below and above its branches spread, nourished by the *gunas*. Sense objects are its shoots and below, the roots are stretched forth in the world of men, bringing about action.

The higher up the tree, the higher the plane of existence, the more superior god-like planes being nearer to the top. The branches coming down represent the more inferior beings and life-forms. But in the whole of the tree is the life sap that causes the shoots, sprouts, buds and twigs to form and become manifest. This is a symbol of *prakriti* with the *gunas* being the sap that enable the manifestation of sense objects. The more complex the branches, twigs, shoots and buds, the more complex the *gunic* combinations and the greater the involvement of individuals with their counterpart as life, of which the twigs, shoots and so on are a symbol, so *bringing about action (karma)* at the human level. Thus, the less-evolved individual is concerned with the external trappings of life, the *sense objects*, with the twists and turns of daily events – things wanted, things to be hung on to, goals to be achieved, things to avoid and things to do. The chances here of perceiving the *atman* within are remote. It is the mass of roots that symbolize the entanglement of the individual in *prakritic* living, and it is here that individuals search out their desires and avoid their aversions without ever knowing the main roots that reach up to transcendent Reality. The *shoots* of the fig tree are also sticky: thus, when the verse says that *sense objects* are its shoots, it is perhaps aptly implying that one gets stuck in the world of the senses.

VERSE 3

Its form is not perceived as such here, neither its ends, nor its origin, nor its foundation. Cut asunder this firm-rooted *ashvattha* with the strong axe of non-attachment.

The tree symbolizes the ever-changing state of life, beyond which, humanity too frequently does not care to look. Thus, ultimate Reality *is not perceived as such*, while individuals are trapped in *prakriti*, attached to the sense objects caused by the *gunas*. If they can dissociate themselves from the *prakritic* world by non-attachment to sense stimuli, it would be as if the tree were cut down, the *gunas* would have no affect. Non-attachment, then, is the means by which *samsara* can be overcome. As in the last chapter, *prakriti*, which is the subject of the present verse, has no end and no beginning. The process of its manifestation and non-manifestation brought about by Brahman is eternal. But, clearly, most have no knowledge of the workings of *prakriti*, which is what is meant by *not perceived as such here*, or of Brahman as the *foundation* of *prakriti*. *To cut asunder* here is to break contact with the world of *prakriti*, cutting those aerial and adventitious roots that prevent ascent of the tree.

VERSE 4

Then, that goal should be sought for whither, having gone, none return again. "I seek refuge in that primeval Purusha from which streamed forth the ancient energy."

The sudden use of the first person in the verse suggests that part of it is meant as a meditative statement. *Ancient energy (pravritti purani)* is variously interpreted, with energy sometimes translated as action, endeavour, effort, creativity or current. Indeed, *pravritti* normally means "action" or "activity". Richard Gotshalk has "manifestation", which captures the sense of the expression well,[6] and Aurobindo referred to the "coils of Pravritti" which he described as "the movement of birth and action",[7] or "urge to action", which encompass all these ideas. Taking the analogy of the *ashvattha* further, Aurobindo stated that the goal is to scale its heights in "the path of Nivritti or cessation from the original urge to action, and the consummation of this way is the cessation of birth itself and a transcendent status in the highest supra-cosmic reach of the Eternal".[8] Such is the aptly described *goal* in the verse. Such a goal is much higher than the tree itself: from the darkness, the *tamas* of aerial roots, to the middle *rajasic* realms, to the highest *sattvic* branches, the individual must eventually transcend even the tree itself, so loosening the Self, the *atman* from the hold of *prakriti*. *Streamed forth* depicts rather well the creative energy of *prakriti*, which, stemming from Brahman, bursts out into manifest creation, the *gunas* that compose it combining in temporary liaisons and equations to provide the complexities of life. The goal is to transcend *samsara* by non-involvement with the *gunas* and to recognize the Source of all as Brahman.

VERSE 5
Free from pride and delusion, having conquered the evil of attachment, dwelling constantly in the intrinsic Self, having completely turned away desires, liberated from the pairs of opposites known as pleasure and pain, the undeluded reach that imperishable goal.

There is much here that summarizes the teachings of earlier parts of the *Gita* – fixing the mind on *atman* and achieving detached action, freedom from attachment to sense objects, loss of ego, loss of *dvandvas*, the *pairs of opposites* or dualities, and the loss of the deluded perspective of reality as consisting of *prakriti* and the three *gunas*. All these facets are necessary for liberation from *samsara*. There is a contrast here between the busy occupation with the world of *prakriti* that is the life of the deluded, the life of those lower down on the tree of life amongst its roots, and the life of the enlightened one that experiences only the *sattvic* heights and the essence that is Brahman. *Evil*, *dosha*, is meant in the sense of a defect, a *delusion* (*moha*). The *intrinsic Self* is the *adhyatma* that Krishna described at the beginning of CHAPTER EIGHT.

The *Gita* has consistently used the opposites of *pleasure* or happiness, *sukha*, and *pain* or suffering, *duhkha*, because both are motivators of normal living, the former encouraging our desire, *kama* – about which the *Gita* has had much to say – and the latter engendering aversion. There is an equanimity beyond these opposites that is the *imperishable* (*avyaya*) *goal*, that is to say, total liberation, which Krishna now describes.

VERSE 6
That the sun illumines not, nor the moon, nor fire; that is my supreme abode, having gone to which, they do not return.

Since Brahman is *guna*-less, *nirguna*, it is beyond qualities and dualities. When *moksha* is attained and an individual merges with Brahman then that individual, too, loses all dualities: light and darkness, fire, cold, or any of the elements, are left behind. Only the egoistic *jiva* experiences such dualities; when this is lost, pure *atman*, devoid of *gunas*, remains. But, as the next verse will make clear, the individual *atman* is not lost. The verse reflects the *Katha Upanishad* (5:15) in its description of the *supreme abode* (*dhama*): "There the sun does not shine, nor the moon and stars", and also the *Shvetashvatara Upanishad*: "There the sun does not shine, nor the moon and stars; there lightning does not shine, of this common fire need we speak! Him alone, as he shines, do all things reflect; this whole world radiates with his light."[9]

VERSE 7
An eternal part of me becomes a *jiva* in the world of *jivas*, drawing the five senses and the mind as the sixth, abiding in *prakriti*.

Although the egoistic *jiva* is lost when *moksha* is attained and only the *atman* remains, the *jivatman* is not totally separate from Brahman while it exists. At the material level, the *jivatman* is part of *prakriti*, and *prakriti* is inseparable from

Brahman for it is caused by Brahman as its Source. Thus, Brahman becomes the individual life-element, the *jiva*, of each being. We are more familiar with the *atman* being expressed as a part of Brahman but the verse is clearly talking about the material *jivatman* being a part, given that it mentions *prakritic senses* (*indriyas*) and *mind* (*manas*). Yet, *the eternal part of me* is more suggestive of the *atman*. Such seems to be the way Aurobindo understood it: "This is an epithet, a statement of immense bearing and consequence. For it means that each soul, each being in its spiritual reality is the very Divine, however partial its actual manifestation of him in Nature . . . each manifesting spirit, each of the many, is an eternal individual, an eternal unborn undying power of the one Existence."[10] Although the *jivatman* is often associated with the self of personality and individuality, the distinction between *jivatman* as such and *atman* was less clear at the time the *Gita* was written and this verse seems to exemplify such a lack of clarification.

Verse 8

When the lord obtains a body and also when he leaves he takes these and goes like the wind takes scent from their places.

Most commentators understand *lord, ishvara*, here to refer to the *jiva*, the reincarnating self of the previous verse. *Ishvara* can mean "sovereign" suggestive of the individual being sovereign or lord of the body, mind and senses, the *these* of the present verse. The wind has no scent of its own, it can only gather it from material sources. Similarly, the *jivataman* gathers its personality from *prakriti* and from its past actions, taking that personality with it at death into the next existence like the wind carries scents. But, just as the wind is really free from any scent, so also the *jivatman* has the potential to be free of its attachments to the world and its sense of "I". On the other hand, other commentators like Aurobindo[11] believe *lord* to refer to the *atman*, which is that by which the *jiva* can become involved in *prakriti* and which must always be present for any matter to exist. The analogy of the wind here would be equated with the *atman* which, when trapped in *prakriti*, continues to be associated with fruitive *karma*, the *scents*, in the next birth. However, the previous verse clearly referred to the ordinary body, which suggests here, in this verse, that it is the *karmic* personality that *obtains the body*. Nevertheless, The *Katha Upanishad* has a similar thought to this verse, but refers to the *atman*: "The senses, they say, are the horses, and sense objects are the paths around them; He who is linked to the body (*atman*), senses, and mind, the wise proclaim as the one who enjoys."[12] Here, the wise would have knowledge of the passive *atman* that is within each rebirth and which lends to the personality the ability to experience. The subject in verse 11 below is more clearly the *atman* that is the real Self, and verse 10, too, makes more sense if it is the *atman* that is the implied subject. However, the *atman* takes nothing with it when the body ceases to exist; only the *jivatman* can take *prakritic* characteristics with it after death, again, the *these* – the senses and mind of verse 7.

VERSE 9

Presiding over the ear, the eye, touch, taste, smell and also the mind, he enjoys objects of the senses.

Strictly speaking, the *atman* has always been the "enjoyer" or "experiencer" within the material body, which is why it is trapped. Thus, as with the last verse, it is none too clear whether what does the *presiding over* here is the personality self or the trapped *atman*. *Mind* (*manas*) is the interpreter of sense data but, like the other senses, is matter. The inner Self is the true non-material entity that really presides over these senses by becoming involved with them and positing a false self that controls them, *enjoys* or experiences them and "cultivates", to use the term favoured by Gotshalk,[13] the likes and dislikes of sense experience conveyed by the senses. Thus, the verse would make more sense if the implicit subject in this case were to be the *atman*.

VERSE 10

The deluded do not see him who departs, stays and enjoys, who is united with the *gunas*. Those see, who possess the eye of knowledge.

Again, we have the difficulty of *him who departs, stays and enjoys*: is it the *atman* which, strictly speaking, is the only conscious spirit that can enjoy and experience? Or is it *the deluded* (*mudha*) who see reality as sense stimuli. So, in the latter case, they remain in the body, enjoy what they can and then depart, only to set up the same system for themselves in the next life. Without knowledge of what involvement of *prakriti* is, and of the *atman* within, *samsara* is inevitable. I am inclined to think that *him* in the verse is probably the non-material *atman*, that which has to be present in every passage from one life to the next in order for life to take place and the only means by which sense experience can occur. Thus, the *him* of the following verse is clearly the *atman* as Brahman.

VERSE 11

The *yogins* who strive perceive him dwelling in the self; the unrefined and unintelligent, though striving, see him not.

Here, that which dwells in the self is certainly the non-*prakritic atman*. Although both the *yogin* and the ordinary being strive and labour in life, the labour of the former is rooted in *atman*, of the latter in ego: God remains remote without experience of the *atman* within. *Unrefined* may mean unpurified. Shankara believed the term referred to those who had not purified themselves through *tapas*, austerities,[14] but the meaning is probably wider and indicative of not having purified the self in terms of self-control, loss of egoism, non attachment to the fruits of actions – in short, all that the *Gita* has taught thus far. The distinction in perception here is, according to Ramanuja, dependent on *prapatti*, "total surrender" to God (though he does not mention *prapatti* explicitly). Those who practise it through *karma-yoga* are able to realize, unlike others, that *atman* and *prakriti* are different. However, he said of Krishna: "The *yogins* who strive in regard to *karma-yoga* and such other ways of realisation, after surrendering themselves to Me, have their internal organ of perception cleared of all stains thereby; they see with the eye called *yoga* this (self) as abiding in its own form as separate from the body."[15] Importantly, Ramanuja said: "Thus, it has been taught that the self, both in the emancipated condition and in the condition of bondage, is owned and ruled over by the Lord."[16]

VERSE 12

The radiance that, residing in the sun, illumines the whole world, know that radiance that is in the moon and the fire to be mine.

Krishna now turns to describing something of his nature as Brahman, his *vibhutis*. Here, he is the *Purushottama*, "Supreme Purusha", of the title of the chapter. *Radiance*, or light, *tejas*, sometimes translated as "splendour" or "brilliance" is associated with the *sattva guna*. Without such radiance, all awareness and knowledge is impossible. Ishvara makes possible this knowledge by being the essence in all forms of light. Matter cannot perceive itself; it is only spirit that can know and experience, and knowledge may be of the *prakritic* world in which the Self becomes trapped or of Brahman, by which the Self is liberated.

VERSE 13

Permeating the earth, I support all beings by energy. I nourish all the herbs being the sapid moon.

The verse refers to the manifest *energy* or power of Ishvara, known as *ojas*, which pervades the whole universe, present in both animate and inanimate phenomena. It is the life-force, the vital force of every individual being and the highest form of energy. The moon, here *soma*, is thought to be the medium by which such energy, *rasatmaka soma*, or "life-giving nourishment", is passed to herbs and plants, though they also gain energy through the sun.[17] Both sun and moon are believed to contain different energies. Since the moon in the verse is *soma*, some prefer to translate the word as a plant. However, the moon was believed to be the source of all fluids and savours, and is the better translation. Barbara Stoler Miller thus translated "the liquid of moonlight",[18] suggestive that sap was believed to be infused into plants, so nourishing them. The use of *rasa*, "sap", takes us back to the symbolism of the *ashvattha* tree.

VERSE 14

Abiding in the body of living beings, having become Vaishvanara, associated with *prana* and *apana*, I digest the fourfold food.

Without fire and heat, humanity cannot survive. In particular, the process of combustion within a person turns food into energy, a change of gross material to subtle. This energy is known as *vaishvanara*. In the *Brihad-aranyaka Upanishad*, we find the words: "The fire common to all men is the one within a person, the one through which the food he eats is digested."[19] In the *Vedanta*, too, *vaishvanara* is a term used for the waking state of all human beings. In the earlier *Rig Veda*, however, *vaishvanara* was associated with Agni, the god of fire, who was responsible for transforming gross sacrificial food offered to the gods into the subtle form that they could absorb; hence the transformation of food into energy in the living being. *Prana* and *apana* refer to the breathing process that aids digestion. *Fourfold food* refers to the different ways (and therefore different types of food) in which food can be eaten — masticated, sucked, licked and swallowed.

Verse 15

And I am seated in the heart of all. From me are memory, knowledge and their loss. I am that which is to be known by all the *Vedas*, I am indeed the author of the *Vedanta* and even the knower of the *Veda*.

Seated in the heart of all is a reference to the essence of the divine as the *atman* within, to the consciousness it permits, and to its being the source of what is, or is not, known or remembered. However, the reference to *memory*, Sanskrit *smriti*, is likely to be to intuitive memory and thus has a far stronger connotation than simply factual memory, what Miller called "the awakening of latent impressions left by prior perceptions; essential to the aesthetic experience of Krishna's revelation",[20] Similarly, *knowledge (jnana)* is of the intuitive kind, too, that which brings knowledge of the *atman* and of Brahman. *Loss* is sometimes translated as "disputation" or "debate", which would not suit the context if memory and knowledge are given deeper meanings.

The consciousness that arises through memory and knowledge is the manifestation of Ishvara as the spirit, the *purusha* of all beings that passively witnesses all that takes place in the world of *prakriti*. If an individual retains such passive witnessing then consciousness is pure with knowledge only of Brahman. If that consciousness becomes actively engaged in what it witnesses, then the whole psychological and material being accumulates *prakritic* knowledge and memory function to create order and personal identity in the surrounding world. But it can only be the *purusha* within that can be the source of any knowledge. The supreme Purusha, the Purushottama, is also the essence of *Veda* and *Vedanta* which are the sources by which Brahman can be known. Brahman as supreme Purusha is also knower (*Kshetrajna*) and that which is to be known (*prakriti* or *kshetra*). The truth that is held in the *Veda* and *Vedanta* is revealed by Brahman at the beginning of each new manifestation of the universe.

Verse 16

There are these two *purushas* in the world – the perishable and the imperishable. All beings are the perishable and the immutable is called the imperishable.

When consciousness occurs as a *jivatman*, an individual being, it is a *perishable (kshara) purusha*, an ordinary being. It is a *purusha* that is bound in *prakriti* where it finds itself part of a transient world, the result of which is the cycle of births and deaths in which it revolves. The *jivatman* here is the perishable *purusha*, but not the true Self, the *atman* within, which is *imperishable (akshara)*. The perishable *purusha* has linked itself with a material ego, mind and intellect, whereas pure *purusha* is the true Self, identifiable in part with Brahman.

Immutable in the verse is *kuta-stha*, which we first met in 6:8 and again in 12:3. It means something like "standing on the mountain top", "being at the peak", "one on the peak" and, therefore, is usually translated as "immutable", "unmoving", "unchangeable". It is rather apt here, in the light of the *ashvattha* image, since the aim is to reach the apex of the tree, albeit ultimately transcending even that. By extension, then, this *kuta-stha* is the still point of consciousness, pure consciousness that is the pinnacle, the goal, and passive, again, like the bird silently and passively witnessing another flitting from fruit to fruit and tree to tree. Sri Krishna Prem graphically wrote: "To Its calm, impassive gaze, all things are equal, all yesterdays are one with all tomorrows, action and flowing movement can exist no more. This is the unmoved Witness of the Cosmos, the stainless Light that naught can ever move. Many have viewed It as the Goal of all and sought a refuge in Its changeless peace beyond a world of constant change and sorrow."[21] And yet, as the following verse will state, this is not the ultimate Reality.

VERSE 17

But there is another superior Purusha: this is called the *Param-Atman,* the imperishable Ishvara who pervades and sustains the three worlds.

If the previous verse depicted two *purushas* as the perishable *jivatman* and the imperishable *atman*, as I think they do, the highest Brahman is beyond both. Yet even here, Purusha is Brahman manifest, *saguna* Brahman, indicated by the use of *Ishvara*, "Lord". It is this *saguna* aspect that is the panentheistic, transcendent Cause of the continued manifestation of *prakriti* and yet is that which also continues to exist when *prakriti* ceases to be manifest. Since it is higher than the imperishable *purusha* of the previous verse, where it is probably the *atman*, this *Param-Atman* is greater than its own essence in all beings and all things: Krishna is *prakriti* and *atman* and yet transcends both. The *three worlds* are Heaven, Earth and the middle regions between the two or perhaps Heaven, Earth and the hells.[22]

VERSE 18

Since I transcend the perishable and am superior to the imperishable also, I am therefore declared Purushottama in the world and in the *Veda.*

This could be a reference to *saguna* or to *nirguna* Brahman. The previous verse mentioned Ishvara, suggesting that there it was *saguna* Brahman that was being referred to. This verse may be continuing that idea or referring to *Purushottama*, "Supreme Purusha", as *nirguna* Brahman. But, again, since Brahman is greater than the *atman*, which is the true nature of each being, there is a distinct dualism and panentheism in the concept that is consonant with so much of the *Gita's* teaching.

VERSE 19

Who thus, undeluded, knows me as the Purushottama, he is all-knowing and worships me with his whole being, Bharata.

When the individual is able to understand the Self as part of this cosmic Purusha, then there is no longer delusion about the true nature of the world. With such realization, total concentration on what is real ensues and the *jivatman* no longer becomes the centre of reality and attached to *prakriti*. Self-importance is lost and *prakriti* is given up in favour of Purusha. Again, *worships* (*bhajati*) suggests a dual relationship between worshipper and even this highest, supreme Purusha. The verse combines *jnana* with *bhakti* rather well.

VERSE 20

Thus, this most secret *shastra* has been taught by me, sinless one. Knowing this he becomes wise and has accomplished all duties, Bharata.

The final verse refers to a special secret teaching, a *shastra*. This word means "instruction", "treatise", "law book", "rule" or "scripture" and so has a formal connotation, thus lending a formal character to the teaching expounded in the *Gita*. Since this *shastra* is *this most secret* (*guhya*) one, it is suggestive that it is one that transcends other teachings, though it would be in line with much *Vedantic* thought in saying that knowledge of Brahman is the ultimate knowledge by which every possible duty is fulfilled and there is no longer any need for ritual action. Thus, *accomplished all duties* can be variously interpreted – done all that has to be done, fulfilled all things, what ought to be done is done, fulfilled his purpose. The *dharmas*, the duties, laid down in the scriptures dictating class, caste, stage of life, religious ritual and so on, are all considered to be accomplished when one understands this most secret teaching of the *Gita*, when one, to use Aurobindo's phrase, arrives at "an ether of dispassionate equality".[23]

In the *Upanishad* of the *Bhagavad Gita*, the knowledge of Brahman, the teaching of *Yoga* and the dialogue between Shri Krishna and Arjuna, this is the fifteenth chapter called *Purushottama Yoga*.

CHAPTER SIXTEEN

Daivasura Sampad Vibhaga Yoga

The *Yoga* of the Differentiation of the Divine and the Demonic

As its title suggests, what follows deals with the virtues of the godly, *daiva*, those of divine nature, contrasted with the depravities of the ungodly, *asura*, those of a demonic nature. In dealing with such a topic, the chapter contains much moral teaching in terms of proximate goals. It has nothing to do with the subject of gods and demons *per se*, but with the godly and demonic qualities of humanity. The bulk of the chapter launches into a castigation of the unorthodox believers like the materialists overlapping with the ostentatious wealthy. In short, there is less of the divine and more of the demonic, which rather detracts from the loftier heights of much other material in the *Gita*. Thus, when the content turns to examine the nature of the ungodly, we find it pointing to one who "is essentially an atheist, a libertine, a braggart, a murderer, and a hypocrite", to use Robert Zaehner's description.[1] However, in the context of the whole of the *Gita*, where the qualities of the *yogin* have featured widely in chapters TWO, TWELVE, THIRTEEN and FOURTEEN, this diatribe against what are deemed evil individuals is perhaps a small slice of the overall content.

VERSE I
Fearlessness, purity of heart, steadfastness in *jnana* and *yoga*, giving, control of the senses, *yajna*, study of the *Shastras*, austerity and uprightness . . .

The first three verses list the *sattvic* qualities that are characteristic of one who is in, or destined for, the divine state. For the most part, it seems to me that they should be interpreted according to the content of the *Gita* as a whole, rather than looking for their general interpretation beyond. Most of the qualities listed in these verses have been mentioned already in 13:7–11. *Fearlessness* is *abhyaya*; it is characteristic of godliness because the closer to God one is, the less one experiences fear or any kind of dualities. Fear comes about when one is attached to the material body, mind and intellect and to the egoistic "I". The *purity* mentioned is actually *sattva*, the enlightening and evolving quality. *Steadfastness in jnana and yoga* could mean simply steadfastness in *jnana-yoga*, the path of knowledge, and so steadfastness in the *yoga* of knowledge. This would refer to knowledge of the true nature of life as *prakritic* and impermanent contrasted with the permanent *atman* within. But since *jnana* and *yoga* are not separated elsewhere like this, the term may refer to *jnana-yoga* and another *yoga*, presumably, *karma-yoga*. *Giving* is *dana*, meant in the broad sense of giving without thinking of one's self, rather than simply giving to the poor: it is, thus, altruistic giving and will be taken up at some length in CHAPTER SEVENTEEN of the *Gita*. Similarly, *yajna* is "sacrifice", but not only in the narrow sense of religious ritual, but in the *Gita*'s wider sense of the term as self-sacrifice. *Study of the Shastras, svadhyaya*, is study of the scriptures, the wider scriptures that stretch beyond the *Veda*. Here, this is presented as a proximate goal, even though ultimately the scriptures are transcended when *moksha* is realized. Ramanuja's comments on this verse show clearly that he endorsed the maintenance of *Vedic* ordinances even for the divinely characterized individual.[2] *Austerity, tapas*, may mean, narrowly, the austerities of bodily mortification, as Shankara understood the term[3] or, in a wider sense, the curtailing of the slavery of the mind to sense stimuli, which is more in line with the general teaching of the *Gita*, in the same way that *dana* and *yajna* are given wider contexts of application. All three – *dana, tapas* and *yajna* – will feature in this wider sense in CHAPTER SEVENTEEN. The goals of the verse represent the *sattvic* path in life and are the proximate goals of the *yogin*, the means to *moksha* as the ultimate goal.

VERSE 2
. . . non-violence, truth, absence of anger, renunciation, peacefulness, absence of crookedness, compassion to beings, non-covetousness, gentleness, modesty, absence of fickleness . . .

Non-violence here is the proximate goal of *ahimsa*. *Truth* is *satya*, an ultimate goal to be achieved. *Absence of anger* is *akrodha* and reflects the earlier teaching of the *Gita* that the mind should be still in situations that would normally cause pleasure or anger. *Renunciation, tyaga*, in the *Gita*'s teachings is renunciation of desire and of the fruits of actions and not renunciation of the world. *Peacefulness (shanti)* is the serenity of mind that promotes equilibrium, stilling reactions to senses. *Absence of crookedness* is meant in the sense of not fault-finding, not back-biting and lacking in calumny. *Non-covetousness* probably refers to the necessity for stilling the senses when they are in contact with sense objects so that desires for what one does not have are overcome. *Absence of fickleness* is often seen as bodily, physical stillness[4] as opposed to the fidgeting that is characteristic of the restless person who is constantly ill at ease. More generally, it would point to reliability.

VERSE 3
. . . vigour, patience, firmness, purity, absence of hatred and exaggerated pride belong to those born for the divine state, Bharata.

Vigour here is *tejas*, the word also for "burning power", or "fire", suggesting energy, ardour and the like, though it can also mean "splendour", "radiance" "majesty" or "effulgence." Ramanuja saw *tejas* as invincible power, "the quality of not being overcome by wicked persons".[5] *Patience, kshama*, is meant in the sense of forbearance, while *firmness, dhriti*, is suggestive of steadfastness and sustained effort. *Purity* (*shauca*) refers to both an outward and an inward state of mind. Again, the qualities are *sattvic* and therefore those that bear them are destined for a godly existence or birth in a good womb. The use of the word *born* is a reminder that it is past actions and character that determine the next life. Thus, the *sattvic* life facilitates a good birth where personal evolution and a divinely-inspired existence can continue.

VERSE 4

Hypocrisy, arrogance, self-conceit, anger, harshness and ignorance are for those born for the demonic state, Partha.

What now follows is a description of the demonic or *asuric* characteristics of those destined for a devilish state or birth. The suggestion is of a fate that acquires a demonic *jivatman* with demonic traits, rather than a life in the hells. *Hypocrisy* is ostentation, being what one is not, as is *arrogance* in thinking oneself superior to others. The *Gita* has mentioned the fault of *anger* (*krodha*) many times, as also, *ignorance* (*ajnana*). Ignorance, according to Ramanuja, is "lack of discrimination between the higher and lower principles, and between what ought to be done and what ought not to be done".[6] Higher and lower here are the Self freed from *prakriti* and the self attached to it respectively. Again, *born* is important here in that it is indicative of the sum total of past actions that brings about being born into the demonic state and the subsequent living of a demonic life.

VERSE 5

The divine state is deemed for liberation, the demonic for bondage. Do not grieve, Pandava, you are born for the divine state.

Ideally, life is an evolutionary process in which a being rises in levels of consciousness until the point of *liberation*, *moksha*, is reached. Thus, in the *samsaric* cycle, the *jivatman* carries its good qualities with it and the evolution of the self is possible. However, evolution of the self may be slow, or even static. *Bondage* to the cycle of rebirth is then inevitable and if individuals' qualities are not particularly good, they may remain for countless lives in the demonic state or be subject to births that cause their involution. Arjuna is one whose past lives have been witnessing the steady evolution necessary on the path to *moksha*.

VERSE 6

There are two types of beings in this world, the divine and the demonic; the divine has been described at length, hear from me, Partha, of the demonic.

We now begin what seems to present a rather black and white perspective of human nature – those who are good and are destined for evolution, and those who are demonic and are destined for involution. However, the *Gita* seems to target mainly a specific group of individuals, which will become clear in verse 8. For *types of beings* many prefer "creations of beings", which adds a somewhat different nuance of thought. "Creation" raises the difficulty of needing a creator, and that makes God the agent and cause of the divine and demonic beings rather than their own inclinations serving to make them *karmically* predisposed to particular births and lives. Perhaps, in terms of creation, the idea underpinning the verse is of the creation of gods and demons and the constant battles between the two that runs through much early Hindu mythology.

Another difficulty is how these two natures relate to the theory of the three *gunas*: such a black and white, good and evil, perspective hardly does justice to the theory of the *gunas*, which allows for multiple nuances of personality, though constantly changing in any one individual. And yet, the lower the class of person, the less *sattva* is to be found and the more *tamasic* the character. The god-like destined for liberation are few, as Krishna has already said (7:19), and the intensely evil at the opposite end of the scale must be few, too. The bulk of humanity is in the multi-charactered middle range with a few or many of the faults that the *Gita* assigns to the demonic. Many will be full of desires and live their lives immersed in them but may hold hope for some spiritual evolution at the same time. Desires and aversions are facets of ordinary lives, it is only when they turn to lust and hate that they become demonic.

VERSE 7

Of action and inaction demonic men do not know; neither purity, right conduct, or truth is in them.

There is little that is *sattvic* in demonic beings, though we should remember that, according to Sankhyan theory, everything must contain at least a grain of each of the *gunas*. The actions of these demonic beings are non-evolutionary and against *dharma*. *Action and inaction, pravritti* and *nivritti*, may simply refer to not knowing which actions to do and which not to do, thus, not being able to discriminate, especially between good and evil. Or, the expression may refer to the egoless action of which the *Gita* has said much – the action in inaction – and of which demonic characters have no concept. Other translations of *pravritti* and *nivritti* vary, for example, "inclination and disinclination",[7] or "activity and rest".[8] However they are translated, *pravritti* is suggestive of involvement in the world and *nivritti* of withdrawal from it, of renunciation, and is a rather neat synthesis by the *Gita* of two seemingly opposing terms by conjoining action with renunciation of its fruits through concentration on the inactive *atman*. Aurobindo took *nivritti* and *pravritti* further in finding the former as the impersonal Brahman, and the latter as the dynamic presence of Brahman in the world in all existences: "It is the essential quality and force, *svabhava*, the self-principle of all their becoming, the inherent principle and divine power behind their phenomenal existence."[9] Again, Ramanuja endorsed *Vedic* praxis as a means to release in his comments on this verse, the demonic not having the *purity* (*shauca*) or ability, the *right conduct*, to engage in such praxis.[10] Purity for Ramanuja represented the cleanliness and, therefore, fitness for performing *Vedic* rites.[11]

VERSE 8

They say "the world is unreal, without a basis. It is without a Lord, brought about by mutual union caused by desire; what else?"

The theistic *Gita* now launches into an attack on the materialists, those who would be opposed to any idea of a spiritual presence. And it looks as though it is such materialists that the author of the *Gita* has had in mind from the beginning of the chapter. Like the materialists, the demonic are portrayed as believing there is no First Cause, no related cause and effect and no ultimate purpose or reality in life. *Unreal* is *asat* what is devoid of reality or truth and probably refers to those who believe that only matter exists and that nothing spiritual can obtain at all. Such was the view of the materialists, of which the Lokayatas and the Charvakas were the main protagonists. As the verse suggests, they believed that the only cause of coming-to-be could be sexual union through *desire, kama*, the *mutual union* of the verse, and nothing could possibly be known beyond the empirical. The self, then, can be the living body and nothing more. Religious beliefs and scriptures were untenable to the materialists and there was definitely no God. Though goodness was believed to lead to happiness and evil to unhappiness, the materialists rejected any belief in *karma* and rebirth, the cause–effect process. *Without a basis* is a rejection of a First Cause and, therefore, of any need for a moral order or any kind of logical progression of evolutionary creation as in the Sankhya evolves of *prakriti*.[12] Perhaps the idea that it is the materialists that is being referred to is perpetuated from Shankara's commentary.

VERSE 9

Holding this view, these ruined selves of little intellect, of dreadful actions, come forth as enemies for the destruction of the world.

Ruined souls are those with great adverse *karma* as a result of lives that are *adharmic*. With *little intellect* (*buddhi*) they live lives totally at the mercy of sense experience, seeing nothing beyond it.

VERSE 10

Filled with insatiable desire, full of hypocrisy, pride and arrogance, holding false ideas through delusion, they act with impure resolves . . .

Desire in this verse and in those that follow is *kama*, which is sensual pleasure, sexual pleasure and gratification of the senses. Thus, it is sometimes translated in these verses as "lust". *Kama* is not, in itself, evil, being one of the four Hindu goals of life, along with *artha*, "wealth", *dharma* and *moksha*, and should always be held in check by *dharma*. The desires of those of demonic nature are totally *adharmic* and their desires have got out of hand and psychologically and physically amplified through total *delusion* (*moha*). As such, these desires become lust.[13] *Impure resolves* may mean incorrect ritual, polluting practices or, more likely, acts undertaken for self-gratification.

VERSE 11

... housed in immeasurable cares, ending only in death, regarding gratification of desires as their highest aim, and feeling sure that that is all
...

Ending only in death does not mean in reality that the cares of the demonic will end, just that they *think* they will. As materialists, they believe that death – here, *pralaya*, "dissolution" – will bring about their complete extinction, for there is nothing beyond it. However, *pralaya* might also refer to the end of the universe, when all becomes unmanifest, for *gratification of desire* points to innumerable rebirths that can only end – and then, temporarily – when time is suspended. *Immeasurable cares* refers to the multitude of desires that fill the minds of the demonic. *Gratification* is *bhoga*, which also means "enjoyment", suggestive of a thoroughly hedonistic attitude to life.

VERSE 12

... bound by a hundred ties of hope, given over to desires and anger, [they] strive by unjust means for hoards of wealth for sensual enjoyment.

Wealth and the pursuit of it is not *per se* regarded as evil in Hinduism. Providing wealth is subject to *dharma*, as was seen in the case of *kama* in verse 10, it can be incorporated into daily living. In fact, *artha*, "wealth" is important at the second stage of life, the householder stage, as is *kama*, when raising a family and acquiring a position in society are considered necessary. But because *dharma* always remains one of the four aims of life, wealth and social successes should not be acquired in an unrighteous way – which is exactly what the *Gita* is accusing the materialists of doing. So what is described here is the non-virtuous pursuit of wealth through means that are *adharmic*, and of incessant *desire* (*kama*) and *anger* (*krodha*) in perpetrating such means.

VERSE 13

"This has been gained by me today; this desire I shall obtain; this is mine and that wealth also shall be mine in time."

Notable here is the emphasis on action undertaken for results, totally full of egoistic desire, as opposed to the egoless action from the still *atman* advocated by the earlier chapters of the *Gita*.

VERSE 14

"That enemy has been slain by me; I shall also slay others. I am lord; I am the enjoyer, I am perfect, powerful and happy."

The egoistic arrogance, pride, self-centredness and domineering nature of the individual here is brought out by the "I", "me" and "mine" of the verse. Since the speaker claims *I am lord*, the demonic is still the materialist, who believed that the empirical self is all there is. Thus, there is no passive *atman* as the pure, spiritual consciousness and *enjoyer*, only the material individual full of ego. Perfection (*siddhi*) and happiness (*sukha*) have hitherto been used in the *Gita* of the liberated Self: here, the terms serve to indicate the false states of the demonic.

VERSE 15

"I am rich and well-born. Who else is equal to me? I shall sacrifice, I shall give gifts, I shall rejoice." Thus deluded by ignorance . . .

We move here, it seems, from the formerly criticized materialists to materialists of another kind – those obsessed with wealth, though given the materialist view that there is nothing beyond matter, the verse may still refer to the former. For *I shall rejoice*, Zaehner had: "I'll have a marvellous time",[14] which suits the hedonistic tone rather well. If a person is rich and well-born, it is as a result of good *karma*, the result of good actions in past lives, the results of causes made elsewhere. Yet the wealthy of the verse have an exaggerated sense of their importance, enhanced egos and believe that they can manipulate further wealth for themselves. *Well-born* would presumably refer to *Brahmins* or *Kshatriyas*. There were learned men who studied materialist treatises, so it was not impossible for *Brahmins* and *Kshatriyas* to court materialist ideas: thus, they could *sacrifice*, but still hold unorthodox notions. Moreover, the *sacrifice*, *yajna*, mentioned here is nothing like the broader meaning of disinterested actions without concentration on results.

VERSE 16

. . . bewildered by many thoughts, entangled in the net of delusion, addicted to the gratification of desires, [they] fall into a foul hell.

The use of *jala*, *net*, suggests that, like fish trapped in a net, there is no escape for those trapped in *delusion* (*moha*) and ignorance. For *bewildered by many thoughts*, Eknath Easwaran had, graphically, "whirled about by a fragmented mind",[15] which captures the sense of the phrase superbly: the *thoughts* (*chitta*) are totally involved in the world of the senses. *Hell* is Naraka, and verse 21 will depict the demonic characteristics of those destined to enter its gates.

VERSE 17

Self-conceited, stubborn, filled with pride and intoxication of wealth, they perform sacrifices in name, with hypocrisy, without regard to scriptural ordinances.

The criticism here is of those who *seem* outwardly righteous – and make a good show of it – but who are inwardly devoid of it. Given the acceptance of orthodoxy in the verse there is certainly a shift away from the materialists who eschewed religious praxis so presumably, here, it is the well-born orthodox of verse 10, those courting materialism, who come under attack.

VERSE 18

Given over to egoism, power, haughtiness, desire and anger, these malicious people hate me in their own bodies and in those of others.

Those with powerful egoism (*ahankara*) find it impossible to relate to God. We would expect little, if any, recognition of the spiritual *atman* within and no recognition of the divine in others. However, there is a sense in the verse of some recognition of the presence of the *atman*, but a conscious hatred of and antipathy to it. Perhaps the people of whom he talks are the *Brahmins* and *Kshatriyas* who court unorthodox ideas. It is cetrainly those against Krishna who are the subject of his vilification: "But those who, contending this my teaching, do not practise it, know them to be deluded in all knowledge, ruined, devoid of discrimination", he says in 3:32. And in 4:40: "The ignorant, faithless and doubting self goes to destruction. The doubting self has not this world, nor the next, nor happiness." Thus, there are stringent criticisms elsewhere; it is their concentration here in this chapter that significantly brings them to the fore.

VERSE 19
Those cruel, hateful men, worst in the worlds; I hurl these polluted ones for ever into only demonic wombs.

For the incessantly evil, it seems, such an entity as an eternal Hell – *for ever*, in the text – is possible. Some translate as "ceaselessly" and Richard Gotshalk's "over and over again"[16] hints, perhaps, that there might be an end to the process. The "for ever" concept is contrary to ideas of the possibility, however remote, of *atman*-realization for *all* entities. But there is no hint of any *sattvic* element, or of any respite for the *worst among men*, according to this verse which, in my view, does not express the greatest of concepts in the *Gita*. The thought has been stated already by Krishna in 7:15, where he says: "Evil doers, the deluded, the lowest of men, do not seek me. Deprived of knowledge by *maya*, they belong to the nature of *asuras*," but this verse is not suggestive of divine agency. Intensely adverse *karma* would cause equally adverse involution anyway as part of the cause–effect process, and *demonic wombs* is often taken to mean births in animal or insect forms. It is, again, the question of agency that is the difficult point, with the statement *I hurl these polluted ones* into demonic states rather than self-agency through adverse *karma* and *adharma* being the cause of involution. Commentators are loathe to accept the "for ever" idea. Aurobindo, for example, went to some length to rescue the evil-doer at the final moment – "even the greatest sinner, the most impure and violent evil-doer is saved the moment he turns to adore and follow after the Godhead within him".[17] But the *Gita* does not even hint at such hope at this point, or in this chapter. Krishna has previously dissociated himself from agency: "The Lord does not create agency nor actions for this world: he does not create union with the fruits of actions. One's nature leads to action", he says in 5:14, implicitly placing good and evil firmly in the *gunic* make-up. And quite incongruous with the present verse are the words: "The Lord takes no note of evil or even merit of anyone", at the beginning of 5:15.

VERSE 20
Entering into demonic wombs in birth after birth, still not attaining me, the deluded fall into an even lower condition than that, Kaunteya.

Involution is even more pronounced in this verse and *still not attaining me* suggests the permanence of these lowest demonic states. Indeed, Zaehner translated "they never attain to me".[18] Perhaps there are the remnants of the older *Vedic* belief in a rewarding Heaven and a retributive Hell in these verses; certainly, eternal damnation is an unfamiliar theme in Hinduism in general. And if, as many commentators believe, birth in these lowest states is as animals and insects – particularly snakes, dogs and hogs – lacking capability for conscious reflection, how can they fall even lower or ever consciously turn to God and begin an evolutionary climb? *Birth after birth* according to the law of cause and effect sees the wicked subject to involution, but only until their adverse *karma* has been exhausted. That would then permit a rise from animal form to human. But no hint of this is to be found here and we are faced with the difficulty of animals and insects having to be capable of choice in changing character. Plenty of hope is given earlier in the *Gita* to those who, even if sinful, turn to Krishna,[19] but not to those who deny him.

VERSE 21

This gate of Hell is triple – desire, anger and greed – destructive of the self. Therefore, renounce these three.

Desire here, as in earlier verses, is *kama*; anger is *krodha* and *greed* is *lobha*. They are the three characteristics that are inimical to evolution of the self and for one subject to all three, involution is likely. *Destructive of the self* must be indicative of destruction to the evolving self, the *jivatman*, since the *atman* is present in all and is indestructible. We have been led to believe earlier in the *Gita* that nothing can come into being without the *atman* as the essence of God within it, and verse 18 of this chapter certainly suggests that God resides even in the most evil of beings, but to no avail for the lowest of the demonic. *Hell*, Naraka, is certainly the fate of those who propagate desire, anger and greed, the *three gates to darkness* of the following verse.

VERSE 22

The man liberated from these three gates to darkness, Kaunteya, practises good for the self and then achieves the supreme goal.

Is there, then, a ray of hope in this verse? Can even the lowest of demonic natures reach out from hellish darkness? Or is Krishna merely speaking of the fate of the juxtaposed divinely-inspired being? *Darkness* here is *tamas* and Zaehner made the point that it cannot be pure *tamas* because desire, anger and greed are *rajasic* not *tamasic* qualities.[20] But this is unlikely: *rajas* is a *guna* of energy and also of equilibrium and therefore of insufficient energy to cause evolution or involution. Thus, only *tamas* could cause involution of individuals, just as *sattva* causes them to evolve. *Goal* here, as in the following verse, may mean "path", which would bring out the idea of the destiny of the good and evil in terms of their *karmic* futures.

VERSE 23

He who, having cast aside the ordinances of the *Shastras*, acts under the impulse of desire, will not attain perfection, nor happiness, nor the supreme goal.

The *ordinances of the Shastras*, the scriptures, prescribe what is and what is not to be done. The demonic, therefore, will not do what *is* to be done and will do what is *not* to be done. In earlier parts of the *Gita* it was stated that the enlightened *yogin* had no need of the *Vedas*. One who is on the path to *moksha*, the *supreme goal*, however, has need of them as a spiritual guide. If Krishna seems over critical of the scriptures elsewhere in the *Gita* – especially of the *Vedas* – this verse suggests the contrary, and their essential need on the path to *moksha* that culminates in true *perfection* (*siddhi*) and *happiness* (*sukha*), not the false perception of these in verse 14. The following verse endorses this.

VERSE 24

Therefore, let the *Shastras* be the authority determining what ought to be done and ought not to be done. Knowing what is said in the ordinance of the *Shastras* you should perform it here.

The *Shastras*, the sacred books of Hinduism, include the *shruti* ("heard" or "cognized") literature of the *Vedas* where, certainly, prohibitions and injunctions form an important part. But the *Shastras* also contain teaching on *dharma* that is separate from the *Vedas*. *Smriti* ("remembered") scriptures are also included in the *Shastras*. Is the reference to *Shastras*, then, deliberate, thus widening the scope of teaching on *dharma*? Indeed, it would soften this rather harsh chapter of the *Gita* by thinking so. In the final analysis, this chapter of the *Gita* does little to further that prickly debate on the nature of good and evil and the fate of those who perpetrate either.

In the *Upanishad* of the *Bhagavad Gita*, the knowledge of Brahman, the teaching of *Yoga* and the dialogue between Shri Krishna and Arjuna, this is the sixteenth chapter called *Daivasura Sampad Vibhaga Yoga*.

CHAPTER SEVENTEEN

Shraddha-traya Vibhaga Yoga

The *Yoga* of the Differentiation of the Threefold *Shraddha*

Shraddha means "faith", or "trust", and this chapter, therefore, is about faith in its various kinds and in relationship to the three *gunas*. Faith is linked with the *gunas* because it is associated with strength of feeling, one's heartfelt tendencies and, thus, what one is inwardly will dictate what one does outwardly. Thus, Radhakrishnan aptly stated that *shraddha* "is not acceptance of a belief. It is striving after self-realization by concentrating the powers of the mind on a given ideal".[1] *Yajna* "sacrifice", *tapas* "austerity" and *dana* "giving, generosity", are also continued in this chapter especially in relation to the *gunas*, but the *gunas* are also discussed in relation to food. The chapter ends with representations of Brahman, *Om*, *Tat* and *Sat*.

VERSE I   Arjuna said:
What is the nature, Krishna, of those who, setting aside the ordinances of the *Shastras*, perform sacrifice endowed with *shraddha*: is it *sattva*, *rajas* or *tamas*?
The previous chapter discussed the nature of those destined for evolution and those for involution. There, verse 16:23 stressed the importance of conforming to the *Shastras*, the scriptures, on the path to *moksha*. Arjuna asks Krishna what the state would be of those who are not really conversant with such ordinances and yet who live their lives with *shraddha*. The previous chapter depicted the demonic as subject to desire, anger and greed. But Arjuna is raising the question we all want to raise; what of the generally unorthodox people who *are* good and who have faith in God? Will they be sufficiently *sattvic* to evolve, or are they to be classed as demonic? The crux of the answer will be that faith and its expression in practice cannot be separated but can be of differing values: in contemporary parlance, we might say intellectual faith, blind faith, or socially accepted faith, with what Sri Krishna Prem termed "nothing more than the instinct for social conformity".[2] In short, individuals may seem full of faith, but the quality of that faith will be dictated by their inner personalities as we shall see as the chapter unfolds. For *endowed with* faith, some prefer "full of faith", but since Krishna is about to qualify the faith practised by different types of people, many faiths are far from being full. Shankara considered that Arjuna is enquiring about those who live a life worshipping the gods in faith but who are unaware of the ordinances in the *Shastras* laying

down how this should be done.[3] Ramanuja seemed to suggest that faith in acts not endorsed by the *Shastras* could have no results:[4] "it is taught how, whatever is not ordained by the *sastras* is fruitless because of its being demoniacal."[5] Presumably, it is not that they bear no results at all, but that their fruits are of less value.

VERSE 2   The Lord said:
Threefold is the *shraddha* inherent in the intrinsic nature of the embodied – *sattvic, rajasic* and *tamasic*. Listen to this.

Although the *gunas* are mixed in an individual, one will be predominant and will dictate the general characteristics – the innate or *intrinsic nature, sva-bhava,* literally "own being" of a person. Such individual nature will be the result of actions of past lives, the cumulative effects of previous causes, and will dictate, too, the various activities, dispositions, likes and dislikes of the individual, and also the kind of *jivatman* that will pass on after death to the next existence. *Karma* from past lives, similarly, will determine the predominant *guna* of the present existence. Arjuna has asked whether someone who conducts non-orthodox *yajna* with faith is *sattvic, rajasic* or *tamasic.* Krishna turns the question around and says that the *gunic* inner nature will determine the kind of faith a person has. In modern terms, it is a reductionist theory that makes behaviour dependent on intrinsic make-up. So whatever nature a person has will dictate the level and nature of his or her faith. The faith of the *rajasic* selfish individual, for example, will be geared to rewards in life or after it. This is why Krishna says over and over again that those who give themselves over to him, are devoted to him, act for him and sacrifice for him, transcend the *gunas. Embodied* is rather difficult. The Sanskrit is *dehin*, which has been used fairly consistently as the passive *atman* within as opposed to *deha*, which is the physical and mental being. Probably, I think, the verse points to the *gunic* personality, the *sva-bhava* in conjunction with, and alongside, the *embodied* (*dehin*) passive *atman.*

VERSE 3
The *shraddha* of everyone, Bharata, is in accordance with their nature. Man consists of his *shraddha*: truly, what his *shraddha* is, that is he.

The type of faith a person has, its degree of intensity, quality, and resulting actions, will be related to the inner personality. A *rajasic* individual, for example, is hardly likely to have the faith or life-style of the mystic: faith and personality are inextricably linked. *Nature* in the verse is actually *sattva*, which is sometimes translated in the context of this verse as "soul" or "mind". It refers here to the innate tendencies of an individual, the individual's inner nature, and that will depend on the unique combination of *gunas* in an individual. Thus, nature here has a much deeper meaning than it does in verse 1. In the present verse it is more like "essence", the deep-rooted nature or being of an individual that drives personality. Aurobindo put it thus: "We create our own truth of existence in our own action of mind and life, which is another way of saying that we create our own selves, are our own makers."[6] The dark, unknown world of the subconscious is stocked full of the residues of past experiences from countless lives. These residues are called *samskaras* and they are constantly being replenished by present experiences. Crucially, both are related, the past latent residues influencing the way we behave here and now and the way we behave here and now reinforcing and building up exactly the same tendencies for the future.[7]

VERSE 4
Sattvic men perform sacrifice to the *devas*; *rajasic* men, the *Yakshas* and *Rakshasas*; the others, the *tamasic* people, the *pretas* and the hosts of *bhutas.*

The level of consciousness of an individual will determine the type of religion a person has, and that level of consciousness will depend on the predominant *guna* in the person. On the basis of like seeks like, a personality predominantly *sattvic* in nature is more likely to focus worship on the more highly evolved concepts of God, though the verse makes this plural, *devas*, gods. Those predominantly *rajasic* would focus more on anthropomorphic concepts of lesser deities or even non-divine beings like *Yakshas* and *Rakshasas* who are classes of demons. These would reward, punish, and slay enemies. Then, too, the *Yakshas*, the demons mentioned in the verse, were followers of the god of wealth, so *rajasic* people have the acquisition of wealth, power and materialism as their goals. *Tamasic* personalities will be more attracted to worship of the ghosts of ancestors, the *pretas*. *Pretas* are sometimes those who depart without proper funeral ritual and who, therefore, cannot become proper ancestors. Thus, they are tied to the earth, cemeteries and inauspicious places.[8] The *bhutas*, nature-spirits or ghosts, are more capricious and wayward in nature.

VERSE 5
Men who practise dreadful austerities not enjoined by the *Shastras* are given to hypocrisy and egoism driven by the force of desire and attach-ment . . .

Force, here, is sometimes added to the characteristics of *desire* (*kama*) and *attach-ment* (*raga*), rather than describing them. The verse is a stringent attack on those sects of Hindu society that engage in extreme austerities (*tapas*). Though to an onlooker their faith appears to be such that they can subject their bodies to acts that would be agonizingly painful to the average person, their practices have no foun-dation in scripture and are abnormal. Those who practise such austerities appear to be focused on God, but the verse actually accuses them of being bound in *egoism* (*ahankara*). The *Shastras* here and in this chapter are spoken of favourably: those engaged in the application of *dharma*, and who are not fully enlightened, clearly have need of them. Indeed, Ramanuja said nothing positive can come from ritual acts that are not enjoined by the *Shastras*.[9]

VERSE 6
. . . senselessly torturing all the elements in the body, and even me who dwells in the body: know them to be of demonic resolves.

Significantly, *senselessly*, *achetas*, is without reason, without proper thought.

Dwells in the body is a reference to the passive *atman* within that witnesses the abnormal, exaggerated austerities that fall under the description of *tapas*. Really speaking, nothing in the *prakritic* world, which includes the body, can have any effect on the *atman*, so perhaps this is simply Krishna's way of saying that he finds the practices offensive. Alternatively, the ordinary *jiva*, too, is a particle of the *prakriti* that is the expression of Brahman, and is capable of obscuring the *atman*, which is perhaps what is meant by *even me who dwells in the body*. Demonic is *asura* as in the previous chapter.

VERSE 7

The food also favoured by all is indeed threefold, also *yajna*, *tapas* and *dana*. Hear now of this, their distinction.

Food is the topic of this and the following three verses. Just as the level of consciousness of an individual dictates the choice of religion as a result of the predominant *guna*, so that same *gunic* influence and resulting consciousness will dictate choices and predispositions in all other aspects of life, even choice in what one eats. Such *gunic* influence will be dictated by habits, *vasanas*, and *karma* in previous lives.

VERSE 8

Those foods that increase life, *sattva*, strength, health, happiness and cheerfulness, what are savoury, oily, substantial and agreeable are dear to the *sattvic*.

Sattva in the first part of this verse is meant in the sense of purity or perhaps *sattvic* quality. *Substantial* food is that which is nourishing and that sustains the body for a long time, energizing it over a long period. *Oily* or fatty, oleaginous food would be milk, butter and cheese rather than animal fat.

VERSE 9

Bitter, sour, saline, excessively hot, pungent, dry, burning foods liked by the *rajasic* bring pain, grief and disease.

The foods described here are those that make the eyes water and the tongue and stomach burn. Shankara commented on this verse to suggest that each quality should be preceded by "excessively" suggesting that bitter, sour food in moderation is perhaps permissible.[10] *Disease* would be food related, like indigestion. Such foods will promote *pain* (*duhkha*) as opposed to its opposite of *happiness* (*sukha*) in the *sattvic* foods of the previous verse.

VERSE 10

Stale, tasteless, putrid, rotten and that which is refuse and impure is the food liked by the *tamasic*.

Stale and *tasteless* food is that which has lost its goodness through being left too long (three hours) after cooking and is powerless in maintaining the body. *Putrid* food has a bad smell. *Rotten* food is that which has been left overnight or longer, and its taste will have changed, while *refuse* is leftovers. *Impure* food could mean food totally lacking in quality or food that is unfit for offering as sacrifice. Ramanuja accepted that traditional remnants left over from sacrifice were legitimate food.[11]

VERSE 11

That *yajna* is *sattvic* which is offered as enjoined by ordinance, by men desiring no fruit and ought to be offered having fixed the mind on *yajna* only.

The text now moves from the relation between food tastes and the *gunas* to the way in which the *gunic* make-up affects *yajna*, "sacrifice". Translations of this verse have almost no correlation at all. J. A. B. van Buitenen's is a sound alternative: "*Sattva* rules a person who offers up sacrifices found in the injunctions which are performed by those who do not covet their fruits, and observes them in the pure conviction that the sacrifice must go on."[12] However, the idea that the "sacrifice must go on" or simply has to be performed, is tainted with mere conformity and lack of inward meaning. True *yajna* is performed without the *mind (manas)* focusing on reward or results, the *fruit (phala)*: it is a pure offering, a divine act, and is thus *sattvic*, and such action without desire for its fruits has been a key message of the *Gita*. So, *having fixed (samadhi) the mind on yajna* means focusing totally on the act and nothing else.

VERSE 12

That *yajna* which is offered seeking for fruits, for ostentation, best of Bharatas, know that as *rajasic*.

True *yajna* is not performed ostentatiously or in order to achieve *fruits (phala)*, as the previous verse stated. If it is conducted in this manner, then the action is *rajasic* rather than *sattvic*. Thus, again, the innate nature of the individual informs the practical outcome of expressions of faith.

VERSE 13

Tamasic yajna is said to be that which does not keep to the ordinances, in which no food is distributed, which is devoid of *mantras*, which is devoid of gifts, which is devoid of *shraddha*.

This verse, like others in the chapter, continues to emphasize the importance of conformity to the *Shastras*, but the emphasis on *shraddha* ensures that the conformity is not merely outward and that any religious action is undertaken with an inner faith. Thus, the prescribed nature of *yajna* here is underpinned by *shraddha*. *Food* refers to the food offered to the deity in worship, in earlier times, animal sacrifice, but here probably rice and the like. Clearly, prescribed ordinances on sacrificial food are endorsed. *Mantras* refers probably to the correct intonation of chants or, more broadly, the *Shastras*, and gifts, *dakshina*, are likely to be fees paid to the priests for sacrifice.

VERSE 14

Worship of the gods, of the twice-born, the teachers and the wise; purity, uprightness, celibacy and non-violence are called the *tapas* of the body.

The next three verses deal with what should be *tapas*, "austerity" of body, speech and mind. *Worship* here is *puja*, which has much more of the idea of respect and honour than worship in the western sense, though the object of such worship in the verse is clearly *gods, devas*. *Puja* can be performed, then, not only to the gods, but also to *teachers, gurus*, and the wise. *Celibacy* is *brahma-charya*, which is also the first stage of the four stages of life in Hinduism, when twice-born males spend time studying the scriptures under the tutelage of a *guru*, remaining celibate and practising continence before the second, householder stage. *Twice-born (dvija)* here, however, is generally considered to be a reference to the *Brahmins*, those who are born specifically for the purpose of leading a spiritual life and conducting ritual though, strictly speaking, twice-born refers to the first three classes. *Non-violence* is *ahimsa*. All these characteristics that are described as *tapas* contrast profoundly with the "dreadful" and "torturing" austerities of verses 5 and 6.

VERSE 15

Speech causing no distress, truthful, pleasant and beneficial, also the constant practice of study, these are called *tapas* of speech.

Study is *svadhyaya*, study of the scriptures. It is often understood here to mean sacred recitation that takes place daily and is done with the correct intonation and as prescribed. More generally, it is taken to mean study of the *Vedas*. *Constant practice, abhyasa*, is normally combined with *yoga* in the *Gita*. *Causing no distress* is causing no excitement, trouble, annoyance, in other words, no agitation or pain to others, as Shankara suggested.[13] The qualities of good speech outlined here are to be practised simultaneously, Shankara suggested; where one is missing, true *tapas* of speech does not occur.[14]

VERSE 16

Serenity of mind, good-heartedness, silence, self-control, purity of being, this is called mental *tapas*.

Serenity (prasada) of mind (manas), rather like *silence* of the mind is a state of equilibrium in which the mind with all its thoughts is still. It is a state of mastery over the mind so that there is no response to sense stimuli. If the mind is still and silent, so is thought and speech.

VERSE 17

This threefold *tapas* practised by steadfast men with the highest *shraddha*, desiring no fruit, they call *sattvic*.

Once again, if action is undertaken in order to avoid or gain a specific *fruit (phala)* a result; it is result driven and it is *karmic*. When body, speech and mind are steadfast, however, detached action is possible, and the individual is unaffected by success or failure. *Threefold* in the verse, then, refers to the bodily actions, speech and mind of the last three verses. This kind of *tapas* is so innate to the individual that it is done with ease and naturalness without thought of gain.

VERSE 18

Tapas that is practised here with the object of gaining respect, honour and reverence and with hypocrisy, is said to be *rajasic*, unstable and transitory.

This continues the thought of the previous verse, that actions should not be undertaken for the results they achieve. But here, there is a strong sense of ego-involvement in addition: indeed, *reverence, puja*, is also used as worship of the gods but these egoistic practitioners want the reverence for themselves. Such *rajasic* individuals appear religious in order to enhance their own status: true austerity is not of this kind. *Here* means in this existence, that is to say, such results that are gained – *respect, honour and reverence* – are only temporary and transitory, for they are pertinent only to the immediate lifetime.

VERSE 19

Tapas that is practised out of a deluded notion of torturing the self, or for the purpose of destroying another, is declared *tamasic*.

Krishna has already criticized the kind of severe austerity practised by some ascetics, and here it is referred to again with the inference that those who practise severe *tapas* are *deluded* (*mudha*) and do not really understand the nature of true *tapas* at all. How such practice can destroy another is not made clear.

VERSE 20

That *dana* that ought to be given is given to one who does no service in return, and in the right place and the right time, and to a worthy person: that *dana* is held to be *sattvic*.

The text turns now to the relationship between *dana*, "giving, beneficence, charity" or "almsgiving" and the *gunic* make-up of individuals. For something to be a true gift, nothing should be expected in return, but even then, the other conditions cited in the verse need to be present for purely *sattvic* giving. Those who interpret the *Gita* as a social text see this verse and the following two as evidence of *loka-sangraha*, "welfare of the world" and *karma-yoga*.[15] Certainly, the *yogin*, it seems, is one who is socially active.[16] There is a hint that it is the inner attitude of the one offering charity that is all-important.

VERSE 21

Indeed, what is given with a view to receive in return, or looking for fruits, and reluctantly, that *dana* is held to be *rajasic*.

Receiving *in return* with an eye on the *fruits* (*phala*) of action encompasses not only giving to those who would benefit one in the future, but also to those who want to receive the reward of Heaven for charitable works, so that even those that appear to be very good and beneficent could reap adverse *karma* from their charitable actions.

VERSE 22

The *dana* given at the wrong place and time, and to unworthy persons, without respect or with contempt, that is declared to be *tamasic*.

Giving that is done inappropriately in time and place and to an unworthy recipient is usually that kind of giving that is done for selfish ends, giving that will be useful for the giver in the future. Then, too, charity is often given condescendingly, which carries lack of *respect* and a certain level of disdain for the recipient.

This verse ends the discussion concerning the relation of *dana* to the three *gunas* and ends this whole section on how *sattvic*, *rajasic* and *tamasic* natures are expressed practically in terms of *yajna*, *tapas* and *dana*. The tone now changes to a more philosophical one with a deeper analysis of *yajna*, *tapas* and *dana*.

VERSE 23

Om, *Tat*, *Sat*; this has been declared the threefold designation of Brahman. By that were formerly created the *Brahmins*, the *Vedas* and the *yajnas*.

Om, *Tat*, *Sat* is itself a meditative *mantra*. *Om* is the symbolic sound of Brahman. It is said to be the first manifestation of existence when the whole of the cosmos came into being and then became the sound of the cosmos. Like Brahman itself, *Om* is vaster than the mind can conceive of: it is, as Robert Zaehner described it, the sacred syllable *par excellence*.[17] A number of times in the *Gita*, Brahman has been referred to as *akshara*, "Imperishable", but *akshara* can also mean "syllable" and can refer to *Om*. Hence, *Om* is the imperishable symbol representing the absolute imperishable Brahman. Zaehner translated the word *Om* as "it is", for in ordinary speech it means "yes", but in relation to Brahman is the syllable of total affirmation, "the Word spoken by the Absolute by and through which men can reach the soundless, silent Brahman which is its crown and apex".[18] As a sacred syllable it is by chanting *Om* that the unmanifest Brahman can be reached. So *Om* is both the symbol of manifest, *saguna* Brahman, and unmanifest, *nirguna* Brahman, making it the most sacred of all chants in the *Vedas* and of all *mantras*. Thus, it is uttered at the beginning of ritual.

Tat is THAT or IT in reference to Brahman as beyond understanding, as nothing, that which is beyond anything the mind can conceive of. Its most famous expression is found in the *Chandogya Upanishad* (6:8–16), in the statement *Tat tvam asi*, "THAT you are", where it indicates the non-dual total identification of the inner *atman* with Brahman and yet its universality. *Sat*, formed from the Sanskrit *as*, "to be",[19] is Truth, Reality, Being and also Goodness, and is constant and unaffected by the transience of life, time or space. "Truth", said Prem, "must be all-inclusive and harmonious. It cannot form into little eddies and closed systems."[20] *Brahmins*, or those who know Brahman, the members of the priestly class, were the only ones entitled to perform certain sacrifices on behalf of the people.

VERSE 24

Therefore, uttering *Om*, the acts of *yajna*, *dana* and *tapas* as enjoined in the scriptures, are always begun by expounders of Brahman.

All action undertaken with any *yajna*, *tapas* or *dana* is preceded by the word *Om*. It has the purpose of removing any grains of evil in the action performed, bearing in mind the pre-requisitions laid down in the previous verses. No one can live without action, but if action is detached from ego and that action is pure, no fruitive *karma* occurs. In popular religion, Ganesha became the deity that removes obstacles before any undertaking, so becoming the embodiment of *Om*.

VERSE 25

With *Tat*, the various acts of *yajna* and *tapas* and the acts of *dana* are perfomed without aiming at fruits by the seekers of *moksha*.

Tat, as was seen above, is Brahman. All actions, if undertaken without ego, without desire for *fruits* (*phala*) and concentrating on *Tat*, will not carry fruitive *karma*. Without any results to be reaped from actions there is no necessity for reincarnation; *samsara* ends and *moksha* is achieved. In the case of Arjuna, who is about to engage in the battle, as long as he concentrates his actions on Krishna, he can incur no evil.

VERSE 26

The word *Sat* is used in the sense of Truth, in the sense of Good and also, Partha, *Sat* is used of a praiseworthy act.

Praiseworthy here might suggest a certain mundane application of the word *Sat*, which is the way Shankara saw it with a translation "auspicious".[21] Praiseworthy suits the context better, I think, and brings out the general tenet of the chapter that inner nature, *sva-bhava*, if a good one, *sadhu-bhava*, will result in good, praiseworthy acts. Having a connotation of goodness brings the reality of *Sat* into functional living.

VERSE 27

Thus, steadiness in *yajna* in *tapas* and in *dana* is called *Sat* and actions performed for these purposes are also called *Sat*.

Although we would expect *Tat* as Brahman and *Sat* as Truth to be identical, *Tat* in fact refers to *nirguna* Brahman and *Sat* to *saguna* Brahman, which is why "praiseworthy" in the previous verse is more readily relatable to *Sat* and not to *Tat*. For those who are touching *moksha*, who are almost at the end of their long journey, *Tat* is the focus. But for those still travelling with far to go, *Sat* will be more relevant to their stage of evolution. Both, nevertheless, focus on the divine. The question might be raised here of an incidence where there is total focus on the divine in an action, but that action is, nevertheless not a good one. Does that action then carry no *karma*? It is perhaps the purpose of the whole of this chapter to address such a question, and the *Gita*'s stance is that it is the inner nature that will dictate the quality of action or devotion, so the question does not really arise. The connection between *Sat* as Truth *and* as Goodness or praiseworthiness necessitates that actions have much wider criteria to make them non-*karmic* as the whole of this chapter has indicated. But even Shankara believed that non-*sattvic* acts could not accrue bad *karma* if they were carried out with total devotion to God.[22] It is easy to see how this could raise considerable ethical problems if a non-*sattvic* action could be changed to a *sattvic* one simply by devoting it to the divine.

VERSE 28
Whatever is sacrificed, given or performed and whatever *tapas* is practised without *shraddha*, it is called *asat*, Partha; it is nothing here or
hereafter.

When *yajna*, *dana* and *tapas* are undertaken with *shraddha*, faith, there is less of an emphasis on the individual self, the ego. Without *shraddha*, however, whatever the outward appearance, the inner ego is paramount and therefore further from God. *Asat* is "non-truth", the total opposite of *Sat* and those who incorporate it in their lives can expect nothing *here or hereafter*, in this world or the next life. And since the previous verse saw *Sat* as good action, *asat* here can mean unworthiness, the opposite of what is praiseworthy and what is devoid of goodness. There is no room here for the good person that acts well and altruistically, but has no faith. But in the context of Arjuna's dilemma, this chapter ends with the necessity for the dual relationship between devotee and divine being fully underpinned by the faith of the devotee. In relation to Arjuna's original question concerning faith and its relation-
ship to the three *gunas*, no faith at all seems to deny any value of being, given the correlation of "own being" and *shraddha*. Here, then, not only are the *yajna*, *tapas* and *dana* denied any efficacy, but the individual with it. Such, it seems, is the *tamasic* nature which, in conjunction with the preceding chapter, is also demonic.

In the *Upanishad* of the *Bhagavad Gita*, the knowledge of Brahman,
the teaching of *Yoga* and the dialogue between Shri Krishna
and Arjuna, this is the seventeenth chapter called
Shraddha-traya Vibhaga Yoga.

CHAPTER EIGHTEEN

Moksha Sannyasa Yoga
The Yoga of Liberation and Renunciation

This very long chapter deals with many aspects but its main theme is that of renunciation of the fruits of actions, thus addressing a constant message put forward in the previous chapters. Two important Sanskrit terms are featured; *sannyasa* and *tyaga*, both meaning "renunciation", or "abandonment" but presented at the outset with different nuances of meaning. The text relates the three *gunas*, the constituents of *prakriti*, to renunciation and to a number of other aspects – knowledge, action, the agent of action, intellect, firmness, and happiness. The final message of the chapter and, indeed, of the *Gita* is God's love for his devotee. Throughout there is implicit advice for Arjuna and a summing up of previous teaching, though Krishna leaves the choice of path entirely in Arjuna's hands. The close brings us back to the battle of Kurukshetra.

VERSE I   Arjuna said:
I should like to know, Mahabaho, the differing aspects of the truth of *sannyasa*, Hrishikesha, and also of *tyaga*, Keshinishudana.

Arjuna is asking to know the difference between *sannyasa* and *tyaga*. These have been dealt with before, but Arjuna wants a synthesis of the earlier teachings and so this last chapter serves the purpose of drawing together many threads. As noted above, both *sannyasa* and *tyaga* mean "renunciation". *Sannyasa* comes from the Sanskrit root *as*, "to cast away" and *tyaga* is from the root *tyaj*, "to give up" or "abandon", "relinquish". J. A. B. van Buitenen's comment here is interesting: *sannyasa*, he says, is "'giving up entirely' (lit., 'throwing it all down'), and *tyaga*, 'giving up with generosity what one could probably have kept'".[1] This rather suggests what the nuances of meaning are between the two terms and yet, even in the *Gita*, they are often used synonymously, and Ramanuja certainly saw the terms as synonymous.[2] *Sannyasa* is the term used of the fourth stage of life, of the life of the wandering ascetic and so, in this context, means renunciation of society, of the general world. In the Sankhya school, *sannyasa* meant the giving up of *all* action, and for Shankara, too, *sannyasa* in the sense of abandoning *all* action, conjoined with knowledge, were the sole means to liberation.

While *tyaga*, too, means "renunciation", it is meant more in the sense of relinquishing and renouncing something and, as the next verse will show, it is the important relinquishment of the fruits of actions rather than the world that is meant. Indeed, the *Gita* does not recommend total non-action in the way that

Sankhya and some *sannyasins* understood it. Thus, Aurobindo saw *sannyasa* as outward renunciation and *tyaga* as inner. And as he rightly pointed out, the *Gita's* idea of renunciation is not fleeing from the world but active involvement in it without being geared to seeking rewards and results.[3] But it is possible, too, to conceive of an inner *sannyasa* in the same way as *tyaga*, so that there are times in the *Gita*, and certainly in this chapter, when this is so. More generally, *sannyasa* is a specialist term, particularly for the path of the *jnana-yogin*. A *sannyasin* might also practise *tyaga*, but *tyaga* is a wider term, so that a *tyagin* would not necessarily be a *sannyasin* and, in the *Gita's* view, would not need to be a *jnana-yogin*. Nevertheless, *sannyasa* is not used in the *Gita* to refer directly to abandonment of the *fruits* of actions: only *tyaga* is used in this sense. Otherwise, it seems *sannyasa* and *tyaga* can be used interchangeably.

Krishna is called by three different names in this verse: *Mahabaho*, "Mighty-armed", *Hrishikesha*, "Lord of the Senses", and *Keshinishudana*, "Killer of the Demon Keshu". The last two names are important in that they express ideas pertinent to the present chapter – mastery of the senses and destruction of the demon of egoism. Arjuna has also been called Mahabaho in previous chapters.

VERSE 2   The Lord said:
Renunciation of *kamya karma* the sages understand as *sannyasa*. The renunciation of the fruits of all action the wise call *tyaga*.

So here we have Krishna's initial distinction between the two terms. *Kamya karma* is action undertaken as a result of desire, as a result of response to sense stimuli. Most action falls into this category, for humankind incessantly reacts to the environment's stimuli. The pursuit of *moksha* also falls into this category of *kamya karma* even though it is an activity engaged in for good rewards. *Sannyasa*, in this verse, is the renunciation of all desires and therefore implies desires for results: it is traditionally accepted as renunciation of all actions that might involve succumbing to desires. *Tyaga*, in the *Gita*, is much more to do with the results of actions, explicitly non-attachment to the *fruits* of actions (*karma-phala*) so, though the terms are closely connected, there is a subtle difference between them as they are presented in this verse. Put succinctly, *sannyasins* give up the desires and actions that lead to results, while *tyagins* abandon the fruits of actions but not the actions themselves. The *Gita's* view is that *sannyasa* that is merely the abandonment of all actions is useless without *tyaga* as the abandonment of the *fruits* of actions. The *Gita* rather neatly harmonizes the traditional ascetic path with action but, alas, it will not remain faithful to its easy differentiation of *tyaga* and *sannyasa* in the verses that follow. In relation to Arjuna, he has to act but not be attached to the results of his actions.

VERSE 3
Some philosophers declare that all action should be renounced as an evil while others say that actions of *yajna*, *dana* and *tapas* should not be renounced.

The abandonment of all actions was a particular feature of the school of Sankhya, the *philosophers* of the verse, who saw all actions (*karma*) as a defect or *evil* (*dosha*), while those who accepted actions – particularly prescribed ritual – were the *karma-yogins*. Shankara considered that true *sannyasins*, the true *jnana-yogins*, transcended both these schools, for they had transcended the *gunas*, though there were some *sannyasins* "but not sanyasa proper", he said, who were still *sattvic*, still held by the *sattva guna* and therefore still bound by some *karma*.[4] *Yajna*, "sacrifice", means *Vedic* ritualistic sacrifice and ceremony, though the *Gita* widened the concept to include any kind of sacrifice. *Dana* is essentially the act of giving, while *tapas* is the practice of austerities and asceticism. All three featured in the last chapter. *Tyaga* is the term used for renunciation in both cases in the verse, though *sannyasa* would have been more appropriate for the renunciation of actions, judging by the differentiation in verse 2. *Tyaga* and its derivatives, indeed, is the term used for renunciation in all the following verses, as far as, and including, verse 11.

VERSE 4

Hear, then, my decision about *tyaga*, best of Bharatas; truly, *tyaga* has been declared to be of three kinds, best of men.

So Krishna's *decision* about *tyaga* is that it is of *three kinds*, in other words it can be related to the three *gunas*. Here, Krishna refers only to *tyaga*, so he is thinking more of the results of actions or the desire to undertake them for the gratification of the ego.

VERSE 5

Actions of *yajna*, *dana* and *tapas* should not be renounced but, indeed, ought to be done. *Yajna*, *dana* and *tapas* are, indeed, purifiers of the wise.

Giving up all actions is not advised, and renunciation here is *tyaga*, suggestive that actions (consistently *karma* in this and the following verses) are necessary as long as the fruits of them are renounced. On the path to liberation, prescribed actions of *yajna*, *dana* and *tapas* are necessary, but while on that path, an individual gradually loses the desire to practise them for rewards in life and their actions become less related to the ego. Disinterested actions become the norm and natural qualities of the devotee, and not actions undertaken with a view to results, as the following verse will say.

VERSE 6

But even these actions should be performed by renouncing attachment and fruits. This, Partha, is my definitive and best belief.

The purity of *yajna*, *dana* and *tapas* will depend on the purity of the actions. If, for example, one gives generously, but praises the self in giving, the act is not as pure as when giving is performed without any involvement of the ego and the mind has no thought of result or reward. In this latter case, no fruitive *karma* can accrue from such an action. Shankara, in contrast, saw such actions as bearing fruitive *karma*, since the previous verse stated that these acts have the result of purifying the wise. Because abstention from *all* action is the prescribed path of the ascetic non-dualist, the *advaitist*, Shankara considered abstention from *all* action to be the superior path. The path of action, the *karma-yoga* path – albeit abandoning fruits of actions – Shankara believed can only produce good *karma*, but not *moksha*.[5]

VERSE 7

Sannyasa of obligatory action is not really proper: such *tyaga* from delusion is declared *tamasic*.

Notably in this verse, *sannyasa* and *tyaga* seem to be used synonymously. Obligatory duty is *niyata-karma*, sacred duty, that prescribed by the scriptures, such as those related to *yajna*, *dana* and *tapas*, to duties of class and stage of life and pertaining to the necessities of life. Such duty will vary from one individual to another. To go against such obligatory duty is considered *adharmic*, against *dharma* and, therefore, characteristic of the *guna* of involution, *tamas*. Implicit in the verse is the message to Arjuna that his obligatory duties as a *Kshatriya* need to be performed. Renunciation, then, as conducted by *sannyasins* who try to perform no actions at all, ritual or otherwise, is not acceptable: such misconception is *delusion* (*moha*).

VERSE 8

He who renounces action from fear of bodily trouble, because it is painful, thus performing *rajasic tyaga*, does not obtain the fruit of such *tyaga*.

The fruit of real *tyaga* is *moksha*. Any pseudo-*tyaga* such as shirking action because of fear or pain will bring results but not the goal of liberation. The action will not be *sattvic*, but *rajasic*. *Bodily trouble* is likely to be hard work, the necessity of physical labour – in Arjuna's case, fighting in the battle.

VERSE 9

Whatever obligatory action is performed, Arjuna, because it ought to be done, renouncing attachment and its fruit, that *tyaga* is regarded as *sattvic*.

All action produces a result: it is essentially an action–reaction process. Both *tamasic* and *rajasic* actions produce results, but so will *sattvic* actions. Even the performance of *obligatory action* (*niyata karma*) laid down in the scriptures including action necessary for daily living will produce results. However, true *sattvic tyaga* is renunciation of the *fruits* (*phala*) of one's action, so the individual acts without any thought at all as to the results. If no ego is involved in this *sattvic* action, no "I" seeking results from it, then there is no "I" to reap any *karma*. So, renunciation is a *sattvic* characteristic if it is not result orientated. If it is result orientated, then, though *sattvic*, results related to the individual will occur – albeit beneficial ones. Any renunciation without letting go of results is not true *tyaga* but simply *rajasic* or *tamasic tyaga*. The important combination is *sattvic* action, doing *what ought to be done* (*karya*), with renunciation of attachment to results.

VERSE 10

The wise *tyagin* pervaded by *sattva*, with his doubts cut asunder, does not hate disagreeable action nor is attached to agreeable action.

The *tyagin* here is one who has renounced or abandoned desire for results of actions. He is also *wise*, possessing *medhavi*, "wisdom", "intelligence" or "steady understanding", and with these ingredients a state of perfect equilibrium is achieved when actions are carried out. The verse, then, depicts the liberated *tyagin* when the *atman* is experienced and *prakriti* merely witnessed, rather like a mirror that reflects images but does not hang on to them and react to them. *Disagreeable action* is *akushala-karma*, the kind of action that reaps an evil or adverse result. Shankara saw *akushala-karma* as evil action, a stronger nuance of meaning than simply disagreeable. For Shankara, any action involving the ego and producing fruitive *karma*, and thus *samsara*, fell into this class of *akushala-karma*. Its opposite is *kushala-karma*, which Shankara saw as the obligatory actions laid down by scriptures.[6] Again, Shankara believed that abandonment of the fruits of action while carrying out prescribed rituals was an inferior path – the *karma-yoga* path – but preparatory to the path of knowledge, *jnana-yoga*.[7] Important in the verse is the equilibrium that is maintained between opposites.

VERSE 11

Indeed, it is not possible for an embodied being to renounce action entirely. But he who renounces the fruits of action is thus called a *tyagin*.

Renunciation of all action is impossible; the body has its own actions independent of the will, and many bodily actions such as eating and sleeping are necessary. But apart from such necessary action, there are many necessary duties to perform in life and it is here that it is important to undertake such duties without attachment to their results. Detached action with no attention on the *fruits of action* (*karma-phala*) is therefore the key to *tyaga*, true renunciation. Once again, Shankara considered that this verse referred only to the *karma-yogin* for whom the renunciation of all actions was impossible. True *sannyasins*, Shankara believed, *could* renounce *all* actions: though they had attained *moksha* while in the body, the body would no longer be regarded as the true self and would virtually be abandoned.[8] *Embodied being* has nothing to do with the true Self here: it merely refers to a being in a body (*deha*).

VERSE 12

The threefold fruit of action, disagreeable, agreeable and mixed, accrues after death to non-*tyagins*, but never to *sannyasins*.

Clearly, *tyaga* and *sannyasa* here are treated synonymously and the verse would make no sense without such synonymy. The *disagreeable, agreeable and mixed* results or *fruits of action* (*karma-phala*) all come from result-driven action. Eknath Easwaran actually combined the three as characteristic of most actions, "when a person acts out of selfish attachment, he must fully partake of the result, the karma, of every thought, word and deed; and although these results may be what was desired, they may also be something not desired at all or a little of both. In this life you can never be sure that things will turn out as planned."[9] The fate of those with evil *karma* was described in CHAPTER SIXTEEN. Those with good *karma* are born in celestial realms and those with mixed *karma* in earthly existence. Those with disagreeable *karma* would be born as *Asuras* or animals. Just as a person goes to sleep and wakes up with the same personality, so like creates like in the new existence after death.

VERSE 13

Learn from me these five causes for the accomplishment of all action, Mahabaho, as declared in Sankhya, which is the end of all action.

Sankhya here is sometimes taken to mean the *Vedanta* of the *Upanishads* rather than the atheistic school of Sankhya, though it is more likely to be a reference to early Sankhyan ideas. *The end* here is sometimes seen as "the end of the *krita* age", the first of the four ages,[10] which was regarded as perfect, and was when original and pure Sankhya doctrines were believed to have been taught.[11] However, it may simply mean the end product of an action, the success or completion of an action, which I think is more the sense of the verse. The *five causes* are given in the following verse.

VERSE 14

The seat, the agent, the various causes, the various sorts of different functions, divine providence also as the fifth . . .

By *seat*, *adhishthana*, is meant the body, that is to say, the seat of emotions of desire, happiness and unhappiness and so the motivating factor of the self. The *agent*, *karta*, is the ego that makes sense of, and responds to, outward stimuli, making it the doer. The *causes* or instruments, *karana*, are the organs of sense: Ramanuja understood them to be the many organs of action, since it is these that do the work – speech, hands, feet, and so on,[12] and the *different functions* are sometimes considered to be the functions of *prana*, the life-giving breath, but may be simply different actions or the functioning of the senses. The fifth entity, *divine providence* as I have it, is more problematic, but is very important. The Sanskrit is *daiva*, which instantly carries some connection with the gods. Some examples of the range of interpretation are pertinent here, given the connotations the word might have for notions of predestination. Chidbhavananda considered that it means the "presiding deity" of the body, which he took to be the *jivatman*,[13] though this does not really differ from the agent, the second cause. Shankara believed *daiva* meant divinity "such as the Aditya and other Gods by whose aid the eye and other organs discharge their functions".[14] Shankara's suggestion is tenable since each sense organ was presided over by a particular deity: Aditya, for example, was connected with the sun, light, and hence the eye. Then, too, human beings were believed to be influenced by all kinds of supernatural and divine forces. Thus, these would be a kind of divine influence or providence – Gandhi termed it the "Unseen"[15] – affecting each individual. We should not exclude the possibility that it could refer to the divine element within the body, the *atman*. Thus, Ramanuja interpreted *daiva* as divine providence but identified it with the Supreme *Atman*, the Inner Ruler and main cause, in line with his interpretation of 15:15 and 18:61.[16] Nevertheless, in his comments on this verse, Ramanuja clearly allowed freewill of individual actions but all the time with the Supreme Self permitting that freedom of action.[17]

Gotshalk's interpretation of *daiva* reflects an interesting view shared by some. He links each of the five causes with *prakriti*, which seems an attractive and workable hypothesis. Thus, the seat is *avyakta prakriti* from which all evolutes come into being. The agent, as I have it, is the intellect (*buddhi*) and ego (*ahankara*), which are the agency of actions. The causes are the mind and organs of perception, the different functions are the five organs of action and *daiva*, which Gotshalk translates as "divine fate", is "the realm of the elements, gross and subtle, presided over by the *devas*". This, thinks Gotshalk, corresponds to the twenty-four evolutes of *prakriti* in the Sankhya system.[18] Douglas Hill had exactly the same analysis.[19] If this is so, then Sankhya of the previous verse is a reference to the unorthodox early school rather than orthodox *Vedanta*.

Robert Zaehner, like many, translated the word as "fate".[20] Zaehner posited the following interesting comment on the relationship between fate and "the load of *karma* that man drags along with him in the samsaric world", in the context of the *Mahabharata*. This text, he said "compares the two to the rain which prepares the ground and the seed that man puts into it (5.78.2–5): the two are interdependent and work in harmony together. Human *karma* is but a fraction of the *karma* of the whole universe, and this totality of *karma* adds up to fate, and fate itself is under the control of God. Fate is the cosmic *dharma* from which man cannot escape."[21] This seems to me an eminently sensible interpretation for this term *daiva* in the *Gita* – God in overall control, human freewill either in line with or antagonistic to that control, but ultimately God has unmitigated control over his creation, though the word "fate", is too suggestive of events external to the individual rather than internal.

Clearly, there is an implication of some kind of divine influence in the word and for my part, I think this might be simply the divine *maya* and binding *karma* that serve to make an individual what he or she is. Similarly, Rohit Mehta translated *daiva* as "personal unconscious",[22] and Radhakrishnan described *daiva* as the "unaccountable element which is called luck, destiny, fate or the force accumulated by the acts of one's past lives".[23] This last also seems a sound interpretation, that is to say, the unknown results of past causes that are coming our way through the divine processes of cause and effect. As Radhakrishnan went on to say: "Daiva or the supernatural fate is the general cosmic necessity, the resultant of all that has happened in the past, which rules unnoticed. It works in the individual for its own incalculable purposes."[24] Nevertheless, Franklin Edgerton's warning needs noting, that "much needless trouble has been caused by this verse", and that: "Each of the five words is to be taken in the simplest possible sense and no comments really needed – except that all existing comments are worthless and misleading".[25]

VERSE 15

. . . whatever action man performs with body, speech or mind, right or wrong, these five are its causes.

The *body* (*sharira*) is able to be used in a variety of ways, for good or evil: the choice is always left to the individual. Such choice is usually exercised in every action, every spoken word and in every thought, and *karma* is produced by all three. If action, speech or thought is right, it is *dharmic*; if it is wrong, it is *adharmic*. While external actions may be brought under some control, spontaneous speech is more difficult to tame, and the most difficult is thought since we cannot still our thoughts for more than a fraction of time and the whole realm of subconscious streams triggers involuntary reactions to the surrounding world: the *mind* (*manas*) thus remains untamed.

VERSE 16

This being so, he sees not who, of untrained intellect and imperfect understanding, sees the self alone as the agent.

All that functions in an individual – actions, speech and thought – is *prakritic* and is the result of *gunic* interplay. It is the *atman* within that lends consciousness to the material processes of thought but the individual is blinded to the reality of it as the source. The *atman* is not affected by *prakriti* and is really separate from it, but the ignorant whose *intellect* (*buddhi*) is *untrained*, cannot see this separation and make the *atman* the doer, the speaker and the thinker. Some see the *self* in the verse as the *atman*, prompted, perhaps, by the expression *self alone*. *Alone* is *kevala* and reminiscent of the ultimate free *purusha* of the Sankhya school, where each *purusha* is isolated at liberation from all others. Thus, Zaehner had "isolated"[26] which, in my view, is too close to Sankhya proper. The *Gita* does accept the separation of *atman* from *prakriti* but rather than the "aloneness" of each *atman*, the union of all *atmans* in the divine. Thus, *alone* need not be given any significance here, and I am inclined to see the *self* of the verse as the material *prakritic* being that believes its own intellect, ego and mind are all there is. Either way, *imperfect understanding* means being unable to see things clearly or properly and having a distorted view of Reality.

VERSE 17

He who is free from the notion of egoism, whose intellect is not tainted, even though he slays these worlds, he does not kill, he is not bound.

Where *egoism* (*ahankara*) is absent there can be no agent and if there is no agent, then there can be no *karma* to be reaped. When an action is undertaken without the involvement of the ego, it is simply an action and nothing else and the *intellect*, the *buddhi*, remains pure. Only the egoistic *jivatman* can be an agent of *karma*, and that agent of *karma* is always *prakritic*. The *atman* is not an agent at all, so being focused entirely on the *atman* within releases one from fruitive *karma* so that one is *not bound* and unlikely to be bound to the chain of *samsaric* rebirths. The teaching in this verse is most appropriate for Arjuna in the forthcoming battle where he must slay, without any trace of ego, his enemies and family, as well as great men such as

Bhishma. Arjuna can only kill if he says "*I* am killing" and maintain the "I" that kills. If he identifies himself with *atman* and not with the five causes of his own personal character, he will have no ego that can slay. Nevertheless, *slays these worlds*, probably referring to the three worlds of Heaven, Hell and Earth, is a strong statement, one that Zaehner termed "a disturbing doctrine"[27] in the *Gita*, and is certainly a problem that the *Gita* continues to bear.

Verse 18

Knowledge, the object of knowledge and the knower are the threefold impulses to action: and the cause, the action and the agent are the three-fold bases of action.

Knowledge, jnana, refers to knowledge acquired by the senses. The *object of knowledge (jneya)* is the sense stimulus and the *knower* is the egoistic *jivatman*. These three closely interrelated and interdependent aspects make up the process of knowledge. The *cause (karana)*, *action (karma)* and *agent (karta)* are similarly interdependent, being the cause of action of body, speech and mind, along with sense organs as in the Sankhya scheme of evolutes. The *jivatman* is both the knower and the agent, the one who acts. All combine in the process of reaction to the sense stimuli of the environment, the involvement in *prakriti* that binds the *jivatman* to the sensory world, to cause and effect and to reincarnation. Shankara saw the bases of action as the organ, the end, and the agent, which are different ways of expressing the three, the organ being "that by which something is done", the end, "that which is sought for" and the agent "he who sets the organs going".[28]

Verse 19

Knowledge, action and agent in the Sankhya *gunas* are said to be of three kinds only, according to the distinction of the *gunas*; duly hear of them also.

The *Gita* accepts the Sankhya theory of matter consisting of the *gunas*, though it departs from atheistic Sankhya in accepting a unifying principle of Brahman. At this point, the text begins an analysis of the nature of *knowledge (jnana)*, *action (karma)* and *agent (karta)* in relation to the three *gunas*.

Verse 20

That knowledge by which one sees the imperishable Reality in all beings, undivided in the divided, know that as *sattvic*.

The first to be analysed in relation to the *gunas* is *knowledge, jnana*, though it is not an easy verse and translations vary considerably. *Prakriti* is diverse and highly differentiated, continually informed by the constantly changing interplay of the *gunas*. But underlying the differentiation of *prakriti* is the One, the *undivided*, the inseparate and *imperishable (avyaya)* Brahman, a point that has already been made in the *Gita* in 9:15, also when Arjuna saw the whole universe existing as one in Krishna in 11:13 and then, again, in 13:16 with the statement "Undivided, yet as if existing divided in beings", this last illustrating clearly the unity that underpins the diversity of *prakriti*. Although the cause of *prakriti*, the One is unaffected by it. It is this kind of knowledge that is *sattvic*. This verse is an immensely important one, what Zaehner termed "the Gita's consistent metaphysical doctrine".[29]

VERSE 21

But knowledge that sees in all beings various entities of distinct kinds as mutually different, know that knowledge as *rajasic*.

Rajasic knowledge sees variation in all entities with each entity essentially different from any other and accepts this as reality. Each self is composed of limiting attributes called *upadhis*, which give the appearance of difference to those who are blinded to the Reality of Brahman as the unifying *Atman* in all things. The *upadhis* are linked with the body, mind, senses and ego, and create incorrect knowledge. *Rajasic* knowledge, then, understands only diversity, plurality, individuation, and the distinct and *mutually different* of the universe, not its true underlying unity.

VERSE 22

But that which is attached without reason, without foundation in truth and trivial, to one single causal object as if it were the whole, that is declared *tamasic*.

The *tamasic* individual cannot understand that there is a real Self beyond the physical form or that there is a God that is beyond matter. Such an individual is blinkered to one particular narrow view that amounts to a very narrow perspective of reality. This is the person who focuses on *one single causal object* – an object such as the material body, a belief or misdirected goal or one small part of existence, which is mistaken for *the whole*. Shankara also included "an external idol" as such an object.[30]

VERSE 23

Action that is ordained, free from attachment, done without passion or with hatred, by one not desirous of the fruit, that is declared to be *sattvic*.

The text now turns to the three kinds of *gunic* action. *Ordained* action is *niyata*, that prescribed by the scriptures, including requirements regarding daily living. The verse reiterates so much that has already been dealt with in the *Gita* and is particularly pertinent to Arjuna who must carry out his personal *dharma* as the scriptures ordain but in a state of detached action that is not result orientated, not *desirous of the fruit* (*aphala*). Even engaged in war, *passion* (*raga*) and *hatred* (*dvesha*) must be absent.

VERSE 24

But action that is performed by one longing for desires or again with egoism, with much stress, that is *rajasic*.

Again, the verse summarizes what has already been said in the *Gita* in different contexts. "Actions are performed by the *gunas* of *prakriti*" we have been told (3:27) and the same verse pointed out that it is only the person with *egoism* (*ahankara*) who thinks "I am the doer". This has been reiterated elsewhere in conjunction with the *atman* as the non-doer (13:29). *Desires* (*kama*) here, are the causes of actions, so the actions are result-driven. Even the *sattvic* person is likely to undertake certain actions for the purpose of personal or social evolution – alleviating the suffering of others and other good works, for example. The actions here are good, but if conducted with a measure of ego would still produce *karmic* effects. Desires at a more materialistic level are more obviously *rajasic*. Then, too, so much action involves egoistic *stress* – mental and physical effort, great strain and trouble. Commenting on this last verse, Gandhi pertinently wrote: "A *rajasic* person is engaged in inventing an aeroplane and is busy the next in discovering how to reach India from England in five hours. Such a person sets apart half an hour out of twenty-four to deceive his atman, and devotes the remaining twenty-three and a half to his body."[31]

VERSE 25

Action that is undertaken from delusion, without regard for the consequence, loss, injury, or one's own capability, that is declared to be *tamasic*.

The verse refers to indiscriminate action, that undertaken without thought of its nature as right or wrong. It could be argued that such action is detached, which is what the *Gita* advocates, but the context of *delusion* (*moha*) or ignorance, of *injury* and *loss* to oneself and others, suggests these actions are *karmically* adverse. *Loss*, Shankara commented, would incur loss of power and wealth,[32] which might seem at odds with other concepts in the *Gita* unless it refers to the householder stage of life, or perhaps to Arjuna's loss of power and kingdom if he does not accept the *sattvic* approach. But if right, Shankara's view here is still at variance with the necessity of remaining unattached to the fruits of actions. And if he is right, then the opposite of loss would be regard for power and wealth, and Arjuna had certainly acquired an abundance of both in his life so far. *One's own capability* is one's own capacity and ability to do the action. *Tamasic* individuals will undertake something for which they are way out of their depth, without preparation, thought, or an eye on the consequences – here, of the adverse results: the verse is not suggesting that they are acting without thinking of results at all. Presumably, the *sattvic* person will need to know the consequences of an action but will not be attached to them.

VERSE 26

An agent who is free from attachment, not self-focused, endued with firmness and enthusiasm, unaffected in success or failure, is called *sattva*.

After relating knowledge and action to the *gunas*, it is now the turn of the *agent* (*karta*) of both to be related to them. *Firmness* (*dhriti*) implies steadfastness and sustained effort. *Free from attachment* here is the reiterated, constant message of the *Gita* concerning detached action. *Enthusiasm* or "zeal", is variously translated; "vigour" or "enterprise" are other suggestions. At first glance, enthusiasm is suggestive of a *rajasic* person, but it is meant more in the sense of confidence, having the knowledge of one's own capability in undertaking a task, unlike the *tamasic* individual of the previous verse. It is also indicative of putting one's energy into the task itself, rather than being half-hearted about it.

VERSE 27
Passionate, desirous of the fruits of action, greedy, cruel, impure, moved by joy and sorrow, is called a *rajasic* agent.

This depiction of the *rajasic* agent is, as other descriptions of *rajas*, a derogatory one. Clearly, *rajas* is not to be considered the middle state between *sattva* and *tamas* with a mixture of positive and negative characteristics; no positive qualities in the *rajasic* individual appear here. This *rajasic* individual is dominated by characteristics inimical to liberation – passion (*raga*) and greed (*lobha*) being so frequently mentioned in the *Gita* and here, the *fruits of action* (*karma-phala*) are motivated by the opposites of desire for *joy* and aversion to *sorrow*.

VERSE 28
Unsteady, vulgar, unbending, cheating, malicious, lazy, despondent, procrastinating, is said to be the *tamasic* agent.

Unsteady is *ayukta*, the exact opposite of the integrated one that is *yukta*. *Vulgar* means unrefined or even illiterate. Notable is that *despondency* is a *tamasic* characteristic and it was heavily criticized by Krishna early on in the *Gita* when Arjuna displayed so much of it. *Procrastinating* is Sanskrit *dirghasutri*, which means something like making a long excuse why one cannot do something – which is what Arjuna did in CHAPTER ONE.

VERSE 29
Listen, Dhananjaya, as I tell fully and distinctly of the threefold division of intellect and firmness, according to the *gunas*.

Dhananjaya means "Conqueror of Wealth" and refers to Arjuna's taking of the wealth of earthly and celestial kings when that wealth was excessive, in order to use it for righteous purposes. *Intellect* is *buddhi*, which is about to be discussed in relation to the three *gunas*. Since it is the reasoning factor, depending on its nature, it will determine so much of how an individual thinks, and what that individual does and says, as well as likes and dislikes and the way in which life is understood and responded to. *Firmness, dhriti*, will be taken up in verses 33–5.

VERSE 30
The intellect that knows action and inaction, what ought to be done and what ought not to be done, fear and absence of fear, bondage and liberation, that, Partha, is *sattvic*.

It is now the turn of the intellect, the *buddhi*, to be related to the three *gunas*. *Action* and *inaction* are *pravritti* and *nivritti* respectively, sometimes translated as work and renunciation. *Pravritti* can be *karmic* action, the type of action that binds one to *prakriti* and to the cycle of *samsara*, or action that is desireless. *Nivritti*, its opposite, can be simply inactivity, or it can be inaction in the sense of withdrawal from result-orientated activity that leads to *moksha*, so it is important for the devotee to know the difference between the two. Shankara, reflecting his non-dualist view, considered *pravritti* to refer to *karma-marga*, the path of action, and *nivritti* to the *jnana-marga*, the superior path of knowledge and of the *sannyasin*.[33] Total inactivity is not endorsed here, since *what ought to be done (karya)* is linked with *pravritti* and, in the light of the following verse, *what ought not to be done (akarya)* – presumably avoidance of *adharmic* action – with *nivritti*. The *sattvic* individual has to have knowledge that transcends *fear* – concerns about life – with the desireless activity that will also transcend *bondage* and bring *liberation, moksha*.

VERSE 31

The intellect that incorrectly understands *dharma* and *adharma*, what ought to be done and what ought not to be done, that, Partha, is *rajasic*.

Rajasic characters have a distorted picture of reality and act accordingly, mistakenly believing they do right, though their actions are *adharmic*. They may be outwardly very successful, since they are goal-driven and have high aspirations, but their lives are always focused on results and the acquisition of aims. Thus, they confuse *what ought to be done (karya)* and *what ought not to be done (akarya)*.

VERSE 32

The intellect that, enveloped in darkness, thinks *adharma* is *dharma* and all things their opposite, that, Partha, is *tamasic*.

Here, the picture of reality is so distorted that the intellect is totally perverted. The *tamasic* individual thinks the opposite of what is right. *Darkness* is *tamasa* suggestive of the individual being swallowed up, *enveloped in tamas*. *All things their opposite* means the kind of confusion in life that gets things the wrong way around so that the opposite of what the *tamasic* person thinks and does is actually correct.

VERSE 33

Firmness that holds the functions of the mind, the breath and the senses in unswerving *yoga*, that firmness, Partha, is *sattvic*.

Firmness in relation to the *gunas* is the subject of this and the next two verses. Its Sanskrit equivalent is *dhriti*, which also means "constancy", "steadfastness", "sustaining effort", "resolve" and "fortitude", so it reflects an inward quality of strength in dedication to something. Breath is *prana*, the life-energy and force. For *dhriti* to be present, the functions of the *mind (manas)* and *senses (indriyas)* as well as the life-energy itself have to be concentrated and harmonized. Firmness is needed to cultivate both control of the mind and senses, and is increased in turn by that control. The verse has strong hints of the formal pathway of *yoga* and *jnana-yoga*.

VERSE 34

But the firmness, Arjuna, which holds fast to *dharma*, *kama* and *artha*, desirous of the fruits of action, that firmness is *rajasic*, Partha.

The verse refers to the *purusharthas*, the four basic proximate goals of life, *dharma*, what is right in terms of duty, class and ritual, *kama*, pleasure, especially sexual pleasure, and *artha*, which is wealth. *Dharma* in the context of this verse may refer to prescribed ritual actions, or to duty, through which one can acquire good results either in the present life or a future one. The fourth, not mentioned here, is *moksha*, liberation. Alongside the *purusharthas* are the *ashramas*, the four stages of life, which allow *artha* and *kama*, for example, to be legitimate goals at the second, householder, stage. Yet it is surprising to see the *purusharthas* classified as *rajasic* here, particularly since *dharma* is included. Indeed, attachment to *dharma* might seem to be thoroughly *sattvic*, albeit resulting in positive *karma*. But what is important is the emphasis on *fruits of action (karma-phala)*. Thus, performing actions that seem *dharmic* and right in order to receive rewards or good results are ultimately *rajasic* actions, however *sattvic* they may appear on the surface.

Verse 35

That firmness by which a stupid man does not abandon sleep, fear, grief, despair and also conceit is *tamasic*, Partha.

Some people are like plants, they hardly move, except to be overcome by their immediate environments. They sleep too much and cannot get going in life. The *stupid man* is one who is deluded (*mudha*). For *conceit*, some translate "intoxication", "inebriation" or "drunkenness". This verse concludes the discussion of *dhriti*, firmness, in relation to the three *gunas* and it is now the turn of *sukha*, "happiness" or "pleasure", to be dealt with in the same way.

Verse 36

Now hear from me, best of Bharatas, of the threefold happiness by constant practice of which one rejoices and attains to the end of suffering.

Abhyasa, *constant practice*, seems to be an important criterion for the goal of *happiness (sukha)*, which is the topic of this and the next three verses. Such practice suggests that happiness is not something that can be grasped at, but something that must be worked at in the sense of controlling the mind. *Suffering* in the verse is *duhkha*, the pain that ensues from living life from the wrong perspectives.

Verse 37

That which is like poison at first in the end is like nectar; that happiness is declared *sattvic* born of the purity of one's Self-understanding.

This verse relates very much to the constant practice, *abhyasa*, of the previous verse. When practice of controlling the mind begins, it is as uncomfortable as any other kind of practice until the activity comes naturally, when it becomes *like nectar* (*amrita*). People become used to a life geared to the senses, to thinking of activities in terms of results and to regarding "I" as the centre of all things. To turn away from such thoughts is difficult and demands practice and perseverance but as these increase, *purity* or clarity of the mind is gained and true happiness is experienced. *Purity*, here, is *prasada*, which also means "serenity" and "peace". The end result of this practice and perseverance is total realization of the Self, the *atman*: true happiness can only be found in the *atman*, within the Self, not outside it. *Self-understanding* is *atma-buddhi* suggesting an intellect that turns in to its real Self, though translations of this last part of the verse vary considerably.

VERSE 38
That happiness which, from the union of the senses with the object is at first like nectar and in the end like poison; that is declared *rajasic*.

Happiness is most usually associated with gratification of the *senses* (*indriyas*) and all such happiness is transient. Yet, the more one clings to this type of happiness, the more it is likely to cause unhappiness mainly because objects of the senses are impermanent. The more one becomes bound to seeking happiness through sense gratification, the more one becomes trapped in the *prakritic* world and the further away from Self-realization. It is, said Chidbhavananda, "like water poured into a leaky pot . . . happiness slips away as quickly as it is sought".[34] From a different perspective, happiness that is sought through the senses is one of a pair of opposites, *dvandva*, which assumes that there is an opposite to be avoided. What brings happiness seems like *nectar* (*amrita*), but that nectar carries with it the sense of its opposite, which is *poison*.

VERSE 39
Happiness that at first and consequently is delusive to the self, arising from sleep, indolence and heedlessness; that is *tamasic*.

The words *and consequently* suggest something like "in the sequel" in the Sanskrit. In the context of the previous verses this might suggest in the end or, as Shankara suggested, after the termination of this life: thus, the *tamasic* would be destined for Hell.[35] For *delusive to the self*, Gandhi had the graphic "stupefies the soul",[36] and Ramanuja saw this as "absence of knowledge of things as they are".[37] Delusion (*moha*) has been mentioned frequently in the *Gita* as an inimical force to personal evolution.

VERSE 40
There is not a being on Earth, or in Heaven among the gods that can be free from these three *gunas*, born of *prakriti*.

The terms *prakriti* and *gunas* are really synonymous. Everything in the cosmos, even divine beings, are composed of the three *gunas* in varying combinations, and everything composed of variations of the *gunas* is *karmic* and subject to *samsara*. Even Brahma, the creator god, like all *gods* (*devas*), is subject to *karma*, though he is at the apex of all *prakriti*, albeit that his *karma* is such that he will not be born again. Brahma will, at the end of existence, transcend the very *gunas* by which he is believed to form creation and which form himself, so he will eventually be liberated. For every other being in whatever realm, it is the *gunas* that make up that being and the existential condition in which it exists. Until the *gunas* are transcended, each being remains bound to rebirth. It is *gunic* make-up that informs behaviour and life patterns – all dictated by *karmic* activity. I see no reason to posit

Krishna as the sole agent in all activity so that "there is no *automatic* or necessary causal connection between behaviour and result", as Will Johnson suggests. He continues: "Actions have results, but neither the actions nor the results are really ours."[38] The *Gita* puts the divine as the creator of *prakriti* but does not suggest that its intricate *gunic* processes in *all* action are the responsibility of the divine as the agent that makes some chosen individuals predestined to know God and to be devoted to him: freewill is not denied by the *Gita*.

VERSE 41
The duties of *Brahmins*, *Kshatriyas*, *Vaishyas* and also *Shudras* are assigned by the *gunas* born of their own nature, Parantapa.

The text now relates each of the *gunas* to members of the four classes. *Own nature* is *sva-bhava*, referring to the innate nature of the individual that is dependent on the combination of *gunas* in the personality, especially on the dominant *guna*. It is this personal *sva-bhava* that is linked so closely to *karma* and, just as earlier it was seen that the *sattvic*, *rajasic* and *tamasic* personalities would show a propensity for certain types of food, religion and lifestyle, so also their profession and their class, *varna*, will be an indication of the predominant *guna*. Class, *varna*, will also be an indication of the *sva-bhava* of persons during their past lives. Every action, whether of body, speech or mind, produces *karmic* results, building up tendencies, *samskaras* and *vasanas*, some lying latent, some already active. These are like collections of characteristics filling up appropriate jars until, at a certain level, some will predominate in an individual, while some are less dominant and some still dormant. In such a way, the individual builds up a future existence for a future life, a complexity of manifest *gunas* that are the results of causes made in previous lives.

The class system outlined here is probably that existing at the time the *Gita* was written and the verse rationalizes it as it was at the time. We have no suggestion of its hereditary nature here – maybe that was simply accepted by the writer – or any idea that one's nature could change in a lifetime so that one could change class. Arjuna has already spoken passionately about any mixture of classes (1:42), so there must have been some belief that birth, generally, dictated class and in an ideal society, each class was thought to be happy with its allotted duties. Hereditary occupation is considered by many to be more a facet of the later caste system. But it is difficult to extricate the nature with which one is born from the profession and duties one is allowed to do. Hereditary criteria seem to be the only possible means by which whoever is born can be classified. *Duties*, here *karma*, amounts to saying that it is one's duty to do the best possible with one's allotted *karmic* life, one's particular *gunic* make-up and one's own *sva-bhava* and *sva-dharma*,[39] and these last two terms are interlinked to the extent that one's nature dictates one's duty. The Sanskrit actually separates the *Shudras* from the other three classes syntactically in order, perhaps, to show their inferiority.

VERSE 42

Serenity, self-restraint, austerity, purity, forgiveness, uprightness, knowledge and realization, religious faith, are the duties of the *Brahmins*, born of their own nature.

Brahmins are *sattva-rajas* with *sattva* dominant. *Austerity* is the familiar *tapas*, while knowledge and realization are *jnana* and *vijnana* respectively, to which the whole of CHAPTER SEVEN was devoted. *Religious faith* is the corollary of the *Brahmin*; it is the religious faith that is necessary for his study of the *Vedas* and for conducting of ritual. Other qualities – *serenity* (*shama*), *self-restraint* (*dama*), *purity* (*shauca*), *forgiveness* (*kshanti*) – have featured hitherto.

VERSE 43

Bravery, boldness, firmness, resourcefulness, unwillingness to flee in battle, generosity and lordliness are the duties of *Kshatriyas*, born of their own nature.

The *Kshatriya* is *rajas-sattva* in nature, with *rajas* dominant, and is the ideal warrior, king or administrator. He is just, and therefore lives life according to *dharma*, protecting society from harm, this being his own personal *dharma*, his *sva-dharma*. *Boldness* is *tejas*, which can also mean "vigour" or even "splendour". *Firmness*, is *dhriti*, which has already occurred earlier in this chapter, and means "sustaining effort". *Generosity*, or "giving", *dana*, has also already featured in this and previous chapters. *Resourcefulness*, *daksha*, is variously interpreted. Shankara had "promptness".[40] The *Kshatriya*, then, has the *Vaishya's* practical energy with the *Brahmin's* spirituality – the qualities necessary for good leadership. The qualities outlined in this verse are especially pertinent to Arjuna's situation, not just as a warrior about to go into battle, but also as a ruler of people.

VERSE 44

Agriculture, cattle-rearing and trade are the duties of the *Vaishyas* born of their own nature, and duty consisting of service is that of the *Shudras*, born of their own nature.

Vaishyas are *rajas-tamas* in temperament, with *rajas* dominant. Their lives are very much involved with the material plane of existence. *Cattle-rearing* is actually cow-rearing. The modern equivalent of *Vaishyas* are those engaged in industry, trade and technology, craftsmen, artisans, doctors, lawyers and teachers. The fourth class, the *Shudras* is one that serves others, the other three classes, in view of their *tamas-rajas* nature and the dominance of *tamas*. Among the four religious paths, *margas*, of *jnana*, *karma*, *bhakti* and *raja*, the *jnana-marga* is linked with the temperament of *Brahmins*, *bhakti-marga* with *Kshatriyas*, *raja-marga* with *Vaishyas* and *karma-marga* with *Shudras*.[41] Any attempt to place a hierarchy on the paths, will place a hierarchy, too, on the classes associated with them. There is still no overt suggestion here that class is hereditary: in fact, it is actions in past lives – the tendencies built up – that inform the *gunic* make-up, and therefore class, of the present life. Even so, such a theory implies a certain degree of reward and retribution that maintains and endorses social value judgements. Evolution of the self was traditionally through the classes, the *varnas*, from one life to the next, just as involution reverses the process. The text of the *Ramayana* casts thought back to a supposed Golden Age, when the class system operated perfectly, each class being valued for its service to society and integral to maintaining social harmony, but with no trace of hierarchical judgement. Importantly, the duties of the four classes involve actions: at best they are *dharmic* actions undertaken without egoistic aims but, broadly speaking, most activities are essential for the mainstay of society, and are goal-related.

VERSE 45
Man attains perfection each delighting in his own duty: hear how he, attentive to his own duty, finds perfection.

Whatever the debate about the unfairness of hereditary class, the *Gita* makes it clear here that liberation is for any class. Each person in life must follow his or her *dharma*, what is right for that person, the personal *dharma* or *sva-dharma* with its concomitant *duty*. This is important because it is the best way in which an individual can work out past *karma*. So each person's *karma* in terms of present existence is prescribed for him or her, but actions done to the best *dharmic* ability in that *karmic* life will ensure evolution and the negating of some past *adharma*. Mehta thought that *sva-dharma* arises naturally out of an individual's *sva-bhava*, the innate nature or "own being", and that conflict occurs by trying to adopt and live by an acquired nature. If this is so, then an acquired nature is inimical to evolution because it disengages the individual from his or her true nature and true path of development, though how such a theory would work in the case of an evil *sva-bhava* is not made clear, for here, a better "acquired nature" might be an evolutionary step. However, Mehta also described the true nature, the *sva-bhava*, as one's true *spiritual* self, which might solve the issue. Either way, he was right to see this closeness between the working out of *sva-bhava* and *sva-dharma*.[42] *Delighting in* contains the word *rata*, "joy", which rather suggests that one is happy in one's own nature and in what one has to do. It is this kind of person that undertakes a task for its intrinsic value rather than for the extraneous results it will bring, an attitude that results in *perfection (siddhi)* of being.

VERSE 46
He from whom is the evolution of beings, by whom all this is pervaded – worshipping him with his own duty, a man attains perfection.

Whatever class an individual belongs to, everyone is pervaded by the same divine essence and has the same Source, the same beginning and the same end. The cosmos is pervaded by an eternal *dharma*, the *sanatana-dharma*, the cosmic norm, and following *sva-dharma* conforms to the cosmic norm. It is Arjuna's *dharma* as a *Kshatriya* to fight in the present war and to maintain righteousness, a righteousness that, at this present time, is being threatened in a very serious way. By following his *sva-dharma*, the *sanatana-dharma*, the eternal *dharma*, will be upheld. *Evolution* in the text is *pravritti*, which really means "action", but is mostly accepted here as the creative divine activity that is evolution. *Duty* – here meaning *karma-yoga*, is combined with *bhakti-yoga* to provide an answer to Arjuna's dilemma.

Clearly, Krishna upholds the class system, which he not only created (4:13), but sees following it as a valid route to himself. His words in the verse may be meant for Arjuna's role in the impending battle, but it seems, too, that he is referring to all classes, suggesting that, whether *Brahmin* or *Shudra*, if one is able to perform one's duty without attachment to results, evolution of the self is guaranteed: *perfection* (*siddhi*) can be the end product, regardless of class.

Verse 47

Better is one's own *dharma* devoid of merits, than the *dharma* of another well performed. Doing duty ordained by his own nature, one incurs no sin.

Again, *one's own dharma* is *sva-dharma*, the personal right and natural path that is specific for an individual. Since it is closely bound to one's *karma*, it is the best possible path for getting rid of negative *karma*. And it is *duty* that is *ordained by* one's *own nature, sva-bhava*, that is the important proximate goal. This famous verse, repeating that of 3:35, raises again, the difficulty of the fully *tamasic* individual whose *sva-bhava* and *sva-dharma* are actually evil, especially if *sva-dharma* is dependent on the *sva-bhava* that is one's innate nature as Mehta suggested above. Such a difficulty is avoided only if the own nature refers to class duty – and this seems to be the context of the verse. A more generalized interpretation would raise a minefield of ethical issues. But I think the verse should be interpreted solely in the context of Arjuna's position, though it certainly links one's *dharma* with one's innate, natural nature. Ramanuja understood *one's own dharma* to be the proper *dharma* of *karma-yoga*, that is to say, abandonment of the results of actions through focus on the *atman*.[43]

The second part of the verse is unlikely to mean that a thoroughly *tamasic* individual will not incur negative *karma* as a result of wrong actions. *Sva-dharma* and *karma* are so closely linked in this respect as to be almost identical, and it is this that raises the difficulty. Here, of course, it is Arjuna's *dharma* to fight in this war. To turn against his own *dharma* would be *adharma* and would be deemed a negative action. Even if he turns his back on a *Kshatriya*'s duty and adopts the *dharma* of a holy man, performing his duties as a holy man very well, the results of this action would be negative *karma* because he failed to carry out his *sva-dharma*. Arjuna's role as a warrior is his *sva-dharma* and is also in line with the eternal *dharma*, the *sanatana-dharma*. It is when we apply the theory to thoroughly *tamasic* beings, to the *Rakshasas*, for example, let alone the *tamasic* amongst humanity, that it is difficult to explain, especially given the dreadful descriptions of the *tamasic* character in earlier chapters. Adopting the well-performed *dharma* of another, better, person, seems the only solution for the thoroughly *tamasic* person, but this is totally against the spirit of the verse.

VERSE 48
One should not abandon the duty for which one was born, Kaunteya, even if defective, for all undertakings are enveloped in defects like fire is by smoke.

For which one was born is actually "born with oneself", *sahaja*, suggesting that one's own being, *sva-bhava*, is natural to the self, portraying the interrelation between *sva-bhava* and *karma* very well. The sum total of *karma* acquired in previous existences dictates the circumstances into which one is born, the nature one is, and the kinds of situations that will occur in life. The *sva-bhava* of an individual will best equip that person to deal with those situations and absolve the *karma* that is carried.

Every action has something adverse about it – even eating and breathing – but it is the degree of intentional evil in the action that dictates whether an action is good or bad for the perpetrator, and will bring the appropriate resulting *karmic* effect. Every individual is composed of the *gunas*, not only physically, but also mentally and psychologically, and all activity is also *gunic* as is *karma* itself, so everything will contain the disharmony of *prakriti* and is flawed, or has *defects* (*doshas*). Only when the *gunas* are transcended can such defects be lost.

VERSE 49
He whose intellect is everywhere unattached, who has subdued his self, whose desires have fled, by *sannyasa* he attains the supreme perfection of freedom from *karma*.

The *Gita* now moves to a summary of its teaching on detached action. The verse depicts the egoless state when the mind is unaffected by sense objects in any way and is *unattached* (*asakta*). This would be true of the *Gita*'s view of *karma-yogins* who, even though engaged in activity are not ego-involved and not result orientated. But the verse specifically cites *sannyasa* not *tyaga*, thus departing from the differentiation between the two at the beginning of the chapter. The use of *sannyasa* here and not *tyaga* is another example of their occasional synonymous use in this chapter. For the *sannyasin*, the *tyagin*, the *yogin*, the self has to be mastered whatever the path: it is the *atman* that must inform the sole identity so that *perfection* (*siddhi*) is reached and *moksha* realized. It is the intellect, the *buddhi*, which has to disengage from sense objects through renunciation. *Karma* is meant here not just in the sense of fruitive *karma* but also in the sense of action that binds one to results. The *supreme perfection of freedom* is *naishkarmya siddhi*, the ultimate goal, the actionless Self, the unattached mind, "a complete inner quietism" in Aurobindo's words.[44] It is liberation from all desire and a total inner renunciation.

VERSE 50
Learn from me briefly, Kaunteya, how, that perfection attained, one may obtain Brahman, which is the highest state of knowledge.

Perfection here is, again, *siddhi* and it is that which allows an individual to attain to Brahman. The verse returns to supreme *knowledge* (*jnana*) at the same time, perhaps suggestive that *jnana* or *vijnana*, "realization", can only be attained after the criteria outlined in the previous verse have been perfected. As Aurobindo put it: "It is only when we lose our limited ego personality in the impersonality of the Self that we arrive at the calm and free oneness by which we can possess a true unity with the universal power of the Divine in his world movement."[45] To *obtain Brahman* in the *Gita*'s view is not to leave the world but to engage in it perfectly focused on, and at one with, Brahman.

VERSE 51
Integrated with a pure intellect, controlling the self by firmness, relinquishing sound and other sense objects, and abandoning attachment and aversion . . .

It is only by means of a *pure intellect*, understanding or wisdom (*buddhi*) that one can hope to understand the true nature of the self. When the intellect is tainted, the perspective of reality is bound to be distorted. *Moksha* involves a pure *atman* and the understanding of the impermanence of *prakritic* existence. It is *buddhi* as the major evolute of *prakriti* that is able to reflect the inner *atman* in the perfected being, but in those not liberated, it serves to bind the self to *prakriti* and obscure the *atman*. The goal is to lose the *buddhi* focused on the world and attain a pure *buddhi*. So, said Sri Krishna Prem, "the wasteful rush of the mind (*atmanam*) must be checked by firmness so that it moves by its own power, and is no longer pulled and pushed by the blind forces of attraction and repulsion".[46] *Integrated*, *yukta*, has been a frequently mentioned quality the *Gita* regards as essential. *Firmness* is, again, *dhriti*, about which much has already been said. It encompasses strict control of the senses, non-reaction to sense stimuli, desirelessness and, therefore, abandonment (*tyaga*) of the opposites of *attachment* (*raga*) and *aversion* (*dvesha*).

VERSE 52
. . . living in solitude, eating lightly, speech, body and mind subdued, always engaged in meditation and *yoga*, taking refuge in detachment . . .

The verse is reminiscent of much of the teaching in CHAPTER SIX. *Meditation and yoga* are both contained in the word for meditation, which is *dhyana*, the advanced stage of *yogic* practice that encompasses both meditation and concentration. The separate reference to *yoga* here may make the implied concentration specific to the *Gita*'s understanding of the term. Otherwise, the reference would be to *dhyana-yoga*, the *yoga* of meditation, which is what some prefer. *Detachment* is *vairagya*, also meaning "dispassion", that is to say, non-involvement in desires and aversions. While detachment from desires and aversions is necessary for Arjuna, the state of being described in this verse is purely *sattvic*. It is the life Arjuna thought might be better for him at the beginning of the *Gita*, but *living in solitude* in a cave or forest in order to subdue the *mind* (*manas*) will in no way cause him to fulfil his *dharma* as a *Kshatriya*.

VERSE 53

... having abandoned egoism, force, arrogance, desire, anger, covetousness, with no sense of "mine", peaceful, he is fit for becoming Brahman.

Desire (kama) and *anger (krodha)* have occurred many times in the *Gita* as two of
the three root evils of humankind. The third is greed, which is captured in the verse
by *covetousness*. This last has the idea of possession, probably of property. For *force*,
Shankara had "strength", which he saw as an internalized emotion that combined
with passion and desire to bind the self.[47] Importantly, the "I" of the self that engenders *egoism (ahankara)* is lost, to leave *peace (shanti)*. *Becoming Brahman* here is
brahma-bhuya, which Ramanuja described as "the state of Brahman"[48] and in the
following verse, he described this as "he to whom the essential nature of the self has
become manifest as consisting of infinite-knowledge and as having the sole character of being absolutely dependent on and subservient to Me".[49]

VERSE 54

Brahman-become, of serene self, he neither grieves nor desires; the same
to all beings, he obtains supreme devotion to me.

Brahman-become, brahma-bhuta, as in similar statements elsewhere, is unlikely to
be meant in the monistic sense of Shankara's non-dualism, but in the dualistic sense
of fusion with Brahman while retaining individuality, given the reference to *devotion, bhakti*, in the last part of the verse. *The same (sama) to all beings* has also occurred
in other parts of the *Gita* and, while Shankara was adamant this had nothing to do
with the one Brahman-become seeing Brahman in all others[50] this is, I think,
exactly what the expression does mean. Thus, Zaehner gave the variant "the same
in all beings" on the basis that one who is Brahman-become is, like Brahman, identifiable with the *atman* of every being,[51] and though *to* all beings is the more widely
accepted, the reason why the one Brahman-become is the same to all beings is that
the same *atman* in all beings is perceived. The verse neatly combines *jnana* and
bhakti, as does the following verse. Ramanuja's comments on this verse bring out
the full expression of devotional Vaishnavism, with depictions of God as, for
example, "the sole ground of innumerable hosts of auspicious qualities the excellence of which is unbounded . . .".[52]

VERSE 55

By devotion he knows me, what and who in truth I am: then, having
known me in truth, he enters me forthwith.

Devotion here is *bhakti*, but whether one's path is *bhakti-yoga* or *jnana-yoga*,
knowledge of Brahman involves knowledge of both *nirguna* and *saguna* Brahman
and realization of the *atman* – *what and who in truth I am*. *Enters me* is in the dual
sense; there will always be a differentiation between the devotee and Brahman,
which is typical of the classical period of Hinduism: individuality is retained, even
though the ego is lost. The *atman* is not the totality of Brahman but can become
panentheistically at one with it, again, rather like the drop of water returning to
the ocean or the grain of sand to the sea shore. Taking the last two verses together

there is a possibility that they depict a progression from devotion to full knowledge of Brahman; yet it seems to me that both verses could also depict the same state, showing a synthesis of both *bhakti-* and *jnana-yoga*. However, Sampatkumaran comments here that, for Ramanuja, the path is one of supreme devotion, which brings supreme knowledge, which then brings the highest *bhakti* of all.[53]

VERSE 56

Continually doing all actions taking refuge in me, by my grace he obtains the eternal, imperishable abode.

It seems to be the path of the *karma-yogin* that is mainly being described here, the path of detached action, inaction in action, to use the *Gita*'s earlier description, while at all times focused on the divine. So we have had devotion, knowledge and now egoless action mentioned in the last three verses. Are they meant to be taken together or separately? Though different sects and schools conclude that the *Gita* upholds one path or another as favoured by Krishna, as far as I can see, the boundaries between the paths remain very blurred. The *karma-yoga* path of this verse would certainly be the most appropriate for Arjuna in his present circumstances, but the verse also maintains that distinct dualism between the human and divine, entrenched by *taking refuge in me* and especially by the use of *grace, prasada,* both of which complement the theme of devotion. And if any one path should come to the fore, it is this last, *bhakti,* but the verse implies a harmony of both *karma-* and *bhakti-yoga.* The *imperishable (avyaya) abode (pada)* that is *eternal (shashvata)* is total liberation.

VERSE 57

Mentally renouncing all actions in me, having me as the highest goal, resorting to *buddhi-yoga,* always have your thoughts fixed on me.

The dualism between divine and human and the idea of focus and devotion to God is continued from the last verse. Now, Krishna addresses Arjuna directly, advising him how to respond to his earlier dilemma. When all actions are resigned in Krishna, there can be no sense of ego, of "I", as the agent of actions or their consequences. The egoistic *jivatman,* then, is lost and without attachment to actions and their results, no fruitive *karma* can be reaped from them. The process for Arjuna will be an inward one, a mentally focused one that is extraneous to the battle. Krishna has already told Arjuna to renounce all actions in him and centre his mind on the *atman* (3:30), and has said that whatever action Arjuna undertakes should be done as an offering to him (9:27): now, that is linked with *buddhi-yoga,* the *yoga* of the intellect – action and devotion that are based in concentrated mental discipline – the synthesis of devotion, *bhakti,* with *karma*-less action, *karma-yoga,* and also with knowledge, *jnana-yoga.*

VERSE 58

Fixing thought on me, by my grace you will overcome all obstacles, but if from egoism you will not hear, you will perish.

Again, the idea of *grace, prasada*, reinforces the dualism between human and divine. Like Buddhism, the teaching here is that the ego causes a false perception of reality and a sense of "I" as the agent in all activities. For the *Gita*, it is the operation of the *gunas* that informs action, underpinned by the *atman* that lends false consciousness to the *buddhi*. Since the ego, *ahankara*, is also *prakritic*, it is matter; it cannot be a real agent of action. To overcome such egoism, *thought (chitta)* needs to be focused totally on Krishna.

VERSE 59

If, having taken refuge in egoism, you think "I will not fight", vain is this your resolve; your nature will compel you.

The reason why Arjuna wants to turn from the battle and against his *dharma* is that his ego (*ahankara*) is involved in the action. He is thinking in terms of results of his actions and therefore his actions will involve him in consequential *karma*. If ego is lost, and the battle is undertaken in a state of detached action, there can be no fruitive *karma*; it is in this state of mind that Arjuna must fight. His *karma* is to fight and his *nature*, here, *prakriti*, will not allow him to escape from it. The use of *prakriti* here as Arjuna's nature may have the double meaning of nature in general and yet refer to Arjuna's nature as a *Kshatriya*; both are really the same thing.

VERSE 60

Bound by your own *karma*, born of your own nature, Kaunteya, that which from delusion you wish not to do, helpless, you will surely do.

The sum total of Arjuna's personality, his *nature, sva-bhava* in the verse, is a result of his past *karma*; he cannot escape this. He is a *Kshatriya* and it is his *karma* to live the life of one. Even if through *delusion* (*moha*) he does not want to fight, he will have to, for the *karma* ahead will create that situation for him and his inherent nature will get caught up in it. The only way to exhaust one's *karma* from past lives is to face it, go through it, and then leave it behind; but it cannot be avoided. Trying to avoid it only reaps more similar *karma*. It would be impossible to avoid the conclusion here that *karma* creates respective births of individuals, that is to say, the best kind of birth in which *karma* can be eradicated, given that *karma* is *born of one's own nature*.

VERSE 61

Ishvara dwells in the hearts of all beings, Arjuna, causing all beings by his *maya* to whir as if mounted on a machine.

This verse combines a number of key concepts in the *Gita*. Krishna dwells in the heart of all as the *atman* and is the cause of the whole process of *prakriti*, the whole complexity of changing processes of cause and effect. And yet he does no action, in the same way that he drives Arjuna's chariot, is the means by which Arjuna will engage in the war, but carries no weapons and does not wage war himself. All *karma*, all *prakriti*, thus belongs to Krishna but he has no active engagement in these: he causes all but is its detached observer. Individuals, conversely, believe themselves to be agents and the centre of their own actions. They are wrapped in *maya*, illusion about the reality of *prakriti*, like parts of some machine being incapable of doing anything other than what they do. Mistakenly, they think they are the only part, while all the time, something else makes the machine work; but all they can do is play their prescribed parts. *To whirl as if mounted on a machine* is, thus, a graphic description of human lives that are bound with the power of *prakritic* illusion. Krishna has already said in 7:14 that trust in him will be the means of escape from it. Juan Mascaró translated the second part of the verse attractively with: "And his power of wonder moves all things – puppets in a play of shadows – whirling them onwards on the stream of time."[54] Similarly, Ramanuja understood *maya* here to be the workings of the *gunas* in *prakriti*: past *karma* and the habits accrued in past lives (*vasanas*) – the latter lying deeply rooted in the psyche – perpetuate the *maya* of God, the *machine* in which all are bound,[55] which captures the sense of the verse very well without resorting to tones of predestination.

Verse 62

Taking refuge in him alone with all your being, Bharata, by his grace you will obtain supreme peace and the eternal abode.

To continue the analogy of the previous verse, the suggestion here is that one should take *refuge in* the owner of the machine, not the machine itself, thus Ishvara and not *prakriti*, so finding *peace* (*shanti*). Instead of being engaged in worldly affairs and believing the self to be the sole agent of all one does, the ego is to be put aside and the entirety of the individual focused on God. Zaehner noted that *being, bhava*, in the verse can be translated as "love",[56] which would make the verse even more theistic in tone. Either way, the use of *grace, prasada*, again, is suggestive of devotional theism and a distinct dualism between human and God.

Verse 63

Thus, to you has been declared knowledge more secret than any secret, by me. Fully reflecting over this, act as you will.

Notably, Krishna does not compel Arjuna to act; he asks him to reflect and to act with *knowledge* (*jnana*), not blindly. *Act as you will* he tells Arjuna, allowing the freedom of choice, the freedom of living according to Arjuna's own conscience and consciousness. Ramanuja believed Krishna was asking Arjuna to choose and act according to either *karma-yoga, jnana-yoga*, or *bhakti-yoga*,[57] but this would fall short of knowledge imparted as the utmost *secret* (*guhya*). I find it impossible to accept the view of Johnson here that Arjuna could have no real choice because Krishna has "divine total agency".[58]

This really ends the knowledge that Krishna gives to Arjuna. What follows is deemed to be the most secret and profound of all possible secrets and is one that will bring the devotee to Brahman.

Verse 64

Hear again my supreme word, most secret of all: you are beloved by me, therefore I shall speak to you what is for your good.

What Krishna now imparts to Arjuna is the great *secret* (*guhya*) of the *Gita* – God's profound love of his devotee. The teaching in this verse and the two that follow are the heart of the theism of the *Gita*. This love of God for the devotee is presented as the *supreme* or highest *word* or utterance. *You are beloved by me* is tantamount to saying "I love you dearly", and is one of the most beautiful statements of Krishna in the *Gita*. The devotional love of the verse implies that it is *bhakti-yoga* that is the supreme path, even if other paths are not discounted elsewhere.

Verse 65

Fix your mind on me, be devoted to me, sacrifice to me, pay homage to me, then, in truth I promise you, you will come to me, for you are dear to me.

Krishna has already described in 12:13–20, those who are dear to him and here we have, again, a profoundly theistic verse. When the whole being is directed towards Krishna, then the whole action is reciprocated by him so that the two are ultimately joined in union: the greater the love of the devotee, the greater the reciprocated love from God. This is a verse exclusively concerned with devotion, promoting it as the path to liberation: devotion (*bhakti*), sacrifice (*yajna*) and homage (*namaskar*) are focused totally on Krishna.

Verse 66

Renounce all *dharmas*; take refuge in me alone. I will liberate you from all evils; grieve not.

Gandhi described this verse as "the essence of all Shastras and of the *Gita*,[59] and it is certainly at the heart of the whole teaching. For Ramanuja and the school of Vishishtadvaita, it was the conclusion to the *Gita*. To *take refuge* is to surrender the entirety of one's being to God, though Ramanuja did not mention *prapatti*, "surrender", specifically, despite its being a main tenet of Vishishadvaita. *Renounce all dharmas* is variously interpreted. At a simple level, it might mean abandonment of all the religious *dharmas* undertaken for results, or it might mean that Krishna transcends all *dharmas*, so taking refuge in him will make all necessary *dharmas* fulfilled. *Dharma* is what is right in terms of action, duty, ritual, class, stage of life and the right *karmic* path through life. Until liberation, *moksha*, those paths have to be followed just as rivers follow their courses until they reach the ocean. Once Brahman-become, the *dharmas* that pertain to life and to the individual cease to be. However, there are other views. Shankara considered renouncing all *dharmas* to mean giving up all good and evil deeds, all *dharma* and *adharma*, believing this to be referring to all action, in line with his *advaitist* view that *all* action has to be abandoned for liberation.[60] But the *Gita* is adamant that all action cannot be abandoned. If all *dharmas* are abandoned, even personal *dharma*, *sva-dharma* is abandoned and Krishna has advocated quite the opposite, upholding Arjuna's *dharma* as a *Kshatriya*. Krishna does not believe that abandoning all action is the right path, just the abandonment of attachment to the results of it. But by taking *refuge* in him *alone*, he will assist the process and the path to liberation.[61]

Ramanuja interpreted *all dharmas* as *karma-*, *jnana-* and *bhakti-yoga* by relinquishing any sense of "I", thus seeing God as "the agent, the object of worship, the goal of attainment and the means". Such "has been firmly established as the renunciation, in accordance with the *sastras*, of all *dharmas*".[62] Easwaran thought that *dharmas*, used in the plural in the verse, has the rarer meaning of "a thing's attribute, condition, or conditioning", so "dharmas are the innumerable beings, things, emotions and mental states that make up everyday existence as we experience it".[63] The idea is attractive and suits the context of Krishna telling Arjuna to abandon externalities. The *Gita* has had much to say on the necessity of transcending *prakriti* and the desires and aversions, the good and the bad, which come one's way. The pairs of opposites in life cause reaction physically or mentally in response to how one feels about something and herein lies the attachment and the consequent *karma*.

The *Gita's* point, as far as I can see, is that taking refuge totally in Krishna helps an individual to transcend *prakriti* and be grounded in the passive *atman* within. Then, one's *sva-bhava*, "own being", is elided into pure *atman* and one automatically does what is right. Arjuna has been told earlier that it is his *dharma* as a *Kshatriya* to fight, supported by his *sva-bhava*, his innate nature as a *Kshatriya*. Taking refuge in Krishna will not mean that he can give up the actions to which his *dharma* bind him; rather, immersed in Krishna, he will fulfil them without ego-involvement and without attachment to results. Detached action and devotion to Krishna seem to be the best possible path for Arjuna. This way, no *evils* (*papa*) can befall him. Sometimes translated as "sins", "evils" tends to bring out the more subtle notions of incorrect knowledge and false perceptions that attachment to the *gunas* of *prakriti* entail, rather than simply negative *karmic* results, which is how Ramanuja understood *papa*. Thus, for *I will liberate you*, which is tantamount to God's grace towards his devotee. Ramanuja's understanding of the phrase was: "That is, I will release you from all sins which stand in the way of attainment of Myself, and which consist of countless acts of doing what ought not to be done and omissions to do what ought to be done, piled up from time without beginning."[64] However, *grieve not*, here, is suggestive of Arjuna having some concerns about his fitness for, and deserving of, the path of devotion.

At this point, Krishna has finished his teaching, and we have had in this verse what is called a *carama-shloka*, a last, final and important stanza, summarizing the central tenet of the whole of the *Gita*.

VERSE 67

This should not be spoken by you to one devoid of *tapas*, to one who is not devoted, and never to one who does not do service [or who does not listen], and to one who speaks ill of me.

People can only understand what their levels of consciousness allow them to, and that level of consciousness is dictated by past *karma*, so they really create themselves. Each person is at a different point on his or her evolutionary path and what is right for one would not be right for another. The *atman* may exist in all beings but some are so far from its realization as to find spiritual teaching wholly alien, and the *Gita* has had much to say about such truly *tamasic* individuals. Then, too, at the time of the *Gita*, there were many opposing schools of thought, some orthodox and some unorthodox, so the verse may well be aimed at antagonists to Krishna, those who are *not devoted (abhakta)*. *One who does not do service* is *ashushrushava* in the Sanskrit and it has the alternative meaning of "one who does not listen", which is found in some translations.

VERSE 68

Whoever declares this supreme secret to my devotees and shows supreme devotion to me will doubtless come to me.

In contrast to those whose consciousness is not yet fit for the spiritual teaching of the *Gita*, or those who are antagonistic to it, there are those whose consciousness is right. To be the instrument of such teaching, while devoted to Krishna, this verse states, is a sure means to reaching enlightenment. Here, then, is a verse that praises both *karma* and *bhakti* paths. The word *devotion* features frequently in the verse, emphasizing the importance of *bhakti*. So the *secret (guhya)* is not to be kept but to be shared.

VERSE 69

And nor is there any among men who does dearer service to me than he, nor shall there be another on Earth dearer to me than he.

This continues the sense of the previous verse, the subject being he who teaches or declares the supreme secret, with the notable reciprocal love between divine and human.

VERSE 70

And whoever studies this sacred dialogue of ours, by him I shall have been worshipped by *jnana-yajna*, so I believe.

Studying this scripture is deemed to be an act of *jnana-yajna*, "sacrifice of knowledge". Shankara claimed that *yajna* is of four types; *vidhi*, which is ritual, *japa*, which is loud prayer, *upamsu*, which is prayer uttered in a low voice, and *manasa*, which is prayer offered with the mind. Worship by *jnana-yajna*, he believed, would be placed in this last category and is the highest form.[65] But a key word in the verse is *dialogue*, the two-way instruction of the teacher and the questioning by the pupil. It is, again, indicative of the dual relationship between devotee and God and this must surely be, I think, the heart of the message of the *Gita*: knowledge is crucial, detached action is crucial, but the underpinning concept to both as we reach the end of the *Gita* is devotion to Krishna.

VERSE 71

And the man who hears, full of *shraddha*, free from malice, he too will be liberated and will attain the happy worlds of those of righteous actions.

Shraddha, "faith", and *actions* (*karma*) give the impression that the practice of *bhakti* and of *karma-yoga*, particularly the former, in following and living by the teachings of the *Gita*, are sufficient for liberation. But *liberated* (*mukta*) here is qualified as a heavenly existence – the *happy worlds* – as a result of good *karma*, rather than a loss of *karma*. That is not the liberation that achieves total release from *samsara*, and when good *karma* is exhausted in such happy lands, rebirth on Earth is inevitable – albeit in a good position for imminent and true liberation.

VERSE 72

Have you heard this, Partha, with one-pointed thought? Has the delusion of ignorance been destroyed, Dhananjaya?

Krishna surely knows the answer to his question, but wishes Arjuna to articulate it. *Thought* (*chetas*) is indicative of the whole reasoning process, the whole of the mind and consciousness, since *one-pointed*, *ekagrena*, is "single-minded concentration", an important facet of *yogic* practice, the kind that dissolves *ignorance* (*ajnana*).

VERSE 73   Arjuna said:

Delusion is destroyed. Through your grace, memory has been regained, Achyuta. I stand firm, freed from doubts. I shall do your word.

Arjuna's ignorance is now totally dispelled, and his egoistic individuality is surrendered to Krishna. With such surrender of the ego, no *delusion* (*moha*) can remain, and Arjuna loses all the self-originated problems with which the *Gita* began. He addresses Krishna as Achyuta, "Immortal, Immovable", One who does not change from a supreme state, and it is to this supreme state that Arjuna has surrendered himself. The words *memory has been regained* are interesting, for they suggest a return to an original state – perhaps the state of identification of the *atman* with Brahman which, in the intermediate years has been forgotten: they suggest a return to the norm, to the beginning. *Memory*, *smriti*, which literally means "remembered", however, is variously translated; recognition is an apt alternative, especially if broken down to re-cognition. But Barbara Stoler Miller had, I think, the right idea of the meaning when she described it thus: "Not discursive recollection of past events, but the awakening of latent impressions left by prior perceptions; essential to the aesthetic experience of Krishna's revelation."[66] It is an understanding of one's very nature as *atman*.

The medium for such recollection, recognition or regaining of memory is the grace, *prasada*, of Krishna. Arjuna would not have gained such a state without

Krishna's guidance, without his grace. Once again, the idea of the grace of God brings to the fore the dual relationship between devotee and the divine; self-effort is necessary on the path to *moksha* but it is effort that is rewarded by God much more when the devotee turns towards God and is fully focused on him. Arjuna's statement that he is *firm* (*sthita*) suggests the certainty of his knowledge of Brahman, of his focus on Ishvara and his state in which all his doubts have vanished. Arjuna has reached the deepest essence of himself as the *atman*. He can now face the battle, free from his own ego, detached, rooted in *atman*. *I shall do your word* represents his total surrender to Krishna.

VERSE 74   Sanjaya said:
Thus I have heard this wonderful, hair-raising dialogue of Vasudeva and great-souled Partha.

The whole of the *Gita*, we should remember, is being related to Dhritarashtra by his enlightened sage, Sanjaya, who "hears", "sees" and cognizes all the events that are taking place on the battlefield. His hair is standing on end because of the nature of the religious content, not because of fear. *Hair-raising*, literally, "that causes one's hair to stand up", is variously interpreted. Zaehner had "I shuddered with delight",[67] van Buitenen "marvellous and enrapturing"[68] and Johnson, "shivers running down my spine".[69] Such descriptions are meant to emphasize the impact of the *Gita* on its listeners. The *dialogue* that *Sanjaya* hears is *sanvada*, sometimes translated as "colloquy", which van Buitenen thought may have once formed part of, or the whole of, the original title of the *Gita*.[70] Sanjaya has no delusions about the nature of the battle and its outcome, but Dhritarashtra, blind physically, is also blind to wisdom. Sanjaya refers to Arjuna as a *great-soul*, a *mahatma*, which should forewarn Dhritarashtra that righteousness is on the side of the Pandavas.

VERSE 75
Through the grace of Vyasa, I have heard this secret and supreme *yoga* directly from Krishna, the Lord of *Yoga* himself, declaring it.

It was the sage Vyasa who blessed Sanjaya with the divine eye. As a result, he could intuit or cognize all that took place between Krishna and Arjuna, has heard the same *secret* (*guhya*). Krishna is called *Lord of Yoga*, *Yogeshvara*, the Lord of the distinctive *Yoga* of the *Gita*.

VERSE 76
O King, remembering again and again this holy, wonderful dialogue between Keshava and Arjuna, I rejoice again and again.

Sanjaya is at one with Krishna and Arjuna, not with Dhritarashtra. Hearing and understanding the whole dialogue is a total delight and wonder to the privileged sage.

VERSE 77

And remembering again and again that most wonderful form of Hari, great is my wonder, O King, and I rejoice again and again.

Hari, "Lord", which occurred also in 11:9, is another name for Krishna. Sanjaya, too, was privileged to see that which Arjuna saw in CHAPTER ELEVEN, the vision of the resplendent Krishna, but also the terrifying aspects.

VERSE 78

Wherever Krishna the Lord of *Yoga* is, wherever Partha the archer is, there is fortune, victory, happiness, firmness and firm conduct, I believe.

Sanjaya concludes with the fact that everything is on the side of the Pandavas. Arjuna began the *Gita* by laying down his bow, Gandiva, but now, at the close of the *Gita* he again becomes Partha the archer.

In the *Upanishad* of the *Bhagavad Gita*, the knowledge of Brahman, the teaching of *Yoga* and the dialogue between Shri Krishna and Arjuna, this is the eighteenth chapter called *Moksha Sannyasa Yoga*.

Epilogue

The conch shells had been blown and the Battle of Kurukshetra began, lasting for eighteen days. Every one of the Kauravas was killed in terrible warfare. The five Pandava brothers, along with Krishna, survived; though they lost relatives, children and friends in the slaughter. Bhishma died on a bed of arrows and in the final stages of the battle, Duryodhana was slain by Bhima who himself died the following day. Blind Dhritarashtra survived all and, after the war, became reconciled with the Pandavas when the firstborn of them, Yudhishthira, became king. Dhritarashtra later left for a reclusive life in the forest and died in a fire.

For thirty-six years, Yudhishthira ruled the kingdom at Hastinapura, *but the* Mahabharata *has no ending of happiness and peace. At the close of the great epic, the Yadavas resorted to* adharmic *actions – depravity, drunkenness, abuse of gods and Brahmins, and self-destruction – and brought about the ruin of the Vrishni race. We do not find greatness in the death of any of the Pandava heroes, not even in the death of Krishna, for while sitting deep in meditation he was killed accidentally by a hunter. As the* Mahabharata *puts it,* Time is that which gives and that which takes away. *Within its confines one day we are inspired and on another frustrated: one period we are masters only to find ourselves servants at another. And Time,* Kala, *caught up one by one with the Pandavas: each died because of a fault in his or her nature. Arjuna, the magnificent archer, suddenly found himself impotent, his great bow,* Gandiva, *ceasing to have any power, and his formerly inexhaustible quiver of no use.*

Saddened by events, Yudhishthira, his brothers, their wife Draupadi and a faithful dog who attached itself to them, set out in the direction of the Himalayas to find the heaven of the god Indra at the peak of Mount Meru. Draupadi was the first to die on the ascent, then Sahadeva, then Nakula. The next to fall and die was Arjuna, punished because he held all other archers in contempt. His vanity was the reason he could not reach Indra's heaven. Bhima, too, died on the ascent, leaving only Yudhishthira and the dog who was deeply devoted to him. When Indra, driving his chariot, met Yudhishthira and invited him into his heaven, Yudhishthira refused to enter without his faithful dog. When he was told that heaven had no space for the dog, and that renunciation of all attachments was the key to heaven, Yudhishthira said he would die rather than forsake one who was so devoted to him. But the dog then transformed itself to its true nature as the god of Dharma and led Yudhishthira into Indra's heaven, though even then, Yudhishthira wanted only to be wherever his four brothers and their wife Draupadi were. Assured that he would see his brothers and his wife, Yudhishthira entered Indra's heaven. But there he found the villain Duryodhana enjoying its delights despite having caused so much suffering. Yet Duryodhana had fulfilled his duty as a Kshatriya *by dying in battle, and had, therefore, earned the right to be there. Yudhishthira again refused to remain in that heaven and requested that he be taken to his brothers. His wish was granted and he was guided to a hell where he heard only their voices wailing at him to stay to soothe their agonies. Such was his compassion that Yudhishthira, despite the promise of the delights of a heaven, resigned himself to a hell. It was then that all the horror vanished and Yudhishthira found himself reunited with his loved ones in a perfect heaven. His compassion for the dog had overruled his own happiness, as had his compassion for his brethren: both were tests of his incorruptibility. A life of utter happiness awaited the Pandavas and Draupadi as a result of their good* karma *– until, that is, their merit is exhausted and they are reborn on Earth.*

Notes

Introduction

1 The ancient language of these Aryans is linked to a wide spectrum of other languages like Greek, Latin and Persian, as well as Germanic and Slavonic languages. There is also a link with Celtic languages: indeed, the old name for Ireland as Eire is likely to be a cognate of the Sanskrit word Aryan.

2 Strictly speaking, the Sanskrit term for the priestly class is *Brahmana*. But since this is also the term for a commentary on a *Samhita* or *Veda*, and might be confusing for the reader, I shall retain the anglicized and better-known transliteration, *Brahmin*, for a priest/the priestly class.

3 The *Atharva Veda* and its associated traditions are probably an exception here since it is the latest of the *Vedas*, see P. Olivelle, *Upanisads* (Oxford and New York: Oxford University Press, 1996), p. xxx, note 11.

4 See Surendranath Dasgupta, *A History of Indian Philosophy, Vol. 1* (Delhi, Varanasi, Patna, Bangalore, Madras: Motilal Banarsidass, 1988 reprint of first Indian edn 1975, first published 1922), p. 26.

5 *Rig Veda* 1:164:46 see R. T. H. Griffith, translator, *The Hymns of the Rg Veda* (Delhi: Motilal Banarsidass, 1991 reprint of 1973 new, revised edn), p. 113.

6 Suggested by Sarvepalli Radhakrishnan, translator, *The Principal Upanisads* (New Delhi: Indus, 1994, first published 1953), p. 35.

7 M. Hiriyanna, *Outlines of Indian Philosophy* (Delhi: Motilal Banarsidass Publishers Private Limited, 1993), p. 42.

8 While there are about a hundred and twelve *Upanishads* of various dates, there are thirteen main ones with the addition of perhaps five more that also can be considered important. None has any author. The term *Upanishad* is usually taken to mean something like "sitting down near", that is to say, near to a teacher.

9 *Brihadaranyaka Upanishad* 1:3:28, translator Radhakrishnan, *The Principal Upanisads*, p. 162.

10 Juan Mascaró, *The Bhagavad Gita* (London, New York, Victoria, Ontario, Auckland: Penguin, 1962), p. 22.

11 J. A. B. van Buitenen, translator, *The Bhagavadgita in the Mahabharata* (Chicago and London: Chicago University Press, 1981), p. 39.

12 Kashi Nath Upadhyaya argues for a more genuine placement of the *Gita* in the *Mahabharata*, pointing out synonymy of language, phrases and ideas between both, as well as places in the *Mahabharata* in which the *Gita* is mentioned. He suggests that the *Gita* is "an integral part of the *Mahabharata*". See his *Early Buddhism and the Bhagavadgita* (Delhi, Varanasi, Patna: Motilal Banarsidass, 1983 reprint of 1971 edn), pp. 6–7.

13 Alexandre Piatigorsky in his introduction to J. A. B. van Buitenen, translator, *The*

Bhagavad Gita (Rockport, Massachusetts, Shaftesbury, Dorset, Brisbane, Queensland: Element, 1997), p. 3.

14 See John Brockington, "The Sanskrit Epics". In Gavin Flood, ed., *The Blackwell Companion to Hinduism* (Malden, Massachusetts, Oxford, Victoria: Blackwell Publishing, 2005 reprint of 2003 edn), p. 116.

15 The Purva or Karma Mimamsa school, or at least its developing strands, possibly predates the *Gita*.

16 For example, Sarvepalli Radhakrishnan, translator, *The Bhagavadgita, with an Introductory Essay, Sanskrit Text, English Translation and Notes* (New York: Harper, 1973, and London: George Allen & Unwin, 1948), p. 14.

17 See Upadhyaya, *Early Buddhism and the Bhagavadgita*, p. 21.

18 See Gavin Flood, *An Introduction to Hinduism* (Cambridge, New York and Melbourne: Cambridge University Press, 1996), p. 119.

19 Flood, *ibid.*

20 For a lengthy account of the possibilities and complexities of Krishna's origins, see W. Douglas P. Hill, *The Bhagavadgita: Translated from the Sanskrit with an introduction an argument and a commentary* (London: Oxford University Press, 1928, reprinted 1966), pp. 1–10.

21 Or, perhaps, "Attractor", see E. Osborn Martin, *The Gods of India* (New Delhi: Cosmo, no date), p. 130, and Arvind Sharma, *The Hindu Gita: Ancient and classical interpretations of the Bhagavadgita* (London: Duckworth, 1986), p. xiii.

22 Hill, *The Bhagavadgita*, p. 7.

23 See, for example, George Thompson, translator, *The Bhagavad Gita: A new translation* (New York: North Point Press, 2008), p. xxiii, Barbara Stoler Miller, translator, *The Bhagavad-Gita: Krishna's counsel in time of war* (New York, Toronto, London, Sydney, Auckland: Bantam Books, 1986), p. 3, and John L. Brockington, "The Bhagavad Gita: Text and Context". In Julius Lipner, ed., *The Fruits of Our Desiring: An enquiry into the ethics of the Bhagavadgita for our times* (Calgary, Canada: Bayeux, 1997), p. 32.

24 Miller, *ibid.*

25 See Richard Gotshalk, translator, *Bhagavad Gita: Translation and commentary* (Delhi: Motilal Banarsidass Publishers Private Limited, 1993 reprint of 1985 edn), p. ix.

26 Will J. Johnson, *The Bhagavad Gita: A new translation* (Oxford and New York: Oxford University Press, 1994), p. x.

27 Franklin Edgerton, *The Bhagavad Gita* (Delhi: Motilal Banarsidass Publishers Private Limited, 1994, first published 1944), p. xiii.

28 Charles Wilkins *The Bhagvat Geeta, or Dialogues of Kreeshna and Arjoon in Eighteen Lectures with Notes* (London, 1785).

29 Eric J. Sharpe, *The Universal Gita: Western images of the Bhagavad Gita* (La Salle, Illinois: Open Court Publishing Company, 1985), p. xi. Sharpe's book deals critically with translations of the *Gita* into English from the eighteenth to the twentieth centuries, subject matter that is beyond the remit of this present book but which the interested reader might wish to take up.

30 Poona: Bhandarkar Oriental Research Institute, pp. 114–88.

31 Another commentator, Bhaskara, also refers to variant readings in his commentary on the first nine chapters of the *Gita*. His dates are uncertain and he could have written his commentary some time before or after Shankara. After the *Mahabharata* war was over, at a time of relative tranquillity, Arjuna seems to have forgotten a good deal of

Krishna's teaching and requests that Krishna iterates it. Krishna refuses a word-by-word repetition, but does recapitulate his teaching. This teaching and Arjuna's request for it are recorded in the *Anugita*, dated somewhere around the third century CE. The *Anugita* is interesting in that it gives prominence to the path of knowledge and little emphasis to devotion, unlike the *Gita*. Arvind Sharma thinks this text is indicative of a trend to interpret the *Gita* monistically, well before Shankara's famous non-dual perspective of it, see *The Hindu Gita*, p. 7.

32 Most notably, the *Chandogya Upanishad* 6:8:7 with its *Tat tvam asi*, "That you are", and also the *Brihadaranyaka Upanishad* in a number of places (1:4:10; 3:4:1; 3:7:15).

33 Sri Krishna Prem, *The Yoga of the Bhagavat Gita* (Shaftesbury, Dorset: Element Books, 1988), pp. xix–xxix.

34 Trevor Leggett, *Realization of the Supreme Self: The Bhagavad Gita Yoga-s* (London and New York: Kegan Paul International, 1995).

35 Alan Jacobs, *The Bhagavad Gita* (Winchester, UK and New York: O Books, 2003), p. xiii.

36 *Ibid.*, p. xv.

37 "It was at this time that, coming into contact with two Englishmen, I was induced to read the *Gita*: I say "induced" because I had no particular desire to read it. When these two friends asked me to read the *Gita* with them, I felt rather ashamed. The consciousness that I knew nothing about our holy books made me feel miserable. The reason, I think, was my vanity. I did not know Sanskrit well enough to be able to read the *Gita* without help. The two English friends, on their part, did not know Sanskrit at all. They gave me Sir Edwin Arnold's excellent translation of the poem. I went through the whole of it immediately and was fascinated by it. From that time until now, the last nineteen stanzas of Chapter II have ever remained engraved in my heart. For me, they contain the essence of dharma. They embody the highest knowledge. The principles enunciated in them are immutable." Mohandas Gandhi in Mahendra Kulasrestha, ed., *Mahatma Gandhi, The Bhagavadgita: A book of ethics for all religions* (New Delhi: Lotus Press, 2008), p. 11.

38 Satya P. Agarwal, *The Social Role of the Gita: How and why* (Delhi: Motilal Banarsidass Publishers Private Limited, 1997 reprint of 1993 edn), *passim*.

39 Sri Aurobindo, *Essays on the Gita* (Pondicherry: Sri Aurobindo Ashram, 1987 impression of eighth edn 1970, first published 1916–20), p. 8.

40 A few more examples will suffice: Radhakrishnan's *maha-vakya* was 2:16, indicative of his *advaitist* stance. Aurobindo's was 15:16–17.

41 See, for example, Miller, *The Bhagavad-Gita*, and Geoffrey Parrinder, *The Bhagavad Gita: A verse translation* (Oxford: Oneworld, 1996, first published 1974).

42 E. Gough, *The Philosophy of the Upanishads: Ancient Indian metaphysics* (New Delhi: Cosmo, 1979), p. 38.

43 See J. C. Heesterman, "Brahman" in *Encyclopedia of Religion*, vol. 2, edited by Mircea Eliade (New York: Macmillan Publishing Company and London: Collier Macmillan, 1987), p. 295.

44 Some, however, believe otherwise. See, for example, Aurobindo, *Essays on the Gita*, p. 16.

45 Radhakrishnan, *The Principal Upanisads*, p. 73.

46 *Ibid.*

47 Edgerton, *The Bhagavad Gita*, p. 37.

48 W. Halbfass, *On Being and What There Is: Classical Vaisesika and the History of Indian Ontology* (Albany, New York: State University of New York Press, 1992), p. 26.
49 Radhakrishnan, *The Principal Upanishads*, p. 90.
50 Gotshalk, *Bhagavad Gita*, p. 86.
51 Thus, the *jivatman* is sometimes understood as equating with the *atman*. Aurobindo, for example, understood *jiva* as spirit, "a higher, a supreme, a conscient and divine Nature, and it is that which has become the individual soul". *Essays on the Gita*, p. 80. More frequently, the *jivatman's* involvement in the world divorces it from the passive *atman*.
52 Chandradhar Sharma, *A Critical Survey of Indian Philosophy* (Delhi: Motilal Banarsidass Publishers Private Limited, 1987 reprint of 1960 edn), p. 19.
53 Radhakrishnan, *The Principal Upanisads*, p. 92.
54 Radhakrishnan, *The Bhagavadgita*, p. 52.
55 Robert Charles Zaehner, *The Bhagavad-Gita* (Oxford, London, New York: Oxford University Press, 1973, first published 1969), p. 18.
56 S. Chatterjee and D. Datta, *An Introduction to Indian Philosophy* (Calcutta: University of Calcutta, 1984), pp. 21–22.
57 Radhakrishnan, *The Bhagavadgita*, p. 70.
58 Aurobindo, *Essays on the Gita*, p. 108.
59 Ursula King, "Who is the Ideal Karmayogin? The Meaning of a Hindu Religious Symbol". In *Religion*, 1980, p. 47.
60 See Jeaneane Fowler, *Perspectives of Reality: An introduction to the philosophy of Hinduism* (Brighton, Sussex and Portland, Oregon: Sussex Academic Press, 2002), pp. 199–200.
61 Sharma, *The Hindu Gita*, pp. 12–14.
62 Aurobindo, *Essays on the Gita*, p. 69.
63 *Ibid.*, p. 337.
64 Sharma, *The Hindu Gita*, p. xx.
65 *Ibid.*, p. xxiii.
66 Hill, *The Bhagavadgita*, p. 71.

CHAPTER ONE Arjuna's Despondency

1 J. A. B. van Buitenen, translator, *The Bhagavadgita in the Mahabharata* (Chicago and London: University of Chicago Press, 1981), p. 47.
2 Sri Aurobindo, translator, *The Message of the Gita* (Pondicherry: Sri Aurobindo Ashram, 1993 fifth edn, first published 1938), p. 1.
3 Sarvepalli Radhakrishnan, translator, *The Bhagavadgita, with an Introductory Essay, Sanskrit Text, English Translation and Notes* (New York: Harper, 1973, first published 1948), p. 79.
4 See George Thompson, translator, *The Bhagavad Gita: A new translation* (New York: North Point Press, 2008), p. x1.
5 Some commentators translate "Purujit from the Kuntibhoja clan" here, see for example J. A. B. van Buitenen, translator, *The Bhagavad Gita* (Rockport, Massachusetts, Shaftesbury, Dorset and Brisbane, Queensland: Element, 1997), p. 25, and Bibek Debroy, translator, *The Bhagavad Gita* (London, New York, Toronto, Paris: Penguin Books, 2005), p. xviii. There is also a possibility that the two names refer to one person. Hill, however, distinguished between them and added that Kuntibhoja adopted Kunti, Arjuna's mother. See W. Douglas P. Hill, translator, *The Bhagavad Gita: Translated from*

the Sanskrit with an introduction an argument and a commentary (Oxford: Oxford University Press, 1966, first published 1928), p. 100 note 9.

6 So, van Buitenen, *ibid.*, and Robert Charles Zaehner, translator, *The Bhagavad-Gita* (Oxford, London, New York: Oxford University Press, 1966), p. 45.

7 See Hill, *The Bhagavad Gita*, p. 101 note 2.

8 Geoffrey Parrinder, translator, *The Bhagavad Gita: A verse translation* (Oxford: Oneworld, 1996 reprint of 1974 edn), p. 4.

9 van Buitenen, *The Bhagavadgita in the Mahabharata*, p. 69.

10 See, for example, Will J. Johnson, translator, *The Bhagavad Gita* (Oxford, New York: Oxford University Press, 1994), p. 83 and Radhakrishnan, *The Bhagavadgita*, p. 83. There is some justification for this in that Bhaskara's commentary way back in the past also made such a change.

11 Hill, *The Bhagavad Gita*, pp. 101–2.

12 van Buitenen translated the name as "Honey-like", *The Bhagavad Gita*, p. 82 note 15. Alternative names for Krishna and Arjuna will receive comment and translation at the first citation, though not thereafter. The *Glossary and Index of Sanskrit Terms*, however, will supply an easy reference.

13 Later in the *Gita*, Krishna will reveal that this is his purpose on Earth; it will be the rationale for his "descent" or *avatara*. There is no mention of the word *avatara* in the *Gita*, though the concept is implicit, especially in the theophany of CHAPTER ELEVEN. Vishnu is the deity associated with such descents – mainly ten, the Fish, Tortoise, Boar, Man-Lion, Dwarf, Rama with the Axe, Rama of the *Ramayana*, Krishna, the Buddha, and one to come, the Kalkin. I doubt, however, that the full developed *avatara* doctrine is present in the *Gita*. Indeed, there is no reference to the other descents and the deity Vishnu hardly features in the *Gita* until CHAPTER ELEVEN, and then has to be very much assumed. It is with Krishna that the concept of *avataras* was born, but has been subsequently interpreted as fundamental to the nature of Krishna in the *Gita*.

14 See, for example, Franklin Edgerton, translator, *The Bhagavad Gita* (Delhi: Motilal Banarsidass, 1994, first published 1944), p. 7. Hill, keeping close to the Sanskrit had, "when now the arrows had begun to fly", *The Bhagavad Gita*, p. 104.

15 van Buitenen, *The Bhagavad Gita*, p. 82 note 25.

16 Hill, *The Bhagavad Gita*, p. 105 note 2.

17 See, for example, van Buitenen, *The Bhagavadgita in the Mahabharata*, p. 71.

18 So, Johnson, *The Bhagavad Gita*, p. 5 and van Buitenen, *The Bhagavad Gita*, p. 27.

19 Hill, *The Bhagavad Gita*, p. 108 note 1.

CHAPTER TWO **The *Yoga* of Sankhya**

1 Jeaneane Fowler, *Perspectives of Reality: An introduction to the philosophy of Hinduism* (Brighton, Sussex and Portland, Oregon: Sussex Academic Press, 2002), p. 160.

2 Krishna is described here as *Shri Bhagavan*, sometimes translated as "The Blessed Lord". The description is indicative of the devotionalism surrounding a personal deity, perhaps typical of the monotheistic *Bhagavata* religious sect: see Kashi Nath Upadhyaya, *Early Buddhism and the Bhagavadgita* (Delhi, Varanasi, Patna: Motilal Banarsidass, 1983 reprint of 1971 edn), pp. 136–7.

3 Alan Jacobs, translator, *The Bhagavad Gita: A transcreation of The Song Celestial* (Winchester, UK and New York: O Books, 2003), pp. 12–13.

4 Mahendra Kulasrestha, ed., Mahatma Gandhi, *The Bhagavadgita: A book of ethics for all*

religions (New Delhi: Lotus Press, new first edn 2008), p. 30.

5 Gavin Flood, "The Meaning and Context of the Purusarthas". In Julius Lipner, ed. *The Fruits of Our Desiring: An enquiry into the ethics of the Bhagavadgita* (Calgary: Bayeux, 1997), p. 12.

6 *Ibid.*, p. 19.

7 W. Douglas P. Hill, *The Bhagavadgita: Translated from the Sanskrit with an introduction an argument and a commentary* (London: Humphrey Milford, 1928, and Oxford, Oxford University Press, 1966), p. 112.

8 There are four stages of life (*ashramas*) laying down what is right for each stage of life for the Aryans. The first stage is the student one, when boys are attached to a teacher and taught the scriptures. The second stage, that in which Arjuna now finds himself, is the householder, the stage of life in which the man puts his efforts into raising a stable family and contributes to society at large. The two proximate goals of wealth and pleasures mentioned by Arjuna in verse 5 are applicable to this stage of life. At the third stage, the man leaves his family and society, when his hair is greying, and partially retreats to contemplate more spiritual things until the final stage in old age when he becomes a wandering beggar, totally immersed in the divine.

9 Sri Aurobindo, translator, *The Message of the Gita* (Pondicherry: Sri Aurobindo Ashram, 1993 fifth edn, first published 1938), pp. 16–17.

10 Richard Gotshalk, translator, *Bhagavad Gita: Translation and commentary* (Delhi: Motilal Banarsidass Publishers Private Limited, 1993 reprint of 1985 edn), p. 143 note 6.

11 Will J. Johnson, translator, *The Bhagavad Gita* (Oxford and New York: Oxford University Press, 1994), p. 8.

12 Robert Charles Zaehner, translator, *The Bhagavad-Gita* (London, Oxford, New York: Oxford University Press, 1973, first published 1969), p. 124.

13 Gotshalk, *Bhagavad Gita*, p. 78.

14 J. A. B. van Buitenen, translator, *Ramanuja on the Bhagavadgita: A condensed rendering of his Gitabhasya with copious notes and an introduction* (Delhi: Motilal Banarsidass, 1968), p. 50.

15 Ramanuja in van Buitenen, *ibid.*, pp. 20–21.

16 The senses that make contact with objects in the Sankhyan scheme are *tanmatras* – sound, touch, colour, taste and smell – and will be dealt with in the context of Sankhya philosophy in CHAPTER THREE, especially verse 28.

17 The Sanskrit has something like "Being (*bhava*) is not of the unreal (*asat*): non-being (*abhava*) is not of the real (*sat*)".

18 Zaehner, *The Bhagavad-Gita*, p. 129.

19 Sri Sankaracharya, *The Bhagavad Gita*, translated by Alladi Mahadeva Sastry (Madras: Samata Books, 1985 reprint of 1979 edn first published 1897), pp. 34–7.

20 Hill, *The Bhagavadgita*, pp. 114–15, my parentheses.

21 There were strict laws laid down in the old Law Book, the *Laws of Manu*, for a righteous war. No warrior could use poisonous weapons or deceitful means in fighting and a warrior that surrendered, lost his weapons or was already engaged in fighting another was not to be attacked. In short, in a righteous war, it was not permissible to take unfair advantage of an opponent.

22 See, for example, Zaehner, *The Bhagavad-Gita*, p. 138.

23 Satya P. Agarwal, *The Social Role of the Gita: How and why* (Delhi: Motilal Banarsidass, 1998), p. 279.

24 See J. A. B. van Buitenen, translator, *The Bhagavad Gita* (Rockport, Massachusetts, Shaftesbury, Dorset, Brisbane, Queensland: Element, 1997), p. 86.

25 Arvind Sharma, "Buddhiyoga in the Bhagavadgita". In Krishna Sivaraman, ed., *Hindu Spirituality: Vedas through Vedanta* (London: SCM, 1989), p. 197.

26 See Fowler, *Perspectives of Reality*, p. 199.

27 Jean Varenne, *Yoga and the Hindu Tradition* (Chicago and London: University of Chicago Press, 1976, first published in French in 1973), p. 120.

28 Arvind Sharma, *The Hindu Gita: Ancient and classical interpretations of the Bhagavadgita* (London: Duckworth, 1986), p. xxii.

29 See Franklin Edgerton, translator, *The Bhagavad Gita* (Delhi: Motilal Banarsidass, 1994, first published in two volumes in 1944), *Second Part*, p. 39 note 8.

30 Sri Aurobindo, *Essays on the Gita* (Pondicherry: Sri Aurobindo Ashram, 2000 third impression of 1996 ninth edn, first published between 1916 and 1920), p. 181.

31 J. A. B. van Buitenen, translator, *The Bhagavadgita in the Mahabharata* (Chicago and London: The University of Chicago Press, 1981), p. 163.

32 Zaehner, *The Bhagavad-Gita*, p. 146.

33 *Ibid.*, p. 51.

34 *Ibid.*, p. 149.

35 Gandhi, *The Bhagavadgita*, pp. 11–12.

36 *Ibid.*, p. 54.

37 Sarvepalli Radhakrishnan, translator, *The Bhagavadgita, with an Introductory Essay, Sanskrit Text, English Translation and Notes* (New York: Harper 1973, first published 1948, London: George Allen & Unwin), p. 124.

38 See Zaehner, *The Bhagavad-Gita*, p. 152.

39 Edgerton, *The Bhagavad Gita*, p. 181 note 10.

40 van Buitenen, *The Bhagavad Gita*, p. 90.

41 For a full discussion of *samskaras*, *vasanas* and the *yogic* path to overcome them, see Fowler, *Perspectives of Reality*, pp. 222–7.

42 Zaehner believed that the verse is professing this kind of focus of attention on a divine figure as an aid to liberation and that there is no hint of a permanent union with the divine. There seems to be no reason for such a claim other than a comparison with classical Yoga. The *Gita* departs from both Sankhya and Yoga in accepting a supreme Brahman and probably reflects a time when formative Sankhya and Yoga were traditionally theistic.

43 Radhakrishnan, *The Bhagavadgita*, p. 126.

44 Aurobindo, *The Message of the Gita*, p. 46 note 2.

45 Zaehner insisted on "development", for the word in both Sanskrit and Pali normally means "nourish" or "develop". Such meanings, however, do not appear to suit the context. Zaehner, *The Bhagavad Gita*, p. 155.

46 Bibek Debroy, translator, *The Bhagavad Gita* (London, New York, New Delhi: Penguin, 2005), p. 274 note 63.

47 Sankaracharya, *The Bhagavad Gita*, p. 77.

48 Zaehner, *The Bhagavad-Gita*, p. 158.

49 *Ibid.*, p. 159.

50 Johnson, *The Bhagavad Gita*, p. 84.

51 van Buitenen, *The Bhagavad Gita*, p. 90 note 34.

CHAPTER THREE The *Yoga* of Action

1   Rohit Mehta, *From Mind to Super-Mind: A commentary on the Bhagavad Gita* (Delhi: Motilal Banarsidass Publishers Private Limited, 1995 reprint of second, revised edn 1972), p. 34.

2   See for example Robert Charles Zaehner, *The Bhagavad-Gita* (London, Oxford, New York: Oxford University Press, 1973, first published 1969), p. 161.

3   J. A. B. van Buitenen, translator, *Ramanuja on the Bhagavadgita: A condensed rendering of his Gitabhasya with copious notes and an introduction* (Delhi: Motilal Banarsidass, 1968), p. 67.

4   Sri Aurobindo, *The Message of the Gita*, edited by Anilbaran Roy (Pondicherry: Sri Aurobindo Ashram, 1993 reprint of 1938 edn), p. 51.

5   For example Zaehner, *The Bhagavad-Gita*, p. 163.

6   Sri Sankaracharya, *The Bhagavad Gita*, translated by Alladi Mahadeva Sastry (Madras: Samata Books,1985 reprint of 1979 edn first published 1897), pp. 93–4.

7   *Ibid.*, p. 96.

8   Mahendra Kulasrestha, ed., Mahatma Gandhi, *The Bhagavadgita: A book of ethics for all religions* (New Delhi: Lotus Press, 2008), p. 76.

9   van Buitenen, *Ramanuja on the Bhagavadgita*, p. 67.

10 Aurobindo, *The Message of the Gita*, p. 53.

11 M. R. Sampatkumaran, translator, *Ramanuja's Commentary on the Gita* (Bombay: Ananthacharya Indological Research Unit, 1985), p. 74.

12 W. Douglas P. Hill, translator, *The Bhagavad Gita: Translated from the Sanskrit with an introduction an argument and a commentary* Oxford: Oxford University Press, 1966, first published 1928), pp. 128–9 note 3.

13 Lars Martin Fosse, *The Bhagavad Gita* (Woodstock, New York: YogaVidya.com, 2007), p. 30.

14 Vimala Thakar, *Insights into the Bhagavad Gita* (Delhi: Motilal Banarsidass Publishers Private Limited, 2005), p. 63.

15 Gandhi, *The Bhagavadgita*, pp. 78–9.

16 Eknath Easwaran, translator *The Bhagavad Gita* (Tomales, California: Nilgiri Press, 1985), p. 217.

17 Sampatkumaran, *Ramanuja's Commentary on the Gita*, p. 75.

18 Maharishi Mahesh Yogi, *Bhagavad Gita: A new translation and commentary chapters 1–6* (London, Frankfurt, Oslo, Geneva, Toronto, Los Angeles, Rishikesh: International SRM Publications, 1967), p. 144.

19 van Buitenen, *Ramanuja on the Bhagavadgita*, p. 70.

20 For an excellent discussion of the wider meanings of *yajna*, see John M. Koller, *The Indian Way: An introduction to the philosophies and religions of India* (Upper Saddle River, New Jersey: Pearson, Prentice Hall, 2006 revised edn, first published 1982), pp. 40–44.

21 Sampatkumaran, *Ramanuja's Commentary on the Gita*, p. 78.

22 Gandhi, *The Bhagavadgita*, pp. 88–9.

23 Translator S. Radhakrishnan, *The Principal Upanisads* (New Delhi: Indus, 1978 reprint of 1953 edn), p. 713.

24 J. A. B. van Buitenen, translator, *The Bhagavad Gita* (Rockport, Massachusetts, Shaftesbury, Dorset and Brisbane, Queensland: Element, 1997), p. 91 note 9.

25 Swami Chidbhavananda, *The Bhagavad Gita* (Tamil Nadu: Sri Ramakrishna Tapovam, 1982), p. 237.

26 van Buitenen, *Ramanuja on the Bhagavad Gita*, p. 70.

27 A few commentators point out that there are a number of celebrated kings called Janaka. Bibek Debroy, for example, thinks the Janaka cited in this verse is the son of Mithi. See Bibek Debroy, *The Bhagavad Gita* (London, New York, Ontario, New Delhi: Penguin, 2005), p. xxxvi and p. 275 note 23. The case of Janaka, King of Videha, however, suits Arjuna's predicament rather well.

28 van Buitenen, *Ramanuja on the Bhagavad Gita*, p. 71.

29 Sarvepalli Radhakrishnan, translator, *The Bhagavadgita, with an Introductory Essay, Sanskrit Text, English Translation and Notes* (New York: Harper, 1973, first published 1948 London: George Allen & Unwin Ltd.), p. 139.

30 Thakar, *Insights into the Bhagavad Gita*, p. 78.

31 Robert Minor, "Introduction". In Robert Minor, ed., *Modern Indian Interpreters of the Bhagavad Gita* (Delhi: Sri Satguru Publications, 1986), p. 4.

32 Radhakrishnan, *The Bhagavad Gita*, p. 142.

33 van Buitenen, *Ramanuja on the Bhagavadgita*, p. 72.

34 Sampatkumaran, *Ramanuja's Commentary on the Gita*, p. 86.

35 van Buitenen, *Ramanuja on the Bhagavadgita*, p. 73.

36 Aurobindo, *The Message of the Gita*, p. 63.

37 Zaehner, *The Bhagavad-Gita*, p. 173.

38 We are left to ponder here how far Krishna supports the fourth *ashrama*, the fourth stage of life of the wandering ascetic who has given up all action, even prescribed ritual action, let alone social altruism.

39 Mehta, *From Mind to Super-Mind*, p. 41.

40 van Buitenen, *Ramanuja on the Bhagavadgita*, p. 73.

41 Zaehner, *The Bhagavad-Gita*, p. 174.

42 Chidbhavananda, *The Bhavagad Gita*, p. 256.

43 van Buitenen, *Ramanuja on the Bhagavadgita*, p. 74.

44 Sankaracharya, *The Bhagavad Gita*, p. 112.

45 van Buitenen, *Ramanuja on the Bhagavadgita*, p. 75.

46 Sampatkumaran, *Ramanuja's Commentary on the Gita*, p. 97.

47 Chidbhavananda, *The Bhagavad Gita*, p. 265.

48 Aurobindo, *The Message of the Gita*, p. 67.

49 Sankaracharya, *The Bhagavad Gita*, p. 116.

50 Maharishi Mahesh Yogi, *Bhagavad Gita*, p. 177.

51 See van Buitenen, *Ramanuja on the Bhagavadgita*, p. xxix

52 *Katha Upanishad* 10:3, translater Patrick Olivelle, *Upanisads* (Oxford, New York: Oxford University Press, 1996), p. 239.

CHAPTER FOUR The *Yoga* of Knowledge

1 Sri Aurobindo, translator, *The Message of the Gita* (Pondicherry: Sri Aurobindo Ashram, 1993 reprint of 1938 edn), p. 70 note 3.

2 The Sanskrit root *man*, "to think", informs both the name Manu and the word for mind, *manas*.

3 According to van Buitenen, he was Manu's great-grandson. J. A. B. van Buitenen, translator, *The Bhagavad Gita* (Rockport, Massachusetts, Shaftesbury, Dorset, Brisbane, Queensland: Element, 1997), p. 91 note 3. The number of Manus is problematic. Later, in 10:6, only four are mentioned, which may be representative of an earlier tradition.

4 Robert Charles Zaehner, translator, *The Bhagavad-Gita* (London, Oxford, New York: Oxford University Press, 1969), p. 181.

5 Bibek Debroy, translator, *The Bhagavad Gita* (London, New Delhi: Penguin, 2005), p. 278 note 8.

6 Maharishi Mahesh Yogi, translator, *The Bhagavad Gita: A new translation and commentary chapters 1–6* (London, Toronto, Los Angeles, Rishikesh, Frankfurt, Oslo, Geneva, Toronto: International SRM Publications, 1967), p. 189.

7 Sri Sankaracharya, *The Bhagavad Gita*, translated by Alladi Mahadeva Sastry (Madras: Samata Books, 1985 reprint of 1977 edn, first published 1897), p. 121.

8 J. A. B. van Buitenen, translator, *Ramanuja on the Bhagavadgita: A condensed rendering of his Gitabhasya with copious notes and an introduction* (Delhi, Varanasi, Patna: Motilal Banarsidass 1968), p. 77.

9 Maharishi Mahesh Yogi, *The Bhagavad Gita*, p. 182.

10 Rohit Mehta, *From Mind to Super-Mind* (Delhi: Motilal Banarsidass Publishers Private Limited, 1995 reprint of 1972 edn), p. 46.

11 B. Srinivasa Murthy, translator, *The Bhagavad Gita* (Long Beach, California: Long Beach Publications, 1985), p. 52.

12 Mehta, *From Mind to Super-Mind*, p. 45.

13 Hill, indeed, suggested that the completion of such an identification did not occur until the early first century CE, see W. Douglas P. Hill, translator, *The Bhagavad Gita: Translated from the Sanskrit with an introduction, an argument and a commentary* (Oxford: Oxford University Press, 1966, first published 1928), p. 12.

14 van Buitenen, *Ramanuja on the Bhagavadgita*, p. 78.

15 M. R. Sampatkumaran, translator, *Ramanuja's Commentary on the Gita* (Bombay: Anantacharya Indological Research Unit, 1985), p. 106.

16 Sankaracharya, *The Bhagavad Gita*. p. 123.

17 Zaehner, *The Bhagavad-Gita*, p. 186.

18 Richard Gotshalk, translator, *Bhagavad Gita* (Delhi: Motilal Banarsidass Publishers Private Limited, 1993 reprint of 1985 edn), p. 186 note IV.11.

19 Mahendra Kulasrestha, ed., Mahatma Gandhi, translator, *The Bhagavadgita: A book of ethics for all religions* (New Delhi: Lotus Press, 2008 edn), p. 120.

20 Aurobindo, *The Message of the Gita*, p. 75.

21 Notably in this verse, class is dictated by *gunic* make-up and past actions and for the moment, birth does not seem to be an indicator as became the custom. But, presumably, *gunic* make-up and *karma* would, in any case, inform the nature of the birth which, therefore, is likely to be implicit in the verse.

22 Zaehner, *The Bhagavad-Gita*, p. 187.

23 Mehta, *from Mind to Super-Mind*, p. 47.

24 Aurobindo, *The Message of the Gita*, pp. 77–8.

25 Maharishi Mahesh Yogi, *The Bhagavad Gita*, p. 203.

26 Sankaraharya, *The Bhagavad Gita*, p. 131.

27 Mehta, *From Mind to Super-Mind*, p. 48.

28 Maharishi Mahesh Yogi, *The Bhagavad Gita*, p. 209.

29 Swami Chidbhavananda, translator, *The Bhagavad Gita* (Tamil Nadu: Sri Ramakrishna Tapovanam, 1982), p. 296.

30 Sankaracharya, *The Bhagavad Gita*, p. 137.

31 van Buitenen, *Ramanuja on the Bhagavadgita*, p. 81.

32 Sankaracharya, *The Bhagavad Gita*, p. 141.

33 Aurobindo, *The Message of the Gita*, p. 81 note 1.

34 Sankaracharya, *The Bhagavad Gita*, pp. 141–3.

35 van Buitenen, *Ramanuja on the Bhagavadgita*, p. 82.

36 Sankaracharya, *The Bhagavad Gita*, p. 144.

37 Chidbhavananda, *The Bhagavad Gita*, p. 303.

38 Debroy, *The Bhagavad Gita*, p. 281 notes 37 and 38.

39 See also George Thompson, *The Bhagavad Gita* (New York: North Point Press, 2008), p. 24, who has a similar interpretation; van Buitenen, *The Bhagavadgita in the Mahabharata*, pp. 89 and 164 notes 11 and 12; Gotshalk, *Bhagavad Gita*, p. 151 notes 21 and 22; Franklin Edgerton, translator, *The Bhagavad Gita* (Delhi: Motilal Banarsidass Publishers Private Limited, 1994, first published 1944), p. 182 note 4.

40 van Buitenen, *The Bhagavadgita in the Mahabharata*, p. 164 note 14.

41 Sankaracharya, *The Bhagavad Gita*, p. 147.

42 Debroy, *The Bhagavad Gita*, p. 282 note 50.

43 Gotshalk, *Bhagavad Gita*, p. 188.

44 Sri Krishna Prem, *The Yoga of the Bhagavat Gita* (Shaftesbury, Dorset: Element, 1988), p. 35.

45 Mehta, *From Mind to Super-Mind*, p. 52.

46 Veeraswami Krishnaraj, translator, *The Bhagavad-Gita* (San Jose, New York, Lincoln, Shanghai: Writers Club Press, 2002), p. 93.

47 Sankaracharya, *The Bhagavad Gita*, p. 149.

48 van Buitenen, *Ramanuja on the Bhagavadgita*, p. 84.

49 For a full discussion of different kinds of *karma*, see Jeaneane Fowler, *Perspectives of Reality: An introduction to the philosophy of Hinduism* (Portland, Oregon and Brighton, Sussex: Sussex Academic Press, 2002), pp. 221–2.

50 See the *Chandogya Upanishad* 5:24:1–3, and the *Shvetashvatara Upanishsd* 2:6–7.

51 Maharishi Mahesh Yogi, *The Bhagavad Gita*, p. 227.

52 Aurobindo, *The Message of the Gita*, p. 87.

53 Sarvepalli Radhakrishnan, translator, *The Bhagavadgita, with an Introductory Essay, Sanskrit Text, English Translation and Notes* (London: George Allen & Unwin, 1948), pp. 171–2.

54 Prem, *The Yoga of the Bhagavat Gita*, p. 37.

CHAPTER FIVE **The *Yoga* of Renunciation**

1 From the root *as* meaning "to cast down".

2 Robert Charles Zaehner, translator, *The Bhagavad-Gita* (London, Oxford, New York: Oxford University Press, 1973, first published 1969), p. 200.

3 Rohit Mehta, *From Mind to Super-Mind* (Delhi: Motilal Banarsidass Publishers Private Limited, 1995 reprint of 1972 second revised edn), p. 54.

4 J. A. B. van Buitenen, translator, *Ramanuja on the Bhagavadgita: A condensed rendering of his Gitabhasya with copious notes and an introduction* (Delhi: Varanasi, Patna: Motilal Banarsidass, 1968), p. 85.

6 Sri Sankaracharya, translator, *The Bhagavad Gita*, translated by Alladi Mahadeva Sastry (Madras: Samata Books, 1985 reprint of 1979 corrected and reprinted 1977 edn, first published 1897), chapter 5 *passim*.

7 *Ibid.*, p. 160.

8 *Ibid.*, p. 163.

9 Vimala Thakar, *Insights into the Bhagavad Gita* (Delhi: Motilal Banarsidass Publishers Private Limited, 2005), p. 154.

10 *Ibid.*, p. 166.

11 Barbara Stoler Miller, translator, *The Bhagavad-Gita* (New York, Toronto, London, Sydney, Auckland: Bantam Books, 1986), p. 58.

12 Franklin Edgerton, translator, *The Bhagavad Gita* (Delhi: Motilal Banarsidass Publishers Private Limited, 1994, first published 1944), p. 55.

13 *Ibid.*, p. 182 note 2.

14 Zaehner, *The Bhagavad-Gita*, p. 207.

15 Sarvepalli Radhakrishnan, translator, *The Bhagavadgita, with an Introductory Essay, Sanskrit Text, English Translation and Notes* (New York: Harper, 1973, first published London: George Allen & Unwin, 1948), p. 178.

16 Richard Gotshalk, translator, *Bhagavad Gita* (Delhi: Motilal Banarsidass Publishers Private Limited, 1993 reprint of 1985 edn), p. 22.

17 *Ibid.*, p. 153 note 9.

18 Sankaracharya, *The Bhagavad Gita*, p. 166.

19 Bibek Debroy, translator, *The Bhagavad Gita* (London, New York, Toronto, New Delhi: Penguin Books, 2005), p. 79, my italics.

20 *Ibid.*, p. 283 note 17.

21 Mahendra Kulasrestha, ed., Mahatma Gandhi, translator, *The Bhagavadgita: A book of ethics for all religions* (New Delhi: Lotus Press, 2008), p. 154.

22 See, for example, Debroy, *The Bhagavad Gita*, p. 283 note 19; Geoffrey Parrinder, translator, *The Bhagavad Gita: A verse translation* (Oxford: Oneworld, 1996 reprint of 1966 edn), p. 38; Lars Martin Fosse, translator, *The Bhagavad Gita* (Woodstock, New York: YogaVidya.com), p. 53; Zaehner, *The Bhagavad-Gita*, p. 208.

23 Hill, however, found the complete opposite of a definite determinism in this and the following verse: W. Douglas P. Hill, translator, *The Bhagavad Gita: Translated from the Sanskrit with an introduction an argument and a commentary* (Oxford: Oxford University Press, 1966, first published 1928), p. 37.

24 Zaehner, *ibid.*, p. 209, see also Parrinder, *ibid.*, p. 38 and Edgerton, *The Bhagavad Gita*, p. 55, who thought the same.

25 Zaehner, *ibid.*

26 Sankaracharya, *The Bhagavad Gita*, p. 169.

27 For example Debroy, *The Bhagavad Gita*, p. 283 note 19.

28 Thakar, *Insights into the Bhagavad Gita*, p. 166.

29 van Buitenen, *Ramanuja on the Bhagavadgita*, p. 88.

30 M. R. Sampatkumaran, translator, *Ramanuja's Commentary on the Gita* (Bombay: Ananthacharya Indological Research Unit, 1985), p. 138.

31 Sri Aurobindo, translator, *The Message of the Gita* (Pondicherry: Sri Aurobindo Ashram, 1993 reprint of 1938 edn), p. 94.

32 Sampatkumaran, *Ramanuja's Commentary on the Bhagavad Gita*, p. 139.

33 Radhakrishnan, *The Bhagavadgita*, p. 180.

34 See, for example, Parrinder, *The Bhagavad Gita*, p. 38.

35 For example Zaehner, *The Bhagavad-Gita*, p. 209 and Fosse, *The Bhagavad Gita*, p. 54.

36 Gandhi, *The Bhagavadgita*, p. 155.

37 Veeraswami Krishnaraj, translator, *The Bhagavad-Gita* (San Jose, New York, Lincoln,

Shanghai: Writers Club Press, 2002), p. 107.

38 Mehta, *From Mind to Super-Mind*, p. 58.

39 Maharishi Mahesh Yogi, translator, *Bhagavad-Gita: A new translation and commentary, chapters 1–6* (London, Frankfurt, Oslo, Geneva, Toronto, Los Angeles, Rishikesh: International SRM Publications, 1967), p. 271.

40 *Ibid.*, p. 272.

41 Zaehner, *The Bhagavad-Gita*, pp. 212–13.

42 *Ibid.*, p. 214.

43 *Sanyutta Nikaya* 4:94–5.

44 Zaehner, *The Bhagavad-Gita*, p. 213.

45 Aurobindo, *The Message of the Gita*, p. 97.

46 *Ibid.*, p. 98.

47 *Ibid.* (my upper case for Self).

48 Aurobindo, *The Message of the Gita*, p. 99.

CHAPTER SIX The *Yoga* of Meditation

1 See, for example, Will J. Johnson, translator, *The Bhagavad Gita* (Oxford, New York: Oxford University Press, 1994), p. 27.

2 Alan Jacobs, translator, *The Bhagavad Gita* (Winchester, UK and New York: O Books, 2003), p. 87.

3 Rohit Mehta, *From Mind to Super-Mind* (Delhi: Motilal Banarsidass Publishers Private Limited, 1995 reprint of 1972 second, revised edn), p. 62.

4 *Ibid.*, p. 63.

5 Aurobindo, translator, *The Message of the Gita* (Pondicherry: Sri Aurobindo Ashram, 1993 fifth edn, first printed 1938), p. 101.

6 W. Douglas P. Hill, translator, *The Bhagavad Gita: Translated from the Sanskrit with an introduction an argument and a commentary* (Oxford: Oxford University Press, 1966, first published 1928), p. 156.

7 Shankara interpreted the verse in this way, Sri Sankaracharya, translator, *The Bhagavad Gita* translated by Alladi Mahadeva Sastry (Madras: Samata Books, 1985 reprint of 1979 corrected edn), p. 187, and amongst modern translators, Swami Chidbhavananda, translator, *The Bhagavad Gita* (Tamil Nadu: Sri Ramakrishna Tapovam, 1982), p. 362; Johnson, *The Bhagavad Gita*, p. 27; J. A. B. van Buitenen, translator, *The Bhagavad Gita* (Rockport, Massachusetts, Shaftesbury, Dorset, Brisbane, Queensland: Element, 1997), p. 43; Richard Gotshalk, translator, *Bhagavad Gita* (Delhi: Motilal Banarsidass Publishers Private Limited, 1993 reprint of 1985 edn), p. 24. For an example of the variety of possible translations here and the choices between self and Self, see also Gotshalk p. 189 note VI:6.

8 See, for example Robert Charles Zaehner, translator, *The Bhagavad-Gita* (London, Oxford, New York: Oxford University Press, 1973, first published 1969), p. 221, and Gandhi had: "By one's Self should one raise oneself, and not allow oneself to fall; for *Atman* (self) alone is the friend of self and Self alone is self's foe." Mahendra Kulasrestha, ed. Mahatma Gandhi, translator, *The Bhagavadgita: A book of ethics for all religions* (New Delhi: Lotus Press, new edn 2008), p. 164.

9 Maharishi Mahesh Yogi, translator, *Bhagavad-Gita: A new translation and commentary, chapters 1–6* (London, Frankfurt, Oslo, Geneva, Toronto, Los Angeles, Rishikesh: International SRM Publications, 1967), p. 294.

10 *Ibid.*

11 So, Zaehner, *The Bhagavad-Gita*, p. 221.

12 *Ibid.*

13 *Ibid.*, p. 222.

14 Sri Aurobindo, *The Message of the Gita*, p. 103, see also Sri Aurobindo, *Essays on the Gita* (Pondicherry: Sri Aurobindo Ashram, 2000 third impression of 1996 ninth edn, first published between 1916 and 1920), p. 241.

15 So, Hill, *The Bhagavad Gita*, p. 191 and Sarvepalli Radhakrishnan, translator, *The Bhagavadgita, with an Introductory Essay, Sanskrit Text, English Translation and Notes* (London: George Allen & Unwin, 1948), p. 156 note 3.

16 Vimala Thakar, *Insights into the Bhagavad Gita* (Delhi: Motilal Banarsidass Publishers Private Limited, 2005), p. 200.

17 Zaehner, *The Bhagavad-Gita*, p. 219.

18 See the comments on 14:27.

19 J. A. B. van Buitenen, translator, *The Bhagavadgita in the Mahabharata* (Chicago and London: University of Chicago Press, 1981), p. 95.

20 *Ibid.*, p. 165 note 6, my italics.

21 van Buitenen, *The Bhagavad Gita*, p. 93 note 2.

22 Bibek Debroy, translator, *The Bhagavad Gita* (London, New York, New Delhi, Toronto, Dublin, Victoria, Aukland, Johannesburg: Penguin, 2005), p. 95 note 4.

23 Mehta, *From Mind to Super-Mind*, p. 66.

24 Gandhi, *The Bhagavadgita*, p. 172.

25 Veeraswamy Krishnaraj, translator, *The Bhagavad-Gita* (San Jose, New York, Lincoln, Shanghai: Writers Club Press, 2002), p. 120, my upper case for Self.

26 For a detailed discussion of both terms see Jeaneane Fowler, *Perspectives of Reality: An introduction to the philosophy of Hinduism* (Brighton, Sussex and Portland, Oregon: Sussex Acdemic Press, 2002), pp. 207–10, 197, 209 and 235.

27 Gandhi, *The Bhagavadgita*, p. 172.

28 Zaehner, *The Bhagavad-Gita*, p. 228, my italics.

29 *Ibid.*, p. 229.

30 Hill, *The Bhagavad Gita*, p. 159.

31 Krishnaraj, *The Bhagavad Gita*, p. 122.

32 Chidbhavananda, *The Bhagavad Gita*, p. 389.

33 Sankaracharya, *The Bhagavad Gita*, p. 198.

34 Johnson, *The Bhagavad Gita*, p. 29.

35 So, van Buitenen, *The Bhagavadgita in the Mahabharata*, p. 97.

36 Sankaracharya, *The Bhagavad Gita*, p. 198.

37 *Isha Upanishad* 6–7, translator Patrick Olivelle, *Upanisads* (Oxford and New York: Oxford University Press, 1996), p. 249.

38 For a full discussion of terms like monism, pantheism and panentheism see Fowler, *Perspectives of Reality*, chapter 1, *passim*.

39 J. A. B. van Buitenen, translator, *Ramanuja on the Bhagavadgita: A condensed rendering of his Gitabhasya with copious notes and an introduction* (Delhi: Motilal Banarsidass, 1968), p. 95.

40 M. R. Sampatkumaran, translator, *Ramanuja's Commentary on the Gita* (Bombay: Ananthacharya Indological Research Unit, 1985), p. 162.

41 *Ibid.*

42   Zaehner, *The Bhagavada-Gita*, p. 219.
43   *Ibid.*
44   Debroy, *The Bhagavad Gita*, p. 33.
45   Thakar, *Insights into the Bhagavad Gita*, p. 203.
46   Sankaracharya, *The Bhagavad Gita*, p. 202.
47   *Ibid.*, p. 204.
48   *Ibid.*
49   *Ibid.*, p. 205.
50   Hill, *The Bhagavad Gita*, p. 163 note 2.
51   Sampatkumaran, translator, *Ramanuja's Commentary on the Gita*, p. 174.
52   Maharishi Mahesh Yogi, *Bhagavad-Gita*, p. 345.
53   Aurobindo, *The Message of the Gita*, p. 114.

CHAPTER SEVEN The *Yoga* of Knowledge and Realization

1   Rohit Mehta, *From Mind to Super-Mind* (Delhi:Motilal Banarsidass Publishers Private Limited, 1995 reprint of 1972 second, revised edn), p. 75.
2   Sri Aurobindo, translator, *The Message of the Gita* (Pondicherry: Sri Aurobindo Ashram, 1993 fifth edn, first printed 1938), p. 115.
3   Robert Charles Zaehner, translator, *The Bhagavad-Gita* (London, Oxford, New York: Oxford University Press, 1973, first published 1969), p. 244.
4   Richard Gotshalk, translator, *Bhagavad Gita: Translation and commentary* (Delhi: Motilal Banarsidass, 1993 reprint of 1985 edn), p. 29.
5   J. A. B. van Buitenen, translator, *Ramanuja on the Bhagavadgita: A condensed rendering of his Gitabhasya with copious notes and an introduction* (Delhi, Varanasi, Patna: Motilal Banarsidass, 1968), p. 100.
6   Aurobindo, *The Message of the Gita*, p. 116.
7   See Arvind Sharma, "Buddhiyoga in the *Bhagavadgita*". In Krishna Sivaraman, ed., *Hindu Spirituality: Vedas through Vedanta* (London and New York, 1989), p. 196.
8   Vimala Thakar, *Insights into the Bhagavad Gita* (Delhi: Motilal Banarsidass Publishers Private Limited, 2005), p. 210.
9   Aurobindo, *The Message of the Gita*, p. 118.
10   Mehta, *From Mind to Super-Mind*, p. 77.
11   Sri Aurobindo, *Essays on the Gita* (Pondicherry: Sri Aurobindo Ashram, 2000 third impression of 1996 ninth edn, first published between 1916 and 1920), p. 421.
12   Aurobindo, *The Message of the Gita*, p. 119.
13   Trevor Leggett, *Realization of the Supreme Self* (London and New York: Kegan Paul International, 1995), p. 62.
14   Sri Sankaracharya, *The Bhagavad Gita*, translated by Alladi Mahadeva Sastry (Madras: Samata Books, 1985 reprint of 1979 corrected edn), p. 211.
15   Eknath Easwaran, *The Bhagavad Gita* (Tomales, California: Nilgiri Press, 1985), page 113.
16   Alan Jacobs, *The Bhagavad Gita: A transcreation of The Song Celestial* (Winchester, UK and New York: O Books, 2003), p. 107.
17   Aurobindo, *The Message of the Gita*, p. 121.
18   Thakar, *Insights into the Bhagavad Gita*, p. 228.
19   Mehta, *From Mind to Super-Mind*, pp. 78–9.
20   van Buitenen, *Ramanuja on the Bhagavadgita*, p. 102.

21 M. R. Sampatkumaran, translator, *Ramanuja's Commentary on the Gita* (Bombay: Ananthacharya Indological Research Unit, 1985), p. 187.

22 Gotshalk, *Bhagavad Gita*, p. 30.

23 Thakar, *Insights into the Bhagavad Gita*, p. 223.

24 Sri Krishna Prem, *The Yoga of the Bhagavat Gita* (Shaftesbury, Dorset: Element Books, 1988), p. 63 and note 1.

25 Gotshalk, *Bhagavad Gita*, p. 30.

26 Zaehner, *The Bhagavad-Gita*, p. 250.

27 J. A. B. van Buitenen, translator, *The Bhagavadgita in the Mahabharata* (Chicago and London: University of Chicago Press, 1981), p. 99.

28 Thakar, *Insights into the Bhagavad Gita*, p. 225.

29 van Buitenen *Ramanuja on the Bhagavadgita*, p. 104.

30 Sankaracharya, *The Bhagavad Gita*, p. 215.

31 Zaehner, *The Bhagavad-Gita*, p. 251.

32 Sampatkumaran, *Ramanuja's Commentary on the Gita*, p. 191.

33 See, for example, van Buitenen, *The Bhagavadgita in the Mahabharata*, p. 99.

34 van Buitenen, *Ramanuja on the Bhagavadgita*, p. 104.

35 Sampatkumaran, *Ramanuja's Commentary on the Gita*, p. 191.

36 van Buitenen, *Ramanuja on the Bhagavadgita*, p. 105.

37 Zaehner, *The Bhagavad-Gita*, p. 253.

38 For a sample of the wide possibilities in translation, see Gotshalk, *Bhagavad Gita*, pp. 192–3 note VII:3.

39 Sarvepalli Radhakrishnan, translator, *The Bhagavadgita, with an Introductory Essay, Sanskrit Text, English Translation and Notes* (New York: Harper, 1973, first published 1948), p. 223, my parentheses.

40 See, for example, Gotshalk, *Bhagavad Gita*, p. 31.

41 Aurobindo, *The Message of the Gita*, p. 128.

42 The verse is reminiscent of the Christian God in the biblical *Revelations* 1:8: "'I am the Alpha and the Omega' says the Lord God, who is and who was and who is to come, the Almighty."

43 Zaehner, *The Bhagavad-Gita*, p. 254.

CHAPTER EIGHT **The *Yoga* of the Imperishable Brahman**

1 Sri Krishna Prem, *The Yoga of the Bhagavat Gita* (Shaftesbury, Dorset: Element Books, 1988), p. 68.

2 Sarvepalli Radhakrishnan, translator, *The Bhagavadgita, with an Introductory Essay, Sanskrit Text, English Translation and Notes* (New York, Harper 1973, first published 1948 London: George Allen & Unwin), p. 227.

3 J. A. B. van Buitenen, translator, *Ramanuja on the Bhagavadgita: A condensed rendering of his Gitabhasya with copious notes and an introduction* (Delhi, Varanasi, Patna: Motilal Banarsidass, 1968), p. 107.

4 Sri Sankaracharya, translator, *The Bhagavad Gita*, translated by Alladi Mahadeva Sastry (Madras: Samata Books, 1985 reprint of 1979 corrected edn), p. 223.

5 W. Douglas P. Hill, translator, *The Bhagavad Gita: Translated from the Sanskrit with an introduction an argument and a commentary* (Oxford: Oxford University Press, 1966, first published 1928), p. 174 note 1.

6 Franklin Edgerton, translator, *The Bhagavad Gita* (Delhi: Motilal Banarsidass, 1994 first Indian edn, first published 1944), p. 184 note 2.

7 *Ibid.*, p. 184 note 4.

8 Sankaracharya, *The Bhagavad Gita*, p. 224.

9 Bibek Debroy, translator, *The Bhagavad Gita* (New York, London: Penguin, 2005), pp. 289–90.

10 Richard Gotshalk, translator, *Bhagavad Gita* (Delhi: Motilal Banarsidass Publishers Private Limited, 1993 reprint of 1985 edn), p. 31, with my italics.

11 *Ibid.*, p. 32. Gotshalk notes the similarity with the *Katha Upanishad* 2:3:13 here: "he is to be apprehended precisely in 'he is' and by his true nature (*tattva-bhavena*) both; apprehended precisely in 'he is', his true nature becomes clear", p. 155, note 1. It is worth noting here that Gotshalk considers all the terms discussed here as adjectives or adverbs agreeing with Brahman rather than nouns.

12 *Ibid.*, p. 32.

13 See on this point the comments of Robert Charles Zaehner, translator, *The Bhagavad-Gita* (London, Oxford, New York: Oxford University Press, 1973, first published 1969), p. 244.

14 Radhakrishnan, *The Bhagavadgita*, p. 229.

15 Sri Aurobindo, translator, *The Bhagavad-Gita* (Pondicherry: Sri Aurobindo Ashram, 1993 fifth edn, first printed 1938), p. 134 note 1.

16 Sankaracharya, *The Bhagavad Gita*, p. 228.

17 The *Brihadaranyaka Upanishad* 4:4:1–2 also gives a detailed description of this process.

18 Swami Chidbhavananda, translator, *The Bhagavad Gita* (Tamil Nadu: Sri Ramakrishna Tapovam, 1982), p. 468.

19 Rohit Mehta, *From Mind to Super-Mind* (Delhi: Motilal Banarsidass Publishers Private Limited, 1995 reprint of 1972 second, revised edn), p. 88.

20 For a finely detailed account and tabulated details of the numbers here, see Veeraswamy Krishnaraj, translator, *The Bhagavad-Gita* (San Jose, New York, Lincoln, Shanghai: Writers Club Press, 2002), pp. 156–9.

21 Vimala Thakar, *Insights into the Bhagavad Gita* (Delhi: Motilal Banarsidass Publishers Private Limited, 2005), p. 250.

22 Zaehner, *The Bhagavad-Gita*, pp. 267–9 and 269–70.

23 J. A. B. van Buitenen, translator, *The Bhagavad Gita* (Rockport, Massachusetts, Shaftesbury, Dorset and Brisbane, Queensland: Element, 1997), p. 50.

24 Gotshalk, *Bhagavad Gita*, p. 33.

25 Zaehner, *The Bhagavad-Gita*, p. 270.

26 *Ibid.*, p. 268.

27 van Buitenen, *Ramanuja on the Bhagavadgita*, p. 111.

28 Sankaracharya, *The Bhagavad Gita*, p. 234.

29 See also the *Chandogya Upanishad* 4:15:5, the *Prashna Upanishad* 1:9–10, and the *Mundaka Upanishad* 1:2:11.

30 Sankaracharya, *The Bhagavad Gita*, p. 236.

31 *Ibid.*

CHAPTER NINE **The *Yoga* of Royal Knowledge and Royal Mystery**

1 Robert Charles Zaehner, translator, *The Bhagavad-Gita* (London, Oxford, New York: Oxford University Press, 1973, first published 1969), p. 274.

2   Rohit Mehta, *From Mind to Super-Mind* (Delhi: Motilal Banarsidass Publishers Private Limited, 1995 reprint of 1972 second, revised edn), p. 91.
3   *Ibid.*
4   *Ibid.*
5   Sri Aurobindo, translator, *The Message of the Gita* (Pondicherry: Sri Aurobindo Ashram, 1993 fifth edn, first printed 1938), p. 143.
6   J. A. B. van Buitenen, translator, *Ramanuja on the Bhagavadgita: A condensed rendering of his Gitabhasya with copious notes and an introduction* (Delhi, Varanasi, Patna: Motilal Banarsidass, 1968), p. 113.
7   Sri Sankaracharya, translator, *The Bhagavad Gita*, translated by Alladi Mahadeva Sastry (Madras: Samata Books, 1985 reprint of 1979 corrected edn), p. 238.
8   M. R. Sampatkumaran, translator, *Ramanuja's Commentary on the Gita* (Bombay: Ananthacharya Indological Research Unit, 1985), p. 224.
9   *Ibid.*
10 *Ibid.*
11 *Ibid.*, p. 225.
12 Sankaracharya, *The Bhagavad Gita*, p. 241.
13 *Ibid.*
14 Zaehner, *The Bhagavad-Gita*, p. 274.
15 Aurobindo, *The Message of the Gita*, p. 144.
16 van Buitenen, *Ramanuja on the Bhagavadgita*, p. 114.
17 Sampatkumaran, *Ramanuja's Commentary on the Gita*, p. 226.
18 J. A. B. van Buitenen, translator, *The Bhagavadgita in the Mahabharata* (Chicago and London: University of Chicago Press, 1981), p. 166 notes 1 and 2.
19 Lars Martin Fosse, translator, *The Bhagavad Gita* (Woodstock, New York: YogaVidya.com, 2007), p. 85.
20 Vimala Thakar, *Insights into the Bhagavad Gita* (Delhi: Motilal Banarsidass Publishers Private Limited, 2005), p. 287.
21 Aurobindo, *The Message of the Gita*, p. 145 note 1.
22 W. Douglas P. Hill, translator, *The Bhagavad Gita: Translated from the Sanskrit with an introduction an argument and a commentary* (Oxford: Oxford University Press, 1966, first published 1928), p. 182.
23 Zaehner, *The Bhagavad-Gita*, p. 285.
24 Sankaracharya, *The Bhagavad Gita*, p. 243.
25 Zaehner, *The Bhagavad-Gita*, pp. 276–7.
26 Sankaracharya, *The Bhagavad Gita*, p. 243.
27 Swami Chidbhavananda, translator, *The Bhagavad Gita* (Tamil Nadu: Sri Ramakrishna Tapovam, 1982), p. 493.
28 See *ibid.*
29 Mahendra Kulasrestha, ed., Mahatma Gandhi, translator, *The Bhagavadgita: A book of ethics for all religions* (New Delhi: Lotus Press, 2008), p. 212.
30 The *Asuras* were originally deities like Indra, Varuna and Agni but, over time, the term came to be associated with anti-gods.
31 Will J. Johnson, translator, *The Bhagavad Gita* (Oxford, New York: Oxford University Press, 1994), p. 42.
32 George Thompson, translator, *The Bhagavad Gita* (New York: North Point Press, 2008), p. 45.

33 van Buitenen, *The Bhagavadgita in the Mahabharata*, p. 105.

34 van Buitenen, *Ramanuja on the Bhagavadgita*, p. 116.

35 Sampatkumaran, *Ramanuja's Commentary on the Gita*, p. 233.

36 J. A. B. van Buitenen, translator, *The Bhagavad Gita* (Rockport, Massachusetts, Shaftesbury, Dorset and Brisbane, Queensland: Element, 1997), p. 95 note 9.

37 Zaehner, *The Bhagavad-Gita*, p. 281.

38 *Ibid.*

39 Sankaracharya, *The Bhagavad Gita*, p. 250.

40 van Buitenen, *Ramanuja on the Bhagavadgita*, p. 117.

41 B. Srinivasa Murthy, translator, *The Bhagavad Gita* (Long Beach, California: Long Beach Publications, 1985), p. 84.

42 Zaehner, *The Bhagavad-Gita*, p. 282.

43 van Buitenen, *The Bhagavadgita in the Mahabharata*, p. 166 note 6.

44 Murthy, *The Bhagavad Gita*, p. 84.

45 Sankaracharya, *The Bhagavad Gita*, p. 253.

46 Johnson, *The Bhagavad Gita*, p. 42.

47 van Buitenen, *Ramanuja on the Bhagavadgita*, p. 118.

48 Zaehner, *The Bhagavad-Gita*, p. 279.

49 Chidbhavananda, *The Bhagavad Gita*, p. 515.

50 Eknath Easwaran, translator, *The Bhagavad Gita* (The Blue Mountain Center of Meditation: Nilgiri Press, 1985), p. 131.

51 The inclusion of women here reflects the post-*Vedic* period when the status of women had declined from their more elevated position in *Vedic* Aryan culture. Even a few of the *Rig Vedic* hymns were written by women, and they were never precluded from studying the *Vedas* in Aryan times. Only later was their status vastly diminished. Perhaps this was because Aryan men married non-Aryan women.

52 Aurobindo, *The Message of the Gita*, p. 155.

53 Sampatkumaran, *Ramanuja's Commentary on the Gita*, p. 248.

54 Aurobindo, *The Message of the Gita*, p. 156.

55 Sri Krishna Prem, *The Yoga of the Bhagavat Gita* (Shaftesbury, Dorset: Element Books, 1988), p. 79.

CHAPTER TEN The *Yoga* of Manifestation

1 Vimala Thakar, *Insights into the Bhagavad Gita* (Delhi: Motilal Banarsidass Publishers Private Limited, 2005), p. 313.

2 J. A. B. van Buitenen, translator, *The Bhagavad Gita* (Rockport, Massachusetts, Shaftesbury, Dorset and Brisbane, Queensland: Element, 1997), p. 95 note 2.

3 Robert Charles Zaehner, translator, *The Bhagavad-Gita* (London, Oxford, New York: Oxford University Press, 1973, first published 1969), p. 291.

4 For example Lars Martin Fosse, translator, *The Bhagavad Gita* (Woodstock, New York: YogaVidya.com, 2007), p. 93 and J. A. B. van Buitenen, translator, *The Bhagavadgita in the Mahabharata* (Chicago and London: University of Chicago Press, 1981), p. 109.

5 Sri Aurobindo, translator, *The Message of the Gita* (Pondicherry: Sri Aurobindo Ashram, 1993 fifth edn, first printed 1938), p. 157.

6 Sri Sankaracharya, translator, *The Bhagavad Gita*, translated by Alladi Mahadeva Sastry (Madras: Samata Books, 1985 reprint of 1979 corrected edn), p. 260.

7 *Ibid.*, p. 261.

8   Mahendra Kulasrestha, ed., Mahatma Gandhi, translator, *The Bhagavadgita: A book of ethics for all religions* (New Delhi: Lotus Press, 2008), p. 223. See also Richard Gotshalk, translator, *Bhagavad Gita* (Delhi: Motilal Banarsidass Publishers Private Limited, 1993 reprint of 1985 edn), p. 38.

9   Aurobindo, *The Message of the Gita*, p. 159.

10 Franklin Edgerton, translator, *The Bhagavad Gita* (Delhi: Motilal Banarsidass Publishers Private Limited, 1994, first published 1944), p. 184 note 1.

11 Zaehner, *The Bhagavad-Gita*, p. 293.

12 van Buitenen, *The Bhagavadgita in the Mahabharata*, p. 167 note 2.

13 Aurobindo, *The Message of the Gita*, p. 160.

14 Zaehner, *The Bhagavad-Gita*, p. 294.

15 Bibek Debroy, translator, *The Bhagavad Gita* (London, New York, New Delhi: Penguin, 2005), p. 143.

16 B. Srinivasa Murthy, translator, *The Bhagavad Gita* (Long Beach, California: Long Beach Publications, 1985), p. 88.

17 W. Douglas P. Hill, translator, *The Bhagavad Gita: Translated from the Sanskrit with an introduction an argument and a commentary* (Oxford: Oxford University Press, 1966, first published 1928), p. 192.

18 Zaehner, *The Bhagavad-Gita*, p. 294.

19 Sankaracharya, *The Bhagavad Gita*, p. 264.

20 Swami Chidbhavananda, translator, *The Bhagavad Gita* (Tamil Nadu: Sri Ramakrishna Tapovam, 1982), p. 536.

21 M. R. Sampatkumaran, translator, *Ramanuja's Commentary on the Gita* (Bombay: Ananthacharya Indological Research Unit, 1985), p. 258.

22 Zaehner, *The Bhagavad-Gita*, p. 294.

23 Sankaracharya, *The Bhagavad Gita*, p. 265.

24 Sampatkumaran, *Ramanuja's Commentary on the Gita*, p. 258.

25 Or perhaps lyre, see Hill, *The Bhagavad Gita*, p. 193 note 1.

26 Debroy, *The Bhagavad Gita*, p. 296 note 15. van Buitenen also accepts the two names as referring to one individual, see *The Bhagavadgita in the Mahabharata*, p. 109. Neither translator, however, cites any source evidence.

27 Hill, *The Bhagavad Gita*, p. 193 notes 2 and 3.

28 Murthy, *The Bhagavad Gita*, p. 89.

29 Sankaracharya, *The Bhagavad Gita*, pp. 267–8.

30 Sarvepalli Radhakrishnan, translator, *The Bhagavadgita, with an Introductory Essay, Sanskrit Text, English Translation and Notes* (New York: Harper, 1973 first published 1948 by George Allen & Unwin), p. 262.

31 J. A. B. van Buitenen, *Ramanuja on the Bhagavadgita: A condensed rendering of his Gitabhasya with copious notes and an introduction* (Delhi, Varanasi, Patna: Motilal Banarsidass, 1968), pp. 124–5.

32 Debroy, *The Bhagavad Gita*, p. 297 note 30.

33 Rohit Mehta, *From Mind to Super-Mind* (Delhi: Motilal Banarsidass Publishers Private Limited, 1995 reprint of 1972, second, revised edn), p. 101.

34 See George Thompson, translator, *The Bhagavad Gita* (New York: North Point Press, 2008), p. 97 note 4.

35 Hill, *The Bhagavad Gita*, p. 198 note 8.

36 Sankaracharya, *The Bhagavad Gita*, p. 272.

37 See Edgerton, *The Bhagavad Gita*, p. 185 note 12.

38 Cf. 2:45; 3:3; 4:22; 7:27, 28.

39 Murthy, *The Bhagavad Gita*, p. 142 note 25.

40 For example, van Buitenen, *The Bhagavad Gita*, p. 98 note 42.

41 See Gotshalk, *Bhagavad Gita*, p. 197 note X 36, and Edgerton, *The Bhagavad Gita*, p. 185 note 14.

42 Sankaracharya, *The Bhagavad Gita*, p. 275.

43 Sri Krishna Prem, *The Yoga of the Bhagavat Gita* (Shaftesbury, Dorset: Element Books, 1988), p. 100.

44 *Ibid.*, p. 101.

CHAPTER ELEVEN **The *Yoga* of the Vision of the Universal Form**

1 The reference to Vishnu in 10:21 is unlikely to be anything to do with the *avatara* doctrine.

2 For example George Thompson, translator, *The Bhagavad Gita: A new translation* (New York: North Point Press, 2008), p. xlvii.

3 Sri Aurobindo, translator, *The Message of the Gita* (Pondicherry: Sri Aurobindo Ashram, 1993 fifth edn, first printed 1938), p. 173.

4 Mahendra Kulasrestha, ed., Mahatma Gandhi, translator, *The Bhagavadgita: A book of ethics for all religions* (New Delhi: Lotus Press, 2008), p. 232.

5 Robert Charles Zaehner, translator, *The Bhagavad-Gita* (London, Oxford, New York: Oxford University Press, 1973, first published 1969), p. 304.

6 Aurobindo, *The Message of the Gita*, p. 174.

7 Geoffrey Parrinder, translator, *The Bhagavad Gita: A verse translation* (Oxford, England and Rockport, MA: Oneworld, 1996 reprint of 1974 edn), p. 73.

8 Sri Sankaracharya, translator, *The Bhagavad Gita*, translated by Alladi Mahadeva Sastry (Madras: Samata Books, 1985 reprint of 1979 corrected edn), p. 281.

9 Lars Martin Fosse, translator, *The Bhagavad Gita* (Woodstock, New York: YogaVidya.com, 2007), p. 106.

10 J. A. B. van Buitenen, translator, *The Bhagavadgita in the Mahabharata* (Chicago and London: University of Chicago Press, 1981), p. 113.

11 Parrinder, *The Bhagavad Gita*, p. 72.

12 Sankaracharya, *The Bhagavad Gita*, p. 282.

13 W. Douglas P. Hill, translator, *The Bhagavad Gita: Translated from the Sanskrit with an introduction an argument and a commentary* (Oxford: Oxford University Press, 1966, first published 1928), p. 205 note 2.

14 Zaehner, *The Bhagavad-Gita*, p. 307.

15 Aurobindo, *The Message of the Gita*, p. 177.

16 Sankaracharya, *The Bhagavad Gita*, p. 285.

17 Zaehner, *The Bhagavad-Gita*, p. 309.

18 *Ibid.*

19 B. Srinivasa Murthy, translator, *The Bhagavad Gita* (Long Beach, California: Long Beach Publications, 1985), p. 88.

20 Rohit Mehta, *From Mind to Super-Mind* (Delhi: Motilal Banarsidass Publishers Private Limited, 1995 reprint of 1972, second, revised edn), p. 112.

21 Sri Krishna Prem, *The Yoga of the Bhagavat Gita* (Shaftesbury, Dorset: Element, 1988), p. 105.

22 Eknath Easwaran, translator, *The Bhagavad Gita* (Tomales, California: Nilgiri Press, 2003 reprint of 1985 edn), p. 148.

23 Aurobindo, *The Message of the Gita*, p. 180. *Ananda* here is "bliss".

24 See, for example, Will J. Johnson, who writes "individual choice is essentially an illusion, since God is the only real chooser, God is the only real actor", in "Transcending the World: Freedom (moksa) & the Bhagavadgita". In Julius Lipner, ed., *The Fruits of Our Desiring: An enquiry into the ethics of the Bhagavadgita for our times* (Calgary, Canada: Bayeux, 1997), pp. 92–103. Douglas Hill wrote, too: "Freedom, in the Gita, is an illusory liberty of choice, working within the bounds of an ultimate determinism", *The Bhagavad Gita*, p. 37.

25 M. R. Sampatkumaran, translator, *Ramanuja's Commentary on the Gita* (Bombay: Ananthacharya Indological Research Unit, 1985), p. 293.

26 J. A. B. van Buitenen, translator, *Ramanuja on the Bhagavadgita: A condensed rendering of his Gitabhasya with copious notes and an introduction* (Delhi: Motilal Banarsidass, 1968), p. 130.

27 Sampatkumaran, *Ramanuja's Commentary on the Gita*, p. 294 note 562.

28 Vimala Thakar, *Insights into the Bhagavad Gita* (Delhi: Motilal Banarsidass Publishers Private Limited, 2005), p. 313.

29 Zaehner, *The Bhagavad-Gita*, pp. 313–15.

30 See Bibek Debroy, translator, *The Bhagavad Gita* (London, New York, New Delhi: Penguin 2005), p. 167.

31 As, also, for example, Franklin Edgerton, translator, *The Bhagavad Gita* (Delhi: Motilal Banarsidass Publishers Private, Limited, 1994, first published 1944), p. 115.

32 Sankaracharya, *The Bhagavad Gita*, p. 293.

33 Edgerton, *The Bhagavad Gita*, p. 115.

34 Richard Gotshalk, translator, *Bhagavad Gita: Translation and commentary* (Delhi: Motilal Banarsidass, 1993 reprint of 1985 edn), p. 211.

35 Sankaracharya, *The Bhagavad Gita*, p. 293.

36 Zaehner, *The Bhagavad-Gita*, p. 315.

37 *Ibid.*, p. 316.

38 Sankaracharya, *The Bhagavad Gita*, p. 298.

39 Zaehner, *The Bhagavad-Gita*, p. 319.

40 Sankaracharya, *The Bhagavad Gita*, p. 299.

41 Prem, *The Yoga of the Bhagavat Gita*, p. 111.

42 Sampatkumaran, *Ramanuja's Commentary on the Gita*, p. 304.

43 *Ibid.*, p. 305.

44 Sankaracharya, *The Bhagavad Gita*, p. 301.

CHAPTER TWELVE **The *Yoga* of Devotion**

1 Robert Charles Zaehner, translator, *The Bhagavad-Gita* (London, Oxford, New York: Oxford University Press, 1973, first published 1969), p. 321.

2 *Ibid.*, pp. 321–2.

3 Sri Sankaracharya, translator, *The Bhagavad Gita*, translated by Alladi Mahadeva Sastry (Madras: Samata Books, 1985 reprint of 1979 corrected edn), p. 303.

4 J. A. B. van Buitenen, translator, *The Bhagavad Gita in the Mahabharata* (Chicago and London: University of Chicago Press, 1981), p. 168.

5   George Thompson, translator, *The Bhagavad Gita* (New York: North Point Press, 2008), p. 60.

6   Zaehner, *The Bhagavad-Gita*, pp. 325–6.

7   *Ibid.*, p. 326.

8   Mahendra Kulasrestha, ed., Mahatma Gandhi, translator, *The Bhagavadgita: A book of ethics for all religions* (New Delhi: Lotus Press, 2008), p. 242.

9   Rabindranath Tagore, *Collected Poems and Plays* (London: Macmillan,1983 reprint of 1939 edn), xxix, p. 275.

10 Swami Chidbhavananda, translator, *The Bhagavad Gita* (Tamil Nadu: Sri Ramakrishna Tapovam, 1982), p. 650.

11 Sankaracharya, *The Bhagavad Gita*, p. 307.

12 W. Douglas P. Hill, translator, *The Bhagavad Gita: Translated from the Sanskrit with an introduction an argument and a commentary* (Oxford: Oxford University Press 1966, first published 1928), p. 85.

13 J. A. B. van Buitenen, translator, *The Bhagavad Gita* (Rockport, Massachusetts, Shaftesbury, Dorset, Brisbane, Queensland: Element, 1997), p. 62.

14 M. R. Sampatkumaran, translator, *Ramanuja's Commentary on the Gita* (Bombay: Ananthacharya Indological Research Unit, 1985), p. 312.

15 See Kees W. Bolle, *The Bhagavadgita: A new translation* (Berkeley, Los Angeles, London: University of California Press, 1979), p. 149.

16 Sankaracharya, *The Bhagavad Gita*, p. 308.

17 *Ibid.*

18 Zaehner, *The Bhagavad-Gita*, p. 329.

19 Richard Gotshalk, translator, *Bhagavad Gita* (Delhi: Motilal Banarsidass Publishers Private Limited, 1993 reprint of 1985 edn), p. 199.

20 Sri Aurobindo, translator, *The Message of the Gita* (Pondicherry: Sri Aurobindo Ashram, 1993 fifth edn, first printed 1938), pp. 195–6.

21 Hill, *The Bhagavad Gita*, pp. 219–20 note 2.

22 Zaehner, *The Bhagavad-Gita*, p. 329.

23 Though see Upadhyaya who sees heavy influence of Buddhism here and elsewhere. Kashi Nath Upadhyaya, *Early Buddhism and the Bhagavadgita* (Delhi, Varanasi, Patna: Motilal Banarsidass, 1983 reprint of 1971 edn), pp. 128–31.

24 Rohit Mehta, *From Mind to Super-Mind* (Delhi: Motilal Banarsidass Publishers Private Limited, 1995 reprint of 1972, second, revised edn), p. 127.

25 *Ibid.* p. 119.

CHAPTER THIRTEEN The *Yoga* of Differentiation of the *Kshetra* and the *Kshetrajna*

1   Zaehner described this chapter as "the most confused in the whole of the *Gita*" because he believed it contradicts ideas elsewhere in the work. Given that his thesis that the personal God is higher than the indescribable Brahman, it is small wonder that he found the stress on the highest Brahman as the true object of knowledge in this chapter contradictory to his own interpretations. See Robert Charles Zaehner, translator, *The Bhagavad-Gita* (London, Oxford, New York: Oxford University Press, 1973, first published 1969), p. 332.

2   Rohit Mehta, *From Mind to Super-Mind* (Delhi: Motilal Banarsidass Publishers Private Limited, 1995 reprint of 1972, second, revised edn), p. 129.

3 J. A. B. van Buitenen, translator, *Ramanuja on the Bhagavadgita: A condensed rendering of his Gitabhasya with copious notes and an introduction* (Delhi: Motilal Banarsidass, 1968), p. 137.

4 Sri Sankaracharya, translator, *The Bhagavad Gita*, translated by Alladi Mahadeva Sastry (Madras: Samata Books, 1985 reprint of 1979 corrected edn), p. 317.

5 A few commentators, however, take *body* to be *prakriti*, for example W. Douglas P. Hill, translator, *The Bhagavad Gita: Translated from the Sanskrit with an introduction an argument and a commentary* (Oxford: Oxford University Press, 1966, first published 1928), p. 222 note 2.

6 Sarvepalli Radhakrishnan, translator, *The Bhagavadgita, with an Introductory Essay, Sanskrit Text, English Translation and Notes* (New York: Harper, 1973, first published 1948 by George Allen & Unwin), pp. 301–2.

7 van Buitenen, *Ramanuja on the Bhagavadgita*, p. 138.

8 *Ibid.*, p. 139.

9 *Ibid.*

10 Sankaracharya, *The Bhagavad Gita*, p. 336.

11 From early commentators of the *Gita* it seems that Badarayana may have used the *Gita* as a source for two of his *sutras* (2.3.45 and 4.1.10), which refer to what is declared in *smriti* scripture. See J. A. B. van Buitenen, translator, *The Bhagavadgita in the Mahabharata: Text and translation* (Chicago and London: University of Chicago Press, 1981), p. 11.

12 These are the *tanmatras*, the five subtle and imperceptible elements and are the medium by which the earlier evolutes are connected to the physical world. For a detailed explanation of these and the other evolutes in classical Sankhya, see Jeaneane Fowler, *Perspectives of Reality: An introduction to the philosophy of Hinduism* (Brighton, Sussex and Portland, Oregon: Sussex Academic Press, 2002), pp. 166–76.

13 van Buitenen, *Ramanuja on the Bhagavadgita*, p. 142.

14 Franklin Edgerton, translator, *The Bhagavad Gita* (Delhi: Motilal Banarsidass Publishers Private Limited, 1994), pp. 127 and 187 note 3.

15 Hill, *The Bhagavad Gita*, pp. 223–4 note 9.

16 Swami Chidbhavananda, translator, *The Bhagavad Gita* (Tamil Nadu: Sri Krishna Tapovam, 1982), p. 680.

17 Zaehner, *The Bhagavad-Gita*, p. 336.

18 *Ibid.*

19 Mahendra Kulasrestha, ed., Mahatma Gandhi, translator, *The Bhagavadgita: A book of ethics for all religions* (New Delhi: Lotus Press, 2008), p. 251.

20 Sankaracharya, *The Bhagavad Gita*, pp. 345–6. The *supreme Brahman, beginningless* in the Sanskrit is *anadimat param*, which is sometimes divided differently – *anadi matparam brahma*, to render something of the nature "the beginningless Brahman, to which I am superior". Such is the way Ramanuja interpreted the verse, the "beginningless" referring to the individual Self, and God as "what has Me for its superior": see M. R. Sampatkumaran, translator, *Ramanuja's Commentary on the Gita* (Bombay: Ananthacharya Indological Research Unit, 1985), p. 340. *Brahman* of the verse is for Ramanuja the individual Self, the essential nature of the self, and it is this that, as the body of Brahman is neither existent nor non-existent: *ibid.*, pp. 340–42.

21 Once again, Zaehner gave a lengthy discourse on this verse in order to support his contention that Krishna is a "Person" beyond the "unmanifest beyond the unmanifest",

The Bhagavad-Gita, pp. 338–40. The idea, as I noted in 11:37, is hardly credible.

22 Sri Aurobindo, translator, *The Message of the Gita* (Pondicherry: Sri Aurobindo Ashram, 1993 fifth edn, first printed 1938), p. 203.

23 Eknath Easwaran, *The Bhagavad Gita* (Tomales, California: Nilgiri Press, 1985), p. 203.

24 Zaehner, *The Bhagavad-Gita*, p. 341.

25 Aurobindo, *The Message of the Gita*, p. 204.

26 See, for example, Chidbhavananda, *The Bhagavad Gita*, p. 693 and B. Srinivasa Murthy, translator, *The Bhagavad Gita* (Long Beach, California: Long Beach Publications, 1985), p. 107.

27 Zaehner continued to see Krishna as the ultimate personal deity beyond the *nirguna* Brahman in this verse, *The Bhagavad-Gita*, p. 342.

28 Aurobindo, *The Message of the Gita*, p. 205 note 2.

29 Cf. *Shvetashvatara Upanishad* 3:8, 16; the *Isha* 5; the *Mundaka* 13:1, 7; the *Brihadaranyaka* 4:4, 16.

30 Sankaracharya, *The Bhagavad Gita*, p. 358.

31 van Buitenen, *Ramanuja on the Bhagavadgita*, p. 144.

32 Sankaracharya, *The Bhagavad Gita*, p. 367.

33 Zaehner considered here that the *kshetrajna* refers to the "spiritual monad" that is the enlightened separated entity of Sankhya philosophy, *The Bhagavad-Gita*, p. 347. This seems an unnecessary assumption that does not fit the context.

34 Purusha is considered male and *prakriti* female.

35 Sampatkumaran, *Ramanuja's Commentary on the Bhagavad Gita*, p. 354.

36 See Hill, *The Bhagavad Gita*, p. 228 note 4.

37 Richard Gotshalk, translator, *Bhagavad Gita* (Delhi: Motilal Banarsidass Publishers Private Limited, 1993 reprint of 1985 edn), p. 163 note 24.

38 Compare 3:22 and the *Shvetashvatara Upanishad* 6:11.

39 M. R. Sampatkumaran, translator, *Ramanuja's Commentary on the Gita* (Bombay: Ananthacharya Indological Research Unit, 1985), p. 356.

40 Aurobindo, *The Message of the Gita*, p. 210.

CHAPTER FOURTEEN **The *Yoga* of Differentiation of the Three Gunas**

1 Sri Sankaracharya, translator, *The Bhagavad Gita*, translated by Alladi Mahadeva Sastry (Madras: Samata Books, 1985 reprint of 1979 corrected edn), p. 379.

2 Sri Aurobindo, translator, *The Message of the Gita* (Pondicherry: Sri Aurobindo Ashram, 1993 fifth edn, first printed 1938), p. 211 and 211 note 1.

3 Franklin Edgerton, translator, *The Bhagavad Gita* (Delhi: Motilal Banarsidass Publishers Private Limited, 1994), p. 135.

4 M. R. Sampatkumaran, translator, *Ramanuja's Commentary on the Gita* (Bombay: Ananthacharya Indological Research Unit, 1985), p. 359.

5 Sankaracharya, *The Bhagavad Gita*, p. 379.

6 J. A. B. van Buitenen, translator, *The Bhagavad Gita* (Rockport, Massachusetts, Shaftesbury, Dorset and Brisbane, Queensland: Element, 1997), p. 100 note 14:2.

7 Sri Krishna Prem, *The Yoga of the Bhagavat Gita* (Shaftesbury, Dorset: Element Books Limited, 1988), p. 135.

8 For a superb analysis of the *shakti* force in Hinduism, see Lynn Foulston and Stuart Abbot, *Hindu Goddesses: Beliefs and Practices* (Eastbourne, Sussex and Portland, Oregon: Sussex Academic Press, 2009), Part 1, chapter 1, pp. 9–43.

9 Sampatkumaran, *Ramanuja's Commentary on the Gita*, p. 361.

10 Rohit Mehta, *From Mind to Super-Mind* (Delhi: Motilal Banarsidass Publishers Private Limited, 1995 reprint of 1972, second, revised edn), p. 139.

11 Sankaracharya, *The Bhagavad Gita*, p. 383.

12 Traditionally, there are nine gates – two eyes, ears and nostrils, the nose, the mouth, the genitals and the anus.

13 Aurobindo, *The Message of the Gita*, p. 217 note 1.

14 Sankaracharya, *The Bhagavad Gita*, p. 387.

15 This, in fact, is part of the rationale for the class system that finds the lowest class, or worse, those beyond the class system, as incapable of higher knowledge. *Shudras* are *tamas-rajas* in nature, destined not to ascend to evolutionary spiritual planes since they do not have the *gunic* make-up. The *Dalits*, the former Outcastes, beyond the class system, are considered wholly *tamasic* and so placed through cumulative sins in past lives. Women may be viewed in the same way, too.

16 J. A. B. van Buitenen, translator, *Ramanuja on the Bhagavadgita: A condensed rendering of his Gitabhasya with copious notes and an introduction* (Delhi: Motilal Banarsidass, 1968), p. 149.

17 Mehta, *From Mind to Super-Mind*, p. 137.

18 Sankaracharya, *The Bhagavad Gita*, p. 390.

19 Mehta, *From Mind to Super-Mind*, p. 144.

20 See also, 2:54–72, 6:7–9 and 12:13–19 where the thought is similar to the current verses.

21 Eknath Easwaran, translator, *The Bhagavad Gita* (Tomales, California: Nilgiri Press, 1985), p. 176.

22 van Buitenen, *Ramanuja on the Bhagavadgita*, p. 151.

23 In commenting on these last two verses, Chidbhavananda considered that all four paths, four *yogas*, have been dealt with and harmonized. The previous verse upheld *bhakti* and the path of attaining the personal, *saguna*, God. The present verse speaks of the Imperishable and Immortal Brahman or *nirguna* Brahman, reached by the path of knowledge, *jnana*, and the reference to the *eternal* or everlasting *Dharma*, the *sanatana-dharma* he thought relates to the path of egoless action, *karma-yoga*. *Raja-yoga* is the fourth path which, he said, has as its goal *amrita dhara*, divine nectar that brings the absolute bliss spoken of in the verse. Chidbhavananda's point is that Brahman is all these paths so they are all equal in the goal of transcending the *gunas* albeit by different methods. Swami Chidbhavananda, translator, *The Bhagavad Gita* (Tamil Nadu: Sri Krishna Tapovam, 1982), pp. 747–8.

24 Robert Charles Zaehner, translator, *The Bhagavad-Gita* (London, Oxford, New York: Oxford University Press, 1973, first published 1969), p. 358.

25 Geoffrey Parrinder, translator, *The Bhagavad Gita* (Oxford: Oneworld, 1996 reprint of 1974 edn), p. 95.

26 Edgerton, *The Bhagavad Gita*, p. 49 and p. 49 note 28.

27 Sri Aurobindo, *Essays on the Gita* (Pondichery: Sri Aurobindo Ashram, 2000 third impression of 1996 ninth edn, first published between 1916 and 1920), p. 91.

28 Richard Gotshalk, translator, *Bhagavad Gita* (Delhi: Motilal Banarsidass Publishers Private Limited, 1993 reprint of 1985 edn), p. 163 note 9.

29 John Grimes, *A Concise Dictionary of Indian Philosophy* (Albany, New York: State University of New York Press, 1989), p. 271.

CHAPTER FIFTEEN The *Yoga* of the Seprume *Purusha*

1 See W. Douglas P. Hill, translator, *The Bhagavad Gita: Translated from the Sanskrit with an introduction an argument and a commentary* (Oxford: Oxford University Press, 1966, first published 1928), pp. 236–7.

2 *Rig Veda* XXIV:24:7, translator Ralph T. H. Griffith, *The Hymns of the Rgveda* (Delhi: Motilal Banarsidass Publishers Private Limited, 1991 reprint of 1973 new revised edn), p. 14.

3 *Katha Upanishad* 6:1, translator Patrick Olivelle, *Upanisads* (Oxford, New York: Oxford University Press, 1996), p. 244.

4 Hill, *The Bhagavad Gita*, p. 236 note 1.

5 Arvind Sharma, *The Hindu Gita: Ancient and classical interpretations of the Bhagavadgita* (London: Duckworth, 1986), p. 76.

6 Richard Gotshalk, translator, *Bhagavad Gita* (Delhi: Motilal Banarsidass Publishers Private Limited, 1993 reprint of 1985 edn), p. 55.

7 Aurobindo, translator, *The Message of the Gita* (Pondicherry: Sri Aurobindo Ashram, 1993 fifth edn, first printed 1938), p. 223.

8 *Ibid.*

9 *Shvetashvatara Upanishad* 6:14, translator Olivelle, *Upanisads*, p. 264.

10 Aurobindo, *The Message of the Gita*, p. 225. Some, however, place "eternal" with *jiva* to give: "A part of me becomes an eternal *jiva* in the world of *jivas*", which is perhaps more clearly indicative of the spiritual *atman* within the material self.

11 *Ibid.*, p. 226.

12 *Katha Upanishad* 1:3:4, translator Olivelle, *Upanisads*, p. 239.

13 Gotshalk, *Bhagavad Gita*, p. 55.

14 Sri Sankaracharya, translator, *The Bhagavad Gita*, translated by Alladi Mahadeva Sastry (Madras: Samata Books, 1985 reprint of 1979 corrected edn), p. 405.

15 M. R. Sampatkumaran, translator, *Ramanuja's Commentary on the Gita* (Bombay: Ananthacharya Indological Research Unit, 1985), p. 386.

16 *Ibid.*

17 While staying in south-west France recently, I was surprised to find in the village where I stayed, Saint Germain Du Bel Air, that the local people planted their garden crops in accordance with the cycles of the moon and would not dream of planting crops at an inauspicious time for the plants.

18 Barbara Stoler Miller, *The Bhagavad-Gita: Krishna's counsel in time of war* (New York, Toronto, London, Sydney, Auckland: Bantam Books, 1986), p. 130.

19 *Brihadaranyaka Upanishad* 5:9:1, translator Olivelle, *Upanisads*, p. 75.

20 Miller, *The Bhagavad-Gita*, p. 160.

21 Sri Krishna Prem, *The Yoga of the Bhagavat Gita* (Shaftesbury, Dorset: Element Books Limited, 1988), p. 153.

22 Or perhaps three systems of world, see Kashi Nath Upadhyaya, *Early Buddhism and the Bhagavadgita* (Delhi, Varanasi, Patna: Motilal Banarsidass, 1983 reprint of 1971 edn), p. 383.

23 Sri Aurobindo, *Essays on the Gita* (Pondicherry: Sri Aurobindo Ashram, 2000 third impression of 1996 edn, first published between 1916 and 1920), p. 453.

CHAPTER SIXTEEN The *Yoga* of the Differentiation of the Divine and the Demonic

1 Robert Charles Zaehner, translator, *The Bhagavad-Gita* (London, Oxford, New York: Oxford University Press, 1973, first published 1969), p. 369.

2 J. A. B. van Buitenen, translator, *Ramanuja on the Bhagavadgita: A condensed rendering of his Gitabhasya with copious notes and an introduction* (Delhi, Varanasi, Patna: Motilal Banarsidass, 1968), p. 155.

3 Sri Sankaracharya, translator, *The Bhagavad Gita*, translated by Alladi Mahadeva Sastry (Madras: Samata Books, 1985 reprint of 1979 corrected edn), p. 415.

4 So, Shankara, *ibid.*, p. 416.

5 M. R. Sampatkumaran, translator, *Ramanuja's Commentary on the Gita* (Bombay: Ananthacharya Indological Research Unit, 1985, first published 1969), p. 397.

6 *Ibid.*, p. 398.

7 Bibek Debroy, translator, *The Bhagavad Gita* (New York, New Delhi, London: Penguin Books, 2005), p. 215.

8 Barbara Stoler Miller, translator, *The Bhagavad-Gita* (New York, Toronto, London, Sydney, Auckland: Bantam Books, 1986), p. 134.

9 Sri Aurobindo, *Essays on the Gita* (Pondicherry: Sri Aurobindo Ashram, 2000 third impression of 1996 ninth edn, first published between 1916 and 1920), p. 268.

10 van Buitenen, *Ramanuja on the Bhagavadgita*, p. 156.

11 Sampatkumaran, *Ramanuja's Commentary on the Gita*, p. 400.

12 Upadhyaya considers that this verse, along with verses 14 and 23, are referring not to materialists, but to Buddhists. The point is not without merit, given, as Upadhyaya says, that materialists accepted the reality rather than unreality of the world. See Kashi Nath Upadhyaya, *Early Buddhism and the Bhagavadgita* (Delhi, Varanasi, Patna: Motilal Banarsidass, 1983 reprint of 1971 edn), p. 127.

13 The tone of the chapter rather suggests that lust may be the better translation but I have retained the normal sense of *kama* throughout the chapter.

14 Zaehner, *The Bhagavad-Gita*, p. 372.

15 Eknath Easwaran, translator, *The Bhagavad Gita* (Tomales, California: Nilgiri Press, 1985), p. 192.

16 Richard Gotshalk, translator, *Bhagavad Gita* (Delhi: Motilal Banarsidass Publishers Private Limited, 1993 reprint of 1985 edn), p. 576.

17 Sri Aurobindo, translator, *The Message of the Gita* (Pondicherry: Sri Aurobindo Ashram, 1993 fifth edn, first printed 1938), p. 239.

18 Zaehner, *The Bhagavad-Gita*, p. 373.

19 See for example 6:36, 9:31 and 12:7.

20 Zaehner, *The Bhagavad-Gita*, p. 374.

CHAPTER SEVENTEEN The *Yoga* of the Threefold *Shraddha*

1 Sarvepalli Radhakrishnan, translator, *The Bhagavadgita, with an Introductory Essay, Sanskrit Text, English Translation and Notes* (New York: Harper, 1973, first published 1948 London: George Allen & Unwin), p. 343.

2 Sri Krishna Prem, translator, *The Yoga of the Bhagavat Gita* (Shaftesbury, Dorset: Element Books, 1988), p. 166.

3 Sri Sankaracharya, translator, *The Bhagavad Gita*, translated by Alladi Mahadeva Sastry (Madras: Samata Books, 1985 reprint of 1979 corrected edn), pp. 427–8.

4 J. A. B. van Buitenen, translator, *Ramanuja on the Bhagavadgita: A condensed rendering of his Gitabhasya with copious notes and an introduction* (Delhi, Varanasi, Patna: Motilal Banarsidass, 1968), p. 158.

5 M. R. Sampatkumaran, translator, *Ramanuja's Commentary on the Gita* (Bombay: Ananthacharya Indological Research Unit, 1985), p. 410.

6 Sri Aurobindo, translator, *The Message of the Gita* (Pondicherry: Sri Aurobindo Ashram, 1993 fifth edn, first printed 1938), p. 243 note 1.

7 For a full discussion on *samskaras* and the way these affect the self, see Jeaneane Fowler, *Perspectives of Reality: An introduction to the philosophy of Hinduism* (Brighton, Sussex and Portland, Oregon: Sussex Academic Press, 2002), pp. 219–25.

8 See W. Douglas P. Hill, translator, *The Bhagavad Gita: Translated from the Sanskrit with an introduction an argument and a commentary* (Oxford: Oxford University Press, 1966, first published 1928), p. 250 note 1.

9 van Buitenen, *Ramanuja on the Bhagavadgita*, p. 159.

10 Sankaracharya, *The Bhagavad Gita*, p. 432.

11 van Buitenen, *Ramanuja on the Bhagavadgita*, p. 160.

12 J. A. B. van Buitenen, translator, *The Bhagavad Gita* (Rockport, Massachusetts, Shaftesbury, Dorset, Brisbane, Queensland: Element, 1997), p. 72.

13 Sankaracharya, *The Bhagavad Gita*, p. 434.

14 *Ibid.*

15 See Satya P. Agarwal, *The Social Role of the Gita: How and why* (Delhi: Motilal Banarsidass, 1998), p. 377.

16 See Agarwal, *ibid.*, p. 383.

17 Robert Charles Zaehner, translator, *The Bhagavad-Gita* (London, Oxford, New York: Oxford University Press, 1973, first published 1969), p. 379.

18 *Ibid.*, p. 380.

19 Cf. the related English *is*.

20 Prem, *The Yoga of the Bhagavat Gita*, p. 167.

21 Sankaracharya, *The Bhagavad Gita*, p. 835.

22 *Ibid.*, pp. 836–7.

CHAPTER EIGHTEEN The *Yoga* of Liberation and Renunciation

1 J. A. B. van Buitenen, translator, *The Bhagavadgita in the Mahabharata* (Chicago and London: University of Chicago Press, 1981), p. 170 note 2.

2 J. A. B. van Buitenen, translator, *Ramanuja on the Bhagavadgita: A condensed rendering of his Gitabhasya with copious notes and an introduction* (Delhi, Varanasi, Patna: Motilal Banarsidass, 1968), pp. 165 and 169.

3 Sri Aurobindo, translator, *The Message of the Gita* (Pondicherry: Sri Aurobindo Ashram, 1993 fifth edn, first printed 1938), p. 252.

4 Sri Sankaracharya, translator, *The Bhagavad Gita*, translated by Alladi Mahadeva Sastry (Madras: Samata Books, 1985 reprint of 1979 corrected edn), pp. 444–5.

5 *Ibid.*, pp. 447–8.

6 *Ibid.*, p. 451.

7 *Ibid.*, p. 450.

8 *Ibid.*, p. 452.

9 Eknath Easwaran, *The Bhagavad Gita* (Tomales, California: Nilgiri Press, 1985), p. 202.

10 See, for example, Sarvepalli Radhakrishnan, translator, *The Bhagavadgita, with an*

Introductory Essay, Sanskrit Text, English Translation and Notes (New York: Harper, 1973, first published 1948, George Allen & Unwin), p. 355.

11 So, Richard Gotshalk, translator, *Bhagavad Gita* (Delhi: Motilal Banarsidass Publishers Private Limited, 1993 reprint of 1985 first edn), p. 166 note 9 and p. 207 XVIII.13.

12 M. R. Sampatkumaran, translator, *Ramanuja's Commentary on the Gita* (Bombay: Ananthacharya Indological Research Unit), p. 440.

13 Swami Chidbhavananda, translator, *The Bhagavad Gita* (Tamil Nadu: Sri Ramakrishna Tapovam, 1982), p. 864.

14 Sankaracharya, *The Bhagavad Gita*, p. 455.

15 Mahendra Kulasrestha, ed., Mahatma Gandhi, translator, *The Bhagavadgita: A book of ethics for all religions* (New Delhi: Lotus Press, 2008), p. 296.

16 van Buitenen, *Ramanuja on the Bhagavadgita*, p. 165.

17 Sampatkumaran, *Ramanuja's Commentary on the Gita*, p. 441.

18 Gotshalk, *Bhagavad Gita*, pp. 207–8 note XVIII.14

19 W. Douglas P. Hill, translator, *The Bhagavad Gita: Translated from the Sanskrit with an introduction an argument and a commentary* (Oxford: Oxford University Press, 1966, first published 1928), p. 259 note 2.

20 Robert Charles Zaehner, translator, *The Bhagavad-Gita* (London, Oxford, New York: Oxford University Press, 1973, first published 1969), p. 388.

21 Robert Charles Zaehner, *Hinduism* (Oxford: Oxford University Press, 1966 reprint of 1962 edn), p. 106.

22 Rohit Mehta, *From Mind to Super-Mind* (Delhi: Motilal Banarsidass Publishers Private Limited, 1995 reprint of second revised edn 1972, first published 1966), p. 176.

23 Radhakrishnan, *The Bhagavadgita, with an Introductory Essay, Sanskrit Text, English Translation and Notes*, p. 356.

24 *Ibid.*

25 Franklin Edgerton, translator, *The Bhagavad Gita* (Delhi: Motilal Banarsidass Publishers Private Limited, 1994 Indian edn, first published 1944), p. 159 note 2.

26 Zaehner, *The Bhagavad-Gita*, p. 388.

27 *Ibid.*

28 Sankaracharya, *The Bhagavad Gita*, p. 460.

29 Zaehner, *The Bhagavad Gita*, p. 389.

30 Sankaracharya, *The Bhagavad Gita*, p. 463.

31 Gandhi, *The Bhagavadgita*, p. 298.

32 Sankaracharya, *The Bhagavad Gita*, p. 464.

33 *Ibid.*, p. 467.

34 Chidbhavananda, *The Bhagavad Gita*, p. 902.

35 Sankaracharya, *The Bhagavad Gita*, p. 471.

36 Gandhi, *The Bhagavadgita*, p. 300.

37 Sampatkumaran, *Ramanuja's Commentary on the Gita*, p. 455.

38 Will Johnson, "Transcending the World?: Freedom (moksa) & the Bhagavadgita". In Julius Lipner, ed., *The Fruits of Our Desiring: An enquiry into the ethics of the Bhagavadgita for our times* (Calgary, Canada: Bayeux Arts, 1997), p. 100.

39 My students have had heated debates about one whose *karma*, *gunic* make-up and *sva-dharma* result in that person being a murderer. If it is one's nature to be seriously *adharmic* – a murderer – then, seemingly, that is what one must be, and that would seem to be right! Presumably, involution would have to continue until a glint of right

action occurred but, according to the *Gita*, it would be wrong for the murderer to adopt the *dharma* of another, even if a better one, which could offer that glint of right action.

40 Sankaracharya, *The Bhagavad Gita*, p. 474.

41 *Shudras* could not be taught the scriptures: indeed, a Brahmin would end up in Hell should he deem to impart knowledge to a *Shudra*. A *Shudra* was traditionally alienated from liberation, so the *Gita* was flouting tradition by saying that a *Shudra* performing servile duties could reach perfection. While barred from many religious observances, the ultimate goal of liberation became a possibility.

42 Mehta, *From Mind to Super-Mind*, pp. 192–3.

43 van Buitenen, *Ramanuja on the Bhagavadgita*, p. 171.

44 Aurobindo, *The Message of the Gita*, p. 276.

45 *Ibid.*, p. 277. My upper case for Self.

46 Sri Krishna Prem, translator, *The Yoga of the Bhagavat Gita* (Shaftesbury, Dorset: Element Books, 1988), p. 183.

47 Sankaracharya, *The Bhagavad Gita*, p. 490.

48 Sampatkumaran, *Ramanuja's Commentary on the Gita*, p. 465.

49 *Ibid.*, p. 466.

50 Sankaracharya, *The Bhagavad Gita*, p. 492.

51 Zaehner, *The Bhagavad-Gita*, p. 397.

52 Sampatkumaran, *Ramanuja's Commentary on the Gita*, p. 466.

53 *Ibid.*, p. 467 note 921.

54 Juan Mascaró, translator, *The Bhagavad Gita* (London, New York, Victoria, Auckland, Ontario: Penguin, 1962), p. 120.

55 Sampatkumaran, *Ramanuja's Commentary on the Gita*, p. 471.

56 Zaehner, *The Bhagavad Gita*, p. 400.

57 Sampatkumaran, *Ramanuja's Commentary on the Gita*, p. 472.

58 Johnson, "Transcending the World?: Freedom (moksa) & the Bhagavadgita", p. 99.

59 Gandhi, *The Bhagavadgita*, p. 305.

60 Sankaracharya, *The Bhagavad Gita*, p. 499.

61 Shankara's commentary at this point launches into a very long discourse that attempts, as at many points of his commentary, to set out *karma-yoga*, the path of detached action as inferior to the path of *jnana*, knowledge, though he concedes it may be a way of reaching the true path, *ibid.*, pp. 499–516. For Shankara, total renunciation of action and intuitive knowledge of Brahman – *jnana-yoga* – was the only possible path to liberation.

62 Sampatkumaran, *Ramanuja's Commentary on the Gita*, pp. 474–5.

63 Easwaran, *The Bhagavad Gita*, p. 223.

64 Sampatkumaran, *Ramanuja's Commentary on the Gita*, p. 475.

65 Sankaracharya, *The Bhagavad Gita*, p. 518.

66 Barbara Stoler Miller, translator, *The Bhagavad-Gita: Krishna's counsel in time of war* (New York, Toronto, London, Sydney, Auckland: Bantam Books, 1986), pp. 159–60.

67 Zaehner, *The Bhagavad-Gita*, p. 402.

68 van Buitenen, *The Bhagavadgita in the Mahabharata*, p. 145.

69 Will Johnson, *The Bhagavad Gita* (Oxford and New York: Oxford University Press, 1994), p. 81.

70 van Buitenen, *The Bhagavadgita in the Mahabharata*, p. 170 note 8.

Further Reading

Primary sources

The standard Sanskrit text of the *Gita* accepted today is that edited by S. K. Belvalkar as volume 7 of the *Mahabharata*. This standard text today was the one used by Shankara, and the reader who wishes to use the actual Sanskrit text would do well to obtain Alladi Mahadeva Sastry's translation of Shankara's work, *The Bhagavad Gita: With the commentary of Sri Sankaracharya*. This was first published in 1897 and the edition I have used is the 1985 reprint of the 1979 corrected and reprinted 1977 edition, published in Madras by Samata Books. A more recent edition was produced in 1998 by Arcana Publishing.

There are a number of recently published works that will supply the Sanskrit text along with a translation. Bibek Debroy has a Sanskrit text and translation with useful notes to the text in *The Bhagavad Gita* (London, New York, Toronto, Paris: Penguin Books, 2005), as does Lars Martin Fosse's very recent *The Bhagavad Gita* (Woodstock, New York: YogaVidya.com) in 2007. Swami Chidbhavananda's *The Bhagavad Gita* (Tamil Nadu: Sri Ramakrishna Tapovam, 1982 reprint of 1951 edn) has a useful arrangement of each verse in the Sanskrit script, a transliteration of the verse, a word-by-word translation of the Sanskrit, an English translation and then a commentary. A much older translation that gives the Sanskrit script, English translation and very full notes, is that of W. Douglas P. Hill. His work, first published in 1928 and reproduced at Oxford by Oxford University Press in 1966, is entitled *The Bhagavad Gita: Translated from the Sanskrit with an introduction an argument and a commentary*. While an older source, it is an eminent one. Another older source, but an important one, is Sarvepalli Radhakrishnan's translation, which, as its title suggests, is very full – *The Bhagavadgita, with an Introductory Essay, Sanskrit Text, English Translation and Notes*. It was published in London by George Allen & Unwin in 1948 and more recently in New York, by Harper in 1973.

Maharishi Mahesh Yogi did an extensive commentary of the first six chapters of the *Gita* that is interspersed with his teaching on transcendental meditation. This text provides the Sanskrit script with a translation and is *The Bhagavad Gita: A new translation and commentary, chapters 1–6* (London, Frankfurt, Oslo, Geneva, Toronto, Los Angeles, Rishikesh: International SRM Publications, 1967). The Sanskrit script with a translation and an extensive commentary was also provided by Sri Aurobindo in *The Message of the Gita*, published at the Sri Aurobindo Ashram in Pondicherry and edited by Anilbaran Roy. It was first published in 1938 with a later edition in 1993. Highly respected is Franklin Edgerton's *The Bhagavad Gita*, first published in Cambridge in 1944 and brought out in an Indian edition in 1994 by Motilal Banarsidass Publishers Private limited, in Delhi. Edgerton provided a transliterated Sanskrit text and a verse translation with extensive notes and very full chapters on themes that arise in the *Gita*. Mahendra Kulasrestha is the editor of a recent publication in 2008, which gives a Sanskrit text followed by a verse translation and commentary by Mahatma Gandhi. This is Gandhi's *The Bhagavadgita: A book of ethics for all religions*, published in New Delhi by Lotus Press.

For an academic source that deals with the technicalities of the Sanskrit along with a commentary, Robert Charles Zaehner's *The Bhagavad-Gita* is still hailed as a standard work. This work, published by Oxford University Press (London, Oxford and New York, 1973 reprint of 1969 Clarendon Press edition) supplies transliterated Sanskrit. For specifically a translation without a commentary, easily obtained is Will J. Johnson's *The Bhagavad Gita: A new translation*, published by Oxford University Press (Oxford and New York, 1994). George Thompson has also produced a very recent translation in 2008, *The Bhagavad Gita: A new translation* published in New York by North Point Press.

An easy verse translation has been done by Geoffrey Parrinder (Oxford: Oneworld, 1996 reprint of 1974 edn). Kees W. Bolle also has a verse translation published in 1979 by the University of California Press (Berkeley, Los Angeles and London). This work, *The Bhagavadgita: A new translation*, has a useful concordance of Sanskrit words at the end. Another verse translation was done by Barbara Stoler Miller in *The Bhagavad-Gita: Krishna's counsel in time of war* (New York, Toronto, London, Sydney, Auckland: Bantam Books, 1991, first published 1986).

Richard Gotshalk's translation is very sound, as are his extensive notes to the translation, if rather oddly arranged, making it difficult for the reader to access several pages at once. The translation and notes, however, are well worth the effort. The work is published by Motilal Banarsidass Publishers Private Limited in Delhi and the first 1985 edition has been reprinted in 1993. Eknath Easwaran's translation, *The Bhagavad Gita*, is generally sound, with introductions to each chapter by Diana Morrison. B. Srinivasi Murthy also provides a reliable translation in his *The Bhagavad Gita*, which was published in 1985 in California, by Long Beach Publications. Older translations include the English translation of J. A. B. van Buitenen, *The Bhagavad Gita* (Rockport, Massachusetts, Shaftesbury, Dorset and Brisbane, Queensland: Element, 1997), which has useful notes to the translation, and his lengthier *The Bhagavadgita in the Mahabharata: Text and translation* (Chicago and London: University of Chicago Press, 1981), which, as its title suggests, has a transliteration of the Sanskrit text.

Two sources are invaluable for examination of Ramanuja's comments on the *Gita*. These are J. A. B. van Buitenen's translation published in 1968, *Ramanuja on the Bhagavadgita: A condensed rendering of his Gitabhasya with copious notes and an introduction*, published in Delhi by Motilal Banarsidass, and M. R. Sampatkumaran's translation of 1969, *Ramanuja's Commentary on the Gita*, published in Madras by the M. Rangacharya Memorial Trust. This work is now also available in a 1985 edition published in Bombay by Ananthacharya Indological Research Unit. Arvind Sharma's work, *The Hindu Gita: Ancient and classical interpretations of the Bhagavadgita* (London: Duckworth, 1986), examines material taken from the oldest commentators of Bhaskara, Shankara, Ramanuja and – often neglected – Madhva.

Secondary sources

Vimala Thakar's *Insights into the Bhagavad Gita* now in an Indian edition of 2005 (Delhi: Motilal Banarsidass Publishers Private Limited) is, as the title suggests, "insightful" and a thoughtful perception of the *Gita*. Rohit Mehta also provided a powerful philosophical commentary on the *Gita* entitled *From Mind to Super-Mind: A commentary on the Bhagavad Gita*. This was first published in 1966, but there is a 1995 reprint of the 1972 edition published in Delhi by Motilal Banarsidass. Sri Krishna Prem's *The Yoga of the Bhagavat Gita* published in Shaftesbury, Dorset by Element Books in 1988 also provides a comprehensive commentary on the *Gita*. Sri Aurobindo's *Essays on the Gita* is a lengthy work that he wrote for the monthly review, *Arya*, between 1916 and 1918. In 1922, Aurobindo revised these essays to form a book, now in its third impression of 2000 and produced by the Aurobindo Ashram at Pondicherry.

The Fruits of Our Desiring: An enquiry into the ethics of the Bhagavadgita (Calgary: Bayeux, 1997) is an edited work by Julius Lipner containing a number of articles that deal with selected themes in the *Gita* related to one of its central tenets of action that has desire and action that is desireless. *The Social Role of the Gita: How and why* is a very interesting work by Satya P. Agarwal that takes up the social aspects of the *Gita* and the *karma-yoga* theme that inspired India's social and political reformers. Again, published in Delhi by Motilal Banarsidass, it was originally published in 1993 and reprinted in 1997. Similarly, Robert Minor has examined the ways in which some of these reformers and religious leaders have interpreted the *Gita* in *Modern Indian Interpreters of the Bhagavda Gita* (Delhi: Sri Satguru Publications, 1986), and Eric J. Sharpe has examined the different ways in which the *Gita* has been interpreted in a critical, precise and very readable manner, *The Universal Gita: Western images of the Bhagavadgita* (La Salle, Illinois: Open Court Publishing Company, 1985).

Glossary and Index
of Sanskrit Terms

References to the main *Introduction* are in Roman numerals (xiv). Other references in bold are to chapters, followed by the verses in normal font (6:20). The introduction to each chapter is referenced as :*intro*, and the notes (page 306 et seq.) to that chapter as 6: *notes*. The same format is adopted for the *Index of English Words* that follows. In consideration of space, entries are put only in the main Sanskrit forms in which they occur: other forms, for example adjectival, participial etc., are subsumed under the main form. The following abbreviations are used: n. pr. m.– noun proper masculine; n. pr. f. – noun proper feminine; and n. pr. loc. – noun proper location.

abhava/abhāva	non-being, non-existence, non-becoming 2:16; 4:4; 10:4
Abhimanyu	n. pr. m. *see* Subhadra
abhyasa/abhyāsa	constant practice, endeavour, repetition 6:35, 44; 12:10, 12; 17:15; 18:36, 37; -*yoga* the *yoga* of constant practice 8:8, 10; 12:9
achala	immovable, steady, firm 2:24, 53; 6:13; 7:21; 8:10; 12:3; -*pratishtha* settled in stillness 2:70
acharya/āchārya	teacher 1:2, 3, 26, 34
achintya	unthinkable, inconceivable 2:25; 8:9; 12:3
Achyuta	n. pr. div. "Immortal, Immovable, One who has not fallen", a name of Krishna 1:21; 11:42; 18:73
adharma	unrighteous; against what is right 1:1, 40, 41, 44; 3:35; 4:8, 23; 6:44; 4:7; 11:32; 14:16; 16:7, 9, 10, 12, 19; 18:7, 15, 30, 31, 32, 45, 47, 66, *notes* 38
adhibhuta/adhibhūta	the five elements 7:30; 8:1, 4
adhidaiva	the divine Purusha; the *atman* 7:30; 8:*intro*, 1, 4, 8
adhiyajna/adhiyajña	presence of a deity at a sacrificial ceremony 7:30; 8:2, 4; 9:24
adhyatma/adhyātma	the *atman*/Self; pertaining to the Self 3:30; 7:29; 8:*intro*, 1, 3, 4; 10:32; 11:1; 15:5; -*jnana/jñāna* knowledge of the intrinsic Self 13:11; -*vidya/vidyā* knowledge of the Self 10:32
adideva/ādideva	Primal God 11:38
Adityas/Ādityas	*Vedic* celestial deities 4:1; 10:21; 11:6, 22
advaita	non-dual xxvii, xl; 5:1; 14:2; 18:6, 66
Agni/*agni*	*Vedic* god of fire xiv, xv, xviii; 1:30; 4:32; 10:23; 11:39; fire 6:1; 8:24; 9:16; 15:14
ahankara/ahaṃkāra	literally "I-maker", ego/egoism 2:71; 3:27, 28, 42; 7:4;

13:*intro*, 5, 8, 20; 16:18; 17:5; 18:14, 17, 24, 53, 58, 59; *nir-* without ego, non-egoism 2:71; 12:13

ahimsa/ahiṃsā — non-injury, non-violence 2:6; 10:5; 13:7; 16:2 ; 17:14

Airavata/Airāvata — the *Vedic* god Indra's elephant 10:27

aja — unborn 2:20, 21; 4:6; 7:25; 10:3, 12

ajnana/ajñāna — ignorance 3:26; 4:40, 42; 5:15, 16; 10:11; 13:11; 14:8, 16, 17; 16:4, 15; 18:72

akarma — inaction 2:47; 3:4, 8; 4:16, 17, 37

akasha/akaśa — space, ether, one of the five elements and the most subtle of them 9:6, 11; 13:32

akshara/akṣara — imperishable, indestructible 8:4; 11:18; 15:16, 18; as the syllable *Om* 3:15; 8:13; 10:25; *as* Brahman 3:43; 8:3, 4, 11, 21, 28; 11:37; 12:1, 3; 17:23

amrita/amṛta — nectar; immortality 2:15; 4:31; 9:19; 10:27; 12:20; 13:12; 14:20, 27; 18:37, 38

amsha/aṃśa — particle, atom 10:41; 15:7

Ananta — "Infinite", "Endless" a description of Krishna 11:19, 37, 47; the cosmic serpent 10:29

Anantavijaya — name of Yudhishthira's conch shell 1:16

ananya — single-minded, exclusive -*bhakti* exclusive devotion to one deity 8:22; 9:30; 11:54; -*chinta* thought 9:22; -*manasa* mindedness 9:13; -*yoga* 12:6; 13:10

anta — final truth, end 2:16; 11:16

antah-karana/ antaḥkarana — intellect, ego and mind 3:42

aprameya — unfathomable, immeasurable 2:18; 11:17, 42

Aranyaka/Āraṇyaka — forest writing of the *Vedas* xiv, xviii

Arisudana/Arisūdana — n. pr. div. "Destroyer of Enemies" one of the names of Krishna 2:4

artha — wealth 2:5; 7:16; 16:10, 12; 18:34

Aryaman/Aryamān — n. pr. m. "Noble One", King of the ancestors 10:29

asakta — without attachment, unattached 3:9,19, 25; 5:21; 9:9; 13:9; 18:49

asat — non-being, non-existence, unreal, without truth 2:16; 9:19; 11:37; 13:12, 21; 16:8, 10; 17:28

ashrama/āśrama — stage of life xlii; 1:37; 2: *notes* 8; 3: *notes* 38; 4:7, 21; 5:1, 6, 14; 18:34

ashvattha/aśvattha — tree of the fig family 10:26; 15:1, 2, 3, 4, 13

Ashvatthama/ Aśvatthāma — n. pr. m. "Horse-voiced", a great archer, son of Drona 1:8

Ashvins/Aśvins — celestial twins 11:6, 22

Asita-Devala — a seer 10:13

asura/Āsura — demonic, ungodly 16:4, 5, 6, 7, 19, 20; 17:6

Asuras/Āsurā — demons, devils, demonic forces 7:15; 9:12; 10:14, 18, 27, 30, 37; 11:22; 18:12

A/atman/Ā/ātman — *as* Supreme Purusha, Brahman 4:6, 7; 7:1, 18; 8:4; 9:4, 5 9, 11, 29, 34; 10:15, 16, 20, 32, 40, 42; 11:3, 4; 13:2, 31, 32;

18:21; *as* true Self xviii, xx, xxvii, xxviii, **xxxvi–vii**, xxxvii, xxxviii, xxxix, xli, xlvi; 2:11, 12, 16, 18, 19, 20, 21, 22, 25, 39, 55, 56, 57, 58 59, 61, 72; 3:*intro*, 1, 2, 17, 43; 4:35, 38, 42; 5:16, 21, 26; 6:5, 6, 7, 18, 19, 20, 25, 26, 29; 7:*intro*, 1, 5, 11, 12, 18, 29; 8:3, 4, 21; 9:9; 10:11, 20, 32; 11:1, 24; 12:15; 13:*intro*, 1, 2, 9, 11, 15, 16, 17, 20, 21, 22, 23, 25, 26, 28, 29, 31, 33, 34; 14:3, 5, 6, 8, 9, 18, 19, 20 23; 15:*intro*, 2, 4, 5, 6, 7, 8, 9, 10, 11, 15, 16, 17, 18, *notes* 11; 16:1, 14, 18, 19, 21; 17:2, 6, 23; 18:37; *as* ordinary self 2:43, 55, 64; 3:1, 2, 3, 6, 7, 13, 17, 20, 25, 26, 27, 29, 30, 42, 43; 4:5, 6, 9, 14, 16, 17, 18, 20, 21, 23, 24, 27, 33, 35, 36, 37, 38, 40, 41, 42; 5:*intro*, 3, 4, 5, 6, 7, 11, 12, 14, 15, 16, 17, 18, 19, 21, 22, 25; 6:3, 5, 6, 8, 10, 11, 14, 15, 18, 19, 20, 21, 25, 26, 28, 29, 30, 33, 34, 36, 37; 8:2, 12; 9:28, 34; 10:11; 12:14; 13:24, 28; 16:9, 17, 21, 22; 17:16, 19; 18:10, 14, 16, 17, 24, 37, 39, 47, 49, 51, 54, 55, 57, 58, 61, 66, 67, 73; *atmavan/ātmavān* established in the Self 2:45; *atma/ātma* realization of the *atman*, Self-understanding 18:37; *-samyama/saṃyama* self-restraint, self-control 4:26, 27; *-samyama-yoga* the *yoga* of self-restraint 4:27; *-vidya* knowledge of the Self 10:32; *Atma/Ātma-Yoga* Krishna's *Yoga* of the Self 11:47; *yatatma/yatātma* self-controlled 5:25; 12:11, 14

avatara/avatāra	divine descent xxiv, xxv, xxvi, xxxiv–v, xliii; 1:20, *notes* 13; 4:5, 7; 10:18, 21, 23, 27, 30, 31; 11:*intro*; 14:3
avinashi/avināśi	indestructible, imperishable (*as* Brahman or *atman*) 2:17, 21; 13:27
avyakta	unmanifest 2:25, 28; 8:18, 20; 9:5, 7, 18, 19; 13:5, 12; *as* Brahman 7:24; 8:18, 20, 21; 9:4, 5, 7; 12:1, 3, 5
avyaya	imperishable, immutable, indestructible, changeless 2:17, 21, 34; 4:1, 6, 13; 7:13, 24, 25; 9:2, 13, 18; 11:2, 4, 18; 13:31; 14:5, 27; 15:1, 5, 17; 18:20, 56; *avyayatman/avyayātman* Imperishable Self 4:6
bhaj	to worship, serve 6:31, 47; 7:16, 28; 9:13, 29, 30, 33; 10:8, 10; 15:19
bhakti	loving devotion xxiii, xxix; 3:30; 4:3, 9, 11; 6:31, 46, 47; 7:*intro*, 16; 8:10, 20, 22; 9:*intro*, 3, 6, 13, 14, 26, 27, 29, 33; 10:10, 22; 11:*intro*, 55; 12: *passim*; 13:10, 24; 14: *notes* 23; 15:19; 18:54, 55, 57, 65, 68, 71; *ananya-* exclusive 8:22; 9:30; 11:54; *para-* supreme 9:14; *-marga* path of xxviii, xl, **xlii–iii**, xliv, xlv, xlvii; 9:31; 18:44, 68; *-yoga* the *yoga* of 7:28; 9:27; 10:10; 12: *passim*; 13:25; 14:26, 27; 18:46, 55, 56, 63, 64, 66; *bhakta* devotee 4:3; 7:17, 21, 23; 8:10, 22; 9:23, 31, 33; 10:30; 11:55; 12:*intro*, 1, 16, 20; 13:24; 18:65, 68; *mad-* my devotee 12:14, 18–19; 13:18; *abhakta* not devoted 18:67
Bharata/Bhārata	n. pr. m. "Descendant of Bharata", Arjuna's tribal name 2:14, 18, 28, 30; 3:25; 4:7, 42; 7:27; 13:2, 33; 14:3, 8, 9, 10;

15:19; 16:3; 17:3; best of Bharatas 3:41; 14:12; 17:12; 18:4, 36; Dhritarashtra's tribal name xxii; 1:24; 2:10; chief, lord of 7:11; 8:23; kingdom of xlviii

bhava/bhāva state of being, existence, nature, intrinsic nature, aspect 2:7, 16; 7:12, 13, 15; 8:6, 20; 9:11; 10:4, 11; 11:49; 15:19; 17:16, 26; 18:7, 20, 21, 43, 62; *mad-* my being 3:10; 4:10; 8:5; 10:5, 6, 17; 13:18; 14:19; *param-* higher nature (of Krishna) 9:11; *sva-* intrinsic essence, own nature, own being 2:16; 5:14; 8:3, 4; 12:11; 14:23; 16:7; 17:2, 26; 18:41, 42, 43, 44, 45, 47, 48, 60

bhavana/bhāvāna contemplation, steady thought, meditation 2:66

Bhima/Bhīma n. pr. m. "The Terrible One", one of the five Pandu brothers xlviii; 1:1, 4, 10, 15

Bhishma/Bhīma n. pr. m. "Awesome", "Terrible" a great warrior of the Kaurava clan xxi, xxii, xxvi, xlviii, xlix; 1:8, 10, 11, 12, 17, 19, 25, 31, 36; 2:4, 5, 11; 11:21, 26, 32, 33, 34; 16:11; *Book of* xxi

bhoga enjoyment, pleasure 1:32, 33; 2:5, 37, 43; 5 :22 ; 9:20; 16:11

Bhrigu/Bhṛgu n. pr. m. a great seer 10:2, 25, 26;

bhuta/bhūta being between humans and gods; ghost; nature spirit 9:25; 17:4

bija/bīja seed 7:10; 9:18; 10:39; 14:4

Brahma/Brahmā creator god, one of the Hindu *trimurti* or trinity of Gods 1:31; 3:10, 15; 4:8, 35, 38; 8:16, 17 18, 21, 24; 9:4, 7, 20; 10:6, 13, 25; 11:15, 22, 37, 39; 14:14, 18; 18:40; *-loka* world of 8:16

Brahma-charya/ celibate student of the *Vedas* 6:14; 8:11; 17:14
Brahmachārya

Brahman/Brāhman the Absolute, ultimate Reality xx, xxiii, xxv, xxvii, xxvii–viii, **xxxiii–v, xxxvi–vii,** xxxviii, xxxix, xl, xli, xliii, xlvi, xlvii, xlviii; v 2:*intro*, 17, 20, 24, 25, 29, 38, 39, 45, 54, 59, 70, 71, 72 *notes* 40; 3:2, 9, 10, 15, 16, 29, 30, 42; 4:*intro*, 6, 7, 10, 14, 21, 23, 24, 25, 30, 31, 32, 33, 34, 35, 42; 5:4, 5, 6, 7, 8– 9, 10, 11, 12, 15, 16, 17, 19, 20, 21, 22, 24, 29; 6:3, 4, 7, 8, 14, 15, 21, 27, 28, 29, 30, 38; 7:*intro*, 1, 5, 6, 7, 8, 9, 10, 12, 13, 17, 18, 19, 20, 21, 22, 23, 24, 25, 26, 27, 29, 30; 8:*intro*, 1, 3, 4, 10, 11, 13, 18, 21, 22, 24; 9:*intro*, 2, 4, 6, 7, 9, 10, 11, 12, 13, 15, 17, 18, 21, 24, 25, 29, 34; 10:*intro*, 3, 5, 6, 7, 15, 17, 20, 21, 25, 33, 38, 39, 42; 11:*intro*, 5, 8, 13, 18, 24, 37, 40; 12:*intro*, 3; 13:*intro*, 1, 2, 4, 12, 13, 14, 16, 17, 18, 19, 20, 22, 23, 25, 26, 30, 31, 32, 33, *notes* 1, 20; 14:1, 2, 3, 4, 24, 26, 27; 15:1, 3, 4, 5, 6, 7, 10, 12, 15, 16, 17, 20; 17:*intro*, 6, 23, 24, 25; 18:19, 21, 50, 51, 53, 54, 55, 63, 73; *as prakriti* 3:15; *nirguna/nirguṇa* without attributes xxviii, xxix, xxxiii, xxxiv, xxxv, xxxvii, xxxix, xlvii; 3:15, 22, 23; 4:9, 13; 5:10, 14; 7:5, 6, 7, 8, 12, 13, 18, 24, 25; 8:4, 10, 20, 22; 9:*intro*, 4, 5, 7, 8, 11, 15, 27, 34; 10:2, 12, 33; 11:*intro*, 1, 3, 37, 38; 12:*intro*, 1, 3, 4, 5; 13:12, 14, 15, 26, 31, *notes* 27; 14:3, 19, 27, *notes* 23; 15:6, 18; 16:7; 17:23, 27; 18:56; *saguna/saguṇa* with attributes xxviii, xxix, xxxiii, xxxiv, xxxix, xlvii; 3:15, 22, 2; 4:9, 13; 6:31; 7:6, 8, 22; 8:4, 10, 20, 22; 9:*intro*, 4, 5, 7, 9, 11, 27, 34; 10:12; 11:*intro*, 3, 37; 12:*intro*, 1, 6–7; 13:12; 14:3, 27, *notes* 23; 15:17, 18; 17:23, 27; 18:56; -*atman* partial or total identification of the *atman* within with Brahman; *Brahma-bhuta/bhūta* Brahman-become 5:24; 6:27; 18:54; -*bhuya/bhūya* becoming Brahman xlvii; 14:26; 18:53; -*jnana/jñāna* knowledge of Brahman 9:2; -*jnanin/jñānin* one knowing Brahman 2:54, 55; -*nirvana/nirvāna* oneness with Brahman that is liberation xlvii; 2:72; 5:24, 25, 26; -*sutra/sūtra* a collection of aphorisms about Brahman xxiii; 13:4; -*vidya/vidyā* knowledge of Brahman xxiii; 2:*intro*; 8:24; 10:32; -*yoga* the *Yoga* of Brahman 8:*intro*; *Brahmani-sthita* established in Brahman, liberated 5:19, 20; *Para*- Supreme Brahman 8:20; 10:12, 40; *shabda/śabda-brahma* word of Brahman = the *Vedas* 6:44

Brahmanas/Brāhmaṇas commentaries on the *Vedas* xiv, xvi, xviii, xxxiii

Brahmin/Brāhmaṇa priest and member of the highest class xiv, xxv, xvi–xvii, xxiv, xxxiii, xliii; 1:7; 2:31, 46; 3:9, 20; 4:2, 13; 5:18; 6:2; 8:4; 9:*intro* 33; 10:6, 27; 14:10, 17; 16:15, 18; 17:14, 23; 18:41, 42, 43, 44, 46, *notes* 40

Bhrigu/Bhṛgu n. pr. m. a famous legendary great sage 10:25, 26

Brihaspati/Bṛhaspati chief priest of the *Vedic* god Indra 10:24

Brihatsama/Bṛhatsāma the best part of the *Sama Veda* 10:35

buddhi intellect, wisdom, understanding, knowledge, reason, discrimination, discernment xxxviii; 1:23; 2:39, 41, 44, 45, 49, 52, 53, 54, 57, 63, 64, 65, 66, 71; 3:2, 8, 26, 28, 40, 42, 43; 4:18; 5:11, 17, 20, 28; 6:9, 12, 21, 25, 43; 7:4, 9, 10, 24; 8:7; 10:4, 9, 22; 12:4, 8, 14; 13:*intro*, 5, 20; 14:6; 16:9; 18:16, 17, 29, 30, 31, 32, 37, 49, 51, 58; -*bheda* split intellect 3:26; -*samyoga* union of intellect 6:43; -*yoga* yoga of intellect 2:39, 49, 53; 4:42; 10:10; 18:57; -*yukta* one integrated in intellect/wisdom 2:50, 51

budha the wise, wise person 4:19; 5:22; 10:8

Chekitana/Chekitāna n. pr. m. warrior of the Vrishni clan in the Pandava army 1:5

chela pupil, disciple xx; 4:2, 34; 6:40

chetas reason, thought, consciousness 1:38; 2:7, 44, 65: 3:30; 4:23; 5:26; 6:14, 23; 7:30; 8:8, 14; 10:9, 22; 12:5, 7; 18:57, 72; *chitta* thought, actions of the mind, consciousness 4:21; 6:10, 12, 18, 19, 20, 23; 10:9; 12:9; 13:9; 16:16; 18:57, 58; *chetana/chetanā* consciousness 10:22; 13:6

Chitraratha King of the *Gandharvas*, the celestial physicians and musicians 10:26

Daityas demons 10:21, 30

daiva	godly 16:*intro*, 1, 2, 3, 5, 6; divine providence 18:14
dama	control of the senses, self-restraint 10:4; 16:1; 18:42
dana/dāna	giving, beneficence 10:5; 8:28; 11:48, 53; 16:1; 17:*intro*, 7, 20, 21, 22, 24, 25, 27, 28; 18:3, 5, 6, 7, 43
Danavas/Dānavas	anti-gods 10:14
deha	body 2:13, 18, 30; 4:9; 8:2, 4, 13; 12:5; 13:22, 32; 14:5, 11, 20; 15:14; 16:18; 17:2; 18:11; embodied one, the individual being 8:4; 12:5; 14:14, 20; of God 11:7, 15
dehin	embodied Self, *atman* 2:13, 18, 22, 30, 55, 59; 3:40; 14:5, 7, 8, 14, 20; 17:2
Devadatta	name of Arjuna's conch shell 1:15
devas	gods, divine beings 3:11, 12; 4:12, 25; 7:20, 23; 9:20, 23, 25; 10:2, 14, 22, 27; 11:15, 21, 25, 33, 45, 52; 17:4, 14; 18:40; *as* Krishna 11:13, 14, 15, 44, 45; *adi-deva* Primal God 11:38; *devesha* Lord of gods 11:25, 45
dhama/dhāmā	abode, home 8:21; 11:38; 15:6
Dhananjaya/ Dhanaṃjaya	n. pr. m. "Conqueror of Wealth", another name of Arjuna 1:15; 2:48, 49; 3:1; 4:41; 7:7; 9:9; 10:37; 18:29, 72
dharana	concentration 8:12
dharma	what is right, righteousness, duty xvi, xx, xxxii, *notes to Introduction* 37; 1:1, 36, 37, 40, 41, 43, 44, 45, 46; 2:2, 5, 7, 31, 32, 33, 34, 37, 38, 40, 45, 47, 54; 3:2, 15, 35; 4:2, 7, 8, 23; 6:44; 7:11, 16; 9:2, 3, 31; 11:1, 18, 31, 32, 33, 34, 45; 12:20; 14: *notes* 23; 16:7, 10, 12, 24; 17:5; 18:7, 14, 15, 23, 31, 32, 34, 43, 44, 45, 46, 47, 52, 59, 66, *notes* 38; *amrita/amṛta-* eternal 12:20; 14:27; *ashrama/aśrama-* the four stages of life 2: *notes* 4; family 1:39, 43; *sanatana/sanātana-* eternal, ancient, primeval 1:1, 26, 36, 39, 40; 2:31; 11:18; 12:20; 14: *notes* 23; 15:7; 18:46, 47; *sva-* one's own *dharma* 1:26, 36, 37, 38, 41, 44; 2:31, 32, 33; 3:35; 8:7; 18:41, 43, 45, 46, 47, 66, *notes* 38; *varna-* class 1:37, 39, 41, 45; 2:31, 32, 37, 47; *dharmas* 1:40, 43, 44; 13:6; 15:20; 18:66; as the three *Vedas* 9:20, 21
Dharmakshetra/ Dharmakṣetra	n. pr. loc. "Field of Dharma" 1:1, 2
dhira/dhīra	one who is wise, firm, steadfast, sober 2:13, 15; 6:42; 14:24
Dhrishtadyumna/ Dhṛṣtadyumna	n. pr. m. "He Who Cannot Be Successfully Encountered" a warrior and son of Drupadi 1:3, 4, 17
Dhrishtaketu/ Dhṛṣtaketu	n. pr. m. "Audacious Leader", King of Chedi 1:5
Dhritarashtra/ Dhṛtarāṣtra	n. pr. m. King of the Kauravas xxi, xxii, xlvii, xlix; 1:1, 2, 8, 10, 11, 16, 18, 19, 20, 23, 24, 37, 46; 2:6, 9; 11:9, 26, 32, 34, 35, 47; 18:74, 76
dhriti/dhṛti	firmness, steadfastness, sustained effort 13:6; 16:3; 18:26, 29, 33, 34, 35, 43, 51
dhyana/dhyāna	meditation 5: *passim*; 12:6, 12; 13:24; 18:52; -*yoga* 18:52
dosha/doṣa	defect, fault 1:38, 39, 43; 2:7; 13:8; 15:5; 18:3, 48

Draupadi/Draupadī — n. pr. f. the common wife to all five Pandava brothers 1:3, 6, 8, 18

Drona/Droṇa — n. pr. m. a learned Brahmin and warrior and leader of the Kaurava army xxii, xlix; 1:2, 3, 4, 7, 8, 25, 36; 2:4, 5, 11; 11:21, 26, 32, 33, 34

Drupada — n. pr. m. King of Panchala and father of Draupadi 1:3, 4, 6, 17, 18

duhkha/duḥkha — suffering, pain 2:14, 15, 36, 38, 56, 65; 5:6, 22, 23, 32; 6:7, 17, 23; 8:15; 10:4; 12:5, 13, 18; 13:6, 8, 20; 14:16, 20, 24; 15:5; 17:9; 18:8, 36; *and sukha* happiness 2:14, 15, 38

Duryodhana — n. pr. m. "He Who Is Hard To Overpower" Dhritarashtra's oldest son and enemy of the Pandavas xxi, xlix; 1:1, 2, 3, 4, 7, 9, 10, 11, 12, 15, 16, 23; 2:32 ; 11:34

dvaita — dualism

dvandva — pairs of opposites; two words of equal importance joined together 2:45; 4:22; 7:27, 28; 10:33; 13:6; 15:5; 18:38; *nir-* absence of opposites 2:45; 5:3

dvesha/dveṣa — aversion, hatred 2:64; 3:34; 5:3; 6:9; 7:27; 9:29; 12:13, 17; 13:6; 14:22; 16:18, 19; 18:10, 23, 51

dvija — twice-born xxiii; 1:7; 17:14

eka — one, oneness, unity 2:41; 6:31; 7:17; 9:15; 11:7, 13; 13:30; - *akshara* the one syllable *Om* 10:25; *ekagra* one-pointed 6:12; 18:72

Gandharvas — celestial physicians and musicians 10:13, 26; 11:22

Gandiva/Gāṇḍīva — Arjuna's bow, a gift from Agni, the god of fire 1:30; 18:78

Ganesha/Gaṇeśa — n. pr. div. 10:24; 17:24

Garuda/Garuḍa — celestial bird 10:30

Garutmat — = Vainateya, a celestial bird 10:30

Gayatri/Gāyatri — metre of *Vedic* verse and a prayer to the sun 10:35

Govinda — n. pr. div. "Knower of Living beings", "Master of the Senses" or "Cattle-Finder" 1:32; 2:9

Gudakesha/Guḍākeśa — n. pr. m. "Lord/Conqueror of Sleep", another name for Arjuna 1:24; 2:9; 10:20; 11:7

guhya — mystery, secret 9:*intro*, 1; 10:38; 11:1; 15:20; 18:62, 63; *raja-* 9:2

gunas/guṇas — literally "strands", attributes, constituents, modes, tendencies, forces, qualities 2:45; 3:3, 5, 15, 22, 25, 26, 27, 28, 29, 30, 33, 37, 39, 40; 4:8, 13, 14, 19, 21, *notes* 20; 5:4, 8–9, 14, 15, 18, 19, 20; 6:19, 27; 7:7, 11, 12, 13, 14, 20, 25; 8:3; 9:9, 12, 13, 25, 28, 32, 33; 10:5, 11, 27; 13:1, 6, 12, 14, 19, 21, 22, 23, 26, 29, 31; 14: *passim*; 15:2, 3, 4, 5, 6, 10, 12; 16:6, 7, 19, 22; 17:*intro*, 1–22, 28; 18:*intro*, 3, 4, 7, 16, 19, 20, 23, 24, 26, 29, 30, 35, 40, 41, 44, 48, 58, 61, 64, 66 *notes* 38; *gunatita/guṇātīta* one who is without the *gunas* 14:25; *nirguna* without *gunas* 2:45; 3:22; 13:14, 31

guru	a spiritual teacher xx, xli; 2:5; 4:2, 34, 35; 6:40; 13:7; as Krishna 11:43
Hari	n. pr. m. "Lord" one of the names for Krishna and Vishnu 11:9; 18:77
Hastinapura	n. pr. loc. xlviii
hetu	cause 9:10; 13:20, 21; 18:15
Hiranyagarbha Hiraṇyagarbha	*Vedic* creator deity xix; 8:4; 11:39
Hrishikesha/Hṛṣīkeśa	n. pr. div. "Lord of the Senses" one of the names of Krishna 1:15, 20, 24, 36; 2:9, 10; 11:36; 18:1
Ikshvaku/Ikṣvāku	n. pr. m. first King of the solar dynasty and son of Manu 4:1
Indra	n. pr. div. *Vedic* deity, the god of thunder, storms and battles and chief of the *Vedic* gods xiv, xv, xviii; 1:16; 9:20; 10:21, 22, 23, 24, 28, 37; 11:22, 34, 39
indriyas	senses; the organs of perception (seeing, hearing, touching, smelling and tasting) and of acting (hands, grasping; feet, walking; tongue, speaking; excretion, anus; reproduction, genitals) 2:8, 58, 60, 61, 64, 67, 68; 3:6, 7, 16, 28, 34, 40, 41, 42; 4:26, 27; 5:7, 8–9, 11, 28; 6:8, 12, 21, 24; 7:4; 10:22; 12:4; 13:5, 8, 14; 15:7; 18:33, 38
Ishvara/Īśvara	Lord; *as* Krishna xxxiii, xxxiv; 2:39, 61; 3:30; 4:6, 10; 6:23; 8:10; 9:11; 10:12; 11:3, 7, 8, 9, 15, 18, 19, 21, 44; 13:28; 15:12, 13, 17; 16:8; 18:61, 62: *as atman* 15:8, *Maheshvara/Maheśvara* "Great Lord" 9:11; 13:22; *Loka-Maheshvara* "Great Lord of the Worlds" 5:29; 10:3; *Maha-Yogeshvara/Mahāyogeśvara* "Great Lord of Yoga" 11:9; Parameshvara/Parameśvara "Supreme Lord" 11:3; 13:27; *Yogeshvara/Yogeśvara* "Lord of Yoga" 11:4; 18:75, 78; *Vishveshvara/Viśveśvara* "Lord of the Universe" 11:16; lord 16:14; 18:43
Jahnavi/Jāhnavī	n. pr. river the Ganges 10:31
Janaka	n. pr. m. a king who was a holy sage and a sound ruler 3:20, *notes* 27
Janardana/Janārdana	n. pr. div. "Slayer of Jana" or "One Worshipped for Prosperity and Freedom" or "Liberator of Men" one of the names of Krishna 1:36, 39, 44; 10:18; 11:51
Jayadratha	n. pr. m. a king, one of the Kaurava warriors 11:34
janma	rebirth 2:51; 4:5; 7:19; 8:15, 16; 13:8; 14:20; 16:20
jati	birth, caste 1:41, 43; 2:27; 10:6
jiva/jīva	a living soul, living being, the finite self, the individual self xxxvii–ix, *notes* 51; 13:20, 28; 15:6, 7, 8; 17:6; -*atman/jivātman* the whole self xxxviii–ix, xliii, *notes* 51; 2:22; 5:14; 8:3; 13:1, 2, 21, 22, 28; 15:*intro*, 7, 8, 16, 17, 19; 16:4, 5, 21; 17:2; 18:14, 17, 18, 57; -*bhuta/bhūta* life-element 7:5; 15:7

jivan-mukta/jivan-mukta   one liberated while still in the body xlvi; 14:21, 22, 23, 25; -mukti liberation while still in the body 5:19, 23, 26; 6:30; 14:20, 21, 25

jnana/jñāna   knowledge, wisdom, understanding xiv, xliv, xlvii; 2:51; 3:intro, 32, 39, 40, 41, 49; 4:19, 23, 27, 28, 30, 33, 34, 36, 37, 38, 39, 41, 42; 5:15, 16, 17; 6:8; 7:intro, 2, 5, 15, 17, 19 20; 9:1, 12, 13; 10:4, 10, 38; 12:8, 9, 11, 12; 13:intro, 2, 11, 17, 18, 34; 14:intro, 1, 2, 6, 9, 11, 17; 15:10, 15, 19; 16:1; 18:18, 19, 20, 21, 42, 50, 54, 63, 70, notes 59; -kanda knowledge portion of the Veda xiv; 2:2, 42; -marga the path of knowledge xxviii, xl, xl–ii, xlii, xlvii; 2:51; 4:intro; 6:31, 46; 7:2; 18:30, 44; -nishtha/-niṣṭhā established in knowledge; -vi-jnana/-vijñāna knowledge and realization 3:41; 7: passim; 18:42, 50; -yajna/-yajña sacrifice of knowledge 4:28, 33: 9:15; 18:70; -yoga the yoga of knowledge xx, xxviii, xli–ii, xlv; 2:49; 3:intro, 3, 7, 20, 26, 29, 35; 4: passim; 5:intro, 1; 6:1; 16:1; 8.7, 10:10; 12:1, 4, 9, 14; 13:10, 24, 25; 16:1; 18:10, 33, 57, 63, 66, notes 59; -yogin 7:2; 18:1, 3; jnanin/ jñānin one adept in knowledge of the atman; one who is wise 3:39; 4:34, 41; 5:18; 6:9, 46; 7:16, 17, 18, 19; 13:7

jneya/jñeya   object of knowledge 13:12, 16, 17, 18; 18:18

kala/kāla   time 4:2; 8:23; 10:30; akshaya- everlasting 10:33; maha- great 11:32

kalpa/kālpa   an eon, a period of cosmic time 4:8; 9:7

kama/kāma   desire, pleasure, lust 2:5, 43, 55, 62, 70, 71; 3:37, 39, 42, 43; 4:19; 5:12, 23, 26; 6:18, 24; 7:11, 20, 22, 27; 9:21; 10:28; 15:5; 16:8, 10, 11, 12, 16, 18, 21, 23; 17:5, 11; 18:23, 24, 34, 53; kama-kami/kāma-kāmi desirer of desires 2:70

Kamadhuk/Kāmadhuk   also Kama-dhuh or Kama-dhenu, divine cow of plenty 3:10; 10:28

Kandarpa   n. pr. div. the god of love 10:28

Kapila   n. pr. m. a sage, the reputed founder of classical Sankhya 2:intro 10:26

karana/kāraṇa   cause, instrument 6:3; 13:21; 18:13, 14, 18

karma/karman   action xliii; 1:1, 36, 42, 43, 44; 2:21, 38, 43, 47, 48, 49, 50, 51; 3:intro, 1, 4, 5, 8, 9, 14, 15, 19, 20, 22, 23, 24, 25, 26, 27, 29, 30, 31; 4:9, 12, 15, 16, 17, 18, 19, 20, 21, 23, 27, 32, 33, 41; 5:10, 11, 13, 14; 6:3; 7:28, 29; 9:9, 12; 12:10; 13:29; 14:7, 9, 12, 15; 15:2; 16:9, 24; 17:26, 27; 18:3, 5–13, 15, 18, 19, 23, 24, 25, 56, 57, 71; as ritual xiv, xvi, xliii; fruitive xvi, xvii, xx, xxviii, xxxii, xxxvii, xlii, xlvi; 2: 21, 22, 38, 39, 43, 45, 47, 49, 51; 3:intro, 4, 5, 6, 8, 9, 12, 14, 15, 17, 19, 20, 22, 23, 24, 25, 26, 27, 28, 30, 31, 33, 34, 35, 37; 4:13, 14, 17,18, 23, 32, 36, 37, 41, notes 20; 5:7, 8–9, 10, 12, 15, 16; 6:27, 41, 44; 7:20, 23, 28, 29; 8:1, 3, 6, 16, 19, 24, 28; 9:1,

2, 3, 8, 20, 28, 29, 30; 10:5, 11; 11:31, 32, 33, 52; 12:5, 11, 16; 13:*intro*, 6, 9, 23, 31; 14:*intro*, 5, 6, 12, 14, 16, 19, 25; 15:8; 16:6, 8, 9, 15, 19, 20, 22; 17:2, 7, 21, 24, 25, 27; 18:3, 6, 9, 10, 12, 14, 15, 17, 24, 25, 30, 34, 40, 41, 45, 47, 48, 49, 59, 60, 61, 66, 67, 71, *notes* 38; duty 6:1; 18:41, 42, 43, 44, 45, 46, 47, 48; non-fruitive 12:16; 14:2; 18:57; *-kanda* the ritual action portion of the *Veda* xiv; 2:42, 44; 4:*intro*, 1, 12, 14, 21, 23, 25, 33, 36, 42; 5:*intro*, 1, 2, 3, 5, 6, 10, 12; 6:1, 29; *-marga* xl, **xliii–iv**, xlvii, *notes* 31; 18:30, 44, 56, 68; *-phala* fruits of 2:43, 47, 51; 4:14, 20; 5:12, 14; 6:1; 12:11, 12; 18:2, 11, 12, 27, 34; *-phala-tyaga* renunciation of the fruits of 12:12; 18:2; *-sannyasa* renunciation of 4:41; 5:1, 2, 13; 12:6; 18:57; *akushala/akuśala-* disagreeable 18:10; *kaushala /kauśala-* skill in agreeable 2:50; 18:10; *niyata-* obligatory 3:8; 18:7, 9, 23; *kamya/kāmya-* undertaken from desire 18:2; *nishkama/niṣkāma-* desireless xxx, **xliii–iv**; 3:25; 4:24; *-yoga* the *yoga* of desireless action xxviii, xxx, xxxi, **xliii–iv**, xlv, xlvii; 2:39 49; 3:1, 3, 7, 19, 20, 26, 29, 35; 4:16–23, 41; 5:2; 7:17, 28; 8:7; 9:27; 10:10; 12:4, 10, 11, 12, 15, 16; 13:25; 14: *notes* 23; 15:11; 16:1; 17:20; 18:6, 10, 46, 47, 56, 63, 66, 71, *notes* 59; *-yogin* 2:50; 3:2, 5, 23; 5:6, 11, 12; 6:1, 46; 8:26; 18:3, 11, 49; *as* divine creative action 8:1, 3, 4

Karna/Karṇa   n. pr. m. a warrior, also called Sutaputra, "Son of a Charioteer". He is the Pandavas' half brother xlviii; 1:8; 11:34

karta/kartā   agent, doer 18:18, 19, 26, 27, 28

karuna/karuṇa   compassion 12:13

karya/kārya   what should be done 3:17, 19; 6:1; 16:24; 18:5, 9, 30, 31; effect 13:20

Kashya/Kāśya   n. pr. m. King of Kashi 1:5, 17

Kaunteya   n. pr. m. "Son of Kunti", another name of Arjuna 1:27, 28; 2:14, 37, 60; 3:39; 5:22; 6:35; 7:8; 8:6, 16; 9:7, 10, 23, 27, 31; 13:1, 31; 14:4, 7; 16:20, 22

Kauravas/Kurus   dynastic title of the sons of Kuru xxi, xlviii; 1:1, 2, 8, 10, 12, 13, 19, 23, 24, 25, 36, 38, 44; 2:41; 3:36; 10:37; 11:21, 26–7.

kavi   a poet, seer 8:10; 10:37

Keshava/Keśava   n. pr. div. "One Who Has Destroyed the Demon Keshin", or "One Who Has Long Hair" one of the names of Krishna 1:31; 10:14; 11:35; 13:(1); 18:76

Keshinishudana
  Keśiniṣūdhana   n. pr. div. "Slayer of Keshi" another name for Krishna 18:1

kevala   alone, aloneness 18:16

Kripa/Kṛpa   n. pr. m. a teacher and warrior, the brother-in-law of Drona xxii; 1:8

krodha   anger 2:56, 62, 63; 3:37; 4:10; 5:23, 26, 28; 16:4, 12, 18, 21; 18:53; *akrodha* absence of anger 16:2

kshama/kṣama   forbearance, patience 10:34; 16:3

kshanti/kṣānti	forgiveness, patience 13:7; 18:42
Kshatriya/Kṣatriya	warrior, one of the second, ruler class xxiv; 1:7, 21, 37, 46; 2:2, 3, 5, 31, 32, 36, 38; 3:3, 20, 35; 4:2, 13; 5:5, 18; 6:1; 7:11; 8:4; 9:*intro*, 33; 10:27, 31; 14:10, 17; 16:15, 18; 18:7, 41, 43, 44, 46, 47, 52, 59, 60, 66
kshetra/kṣetra	field, *prakriti* 13:*intro*, (1), 1, 2, 3, 6, 7, 8, 12, 14, 18, 19, 20, 23, 26, 27, 29, 33, 34; 14:*intro*, 4, 5; 15:15
kshetrajna/kṣetrajña	knower of the field, Brahman 13:*intro*, 1, 2, 3, 7, 8, 14, 15, 16, 17, 18, 19, 20, 22, 23, 26, 27, 28, 29, 31, 34; 14:*intro*, 4; 15:15
Kubera	*see* Vittesha
Kunti/Kuntī	n. pr. f. Pandu's first wife and mother of three of the Pandavas xlviii; 1:8, 16, 25; 11:26–7
Kuntibhoja	n. pr. m. Bhishma's maternal uncle 1:5, *notes* 5
Kurukshetra	n. pr. loc. "Field of the Kurus" xxi, xlviii; 1:*intro*, 1, 3; 2:27, 31; 3:22; 13:*intro*; 18:*intro*
Kuru-Nandana	n. pr. m. "Joy of the Kurus", or "Descendant of the Kurus" another name for Arjuna 2:41; 14:13
kuta-stha/kūṭastha	unchanging, unmoved, unshaken, unwavering 6:8; 12:3; 15:16
lobha	greed 1:38, 45; 14:12, 17; 16:21; 18:27
loka-sangraha/ lokasaṃgraha	welfare of the world xxx, xxxi; 3:20, 25; 17:20
Madhava/Mādhava	n. pr. div. "Lord of Fortune",or "Descendant of Madhu" one of the names of Krishna 1:14, 37
Madhusudana/ Madhusūdana	n. pr. div. "Slayer of the Demon Madhu", one of the names of Krishna 1:14, 35; 2:1, 4; 6:33; 8:2
Mahabaho/Mahābāho	n. pr. m. "Mighty-Armed", another name for Arjuna 2:26, 68; 3:28, 43; 5:3; 6:35, 38; 7:5; 10:1; 14:5; 18:13; *also* of Krishna 11:23; 18:1
Mahabharata Mahābhārata	the "Great Indian Epic" in which the *Bhagavad Gita* occurs xxi, xxii, xxiii, xxiv, xxv, xxvi, xxvii, xxxii, xxxv, xlviii, xlix, *notes* 12 and 31; 1:*intro*, 1, 5, 25, 36
maharatha/mahāratha	"great warrior", a highly-skilled warrior and chariot driver 1:4, 17; 2:35
Mahat Brahma	*prakriti* 14:3, 4
mahatma/mahātma	great soul 7:19; 8:15; 9:13; 18:74; as Krishna 11:12, 20, 37, 50
makara	a shark 10:31
manas	mind 1:30, 47; 2:43, 55, 56, 60, 67, 71; 3:6, 7, 28, 40, 42; 5:11, 13, 19, 28; 6:12, 14, 15, 24, 25, 26, 27, 34, 35, 37; 7:1, 4; 8:7, 10, 12, 22; 9:13, 34; 10:6, 22; 11:45; 12:2, 8, 14; 13:*intro*, 5, 20; 15:7, 9; 17:11, 16; 15:7, 9; 17:11, 16; 18:15, 33, 52, 65
Manipushpaka Maṇipuṣpaka	the name of Sahadeva's conch shell 1:16

mantra	meditation chant of a name, phrase or formula xvii; 9:16; 10:22, 33; 17:13, 23
Manu, Manus	first being(s) in an eon 4:1, 8; 10:6; *Laws of* 2: *notes* 21; 4:1; 10:6
Margashirsha/ *Mārgaśīrṣa*	the lunar month, November – December (January) 10:35
Marichi/Marīci	n. pr. div. "Atom of light", a *Vedic* demi-god or a seer 10:21
Maruts	gods of the winds and storms 10:21, 23; 11:6, 22
maya/māyā	qualified reality; *prakriti*; delusion; the power of Brahman xl; 2:16; 3:38; 4:6, 10; 7:14, 15, 25, 26, 27; 9:12; 16:19; 18:14, 61; *atma-* my own power (of Krishna) 4:6; *yoga-* 7:25
Meru	n. pr. loc. a sacred mythical mountain 10:23, 28
moha	delusion, confusion xl; 2:52, 72; 3:2, 6, 27, 32, 34, 40; 4:16, 35; 5:15; 6:38; 7:13, 27, 28; 9:12; 11:1; 14:8, 13, 17, 22; 15:5; 16:10, 15, 16; 17:19; 18:7, 25, 39, 60, 72, 73; *mudha/mūḍha* the deluded 3:32; 6:38; 7:15, 25; 9:11; 14:15; 15:10; 16:20; 17:19; 18:35
moksha/mokṣa	release, liberation, enlightenment xx, **xlv–viii**; 2:5, 15, 61; 4:10, 15, 16, 32; 5:16, 17, 23, 24, 28; 6:15, 19, 30; 7:2, 11, 29; 8:17, 27; 9:1, 2, 25, 28; 10:18; 13:7, 12, 34; 14:1; 15:6; 16:1, 5, 10, 23; 17:25, 27; 18:2, 6, 8, 11, 30, 34, 49, 51, 66, 73; *mukta* one liberated, released xlvi; 2:51; 4:23; 5:28; 7:28; 9:28; 12:15; 14:20; 16:22; 18:26, 71; to be released 4:16; 8:5; 9:1, 28; 18:66, 71; *mukti* release, liberation xlvi; 4:15; 7:16
muni	sage, seer 2:56, 58, 69, 70; 5:6, 8–9, 28; 6:3, 4, 8; 10:26, 37; 14:1
Nagas/Nāgas	snake creatures 10:29
naishkarmya/ naiṣkarmya	non-activity, actionlessness 3:4, 5; 18:49
Nakula	n. pr. m. one of the five Pandava brothers, half-brother to Arjuna xlviii; 1:1, 5, 11, 16
namaskar/namaskṛ	to pay homage to, bow to, revere 9:14, 34; 11:36; 18:65
Narada/Nārada	n. pr. m. a divine seer 10:13, 26
Naraka	n. pr. loc. Hell 1:42, 44; 16:16, 21
Narayana/Nārāyaṇa	n. pr. div. another name for Krishna xxiv
neti neti	not this, not that 2:15, 29; 13:14
nirodha	cessation, negation 6:20
nirvana	liberation 2:72; 5:24, 25, 26; 6:15
nitya	eternal, everlasting, permanent 2:18, 20, 21, 24, 26, 30, 45; 5:3; *-yukta* ever-integrated, steadfast 7:17; 8:14; 9:14, 22; *anitya* impermanent 2:14; 9:33
nivritti/nivṛtti	inaction, withdrawal xlii; 15:4; 16:7; 18:30
niyamya	controlled, restrained 3:7, 41; 6:24, 26; 18:51
niyata	actions that include regular and occasional prescribed religious actions, class duties, necessary and inevitable actions and other actions 3:8; 4:30; 7:20; 18:7, 9, 23, 47

ojas	energy, power, life-force 15:13
Om/Oṃ	*also Oṃkara* a symbol of Brahman, a cosmic sound and a *mantra* 3:15; 7:8; 8:3, 11, 13; 9:17; 10:33; 17:23, 24
pada/pāda	abode, state 2:51; 18:56
Panchajanya/ Pāñcajanya	name of Krishna's conch 1:15
Pandavas/Pandus Pāṇḍavas/Pāṇḍus	sons of Pandu, the five brothers of the Pandu clan xxi, xlviii, xlix; 1:*intro*, 1, 2, 3, 4, 6, 8, 14, 16, 17, 19, 20, 22, 24, 25, 36; 2:5, 32; 10:36, 37; 11:26–7; 18:74, 78; Pandava, Arjuna's clan name 4:35; 6:2; 11:13, 55; 14:22; 16:5
pandit/paṇḍit	wise one 2:11; 4:19; 5:18
Pandu/Pāṇḍu	n. pr. m. one of the sons of Vyasa, the deceased brother of Dhritarashtra and the acting father of the five Pandavas xlviii; 1:8; 11:26–7
papa/pāpa	evil 1:1, 36, 39, 45; 2:33, 38; 3:13, 36, 37, 41; 4:36; 5:10, 15; 6:9; 7:28, 9.20, 32; 10.3; 18:66; -*yoni* evil birth 9:32
Para	Supreme, Greatest, Highest (of Brahman) 2:59; 3:19; 8:3; 11:18, 37, 38, 47, 55; 12:20; 13:34
Param-Atman/ Paramātmān	n. pr. div. Brahman xxxiv; 2:*intro*; 5:15; 6:29; 7:5; 9:11; 11:37; 13:*intro*, 22, 31, 32; 15:16; as individual *atman* 6:7
Parantapa/Paraṃtapa	n. pr. m. "Scorcher of Enemies", another name of Arjuna 2:3; 4:5, 33; 7:27; 9:3; 10:40; 11:54; 18:41
Partha/Pārtha	n. pr. m. "Son of Prithi", another name for Arjuna 1:25, 26; 2:3, 21, 32, 39, 42, 55, 72; 3:16, 22; 4:11, 33; 6:40; 7:1, 10; 8:8, 14, 22, 27; 9:13, 32; 10:24; 11:5, 9; 12:7; 16:4, 6; 17:26, 28; 18:6, 30, 31, 32, 33, 34, 35, 72, 74, 78
Paundra/Pauṇḍra	name of Bhima's conch shell 1:15
Pavaka/Pāvaka	n. pr. m. "The Purifier" one of the *Vasus* or elements, often associated with Agni, the god of fire 10:23
Pavana	the wind god 10:31
Pavitra	Purifier (of Krishna/Brahman) 10:12
phala	fruit (of action) 2:47, 49, 51; 7:23; 8:28; 14:16; 17:11, 12, 17, 21, 25; 18:6, 8, 9, 12, 34; *aphala* non-fruitive (action) 17:11, 17; 18:23
pindodaka/piṇḍodaka	*Vedic* rites for the dead 1:42
pitri/pitṛ	ancestor, father 1:26, 34, 42; 9:25; 10:29; 11:22; -*yana* way of 8:25
prabhava	origin, source 7:6; 9:18; 10:2, 8; 13:3, 16
prabhu	Lord (of Krishna) 9:24; 11:4
Prahlada/Prahlāda	n. pr. m. a devotee of Vishnu, despite being a demon prince 10:30
Prajapati/Prajāpati	n. pr. div. "Lord of Creatures", so a creator god xix; 3:10; 9:39; 11:39
prajna/prajñā	knowledge, wisdom 2:11, 54, 57, 58, 61, 67, 68; 18:31
prakasha/prakāśa	manifest, illuminated, revealed 7:25; 14:22; *aprakasha/ aprakāśa* darkness, indiscrimination 14:13

rajas	energy, dynamism, passion, one of the three *gunas* 2:45; 3:3, 5, 20, 37, 39, 40; 4:2, 8, 13; 6:27; 7:12; 9:12, 33; 10:27; 14:*intro*, 5, 7, 9, 10, 12, 15, 16, 17, 18, 22, *notes* 15; 15:4; 16:22; 17:1, 2, 3, 4, 9, 12, 18, 21, 22; 18:8, 9, 21, 24, 26, 27, 31, 34, 38, 41, 42, 43, 44
Rakshasas/Rakṣasas	demons, monsters 9:12; 10:23; 11:36; 17:4; 18:47
Rama/Rāma	n. pr. div. another "descent" of Vishnu and the hero of the *Ramayana* 1:20, *notes* 12; 3:20; 10:21, 23, 31
Rama with the Axe	10:31
Ramayana/Rāmāyaṇa	a Hindu epic with a "descent" of Vishnu as its hero xxiii; 1:20, *notes* 12; 3:20, 35; 10:21, 23, 31; 18:44
rasa	taste, enjoyable essence of something 2:59; 7:8; sapidity 15:13
rishi/ṛsi	seer xiv; 4:2; 5:25; 10:6, 13, 26 37; 11:15; 13:4; *deva-* divine 10:13; *maha-* great 10:2, 6, 25; 11:21; *raja-* royal 4:2; 9:33;
Rudras	demi-gods of storms and destruction 10:23; 11:6, 22
Sadhyas/Sadhya	inferior celestial deities 11:??
Sahadeva	n. pr. m. the youngest of the Pandava brothers xlviii; 1:1, 16
sama	same, equal, sameness, equanimity 1:4; 2:15, 38, 48; 4:22; 5:18, 19; 6:7, 8, 32, 33; 9:29; 10:5; 12:4, 13, 18; 13:27, 28; 14:24; 18:54; *-bhava* equality; *-buddhi* even-minded 6:9; 12:4; *-chittatva* even-consciousness 13:9; *-darshina* seeing the same 5:18; 6:29; *-duhkha/-duhkha-sukha* same in pain and sorrow 2:15; *samata* equanimity, evenness of mind 2:48; 10:5
samadhi/samādhi	contemplation, absorption in Brahman in meditation 2:44, 53, 54, 55, 64; 4:24, 30; 6:4, 7; 8:10; 12:9; 17:11; *samadhi-stha/samādhistha* one immersed in *samadhi* 2:54
sanghata/saṃghāta	"aggregate" of the body 13:6
Samhitas/Saṃhitas	literally "collection", commentaries on the *Vedas* xiv, xvi, xvii
sammoha/sammoha	delusion 2:63; 7:27; 18:72
sammudha/saṃmudha	confusion, delusion 2:7, 63; 3:29
samsara/saṃsāra	the chain of rebirth xxxviii, xlvi; 2:12, 13, 22, 26, 28, 50, 51; 4:9, 16; 5:3, 16, 19; 8:19, 27; 9:3, 8, 10, 21; 12:7; 13:21, 28; 14:1, 18, 19; 15:*intro*, 1, 3, 4, 5, 10; 16:5; 17:25; 18:10, 17, 30, 40, 71
samskaras/saṃskāra	latent impressions in the mind that inform current behaviour and present karmic results 2:59; 18:41
samyama/saṃyama	self-control, restraint 2:61, 69; 3:6; 4:22, 26, 27, 39; 6:14; 8:12; 12:4
samyoga/saṃyoga	union 5:14; 6:23, 43; 13:26; 18:38
sanatana/sanātana	eternal, ancient, primeval *of atman* 2:24; *of* Brahman 4:31; 7:10; 8:20; 11:18; 15:7
Sanjaya/Saṃjaya	n. pr. m. "One of Complete Victory" the sage who can perceive the dialogue between Krishna and Arjuna xxi–xxii; 1:1, 2, 18, 24, 27, 47; 2:1; 11:8, 9, 14, 35, 47, 48, 50; 18:74–78
sankalpa/saṃkalpa	intention 4:19; 6:2, 4, 6, 24, 25

Sankara/Śankara   n. pr. div. a name of Shiva, the deity of dissolution 10:23; for the seventh century philosopher, *see Index of English Words*

sannyasa/saṃnyāsa   renunciation xli, xlii; 3:4, 30; 4:23, 41; 5:*intro*, 1, 2, 4, 6, 13, 26; 6:1, 2, 4, 14; 9:28; 12:6; 13:10, 24; 18:*intro*, 1, 2, 7, 12, 49, 57; *-yoga* the yoga of renunciation 5:1; 9:28

sannyasin/saṃnyāsin   one who renounces 5:1, 3, 18; 6:1, 2, 3, 4, 9, 46; 12:18–19; 18:1, 2, 3, 7, 11, 12, 30, 49

sarva-gata   all-pervading 2:24; 3:15; 13:32; the Omniscient 12:3

sat   being, existence, reality, truth 2:16; 9:19; 11:37; 13:12, 21; 16:2, 7; 17:23, 26, 27; *satya* truth 10:4; 16:2

Satyaki/Sātyakī   n. pr. m. 1:17 = Yuyudhana 1:4

sattva   light, evolution, goodness, radiance, one of the three *gunas* 2:45, 49, 54; 3:5, 26, 27, 40: 4:8, 13; 6:12, 21; 7:12; 9:13, 14, 28, 32, 33; 10:27, 36; 13:17; 14:*intro*, 5, 6, 8, 9, 10, 11, 13, 14, 16, 17, 18, 19, 22; 15:4, 5, 12; 16:1, 3, 6, 7, 19, 22; 17:1, 2, 3, 4, 8, 11, 12, 17, 20, 22; 18:3, 8, 9, 10, 20, 23, 24, 25, 26, 30, 33, 37, 41, 43, 52; courage 10:36

Saubhadra   n. pr. m. matronymic from Subhadra = Abhimanu, the son of Arjuna and Subhadra 1:6

Savyasachin/ Savyasācin   a name for Arjuna meaning ambidextrous 11:3

Shaibya/Śaibya   n. pr. m. King of the Shibis 1:5

shakti/śakti   female divine energy xxxv; 14:3

shama/śama   serenity, quiescence, calmness 6:3; 10:4; 18:42

shanka/śaṅkha   a conch shell 1:12, 13, 14, 15, 16, 17, 18

shanti/śanti   peace, quiescence, serenity 2:65, 66, 70, 71; 4:39; 5:12, 29; 6:7, 14, 15, 27; 9:31; 11:24; 12:12; 16:2; 18:53, 62

sharira/śarīra   body 1:29; 2:20, 22; 3:8; 4:21; 5:23; 13:1, 31; 15:8; 17:6, 14; 18:15; of God 11:13; *sharirin/śarīrin* embodied Self 2:18, 55

Shashanka/Śaśānka   the moon 11:39

shashvata/śāśvata   changeless, eternal, immortal 1:43; 2:20; 8:26; 10:12; 11:18; 14:27; 18:56, 62

Shastra/Śāstra   authoritative scripture, teaching xlvii; 3:14, 41; 11:54; 15:20; 16:1, 23, 24; 17:1, 5, 13; *ashastra/aśāstra* not enjoined by the scriptures 17:5

shauca   purity 13:7; 16:3, 7; 17:14; 18:42

Shikhandin/Śikhaṇḍin   n. pr. m. a son of Drupadi, born female but changed to a male by a *Yaksha*; he will kill Bhishma xxii; 1:17

shishya   disciple, pupil 1:3; 2:7

Shiva/Śiva   n. pr. div. one of the major deities of Hinduism 2:35; 3:15; 10:23, 24; 11:30

shraddha/śraddhhā   faith, trust xlii; 3:31; 4:39; 6:37, 47; 7:21, 22; 9:3, 23, 24; 12:2, 20; 13:24; 17:*intro*, 1, 2, 3, 13, 17, 28; 18:71; *ashraddha/aśraddhā* without faith 4:40; 9:3; 17:28

shruti/śruti   sacred, revealed "heard" scriptures xiii–xiv, xvi, xix–xx, xxiii; 2:52, 53; 13:25; 16:24

Shudra/Śūdra   member of the fourth and lowest class of servants in Hinduism xxviii; 1:7; 4:13; 8:4; 9:32, 33; 14: *notes* 15; 18:41, 44, 46, *notes* 40

siddhi/siddha perfection, accomplishment, success/perfected one 2:48; 3:4, 20; 4:12, 22, 38; 6:37, 43, 45; 7:3; 8:15; 10:26; 11:21, 22, 36; 12:10; 14:1; 16:14, 23; 18:13, 26, 45, 46, 49, 50

Skanda n. pr. div. god of war and son of Shiva, also called Kartikeya 10:24

smriti/smṛti scriptures that are "remembered" xiv, xxiii; 15:15; 16:24; memory 18:73

Soma *Vedic* deity and ritualistic drink; the moon xiv; 9:20; 10:26; 15:13

Somadatta n. pr. m. King of the Bahikas 1:8

sthanu/stānu stable 2:24; *sthāna* abode 8:28

sthira steady, firm 5:20; 6:11, 13, 33; 12:19; 17:8

sthita/sthitā firm, steadfast, established, steady 2:65, 72; 6:14, 22, 31; 8:12; 17:27; 18:73; *-dhi* thought/wisdom 2:54, 56; *-prajna/prajña* one who is steady, firm in wisdom or knowledge and, hence, is liberated 2:54, 55; *sthiti* steadiness 17:27

Subhadra/Subhadrā n. pr. f. Arjuna's wife 1:6, 14, 18

Sughosha/Sughoṣa name of Nakula's conch 1:16

sukha happiness, pleasure, joy 1:32, 33, 37, 45; 2:14, 15, 32, 38, 56, 66; 4:40; 5:13, 21, 24; 6:7, 17, 21, 27, 28, 32; 10:4; 12:13, 18; 13:6, 20; 14:6, 9, 24, 27; 15:5; 16:14, 23; 17:8, 9; 18:36, 37, 38, 39

suras gods 11:21

Surya n. pr. div. the sun deity xv; 5:14

Sutaputra/Sūtaputra n. pr. m. "Son of a Charioteer", also called Karna, a half-brother to Arjuna 11:26

svarga Heaven 2:2, 32, 37, 43; 9:21

tamas inertia, darkness, one of the three *gunas* 2:45; 3:5, 27; 4:8, 13; 7:12; 8:9; 9:12; 10:11; 13:17; 14:*intro*, 5, 8, 9, 10, 13, 15, 16, 17, 18, 22, *notes* 15; 15:4; 16:6, 22; 17:1, 2, 4, 10, 13, 19, 22, 28; 18:7, 9, 22, 25, 27, 28, 32, 35, 39, 41, 44, 47, 67

tanmatras subtle elements 3:28; 7:4; 13: *notes* 12

tapas literally, "heat", austerity xix; 4:10, 28; 5:29; 6:46; 7:9; 8:28; 9:27; 10:5; 11:48, 53; 15:11; 16:1; 17:*intro*, 5, 6, 7, 14, 15, 16, 17, 18, 19, 22, 24, 25, 27, 28; 18:3, 5, 6, 7, 42, 67

Tat THAT/Brahman 5:16, 17; 13:15; 17:23, 25

tattva reality, truth 2:16; 3:28; 4:9, 34; 6:21; 9:24; 18:1, 55; *-darshana* seeing the real, the essence of; knower of the truth 2:16, 17

tat tvam asi "THAT you are" xxxvii; 2:17; 5:17; 6:30; 13:15; 17:23

tejas splendour; vigour, radiance, light 7:9, 10; 10:36; 11:17, 47; 15:12; 16:3; 18:43

tyaga/tyāga renunciation, abandonment 1:33; 2:3, 48, 51; 4:9, 20, 21; 5:10, 11, 12; 6:24; 12:11, 12, 16; 16:2, 21; 18:*intro*, 1, 2, 3,

4, 5, 6, 7, 8, 9, 11, 12, 49, 51; *tyagin/tyāgin* one who renounces the fruits of actions 1:9; `12:16, 17; 14:25; 18:1, 10, 11, 49, 66

Ucchaihshravas *Ucchaiḥśravas*	Indra's horse 10:27
upadhi/upādhi	limiting attribute of *prakriti* 18:21
upanayama	sacred thread ceremony 1:7
Ushanas/Uśanas	Vedic sage and poet 10:37
Ushmapas/Ũśmapā	class of ancestors 11:22
Uttamaujas	n. pr. m. a famous charioteer in Duryodhana's army 1:6
Vainateya	Garuda, a divine bird and the vehicle of Vishnu 10:30
vairagya/vairāgya	detachment, dispassion 6:35; 13:8; 18:52
vaishvanara *vaiśvānara*	energy that arises from the combustion of food 15:14
Vaishya/Vaiśya	member of the third class in Hinduism 1:7; 4:13; 8:4; 9:32, 33; 18:41, 44
varna/varṇa	class, literally "colour" 1:37, 39, 41, 42, 43; 18:41, 61; -*dharma* 4:7; *chatur-/chātur-* the four classes 4:13
Varshneya/Vārṣṇeya	n. pr. div. "Descendent of Varshni" a patronym for Krishna 1:41; 3:36
Varuna/Varuṇa	n. pr. div. an ancient *Vedic* deity 10:29; 11:39; 15:1
vasanas	*karmic* habits 2:59; 3:9, 33, 34; 5:15; 17:7
Vasava/Vāsava	n. pr. div. Indra 10:22
Vasudeva/Vāsudeva	n. pr. m. "Son of Vasudeva", patronymic for Krishna xxiv–v; 1:25; 7:19; 10:37; 11:50; 18:74
Vasuki/Vāsuki	one of the three kings of serpents 10:28, 29
Vasus	a class of divine beings 10:23; 11:6, 22
Vayu/Vāyu	n. pr. div. god of the wind 2:67; 11:39
Veda	knowledge, wisdom xiii–ix; 3:15; 8:11; injunctions 1:36; scriptures/hymns xiii–xv, xiv, xix, xxiii, xxxiii, xli; 1:1, 7, 42; 2:2, 7, 42, 43, 44, 46, 52, 53; 6:44, 46; 8:28; 11:39, 48, 53; 13:4, 25; 14:17; 15:1, 15; 16:20, 23; 17:15, 23; 18:42; *Rig/Ṛg-* "Royal Knowledge" xiv, xv, xvii, xix; 9:17; 10:22, 24, 37, 42; 15:1, 14; *Sama/Sāma* "Knowledge of Chants" xiv; 9:17; 10:22, 35; *Yajur-* "Ritual Knowledge" xiv; 9:17; *Atharva-* "Knowledge of Incantations" xiv, xv, xxxvi; deities xlii; 8:4; 10:21, 29; 11:22; praxis and rituals xv–xix; 1:42; 2:45, 46, 49; 3:9, 10, 11, 12, 14, 15, 17; 4:12; 6:2; 7:8, 16, 20; 9:16, 17, 23; 10:13, 35; 16:7, 20; 18:3
vibhaga/vibhāga	differentiation, discrimination, division, separation 13:*intro*, 2
vibhu	omnipresent, all-pervading 5:15; 10:12
vibhuti/vibhūti	manifestation; divine glory 10: *passim*; 11:*intro*, 40; 13:13; 15:12
vidya/vidyā	knowledge, science, wisdom 2:6, 17, 19, 21, 25, 29; *Raja-* 9: *passim*

30; 5:5, 8–9, 10, 11, 20, 23, 24, 26; 6:*intro*, 1, 2, 6, 7, 8, 10, 11, 12, 13, 15, 17, 19, 22, 27, 28, 31, 32, 36, 41, 42, 44, 45, 46, 47; 8:10, 12, 13, 14, 23, 25, 26, 27, 28; 9:2, 14, 29, 31; 10:3, 7; 12:14, 17; 13:*intro*, 7, 29; 15:11; 16:*intro*, 23; 17:20; 18:49; *as* Krishna 10:17

Yudhamanyu/
Yudhāmanyu
n. pr. m. a warrior who fought with the Pandava army 1:6

Yudhishthira
Yudhiṣṭhira
n. pr. m. Arjuna's brother and the eldest of the five Pandavas xlviii, xlix; 1:1,16; 2:32; 10:37

yuga
age, eon, period of time 4:8; 8:17; 10:6; *maha-* great eon 10:6

yukta
integrated, steadfast, balanced, united, in unison with 2:39, 50, 51, 61, 66; 3:26; 4:18; 5:8, 12, 13, 21, 23; 6:8, 14, 17, 18, 29, 47; 7:22, 30; 8:8, 10, 14, 27; 9:28; 10:3, 7, 10; 12:1, 2, 4; 13:7; 17:17; 18:28, 51; *nitya-* ever-integrated 7:17; 9:14; 12:2; *yuktatma/yuktātmā* integrated in the Self 5:21; 6:29, 47; 7:18; 9:28, 34; *ayukta* non-integrated, undisciplined, unsteady 2:66; 5:12; 18:28

Yuyudhana/
Yuyudhāna
n. pr. m. = Satyaka, a warrior who fought in the Pandava army 1:4, 17

Index of English Words